The New York Times

BOOK OF

WINE

The New York Times

BOOK OF

WINE

MORE THAN 30 YEARS OF VINTAGE WRITING

Edited by **HOWARD G. GOLDBERG**

Foreword by **ERIC ASIMOV**

STERLING EPICURE
New York

STERLING EPICURE
New York

An Imprint of Sterling Publishing
387 Park Avenue South
New York, NY 10016

ISBN 978-1-4027-8184-1 (hardcover)
ISBN 978-1-4027-9381-3 (ebook)

Library of Congress Cataloging-in-Publication Data
The New York Times book of wine / edited by Howard G. Goldberg.
   p. cm.
 ISBN 978-1-4027-8184-1 (hardcover) -- ISBN 978-1-4027-9381-3 (ebook) 1. Wine and wine
making. 2. Food and wine pairing. I. Goldberg, Howard G. II. New York times. III. Title: Book
of wine.
 TP548.N49 2012
 641.2'2--dc23
                             2011052425

Distributed in Canada by Sterling Publishing
^{c}/o Canadian Manda Group, 165 Dufferin Street
Toronto, Ontario, Canada M6K 3H6
Distributed in the United Kingdom by GMC Distribution Services
Castle Place, 166 High Street, Lewes, East Sussex, England BN7 1XU
Distributed in Australia by Capricorn Link (Australia) Pty. Ltd.
P.O. Box 704, Windsor, NSW 2756, Australia

For information about custom editions, special sales,
and premium and corporate purchases, please contact Sterling Special Sales
at 800-805-5489 or specialsales@sterlingpublishing.com.

Manufactured in the United States of America

2 4 6 8 10 9 7 5 3 1

www.sterlingpublishing.com

Contents

Foreword *Eric Asimov* xi
Introduction *Howard G. Goldberg*. xiv

CHAPTER 1
For Openers . . .

The $410 Corkscrew *Eric Asimov*. 1

CHAPTER 2
Wine Writing and Writers

Words, Words, Words *Frank J. Prial* 6
Wine in Two Words *Eric Asimov* 9
Affairs to Remember *Frank J. Prial* 13
A Reporter's Reporter *Frank J. Prial*. 16
A Beguiling Master of Food, Wine and Words *Frank J. Prial*. 19
Man of the Left Who Put Wines to Right *Frank J. Prial* 23
Pop Goes the Critic *Eric Asimov*. 26
Bronx Cheer of a Wine Guide *William Grimes*. 31

CHAPTER 3
The Jungle of Winespeak

Talk Dirt to Me *Harold McGee and Daniel Patterson*. 34
A Short Course in Wine Tactics *Frank J. Prial*. 40
Rolling Out Those Chewy Behemoths *Frank J. Prial* 43
Guessing Games *Frank J. Prial*. 46

CHAPTER 4
What You Drink With What You Eat

Big and Beautiful: Lafite for 12 *Eric Asimov* 50
A Rule Just Waiting to Be Broken *Eric Asimov* 54
Oysters With Miso Glaze *Florence Fabricant* 57
Three Meals Point the Way to Fish in Red Wine Sauce *Florence Fabricant* 58

How I Spent My Summer of Riesling, by Terroir *Frank Bruni* 60

Not So Cold . . . Doctor's Order *Eric Asimov* 63

Chill Out *Frank J. Prial* 66

A Sturdy Red for Winter *Eric Asimov* 68

12 Reasons to Look Beyond the Usual Wine Selections *Eric Asimov* 71

Wine Enough to Please Them All *R. W. Apple Jr.* 74

In a Season of Memory, a Toast to What Endures *Alex Witchel* 77

Pairing Wine With Chinese Food *Jen Lin-Liu* 80

Enlisting Radicchio's Bitterness to Balance the Fruitiness *Florence Fabricant* . . 83

A Rustic European Treat of Prunes Poached in Wine *Florence Fabricant* 85

A Piquant Appetizer That Brings Out the Best in a Wine *Florence Fabricant* . . 87

America's Love of Sherry Smolders *Eric Asimov* 89

Why Red Wine and Cheese Have Stopped Going Steady *Florence Fabricant* . . . 94

Serendipity in the Cellar *Frank J. Prial* 96

Excellent Box, Sir *Frank J. Prial* 99

Scratch an American, Find an Immigrant *Frank J. Prial* 102

Ancient Messages, Hidden in a Dusty Bottle From Long Ago *Eric Asimov* . . . 105

Memories Are Made of This *Terry Robards* 109

Wine Flavored by the Wind *Terry Robards* 112

A Wine Critic's Feast *Terry Robards* 115

The Tastes of Walla Walla, Secret No More *R. W. Apple Jr.* 119

CHAPTER 5

After the Meal, Treats That Are Sweet, Semisweet—and Powerful

From the Thinnest of Wines, the Richest Spirit: Cognac *R. W. Apple Jr.* 125

In a Glass, a Swashbuckler Called Armagnac *R. W. Apple Jr.* 131

Grappa, Fiery Friend of Peasants, Now Glows With a Quieter Flame
R. W. Apple Jr. 136

A Fine Roughness: On the Trail of a Spirit Called Marc *R. W. Apple Jr.* 141

Port Is a Welcome Guest at Cocktail Parties *Eric Asimov* 145

Vintage Madeira's Enduring Charms *Eric Asimov* 150

Hidden in Hungary, Treasures on the Vine *Evan Rail* 153

A Dessert Wine That's a Public Secret *Florence Fabricant* 160

Frozen Vines (and Fingers) Yield a Sweet Reward *Julia Lawlor* 163

CHAPTER 6
A Magnum of Miscellany

Natural Winemaking Stirs Debate *Eric Asimov* 168
New Wine in Really Old Bottles *Eric Asimov* 171
A Thinking Man's Wines *Eric Asimov* 176
The Truth About "Suitcase Clones" *Eric Asimov* 179
Lack of Sex Among Grapes Tangles a Family Vine *Nicholas Wade* 182
The Earliest Wine: Vintage 3500 B.C. and Robust *John Noble Wilford* 185
Cave Drops Hints to Earliest Glass of Red *Pam Belluck* 189
In Wine Country, Pruning Isn't Just Part of the Job *Jesse McKinley* 191
When Velvety Red Is Only Skin Deep *Eric Asimov* 195
A Zin Oasis in Mexico's Dusty Hills *Eric Asimov* 198
Illegal Sale of Rice Wine Thrives in Chinese Enclaves
    Kirk Semple and Jeffrey E. Singer 202
Japanese Wineries Betting on a Reviled Grape *Corie Brown* 205
Wines Have Feelings, Too *Eric Asimov* 209
Too Broad a Stroke for Labeling Wines *Eric Asimov* 212
The Rites of Vintage Assembly *Frank J. Prial* 215

CHAPTER 7
Made in the U.S. of A.

Pickers to Vintners: A Mexican-American Saga *Eric Asimov* 218
Gratification, but Not the Instant Kind *Eric Asimov* 222
A Cult Winemaker Tinkers With Success *Eric Asimov* 225
Garages for Chardonnays, Not Camrys *Patricia Leigh Brown* 229
Growing in Napa: Club, and Camp, for Wine Lovers *Patricia Leigh Brown* . . . 233
Too Sweet to Be Invited to Dinner *Eric Asimov* 237
Finessed and Light: California Pinot Noirs With a Manifesto *Eric Asimov* . . . 240
Letting a Grape Be a Grape *Eric Asimov* 246
Is There Still Hope for Syrah? *Eric Asimov* 250
The Hard Stuff Now Includes Wine *Eric Asimov* 255
The Day California Shook the World *Frank J. Prial* 259
A Dissenter's View of California Wine *Frank J. Prial* 262
An Actress's Presence Is Still Felt *Terry Robards* 265
A Farewell to the Baron of Bully Hill *Frank J. Prial* 268

CHAPTER 8
You're Feeling Continental? This Is For You.

In a World of Fine Wine, There'll Always Be a France *Eric Asimov* 272

The Paler Shade of Bordeaux *Eric Asimov* 276

The Soulful Side of Bordeaux *Eric Asimov* 279

The 1855 Ratings, Etched in Stone (Almost) *Frank J. Prial* 285

Bordeaux Family Values *Frank J. Prial* 288

Stealing From Thieves *Frank J. Prial* 292

Bordeaux Loses Prestige Among Younger Wine Lovers *Eric Asimov* 295

Burgundy Learns to Bottle Consistency *Eric Asimov* 299

An American Hears the Call of Burgundy *Eric Asimov* 304

For Chablis Fanatics, Ah, 2007 *Eric Asimov* 308

What's New in Beaujolais Is Not Nouveau *Eric Asimov* 311

A Potion From a Town Named for Love *Frank J. Prial* 316

Surprises From the Jura, Jagged in a Velvet-Smooth Universe *Eric Asimov* . . 318

The Rewards of the Pampered Grape *Eric Asimov* 322

Modern Love for Ancient Vines in Southern Italy *Eric Asimov* 326

A Rare Tasting of Conterno Barolos *Eric Asimov* 331

An Italian Prince and His Magic Cellar *Eric Asimov* 334

Some See a Wine Loved Not Wisely, but Too Well *Eric Asimov* 338

In Apulia, Emancipation for the Grapes *R. W. Apple Jr.* 343

In Spain, These Hills Are Alive (Again!) *Eric Asimov* 347

Rooted in Rioja, Traditions Gain New Respect *Eric Asimov* 352

Txakolina, a Tongue-Twisting Name for Simple Pleasure *Eric Asimov* 357

German Rieslings, Light and Dry *Eric Asimov* 361

Austrian Wines Have a Voice, and It's Excited *R. W. Apple Jr.* 364

An Honest Day's Work From Vienna *Eric Asimov* 369

Meanwhile, Back in Alsace *Frank J. Prial* 372

Hungarian Dry Wines? Forge Ahead *Eric Asimov* 375

CHAPTER 9
South of the Equator

New Heights for Andean Wine *R. W. Apple Jr.* 379

South African Goes From Never a Sip to Vineyard Fame *Barry Bearak* 384

A Winemaker, Transplanted *R. W. Apple Jr.* 387

Meals in the Bush, Now With Fine Wines *R. W. Apple Jr.* 392

An Australian Sibling Comes Into Its Own *Eric Asimov* 396

CHAPTER 10
The Night (and Day) They Invented Champagne (and Sparkling Wine)

Taking Champagne Back to Its Roots *Eric Asimov* 400
In Small Houses, Champagne Finds Its Soul *Eric Asimov* 403
Champagne's Servants Join the Masters *Eric Asimov* 409
Buried Treasure in Baltic Has Vintage Taste *John Tagliabue* 414
A Greener Champagne Bottle *Liz Alderman* 418
Spring Comes for a Prince of Champagne *Frank J. Prial* 422
They Make the Champagne of Champagnes *Frank J. Prial* 425
A Drink With Drama *Frank J. Prial* 428
Royal Wedding Wine May Be Bubbly and English *Eric Asimov* 431
In Albuquerque, French-Style Wines That Sparkle *Sarah Kershaw* 433
Produced in Champagne, but What Do You Call It? *John Tagliabue* 437
A Second Life in Champagne *Roger Cohen* 440

CHAPTER 11
Wherein Contrarianism Bursts Forth

Taking a Closer Look at Wine's Conventional Wisdom *Eric Asimov* 443
Berkeley's Wine Radical, 35 Years Later *Eric Asimov* 446
A Rosé Can Bloom in Winter, Too *Eric Asimov* 449
So Who Needs Vintage Charts? *Frank J. Prial* 452
Three Cheers for the Also-Rans *Eric Asimov* 455
Screw Tops Gain Acceptance Worldwide *Frank J. Prial* 458
A Musty Myth *Frank J. Prial* 461
A Sommelier's Little Secret: The Microwave *William Grimes* 463
For a Tastier Wine, the Next Trick Involves . . . *Harold McGee* 467

CHAPTER 12
They Don't Make 'Em Like That Anymore

His Big Idea Is to Get Small *Eric Asimov* 471
The Tastes of a Century *Frank J. Prial* 475
A Twilight Nightcap With Alistair Cooke *Frank J. Prial* 479
A Wine Man Who Vowed to Drain the Cup *Frank J. Prial* 481
Remembrances of a Champion of the Champagne World *Frank J. Prial* 484
The Greatest Vintages of Alfred Knopf, 90 *Terry Robards* 487

By Wine Besotted: A Fantasy Fulfilled *Eric Asimov* 491
A Wine Spree Worth Savoring *Frank J. Prial* 494
A Restaurateur Who Bought for Himself *Frank J. Prial* 497
Naked Came the Vintner *Warren St. John* 500
He Can Bring the Wine and the Music *Eric Asimov* 504
Alois Kracher, Austrian Winemaker and Advocate, Is Dead at 48 *Eric Asimov* . . 507
Nelson Shaulis, 86, Is Dead; Toiled to Improve Vineyards *Howard G. Goldberg* . 509
Joe Dressner, an Importer With No Use for Pretense, Dies at 60 *Eric Asimov* . . 511

CHAPTER 13

So, There You Are in a Restaurant

Postcard From Paris: We Drank! We Ate! *Frank J. Prial* 514
If the Wine Is Off . . . *Frank J. Prial* 517
Just Pour, He Said, and Put a Cork in It *Frank J. Prial* 519
Americans Prefer It by the Glass *Frank J. Prial* 522
On Tap? How About Chardonnay or Pinot Noir? *Eric Asimov* 525
Sometimes, Half a Bottle Is Better Than One *William Grimes* 528
Of Wine, Haste and Religion *Roger Cohen* 531
A Stroll Through the "21" List, Circa 1945 *Frank J. Prial* 533

CHAPTER 14

With Your Kids at the Table

Can Sips at Home Prevent Binges? *Eric Asimov* 537

CHAPTER 15

The Last Drops

The Driest Wines (and the Drollest) Are in the Museum *Howard G. Goldberg* . . 542
The Big Grape: Nouveau York City *Howard G. Goldberg* 546
Jefferson on Wine: "The Only Antidote to the Bane of Whisky"
  Howard G. Goldberg 549
The Spirit of Giving *Frank J. Prial* 553

Contributors' Biographies 555
Photography and Illustration Credits 559
Index 560

FOREWORD

Back in 1972, Abe Rosenthal, then the managing editor of *The New York Times*, assigned Frank J. Prial, a city reporter, to write a weekly column on wine. It would be the first regular coverage of wine in a general-interest American newspaper, though nobody was certain a desire for such reporting actually existed.

"We'll try it for a couple of months," Prial recalled Rosenthal saying.

A couple of months turned into 40 years and counting, and the scope of wine coverage has grown immensely. What started as a sideline for Prial, who crammed his wine writing into moments spared from his general assignment duties, evolved into a full-time job. He, along with other writers and correspondents, traveled the world, visiting wine regions ancient and new, reporting on personalities and politics, economics and conflict, issues, trends and, of course, the liquid in the bottle that was the source of it all.

The story of wine is as old as recorded history. Looking back to its ancient origins, 40 years may not seem like such a long time. Yet in those scant few decades Americans have achieved an entirely new and different understanding of wine. When Prial began writing his Wine Talk column, Americans bought what little wine they drank largely in jugs. Many of these jug wines were assigned names that connoted the Old World—Chablis, Chianti, Rhine Wine, Hearty Burgundy—because, after all, wine was thought to be European in nature. Indeed, many of California's historic vineyards had been planted by European immigrants who were not about to let thousands of miles stand between them and their daily beverage.

Back then, the California wine regions that today are among the most prestigious in the world were hardly known. Napa Valley had barely begun its ascent to glittering stardom. The Russian River Valley was apple country. Glossy magazines had not yet begun to exalt wine as an essential element of "the good life." Robert M. Parker Jr. had not yet introduced the 100-point scale that would give consumers an easy-to-understand tool for making buying decisions. The few scattered American wine connoisseurs of the time looked to Bordeaux as the epitome of fine wine, Burgundy to a lesser degree, and, of course, Champagne, which, if one knew nothing else about wine, one at least understood that Champagne was the beverage of celebrations.

Oh, how the world of wine has evolved since then. The United States is now the world's largest consumer of wine. While it cannot rightly be called a wine-drinking country—a surprisingly small percentage of the American population accounts for an inordinately large percentage of the wine consumed—the United States now has a thriving wine culture, several distinct ones, in fact.

These 40 years have seen not only a revolution in the American perception of wine, but sweeping changes the world over. For centuries the vast amount of wine produced in Europe was sold locally, to nearby villages and occasionally to a city up the river. Now, grape varieties that few people knew existed 40 years ago—savagnin, nerello mascalese, mencía, grüner veltliner—are sold globally, and in good wine shops the nation over.

Thirst for the benchmark wines, like first-growth Bordeaux and grand cru Burgundy, has risen exponentially, as, of course, have prices. No longer will a generation of wine lovers, like Prial's, be able to hone their understanding on fine old Bordeaux and well-aged Burgundy, not when these older bottles are auctioned off for thousands of dollars apiece and the Chinese are paying equivalent amounts for the most recent vintages.

Yet wine lovers coming of age in the 21st century have a wealth of choices that were undreamed of 40 years ago. American stores are jammed with great alternatives to the benchmark wines from all over Italy and Spain, France and Germany. Portugal is coming on strong, as are Austria and Greece. Eastern Europe is playing catch-up, but the fall of the Iron Curtain has allowed ancient wine cultures in Hungary and Georgia, Slovenia and Croatia, to begin the long process of rejuvenation.

What of the United States and other New World wine regions? Napa Valley led the American charge away from jug wines, culminating in the cult cabernets, expensive status bottles that were a world away from the jugs but had less to do with the joy of wine drinking than the jugs did. Still, great wine now comes from California and Oregon, Washington and New York State, with high hopes for areas in between, like Michigan and New Mexico. Australia and New Zealand have changed the way the world buys wine, while Argentina and Chile have become important sources of good, inexpensive wine, and can produce far better. South Africa and Uruguay have leapt into the global wine business. Can China, India and Brazil be far behind?

The articles in this anthology tell the story of this revolution in wine, sometimes in close-ups, and other times in sweeping panoramas. The storytelling has evolved as well. Earlier on, readers required plenty of introductory information, spoon-fed in digestible doses. Now, Americans are far more knowledgeable about wine, even as many people remain far from comfortable with it.

Wine is now a significant component of American culture, to be evaluated, analyzed and parsed just as with other cultural expressions, whether restaurants, architecture, pop music or films. What was once an additional beat for Frank Prial to try for a couple of months is now a field firmly established at The New York Times, 40 years and counting, with its own full-fledged critic. This anthology chronicles wine's coming of age in the United States, from an American point of view. We've been through childhood innocence and adolescent hiccups, and if we have not yet reached confident adulthood, we seem to be heading there.

Eric Asimov
Chief Wine Critic, The New York Times

INTRODUCTION

Think of this anthology of *New York Times* wine articles as a feast of tapas and sherries: small, savory bites and short sips. Check the table of contents as if it were a chalkboard list of specials. Start where you wish; jump around; cater to your mind's momentary appetite, its whimsy. Two or three "plates" washed down by a few "ounces" can satisfyingly fill a half-hour breather; return for a bedtime "snack."

A sampler, by definition, cannot be comprehensive. Rather, you have in hand a representative collection of some of the most rewarding wine topics and articles echoing the circumstances and interests of their periods that *Times* writers (and others) have addressed, mainly in the Living section and its successor, the Dining section. Some have been published in the Sunday Magazine. Longtime readers of *The Times*'s wine and food columns and wine-news reports may recognize bylines that, dating from the early 1980s, sweep across three decades.

Most of the articles have appeared under separate rubrics: Wine Talk, by Frank J. Prial (and Terry Robards and myself), and The Pour, written by Eric Asimov. (Drawing weightily on Wines of the Times, a title under which Asimov's tasting panel makes recommendations, would be impractical because the vintaged bottles and prices cited have limited shelf lives.)

A dyed-in-the-Tricolor Francophile, the street-smart Prial, a genial and benign observer of the Human Comedy, has zero tolerance for pretentiousness, and punctures it without inflicting pain. His nonpareil storytelling is redolent of collegial schmoozing in yesterday's smoke-drenched City Room.

I have always admired Prial's down-to-earth manner and writing, and consider "A Twilight Nightcap With Alistair Cooke" (2004), a highlight of this collection, one of the most heartfelt wine articles I have read by anyone, anywhere, anytime.

When Prial's Wine Talk column carried the headline "So Who Needs Vintage Charts" (2000) wine lovers might have read it as an obituary, in an era of proliferating appellations and terroir-oriented winegrowing.

"Over the years," he wrote, "I have produced vintage chart after chart, always adding enough qualifications and caveats to make the reader wonder why I bothered in the first place." He continued: "In the final frames of *Little Caesar*, Edward G. Robinson snarls, 'Is this the end of Rico?' To my way of thinking, that sacred talisman of the wine buff, the vintage chart, is just as dead as Rico was when the screen went to black."

Eric Asimov, who holds the title chief wine critic, approaches wine as a staple of the dining table and a cultural object. His work forms the leading edge of this volume. He is an informal, scrupulously observant, politely skeptical, exceptionally pro-consumer commentator whose conversational prose conveys a strong aversion to geekiness. His basic tasting vocabulary is an antidote to the over-the-top tasting notes that spring up like Everglades grasses around the quicksands of winedom.

One of my favorite Asimov articles is "Pickers to Vintners: A Mexican-American Saga." In 2004 he told readers: "Over the past few years the first fine wines made by former migrant workers, the children of those workers and other Mexican-Americans have been released, winning good reviews. All told, there are more than a dozen such labels. Fifteen years ago there were none. Mexican-Americans have also become managers or winemakers for important vineyards."

Gastronomic orthodoxy was jolted in 2008 in "A Rule Just Waiting to Be Broken." As Asimov wrote: "I know oysters and red wine sounds bizarre, but 20 years ago white wine with cheese sounded strange. Now, white wine is accepted as a delicious companion for many cheeses."

Not every wine that Asimov and his predecessors have addressed has been readily findable. Still, learning about them is valuable. Take, as he put it, "idiosyncratic" Jacques Selosse Champagnes, made by Anselme Selosse, Jacques's son.

"Anselme Selosse, 54, is not the usual emissary from Champagne, a smooth guy in a suit, talking about product positioning, luxury brands and lifestyles," Asimov said in "Taking Champagne Back to Its Roots" (2008). "To hear them tell it, Champagne pops into this world like a genie from a lamp, ready to make magic."

"But to Mr. Selosse, the magic occurs long before there is a wine. It takes place deep underneath Champagne's chalky soil, where the roots of the vines take hold of what Mr. Selosse calls the essence of the earth."

In 2005 Asimov focused on "New Wine in Really Old Bottles." His absorbing subject was Josko Gravner, an Italian producer. "Rejecting the modern trappings of the cellar, Mr. Gravner has reached back 5,000 years," he wrote. "He now ferments his wines in huge terra-cotta amphorae that he lines with beeswax and buries in the earth up to their great, gaping lips. Ancient Greeks and Romans would be right at home with him. . . ."

In her column called Pairings, Florence Fabricant, a thorough, straightforward, bedrock, no-frills writer, is a fount of sophisticated food and wine combos. Hers are the plates that have launched a thousand sips.

Fabricant brought "A Dessert Wine That's a Public Secret"—Monbazillac—to readers' attention (2003). Less expensive than Sauternes, which also comes from southwestern France, "Monbazillac delivers exotic touches of honeyed mango, quince, passion fruit and citrus, often with a distinctive nuttiness in the aftertaste," she wrote.

In 2007 she presented "A Rustic European Treat of Prunes Poached in Wine," a dessert "rarely offered in the United States. Except at my house." The introduction to her recipe says she prefers "everyday merlot or Chianti" but that Navarre reds recently tasted "suggested they could easily suit this purpose, too," and in the recipe she recommended Navarre.

The cosmopolitan, larger-than-life R. W. Apple Jr.,—Johnny to one and all—ate, drank and wrote on a prodigious scale that even *The New Yorker* magazine's legendary A. J. Liebling, a gourmand for all seasons, might have envied. This hunger gave birth to a thirst for illuminating such digestifs as Cognac, Armagnac, grappa and marc.

While at *The Times* Terry Robards, ruddy and wearing a mustache, resembled an Edwardian Englishman who relished his London club and its cellar groaning with rare claret. He had a gift for being invited to memorable dinners and capturing them and their principals, as, in 1983, "The Greatest Vintages of Alfred Knopf, 90."

Robards wrote of his host: "Rarely acknowledged in all the accolades he has won over the years is that he was the dominant influence in gastronomic publishing in this country.

"He had the temerity to publish P. Morton Shand's classic *Book of French Wines* in 1928, during Prohibition, and to come out with Julian Street's *Wines* in 1933, the year Prohibition ended, when the public's interest in wines was sharply curtailed by the Depression. . . .

"The roster of food and wine authors published by Alfred A. Knopf, Inc. includes James Beard, Julia Child, M.F.K. Fisher, Marcella Hazan, Maida Heatter, Alexis Lichine and Michael Broadbent."

In "Memories Are Made of This" (1982), Robards describes a seven-hour dinner in a mansion on the North Shore of Long Island—"a gastronomic event of gargantuan proportions that might have stirred envy if not outrage even in Rabelais himself.

"Nearly all of the wines for this occasion have been hand-carried, bottle by bottle over a period of months, from the private cellars of the Cartier jewelry concern beneath the cobblestones of the Place Vendôme in Paris," he recounted.

"Louis Cartier, the firm's founder, established one of the finest wine collections in France."

One of my contributions to this collection was a 1987 "interview" titled "Jefferson on Wine: 'The Only Antidote to the Bane of Whisky.'" Tom invited me, so to speak, to lunch at his pied-à-terre at Monticello, to explore our shared interest in Bordeaux.

I left thinking that Jefferson's place in history was unquestionably nailed down, first and foremost, by having been a wine adviser to our first five presidents, himself included.

Howard G. Goldberg

CHAPTER ONE

For Openers . . .

The $410 Corkscrew

By ERIC ASIMOV

They come in all shapes and sizes. Most often, they can be found stuffed into kitchen drawers alongside potato mashers, melon ballers and other seldom-used essentials of the kitchen. Wine lovers take them for granted, except when nobody can find one. Call a Boy Scout! He's sure to be prepared with a handy multifunction pocket knife that includes one.

I'm talking, of course, about corkscrews, which, regardless of the screw cap, remain indispensable for achieving access to the wine within. But would you pay $410 for one?

Oh, please, why even ask? In an era when people pay hundreds of dollars for a bottle of mediocre Champagne, not to mention thousands for a bottle at auction, who would begrudge the Code-38 wine knife from Australia its retail price of $220 to $410? No, it's not made of gold.

The fact is most people pay corkscrews little mind. They're perfectly content with the gimme corkscrew from the local wine shop; or the cheap double-winged corkscrew, in which you squeeze the arms together to extract the cork; or even the Swiss army knife. Ambitious types can find battery-operated corkscrews or tapered yet cumbersome models the size of restaurant pepper mills, which operate not on the principle of twisting the worm into the cork, but with a press and a pull.

In restaurants the world over, sommeliers, those exacting, extracting professionals, rely overwhelmingly on a simple, handy device known as the waiter's friend or, sometimes, as the wine key. Essentially a knifelike handle with a spiral worm for inserting into the cork and a hinged fulcrum for resistance, the waiter's friend has largely stood the test of time, with modest tweaks and improvements, since it was patented in Germany in 1882. Basic versions go for less than $10.

No product, though, no matter how successful, is immune to the fertile imagination of industrial designers. Enter the Code-38, in which the waiter's friend is re-engineered, using the highest principles of design and top-flight materials. What does that get you?

Well, when I pick up my standby home corkscrew, a Pulltap's double-hinged waiter's friend, I'm not wowed by the black plastic handle, flimsy metal fulcrum and serrated foil cutter. It works fine, but I confess I don't feel much of anything about it. When it breaks, I have others lined up ready to go.

The Code-38, by contrast, offers the satisfying, solid heft of a fine tool. It feels good in the hand, like a well-balanced kitchen knife, and it inspires a sort of confidence that I had been unaware of lacking. The basic $220 model, which I bought and tested for several weeks, is made of solid stainless steel, with a thick, strong worm. The foil blade is a curved steel arc that can be opened with one hand and resharpened on a stone.

The fulcrum is smooth and shiny. It's a single-hinge design rather than the double-hinge I have on my Pulltap's. The double-hinge is intended as a safety net for amateurs like me, who can't always get the corkscrew in the right spot for a smooth, continuous extraction. Instead, the double-hinge allows you to pull a cork partway out, and then reset the fulcrum to complete the maneuver.

The Code-38's single-hinge, though, is so precisely engineered that I have yet to meet the cork I could not extract effortlessly, while (in my would-be sommelier's imagination) bantering wittily with the table in front of me and simultaneously surveying the rest of the dining room for trouble.

That's the basic $220 model. For $410, you can have the Code-38 Pro Stealth, the flagship model, "a complete blend of blasted textures and vaporized titanium-based finishes," as the Web catalog puts it.

Ah, well, a fellow can dream. Of course, it's fine for me, a writer with a (limited) expense account, to sing the praises of the Code-38. What would a professional say?

I lent mine to Michael Madrigale, the sommelier at Bar Boulud, a wine-oriented bistro near Lincoln Center. He liked it well enough, especially the way it felt in the hand, but paused when I told him what it cost.

"What, $220?" he said. "It's like the $200 hamburger. It's like reinventing something that's already perfect."

He added that he was quite happy with his waiter's friend, a French model, the Cartailler-Deluc, which sells for under $30. Like me, he also has backups on hand.

Not all professionals were as unappreciative. Chaad Thomas, a partner in

U.S. Wine Imports and a former sommelier in Ann Arbor, Mich., read about the Code-38 on an Internet chat board and was so intrigued that he wrote to the designer, Jeffrey Toering, who sent him one to try.

"It's a gorgeous piece," he told me. "It was superb to be able to extend the knife with just one hand. You could use it really quickly, and it's very durable. As a sommelier, I would actually wear wine keys out."

He said he plans to buy 10 or so to offer to top clients.

It's not that the world of cork extractors has lacked high-end devices, or even expensive waiter's friends. Laguiole, a French cutlery brand, has been renowned for its corkscrews for more than a century. Its waiter's friends are lovely designs in an older, more ornate style than the minimalist Code-38. Laguiole also fills custom orders. Aldo Sohm, the sommelier at Le Bernardin in New York, designed a personalized Laguiole with an Austrian flag design, which also sells for $220. It's an elegant corkscrew, and works beautifully, though it differs from the Code-38 in materials and in its serrated knife, which is more difficult to extend with one hand.

What drives a man to try to create the perfect corkscrew? Mr. Toering, the designer, was not in the wine business. He had learned about design as an instrument fitter in the Australian Air Force, which he likened to being a watchmaker, and he previously designed a portable massage table. The idea for the Code-38 came to him in a restaurant in the 1990s.

"I had ordered a nice bottle of something and was observing the waiter's removal of the cork," he said in an e-mail from Australia. "He was using a cheap plastic wine key. It was in this moment that it occurred to me that the caliber of corkscrew did not match the level of the wine or the restaurant."

So began an odyssey of trial and error, of testing designs and materials, and comparing sources. He inspected worms from around the world before settling on one made in France. Along the way he became the Australian distributor for Laguiole, but he had concerns about its durability in the heavy-duty use of the restaurant world.

"I have designed the product to withstand continual use over many years," he said. "I've been testing prototypes of the product for over five years and many thousands of bottles, and all I've seen is the odd bent spiral, which is more a matter of technique than the product's ability to survive the professional hospitality environment." He says the Code-38 is "fully rebuildable" and covered by a lifetime warranty.

Mr. Toering assembles each one individually in his workshop. So far, he says, he has sold 137 Code-38s, each one to a sommelier (and apparently one wine writer). It's not a lot, but he says the response has been great.

"I think the Laguiole and similar products from that region are brilliant, and I'd like to think that the Code-38 can sit among them as an equal," he said. "In our world of cheap throwaway products, it's just nice to use something that has been designed and made without consideration for just meeting a price point."

April 2011

CHAPTER TWO

Wine Writing and Writers

Words, Words, Words

By FRANK J. PRIAL

Every so often, it is meet and proper to once again examine a peculiar subgenre of the English language—and of the American language as well—that has flowered wildly in recent years, like some pulpy jungle plant. It's called winespeak.

Winespeak is a branch (tendril?) of the mother tongue that seeks to render the sensory experiences triggered by wine into comprehensible words. You know—explain what it tastes like. Winespeak leans heavily on metaphor. Or is it analogy? Or both? Whatever.

A wine esthete pokes his sensitive beak into a glass of Champagne. Then, head thrown back, eyes closed and visage wreathed in an otherworldly smile, he incants: "I see—I see—yes, I see a young girl in white, barefooted, running across a vast green lawn, long hair flowing." That's metaphor. Another initiate sniffs a white wine of questionable provenance. "Broccoli," he says, and tosses it out. That's analogy.

Winespeak—modern winespeak—can be traced to the Gothic piles of Oxbridge, where, in the 19th century, certain dons, addled by claret, bested one another in tributes to the grape. There is, of course, a much older winespeak. Here from the Prophets is Joel 1:5, commenting, one suspects, either on an early-closing law or on a shortage of the nouveau Beaujolais of his time, when he cries, "Awake, ye drunkards, and weep; and howl, all ye drinkers of wine, because of the new wine; for it is cut off from your mouth." Maybe it's better in Aramaic.

The Oxbridge worthies, steeped in Homer and Tacitus, as well as Madeira, leaned on antiquity for their prose. It would be unfair to say that Bacchus and Dionysus were the Bartles and Jaymes of Magdalen and Christ Church in Victorian days, but I think you get my drift. Wines were forever reaching Parnassian, if not Olympian, heights, and a third-rate Médoc could transport even a red-brick lecturer in Greek to the Elysian Fields.

We Americans, not entirely convinced that anything happened before 1930, have little of either history or tradition on which to draw to describe a wine. There is, of course, an argument to be made that it's inappropriate to summon up some lecherous Roman deity to illustrate a wine made by a 20-year-old Californian in a place where lately lettuce grew.

So we're not erudite. We're inventive, which is just as good. When a situation cries out for purple prose, we are not found wanting. Well, not usually. My friend Roger Yaseen, who is in investment banking but knows a bizarre turn of phrase when he sees it, offers the wine list from a restaurant called—sorry—Anotherthyme, in Durham, N.C. It's an O.K. list; someone there knows wine. But, oh, the descriptions.

A 1979 Pol Roger is $35, and at Anotherthyme this is what you're going to get for your money: "Frail lilies blessed with the permanence of granite. Fabulous, timeless vintage Champagne." "Timeless vintage" is probably an oxymoron, but, after the lilies and the granite, oxymorons just don't seem to matter.

The next Champagne, Dom Ruinart, has "exceptionally bright flavors and a stimulating spritz," and drinking it, we are told, is "like pouring diamonds into a tulip."

Krug's Grande Cuvée has "mysticism, erudition and taste," but what are they compared to Schramsberg's 1981 Blanc de Noirs, a "glorious flesh-colored fluid."

When it comes to simple white wines at Anotherthyme, I couldn't decide between Château Guiraud's Château "G," "like cool wet sand under pearly seaside light," or a Montagny Les Coeres from "the scrubby hillsides south of Beaune . . . whose lithe powerful body is insulated by soft tender curves."

Tender curves are hard to pass up, but how could I ignore the Piesporter Hoffburger spätlese with its "Smirking beauty of fruit without pride." No, really; that's what it says.

A Fleurie, which is, after all, just a high-class Beaujolais, has "a texture like the sinful strokes of a feather boa," and Chiroubles, another Beaujolais, at Anotherthyme is "Flashy Chiroubles, adored by cafe society Parisians, with Beaujolais' renowned soft juiciness and a provocative nip."

There is a white Graves, La Louvière, "whose sound architecture aptly frames its core of minerals which seems to have been mined from the bowels of the earth," and there is a Gevrey-Chambertin that is "fathoms deep and as pleasingly prickly as a kitten's tongue."

There is a Firestone cabernet "juicy and ripe with a flexible spine," a Franciscan merlot of "smooth soft body with ample underlying muscle," and a Kalin pinot noir with "a woolly welcoming feel." Along the way, one gets the feeling that Ben Jonson or John Marston, or even Gerard Manley Hopkins, 250 years later, would have loved this crazy imagery. After all, wasn't it just a few years ago that some California fellow, actually a screenwriter seeking an honest dollar, became immortal describing some clunky big zinfandel as "a roller derby in the mouth?"

When it comes to adjectives, I prefer something a little drier myself. Still, I'd love to eat sometime at Anotherthyme. I wouldn't be at all surprised to find Alice, the Mad Hatter and the Rabbit at the next table. And not drinking tea.

March 1987

Wine in Two Words

By ERIC ASIMOV

I'm not one to go overboard in describing the myriad aromas and flavors in a glass of wine. In fact, most of the gaudy descriptions found in tasting notes will not help a whit to understand the character of a bottle of wine or to anticipate the experience of drinking it.

While it may seem heretical to say, the more specific the description of a wine, the less useful information is actually transmitted. See for yourself. All you have to do is compare two reviewers' notes for a single bottle: one critic's ripe raspberry, white pepper and huckleberry is another's sweet-and-sour cherries and spice box. What's the solution? Well, if you feel the urgent need to know precisely what a wine is going to taste like before you sniff and swallow, forget it. Experience will give you a general idea, but fixating on exactitude is a fool's errand. Two bottles of the same wine can taste different depending on when, where and with whom you open them.

Besides, the aromas and flavors of good wines can evolve over the course of 20 minutes in a glass. Perhaps they can be captured momentarily like fireflies in a child's hands, yet reach for them again a minute later and—whiff!—they're somewhere else.

But the general character of a wine: now, that's another matter. A brief depiction of the salient overall features of a wine, like its weight, texture and the broad nature of its aromas and flavors, can be far more helpful in determining whether you will like that bottle than a thousand points of detail. In fact, consumers could be helped immeasurably if the entire lexicon of wine descriptors were boiled down to two words: sweet or savory.

These two simple words suggest the basic divide of all wines, the two grand categories that explain more about the essence of any bottle than the most florid, detailed analogies ever could. Just as important, thinking of wine in this more streamlined fashion is an efficient method for clarifying your own preferences.

First, though, let's define our terms, beginning with sweet, one of the more alarming words to American wine drinkers. Alarming? Naturally. For years, the cliché in the wine trade has been, "Americans talk dry but drink sweet." Some of the most popular American wines, like Kendall-Jackson Vintner Select chardonnay, are made with unannounced residual sugar in them.

But when I use the word "sweet," I'm thinking not only of actual sugar in the wine, but also (more often) of the impression of sweetness. This impression can be provided by dominant fruit flavors and high concentrations of glycerol, a product of fermentation that is heavy, oily and slightly sweet.

Zinfandel, for example, is usually dry, but I would categorize it as sweet because of its intense fruitiness. I would also include plush, opulent California pinot noirs, many Châteauneuf-du-Papes from the ripe 2007 vintage, Côtes du Rhône from the 2009 vintage, Amarones and a number of Spanish reds.

Among whites I would classify as sweet are California chardonnays from the tutti-frutti school, with their tropical flavors and buttery notes, although the term does not fit leaner, more structured examples. Voluptuous viogniers, wherever they come from, typify sweet. Gewürztraminer and pinot gris, especially in their unctuous Alsatian modes, qualify, as do the more flowery torrontés from Argentina.

Savory wines, as you would imagine, are the ones that don't leave the impression of sweetness. In fact, they may not taste like fruits at all, with the exception of citrus and possibly apple flavors, which are more acidic than sweet.

Fino sherries, especially manzanillas, are saline rather than sweet, for example. Good Muscadet and Sancerre? Chablis and other white Burgundies? They may offer suggestions of fruit flavors but they are far more likely to convey herbal or smoky flavors along with the stony, chalky, slate and flint qualities that come under the vague, all-encompassing term "mineral."

Mineral flavors often go hand in hand with lively acidity. Indeed, many of the wines in the savory category also have a freshness that comes with acidity. Good examples of Soave and dry rieslings would also fit in.

Can reds be savory? Of course. In the world of tasting notes, good syrah wines from the northern Rhône Valley are often said to have aromas and flavors of herbs, olives and bacon fat—prime savory material. Yet if you pick the grapes riper and lavish the wine with oak, northern Rhône wines can become sweet. Australian shiraz and California syrahs are more in the sweet category, although some producers in both places make excellent savory examples. Young Riojas are more sweet than savory, but as they get older—especially old-school gran reservas—they turn smoky, spicy and almost leathery, savory for sure.

Naturally, generalizing like this is dangerous. Many categories of wine are too hard to consign to either sweet or savory, and anybody can offer exceptions and counterexamples. Often you have to go bottle by bottle and producer by producer to figure out where a wine fits. Commercial Beaujolais, for example, is often produced to amplify the fruitiness of the gamay grape, and so would be classified as sweet. But serious, small-production Beaujolais often shows more acidity and mineral flavors. The inherent fruitiness is there, but a fine Morgon or Moulin-à-Vent? Arguably savory, but again, it depends on the producer.

Red Burgundy can also go both ways, especially when young. Good examples charm and seduce with their gorgeous, sweet perfumes, but the sweetness is often leavened with earthy mineral qualities. As good red Burgundies age, their savory side becomes more pronounced. Indeed, aging does bring out the savory elements in many wines.

How about Bordeaux? Classic Pauillac is renowned for flavors often described as currant, graphite and cigar box. To me, they are savory. Wines from the Right Bank, with their higher percentage of merlot, are harder to classify. They may have more fruit aromas, but they, too, often have an underlying mineral quality along with a purity of fruit.

Of course, a producer's intent can completely change the character of a wine. The riper the grapes, the sweeter the juice, and the more likely the wine will end up on the sweet side, whether from Pauillac, St.-Émilion or anywhere else. Many sought-after Napa cabernets like Bryant Family are sweet, even as great counterexamples like Dominus and Mayacamas have pronounced savory elements.

Finally, let's turn to German rieslings. Bottles with residual sugar would obviously seem to be sweet. Indeed, it would be perverse to classify sweet German rieslings as savory. Yet, I have to admit I'm tempted, especially by good Mosels, which, with their energy, taut acidic structure and penetrating minerality, can come across as exactly that.

But perhaps that's going too far. I'll leave it to you to decide. The point of this exercise, after all, is not so much to label every wine as one or the other, as it is to suggest a different, simpler way of thinking about these wines. And, perhaps, to help people make their own discoveries.

For example, if you like Australian shiraz, you might assume you would also like northern Rhône reds, as they're made from the same grape. But the sweet-and-savory method would suggest a greater affinity for ripe Châteauneuf-du-Papes—made from a blend of grapes rather than straight syrah, but bold and full of fruit like shirazes.

Or say you were partial to savory wines, and were faced with a selection of Brunello di Montalcinos, which can fall into both categories. Knowing your own preference would help you rule out those with amplified oak or sweet fruit in favor of those higher-acid, bitter cherry and spice flavors.

Of course, this scheme may not have an immediate practical application until more of us speak the same language. Only the rare wine shop or sommelier might respond to a request for a savory wine, and you might not want to ask anybody for a sweet wine, unless you are certain they know what you mean.

Some might object that I am dumbing down wine, but the reverse is true. Simplicity, as designers, cosmologists and philosophers know, is a virtue. As the writer Antoine de Saint-Exupéry once put it, "Perfection is reached not when there is nothing left to add, but when there is nothing left to take away."

It's One or the Other

All wines may be separated into two broad categories, sweet and savory, depending on the grapes, where they were grown and the intent and techniques of the producer. While there are many exceptions, and each wine should be evaluated individually, it's possible to generalize by genre:

Sweet: Zinfandel, grenache, Amarone, commercial Beaujolais, California pinot noir, viognier, modern Barolo, Napa cabernet

Savory: Fino sherry, Muscadet, serious Beaujolais, white Burgundy, dry riesling, Rhône reds, old-school Barolo, extra brut Champagne

February 2011

Affairs to Remember

By FRANK J. PRIAL

Wine drinking goes back at least 6,000 years. Wine writing probably began a year or two later.

The Sumerians wrote about wine; so did the Babylonians and the Egyptians. Then came Homer and his wine-dark sea. In our own epoch, the monks kept vineyard and vintage records at Cluny and the Clos de Vougeot, Pepys praised the "Ho-Bryan" he drank at the Pontac Head in London, and Jefferson, in Paris, reported on his trips to Bordeaux and Burgundy. But bookkeeping, diary entries and an ambassador's reports are one thing. Celebrating wine as a cultural phenomenon is something else. The British seem to have invented it, along with port and sherry. Wine journalism is an even younger enterprise.

Which brings us to G. Selmer Fougner.

Never heard of him? Well, he was a journalist, and fame in that line of work is, as they say, fleeting. G. Selmer Fougner was probably New York's first newspaper wine writer. From the end of Prohibition in 1933 until his death in 1941 he wrote a daily—yes, daily—wine column in *The New York Sun*. The column, called Along the Wine Trail, regularly ran to 3,000 words and was often longer. Fougner rarely confined himself to wine; he gossiped about New York restaurants, described special dinners in loving detail, provided long and complicated recipes and answered readers' questions. He once estimated that he had replied to more than 300,000 mail queries during the eight years that he wrote the column.

After his death from a heart attack in April 1941, at the age of 56, *The New York Times* said in an obituary: "No research was too obscure in answering any question from readers interested in the history or validity of any fine point of eating or drinking."

Fougner presented the classic image of a connoisseur of the good life. Portly, balding and always impeccably dressed, he was known as "The Baron" among friends and in the larger world of food and wine that was his daily beat. During the years that he wrote Along the Wine Trail, he founded or co-founded no less than 14 wine and food societies, most notably Les Amis d'Escoffier, named after the French chef Auguste Escoffier. He made it a point to preside at the society dinners that were the only reason the clubs existed.

He often said that *The Sun* started the column to instruct the public in the finer points of eating, and especially drinking, that had been lost during the years of Prohibition. He went further, judging culinary contests and advising on the training of waiters and bartenders. At the time of Repeal, he described New York as a gustatory wasteland, but in December 1940, four months before he died, he noted proudly that he needed an entire column just to list what he considered "the greatest gastronomic events of the year."

A typical Fougner column, that of Feb. 21, 1940, begins, like many journalistic endeavors, with a lament about how hard the work is: "In one of the most strenuous weeks on record, so far as wining and dining activities are concerned, three dinners had to be cancelled owing to overcrowding of the Trail calendar."

The most regrettable omission, he goes on to say, was a golden wedding celebration for an old friend at the Hotel Kentucky in Louisville. The dinners that prevented the Baron from dashing off to Louisville included "an extraordinarily brilliant" one at the Lotos Club that featured pressed duck and Château Latour 1923, a "rousing sendoff" aboard the Cuba Mail S.S. *Oriente* for a member of the Society of Restaurateurs, a wine-tasting lunch featuring Napa Valley wines made by the Christian Brothers, a Champagne tasting with the managing director of the St. Regis and a "great dinner staged by French Veterans of the World War" at the Hotel Pennsylvania for which he published the entire menu. (They drank a 1934 Sylvaner with the sole Marguery and Château Margaux 1928 with the poussin Pennsylvania.)

The rest of the column is an exchange with a reader from Larchmont, N.Y., who writes: "I have perfected a variation of your 'Lord Botetourt Punch,'" offering it in exchange for "a set of directions for the making of Sherry-wine jelly." Fougner supplies the reader's version of the punch, which involves red wine, brandy, seltzer and fruit, then goes on to give the instructions for making the jelly.

In spite of his impressive food and wine credentials, Fougner listed himself in *Who's Who* as a newspaperman. He was born in Chicago and came to New York to take a job as a reporter for *The New York Herald* in 1906. He later worked for *The New York Press* and joined *The Sun* in 1912. Shortly thereafter, *The Sun* sent him to London as chief correspondent and European manager. He covered World War I until 1917, when he returned to New York, joined the United States Treasury Department and handled publicity for Liberty Loans. He rejoined *The Sun* in 1920, left to do public relations and freelance writing, then went back to newspapering once again in 1931.

Accepted wisdom attributes America's current interest in food and wine to tastes our troops acquired overseas in World War II, to easier travel and more leisure time in the postwar years and to the emergence of a new middle class with money to spend on luxuries. But the Fougner columns indicate that wine affairs, gourmet societies and a taste for the good life were part of the New York scene in the depths of the Depression.

February 1992

A Reporter's Reporter

By FRANK J. PRIAL

Pierre-Marie Doutrelant died earlier this year while jogging in the Bois de Boulogne, in Paris. He was 46 years old, left a wife and a couple of kids, and may have been the best wine journalist of our time.

Most of what you read on the subject is the work of wine writers. There are some good ones, but they are, for the most part, committed. One expects them to tell us nice things, and they rarely disappoint. Philosophically, wine writers are much alike; they vary only in degrees of felicitousness.

The reporter's job is different, or should be. The reporter's tools are an eye for detail and a supply of skepticism. He might love wine—no harm in that—but he should love a good story more. Here is Doutrelant quoting a Beaujolais public relations man: "'We don't bribe the papers, but we do have good journalist friends who never miss an opportunity to come see us when they're in the neighborhood.'"

Or a government inspector on the illegal use of sugar to boost the alcoholic content of Beaujolais Villages: "'If the law had been enforced in 1973 and 1974, at least a thousand producers would have been put out of business.'"

These unchauvinistic remarks were published in 1975, a time when hard reporting on wine was almost nonexistent in France. Food and wine scribes in La Belle France routinely cross the line, working as much for the industry as they do for the press. This kind of talk was sacrilegious.

Fifteen years ago, Doutrelant disclosed that many famous Champagne houses, when short of stock, bought bottled but unlabeled wine from cooperatives or one of the big private-label producers in the region, then sold it as their own. He explained how the growers of Côtes du Rhône planted mourvèdre and syrah, two low-yield grapes that give the wine finesse, strictly for the benefit of government inspectors. Then, when the inspectors left, they grafted cheap, high-yield vines—grenache and carignan—back onto the vines.

Pierre-Marie Doutrelant came from Hazebrouck, in the north, near Lille. He worked on a paper in Angers, then moved to Paris and *Le Monde*, where for eight years he covered politics, urban affairs and, now and then, wine. Some of his wine articles, including those mentioned above, appeared in his first book, *Les Bons Vins et Les Autres* (*The Good Wines and the Others*). His article in the book on

Chablis is subtitled: "Or how the public authorities decided that the best way to combat fraud was to make its practice legal."

He did politics for the weekly *Le Nouvel Observateur*, then moved to the weekly *l'Express*, where he took over the section called Portraits, a series of profiles he wrote on people in the news. According to another Paris journalist, Doutrelant was slated shortly to take over *l'Express Paris*, a sort of grown-up *New York Magazine* for the City of Light.

While he covered economics, politics, lifestyles and everything else from week to week, his not-so-secret passion was food and wine. His acerbic comments on the pompous three-star chefs appeared regularly in *Cuisine & Vins de France* and were compiled in his second book, *La Bonne Cuisine et les Autres*. Among the immortals he skewered like a brochette d'agneau was the great Paul Bocuse himself.

French reporters tell the story of Bocuse about to meet a journalist of whom he had never heard.

"Is he," asked the master, nervously, "du genre Doutrelant?"—a Doutrelant type?

One of Doutrelant's best pieces is a profile of the publicity-hungry Bernard Loiseau, a two-star chef and restaurateur at La Côte d'Or in Saulieu, on the northern edge of Burgundy. Not a few observers of the cutthroat world of big-time French cooking credit—or blame—the Doutrelant profile for delaying Mr. Loiseau's third Michelin star.

Mr. Loiseau, the spiritual heir of the great Alexandre Dumaine, who ran La Côte d'Or before World War II (and taught Bocuse), has come up with something he calls "la cuisine du vapeur"—steam cooking. The result, according to Pierre-Marie Doutrelant, is sauces that look and taste like water. He suggested that the money Mr. Loiseau invested in a heliport to lure fat Parisian cats—and impress the Michelin inspectors—might better have been spent on more substantial food.

Doutrelant was of the school of French reporters who came up in the 1960s, who were on the barricades in 1968, emotionally if not literally. They saw through the ossified political establishment the students hoped to bring down and the hypocrisy of the students themselves, who rioted on weekends and after exams. I don't think I ever saw him wear a tie or, for that matter, a suit, even when, briefly, he wandered through the halls of this newspaper en route to the vineyards of California. Typically, the Napa Valley scene, half work and half chichi, amused more than it impressed him.

We never worked a wine story together. I saw him from time to time at political events, especially during the French presidential campaign in 1980. When the Socialists won, their headquarters in the upper-crust Rue Solferino became one big victory party. Pushing through the crowd, I suddenly came face to face with Pierre-Marie Doutrelant, his hair more disheveled than ever, his face crinkled into a huge smile that virtually closed his eyes.

There was no doubt where his sympathies lay. But his writing on those events was cool and detached. It was the same with wine. He even had some vines at his weekend place in the hauntingly lovely Gers. But that's as far as it went. When he wrote, he was tough and uncompromising, be it on the Médoc or Mitterrand. For a reporter, that's the way it's supposed to be.

November 1987

A Beguiling Master of Food, Wine and Words

By FRANK J. PRIAL

The first thing A. J. Liebling did on arriving in Paris in 1939 was to have lunch. "A wartime lunch," he reported dismissively, "just marennes, Pouilly-Fuissé, caille vendangeuse, and Grands-Échezeaux."

Oysters, quail and two Burgundies; not a bad way to get started on a war.

Liebling wrote for *The New Yorker* from 1935 until his death in 1963. He wrote about New York, about combat, about boxing and the press. And, more or less en passant, he wrote continually about food and drink. With him, it was not just an academic subject.

"The first requisite for writing about food," he insisted, "was having a good appetite." He qualified. Berton Roueche, who joined *The New Yorker* some years after Liebling, recalled their first meeting:

"I was new and didn't know anyone when he appeared in the door of my cubicle and said: 'Hey, kid, you want to have lunch?'

"We went out to 44th Street, to the old Cortile. I don't remember what I had, but he ordered two roast chickens and he ate them all. Even the bones."

Abbott Joseph Liebling, for such was his full name, intoned descriptions of classic French dishes with the same reverence Thomas Wolfe reserved for the names of railroads. A lunch in Paris in 1955 "began with a truite au bleu—a live trout simply done to death in hot water, like a Roman emperor in his bath. It was served up with enough melted butter to thrombose a regiment of Paul Dudley Whites, and accompanied, as was right, by an Alsatian wine—a Lacrimae Sanctae Odiliae."

There follows a brief digression involving that wine and a girl in Strasbourg. Then he returns to the lunch. "We had a magnificent daube provençale, because we were faithful to la cuisine bourgeoise, and then pintadeaux—young guinea hens, simply and tenderly roasted—with the first asparagus of the year, to show our fidelity to la cuisine classique.

"We had clarets with both courses—a Pétrus with the daube, a Cheval Blanc with the guineas."

His companion had been "discounseled" on Burgundies by a small-minded physician. This gave Liebling momentary pause. He was reassured when the friend drank "a bottle and a half of Krug after luncheon."

"We had three bottles between us," he reported; "one to our loves, one to our countries, and one for symmetry, the last being on the house."

The point here is not to do honor yet again to Liebling's heroic gullet or to his unmatchable prose. They earned him the French Legion of Honor. It is instead to call attention to the fact that he wrote just as engagingly, as perceptively, about wine and liquor as he did about food.

His trenchermen, real and fictional, never fail to accompany their Lucullan meals with great wines, and they invariably work up to their feasts with a variety of other potions. In a memorable passage, Col. John R. Stingo, Liebling's raffish muse and fictionalized boon companion who was featured regularly in his *New Yorker* writing, described one lunchtime itinerary of a turn-of-the century New Orleans newspaper editor named O'Malley. His "prandial relaxation," Stingo related, began "at the bar of the St. Charles Hotel, where he had a three-bagger of Sazeracs," moved on to Hyman's bar on Common Street "where he increased his aperitif by four silver gin fizzes and after that over to Farbacher's saloon on Royal where he had a schooner or two of Boston Club punch."

After this workout, O'Malley strolled on to Antoine's where he consumed an immense meal accompanied by "a magnum of Château La Mission-Haut-Brion of the year of the comet [1811]," a dipper of Calvados from a cask brought to Louisiana from Normandy in 1721, and an espresso fetched by the maître d'hôtel from "a dive operated by the Mafia."

By his own admission and from the testimony of friends, it's clear that Joe Liebling drank a great deal. Said Raymond Sokolov, in his biography *Wayward Reporter* (Harper & Row, 1980), "He was certainly never guilty of the bourgeois virtue of deferred gratification."

George Bernard Shaw once characterized marriage as a remarkable institution because, he said, it combined the maximum temptation with the maximum opportunity. Much the same could be said of Paris in 1926, Liebling's novitiate year as a trencherman and wine lover. At the Restaurant des Beaux-Arts on the rue of the same name, where he did much of his early training, the half-bottle of Tavel rosé that accompanied most of his meals cost about two cents.

On the days he was scheduled to pick up his remittance money at the Crédit Lyonnais across the river, he would stop first for lunch at the Beaux-Arts and move up to CôteRôtie or even Hermitage, either of which cost only a few cents more.

Liebling believed in the value of hardship in the development of the palate.

When first he encountered great Burgundy, he was grateful for those days of Tavel rosé and other Rhône wines at the Beaux-Arts.

"Drinking Richebourg without this training," he wrote, "would have been like a debutant prizefighter's meeting Archie Moore in a feature bout; he would not be up to it and would never know what hit him."

"Burgundy," he said in one disquisition, "has the advantage of a clear, direct appeal, immediately pleasing and easy to comprehend on a primary level. This is a quality compatible with greatness. Shakespeare and Tolstoy, because more accessible, are not necessarily inferior to, say, Donne and Dostoyevsky.

"Burgundy thus has two publics: one (which it shares with Bordeaux) that likes it for its profound as well as its superficial qualities, and one that likes it only because it is easy to like."

It was this double audience, he wrote in the mid-1950s, that was responsible for the outrageous prices of good Burgundy both in Paris and New York. "If you like both clarets and Burgundies," he advised, "you can do as well with two dollars invested in a bottle of claret as with four dollars invested in Burgundy."

Joe Liebling died in 1963. What would he have said of today's wine market where the Richebourg he loved sells for $300 or more a bottle, and second-rate restaurants on both sides of the Atlantic demand $30 for a second-rate cru Beaujolais?

Liebling's comments on wine were disarming and unpretentious. The business of florid wine description had not yet flowered in his time. "Hints of cigarbox," "gobs of fruit," "undertones of toasty oak," and similar excesses had yet to become the lingua franca of cork sniffers. We can only guess at how Liebling would have handled such felonious assaults on the language he loved.

Not that Liebling couldn't discuss an individual wine vividly and intelligently when the need arose. One night in 1955 in Paris, a guest salvaged a boring dinner in the boring 16th Arrondissement by producing two bottles of Veuve Clicquot 1919.

The 36-year-old Champagne, Liebling reported, "was tart without brashness—a refined but effective understatement of younger Champagnes, which run too much to rhetoric, at best. Even so," he continued, "the force was all there, to judge from the two glasses that were a shade more than my share. The wine still had a discreet cordon—the ring of bubbles that forms inside the glass—and it had developed the color known as 'partridge eye.'

"I have never seen a partridge's eye because the bird, unlike woodcock, is served without the head, but the color the term indicates is that of serous blood or a maple leaf on the turn." Liebling's own taste in Champagne seemed to favor a house that has since apparently disappeared, Irroy, of Reims. On meeting a Parisian procurer who claimed to drink nothing but Champagne, the writer wondered whether the sweat he saw dripping from the man's "fat ear" might taste like Irroy '28.

Thrice married, usually broke, plagued by gout and increasingly frequent depression, Liebling's own life was more troubled than his light-hearted reportage ever let on. His friends believed his eating and drinking to excess was in part a reaction to the reality of his life. Consuming fine French food and great vintages, he was the boulevardier, the flaneur, who passed through life effortlessly and with consummate grace.

By all accounts, his third marriage, to the writer Jean Stafford, was mostly a happy one. They spent time at his retreat in the Springs, on Long Island, where he gardened now and then and kept a respectable cellar. "He entertained on the grand scale," said Philip Hamburger, the New Yorker writer. "He really relished being surrounded by people he liked and serving the best of food and drink. He was generous to a fault; he gave a lot more than he got."

What he gave mostly was a body of journalism that remains fresh and deeply moving almost three decades after his death.

One last story. In Paris in the 1950s after a long absence, he discovered that a favorite restaurant had changed hands and that the legendary owner, a Madame G., was gone.

An friend related that she had fallen ill and retired.

"What is the matter with her?" Liebling demanded.

"I think," the friend replied, "it was trying to read Simone de Beauvoir."

January 1992

Man of the Left Who Put Wines to Right

By FRANK J. PRIAL

W hen Edmund L. Penning-Rowsell died at his home in Oxfordshire, England, a generation of wine writers died with him.

At 88, Mr. Penning-Rowsell was the last of a group of English wine writers who came of age in the years after World War II and who combined the literary flair of scholars like Cyrus Redding and classicists like P. Morton Shand and George Saintsbury with the common touch of professional journalism and the reality of the marketplace.

He was the author of the definitive history of the Bordeaux wine trade, *The Wines of Bordeaux*, published in 1969 and reissued six times between then and 1990. For 23 years, he was a wine columnist for *The Financial Times*. For most of his life, he also wrote on wine for *Country Life*, a smaller publication that, to an extent, expressed his own lifelong affection for tweeds, dogs, tea by the fire and his unprepossessing home in the Cotswolds decorated in the William Morris style.

But the self-styled country squire was not always what he seemed. During the Depression years, when his father's business went bankrupt, he was pulled out of his school, Marlborough College, and forced to find work rather than go on to Cambridge University as he had planned. The blow turned him into a committed socialist who refused to visit Spain under the Nationalists and, during World War II, got himself dismissed from an aircraft-factory job for trying to organize workers. Later in life, according to people who knew him well, one of his favorite phrases was "Speaking as a man of the Left," often delivered while twirling a glass of rare old wine.

He joined *The Morning Post* in London in 1930. In 1935 he moved into publishing, a career he was to pursue, along with his growing wine interest, well into the 1950s. In England, many wine writers follow parallel careers in the wine industry. Mr. Penning-Rowsell joined the Wine Society, probably the first mail-order wine club, in 1937, and served as its president for many years. Like many of his contemporaries, he saw no conflict between promoting wines in his columns and selling them through the Wine Society.

His principal rival for wine-writing accolades was the late Cyril Ray, originally of *The Manchester Guardian*, a diminutive former foreign correspondent who had, among other feats, jumped into Germany with British paratroopers during the war. The two men were both Bordeaux enthusiasts. They were friends and shared the same birthday, March 16.

Mr. Penning-Rowsell was a familiar figure in Bordeaux, at vintage time and in early spring when a privileged few outsiders were invited to sample the newly fermented wines of the previous autumn. When England was Bordeaux's most important market and he was one of two or three of England's most important wine journalists, he was a favored and lavishly treated guest at many of the great chateaus, where everyone knew him as Eddie.

For a number of years, he regularly stayed at Château Mouton-Rothschild during the summer when the owner, Baron Philippe de Rothschild, was himself vacationing in Denmark or California. Having the Mouton cellar at his disposal was one of the more formidable perquisites of his work.

Mr. Penning-Rowsell's first book was *Red, White and Rosé* (1967), the wine primer that is almost every wine writer's rite of passage. In 1993, he published "Château Latour: The History of a Great Vineyard 1331–1992," an edited and updated translation of a book first published in France. But his most important work was *The Wines of Bordeaux*, first printed by the Wine & Food Publishing Company and later by Penguin. Mr. Penning-Rowsell regularly attended the Hospice de Beaune auction each November in Burgundy, but he rarely displayed any serious interest in Burgundy wines.

By comparison, he reveled in the wines and history of Bordeaux. He knew, and reproduced in his book, the region's total production in hectoliters in 1922, the opening price per tonneau of Château Pichon-Longueville in 1874 and the average monthly rainfall in millimeters for 1959. He tracked the wine purchases of the kings of England back almost a thousand years, reporting for example that in 1215 King John bought 120 tonneaus of Gascon wine "for his personal use." A tonneau in the 13th century equaled about 1,200 modern bottles. In 1308, according to *The Wines of Bordeaux*, Edward II ordered 1,000 tonneaus of Bordeaux for his marriage to Isabella of France. "Quite a wedding!" wrote the man of the Left.

Not surprisingly, Mr. Penning-Rowsell's own cellar was impressive and, aside from Champagne, almost exclusively Bordeaux. He particularly liked older wines and wines in large bottles. Writing in *The Guardian* last week, Michael Broadbent, for many years the head of Christie's wine auction department, noted that Mr. Penning-Rowsell could appear stern and forbidding but was actually quite charming and extremely hospitable, lavishing Champagne upon his guests, as well as "extremely good bottles of claret—for he was, essentially, a claret man."

And, to the end, apparently, a man of the Left. "Those who stayed the night," Mr. Broadbent recalled, "and Eddie was pressing in this respect—not without reason after so much wine—were somewhat bemused to see at the breakfast table, alongside homemade bread, marmalade and *The Times*, a copy of *The Morning Star*, the only reminder of their host's entrenched far-left views."

Mr. Penning-Rowsell was invariably kind and helpful to me over the years. I hadn't seen him for a long time. I would have enjoyed his comments on the invasion of Britain by Australian, New Zealand and American wines in recent years and the subsequent precipitous drop in the sales of Bordeaux. I think he would have recalled other times over the last 10 centuries when Bordeaux wines were out of favor in England and he would have confidently predicted their triumphant return.

March 2002

Pop Goes the Critic

By ERIC ASIMOV

When the refined British wine writer Jancis Robinson joined the frenetic Gary Vaynerchuk last fall on his video blog Wine Library TV it was as if Helen Mirren had shown up on an episode of *Dog the Bounty Hunter.*

As Mr. Vaynerchuk began shouting his greeting into the camera as if he were hawking cap snafflers at three in the morning, the ever game Ms. Robinson could not help but look appalled. But she hung in there, and together they began tasting wine in the informal studio above Wine Library, his family's wine shop in Springfield, N.J.

As they sniffed a 2006 Ridge Geyserville zinfandel, or "took a sniffy-sniff" in Mr. Vaynerchuk's parlance, Ms. Robinson said she detected the aroma of violets. Mr. Vaynerchuk said it smelled "very candylike."

Ms. Robinson grimaced.

"To me, candy is a negative thing," she said. "Candy is something I get on cheap zinfandel."

"In my mind," he responded, "candy, you know, depending on the candy, for example, Big League Chew or Nerds, could be tremendous, whereas candy I don't like, like Bazooka Joe bubble gum, could be a problem."

Gracefully, Ms. Robinson changed the subject. But a significant audience in the wine world loves Mr. Vaynerchuk's tune.

Ms. Robinson and her peers like Robert M. Parker Jr. and *Wine Spectator* may represent the apogee of the classic wine critic, issuing influential scores and opinions from on high as both arbiters and exemplars of the good life. But Mr. Vaynerchuk's kid-in-a-candy-store approach may represent the future. Mr. Vaynerchuk, 33, has broken through class barriers in a way that no other critic has been able to, making wine a part of popular culture.

He's appeared on Ellen DeGeneres's show, and, on Conan O'Brien's, in the guise of educating the host's palate to wine terms like "sweaty," "mineral" and "earthy," he sniffed Mr. O'Brien's armpit and persuaded him to chew an old sock, lick a rock and eat dirt (topped with shredded cigar tobacco and cherries).

"You're an idiot!" Mr. O'Brien exclaimed.

Perhaps so, but Mr. Vaynerchuk now has a million-dollar 10-book contract with HarperStudio that will focus on wine and marketing. And the wine establishment, which initially saw Mr. Vaynerchuk as a retailer with a novelty act, is taking note. In its July issue, *Decanter*, the leading British wine magazine, anointed him No. 40 in its list of the 50 most powerful and influential people in the world of wine.

"His influence is less as a style dictator than as a new media pioneer, showing how things can and will be done," said Ms. Robinson, who said she had pushed for his inclusion in the *Decanter* list.

Few people had ever heard of Mr. Vaynerchuk in early 2006, when he posted his first episode of Wine Library TV on the Wine Library Web site.

Before long his high-volume, hyper-enunciated delivery, sprinkled with bizarre tasting analogies and unlikely stream-of-consciousness departures, had earned him a rabid Internet following, along with ridicule from detractors in the audience. He was called a clown and the Human Infomercial, whose over-the-top style was dumbing down wine. Yet his fan base kept growing. He estimates his audience for each episode of Wine Library TV (he's just recorded No. 733) at 90,000 people, and he has nearly 900,000 followers on Twitter.

The numbers have made Mr. Vaynerchuk not only a wine industry phenomenon but a social media superstar who's being held up as a role model for using the tools of e-commerce to succeed in any business.

"Gary V. is a one-man social network," said Paul Mabray, chief strategy officer for VinTank, a wine industry think tank and consultancy. "He has the ability to get other people to believe in his product, and act as a megaphone for his message, and he's the only wine writer we've seen adopted by mass culture, like Ellen and Conan."

His persona is as much about marketing as it is about wine. His first book, due out next month, is an entrepreneur's self-help guide called *Crush It*. Future books, Mr. Vaynerchuk said, will focus on a combination of wine, marketing and building one's personal brand.

He hopes to extend his marketing reach beyond wine and self-help books. With his younger brother, A. J., Mr. Vaynerchuk has started Vaynermedia, a marketing agency with a small list of high-profile clients like the New York Jets (Mr. Vaynerchuk is a huge fan) and Jalen Rose, a retired N.B.A. player turned commentator. Not surprisingly, the Jets are now among the most Twitter-happy N.F.L. teams.

For Mr. Vaynerchuk, it's been a most unlikely journey. He was born in Belarus and immigrated to New Jersey as a child. His father, Sasha, ran a liquor store, while young Gary honed his entrepreneurial chops, selling baseball cards, he says, and franchising lemonade stands.

After graduating from Mount Ida College in Newton, Mass., Mr. Vaynerchuk took over his father's shop, Shopper's Discount Liquor, and rechristened it Wine Library, which he has built into what he says is a $60-million-a-year business.

Mr. Vaynerchuk might well have remained a successful but anonymous retailer, but in 2006 he initiated his video blog, Wine Library TV. From his first hesitant episodes, all of which are archived on the Wine Library TV website, Mr. Vaynerchuk quickly gathered steam, unleashing his frenzied delivery. He began wearing wristbands and calling his program "The Thunder Show a.k.a the Internet's Most Passionate Wine Program." He draped his minimalist set with action figures of wrestlers and superheroes, dubbed his audience Vayniacs, and bedecked his spit bucket with decals of his beloved New York Jets.

The unlovely ritual of wine tasting, with its swirling and sipping, punctuated with the slurping noise of air sucked through a wine-filled mouth and culminating in a swift discharge into a bucket, is few people's idea of attractive television. But Mr. Vaynerchuk embraced the unattractive, showing utter disregard for production values.

"Many people who I respected were disappointed when I started Wine Library TV," Mr. Vaynerchuk said in an interview one recent morning. "They thought I was dumbing down wine, but I always knew I was one of the biggest producers of new wine drinkers in the world, and people are realizing it now."

Of course, such extravagant claims are impossible to establish, but Mr. Vaynerchuk's audience on his Internet bulletin board certainly seems to have a higher percentage of novice wine drinkers than in the forums on either the Parker or *Spectator* Web sites.

While Mr. Vaynerchuk does not yet come close to Mr. Parker or the *Spectator* in his ability to move the wine market as a whole, his words do sell bottles. In an episode of Wine Library TV in February, Mr. Vaynerchuk raved about a Sonoma Coast pinot noir from Sojourn Cellars, a small producer.

"We took 500 e-mails and phone calls in 24 hours," said Craig Haserot, an owner of Sojourn. "Nothing has put more people on our database and sold more wine than Wine Library TV, and it's not even close."

Mr. Vaynerchuk's appeal is rooted in his undermining of the old-guard mantle of authority and detachment that wine critics of older generations like Ms. Robinson spent years trying to achieve. In many reviews, he seems to subvert the established vocabulary for describing wine.

He begins with the usual jargon, talking about nose and mid-palate, describing flavors like apricot, buttered popcorn and lilacs, as many wine writers do. But then he departs from the script, saying a wine smells like a sheep butt or that drinking it is like biting into an engine. He might improvise a dialogue with a bottle of riesling, and when he talked about another pinot noir from the Sonoma Coast, a 2006 Kanzler, he seemingly went off the deep end in describing its flavor:

"You hit a deer, you pull off to the side of the road, then you stab the deer with a knife, cut it, and bite that venison, and put a little black pepper and strawberries on it and eat it, like a mean, awful human being. That's what this tastes like."

Audiences love it.

"I immediately identified with his passion and enthusiasm," said Dale Cruse, a Web designer and wine blogger who started watching early on. "But I think it's worth noting that passion and enthusiasm isn't going to get you very far in the wine world without some knowledge to back it up."

Indeed, Mr. Vaynerchuk does know his Pommards from his Pomerols, and he clearly loves wine and wants his audience to love wine, too.

"My mission is to build wine self-esteem in this country," he said. "I want people to know their palate is a snowflake. We all like different things. Why should we all have the same taste in wines?"

Mr. Vaynerchuk's own taste is very hard to pin down. He will say that his palate is very different from most people's, and that given a choice between eating a bowl of fruit and a bowl of vegetables, he'll choose the vegetables every time. He rails against "the oak monster," which can make many wines taste like two-by-fours. He freely acknowledges that his palate has changed over the years, away from big fruity wines to more subtle ones, and said he expected his tastes to continue to change.

While Mr. Vaynerchuk has been lauded for making wine more accessible to younger people through his populist vocabulary, the real achievement of Wine Library TV has been to break down the barriers around the omniscient wine critic handing down thoughts from the mountaintop, and to include the audience in the critical process. As Mr. Vaynerchuk tastes and spits, his brain is seemingly on display as it begins to churn and the words emerge unfiltered from his mouth.

"My natural inclination to be improv rather than an educated character serves me well," he said.

While Mr. Vaynerchuk has done well bringing wine to a wider audience, he's done even better using wine to market himself. For now, he is looking ahead to new ventures, including the leap to Internet marketing guru. With his new company, Vaynermedia, he wants to market commercial products, people, teams and even sports like boxing.

"It's about stories," he said. "If I can tell the story to America, whether it's riesling or a boxer from Harlem, it will sell."

He pauses. "I know on my gravestone it's going to be, 'Storyteller.'"

September 2009

Bronx Cheer of a Wine Guide

By WILLIAM GRIMES

With *The Wine Avenger* (Simon & Schuster, $11), Willie Gluckstern establishes himself as the bleacher bum of wine writers. Mr. Gluckstern, a wine teacher and the wine buyer for Nancy's Wines in Manhattan, looks at a bottle of wine the same way the sun-and-beer-addled guy in the centerfield seats looks at the heart of the Marlins lineup: These guys call themselves baseball players? They make how much? You've got to be kidding.

The Wine Avenger, a slim paperback, promises to transform the reader into "a wine-food genius" in one hour. It doesn't. What it does is to deliver, in a highly entertaining way, randomly clustered opinions, tips, observations and explanations.

Mr. Gluckstern doesn't have likes and dislikes. He has mad love affairs and Balkan-style blood feuds.

Mr. Gluckstern hates chardonnay. It is, in his view, overhyped, overpriced and overoaked. Only Chablis escapes his wrath. As for merlot, don't get him started. American sauvignon blanc he dismisses as "acid-deficient and aromatically bizarre." Australian sauvignon blanc "is for mutants." He likes sulfites and heaps contumely on the super-Tuscans.

It's not just the wines. Mr. Gluckstern regards wine writers, winemakers, wine merchants and restaurant owners as an oppressor class with their jackboots firmly poised on the throat of the customer. He doesn't have a very high opinion of most customers either, come to think of it. They're idiots for not recognizing the sublime perfection of riesling, the world's greatest grape.

Mr. Gluckstern, who excels at concise, vivid sensory descriptions—wine aromas, he writes, can range from "nectar-dripping orchids in a Tahitian paradise to the feral stink of a sun-warmed manure pile"—mounts a convincing case for his favorites. He does tend to go on about riesling, but he argues brilliantly for the virtues of a crisp, acidic, citrusy chenin blanc from the Loire, with its "earthy, green-leaf flavor," over almost any chardonnay.

Unlike many other wine writers, Mr. Gluckstern cannot think about wine without thinking about food, and his policy on matching the two is firm. The big bruisers that win the big prizes at wine competitions he regards as the natural enemies of all but the richest foods. For the meals that most mortals eat most of the time, he puts his money on high-acid, medium-bodied wines like sauvignon blanc (from France and New Zealand only, please), cabernet franc, barbera, gamay and pinot noir.

It's the "sharp crack of acidity," he argues, that gets the salivary glands working and brings flavors on the plate alive. "I have come to believe that a well-made $10 or $12 Saumur-Champigny—with its medium weight, ripe piquant fruit and delicate herbal finish—must be, dollar for dollar, the best of all possible red wines for food," he writes. A hefty section of the book is devoted to matching wines and cuisines.

Some of *The Wine Avenger* is useless filler. Is there a human left on the planet who does not know that a wine glass should be held by the stem or base, and not the bowl? And why insist that readers learn to call pinot noir "pinot" if they want to pass as experts? No one cares.

The real point of *The Wine Avenger* is the opinions, and Mr. Gluckstern is full of them. If you don't agree, tough. You're probably just the kind of "palate-dead homunculus" who would like a chardonnay "Dengue Vineyard" Reserve Lot 3 Cuvée Louise Shmenge.

August 1998

CHAPTER THREE

The Jungle
of Winespeak

Talk Dirt to Me

By HAROLD McGEE AND DANIEL PATTERSON

It's hard to have a conversation about wine these days without hearing the French word "terroir." Derived from a Latin root meaning "earth," terroir describes the relationship between a wine and the specific place that it comes from. For example, many will say the characteristic minerality of wines from Chablis comes from the limestone beds beneath the vineyards (although, when pressed, they generally admit that they've never actually tasted limestone). The idea that one can taste the earth in a wine is appealing, a welcome link to nature and place in a delocalized world; it has also become a rallying cry in an increasingly sharp debate over the direction of modern winemaking. The trouble is, it's not true.

When terroir was first associated with wine, in the 17th-century phrase "goût de terroir" (literally, "taste of the earth"), it was not intended as a compliment. Its meaning began to change in 1831, when Dr. Morelot, a wealthy landowner in Burgundy, observed in his "Statistique de la Vigne Dans le Département de la Côte-d'Or" that all of the wineries in Burgundy made wine essentially the same way, so the reason some tasted better than others must be due to the terroir— specifically, the substrata underneath the topsoil of a vineyard. Wine, he claimed, derived its flavor from the site's geology: in essence, from rocks.

In recent years, the concept that one can taste rocks and soil in a wine has become popular with wine writers, importers and sommeliers. "Wines express their source with exquisite definition," asserts Matt Kramer in his book *Making Sense of Wine*. "They allow us to eavesdrop on the murmurings of the earth." Of a California vineyard's highly regarded chardonnays, he writes, there is "a powerful flavor of the soil: the limestone speaks." The sommelier Paul Grieco, in his wine list at Hearth in New York, writes of rieslings that "the glory of the varietal is in its transparency, its ability to truly reflect the soil in which it is grown." In his February newsletter, Kermit Lynch, one of the most respected importers of French wine, returns repeatedly to the stony flavors in various white wines from a "terroirist" winemaker in Alsace: "When he speaks of a granitic soil, the wine in your glass tastes of it."

If you ask a hundred people about the meaning of terroir, they'll give you a hundred definitions, which can be as literal as tasting limestone or as metaphorical as a feeling. Terroir flavors are generally characterized as earthiness and minerality. On the other hand, wines with flavors of berries or tropical fruits and little or no minerality are therefore assumed not to have as clear a connection to the earth, which means they could have come from anywhere, and are thought to bear the mark of human intervention.

If this seems confusing—especially given that wine is made from fruit—it gets worse when you ask winemakers about how to get the flavors from the rocks into the glass. According to them, a good expression of terroir requires more work in the vineyards, or possibly less; it's the hotter climate in California that leads to its high-alcohol, fruit-forward, terroir-less style, or possibly not; even the oft-heard contention that a winemaker must "work with what the vines give you" is contradicted by Ales Kristancic of Movia winery, whose family has been making wines from vineyards on the Italy-Slovenia border for hundreds of years. "Plants need to understand what the winemaker wants," Kristancic says. "Only a winery with great tradition can make great vineyards."

Since there's so little consensus among winemakers about how to foster the expression of place—what Matt Kramer calls "somewhereness"—in their wines, what are our wine experts tasting? How can a place or a soil express itself through wine? Does terroir really exist?

Yes, but the effects of a place on a wine are far more complex than simply tasting the earth beneath the vine. Great wines are produced on many different soil types, from limestone to granite to clay, in places where the vines get just enough water and nourishment from the soil to grow without deficiencies and where the climate allows the grapes to ripen slowly but fully. It's also true that different soils can elicit different flavors from the same grape. Researchers in Spain recently compared wines from the same clone of grenache grafted on the same rootstock, harvested and vinified in exactly the same way, but grown in two vineyards 1,600 feet apart, one with a soil significantly richer in potassium, calcium and nitrogen. The wines from the mineral-rich soil were higher in apparent density, alcohol and ripe-raisiny aromas; wines from the poorer soil were higher in acid, astringency and applelike aromas. The different soils produced different flavors, but they were flavors of fruit and of the yeast fermentation. What about the flavors of soil and granite and limestone that wine experts describe as minerality—a term oddly missing from most formal treatises on wine flavor? Do they really go straight from the earth to the wine to the discerning palate?

No.

Consider the grapevine growing in the earth. It takes in elemental, inert materials from the planet—air and water and minerals—and, using energy captured from sunlight, turns them into a living, growing organism. It doesn't just accumulate the earth's materials. It transforms them into the sugars, acids, aromas, tannins, pigments and dozens of other molecules that make grapes and wine delicious.

"Plants don't really interact with rocks," explains Mark Matthews, a plant physiologist at the University of California, Davis, who studies vines. "They interact with the soil, which is a mixture of broken-down rock and organic matter. And plant roots are selective. They don't absorb whatever's there in the soil and send it to the fruit. If they did, fruits would taste like dirt." He continues, "Any minerals from the solid rock that vine roots do absorb—sodium, potassium, calcium, magnesium, iron, a handful of others—have to be dissolved first in the soil moisture. Most of them are essential nutrients, and they mainly affect how well the plant as a whole grows."

Most of the earthy and mineral aromas and flavors that we detect in wine actually come from the interaction of the grape and yeast. Yeasts metabolize the grape sugars into alcohol, along the way freeing up and spinning off the dozens of aromatic chemicals that make wine more than just alcoholic grape juice. It's because of the yeasts that we can catch whiffs of tropical fruits, grilled meats, toasted bread and other things that have never been anywhere near the grapes or the wine. The list of evocative yeast products includes an organic sulfur molecule that can give sauvignon blancs a "flinty" aroma. And there are minor yeasts that create molecules called volatile phenols, whose earthy, smoky flavors have nothing to do with the soil but are suggestive of it, especially in wines from the southern Rhône.

Grape minerals and mineral flavors are also strongly influenced by the grower and winemaker. When a vineyard is planted, the vine type, spacing and orientation are just a few of many important decisions. Growers control the plant growth in myriad ways, such as pruning, canopy management or, most obviously, irrigating and replenishing the soil with manures or chemical fertilizers. The winemaker then makes hundreds of choices that affect wine flavor, beginning with the ripeness at which the grapes are harvested, and can change the mineral content by using metal equipment, concrete fermentation tanks or clarifying agents made from bentonite clay. Jamie Goode, a British plant biologist turned wine writer, describes in his superbly lucid book *Wine Science* how techniques that minimize the wine's contact with oxygen can increase the levels of sulfur compounds that may be mistaken for "mineral" character from the soil.

So, if vines absorb only rock that is dissolved in water, if grape and wine minerals are not a reflection of the rocks' minerals, and if earthy aromas in wine come from microbes and not the earth, do soil minerals have any real role in wine flavor?

Hildegarde Heymann, a sensory scientist at U.C. Davis, is skeptical about the usefulness of the terms "terroir" and "minerality" as they're used today. But she is intrigued by "minerality." "People who talk about minerality are describing something they perceive that's hard to grab on to," she says. "My guess is that it's a composite perception, something like 'creaminess' in dairy foods. 'Minerality' might be a way of describing a combination of complexity, balance and a substantial body. We do know that mineral ions can affect wine flavor by affecting acidity, chemical reaction rates and the volatility of aromas. And we're just now looking at whether they can affect the body of wine, its 'mouthfeel.' They might."

It's possible, then, that soil minerals may affect wine flavor indirectly, by reacting with other grape and yeast substances that produce flavor and tactile sensations, or by altering the production of flavor compounds as the grape matures on the vine.

The place where grapes are grown clearly affects the wine that is made from them, but it's not a straightforward matter of tasting the earth. If the earth "speaks" through wine, it's only after its murmurings have been translated into a very different language, the chemistry of the living grape and microbe. We don't taste a place in a wine. We taste a wine from a place—the special qualities that a place enables grapes and yeasts to express, aided and abetted by the grower and winemaker.

In the years following Dr. Morelot's missive on terroir, the quality of a wine became synonymous with the quality of the vineyard where it originated. This meant the value of that wine was tied to the land instead of to the winemaker, which allowed it to be handed down from generation to generation. The French went on to codify their vineyards into legal appellations, creating gradations within those appellations that demarcated clear levels of quality (grand cru, first growth and so on), the economic effects of which are felt to this day. Given that it was landowners who benefited most, the commonly held idea of terroir—wine as proxy for a piece of dirt—looks a lot like one of the longest-running, most successful marketing campaigns of the modern era.

Today, it's easy to ascribe all this terroir talk to commerce, to the European reaction to California's recent rise in viniculture status. It's been suggested that terroir is just the Old World saying to the New: It's the land, stupid—we have it and you don't. But that doesn't explain why so many Americans have embraced the concept with near-religious zeal. To paraphrase the great French wine historian Roger Dion, why have so many brilliant and passionate wine professionals been so eager to attribute solely to nature what is actually the result of hard work by talented winemakers?

The answer lies in the complex relationship between tradition, culture and taste. Those wine professionals have all spent vast amounts of time and energy learning what traditional European wines taste like, region by region, winery by winery, vineyard by vineyard. The version of terroir that many of them hold is that those wines taste the way they do because of the enduring natural setting, i.e., the rocks and soil. These wines taste the way they do because people have chosen to emphasize flavors that please them.

The pioneering French enologist Émile Peynaud wrote nearly 25 years ago: "I cannot agree with the view that 'one accepts human intervention (in vinification) as long as it allows the natural characteristics to remain intact,' since it is precisely human intervention which has created and highlighted these so-called natural characteristics!" Modern European views of terroir recognize that typical local flavors are the creation of generations of growers and winemakers, shaping the vineyard and fine-tuning the fermentation to make what they feel are the best wines possible in their place. Typical flavors are expressions not of nature but of culture.

But culture, unlike nature, isn't static. It evolves in response to shifting tastes and technological advances. Over the past 30 years, the staid world of European winemaking has been roiled by an influx of American consumers, led by their apostle, the writer Robert Parker. In his reviews, Parker has brushed aside the traditional practice of judging wine according to historical context (that is, how it should taste), focusing instead on what's in the bottle. His preference for hugely concentrated, fruit-forward wines—the antithesis of distinctive, diverse terroir wines—has dramatically changed the economic landscape of the wine industry. Throughout the world, more and more winemakers are making wine in the style that Parker prefers, even in Europe, where this means abandoning distinctive local styles that had evolved over centuries. "Somewhereness" is being replaced by "anywhereness."

The simplistic idea of terroir as a direct expression of nature has become a rhetorical weapon in the fight against this trend. Kristancic—who interrupted our interview to raise his fists and shout to the heavens, "They're ruining wine!"— sees an advancing wave of homogenization that will eventually turn wine into a soulless, deracinated commodity. Like many others, he is afraid of losing what is special about the traditional role of wine in human life, its way of connecting people to the land and to one another. Conjuring granite in Alsatian rieslings and limestone in Chablis puts that connection to the land right in the bottle, ours for the tasting.

If rocks were the key to the flavor of "somewhereness," then it would be simple to counterfeit terroir with a few mineral saltshakers. But the essence of wine is more elusive than that, and far richer. Scientists and historians continue to illuminate what Peynaud described as the "dual communion" represented by wine: "on the one hand with nature and the soil, through the mystery of plant growth and the miracle of fermentation, and on the other with man, who wanted wine and who was able to make it by means of knowledge, hard work, patience, care and love." "Somewhereness" is given its meaning by "someoneness": in our time, by the terroirists who are working hard to discover and capture in a bottle the difference that place can make.

May 2007

A Short Course in Wine Tactics

By FRANK J. PRIAL

It seems that everyone wants to learn something about wine these days. Not necessarily to drink it, but to learn about it. There are wine schools cropping up all around. Adult education centers offer wine courses, restaurants have them too. Even conservative universities, nervous about their dwindling enrollments, are coming up with wine courses. Tasting groups are everywhere and wine books are appearing at a rate of one a month. Some fanatics go all the way and take up enology. Others get jobs in wineries. Some prefer hands-on experience, which they gather in a succession of bars.

Unfortunately, these methods all take time. They won't save you from a dull evening when you discover you're having dinner with some alleged wine experts tomorrow night. Most other monomaniacs—the tennis bore, the stock market bore, the hi-fi bore—can be handled. The wine expert is tough. After all, the stuff is inescapable; it's right there on the table in front of you, ready to be opened, perchance to be decanted, to be swirled, sniffed and sipped until you're ready to go right through the wall.

Pleading ignorance is not only cowardly, it's bad tactics. To the committed wine bore, particularly if he is the host, the wine clod is a gift from heaven: a new audience, a possible convert. It's fire with fire, or nothing.

Here, then, is a short course in wine tactics. If you think it's going to get you into the Chevaliers du Tastevin, forget it. It won't even save you from being ripped off in your favorite liquor store. The sole purpose of the following information is to cover your ignorance in polite company.

The expertise offered here consists of a selection of simple words and phrases, all in the mother tongue. This meant eliminating some key terms in the wine experts vocabulary, such as "Mon Dieu," "yech" and "feh"—but how much better to start off modestly.

The most important of these phrases is this: "It dies on the middle palate." Yes. Now repeat it six times. What does it mean? What's the difference what it means? Just say it when the supercilious host asks your opinion. With a bit of practice you can begin building sentences based on this phrase. For example, start with: "Superb, but—" Or you may wish to add, "but it finishes well."

This is the total wine put-down. Your host will have reverted back to sloe gin fizzes by 10 a.m. the next day. After all, even Philippe de Rothschild can't argue with your middle palate.

Then there is the word "bramble." Do you know what a bramble is? It's a bush, right? Do you know what a bramble tastes like? Of course not: who eats bushes? Nevertheless, that's what you're going to say, if the wine is red. "It has a real bramble taste; yes, sir, a real bramble taste." Don't worry. It appears on a dozen different California wine labels and it's a safe bet those guys don't know what it means, either. For sure, your host doesn't.

To carry this kind of thing off you must dance and feint; never let 'em lay a glove on you. Don't start out calling a wine "oaky," even if you do have a vague idea of what you're talking about. The wine expert will hit you with "American oak or Yugoslavian oak?" He is piqued by now because the rest of the party has turned to you, impressed by your incomprehensible jargon.

More terminology: "cab," "zin" and "chard." These are three embarrassing little abbreviations much favored by California wine cultists. They stand for, of course, cabernet sauvignon, zinfandel and chardonnay, and are employed thus: "We had a tasting of 20 zins and every one of them was really super." Or: "He's an O.K. winemaker but there's too much oak in his cab and not enough in his chard." Most Californians can't stand "chard" either, but it does crop up now and then when they talk.

"Chewy" and "fat": These, you should be aware, are legitimate descriptive adjectives in some wine circles. They can be condoned—maybe—because more often than not they are used to convey some sense of wines that are truly indescribable: overpowering red wines that have too much of everything in them but restraint. The kind of wines one finds described as "big, fat, chewy monsters; can be laid down for decades but are perfectly good for drinking right now."

Nose. As in: "The nose is very forward." Bouquet and aroma are two different things where wine is concerned but you need not concern yourself with them. "Nose" is a synonym for smell—and the only acceptable substitute. You can say the wine has a lovely nose or a peculiar nose or even a nonexistent nose. The polite way to say that the wine smells terrible is to remark that it has "an off-nose."

Body. As in: "This wine has excellent body." Note: never say "This wine has an excellent body." That would be gauche. Although someone once got away with—in fact became immortal by—saying of a wine that "it had narrow shoulders but very broad hips." Body simply refers to the substance of a wine.

Wine also has legs. This is determined by swirling a partly filled glass of red wine and waiting for it to settle. If the glass is clear and clean and the wine any good at all, you should be able to see colorless lines still making their way down the inside of the glass. These are called legs, obviously in keeping with our obsessive desire to equate wine with the human body.

The Germans are a bit more elegant on this one. They call the "legs" kirchen-fenster, or church windows, because as the lines come down the sides of the glass they form nearly perfect Gothic arches.

Short. As in: "The wine is pleasant enough but I find it a bit short." This is actually a useful term. It simply means that the taste of the wine does not linger in your mouth. This phenomenon is also referred to as a short finish. A wine whose taste lingers is said, naturally enough, to have a long finish.

You're now ready to handle "oak." As in: "Thank God Mondavi is no longer obsessed with oak." Oak is the taste imparted to wine by the oak barrels in which it is sometimes stored. Enthusiasts argue over oak the way bears fight over territory, but at the moment oak is mostly out in wine circles. Unless, of course, it's subtle oak.

Oak, like short finish and long finish, is a tricky term. You'd better have some idea of what you're talking about when you use it. There is nothing a wine bully likes better than to be able to say to someone who has just pronounced a wine oaky than: "Sorry, but this one was fermented and aged in stainless steel. It's never seen wood."

Alcohol. As in: "What's the alcohol in this stuff?" This is an excellent phrase because it implies that you know what alcohol content means. A table wine that has close to 14 percent alcohol by volume is going to give you a headache if you drink too much and it's probably too strong to go with your meal. But you don't have to know this. Merely posing the question will evoke some response from your host. All you need do is nod, knowingly.

pH. As in: "What's the pH in this stuff?" This term is even better than alcohol because nobody understands it. It has something to do with the intensity of the acid in a wine. Low pH means more intensity, high pH means less. Low would be around 2.85; high would be around 4.

These, then, are just a few of the words and phrases that wine people live by, words and phrases that you can master and use to your benefit without knowing muscatel from Muscadet, or Romanée-Conti from Ripple. It's wrong, probably, to advocate such brazen chicanery, but it will serve to give you breathing time if you choose to really learn something about wine. Also it will get you off unscathed if you choose never to mention or even think about wine again. And, too, as you begin to hear other people using these terms, you will come to realize how many of them know almost nothing about wine either.

July 1983

Rolling Out Those Chewy Behemoths

By FRANK J. PRIAL

In a series of articles in *The New Yorker* beginning in the mid-1930s, the writer Frank Sullivan set out to do battle with the inane and the banal in popular writing. He created a cliché expert, Mr. Arbuthnot, and made him the scourge of triteness.

Mr. Arbuthnot turned up intermittently in the magazine into the 1950s, well before wine writers began to impose themselves on the reading public. Because they are everywhere now, it seemed appropriate to resurrect Mr. Arbuthnot and query him about wine and writing.

Q. Mr. Arbuthnot, do you consider yourself a wine expert?

A. No, I am a cliché expert, but I have looked into the literature and have concluded that my expertise is needed even if I can't distinguish a Bordeaux from a Burgundy.

Q. How so?

A. Let me start with the word "nose." Poking into current wine literature, I found "brilliant" noses, "subtle" noses, "off" noses and "troubling" noses. Some wines, I learned, are said to have memorable noses while others, it is claimed, have no noses at all.

I quickly determined that a wine's "nose" is not a gross physical appendage but its bouquet or aroma. Even so, constant repetition has made a cliché of the word, one of the worst sort because constant use has debased it into argot.

Q. Are there other wine words that upset you as strongly?

A. Indeed there are—if you can call them words. I refer to "chard," "cab" and "zin," nicknames as it were for important grapes. Are the words "chardonnay," "cabernet" and "zinfandel" so difficult to pronounce? Did Baron Rothschild ask, "How much cab have you planted?" when he bought Château Lafite? Is the great white wine of Le Montrachet actually derived from something called chard?

Q. You have forgotten zinfandel.

A. No, it warrants special consideration. The zinfandel appears to be a fine, robust grape that lacks some of the charm of cabernet and chardonnay. For this it has suffered a worse fate than either of them. Its often obstreperous fans delight in referring to it as "zinful" and joke about "mortal zin."

Q. Anything besides wine books you find troubling?

A. The worst offenders are often the winemakers themselves and their spokesmen. They no longer make wine, they "craft" it. "We craft our wines," they write, or "these wines were crafted," or, worse still, "hand-crafted." How else would you "craft" something than with your hands?

From what I gather, winemaking has become a high-tech (another cliché) process and, as the procedure becomes more complex, the language describing it becomes more fanciful.

I found, too, a phrase borrowed from the business world: "roll out." A new wine is no longer introduced, offered or announced; it is rolled out, like an 18-wheel truck. The phrase has nothing to do with barrels, which of course, can be rolled around in a wine cellar. It refers to new airplanes being rolled out of the hangars where they were built to go on display. Does one "roll out" a delicate wine? I hope not.

Q. What about the wines that aren't delicate?

A. Some, it would seem, are anything but. They are "behemoths," "mammoth," "stupendous, large-scale, full-throttle" and "blockbusters." They may have "husky mouthfeel" and can display "massive quantities of fruit, glycerin and alcohol." They can be, as one writer described a California cabernet: "Opulent, as well as tannic, with huge chocolaty, roasted herbs, cassis aromas, magnificent flavor concentration, a big graceful richness on the palate and stunningly focused components that coat the palate with viscous flavors and superlative purity of flavor." All that and "food-friendly" too?

Q. And what about Champagne?

A. Some writers refer to all sparkling wines rather childishly as "fizzies," others desperate for another word for Champagne use "bubble" as a noun, as in "a bottle of the bubbly." But the most overworked Champagne cliché is "vintage." Once, vintage Champagnes—wines from a single harvest—were rare. Blends from two, three or more years were the norm. Now almost every year is a vintage year, and the term "vintage Champagne" has become mostly a cliché.

Q. Dare I ask for your closing thoughts?

A. My brief exploration into the wine world leads me to believe there are almost as many clichés as there are wines.

There are catch phrases that are also clichés. Like "excellent value for everyday drinking" or "perfect now but will last 10 years or more" or "great wines begin in the vineyard."

And lest you think hackneyed stuff is all of recent vintage, here, from Alexis Bespaloff's *Fireside Book of Wine*, is the legendary André Simon, writing in the 1930s on a 1905 Margaux: "The 1905 was simply delightful; fresh, sweet and charming, a girl of 15, who is already a great artist, coming on tiptoes and curt-seying herself out with childish grace and laughing blue eyes."

Q. Thank you, Mr. Arbuthnot and do come back. With wine clichés, it appears that we've only scratched the surface.

January 2006

Guessing Games

By FRANK J. PRIAL

S omeone once asked Harry Waugh, the grand old man of the English wine trade, how long it had been since he'd mistaken a Bordeaux wine for a Burgundy. "Not since lunch," he replied.

No single part of wine lore is more beset by myth and misinformation than the vague area of wine tasting. Fiction is filled with stories about legendary feats of wine detection. At some climactic point, while the rest of the characters hold their breath and the tension is almost painful, the hero, brow furrowed and eyes closed in concentration, swirls his glass a bit and says: "I may be wrong, but I'd say this is a '64 Bordeaux and, because it's a bit light, it was probably one of the chateaux that picked during the awful rain that year. Because of the water, there isn't much body, but the structure is there and the elegance one finds only in Pauillac. I'd say it's the 1964 Château Pontet-Canet." And, of course, it is. In the story, anyway.

Bordeaux wine people play these games from time to time, but only among themselves, because they know the reality of wine tasting. One can pull off astonishing feats of detective work one day and not recognize one's own wine the next.

There are certain things an expert can do. In a now-famous profile of Alexis Lichine, the late Joseph Wechsberg recounted how, on a dare, Mr. Lichine took a glass of wine, tasted it, smelled it, tasted it again and then guessed, correctly, that it was Château Lascombes 1928. Mr. Lichine had an advantage: he once headed a group that owned Lascombes and knew its wines well. But wine guessing is a psychological exercise as much as anything else. Mr. Lichine admitted later that he spent as much time trying to figure out what his host would have been inclined to serve him and what wines he would be unlikely to use. In fact, the process of elimination is probably the most important part of the game.

Not long ago, at a lunch at the "21" Club in New York, the young sommelier, Matthew Siegel, offered us a glass of what he called a mystery wine. We were drinking a 1979 Mercurey, Faively's Clos des Myglands, at the time. The mystery wine was darker, almost smoky and enormously concentrated. I guessed it to be a Rhône wine, a very fine Rioja, or one of the new California wines made in the Rhône style from Rhône grapes.

I was lucky; it was a 1984 Côte-Rôtie, La Landonne, from Étienne and

Marcel Guigal, perhaps the greatest of all CôteRôtie wines, and one I'd never had before. Pressed to expand on my original Rhône guess, I probably would have said Hermitage, although there are distinct differences between the wines of the CôteRôtie and Hermitage. And who knows what made me think of Rioja? Incidentally, there are reasons why very few wine enthusiasts know La Landonne: the vineyards, all of them on terraced, precipitous slopes leading down to the Rhône River, is tiny. The whole CôteRôtie appellation only produces about 20,000 cases, or less than most Bordeaux chateaux—and almost all of it is consumed in luxury restaurants in the Rhône Valley.

But even in that simple little guessing game, elimination was the first step. It wasn't Bordeaux or Burgundy or Beaujolais or California cabernet or zinfandel. That eliminated a lot of wine, but what about a great shiraz from Australia, such as Grange Hermitage, or a big red from Italy, Barbaresco or Barolo? The Italians are too distinctive and the Grange Hermitage is much smoother and more elegant than that wine.

The California Rhône-style would have been a better second guess than a third; a wine such as Bonny Doon's Old Telegram, or one of McDowell Valley Vineyards's Lake County syrahs from very old vines. But that's where psychology comes in. The California Rhône-style wines are much in the news these days, and are the kind of wines a sommelier may try to spring on his hapless client. Mr. Siegel resisted that ploy.

Well aware of the traps awaiting even the experienced taster, most professionals will beg off these guessing games in the company of amateurs. They know, for example, that it's relatively easy to fool even a veteran by offering him or her something truly unexpected and out of context. Steven Spurrier's famous 1976 Paris tasting is a case in point. In that event, a blind tasting, he offered a group of French experts a mix of well-known Bordeaux and—to them—unknown California cabernets. The results—in which an American wine, a Stag's Leap Wine Cellars 1973 cabernet, placed first ahead of all the Bordeaux bottles—did wonders for California's reputation but very little for the sensibilities of the French tasters.

In fact, seeing the California wines triumph was less disturbing to them than the idea that they had been led to believe they were tasting only French wines. They were justifiably irritated. As a rule, California wines are drinkable earlier than top Bordeaux. Having assumed all the wines were French and all more or less from the same period, they chose the ones that were easiest to drink.

When the same tasting was repeated 10 years later in New York, one of the now-10-year-old California wines came in first again: the Clos du Val 1972. But, on the second go-around, Mr. Spurrier made up for his earlier mischief by letting everyone know that the same wines were involved. This made the outcome even more of a compliment to the California wines, because tastings, like unfixed horse races, are very unpredictable.

Which means that, like unfixed horse races, they can also be a lot of fun.

May 1989

CHAPTER FOUR

What You Drink With What You Eat

Big and Beautiful: Lafite for 12

By ERIC ASIMOV

Not just any bottle of wine can compel eight people to hop on planes and fly thousands of miles to drink it. But this was not just any bottle.

When my friend Jason's father died last summer, he left behind what seemed to be the predictable assortment of possessions: his Seattle apartment, a beat-up old car, books and papers. But Jason's father also kept wine in an air-conditioned closet in his un-air-conditioned home. When Jason, a wine lover himself, pored over the bottles, he found one huge surprise: an impériale of 1986 Château Lafite-Rothschild.

Really, you don't just find an impériale. It grips you the way the view of Mount Rainier strikes people here on a clear day.

An impériale is as big as it gets in Bordeaux, big enough to hold six liters of wine, the equivalent of eight ordinary bottles. And Lafite is no ordinary wine. It's one of the great wines of Bordeaux and of the world, and 1986 was an exceptional vintage. Stumbling over an impériale is a free trip to wine heaven, with a first-class upgrade. It just does not happen, except that it did.

Like taxes on a lottery prize, any treasure carries hardships. An impériale cannot be doled out a bit at a time, like eight bottles. To uncork an impériale is to open eight bottles at once. It requires appreciative mouths and plenty of planning. It also requires courage.

Anyone who has ever owned a wine the caliber of an '86 Lafite will appreciate the agony involved in choosing just the right time to open a bottle. Is it too soon or, God forbid, too late? Is the occasion worthy enough of such a wine? It's one thing for a rich collector to break out a bottle, just for kicks. But for wine lovers of modest budgets, who may taste a world-class bottle once or twice in a lifetime, it's a momentous decision.

Fortunately, Jason and his wife, Lisa, who live in New York City, were not stymied by the big bottle burden. They proposed a dinner party at Jason's mother's house in Tacoma, practically on the shore of Puget Sound, where the bottle had been stored in the cellar. The guests would prepare and serve a dinner that would flatter the Lafite. They would toast Jason's father, and celebrate friends and family with a bottle that they hoped would be spectacular.

And so seven people from New York and one from Washington flew to

Tacoma on Columbus Day weekend to share a bottle of wine with Jason's mother, his brother and two more friends from the Seattle area. Twelve people seemed just the right number to do justice to the Lafite.

Three days before we arrived Jason's mother, Patty, had the bottle brought up to her kitchen from her cellar. A remnant of purple tissue paper clung to the label, resembling a broad stain, or perhaps a mark of distinction. This was, after all, one of only 400 impériales produced by Lafite in 1986, and the chateau typically keeps 50 to 100 of them for its own use. By some estimates this impériale might be worth $5,000 now.

The bottle was placed upright in a cool, dark spot and left to settle, an important detail when dealing with an older Bordeaux. Wines like the Lafite, made primarily from cabernet sauvignon, produce sediment as they age. Drinking a wine full of sediment is like getting a mouthful of fine coffee grounds, not at all pleasant. When the bottle was standing upright, the sediment would settle to the bottom, where it would remain after the wine was decanted.

The wine needed to be decanted not only to leave the sediment behind, but because it was so young. An ordinary bottle of '86 Lafite would just about be rounding into shape now. But the bigger the bottle, the less the wine inside is exposed to air, and the slower the wine ages. Decanting it would aerate the wine, softening the still-young tannins and allowing the flavors to open up. A bottle this big would need quite a bit of air. We decided to decant the wine six hours or so before we drank it.

But where do you put six liters of wine? We scoured the cabinets for carafes, pitchers and flagons, managing to assemble a motley assortment of vessels that would do the job. The moment of truth had arrived.

Nothing about an impériale isn't big. The cork was practically as wide as a gas cap and presented a daunting challenge to the typical waiter's corkscrew. Jason pulled gradually at the cork, pausing to wipe the rim. Finally, with a soft pop, it emerged and the bottle was open. Slowly, he poured the wine into the decanters. Gritty sediment clung to the interior of one side of the bottle, on which it had been resting all these years.

As the wine flowed, I tried to banish my fears. Had we opened the bottle at the right time? Had it aged enough, or were we killing a baby? There was no going back now.

We poured one glass. I was struck by its elegant aroma, and relieved that the bottle was not corked. It was beautiful, though very young, with a smell almost like grape juice mixed with the cedar scent typical of a fine Pauillac. We shared a quick taste and could sense the depth and intensity of the wine, but the flavors were locked away in a vault of tannins. Would six hours of air be enough?

As Lisa and another friend, Rafael, spent the late afternoon in the kitchen preparing dinner, anticipation built. The Lafite required a dramatic buildup, and so we started with duck terrine and Champagne as the final touches were put on the dinner. Then we began the meal in earnest.

First came a plate of scallop dishes: piquillo pepper stuffed with scallop, shallot and chorizo; scallop ravioli topped with a butternut squash purée, and a sliced, seared scallop with duck magret, superb with a pure, crystalline 2002 Pouilly-Fumé from Didier Dagueneau. Then tagliatelle in a cream sauce with truffle shavings, rich but delicate and delicious with a rough, fragrant 2001 St.-Joseph from Rochecourbe.

Then finally the main course, roasted lamb with garlic and rosemary, with figs, potatoes and onions, and haricots verts. The Lafite was poured into big goblets, leaving plenty of room for the fragrance to rise.

The wine had evolved beautifully in the seven hours since we opened the bottle. The grape juice quality was gone, but the elegance was all there: intensity and concentration combined with a light, velvety texture, the hallmark of great French wine. It was still a little closed and tannic, but the lamb smoothed out the tannins, leaving the seductive core of the wine in all its glory. The flavors seemed to last forever.

With the luxury of plenty, we savored each mouthful, paying attention to nuances even after the food was finished. Plates pushed away, last crumbs of cheese consumed, we realized we had finished only four of the seven pitchers of Lafite. Perhaps we overdid the buildup. Still there was another night. Given how young the wine seemed, even at dinner, we decided to leave the uncovered pitchers of wine on the cool kitchen counter, exposed to the air.

The next night, encore du vin. We poured it with grilled steak, and darned if it hadn't gotten even better. The tannins were softer, the fruit was clear and sedate and the cedar scent had developed into a complex tobaccolike flavor. Rafael said he had tasted all these elements individually in one Bordeaux or another, but never all together in one wine. The Lafite still seemed young, though, and we debated when this wine would hit its peak. Ten years? Twenty? Properly stored, we decided, this is a hundred-year bottle, perfect for celebrating the turn of the next century.

But could there have been a better time for this bottle than this Columbus Day weekend? We were friends and family, drawn from different parts of the country by the novel allure of this huge bottle. We were healthy and happy in one another's company. We drank to Jason's father, we drank to our friends and families, and we drank to ourselves. This is the point of a great wine. It was the perfect time to drink it.

October 2004

A Rule Just Waiting to Be Broken

By ERIC ASIMOV

"Red wine with oysters? Are you mad?" Quite possibly. And yet the thought excited me. Why would I want to muck with such routinely thrilling combinations as oysters with Muscadet, Chablis or Champagne, not to mention the old Irish standby, Guinness stout?

Well, why not?

Nobody loves the tried-and-true oyster-and-wine pairings more than I do. But doesn't there come a time when the certainties are no longer enough? In a favorite restaurant, do you order the same dish each time? Do you read a favorite book over and over? So it goes with wine and food.

It began when I read a post on Dorie Greenspan's blog at doriegreenspan.com. Dorie is a writer and cookbook author who lives part-time in Paris. In January she reported that in two days, at two bistros, servers recommended red wine with her oysters.

Mind you, this was in Paris, temple of the gastronomic verities. Dorie also wrote of a friend whose server at a seafood restaurant mentioned a preference for red wine with Belon oysters.

I know oysters and red wine sounds bizarre, but 20 years ago white wine with cheese sounded strange. Now, white wine is accepted as a delicious companion for many cheeses.

Of course, red wine with cheese can be a deadly match, while oysters go perfectly with a host of white wines. Still, I was intrigued. I had to try this.

Personally, I don't like to devote too much energy to pondering which wine to serve with which food. I prefer to trust instinct and desire over an analysis of flavor and body matches.

Often precision is the enemy of pleasure as it reduces the enjoyable task of choosing a wine to a system in which you must dissect a dish into its sweet, sour, salty and bitter components and pair it with a wine that has been dismantled into elements of acidity, pH, phenols and diacetylenes. You don't know whether to grab a fork or a piece of litmus paper.

Here, instinct is just another word for experience, and I'm afraid that's the bottom line for pairing wines and foods. Years of trying many dishes with different wines yields preferences that can stand in for any system. Yet red wine with oysters was one experience I had not had.

Instinct took over and I began to think of reds that might go well with oysters. The wine would ideally be fresh and lively, not heavy, brooding or tannic. Reds from the Loire came to mind—a Chinon or Saumur, or a spirited gamay from Clos Roche Blanche.

Beaujolais was a natural, preferably from a snappy vintage like 2006, and I thought of more esoteric wines, like poulsard from the Jura—undersung, earthy, light-bodied, pale beauties that can sit in for whites. Or frappatos from Sicily, wines with a vivacious breeziness, or the agile, spicy zweigelts from Austria.

Not coincidentally, the wines sounded somewhat like what Dorie's servers had recommended. To go with oysters a light-textured wine was imperative. So were wines with mineral, earth or spice flavors rather than overt fruitiness, to complement the saline, cucumber and mineral flavors in oysters.

I dragged along a friend to Balthazar, where the shellfish are superb and the wine list features the sorts of bottles I had in mind. I decided to pick four reds and let it fly with a couple dozen oysters, half East Coast and half West. I was disappointed not to find any Belons on the list, but I rarely do this side of the Atlantic.

Red No. 1 was a 2004 Arbois Trousseau from Jacques Puffeney, a wild red with a kind of funky animal quality. I would have preferred the lighter poulsard, but none was on the list so I settled for the trousseau. The others were a pure, light 2006 Morgon from Marcel Lapierre, a 2002 Chinon Les Picasses from Olga Raffault and a 2005 Givry from Chofflet-Valdenaire. The list offered a dozen other possible choices.

Two of the wines worked beautifully with the oysters. The Morgon, with its dancing lightness and minerality, was delicious with every type of oyster. Often, Morgons are somewhat stolid, but I'd had this wine before and knew what to expect. Otherwise I might have sought out a lighter Chiroubles or Brouilly. The Givry, from the Côte Chalonnaise, surprised me by how well it went with the oysters. The key, again, for this pinot noir was its lightness and freshness. I think reds from Sancerre or Alsace, both light pinot noirs, also might have worked well.

On the other hand, the Chinon surprised me by clashing with the oysters. It was too assertive; perhaps a Saumur-Champigny would have been a better choice. Likewise, the Arbois overpowered the oysters, with one exception. The briniest oyster, a Stingray from the Chesapeake, was great with the funky Arbois. To be honest, I've never seen the pairing of brine and funk on any food and wine matching chart.

Like Dorie, I didn't come away from my experiment feeling as if any of these reds would knock Muscadet off the top of the oyster-and-wine hierarchy. But I took pleasure in the experience.

It was fun, it was tasty, and I thought people who refuse to drink white wine would now have some enjoyable options with oysters. And I had some good wines with my post-oysters steak frites.

The experience reminded me of a dinner eight or nine years ago with a winemaker in the Mosel region of Germany. He made the case for serving aged riesling with steak, venison and hearty game dishes. I thought, "Sure, but why would you?" Now, I'm thinking, why not?

December 2008

Oysters With Miso Glaze

By FLORENCE FABRICANT

In a recent column, my colleague Eric Asimov discussed drinking red wine with oysters on the half shell. My instinct, like his, would have led me to Chinon. But he preferred a Morgon and a Givry, speculating that perhaps the Chinon he tried was too assertive.

I decided to see what I thought about oysters with Chinon, but instead of serving them raw, I broiled them with a simple, creamy glaze that I bolstered with just a dollop of red miso paste.

With oysters done this way, the Chinon I had on hand, the Philippe Alliet 2005, an earthy, spicy wine that was soft and open on the palate, came through as a lovely partner.

My only complaint was that my oysters, bluepoints from Long Island, were a trifle bland. Next time I will try to find Malpeques, Moonstones or Wellfleets, to bring a deeper, brinier flavor to the dish.

Time: 30 minutes   **Yield:** 4 to 6 servings

2 dozen oysters on the half shell, juices reserved
Clam juice or fish stock, as needed
1½ tablespoons unsalted butter
½ cup minced shallots
4 teaspoons flour

1 tablespoon lemon juice
1 tablespoon red miso paste
1 cup heavy cream
Salt and freshly ground white pepper
½ cup fine bread crumbs

1. Arrange oysters on a baking sheet, using crumpled foil or rock salt to keep them steady. A large madeleine pan covered in foil is an excellent alternative. Measure the oyster juices and, if needed, add enough clam juice or fish stock to make ½ cup. Preheat broiler.

2. In a saucepan, melt butter over low heat. Add shallots and sauté until soft. Whisk in flour, cook briefly and add oyster juice and lemon juice, whisking until blended. Whisk in miso, then gradually whisk in cream. Cook 3 to 4 minutes. Season with salt and pepper. Mix in crumbs.

3. Spoon mixture on oysters, covering them completely. Broil 5 minutes until glazed and bubbling. Serve.

March 2008

Three Meals Point the Way to Fish in Red Wine Sauce

By FLORENCE FABRICANT

Fish served with red wine has long stopped being a culinary faux pas. But for this pairing I wanted the fish to be in red wine, not just with it.

Just days after we tasted the alluring 2003 wines from St.-Émilion, I was at a dinner party where bottles of fine Bordeaux were poured.

One of the dishes served with them was a classic matelote, prepared by Ronan Cadorel, who works for Daniel Boulud. A matelote is a stew in which eel is cooked in a wine sauce with fingerling potatoes, button mushrooms and bacon lardons. Though red wine fish dishes are served all over France, matelotes are typical of the southwest, near the Bordeaux region.

Then, dining at Alain Ducasse at the Essex House one night, the menu included a matelote of Thai snapper in red wine.

Shortly thereafter, at Gordon Ramsay at the London, line-caught turbot in St.-Émilion sauce was on the menu. That clinched it. How could I resist the notion of pairing our earthy, complex 2003 St.-Émilions with fish in red wine sauce?

I was surprised to find turbot in a couple of markets, both Canadian wild (fillets) and French farm-raised (whole). Neil Ferguson, Gordon Ramsay's chef de cuisine, said sea bass fillets would be a fine stand-in.

In reproducing the Ramsay recipe, I simplified it somewhat, leaving out the salsify that garnished the fish.

Nevertheless, the dish requires the full attention of the cook the whole time, with nothing suitable for advance preparation.

Though you do not have to use a St.-Émilion for the sauce, a Bordeaux-style wine, especially one with a generous component of merlot, is particularly appropriate. The same goes for your choice to pour at the table.

Turbot Poached in St.-Émilion

Adapted from GORDON RAMSAY AT THE LONDON

Time: 1 hour **Yield:** 4 servings

8 medium-size Yukon Gold
  potatoes, about 1 pound
Salt
7 tablespoons crème fraîche
8 tablespoons unsalted butter,
  preferably high-fat European
  style, diced
Freshly ground black pepper
3 tablespoons extra virgin olive oil

16 pearl onions, peeled
1 large shallot, finely chopped
2 cups St.-Émilion or other dry
  red wine, preferably merlot
2 cups fish stock
1 pound turbot or sea bass fillets,
  skinned, in four pieces
1 tablespoon chopped flat-leaf
  parsley leaves.

1. Place potatoes in boiling salted water and cook until tender, about 15 minutes. Drain, peel and mash in a ricer. Return to pan, heat briefly and add 5 tablespoons crème fraîche and 1½ tablespoons butter. Season with salt and pepper and set aside in pan, covered.

2. Heat 2 tablespoons oil in a small skillet, add onions and sauté over medium heat until lightly browned and tender. Set aside, covered.

3. Heat remaining oil in a wide saucepan or a sauté pan that can hold fish in a single layer. Add shallots and sauté over low heat 5 minutes. Add wine and stock and bring to a simmer. Slip fish pieces into pan. Poach 3 to 4 minutes, until just firm. Remove fish, draining well. Place on a warm plate and cover to keep warm.

4. Boil cooking liquid until reduced to about 1 cup. Whisk in remaining crème fraîche and season to taste with salt and pepper. Over low heat add remaining butter bit by bit, whisking it in. Sauce will thicken somewhat and turn glossy.

5. Reheat potato purée and spoon into center of each of 4 dinner plates. Place a piece of fish on top and place onions around. Gently reheat sauce and spoon over each portion. Sprinkle with parsley and serve.

January 2007

How I Spent My Summer
of Riesling, by Terroir

By FRANK BRUNI

On June 21 the sommelier and restaurateur Paul Grieco did something mischievous, idealistic, provocative, ornery and, in its way, rather sweet. Which is to say he summed up, in one sweeping gesture, what makes him such an indelible character in the New York dining and drinking scene.

He revised the menus at his two Terroir wine bars in downtown Manhattan so that anyone interested in a white by the glass would be channeled—nay, forcefully herded—in a certain direction.

Chardonnay? Not an option, unless you were in for a whole bottle. Sauvignon blanc? Same deal, along with verdicchio, sémillon, grüner veltliner. In their stead you could order riesling, riesling or, if those didn't appeal, riesling. And that will remain so through Sept. 22, when Mr. Grieco ends what he calls the Summer of Riesling, an act of evangelism for a grape he worships and a distillation of his idiosyncratic ways.

Mr. Grieco celebrated his first Summer of Riesling in 2008, but that year and the next it affected only the Terroir in the East Village, with just 24 seats. (The second Terroir, in TriBeCa, with about 75 seats, opened this April.)

He recalls that at the start, the chef Marco Canora, with whom he owns the wine bars and the East Village restaurant Hearth, suggested that he could make his point and have his fun but run less risk of disappointing patrons if he devoted, say, just half of the whites by the glass to riesling.

Mr. Grieco declined.

Some of the servers working for him implored him to consider the awkward position he was putting them in.

Mr. Grieco told them to buck up.

Riesling, he reasoned, deserved uncompromising advocacy, so that its popularity might finally catch up with what he sees as its extraordinary expressiveness, its underrated nimbleness, its food-friendliness and its cool counterpoint to a hot August day.

"There should be no fallback," he said recently at his TriBeCa bar. Actually, he declaimed it. I could almost hear the trumpet blasts bracketing his words.

And this was the corresponding visual: above sneakers and cargo shorts he wore a T-shirt with, front and center, an image of a hokey, oversize, fill-in-the-blank tag that read, "Hello, My Name Is . . . Summer of Riesling." That same image immediately greets visitors to the Terroir Web site (wineisterroir.com).

Mr. Grieco, 44, tends to dress for effect. In a fancy mood he favors seersucker and striped suits, and pairs brightly colored shirts—Paul Smith is his preferred label—with boldly patterned ties. His philosophy when he puts together an outfit, he explained, is that "if, upon first reflection, you look at it and say it clashes, then I've accomplished my goal."

He grooms for effect, too, maintaining a mustache so thin that it prompts a double take—is that lip liner or actual hair?—and a goatee that on this occasion crawled like a spider plant to a destination below his chin. His natty-meets-naughty aesthetic is all his own, and it carries over to his phraseology, which weds scholarly words and cheeky colloquialisms. A little-known wine, for example, is "esoteric juice."

Riesling as a category isn't esoteric, but a by-the-glass list of whites with about two dozen rieslings and nothing else certainly qualifies. I asked him: doesn't it invert, or at least pervert, the usual relationship of restaurant host to guest?

He nodded, pensively.

"I'm taking a somewhat inhospitable view," he conceded, adding, with a sparkle in his eye: "Let's be honest. I'm forcing it down your throat."

He has been building toward this brand of naughty defiance since Hearth's opening in 2003, when the wine list was less a presentation of alternatives than a volume of gonzo literature, thick with messianic riffs and madcap digressions.

Hearth's current list preserves that spirit, presenting this meditation on one of the proprietors of Chateau Musar, a Lebanese winery: "If Jesus and Satan had a son (I guess the first question should be: in which state would Jesus and Satan get married?), he would be called Serge Hochar," Mr. Grieco wrote. "He is my savior and tormentor."

At Insieme, a restaurant in Midtown that Mr. Canora and Mr. Grieco ran from 2007 until late last year, Mr. Grieco used an entire page of the wine list to link a celebrity in the news with a bottle of muscat on the menu.

"I cannot express the joy I felt earlier this week with the release of Paris Hilton from L.A. County jail," he wrote, with gentle sarcasm. "The previous three weeks had been a living hell, wondering how she was doing." This went on for many sentences, concluding with an exhortation that customers "celebrate with a cool little superfluous wine from southern Italy. It sparkles like Paris's eyes, it titillates the soul like Paris's video."

Where in the world did Mr. Grieco come from? Toronto, where his paternal grandfather opened what Mr. Grieco says was that city's first formal Italian restaurant, La Scala, in 1961. It was a true family business, employing Mr. Grieco's father and then Mr. Grieco, who bartended there after dropping out of college.

He relocated in 1991 to New York, where he worked as a waiter or manager in various Manhattan restaurants, starting with Remi. Its general manager at the time, Chris Cannon, says Mr. Grieco stood out for his fierce work ethic and vivid attire, which included a jacket with such broad gold and blue stripes that it called to mind pajamas.

"He likes to stir the pot," Mr. Cannon said.

Mr. Grieco later moved to Gramercy Tavern, where he was named the beverage director in the late 1990s. By then, he said, he had caught the wine bug and, through travel and tasting, educated himself extensively. He largely credits a predecessor at Gramercy, Steven Olson, with opening his eyes (and palate) to the full magnificence of riesling.

I first really talked with him back at Insieme, asking him to choose the wines for my table. He brought us two bottles of red, each label obscured, and challenged us to guess which was from the Old World (Italy, say, or France) and which from the New (e.g. the Americas). This wasn't conventional sommelier behavior, but it perfectly read the table's mood—and captured Mr. Grieco's particular charisma. For him playfulness and passion trump propriety.

At the Terroirs the wine lists, in three-ring binders, are chaotic with stickers, maps, photos, cartoons and, of course, Mr. Grieco's musings, which touch on the Tea Party, Lindsay Lohan, the Emperor Palpatine in the *Star Wars* movies, Eliot Spitzer, global warming, Greek mythology and the Greek debt crisis, for which he proposes an enological palliative: riesling, on account of its "bang for the buck."

The current Summer of Riesling is his most aggressive, and included a recent four-band concert at the Knitting Factory, where the only alcoholic beverage on hand was—you'll never believe this—riesling.

I'm not nearly as mad for it as he is, and have cursed him at times for his stridency. But thanks to him and the two Terroirs, I do appreciate riesling more than ever. In that sense, I guess, Mr. Grieco has saved me—amid a minor measure of torment.

August 2010

Not So Cold . . . Doctor's Order

By ERIC ASIMOV

It could be that I'm a crank. Or a grump. Or maybe I'm anticipating that time in life when I'm not expected to be anything but cranky or grumpy. But I must call attention to an almost reflex practice among many American wine drinkers that troubles me in the extreme.

It's the habit of chilling white wine far too long and drinking it way too cold.

This is perhaps a pointless argument to make in a country that loves things cold. We demand ice cubes in just about any beverage but beer, yet fetishize cold beer to the extent of marketing a brand simply by promising it will offer an icier drinking experience, all while reveling in the shivery goose-flesh chill of over-air-conditioned theaters, restaurants, cars and offices.

Nonetheless, I feel that I must try if only because it is clear to me that drinking overchilled white wine—good white wine—deprives one of fully enjoying the complex aromas and delicious flavors in the glass.

This is not a new discovery. Basic science makes clear that raising the temperature at which a wine is served allows the various flavor compounds in a wine to evaporate and rise, thus adding to a wine's aroma, which contributes greatly to enjoyment on the palate.

In a recent column on Chablis I suggested in passing that the wine should not be served too cold. But now, with summer nearly upon us and the consumption of white wine rising, I think it's worth making the point clearly and explicitly: To enhance the pleasure of drinking a good white wine, please do not serve it too cold.

This suggestion is not so easy to follow if you're in a restaurant. If you order a white wine it may well come to the table straight from the refrigerator and head straight for the ice-water bucket. Many sommeliers know better, but they are accustomed to consumers who want to keep white wine a notch below freezing.

Nonetheless, I appreciate the sommelier who takes the trouble to ask you whether you want the wine on ice or prefer the bottle left on the table. The table, please! Meanwhile, I'm often left cupping the wine glass in the palms of my hands hoping to impart some heat.

I should say right here that wines without much complexity to offer, which might be a bit sweet and out of balance, are best enjoyed with refrigerator temperatures masking their flaws. A one-dimensional pinot grigio, a light rosé devoid of much personality, these are sluicing wines best guzzled cold for their pure icy refreshment.

But what if that rosé were dry and spicy with pleasing mineral and herbal flavors, like a 2008 Edmunds St. John Bone-Jolly gamay noir I had not so long ago? I might not have known it was anything more than a pretty wine the color of pale ruby if I had consumed it at refrigerator temperature.

The other night I pulled a bottle of white Bordeaux from the fridge, a 2006 Blanc de Lynch-Bages. I opened it and poured it right away. It might well have been an anonymous inexpensive white. As it warmed, though, its creamy texture and complexities emerged. It was waxy and floral with depth and detail, even at room temperature.

Not that most whites are best enjoyed at room temperature. That would be too warm. I recently had a 2005 Helfrich riesling from the grand cru vineyard Steinklotz in Alsace. Lightly chilled, it was ideal, full of mineral and floral aromas, steely on the palate. At room temperature, though, it seemed flat, without energy or lift.

Alas, as with so many wine issues, serving temperature is a little complicated. Each white wine probably has its ideal temperature. Yet for me, the starting point ought to be lightly chilled. It's a lot easier to cool a bottle by dunking it in ice water for 15 minutes than it is to warm up an icy bottle, which might take 45 minutes— no, I don't recommend the microwave.

Some people might argue that sparkling wines and sweet wines need to be served colder than dry still whites, but I'm afraid I must take the other side. I feel about sparkling wines the same as I do about still whites—if the wine is complex and balanced its personality will be hidden if served too cold. But if the sparkling wine is not that good, allowing it to warm up from refrigerator temperature will only reveal its flaws.

The same goes for wines with residual sugar in them. If you have a beautiful German riesling, say a spätlese from the Mosel, the wine will be so well balanced that it will be perfectly refreshing lightly chilled or even at room temperature. Too cold, and the subtleties and undertones of the wine will be absent.

You might think by now that I'm a fanatic on this issue. You may well be right. I've come to believe as well that good beer is often served too cold for the same reasons. Not that I'm calling for warm beer—I'm not un-American, after all. But the same principle applies: lightly chilling the beer allows shadings and nuances to emerge.

I fear I may have some splendid isolation ahead of me this summer. I recently had a dinner at a seafood restaurant with a prominent sommelier who seemed generally to agree with my feelings about serving temperature. We were enjoying an excellent Chablis, a 2004 Vaudésir from William Fèvre. The bottle was resting quite comfortably on the table, when, within minutes of turning our attention to other matters, my companion asked the sommelier to put the bottle back on ice.

What? Had he not heard me at all? I was left to splutter as he looked at me defiantly. Apparently this issue is going to require some shouting from the hilltops.

June 2009

Chill Out

By FRANK J. PRIAL

The conventional wisdom is reds at room temperature, whites and rosé chilled. Correct? Not always. And when we do follow the rules, we tend to take them to extremes, serving reds too warm and whites too cold. There must be a course in maître d'hôtel school where students are taught never to serve a white wine until it is so cold that absolutely no taste is discernible.

But what of the reds? Can they be chilled? Not only can be, but in some cases should be. Young, fruity red wines benefit most from chilling, and since 90 percent of the world's wines are drunk when they are young and fruity, chilling emerges as an interesting possibility for many of them. Beaujolais is the prime example, and not just simple Beaujolais and Beaujolais Villages. The bigger, sturdier Beaujolais, like Régnié, Brouilly, Chiroubles, Juliénas and Saint-Amour, all taste better in warm weather if they've spent 20 minutes in the refrigerator or ice bucket.

Over the past few years, a number of Beaujolais cousins have appeared on the market, largely because Beaujolais growers pushed their own prices too high. Most of these wines are made from the same grape, the gamay, but cost a dollar or two less. Some, like the Côtes Roannaise, Côtes du Forez, Gamay de l'Ardèchen and Saint-Pourçain, have turned up in this country. They can be pleasant substitutes for Beaujolais and should be treated the same way—served slightly chilled, particularly in the warm months.

California beaujolais—also called gamay beaujolais—is another candidate for cooling. These wines seem slightly sweeter than their French counterparts, and chilling lessens the impact of the sweetness. Fresh young zinfandels can be enhanced by having their temperature dropped a few degrees, and most red jug wines definitely improve when chilled. Some producers of low-cost varietal wines, like Glen Ellen Winery, leave a touch of residual sugar in their red wines on the tested theory that Americans talk dry but drink sweet. These wines, too, taste more refreshing in the summer when they are cooled.

Italy's dolcetto, made to be drunk young, is yet another type of wine that lends itself to being served cold. Again, these are uncomplicated, fruity varieties at their best with simple Italian meals. In fact, Italy has dozens of wines, including the lighter, inexpensive Chiantis, that benefit from cooler temperatures.

Young wines from the South of France are in this category, too, such as young Côtes du Rhône and Côtes du Ventoux, as well as the rest of the simple reds made in the vast semicircle that is the Midi, from Menton in the east to Collioure, near the Spanish border.

Indeed, wine purists believe that we drink all our red wines too warm. Room temperature is considered the norm, but room temperature when the norm was devised was closer to 60 degrees than the 70 most of us prefer today. "At 70 degrees or over," says Hugh Johnson, the English wine expert, "red wines lose their attractive 'cut.'" This means that even the best red wines probably need a bit of cooling off, unless they came from a wine cellar with the recommended temperature of about 55 degrees.

Most experts say old red Burgundies and Rhône wines should be served the warmest—that is, around 65 degrees. Fine red Bordeaux should be served at about 62 degrees, and young red Burgundies at about 60—the same temperature as important white Burgundies. The proper serving temperature for lighter reds, such as Beaujolais, is actually below that—about 56 degrees.

It's possible to carry all this fine-tuning to absurd lengths. There are even characters who carry their own thermometers along to restaurants. Whether the idea is to impress friends and intimidate waiters or to get the temperature just right, I'll leave to you to decide.

But at any temperature, whatever warm-weather wine you choose should be refreshing. If you feel like cooling off your red wine, do it. If it's too cold, let it warm up. After all, the conventional wisdom is that rules are meant to be broken, particularly wine rules.

May 1992

A Sturdy Red for Winter

By ERIC ASIMOV

In the popular imagination, Provence calls to mind sunny, pastel images of hillside towns climbing up from the sea. For the wine lover, Provence mostly conjures up the tangy, lighthearted spirit of rosé, sipped within earshot of the water. It simply doesn't square that carefree Provence is also home to a superb red wine that practically epitomizes the term "brooding."

But then, anybody who has read the Marseilles-based novels of Jean-Claude Izzo knows that Provence has its dark side, too. As far as wine goes, that would be Bandol. There, in a pocket of terraced hills west of Toulon, within sniffing distance of the Mediterranean, surprisingly sturdy wines made largely from the mourvèdre grape can stun you with their haunting beauty.

Just the other week, I had a 2004 Bandol from Château Pradeaux ($37), one of the most resolutely traditional of Bandol producers. When young, these wines are deep, dark and practically savage, but this one was just emerging from the stranglehold of its tannic embrace. It was decidedly dry and structured yet bewitching, with aromas of licorice, leather and flowers along with something wild and untamed. By its weight, tannins, aromas and flavors, the wine reminded me of nebbiolo, except for that wild element, which is very much mourvèdre's own.

Like many of Mr. Izzo's characters, mourvèdre is an immigrant. It is native to Spain, where it is called monastrell and dominates robust wines like Jumilla and Alicante. These wines are dark and highly aromatic, but often seem, at least to my taste, jammy and coarse-grained.

In the Languedoc, mourvèdre is often used to add structure to wines. It plays a supporting role to grenache in Châteauneuf-du-Pape, although Château de Beaucastel is a notable exception. In Beaucastel's Châteauneuf, and especially in its scarce, high-end cuvée, Hommage à Jacques Perrin, mourvèdre takes the prime role, contributing a characteristically feral, funky note to the wines that differs markedly from the typically sweeter fruitiness of wines dominated by grenache.

In Australia, old-vine mourvèdre is often blended with grenache and shiraz. In California, where mourvèdre is also known as mataró, plantings of Rhône grapes have increased markedly since 1990. Mourvèdre is dwarfed in acreage there by syrah and grenache, but still a few intrepid producers there do make mourvèdre wines.

Not surprisingly, one of them is Tablas Creek in Paso Robles, the sibling winery to Beaucastel, which makes a superb, darkly fruity, mineral-drenched mourvèdre in small quantities ($30 for the 2008 vintage). Its flagship Rhône-style blend, fittingly called Esprit de Beaucastel, is well balanced and pleasing, its 2008 offering some of the dark notes of mourvèdre without the gamy edge ($42). La Clarine Farm also makes an excellent mourvèdre, from Cedarville Vineyard in the Sierra foothills. Its 2008 indeed offers the animal-like musk of a Bandol, combined with an exuberant blackberry fruitiness and a violet aroma ($23).

Bonny Doon Vineyard occasionally makes a mourvèdre, called Old Telegram in homage to the Châteauneuf producer Domaine du Vieux Télégraphe. But Old Telegram is made only when the vintages are exceptional, said Randall Grahm, Bonny Doon's proprietor. "And honestly, the vintages have not been exceptional," he told me recently.

It turns out mourvèdre has a significant problem: it's highly sensitive and not easy to grow. It demands plenty of sun and warmth to ripen properly, preferably with cool nights so that the grapes don't become overly sweet and the wines overblown. It requires a long ripening cycle, and the vines apparently prefer soils rich in limestone.

Nowhere else are the conditions for mourvèdre as right as they are in Bandol, where the wines reach their apogee. Even in Bandol, mourvèdre was almost forgotten. It was the dominant red grape of Provence until phylloxera struck in the late 19th century, and it all but disappeared. Growers grafted their European vines onto American roots, which were resistant to the root-destroying phylloxera aphids, but the first rootstocks they chose were not hospitable to the persnickety mourvèdre vines. Many growers abandoned mourvèdre for more productive grapes.

The rebirth of mourvèdre in the region is largely credited to the efforts of the Peyraud family of Domaine Tempier, which fought in the 1930s to establish the Bandol appellation. When the appellation was officially granted in 1941—some life did go on in the war years—the rules required only that the red wine be 10 percent mourvèdre. That figure was slowly increased over the years until 1977, when it reached its current required level of 50 percent.

Tempier today is the leading name in Bandol and makes the benchmark wine—taming the beast at the heart of mourvèdre and producing about as elegant a wine as you will find in the region, the Cuvée Classique. The 2008 is still dense and chewy but accessible, more floral and licorice than animal.

But the beast lives on in the soul of Château Pradeaux, partly because the Portalis family, which has owned the estate for more than 250 years, has refused to change its methods. Unlike other producers, which remove the stems of the grapes before fermentation to make a softer wine, Pradeaux ferments with stems intact, ages the wine in huge old oak rounds for up to four years and uses at least 95 percent mourvèdre in its blend. The result may come from Provence, but it's a wine at home in the winter.

November 2010

12 Reasons to Look Beyond the Usual Wine Selections

By ERIC ASIMOV

It's entirely possible to go through life eating nothing but the most familiar foods, reading books by the customary best-selling authors or listening to a stock set of composers. Taking great pleasure in the same things over and over is not a bad thing.

Similarly, many people are content to drink only well-known wines. Why not? They satisfy again and again. Alas, producers around the world learned years ago that they could exploit the desire for the familiar, planting a lot of cabernet sauvignon, chardonnay and other international grapes, regardless of the local traditions, to appeal to a global market.

I understand the thinking, yet the world of wine has so much more to offer.

For anybody truly curious about the glorious extent of wine, now is the greatest time in history to be a wine lover. Never before has such a vast diversity of wines been available to so many people. Many are made from unfamiliar grapes, grown in little-known places, yet they offer thrilling drinking for those eager for new experiences.

Like sea creatures discovered at colossal depths, these unfamiliar wines are not new at all. Many represent traditions that reach back centuries. Sadly, in some cases, these traditions barely hang on. The survival of the diversity we now enjoy depends partly on building appreciation of these little-known grapes and wines. In other cases, the grapes, though uncommon, have already gained a following.

Either way, here are a dozen obscure grapes that are the foundation of some wonderful wines and will reward intrepid explorers.

ASSYRTIKO, from the volcanic island of Santorini in the Aegean Sea produces dry, deliciously minerally wines that are superb with seafood and just about any other light dish that smacks of the Mediterranean. If you like assyrtiko, it's worth exploring other Greek white-wine grapes like moschofilero and roditis. Top producers: Gaia, Sigalas and Spyros Hatziyiannis.

BLAUFRÄNKISCH, a red grape grown mostly in the Burgenland region of eastern Austria, can produce gorgeously savory wines that combine the grace of pinot noir and the spice of syrah. Producers worth seeking include Moric,

Paul Achs, Umathum and, from Carnuntum, a region north of the Bergenland, Muhr-Van der Niepoort.

FRAPPATO, from southeastern Sicily, makes lovely, fresh and lively wines that are delicious summer reds, especially when lightly chilled. When frappato is combined with nero d'Avola, it makes the slightly more substantial Cerasuolo di Vittoria, which goes wonderfully with a wide range of foods. Producers to seek out include Arianna Occhipinti, COS and Valle dell'Acate.

FUMIN comes from the Vallée d'Aoste, the peculiar Alpine borderland that is technically Italian, though the language is French. In the hands of a top producer, like Grosjean, fumin makes a spicy, floral red that can be complex and structured. I love these Alpine wines, and a bottle of the Grosjean fumin may cause you to seek out other little-known grapes, like the superb red cornalin and the racy white petite arvine. Around $35 a bottle, these wines are not cheap but are stunningly good.

FURMINT, not to be confused with fumin, is the great white grape of Hungary. It's a crucial constituent in the lavish sweet wine Tokaji aszu, and increasingly is being used in distinctive dry wines with rich textures and complex floral aromas. Look for producers like Kiralyudvar, Royal Tokaji, Dobogo, Oremus and Disznoko.

GRIGNOLINO, mostly from the Piedmont region of Italy, makes a pale, easy-drinking red that is fresh, slightly bitter and somewhat akin to frappato, but even lighter. A delicious wine for casual drinking, perhaps with salumi or pizza. I very much like the grignolino from Cascina 'Tavijn. Strangely, Heitz Cellar in Napa Valley also makes a little from an old eight-acre vineyard. I've yet to find it, but am looking forward to trying it.

LAGREIN from the Trentino-Alto-Adige region of northeastern Italy produces earthy, minerally reds with the flavor of dark fruits that are enjoyably spicy and fresh. Look for wines from J. Hofstätter or Elena Walch.

MENCÍA is the source of excellent red wines from the regions of Ribeira Sacra and Bierzo in western Spain. The dense Bierzo reds have a haunting wild fruit flavor, but I'm partial to the lighter, more minerally wines from the steep, terraced vineyards of Ribeira Sacra. Look for Guímaro, Dominio do Bibei, Raúl Pérez and D. Ventura.

PINEAU D'AUNIS, an ancient red grape from the Touraine region of the Loire Valley, is once more finding favor in the more avant-garde wine bars of France and among discerning wine lovers. The wines can be spicy, peppery and, depending on the producer, attractively funky. Look for Domaine le Briseau, Domaine de Bellivière and Thierry Puzelat.

ROMORANTIN, another ancient grape from the Touraine, can make utterly succulent whites that are perfect balances between sharp citrus freshness and rounded floral, honeyed flavors. Cour-Cheverny is a tiny appellation that has been carved out to showcase Romorantin. François Cazin makes two versions: Le Petit Chambord is dry, while Cuvée Renaissance is slightly sweet.

TREIXADURA, when meticulously grown and vinified in the Ribeiro region of Spain, can make profound whites, richly textured and mineral-flavored, especially in the hands of a producer like Emilio Rojo. Wines from the godello grape are also well worth sampling.

TROUSSEAU, from the Jura region of France, makes lovely reds with a presence at odds with their light body. Top producers include Jacques Puffeney, Ganevat and Philippe Bornard.

Well, that's a dozen, and I'm just starting. We haven't even mentioned poulsard and savagnin from the Jura, or kerner from Germany, or even duras from Gaillac in southwestern France. Cabernet sauvignon and chardonnay, even riesling and syrah, are only the beginning.

July 2010

Wine Enough to Please Them All

By R. W. APPLE Jr.

These next five or six preholiday weeks are the times that try wine lovers' souls.

What, we ask ourselves every year, should we drink with the festive bird or beast? It is a question many of us are called upon to answer repeatedly—first before Thanksgiving, then again before Christmas, and maybe again before New Year's Eve.

There is no pat answer, at least none that goes beyond the sound if rather unhelpful advice "Drink what you like." But there are certain important aspects of celebratory feasting that should be kept in mind because, like candles in the dark, they can provide a flicker of guidance in making choices.

Start with this: Relax. If Cousin Lew, a newcomer to the family table this year, turns out to be allergic to red wine, give him a sherry or a Coke. If Aunt Emily thinks your wine choices are a wee bit pretentious, so be it; she probably thinks the same about your car. If others think you are too cheap to pour something that measures up to their lofty standards, let them take their snobbery to a restaurant next year and exercise it on an overpriced wine list.

This is just wine, not life; a drink, not moral theology.

For hundreds of years, a glass or two of fizz has heralded auspicious events, and both Thanksgiving and Christmas are celebrations of very auspicious events, national in one case, religious in the other, even if that is sometimes forgotten. So consider breaking out the Champagne for a preprandial drink. If you hit the lottery recently, go for the miraculously full-bodied Krug, perhaps the finest of Champagnes. If not, try nonvintage Veuve Clicquot—rich, reliable and attractively priced, a favorite around our house.

Nothing quite matches Champagne, in either quality or price, but a few other bubblies come close, like Roederer Estate, made in California's enigmatic Anderson Valley by the same firm that produces the sumptuous Cristal in France. Iron Horse, from the Russian River, is another winner. Italy provides appealing alternatives, including Franciacorta (Ca' del Bosco is superb but costly) and prosecco (Mionetto, moderately priced, is eminently drinkable).

My wife, Betsey, a Southerner, likes oysters at holiday time; perhaps they are a first-course tradition in your family, too. The Champagne or other sparkling

wine will taste good with them, providing that it is ultradry or brut, but my preference would be for something still and dry, like a fragrant Sancerre from the
great Henri Bourgeois, or a flinty Chablis Premier Cru from one of the several
growers in the Dauvissat family, or a faintly iodinic Muscadet from Louis
Métaireau. California sauvignon blancs from Cakebread (crisp and citrusy) or
Geyser Peak (made in a frankly Antipodean style by an Australian winemaker)
would also serve nicely.

So much for the preliminaries. What about the main course, the enormous
main course, full of contradictory flavors, that tradition dictates for these days of
feasting? Once in a while, like many people, my family rebels, and we eat a rib
roast of beef or even a goose, but it's usually turkey, stuffing, brussels sprouts,
creamed corn, cranberries, pies and the like.

That parade of bland, sweet, fruity, sometimes spicy flavors is hard to
match with wine, and it has produced some outlandish suggestions, including
gewürztraminer, which the Alsatians who make it drink with everything, from
sauerkraut to cheese. Not for me, but I can imagine solving this conundrum with
Conundrum, a Napa Valley blend of five varietals that yields an unusual white
wine, both lush and robust, lively and full of tropical-fruit flavors.

Better though, in my view, a red with good fruit and slight sweetness.

But which? Since holiday meals are usually served to a crowd of people, often
people in a mood to drink more than they usually would, you will want something
that you can afford in quantity. But presuming that neither Robert M. Parker Jr.
nor your favorite sommelier is joining you, people are not likely to spend much
time discussing the wine's pedigree, aroma and maturity anyway.

So unless you are planning to have just three or four at your table, leave the
Beychevelle, the Bonnes-Mares and the Opus One in the cellar.

The most obvious choice, I suppose, is Beaujolais, but not Beaujolais nouveau,
even though its annual release on the third Wednesday in November closely coin-
cides with Thanksgiving. The best bet would be one of the more substantial crus,
like Brouilly, but a good Beaujolais-Villages would be a more than adequate choice
if you're faced with irrigating a crowd.

Among dependable Beaujolais shippers whose wines are widely distributed in
the United States are Joseph Drouhin and, of course, Georges Duboeuf, dubbed
"the Grand Fromage" of Beaujolais by Hugh Johnson, the English writer.

Other affordable, attractive choices might be a good Côtes du Rhône, one
from Guigal or another well-known grower, for instance, or an Old Vine Red

from Marietta Cellars in the Sonoma Valley—a varying but always reliable blend of zinfandel and several various grapes of Rhône Valley origin.

Pinot noir, once considered unmanageable outside France, may be the perfect holiday grape, producing scented, sometimes voluptuous wines in many countries these days. Wines from the fringes of the fabulous Côte d'Or in Burgundy can be bargains; look for St.-Aubin, which comes from a side valley in the more southerly Côte de Beaune, or a Côte de Nuits-Villages.

New Zealand, which first made its name with white wines, is now turning out such vivid and aromatic pinot noirs as Ata Rangi from Martinborough and Felton Road Block 3 from Central Otago, which is not a million miles from Antarctica. Australian pinot noirs from Coldstream Hills, founded by the wine critic James Halliday, and Jeffrey Grosset, who makes the New World's best riesling, Polish Hill, merit consideration if you can manage to find them.

But, hey, we're Americans, and Thanksgiving is a unique American holiday. So you might want to look to Oregon for your pinot—say, Benton Lane, a relatively inexpensive charmer packed with the flavor of cherries. Up the price ladder a bit, I would recommend the Burgundian-style bottlings of David Lett's Eyrie Vineyards, or Brick House, an alluring, more obviously Yankee pinot made by Doug Tunnell.

Betsey and I like to drink the wine of friends on important days. Both Mr. Lett and Mr. Tunnell, who in an earlier life as a CBS News correspondent was a colleague, fall into that category, as does the remarkable Paul Draper, one of whose Ridge zinfandels might make a fine holiday companion, too.

If Rhône-style red seems a good idea, you could hardly do better than the luscious Nine Popes (the name is an awful pun on Châteauneuf-du-Pape), made by Charles Melton, a Marlboro Man look-alike, in Australia's Barossa Valley. Or the toasty, mourvèdre-dominated Bandol produced in Provence by Domaine Tempier, which Alice Waters served at the 30th birthday party of her restaurant, Chez Panisse. Or, for that matter, one of the many successes of the original Rhône Ranger, Randall Grahm—maybe Cigare Volant or Old Telegram.

And to finish? What better than one of the exquisite Cognac-model Germain-Robin brandies made on Ansley J. Coale's mountaintop farm in northern California? No, they're not cheap, but a little drop'll do you.

November 2003

In a Season of Memory,
a Toast to What Endures

By ALEX WITCHEL

September is a month of ghosts, for me, anyway. Back to school conjures once-close friends, now scattered or gone. The memorial service central to Yom Kippur evokes profound loss. And since 9/11, it's almost impossible to look at a late summer blue sky without seeing—and smelling—the smoke.

So it is a bit of a lift that this week brings the publication of the 25th anniversary edition of *Windows on the World Complete Wine Course* (Sterling, $27.95), by Kevin Zraly.

Mr. Zraly was the restaurant's wine director from 1976 to 2001. He was hired by the legendary Joe Baum when he was a 25-year-old wine salesman, a self-educated enophile with a bachelor's degree in education from SUNY New Paltz.

Though he kept the emphasis on French wines, Mr. Zraly embraced the rest of the world as well, turning Windows into an international wine mecca. At the time it was destroyed when the World Trade Center fell, its cellar held close to 100,000 bottles of 1,500 labels. In its final full year, it had the highest wine sales of any restaurant in the world, more than $6 million.

When Windows first opened, Mr. Zraly taught wine classes to members of its private lunch club. By 1980, the course went public, expanding to five eight-week sessions a year for groups of about 100 students each, eventually graduating 19,000 people.

When I took it in 1987, I appreciated Mr. Zraly's populist approach. There were no right or wrong answers when it came to wine; all that mattered was "I like it" or "I don't like it."

I didn't see him again until November 2001, when he relocated the class to the Marriott Marquis in Times Square, where it remains, though in recent years, he has taught only spring and fall sessions.

He was running on adrenaline then, still reeling from the loss of his professional home and so many colleagues. Like Michael Lomonaco, the chef of Windows, Mr. Zraly escaped disaster by default. On the morning of 9/11, Mr. Lomonaco stopped into LensCrafters on the concourse level of the World Trade Center to get his reading glasses fixed, instead of going straight to his office on the 106th floor. Mr. Zraly had taken the day off to celebrate the 10th birthday of his son, Anthony.

Two months later, I sat in on his class again, the first to be held away from Windows. To the usual group of white wines, he had added a Kistler chardonnay from his personal cellar. It was the generous, healing touch of a man whose passion for wine was such that he took a semester off from college to hitchhike to California and educate himself at his own expense about the industry, one winery at a time. After he graduated, he spent another year in Europe doing the same.

"I was obsessed," he told me last month in an interview in New Paltz. "With the taste of wine, the people who made it, everything about it."

This was the first time I had seen Mr. Zraly since 2001. Though he has published an update of the Windows wine course book every year (more than three million copies sold) and still teaches, I hadn't heard much about him. When I visited him, I discovered why.

In 2003, when his daughter Adriana, the youngest of his four children, was 4, her doctors diagnosed leukemia. After some rough years of treatment, she is now 10 and in remission. In 2005, on Palm Sunday, when most of the family was at church, the Zralys' house burned down.

I had thought he and I might sit and talk about it all. Instead, we stayed mostly in the car, driving from the fledgling vineyard he's planted with an organic farmer, to the Depuy Canal House, the site of his first restaurant job and wine class in 1971, then finally to his rebuilt home.

Mr. Zraly spoke haltingly about his family, eloquently about wine. He was sufficiently traumatized by events that he didn't travel for years.

But with the 25th anniversary edition of the book looming, he was inspired to hit the road again, visiting 100 wine regions around the world and tasting 4,000 wines. He expanded his existing chapters and added a new section.

Standing in his wine cellar, Mr. Zraly was the calmest he had been all day. We talked about Mr. Lomonaco (now the executive chef at Porter House New York) and the food he cooked at Windows.

Mr. Zraly said his favorite creation was the appetizer of scallops and capers he first tasted in 1997. With it, he recommends a Puligny-Montrachet, Olivier Leflaive.

"I did all the tasting for those pairings, and even the smell of that dish is so evocative for me," he said.

When I left, I could see him wish he had said, oh, about a million things more. No need. The all-encompassing love for wine that has defined his path, that he has shared with so many people, has remained his salvation. I wish for Mr. Zraly what he wishes for his readers in the dedication for his book's new edition: "May your glass always be more full than empty."

Sea Scallops with Brown Butter, Capers and Lemon
Adapted from MICHAEL LOMONACO

Time: 10 minutes   **Yield:** 4 appetizer servings

12 fresh sea scallops
Sea salt and freshly ground
    black pepper
¼ cup olive oil
3 tablespoons unsalted butter
1 tablespoon finely chopped shallot

2 tablespoons salt-packed capers,
    rinsed of excess salt
Juice of half a lemon
⅓ cup (packed) flat-leaf parsley
    leaves, finely chopped

1. Pat scallops dry with paper towels, and season lightly with salt and pepper. Heat a large sauté pan or nonreactive skillet over medium-high heat, and add oil. After 30 seconds, add scallops; do not crowd pan, work in batches if necessary. Sauté until well browned, about 2 minutes, then turn and cook other side. When second side is dark golden, transfer scallops to a platter; cover and keep warm.
2. Return sauté pan to heat, add butter, and cook until it begins to foam and turn golden. Add shallot and capers, sauté for 1 minute, then add lemon juice (being careful to avoid sputtering butter) and chopped parsley.
3. To serve, place 3 scallops on each of 4 warmed plates. Spoon butter, shallots and capers over scallops, and serve.

September 2009

Pairing Wine With Chinese Food

By JEN LIN-LIU

The red, Sichuan peppercorn-spiked gravy that covered the tender slices of beef served as a warning: This was going to be no easy task. "This is where most people reach for the beer," said Campbell Thompson, a Beijing-based wine importer.

"Or maybe just a glass of water," said another guest.

"Or maybe just white rice," chimed in a third dinner partner.

On a recent Tuesday evening, I gathered a group of eight wine and Chinese cuisine experts in my courtyard kitchen in central Beijing to taste a broad range of 10 Chinese dishes with eight wines. The goal was to test the common perception that it's challenging—or downright impossible—to pair wines with Chinese cuisine.

The Chinese have a dinnertime tradition of drinking baijiu, a high-grade Chinese grain alcohol, but in recent years, more international wines have begun to appear on restaurant menus in China, from the most traditional state-owned Chinese restaurants to trendy ones like Lan and Da Dong in Beijing.

But even as wine lists have emerged at restaurants in Beijing and Shanghai, some wine experts argue that little thought has gone into putting those wine lists together. Burgundies, costly bottles of Lafite, and anything labeled Bordeaux are often served at lavish Chinese meals meant to impress important guests. But some wine experts say that those wines clash with the spice and complex flavors of Sichuanese food and are too heavy to go with the delicate seafood dishes of Cantonese cuisine.

"The young nature of the local wine market is what inhibits creative wine pairings," said Gabriel Suk, the senior representative in Asia for the Chicago-based wine auction house Hart Davis Hart. "Chinese restaurants are told what to purchase by the local distributor, who might be making decisions based on sales margins rather than a concerted effort to find the best pairing."

Another challenge in pairing wines with Chinese cuisine is the complexity of sauces and ingredients that go into the dishes, said Fongyee Walker, who owns the Beijing wine consultancy Dragon Phoenix Wines with her husband, Edward Ragg. In Western cooking, she said, "you can almost think of the wine as a sauce that goes with the dish."

"In Chinese cooking," she continued, "the dishes are already balanced and complete in themselves. For example, a touch of sugar goes into almost every savory Chinese dish."

The upside is that because pairing wine with Chinese cuisine is a relatively new concept, "it's a blank slate," said Mr. Ragg.

I figured my kitchen, where I hold cooking classes and private dinners, would be a good place to discover what works. Joining me for the dinner were Mr. Thompson, Mr. Ragg and Ms. Walker; Melissa Wong and Robert Chu, a Chinese-American couple living in Beijing who are avid wine drinkers; Fiona Sun, the editor of the magazine *Wine in China*; and Vicky Lok, a Guangzhou-based wine broker.

For the occasion, Mr. Thompson, who owns a wine importing company called The Wine Republic, donated four white wines, one pinot noir rosé blend, and three red wines from the New and Old World that retailed from 170 yuan to 520 yuan, or $25 to $75, in Beijing.

Mr. Thompson chose light to medium-bodied wines, and reds with lower tannins, too much of which can clash with salt and spice. Dishes were served in order of their complexity of flavors, beginning with lighter dishes and ending with two dishes loaded with Sichuan peppercorns and dried chili peppers, before moving on to a dessert of candied "basi" apples, a common Beijing dish.

One definite winner of the evening was a semisweet riesling. The 2007 Mount Difficulty Target Gully riesling from Central Otago, New Zealand, stood up to spicy, more complex dishes, including kungpao cashew chicken with its sugar, black Shanxi vinegar, chili peppers, and faint hint of Sichuan peppercorns. With a medium body and high acidity, the riesling balanced the sugar, salt, and even the pickled flavor of the wok-fried bamboo shoots.

By contrast, a 2007 Seresin Estate sauvignon blanc from Marlborough, New Zealand, while slightly effervescent and zingy on its own, was too light to retain its identity when awash with other flavors.

"I love rieslings; they go well with Chinese cuisine because the mouthfeel is quite refreshing," said Ms. Sun, the magazine editor. "The range of dry to sweet rieslings can match all types of Chinese food, plus it's never too heavy, but rather fresh and fruity."

We also discovered two other versatile wines: a 2007 grüner veltliner from Nigl, an Austrian winery, and a 2006 Yering Station pinot noir rosé from the Yarra Valley in Australia. The light pepper and fruity aroma of the grüner velt-liner, a lesser-known white grape that is almost exclusively grown in central

Europe, complemented the steamed sea bass and the stir-fried cabbage hearts with shiitake mushrooms. The soft texture, subtle tannins and floral notes of the extra-dry pinot noir rosé made it go well with nearly everything from the pan-fried pork and pumpkin dumplings to the sweet-and-sour pork (which turned out to be one of the hardest dishes to pair).

One surprise was that the 2006 Te Tera pinot noir from the Martinborough Vineyard in New Zealand worked quite well with several dishes, including twice-cooked pork. The spice, sugar and lightly fermented sauces of the pork dish amplified the pinot noir with light tannins, making it taste more like a full-bodied merlot.

Two wines that did not find a place on the table were the 2006 Miss Harry blend of grenache, shiraz and mourvèdre from Hewitson in South Australia and a 2005 red Burgundy, the Hautes Côtes de Nuits from A. F. Gros. "I can see these going with something heavier, like red-braised pork," Mr. Ragg said.

We also found it difficult to match any of the wines with two dishes laced with Sichuan peppercorns, the oil-braised beef and the Chongqing spicy chicken. They clashed with each sip of even the more elegant wines, like the light-bodied 2007 Chablis Premier Cru from Jean-Marc Brocard and the red Burgundy. Each taste set off an echo chamber of numbing spice in my mouth. "It's a lovely dish on its own," Mr. Ragg said, almost apologetically. He suggested that perhaps a palate-cleansing sparkling wine might be interesting to try with Sichuan peppercorn dishes on another occasion.

The evening demonstrated that pairing wine with Chinese cuisine wasn't as difficult as it seemed, save a few Sichuan peppercorns. Mr. Suk, the wine auction house representative, suggested that if a Chinese restaurant doesn't have a decent wine list, bringing your own bottle is usually an option. Corkage fees at Chinese restaurants in China and abroad are typically low, ranging from $5 to $10, while many hole-in-the-wall eateries may allow you to bring wine for free.

The evening also showed the enthusiasm the Chinese have for wine.

Winemakers should be heartened by the conversion of Ms. Lok, the wine broker from Guangzhou, who had primarily consumed baijiu before tasting her first imported wine in 2006. She soon learned about the difference between New and Old World wines and became an avid drinker of the wines of Spain, Germany and Argentina. But she still vividly remembers her first sip of an imported wine: "It was a south Australian shiraz. It was so much better than the Chinese wines I'd had in the past, and you didn't have to add Sprite to it."

April 2009

Enlisting Radicchio's Bitterness
to Balance the Fruitiness

By FLORENCE FABRICANT

Sometimes a fine pairing comes from contrast: red sling-backs, not black, with the gray tweed.

Recently I had lunch at Esca, an Italian seafood restaurant near the theater district. My fish came with grilled Treviso, an oblong variety of radicchio. My wine was a bright dolcetto from northern Italy.

I was struck by how the berried fruitiness of the wine balanced the bitter salad, taming it. The Treviso brought out some structure and pleasantly tannic nuances in the wine and made the fruit fight a bit to reach the head of the line.

It was a combination of flavors that I remembered as I tasted the Beaujolais crus, thinking that bitterness might do as much for the fruity French wine as it did for the Italian.

Though the 2005 crus from the Beaujolais region were heftier wines than the dolcetto, with less gracious sweetness and more spice, their flavors of crushed berries and sour cherries suggested that they, too, could handle the aggressive Treviso.

So I thought I could take the easy route by starting the dinner with a tossed salad of Treviso, then following it with a classic Beaujolais partner: roast chicken. Instead, I used the Treviso in a stuffing for squid and for a wilted salad on which to bed it.

Treviso is not available in every market, but can easily be replaced by its tight round cousin, regular radicchio.

Pancetta, bread crumbs, chopped squid tentacles and Asian seasonings completed the stuffing.

The one trick to the recipe is to broil the stuffed squid as quickly as possible. That will keep them tender.

Stuffed Squid With Wilted Salad

Time: 45 minutes   **Yield:** 4 to 6 servings

12 squid with tentacles, about
    1½ pounds
2 heads Treviso or regular radicchio,
    quartered and cored
½ cup extra virgin olive oil
2½ ounces pancetta, finely diced
2 cloves garlic, minced

1 tablespoon minced ginger
3 scallions, minced
⅔ cup dry bread crumbs
3 tablespoons Asian fish sauce
2 tablespoons red wine vinegar
Salt and black pepper

1. Remove squid tentacles and chop fine. Rinse and dry squid bodies. Finely chop one head Treviso or radicchio. Shred second head in strips ½-inch wide; keep separate.

2. Heat 1 tablespoon oil in large skillet. Add pancetta and cook over medium heat until starting to brown. Add garlic, ginger and tentacles, and sauté about a minute. Add chopped Treviso or radicchio and scallions. Cook until softened. Stir in bread crumbs and fish sauce, stir about a minute, add a tablespoon or two of water to release crumbs clinging to pan, and transfer to a bowl.

3. Stuff squid bodies with mixture, not packing too tightly and leaving ½-inch headroom. Secure with toothpick. Rub with 1 tablespoon oil. Preheat broiler to very hot.

4. Heat remaining oil in skillet, add shredded Treviso or radicchio, and cook until wilted. Stir in vinegar, toss, season with salt and pepper, and transfer to a platter.

5. Broil squid close to source of heat 1½ to 2 minutes on each side, until barely browned. Place on bed of wilted salad and serve.

October 2007

A Rustic European Treat
of Prunes Poached in Wine

By FLORENCE FABRICANT

Often on a dessert table in a bistro or trattoria in Europe there will be a big bowl of plump prunes poached in wine. It's a dessert I love, but one that is rarely offered in the United States. Except at my house.

Everyday merlot or Chianti are the wines I prefer for poaching prunes. But reds we tasted from Navarre suggested that they could easily suit this purpose, too. Several of them were jammy, with suggestions of rich cooked fruit, spices and earthy tannins on the palate. I also picked up hints of prune in more than one of these wines. And many of them are around $10, making them perfect for poaching prunes to serve at the end of a simple, rustic dinner of grilled flank steak with blistered red peppers and roasted potatoes.

At this time of year, prunes in wine can answer the question of what to serve when the menu calls for a fruit dessert. I prefer to use prunes with pits, which add succulence and nuttiness. And I look for large prunes, like those from Agen, in Southwest France, which are sold in many fancy food shops.

A whiff of orange adds an important flavor dimension. Some spices and a stingy amount of sugar are also needed. Allow the prunes to steep in the wine mixture as they cool. Then present them in the wine sauce in generous stemmed goblets, with a soft cloud of whipped cream or crème fraîche on top.

Prunes in Red Wine

Time: 30 minutes plus cooling   **Yield:** 4 servings

2 cups dry red wine, preferably
    from Navarre
2 3-inch strips orange peel
10 black peppercorns
6 cloves
2 cinnamon sticks
2 whole allspice

¼ cup sugar
1 pound prunes with pits, or
    12 ounces pitted prunes
2 tablespoons triple sec
Softly whipped heavy cream or
    crème fraîche, optional,
    for serving.

1. Combine wine, orange peel, peppercorns, cloves, cinnamon sticks and allspice in a 2-quart saucepan. Bring to a simmer. Stir in sugar. Simmer 10 minutes. Add prunes, simmer 10 minutes more. Remove from heat. Stir in triple sec.

2. Transfer to a bowl, cover and set aside up to 3 hours before serving, turning prunes in wine syrup from time to time. Strain, reserving syrup in a bowl. Return prunes to syrup and discard spices. Serve at once, with a dollop of cream if desired, or refrigerate until ready to serve.

March 2007

A Piquant Appetizer That Brings Out the Best in a Wine

By FLORENCE FABRICANT

L ightly, gracefully, almost teasingly, the chenin blancs from South Africa captivated my palate as I discovered hints of melon, herbs, citrus, minerals and occasionally honey. The best ones displayed admirable consistency. Many were wines that I would gladly open with an array of dishes.

They could be poured throughout a meal that was not excessively rich. I would not think of them with lobster or with scallops in a cream sauce. But they would do the trick as aperitif wines, wines for a chicken salad lunch or wines to pair with a first course of salad or poached seafood.

As a matter of fact, I was drinking South African chenin blanc at lunch at Eleven Madison Park a few months ago and ordered Daniel Humm's tuna confit appetizer. Sometimes a pairing just lands in my lap, figuratively.

Unlike tuna tartare, the ubiquitous raw tuna appetizer, Mr. Humm's dish was made with tuna that had been marinated, gently poached in olive oil, broken up and tossed with piquant seasonings. Served in a nice little mound with a delicate salad alongside, it had a texture of alluring silkiness and a mild flavor enlivened by a dashing spark of capers, peppers and mustard. And it brought the lemon, herb and mineral flavors in the wine into focus.

Though overnight marinating is recommended, about six hours at room temperature is sufficient. The cooking must be at very low heat for just a few minutes, until the pinkness has not quite vanished from the middle of the fish. Then the only trick is to mash the tuna and mix it with the seasonings, using a very light hand. Texture, as much as flavor, is what makes this dish succeed.

And a crisp chenin blanc alongside does a lot for it, too.

Tuna Confit

Adapted from ELEVEN MADISON PARK

Time: 1 hour, plus at least 6 hours' marinating   **Yield:** 6 servings

1 pound fresh tuna

1 cup extra virgin olive oil

2 cloves garlic, smashed

3 sprigs fresh thyme

4 2-inch strips lemon peel

4 teaspoons capers, drained;
    more for garnish

½ tablespoon minced shallots

2 tablespoons Dijon mustard

1 tablespoon sherry vinegar

½ tablespoon chicken stock

3½ tablespoons grape seed oil

Salt and ground black pepper

Toasted country bread for serving

1. Place tuna in a bowl, cutting it into several pieces if necessary. Add olive oil, the garlic, thyme and lemon peel. Cover, and marinate 6 hours, refrigerated or at room temperature, or overnight in the refrigerator.

2. Transfer contents of bowl to a saucepan, bring to a simmer, lower heat and cook 5 minutes. Shut off heat. Tuna will still be pink in middle. Let cool 30 minutes.

3. Remove tuna, drain well, transfer to a bowl and mash coarsely with a fork. Fold capers, shallots, mustard and sherry vinegar into tuna. Whisk 2 table-spoons of the olive oil with chicken stock and grape seed oil. Fold into tuna. Season with salt and pepper. (Mixture should be fairly loose.)

4. To serve at once, place mounds of tuna on each of 6 salad plates, scatter with more capers and serve with toast, as a first course. Otherwise, refrigerate tuna until 30 minutes before serving; then divide onto plates and serve.

March 2007

America's Love of Sherry Smolders

By ERIC ASIMOV

For years, wine writers and other enthusiasts have lamented the public's indifference to the manifest charms and complexities of sherry. Why doesn't everyone love sherry, they asked, celebrating it as the most undervalued, underappreciated wine in the world, as it languished in the back pages of wine lists and on the dustiest of retail shelves.

In the last year or so, the drumbeat seems to have been heard. No, sherry hasn't taken the world by storm. Nobody's bidding up the prices, which remain highly reasonable, with world-class wines starting around $15 a bottle. But in small specialty shops, in restaurants where ardent sommeliers hold sway and in bars mixing creative high-end cocktails, fuddy-duddy sherry is taking its turn as a new hip thing.

At Tinto Fino, a Spanish wineshop in the East Village of Manhattan, four shelves are now devoted to sherries, with a selection at any given time of 35 to 50 different bottles. The shop has started a sherry club, and ships all over the country, said Kerin Auth, a proprietor.

"The cocktail thing has been really, really heavy, and the sherry sippers have been going through the selection quickly," Ms. Auth said, "so I'm constantly trying to offer more and different sherries."

It's one thing for counterculture wine bars like Terroir in New York and restaurant industry hangouts like Nopa in San Francisco to tout the bracingly dry, fragile, seabreeze flavors of cool, crisp manzanilla, or the rounder, nutlike complexity of an aged amontillado. But the fever (all right, call it a mild warmth) is spreading around the country. Much of the interest comes courtesy of the bartending world.

"The sherry cocktail movement is probably the single most meaningful or driving force in the recent resurgence of sherry," said Steven Olson, a former sommelier whose company, aka Wine Geek, has been actively promoting sherry for 12 years.

Sherry cocktails can be delicious, and are historical, dating from the mid-19th century. But for many enthusiasts, the best way to drink sherry is on its own.

In Durham, N.C., Vin Rouge, a bistro, departs from its all-French theme to offer manzanilla on a wine list made for shellfish.

"We don't sell a ton, but people have been putting themselves in our hands to try things they never thought about, like aged Muscadet," said Michael Maller, the general manager. "They develop this trust, and the next time they come in you recommend a glass of manzanilla, and they're receptive."

At the Summit restaurant at the Broadmoor resort in Colorado Springs, Tim Baldwin, the wine director, offers five sherries by the glass, but it hasn't taken off until recently.

"In the last couple of years, it was definitely a hard sell," he said. "But the amount of people now coming in and expressing interest has drastically increased."

Sherry sales remain minute compared with other types of wine. In 2010, just over 1.7 million liters of sherry were exported to the United States from Spain, according to the Consejo Regulador, sherry's regulatory body. That's barely a drip considering Yellow Tail, the inexpensive Australian wine, ships twice that much every month. And about half the shipments were cream sherry, the sweetened commodity that accounts for sherry's proverbial image as the choice beverage of eccentric old aunts.

Yet, strikingly, shipments of cream sherry to the United States dropped by nearly 17 percent in 2010, while shipments of serious sherries shot upward—manzanilla by almost 50 percent, for example, amontillado by nearly 60 percent and oloroso practically tripling.

Sales of these sherries continue to be dominated by big brands like González-Byass Tío Pepe fino and Hidalgo-La Gitana's La Gitana manzanilla, excellent wines despite the scale of production. More enticing to the sherry geeks are the smaller, more artisanal brands. André Tamers of De Maison Selections, which specializes in small sherry producers, says his sherry sales are up around 60 percent this year.

Unlike most wines, sherry is distinguished not by the vineyard so much as by the cellar or warehouse, where yeasts and vintages are mingled together reflecting each cellar's aging system. The bigger brands blend the sherries of many warehouses, creating a house style, just like the large Champagne producers. These can be delicious, but the single-warehouse sherries, like Lustau's almacenista series, or small-lot sherries, like those from Equipo Navazos, which single out particular barrels, can be wildly exciting for sherry devotees.

I count myself among them. I like sherry in a white wine glass, moderately chilled for manzanilla and fino, a little less so for amontillado and just cool for dry oloroso. And almost always, I want to drink it with food, whether manzanilla with olives and almonds, a classic Spanish pairing, or, well, the possibilities seem endless.

At Dovetail on the Upper West Side of Manhattan, which serves an extensive selection of sherries, Amanda Reade Sturgeon, the sommelier, likes to pair roasted filet mignon with dry oloroso. To me, this is brilliance. An oloroso like Sangre y Trabajadero from Gutiérrez Colosia is bone dry and astonishingly complex, with flavors of cream, caramel, nuts and salt that perfectly set off the caramelized beef exterior.

Other excellent small production sherries to look for include manzanillas from La Cigarrera, Gaspar Florido and Herederos de Argüeso, finos from El Maestro Sierra and just about anything from Equipo Navazos.

March 2011

EDITOR'S NOTE:
Mr. Asimov elaborated upon his article in The New York Times
with a sidebar on Diner's Journal on nytimes.com.

A Glossary of Sherries

My column is about how sherry, after years of maddening unpopularity, seems to be catching on among younger wine enthusiasts. Given the usual problem of wanting to include too much information in not enough space, I opted to forgo the array of sherry definitions that seemingly must accompany every such article.

Already, I've gotten puzzled e-mails from both those who don't know their manzanillas from their olorosos, and from those who do, but I think I should have included definitions anyway. Well, here goes. Some brief descriptions on the various kinds of sherry.

Sherry is a fortified wine from the Andalucía region of southern Spain. Dry sherries are made from the palomino grape, and sweet sherries from Pedro Ximénez or moscatel grapes. Dry sherries are notable for two main qualities. First, they are generally made using the solera system, in which newer vintages are blended with older ones year after year, creating a family tree of vintages that can stretch back for decades. Second, sherries are aged in barrels under a film of yeast that occurs naturally, which gives the wine a distinctively fresh, nutlike taste. How the flor reacts with the wine determines its stylistic destiny.

Those that remain content under the flor will eventually become finos, the lightest, palest and freshest sherries. Manzanillas are especially light, fresh finos made around the port of Sanlúcar de Barrameda, noteworthy for an almost saline quality. Those termed manzanilla pasada have undergone extended aging.

Amontillados begin life aging under flor, but then the flor dies, and the wine oxidizes, becoming darker and richer yet retaining a fino character. Olorosos, for a variety of reasons, do not develop under flor but instead gain an oxidative character, richness and a deep complexity. They are naturally dry, but are sometimes sweetened and sold as oloroso dulce. Palo cortados are sherries that have lost their flor and become something between an amontillado and an oloroso.

Or, as Paul Grieco, the wine director of Hearth and Terroir, puts it: "An amontillado is an oloroso trying to be a fino. A palo cortado is a fino trying to be an oloroso."

Finally, sweet sherries. Cream sherries are usually industrial wines that have been sweetened and are not very interesting. By contrast, Pedro Ximénez sherries can be deliciously rich and unctuous, though they have little in common with their dry cousins.

On to other sherry news, one of the best sources for great sherry is De Maison Selections, and its guiding light, André Tamers. With finos in particular, freshness is crucial. Yet how do you tell whether a bottle on the shelf at a wine shop is fresh? All the sherries from De Maison now come with bottling dates on the label, which is a major step. Of course, the houses that De Maison imports—El Maestro Sierra, Gutiérrez Colosia and La Cigarrera—are all very small. It would be great if the big houses would also start adding the bottling dates to their labels.

Finally, much of the growing interest in sherry comes from cocktail enthusiasts, so I would be remiss not to offer a recipe for an excellent sherry cocktail. You can find many other recipes for sherry cocktails at the Sherry Council of America.

Triangulo de Jerez

Adapted from ANDY SEYMOUR.

Time: 5 minutes   **Yield:** 1 serving

1¼ ounces gin

1 ounce blanc or blanco vermouth

¾ ounce manzanilla sherry

1 dash orange bitters

Lemon twist

1. Pour gin, vermouth, sherry and bitters over ice in a mixing glass. Stir thoroughly to chill. Strain over ice in a rocks glass and rub lemon oil from the twist over the rim of the glass.

March 2011

Why Red Wine and Cheese Have Stopped Going Steady

By FLORENCE FABRICANT

The rule of red wine with cheese is as revered as the one dictating basic black and pearls. But in a season when chilled white wine seems so appealing, one of those rules demands to be broken, and not just as a sign of surrender to the weather.

"A majority of our customers drink red wine with the cheese, but my personal preference is for white," said Roger Dagorn, the accredited sommelier at Chanterelle. "Red wine with cheese is an old myth. White wine is livelier and has more acidity, which balances the fattiness of cheese."

Many wine experts agree, although the message seems not to have reached restaurant patrons or dinner party hosts.

"Red wine with cheese? I'd like to debunk that," said Paul Grieco, the beverage director at Gramercy Tavern. His customers usually pair the selection of 15 cheeses with red wine. But he said he might suggest a sweet white wine or an oloroso sherry.

At Picholine, which has the most elaborate cheese selection in New York, Max McCalman, a former sommelier who supervises and serves the cheese, lamented the bias toward red wines. He recalled that the host at a large table of wine buffs not long ago selected a magnum of Château Talbot 1989 to serve with cheese. "There were strong cheeses," Mr. McCalman said. "It was a real clash."

In Paris, Jean-Claude Vrinat, the owner of Taillevent, says he generally prefers white wines with cheese but that most of his customers continue with their red wine when the cheese is served. "Red wines complement very few cheeses," he said.

At a dinner last year at Les Célébrités showcasing the red Burgundies of the Domaine de la Romanée-Conti, Aubert de Villaine, the co-owner of the estate, switched to Le Montrachet for the cheese. "With cheese, I only like white wine," he said to the guests, some of whom had been nursing their red La Tâche for the cheese.

He later said his preference had changed through tasting and experience. "I started drinking white wine with cheese because every time we had a great red with the cheese, it was a disappointment," he said. "Cheese kills the nuances in red wine. In Burgundy now, more and more people are drinking white wine with cheese."

The notion of red wine with cheese appears to be a vestige of sexist, Victorian days. Gerald Asher, a wine writer, explained that in 19th-century England, the consumption of red wine and cheese was not considered ladylike. At the end of dinner, the women retired to the parlor so that the men could get on with serious drinking: claret and port. With Stilton, of course. Mr. Asher believes that in France the habit evolved from a custom of saving the best (red) wines for the end of the meal.

The custom persists for practical reasons. "Often, there's enough red wine left from the main course, so people continue drinking it with the cheese," Mr. Dagorn said. Mr. de Villaine conceded that a white after a big red is not ideal, either. "You need a break," he said. Serve the salad.

Even Mr. McCalman of Picholine said cheese would flatter a light, simple red wine, but most people would not follow the big red wine of the main course with a simple country red any more than they would pop open a white. The one cheese that he believes demands a robust red wine, like a Nebbiolo, is Parmigiano-Reggiano.

If you care only about the cheese, it might not matter what the wine is, but to enjoy the wine and do it credit, it pays to give thoughtful consideration to the pairing.

In the *Pocket Encyclopedia of Wine 1999* (Fireside), Hugh Johnson gives a few easy rules, suggesting that the harder the cheese, the more tannins the accompanying wine can have, as in Nebbiolo with Parmesan. He adds that the creamier the cheese, the more acidity is needed in the wine.

Most cheeses taste of salt and fat. Many are also creamy and pungent. These characteristics often deaden rich, tannic red wines. But refreshing, fruity but dry whites can handle them. Some sweet whites make for brilliant matches, like the classic combination of Sauternes and Roquefort.

Not every wine or cheese aficionado will consent to the marriage of white wine and cheese, of course. Though the notion of white wine with cheese may be gaining ground, it's still not universal.

"I'm hearing many people I respect say the only wine to serve with cheese is white now," said Steven Jenkins, the author of *Cheese Primer* (Workman, 1996). "That's extreme. There are no absolutes."

July 1999

Serendipity in the Cellar

By FRANK J. PRIAL

I t was a good rkatsiteli, not a great rkatsiteli. In fact, quite good, which is more than you can say about most other 18-year-old white wines. It was closer to a golden color than a pale white, but it had lost none of its spicy fruit and little if any of its lively acidity. It paired beautifully with a much younger chicken.

This, or something like it, happens every year around this time. A routine trip to the cellar for a routine wine for dinner morphs into two hours of counting, sorting and rearranging the modest collection of bottles that had been huddled there all winter, minding their own business. Actually, it's a spring cleaning. A dreary business. But then, every so often, something exciting happens. Some long-forgotten gem turns up and makes the whole housekeeping effort worthwhile.

So it was with the rkatsiteli. Most people have never heard of the stuff—it's pronounced er-kotz-uh-TEL-ee—but it's very big in Russia. Also in Bulgaria and the Georgian Republic. It is said to be the second most widely planted white-wine grape in the world after Spain's airén. In the 1950s, Dr. Konstantin Frank, who grew up making wine in the Soviet Union, introduced the grape to the Finger Lakes, where it has thrived. Dr. Frank is gone from us, but his Vinifera Wine Cellars, by Keuka Lake, regularly wins prizes with its wines, including its rkatsiteli, in New York and Midwestern wine competitions. My forgotten 1985 rkatsiteli came from Dr. Frank and, honestly, it was more fun to drink than many an expensive chardonnay that would be hard put to last half as long.

Cheered by my discovery, I hastened back down to the cave, which is what I call the room near the furnace, to see what else might be hidden behind the cases of 1961 Lafite. Sure enough, another rarity appeared: a 1988 chevrier from the Gustave Niebaum Collection, Herrick Vineyard. How had I missed it in all those searches for something, anything, interesting in a white wine? Chevrier is another grape name. It's better known as sémillon, a workhorse white grape that has dropped off the charts in recent years. It once accounted for more than 90 percent of all the grapes in South Africa; now it makes up about 4 percent of the Cape vineyards.

Bordeaux blanc is almost always a blend of sémillon and sauvignon blanc. The great and underappreciated dry Bordeaux whites, like Château Haut-Brion's and the Pavillon Blanc of Château Margaux, are sauvignon-sémillon blends. So too are the legendary sweet Bordeaux like Château d'Yquem. Bordeaux whites can live to remarkably old ages, and that may explain the surprising freshness of my chevrier, which according to the back label was a sémillon-sauvignon blend. In fact, it reminded me of a mature white Graves, if not exactly Haut-Brion.

Gustave Niebaum was a Finnish sea captain and fur trader who established Inglenook in the Napa Valley in 1879. Sold to Allied Grape Growers in 1964, which became Heublein in 1969, the Inglenook name became synonymous with cheap jug blends. In an attempt to upgrade the line, Heublein introduced several premium labels in the late 1980s, including the Gustave Niebaum Collection, a group of vineyard-designated wines produced in limited quantities. Francis Ford Coppola, who had bought a major portion of the Inglenook estate in 1975, bought the rest of the property from Heublein in 1995. Niebaum survives as part of the winery's current name, Niebaum Coppola. My forgotten chevrier may be all that was left of the Heublein days—a still enjoyable wine from a sad time at Inglenook.

Speaking of Inglenook, does anyone remember charbono? It's an obscure red wine grape, probably the corbeau or charbonneau of southwestern France. When John Daniel, Captain Niebaum's nephew, ran Inglenook, he made a specialty of charbono, beginning with the 1941 vintage. Bottles from the '60s still turn up at auctions. It's a sturdy, workaday red wine that developed a cult following—even had its own club for a time. I had my last Inglenook charbono in the '80s.

A few enterprising California winemakers still produce the wine. The best is probably one from Turley Cellars in Napa. The charbono grapes come from the Tofanelli Vineyard, which is also the source of some memorable Turley zinfandels. The critic Robert Parker once suggested that more winemakers should think about charbono rather than waste time on insipid sangioveses. Amen to that.

And then there is valdiguié. Charles H. Shaw spent 10 years in California trying to make Beaujolais. In France, the Beaujolais grape is the gamay, but a specific one, the gamay noir à jus blanc. Translation: the black gamay with white juice. When Mr. Shaw, who would later become famous for his Two-Buck Chuck, came to California around 1980, he found winemakers using two gamay grapes— the gamay Beaujolais and the Napa gamay. Unfortunately, neither was the true Beaujolais grape. Gamay Beaujolais was an undistinguished clone of pinot noir and Napa gamay was identified as a relatively obscure French import called valdiguié. Both made pleasant red wines but not Beaujolais. In the mid-'90s, the government gave the growers 10 years to phase out both names.

What will survive is valdiguié. Even now, quite a few wineries make it. A popular one is J. Lohr's Wildflower valdiguié. Even mighty Gallo has produced it. According to my notes, I stashed away somewhere a 1994 Gallo valdiguié from the Barelli Vineyard in Sonoma, but I couldn't find it. No matter. Valdiguié makes what some people like to call a quaffing, or easy-drinking, wine, something like Beaujolais. But why settle for "something like"? Just as there is little point in drinking a dull California sangiovese when there are delicious Chiantis in any wine shop (at half the price), I see no reason, political correctness apart, for drinking a substitute Beaujolais.

June 2003

Excellent Box, Sir

By FRANK J. PRIAL

"Nice sangria," the woman said, raising her tinkling glass in friendly salute. "Thanks," I said, dumbfounded.

Why dumbfounded? Because she was the third person to compliment the "sangria" that afternoon. And it wasn't sangria. It was something called Delicious Red, made by E.&J. Gallo and sold in a five-liter box for about $9.

Yes, Gallo, and yes, in a box. For the mathematically challenged, a five-liter box holds the equivalent of just under seven standard 750-milliliter bottles of wine. For the culturally incurious, wine in a box is immensely popular, depending on where you hang out. Carriage trade wine shops don't even carry it, but about one in every five glasses of wine consumed in this country comes from a box. We're third; in Australia boxes have half of the wine market, and in Norway, of all places, they claim a third.

Wine boxes come in three sizes: three, five and 18 liters. Americans prefer the five-liter size, Europeans the three. The 18-liter box, the equivalent of two cases of bottled wine, is meant for by-the-glass and by-the-carafe sales in restaurants.

Sometimes called casks, wine boxes are best known by the not particularly mellifluous name bag-in-the-box. In fact, the secret of boxed wine is the bag inside. The box is rectangular, like a big breakfast cereal box. Inside is a triple-layer clear-plastic airtight bag that holds the wine. To pour, punch a hole in the bottom end of the box and pull out a plastic dripless spout. Push the red button and wine jets into the glass.

Because the bag is airtight, and contracts as the wine is poured, the wine will last, in perfect condition, for a surprisingly long time. Jon Fredrikson, a San Francisco wine consultant, once kept a five-liter box of chardonnay in his refrigerator for almost six months as an experiment. "The last glass was a good as the first," he said.

Originally the bag-in-the-box was limited principally to downscale sweet blush wines with names like white zinfandel, white grenache and pink Chablis. More recently, varietal wines, like chardonnay, merlot and cabernet sauvignon have appeared in the bag-in-the-box format. As the fans of those sweet wines moved up in taste the wines went with them.

Australians claim to have invented the bag-in-the-box 30 years ago. An attempt to market the format in this country floundered at first but began to grow as the old, one-gallon jug wine market dwindled in the 1980s. As with other wine innovations, like the screw cap, bag-in-the-box caught on in Europe before it did here and not just with soft generic wines. A recent tasting in London featured 30 bag-in-the-box wines, all of them serious entries from France, Spain, and Italy. In this country, the boxes are popular in supermarkets and working-class liquor stores, which may devote half an aisle to them. Almaden, Franzia and Peter Vella are among the most popular names. Peter Vella is a Gallo line, named after a longtime Gallo winemaker. Overseas, Gallo sells its bag-in-the-box wines under the Sierra Valley and River Crest labels. Gallo's 18-liter box label is William Wycliff. Franzia, which is produced by the Wine Group, makes about a dozen different boxed wines. Most of the American five-liter boxes sell for $8 to $12, or $1.35 to $1.75 a bottle. Some imported five-liter boxes sell for about $16, and one premium-wine California box in the three-liter size sells for about $25.

The big winemaker BRL Hardy is one of the Australian wine producers now found in the market in the United States. The Hardy's Stamp line, now available in some American markets, includes a 2002 chardonnay and, from 2001, a shiraz and a merlot. All are in five-liter boxes priced at around $16.

The Nevada County Wine Guild, in California's Sierra foothills, produces a magnum-size, organic bag-in-the-box wine called Our Daily Red, a saucy riff on the Lord's Prayer. Being organic, the wine is sulfite-free and soon becomes unstable in an opened bottle. But not in the bag-in-a-box, which never admits air. Released in 2001, the wine is slowly moving into national markets.

Many retailers remain skeptical about the future for expensive wines in the bag-in-the-box. Indeed Château Latour in a box sounds far-fetched. Even so, the wine box continues to move up. In Britain, with French imports like Piat d'Or, the market for boxed wine is growing twice as fast as that for bottled wine. The huge Nicolas retail chain in France has been selling Beaujolais and Côtes du Rhône in boxes since the late 1970s.

In California, the first premium-quality bag-in-the-box wine made its appearance last year when Ryan Sproule, a Walnut Creek wine merchant turned winemaker, introduced a Napa Valley 2001 chardonnay in a three-liter box appropriately called Black Box. The wine won a silver medal in a competition sponsored by *The San Francisco Chronicle* and is marketed only in California and Chicago, at about $25.

Mr. Sproule said his Black Box has done well in part because consumers have come to realize that the wine is more important than the packaging. I'm not so sure. Would my guests have been so enthusiastic about that Gallo Delicious Red if they'd seen the box before they drank the wine?

We Americans are still pretty insecure when it comes to wine. We still place undue importance on the bottles, labels and corkscrews. But, as the figures show, we're changing. Next summer, perhaps, the Delicious Red can come out of the refrigerator.

August 2003

Scratch an American, Find an Immigrant

By FRANK J. PRIAL

Thanksgiving is the quintessential American holiday and deserves to be celebrated, at least occasionally, with the bounty of our fields, our farms, our seas
and rivers and, by all means, our vineyards. Hardly anyone is going to argue with
that premise. It's when you get down to particulars, especially where the vineyards
are concerned, that the trouble starts.

For example, just what do we mean by an American wine? The obvious
answer is a wine from California or Oregon or Long Island, instead of a wine
from, well, any other country. But cabernet and chardonnay, just to take two, are
really European grapes transplanted to our shores. There are so-called native
American wines like Concord, Delaware and Niagara, but they all appear to have
some foreign antecedents and, face it, they're not all that great to drink.

There is scuppernong, from the muscadine vine, which has some fans in the
Deep South, and is about as American as a wine can get. But patriotism goes
only so far.

That leaves zinfandel, which has been known for a long time as, yes, the
American wine. There is only one problem: it is not American. Over the last
half century, everyone who has known anything about wine, has known, deep
down, that zinfandel was not native to this land. It was a vinifera vine, just like
cabernet sauvignon and riesling and all the other big names, but there was
always hope.

First it was thought to have come from Italy. An Italian grape called the primitivo was said to be identical. Then we were told it wasn't. Next came something
called plavac mali, a grape from Croatia. That wasn't it, either, but the geneticists
and others who worry about such things were getting warm. Two years ago, in
December, 2001, they finally nailed it down. Zinfandel turned out to be identical
to another Croatian grape, the crljenak kastelanski, which, as you must already
know, is pronounced tsurl-YEN-ak kas-tel-AHN-ski. With that announcement,
primitivo got a reprieve; turns out it really was the same as zinfandel all along.
Plavac mali is a relative; a brother-in-law, perhaps.

The first known documentation of zinfandel in this country was in the 1820s,
when it was offered as a table grape in the catalog of a Flushing, N.Y., nursery.
Planted in California in the 1850s, it became the state's most popular grape by

the 1880s. Now it is second only to cabernet sauvignon among California red wine grapes.

For my money, and in spite of all evidence to the contrary, it is still the American grape. It's been here longer than most of us who think of ourselves as Americans, the Croatians don't seem to want it back and it makes a very American-style wine: intense and excessive in all things if it isn't tightly controlled. What's more, it happens to be the perfect wine for a traditional Thanksgiving dinner. Turkey is not the most delicate of birds; in fact, even a farm-raised turkey can be stronger tasting than many game birds. It calls for a big, aggressive red wine.

Zinfandel specialists have backed away from the hubris of the late 1990s, when vintners like Cecil De Loach were pumping out zins with the alcoholic content of port. Dr. Johnson and Boswell may have downed two bottles of 18 percent alcohol in an evening, but just one bottle of zinfandel of that strength is rather risky these days. Most of the current crop of zinfandels are in the range of 14.5 to 15.5 percent alcohol, high enough when one considers that good Bordeaux rarely pass 13 percent. It's well to bear in mind that the laws allow a 1.5 percent margin in determining the alcohol content of a wine. Thus, a wine listed at 15.5 may well approach 17 percent alcohol.

Among the top zinfandel producers, like Ravenswood, Rosenblum Cellars, Turley Cellars, Storybook Mountain and Ridge Vineyards, alcohol levels range from around 13 percent to 16 percent. Some carry this power better than others. Ridge, for me, has always been the benchmark zinfandel producer, and tasting through a group of Paul Draper's 2001s showed that his wines remain at the top of any zinfandel list, or close to it. Some of this vintage's wines drop below the 75 percent varietal content necessary to use the grape name. Thus the 2001 Three Valleys is listed as simply a red wine although it contains 50 percent zinfandel. The rest is carignane, petite sirah and other red grapes including mataró (mourvèdre) and grenache. The Geyserville and Lytton Springs 2001s are also proprietary reds.

Rosenblum Cellars offers almost a dozen different zinfandels, from vineyards ranging from Paso Robles on the Central Coast to Mendocino in the north. The Richard Sauret Vineyard and the Planchon Vineyard bottlings are worth seeking out.

The winemaker Joel Gott is producing fine zinfandels from various parts of California. A generation ago, his father, Cary Gott, made a name for himself producing striking zinfandels from the Amador County region. Joel Gott's 2002

California Zinfandel, utilizing grapes from Napa, Lodi and Amador, is a delightful wine. He adds to its complexity by blending petite sirah, carignane and barbera into the wine.

Many of the smaller producers' wines never leave California. One not-too-small producer's wines can be found almost everywhere. I'm talking about E.&J. Gallo, which has become a serious fine-wine producer in recent years. Under the Gallo of Sonoma label, the Frei Ranch zinfandel is a good buy.

Under the Rancho Zabaco label there are always several zinfandel bottlings worthy of note, beginning with Dancing Bull and moving up to the Chiotti Vineyard bottling from Dry Creek Valley. At around $12, the Dancing Bull zin is a great introduction to this varietal. Not a subtle wine, it will hold its own with any hearty Thanksgiving dinner.

November 2003

Ancient Messages, Hidden in a Dusty Bottle From Long Ago

By ERIC ASIMOV

The lineup of wines to be served with dinner was extraordinary, including a Montrachet from 1939 and a Volnay Caillerets from 1929. Still, the wine I couldn't wait to try was the '46 Meursault-Charmes.

That would be the 1846.

The dinner was in honor of Bouchard Père & Fils, the venerable Burgundy producer and négociant, which was celebrating its 275th anniversary with a tasting of some very, very old wines. It was held at the historic Château de Beaune, a 15th-century fortress that has been the producer's ceremonial and corporate home since 1810. In addition to the 1846, Bouchard was to pour a relative youngster, the 1865 Beaune Grèves Vigne de L'Enfant Jésus.

Both of these ancient vintages had spent their long lives in the bowels of the chateau, where thick walls keep the cellars cool and the bottles can rest undisturbed. As rare as it is to taste wines this old, it's even more unusual to taste bottles with such an unimpeachable provenance.

Scientists know that the gradual interaction between a fine wine and small amounts of oxygen results in what we call aging. Firm tannins soften and aggressive aromas of fruit mellow and evolve into complex new characteristics. A wine becomes harmonious and shows new dimensions.

That's the ideal, anyway. How the wine is stored and handled and a host of other factors can be the difference between a sublime old bottle and an expired soup. What no one has been able to do is predict when a wine will be at its peak or exactly how it will fare in its descent. What happens after a few decades along the aging trail is a mystery. But wine as old as these bottles borders on the mystical.

"No producer makes a wine to be drunk after 80 years," said François Audouze, a retired French steel executive who now arranges dinners centered on old wines and who was at this dinner. "When a wine is older than that, it is generally not the result of a will but of an accident."

The evening had begun in a nondescript industrial area outside this handsome little city, which has been the center of the Burgundy wine trade for 300 years or more. First, we toured Bouchard's new winery with its great steel tanks, catwalks, lots of oak barrels, the smell of fermented grape juice, even—gasp—a bottling apparatus. Then there was a tasting of Bouchard's 2005 lineup; 2005 was an excellent year in Burgundy, and Bouchard's wines are elegant and pure.

But the luminaries on the tour this soggy late fall evening—including Clive Coates, the British writer; Serena Sutcliffe, the head of Sotheby's international wine department; Allen Meadows of burghound.com, a leading Burgundy critic; and the French writers Thierry Desseauve and Jacky Rigaux—hadn't come to Bouchard to sample unreleased wines. So it was with a discernible eagerness that we dispatched the initial tasting and headed to the chateau. After a Champagne reception (magnums of 1988 Cuvée des Enchanteleurs from Henriot, a corporate sibling of Bouchard), the 49 guests trooped expectantly to the dining tables, where the six wines would accompany six courses.

What's in an ancient bottle almost matters less than the vivid historical images conjured up by the year on the label. An 1865? By the first hint of green on the vines that mid-April, Lincoln was dead, "Hush'd Be the Camps Today," as Walt Whitman wrote that year.

The 1846? Not quite as resonant with me, although the French might have thought of Louis-Philippe, the last king to rule France, who was teetering on the throne before being unseated in 1848. The 1929 brought up the stock market crash and the start of the Great Depression, though I couldn't help thinking of my father, who was born in 1929 at the height of the summer.

Yet none of the wines summoned visions as searing as the 1939 Montrachet. As New Yorkers were enjoying their World's Fair, the French army had just been mobilized with France's entry into World War II. The harvest that fall stretched from days to weeks, Mr. Meadows recounted, as the women and children who were left behind picked grapes when they could, resulting in uneven degrees of ripeness.

Perhaps that explained why the '39 Montrachet, the second wine served after a well-balanced 1992 Chevalier-Montrachet, seemed so odd. It was a dark amber gold, with flavors of sherry and caramel, as if it were slightly oxidized. It smelled sweet yet tasted dry, and truthfully it was slightly disappointing. At first, at least. But an hour later, around the time I might have thought exposure to air would have dried out an older wine, the '39 Montrachet was just coming alive, with a beautiful, brilliant minerality. It was lesson No. 1 of this meal: never give up on a wine.

Lesson No. 2 came from Mr. Meadows, who has made it his business to taste wines from every vintage of the 20th century and before, if he can find them. "Pay attention to the texture," he advised, alluding to the fact that the two 19th-century wines predated the phylloxera epidemic, which devastated European vineyards in the late 1800s. The 1846 and '65 would be those rare Burgundies grown on their own rootstock instead of on grafted American roots, the only protection against phylloxera.

The moment of truth came. The 1846 was poured carefully but generously by the wine stewards, who had opened five bottles. The labels looked almost new, no surprise there. The humidity in a good wine cellar will rot paper, so wineries rarely label bottles until they are ready for shipping. The corks looked fresh, too. With its older bottles, Bouchard replaces the cork every 25 to 30 years, sacrificing one bottle to top off the others, which keeps air from aging the wine more rapidly.

What can one say about a wine 160 years old? It was amber, browner than the 1939, but with wonderfully fresh aromas of lime, grapefruit, chalk and earth, and the slightest overlay of caramel. In the mouth it was vibrant with acidity that was remarkable in a wine this old.

Tasting it blind, I would have guessed it to be 100 years younger—no, make that 130 years younger. And Mr. Meadows was right about texture: this wine was alive and joyous, almost thrusting itself out of the glass. I thought of horse carts, canals and steam engines. Pas mal, as the French say—not a bad little chardonnay. And it got even better over time. What was it served with? I seem to remember chicken in cream sauce. It didn't much matter.

Reds were next, beginning with an appetite-whetter, Le Corton 1990, young and dark with wild berry aromas. Then, with the lamb, the 1929 Volnay Caillerets, Ancienne Cuvée Carnot, was poured. The '29 and '90 vintages were both exceptional in Burgundy, and the '29 was almost as dark as the '90, yet with a sedate sweet fruit aroma balanced by minerals. With time in the glass it developed a smell of truffles.

Finally, the last wine of the evening was poured, the 1865 Beaune Grèves Vigne de L'Enfant Jésus, from a vineyard entirely owned by Bouchard. Like the 1846, it too had the lively texture of youth. Its color was still vibrant, pale ruby with touches of orange around the edges. The fruit was gentle yet striking, reminiscent of the 1929 and even the '90, like a family resemblance seen over generations.

Where I was simply dazzled by the 1846, the 1865 conjured up a feeling of respect and awe. We were tasting a legacy, transmitted long after its makers had died and conveying emotions that might have been inconceivable back then. At a moment like that, I had no doubt that winemaking can rise to the level of an art.

I thought of those bottles deep in the cellar. They had survived the Franco-Prussian War, World War I and World War II, when Bouchard had constructed false walls in the cellars to conceal their older bottles from the Nazis. This year, Bouchard will no doubt put away a few bottles of those promising 2005s. May their passage be somewhat easier.

January 2007

Memories Are Made of This

By TERRY ROBARDS

Our first view of the stone chateau is from above as the three red and white helicopters bank across the beach under cloudy skies, seeking an open space for landing. We settle down on a sand spit jutting into the bay and trudge toward shore as the flying machines whirl upward and away, the beating of their blades vanishing in the distance.

Suddenly there is silence broken only by the lapping of the waves and the occasional screeching of gulls. There are 20 of us in all, and our means of transport is to be surpassed in novelty only by what we face over the next seven hours: an extraordinary repast accompanied by even more extraordinary wines beneath the vaulted cathedral ceiling of the chateau.

We had been named Le Cercle des Vingt, and some of our members have come from as far away as Paris, Florence and Fort Worth to this huge mansion with the moat and the fortresslike tower in Lloyd Neck on the North Shore of Long Island. We are about to participate in a gastronomic event of gargantuan proportions that might have stirred envy if not outrage even in Rabelais himself.

The principal attraction for several of us is an array of wine unrivaled anywhere else, in any other castle or restaurant or private collection—an array that includes three of the greatest vintages of Château d'Yquem harvested in the last century. Twenty-one different wines are to be served, but the ones to make a trip for, to abandon all other commitments for, to savor for years in memory after the last vestiges of flavor have gone from the palate, are the three luscious Yquems.

Devotees of Château d'Yquem are an insatiable and passionate lot, for the object of their attentions is produced only in small quantities at great cost from a hillside vineyard in the Sauternes district of Bordeaux. The grapes are handpicked in late autumn when they have achieved such ripeness that they begin to evolve into raisins yielding a wine of nectarlike intensity and sweetness.

Some vintages of Yquem are better than others, of course, and the best of all are now to be found only in private cellars. So when the word was passed that the Yquem 1893, 1900 and 1921, three of the best ever harvested, were to be served on an autumn Saturday in 1981 at a luncheon only a short helicopter ride from Manhattan, second thoughts did not occur.

As we climb up the hill from the beach toward the chateau, we learn that the meal is being prepared by Georges Perrier, chef and proprietor of Le Bec Fin in Philadelphia, who also has been flown in with some of his staff for the occasion. He has abandoned his restaurant with this vow: "For one day in my life I am going to have fun."

The organizer is a Frenchman named Maurice Renaud, who deals in rare wines in Europe. But nearly all of the wines for this occasion have been hand-carried, bottle by bottle over a period of months, from the private cellars of the Cartier jewelry concern beneath the cobblestones of the Place Vendôme in Paris. Louis Cartier, the firm's founder, established one of the finest wine collections in France, and today some of those wines will be consumed.

"We've calculated that we're going to use 1,000 glasses today for 20 people," says Thomas J. McGrath, our host, a lawyer who with his wife, Diahn, owns Eastfair, the magnificent scene of our debauch.

First we sip icy Krug Champagne 1955 poured into crystal glasses from magnum bottles as we assemble in the bar overlooking Long Island Sound. Just before 2 p.m. we move into Eastfair's main salon, which has been converted for use today as a dining room. One huge square table has been set with white linen for 20, and the bottles are standing upright on a nearby sideboard. "My wish is that we have a thoroughly enjoyable few hours together," says Renaud as soon as we are seated. The onslaught begins.

We receive Perrier's succulent fresh foie gras cooked rare and served with a truffle sauce on a bed of spinach. In a classic accompaniment, we drink Château La Tour Blanche 1923 and 1928, a Sauternes produced not far from the Yquem vineyards, and the flavor combination is a triumph. Eight courses yet to be served, and I take a silent vow to survive by leaving a portion of each on my plate.

Next come filets de rouget, tiny slices of fish marinated in virgin olive oil and bathed in caviar, and the wines are American in a Gallic nod toward our setting. They are also controversial, for the Kistler chardonnay 1980 from California is judged overly oaky and perhaps sulfury, while the Ste. Chapelle chardonnay reserve 1980 from Idaho is also a bit woody, although it will develop richness in time.

Now we move into red wines accompanying slivers of quail breast, and there is Château Pichon-Lalande 1937 in two different bottlings, followed by Château Margaux 1937, 1947 and 1949. Again, there are two bottles of each, as there will be throughout the day—in case one has gone bad.

"For me, Margaux is for smelling and not for drinking," says Dr. Marvin C. Overton III, a Fort Worth neurosurgeon who owns one of America's great wine cellars. But his Margaux glasses are soon empty.

Three renowned 1953s, Château Cheval Blanc, Château Lafite-Rothschild and Château Margaux, come with slices of lobster meat in a delicate fresh tomato and cucumber sauce. All three are firmer and richer than the previous three, but there is disagreement on which is best. My choice is the Lafite, with its classic plummy bouquet and fruity richness that keeps developing in the glass for 30 minutes.

Nearly 5 p.m. and time for a sorbet that we eat standing, as an intermezzo. But soon we are back, sipping Clos Fourtet 1945 and Château Mouton-Rothschild 1945 with tiny mignonettes of lamb wrapped in lettuce leaves. Then Château Pétrus 1950 and 1955 with breast of pigeon. Surprisingly, the '50, an off vintage, is a match for the fruity and textured '55.

With the cheeses come two disappointingly senile Burgundies, a Charmes-Chambertin Vieilles Vignes 1923 from Chevillot and a Bourgogne Vieilles Vignes 1929 from Bouchard Aîné.

It is 7:20 p.m. and the stage is set for the Yquem. André Crispin, a Houston industrialist awed by what is to come, calls for a moment of silence as the 1893 is served with desserts from Le Bec Fin.

The 1893 is obviously in superb condition, displaying a golden amber hue with glints of reddish orange, aromatic and honeyed in bouquet, thick and nectarlike in the mouth, with a long, lingering aftertaste, extremely intense and complex.

The 1900 is virtually the same color as the 1893. Its bouquet is flowery and sweet and its flavor is rich and honeyed, showing strong fruit. But it is a less intense, more elusive, more elegant wine lacking the strength of the 1893. The 1921 is much darker, like an old, barrel-aged sherry. Its aroma is extremely intense and honeyed, with nuances of nectarines and citrus fruits. The wine is big, textured and rich, with the most intense flavor of all, like honey, with a long, rich finish that sticks to the palate, prolonging the sensation. The '21 is superior, if a choice must be made.

Chef Perrier is given a standing ovation at 7:45 p.m. "We clean a lot of glasses—1,500 glasses!" he exclaims. "We will never forget the glasses!" Eastfair has never seen such a feast.

An 1893 Fine Champagne Cognac from Camus has yet to be poured, but nothing can surpass the Yquem, and several of us decide we must depart. We climb into limousines parked near the moat, and soon the headlights are boring into the darkness of the Long Island Expressway. I think of the Cognac that I did not taste, the sacrifice that I made in the name of moderation, and the memory of Yquem '21 remains fresh.

January 1982

Wine Flavored by the Wind

By TERRY ROBARDS

The mistral is the wind that blows down through the Rhône Valley of France, the same wind that turned back the leaves on the trees that Van Gogh painted a century ago, the wind that whistles through the grapevines of the Côtes du Rhône en route to Provence and the Mediterranean Sea. The mistral is a part of everyday life there, and it is especially important to the makers of wine, for it dries out the vineyards after the rain and it is always accompanied by sunshine, which enables the grapes to achieve the great ripeness that is essential for making the intensely flavored wines of the region.

The mistral was sweeping through the trees and rustling the ivy that grows up white stucco walls to the tile roof of Château du Trignon when I met its proprietor, André Roux, a man who makes robust red wines that are typical of the Rhône Valley. We drove from village to village in search of a restaurant for lunch, but it was a Wednesday in November, the tourists were gone from the region, and all of the restaurants were closed. "Alas," said Mr. Roux, "there is only one alternative. You must dine with me."

So we returned to Château du Trignon, and Mr. Roux asked his wife, Collette, if she might put together a meal for us while he served some of his wines and discussed the region where he has been making wine for decades and where his father made wine before him. It is a region whose wines are less fashionable than those of the famous estates of Bordeaux and Burgundy, a region where the production is vast and much of it comes from large, cooperatively owned wineries with huge outdoor tanks—installations that resemble oil refineries. But the wines often are of high quality, especially when made in the old style at a place like Château du Trignon.

Like many lovers of French wines, I was already familiar with the rich and full-bodied Rhônereds called Hermitage, Côte Rôtie and Châteauneuf-du-Pape, wines that are well known among connoisseurs all over the world. What I was seeking from Mr. Roux was an insight into the lesser-known wines of the district, the ones that fall under the general heading of Côtes du Rhône but that also are entitled to their own local appellations. Because Mr. Roux's wines are among the few in this category that reach the United States, he was the appropriate man to see.

We drank an aperitif in a living room with cloth-covered yellow walls and then were invited through an archway into the adjacent dining room, where Mrs. Roux began serving a feast orchestrated to highlight the red wines that her husband poured, wines in moist bottles that still carried the chill of the cellar where they had been stored, for there had been no time for them to reach room temperature.

First there was a salad of corn, hearts of palm, chives, lettuce, green olives and ripe black olives, all tossed in a dressing composed mostly of fresh virgin olive oil. I was astonished that such a splendid salad could be produced on such short notice and helped myself to seconds when the bowl came around again, assuming that this was the entire meal. But I had underestimated Collette Roux's spontaneous culinary artistry.

Next came lamb chops and lean fillet steaks, the ultimate mixed grill served in a pan directly from the stove. I suspected that the meat had been thawed in the oven, but I could not be sure, for it was sprinkled with rosemary and other herbs that gave it a rich Provençal flavor. Again I was encouraged to take seconds, but I was beginning to realize that Mrs. Roux's modest luncheon was much more than I had expected. There followed a cheese course, with wedges of creamy brie, chèvre, Roquefort and reblochon. Finally came a fruit course of apples, tangerines, oranges, pomegranates and cinsault grapes, the same grapes that are used in many wines of the region, all in a basket that was passed repeatedly around the table.

All during the repast Mr. Roux was pouring his wines, and a picture began to emerge not only of the cuisine of the region but of the wines as well. Most of the reds exported to the United States are simply called Côtes du Rhône with no more specific appellation, suggesting that they are blended from a fairly large area, in fact from the entire Rhône region. Some are given brand names, such as Mr. Roux's Cuvée du Bois des Dames, which American consumers are learning to recognize, and there are specific geographical appellations within the region that are not often seen in the United States.

Mr. Roux's chateau, for instance, lies in Gigondas, a part of the Côtes du Rhône that produces especially well-balanced reds, wines of sufficiently pronounced character to merit their own specific name beyond the name Côtes du Rhône. Thus, Mr. Roux produces a Gigondas from grapes harvested within the Gigondas district, a Sablet from vineyards that lie in the nearby Sablet district and a Rasteau from the vineyards of Rasteau. Each carries the name Château du Trignon, with the additional name of the district. Each has its own character that sets it apart from the others.

The wines of Rasteau, for example, are robust and intense, with alcohol levels that sometimes exceed 14 percent, while the wines of Sablet are softer and more elegant. Their individuality is derived from differences in the soil, which is sometimes chalky and sometimes filled with gravel and pebbles, and from minute variations in the weather from vineyard to vineyard. Still, because the climate is basically Mediterranean and because of the unrelenting mistral, differences among vintages are less pronounced in the southern Rhône than in most of the more northern growing areas of France.

The table wines of the area that are classified as Côtes du Rhône tend to be fruity and uncomplicated. They sometimes resemble Beaujolais, although they are made from different grapes, and they tend to taste drier. Like Beaujolais, they are best drunk within three years of the harvest. They are good alternatives to the higher-priced wines from the more fashionable vineyards of France.

At the table of the Roux family in Gigondas, the reds of Château du Trignon tasted as good as the best wines money could buy. We had come to learn about the local wines, but we also learned about hospitality and how an impromptu meal can be transformed into a feast when cooked by Collette Roux for hungry travelers who had the good fortune to find all the restaurants closed on a windy Wednesday afternoon in autumn.

March 1981

A Wine Critic's Feast

By TERRY ROBARDS

People with a passionate devotion to wine are inclined to focus their entertaining on their favorite beverage, and I am no exception. Instead of cocktail parties, I give wine tastings, and planning for my dinner parties begins with deciding which wines I will serve.

Because I managed to establish a cellar back in the 1960s, when the best wines were inexpensive and easy to find, I now have a fairly extensive supply of fully mature bottles that I do not hesitate to uncork under the right circumstances. So my planning involves creating the right circumstances.

At the same time, I plan for relatively simple food, for I do virtually all of my own cooking and have no desire to prepare anything that will either separate me from my guests for long intervals or interfere with the fine wines that I am likely to serve.

My favorite, most special dinner parties always take place at my home in the northern reaches of the Adirondack Mountains of New York State. The area is rugged and wild, with cool nights even in summer, so there is nearly always a fire burning in the fireplace.

The fuel for my fires is hardwood logs from the birch, ash, poplar and maple trees felled on my land, and it creates an extraordinary medium for grilling meats of all kinds. In common with many other enophiles, I have a favorite grilled meat, and it is lamb.

No other readily available meat complements red wines as nicely as lamb, and I am convinced that no lamb could taste better than when it is cooked over hardwood logs in my Adirondack fireplace. The smoky flavor imparted by the wood provides a superb counterpoint to the gamy pungency of the meat, and all that is then needed is a mature red Burgundy from a great vintage.

I recently decided to uncork one of my last remaining bottles of Volnay-Santenots 1959 Hospices de Beaune Cuvée Jehan de Massol, and the feast that was interwoven with the consumption of this wine was splendid—not because I had prepared it, but because it was elegantly relaxed and featured food that would have been special no matter who cooked it.

My guests arrived from across the lake by boat and were handed glasses of icy Taittinger Comtes de Champagne 1973 on my front porch as the evening sun highlighted the leaves that were already taking on the colors of autumn on the opposite shore. The Taittinger is one of several special Champagnes that I serve, and at other times I have used Dom Pérignon, the Perrier-Jouët Fleur de France, Mumm's René Lalou and Louis Roederer Cristal, among others.

No wine launches a festive occasion as perfectly as Champagne, and on this occasion I served fresh caviar as the hors d'oeuvre, a food that not only goes very well with Champagne but that also is capable of enhancing the atmosphere by its mere presence. I also prefer caviar because it is not filling and will not satiate the palate prior to the meal.

After uncorking another bottle of Taittinger for my guests, I disappeared into the kitchen briefly to begin cooking the fish course, smallmouth bass from the lake. I cannot recall ever being served smallmouth bass in a restaurant, and I know that it will be a rarity for most of my guests.

I normally poach the bass in a court bouillon in a large aluminum fish poacher, and this time I had timed the poaching fluid so that it would be reduced to the proper point just after my guests' arrival. The poaching takes only a few minutes, but I do not believe in long preambles before wine-oriented feasts.

The greatest conviviality occurs around the dining table, where the best wines are served, and the sooner I can get my guests there, the better. Moreover, they are in better condition to enjoy the meal and each other if the cocktail period is kept brief.

On this occasion I was serving two California chardonnays with the bass—a Stony Hill 1979 and a Dry Creek 1980 Vintner's Reserve. Both are fairly full-bodied and were superb with the bass, a flavorful fish that is enhanced by a good poaching fluid.

By now the fire in the fireplace had created a bed of crimson embers, and I added two fresh logs, one at the back of the fireplace and one at the front. The two logs serve as props for the heavy wire grilling basket in which I cook the lamb.

I usually buy about a seven-pound leg and ask the butcher to butterfly it, or remove the bone while leaving the meat intact. A butterflied lamb spreads out flat, but is always of uneven thickness.

I consider the unevenness a plus factor; it enables me to serve the meat both rare and well done at the same time. I and most of my guests prefer rare lamb, but many Americans do not, and the butterflying process assures there will be varying degrees of doneness.

I often marinate the lamb in a mixture of vinegar, garlic, basil, pepper and Beaujolais for several hours prior to cooking. This creates a more complex flavor and removes some of the pungency that is normally present in lamb.

The cooking time will vary according to the size of the butterfly and the intensity of the fire. I have cooked butterflied lamb in as little as 10 minutes and as much as 20. The normal time is 12 to 15 minutes in my fireplace, but I have no way of knowing whether this is typical.

While the lamb is cooking, I uncork the red wine—in this case the 1959 Volnay plus a 1964, also from the Hospices de Beaune, for the sake of comparison. Earlier, I had decanted a bottle of Bacigalupi pinot noir 1979, a California wine made from the same grape as the two Volnays.

Comparing California pinot noirs with French Burgundies is not always fair, for the pinot noir is less successful in California than some other French grape varieties. But such comparisons are fun, if not totally valid, and they certainly make for plenty of lively conversation around the table.

This time the Bacigalupi was excellent, although immature, but it could scarcely match the elegant richness of the Volnays. Surprisingly, the 1959 was the biggest, most intensely flavored wine at the table, although it was the oldest. I was reminded of how difficult it is to find Burgundies of that quality any more.

The butterflied lamb came out of the fire precisely on schedule and was transferred to a large, thick wooden carving board. The meat was scorched on the outside and mostly reddish pink on the inside.

With the meat still sizzling from the fire, I carved vertical slices off the butterfly and was able to satisfy everybody at the table both in quantity and degree of doneness. (There was also plenty left over for lamb sandwiches the next day.)

With the lamb I served fresh zucchini, cut lengthwise and broiled with a coating of butter and grated Parmesan cheese. I usually serve whatever green vegetable looks freshest and most interesting at the local market, and zucchini happened to be the one for this occasion.

Sometimes I will also serve potatoes, especially if new potatoes with their transparent pink skins are available or if the so-called salt potatoes, some as tiny as a thumbnail, can be found in the market. I broil them whole in a saucepan with a shallow layer of butter and herbs.

By this point, everybody's calorie quota has usually been surpassed, but I often fail to resist the urge to serve a dessert, especially if I have a luscious

Sauternes or riesling to go with it. This year, the raspberry and blueberry crops in the mountains were abundant, and I simply served a mixture of the two types of berries.

In the absence of fresh fruit, I will often resort to cheesecake, for it is also an ideal dessert with a sweet wine. On this occasion I uncorked a Wehlener Sonnenuhr 1976 beerenauslese from Prüm, a delicious Mosel, with the berries.

The fire was still crackling in the fireplace, taking the chill out of the Adirondack night, as my guests climbed back into their boats. No doubt it was a warm and pleasant voyage across the lake.

October 1982

The Tastes of Walla Walla, Secret No More

By R. W. APPLE Jr.

The landscape that unfolds beneath the little plane as it wends its way east from Seattle is not very welcoming. First come the daunting peaks of the Cascade Range, and then a sparsely populated near-desert. Eventually, it lets down over a series of vast sand dunes that are cloaked during spring and early summer in an emerald-green mantle of winter wheat. Soon the small, ordered city of Walla Walla ("many waters," in the language of the Cayuse Indians) comes into view.

Walla Walla is as improbable as its name. It is a remote yet worldly community of 30,000, famous for sweet onions and more recently for world-class merlot and cabernet sauvignon, near the place where Washington, Oregon and Idaho meet. "The town so nice they named it twice," the Chamber of Commerce rather cloyingly calls it.

It reminded me of St. Helena in the Napa Valley 35 years ago, when that town was just emerging as a wine capital, before it was overrun by Silicon Valley zillionaires and tourists on excursions from San Francisco. It seems safe from that fate; the nearest big city, Spokane, 125 miles away, is short of both tourists and zillionaires.

Like all wine areas, Walla Walla flourishes because of its soils and its climate. The flood waters that once inundated the Walla Walla valley were derived from the failure of an ice-impounded lake known as Glacial Lake Missoula. The unusually deep, well-drained silt, known as loess, in which many vineyards are planted, are the result of winds which eroded and then redeposited some of the flood-deposited sediment. Temperatures are ideal for wine grapes: extremely hot days in summer, nights as much as 25 to 40 degrees cooler.

Two Army Reserve chums, Gary Figgins and Rick Small, put Walla Walla wines on the map. A burly, unpretentious man who likes to laugh, Mr. Figgins started as an amateur winemaker, inspired by holiday visits to California vineyards. He founded Leonetti Cellar in 1977—naming it for his maternal grandparents, who immigrated from Italy—and produced its first wines the next year. A quarter-century later, Leonetti has attained cult status, its name whispered from one aficionado to another.

Even in Seattle, Leonetti is relatively rare in restaurant wine cellars, and it isn't cheap. At Wild Ginger, Rick Yoder's bustling pan-Asian brasserie there, where markups are relatively modest, the 1999 Leonetti cabernet lists for $144 a bottle, and the 2000 vintage will set you back $152.

So what makes Leonetti special? Mr. Figgins opens his cellar to the public only once a year, and then only to those on his mailing list, some of whom come from as far away as Atlanta to pick up their allocations. When he made an exception for me, several things became immediately clear.

More than any other producer I have visited, he emphasizes cleanliness in the winery, believing that even a few germs can spoil a wine. Most winemakers draw wine for tasting from a barrel with a device called a pipette, fill glasses, taste and put what's left back into the barrel. Not Mr. Figgins. He throws away the leftovers.

He uses unusual quantities (17 percent in 2002) of one of the "minor" Bordeaux grapes, petit verdot, along with cabernet and merlot, to add depth to his coveted reserve wine. And he uses barrels of several sizes and ages to control oakiness.

"But it's really all about biological management," he insisted. "Throwing away all those chemicals. The world has to change, and here we already have."

In a pair of tanks, Mr. Figgins brews what he calls earth tea. In goes compost and out comes a liquid for drip irrigation that, he says, "will make anything grow"—vines, lilacs, trees like the oaks and aspens he has planted all over his property. A new Leonetti vineyard, planted on hard, inadequately friable, poorly drained land that had been conventionally farmed, sprang back to life after a few gulps of earth tea.

Mr. Figgins started in a tiny building the size of a one-car garage, which makes him the literal American equivalent, I suppose, of the small-scale "garagistes" of Bordeaux. He dedicated a sparkling new winery in 2000, but still produces only about 6,200 cases a year—"slightly more than Pétrus," he joked.

Mr. Small's Woodward Canyon, founded in 1981, has also limited its output, putting out about 15,000 cases annually. Lean and outgoing, with close-cropped gray hair, Mr. Small gives his old friend full credit for getting him into the game: "He turned me on." Both of them make taut, elegant and boldly flavored wines, and their robust merlots are surely among the best produced anywhere in the United States.

They are neither watery nor hyper-concentrated. Mr. Small has a thing about jammy, overrich wines. "If I wanted jam, I'd go to Smucker's," he said.

Many other producers have followed the lead of Mr. Figgins and Mr. Small. Among the more successful have been Seven Hills, which makes excellent wines under its own name, including a tempranillo, as well as selling grapes to Mr. Figgins; L'Ecole No. 41, named for an old country schoolhouse; and Cayuse, a Rhône-style specialist founded by a Frenchman, Christophe Baron, whose yellow-fronted tasting room on Walla Walla's main drag is open only a couple of weekends a year. Abeja Winery, housed on a 100-year-old wheat farm, with the highly regarded John Abbott as winemaker, is widely seen as a comer.

In 1990, the Walla Walla valley had five wineries. In 2003 the total reached 38, and today there are more than 60.

"We have quite a little secret out here, don't we?" asked Thomas E. Cronin, who recently retired as president of Whitman College, a nationally esteemed liberal arts school. Its most famous alumnus was the Supreme Court justice William O. Douglas, who helped put himself through college by sweeping up at Falkenberg's Jewelers and who kept a cabin in the nearby Blue Mountains during his time on the court.

Actually, Walla Walla is not so secret anymore. For years, such artists as Jim Dine, Louise Bourgeois and the late Edward Kienholz and Nancy Graves have come here to cast sculptures at Mark Anderson's Walla Walla Foundry, one of the foremost establishments of its kind. Mr. Dine even has a house in Walla Walla.

Martin Clubb, the son of a Texas oilman, told me that "this is a town where you can dial a wrong number and get someone you know." But that will not last long. Mr. Clubb, who has a business degree from M.I.T., and his wife, Megan, who used to have a high-powered finance job in San Francisco, came here to run L'Ecole 41, which was founded by Mrs. Clubb's father. She is also the president of the Baker Boyer Bank here.

Family ties brought them to Walla Walla. Others have been lured by good local fly-fishing, hiking, skiing and snowboarding. Still others were seduced by the leisurely pace of life—"We don't have a rush minute, let alone a rush hour," Mr. Cronin said—and the old-fashioned charm of Main Street, lined with low-rise Beaux-Arts storefronts from the 1910s and 1920s, revitalized at a cost of $53 million.

Happily, the town has not been Disneyfied. Old-line businesses survive, like Falkenberg's and the neon-bedecked Italian-American Pastime Café, founded in 1927 and specializing in trend-bucking "ravioli with meatballs or Italian sausage."

Tourists are coming, too, in manageable numbers so far, because Walla Walla is difficult to get to. On Spring Release Weekend early in May, when the pink dogwoods lining the streets are in full bloom, the weather is usually benign and all the wineries are open for tasting, there are often no hotel rooms available within 60 miles.

Come the tourists, come the chefs. When Lewis and Clark passed this way in 1805 and again in 1806, they survived some days on a diet of horsemeat and wild fennel. About a decade ago, when Pierre Rovani, the wine critic, came visiting, things had not improved all that much. A clerk at a local motel recommended that he take his choice of fast-food outlets or, if he insisted on "fine dining," drive south across the Oregon border to a joint that specialized in "blackened prime rib and $10 hookers."

No more. For lunch at Creek Town Café, order a burger made from locally raised beef, and follow with unctuous bread pudding made from the owner's grandmother's recipe. At Nicole Bunker's Grapefields, a wine shop-cum-bistro, pick a wine off the shelves (or, if you're lucky, a local rarity from beneath them) and drink it with your meal, maybe a flank steak with blue-cheese butter or a wild-mushroom pizza.

Mike Davis left the glamorous Salish Lodge near Seattle to open 26 Brix on Main Street, which stars local products. The night my wife, Betsey, and I stopped in, he was offering Washington troll-caught salmon with asparagus from Locati farms outside Walla Walla, which also produces the raw materials for his exquisite caramelized sweet onion consommé with onion ravioli.

As it happens, the Walla Walla region is uncommonly rich in raw materials, unlike Las Vegas, for example, where everything must be flown in. Pierre-Louis and Joan Monteillet—he's from the south of France—produce goat's- and sheep's-milk cheeses near Dayton, just northeast of Walla Walla. Adam and Sarah Sisk grow organic vegetables. Joel and Cynthia Huseby raise steers, sheep and chickens by 19th-century, free-range methods at Thundering Hooves Ranch. Robison Ranch is the nation's largest producer of shallots. Prime lentils (95 percent of American production) come from the Palouse region straddling the Idaho-Washington border. And morels and chanterelles carpet the floors of Blue Mountain forests in spring and fall.

Many of these products come together on the menu of Whitehouse-Crawford, housed in a handsome old planing mill built in 1904 that was restored by Sonia and Carl Schmitt and opened as a restaurant in 2000. The Schmitts brought in Jamie Guerin from Campagne in Seattle as chef, and Mrs. Schmitt has scoured the countryside for scarce ingredients for his kitchen, even distributing golden beet seeds to farmers.

With floors of magnificent red fir two-by-twelves and seating for 110, it quickly developed a big-city buzz and became the canteen for the local wine trade. Tom Olander oversees the region's best wine cellar, with all of the local biggies listed.

Mr. Guerin served the Schmitts, Betsey and me and a tableful of serious local eaters and drinkers a wonderfully balanced, intensely regional and seasonal meal, chock-full of the flavors of here and now. It started with a pork, chile and sweet onion tamal and continued with perfectly pink wild Alaskan king salmon (whose season had opened only a few days before) and local asparagus, greens with Monteillet goat cheese, ribeye steak with local morels, and a dandy rhubarb and ginger cream Napoleon.

No hick-town food, this.

July 2005

CHAPTER FIVE

After the Meal, Treats That Are Sweet, Semisweet—and Powerful

From the Thinnest of Wines,
the Richest Spirit: Cognac

By R. W. APPLE Jr.

"We live very simply," Winston Churchill wrote to his wife in 1915 from his temporary quarters in Surrey, south of London, "but with all the essentials of life well understood and well provided for—hot baths and cold Champagne, new peas and old brandy."

Most of us could think of other essentials. But a lot of people in a lot of countries for a lot of years have agreed with at least the last item on the great man's list. Today brandy, and more specifically Cognac, which is produced here in the Charente region north of Bordeaux, is probably sold in more places than any other spirit.

The leading brands are known all over the world, and have been for centuries, in many cases. Richard Hennessy, the Irish soldier of fortune who founded the firm that bears his name, the largest in the trade, made his first sales trip to the United States in the earliest days of the republic.

Of course other countries, notably Spain and Italy, make brandy, whose name comes from the Dutch word "brandewijn," meaning burnt or distilled wine. But theirs is not Cognac, and Cognac, properly made and aged, is the best brandy in the world. In the chalky soil of this region, with more than ample rainfall, the ugni blanc grape produces wine that is too thin and acid to drink but ideal for distillation—the chalkier the soil, the better the Cognac.

That's a big little word, "best," and there are those who prefer Armagnac or Calvados or Greek or German brandy. But whatever their virtues, those brandies seldom exhibit the satiny sheen and the magical complexity of the very best Cognacs.

As Gilbert Delos writes in *The World of Cognac* (Chartwell Books, 1999), Cognac "owes its place of privilege not to any miracle of good fortune, nor to the unique climate or soil." The decisive factor is the skills in distilling, blending and maturing that have been perfected over 300 years.

Merchandising on a global scale has also played a role. The Cognac trade was developed in large part by Dutch, Irish, English, Scandinavian and German entrepreneurs who set up shop here, starting in the 18th century, often marrying into local families. They sold their products in the countries they came from, moving later into the New World and Asia, where Cognac became a symbol of status and a gift with prestige.

You can read the history in some of the brand names in use today—Larsen, Braastad, Hardy, Hine and Meukow.

And also in one of the place names: Jean Monnet Square in the center of Cognac, named for the scion of a local Cognac-making clan whose wide-ranging travels on behalf of the family firm made him a keen internationalist and eventually led him into diplomacy. He helped to found the European Community.

"The great thing about making Cognac," Monnet said late in a long life, "is that it teaches you above everything else to wait."

Densely planted vines snake in orderly rows up hill and down dale in the tranquil countryside around the main Cognac towns—Cognac itself, Jarnac and Segonzac. There are 190,000 acres planted in white wine grapes, with more than 4,000 growers working plots that average less than 100 acres each. Some big shippers own no vines at all, most own a few and only a handful control large tracts. Frapin, a small but distinguished house, holds 494 acres of vines.

Cognac and Jarnac are austere and rather forbidding places. But the Charente and its tributaries are pretty streams, overhung by willows in places, garlanded with bright flowers in summertime and populated by flotillas of swans.

Rare is the family in these parts whose livelihood does not depend, directly or indirectly, on the amber liquid that lies maturing in the warehouses, or chais, which are marked by a black fungus, *Torula compniacensis*, that feeds on the alcohol in the atmosphere. Every year, as the spirit matures, the equivalent of millions of bottles of Cognac disappears into thin air.

The locals like to describe this as "the angels' share."

Men like René Gombert, a friendly, leathery farmer with silver hair, a large nose and a vigor rare in a man of 82, form the backbone of the industry, producing most of the grapes, doing much of the distilling and sending their eaux de vie off to the great merchants for blending with others.

My wife, Betsey, and I visited him one steamy afternoon in July at his slightly run-down old chateau near Javrezac, west of Cognac, in the Borderies region.

"Borderies is not always as refined as Cognacs from some other areas," Mr. Gombert told us with a sly smile. "But it has real character. As the blenders say, 'Borderies is the salt in our cooking.'"

Like all distillers in the region, he uses the double distillation method. The first run, which lasts 8 to 10 hours, produces a raw spirit known as brouillis; the second, which lasts 12 to 14 hours, rounds off some of the rough edges. Of the resulting bonne chauffe, only the coeur, or heart, is saved, and the tête (head) and queue (tail)—the far less palatable beginning and end of the stream emerging from the still—are discarded.

Mr. Gombert's is not a big operation, with 57 acres in vines and 100 in wheat. He makes the equivalent of 40,000 bottles of Cognac a year. Most, under contract, goes to Hennessy; some goes to Martell as well.

In recent years, the industry has undergone a tremendous consolidation, with the four biggest houses (Hennessy, Martell, Rémy Martin and Courvoisier) swallowing up many smaller firms and themselves passing into the hands of big international combines. The four behemoths, each with sales between 15 and 30 million bottles a year, control 90 percent of the world market. The biggest independent left is Camus, a distant fifth.

Some of the best Cognac comes from none of these but from niche producers like Ragnaud-Sabourin and Normandin-Mercier.

All the big houses offer costly top-of-the-line Cognacs. Rémy Martin sells only Cognac made from grapes grown in the two choicest districts, known as Grande Champagne and Petite Champagne. (Their chalky soil resembles that of the district in far-off northeast France where the world's best bubbly is made.) The smaller houses derive the bulk of their sales from relatively youthful and aggressive-tasting products, labeled VS or three-star, which are meant to be diluted with ice and mixers and not sipped straight after meals.

If it were not for lower-priced grades, the hard times that have persisted here for the last five years, with global sales more or less static between 110 and 120 million bottles a year, would certainly be much worse.

Before World War II, France consumed most Cognac, but as digestifs became less popular, whiskey joined other Anglo-Saxon items like jeans and rock 'n' roll in fashion and Cognac lost its hold. Now 95 percent of Cognac output is exported.

Cognac's biggest market by far is the United States, where 60 brands out of the registered total of 600 are available. And consumption is growing steadily, reaching 3 million cases in 2001 for the first time, while remaining stagnant in most other countries. As Claire Coates of the Bureau National Interprofessionel du Cognac told me: "Most of that is three-star, and the three-star market is ethnic. African-Americans and Hispanics drink Cognac with Coke or with some other mixer."

Not surprisingly, Cognac is big in the popular culture these days. Busta Rhymes has a hit record called "Pass the Courvoisier," and the video for "Without Me" shows the rapper Eminem on an intravenous drip of Rémy Red.

When it comes to Cognac, I'm a traditionalist—strictly an after-dinner man, the older the brandy the better. So I had a field day at La Cognathèque in downtown Cognac, which offers the widest selection in France, including rare vintage Cognacs (at rarefied prices up to $600 a bottle) as well as the products of many smaller distillers.

The region's gastronomic and Cognac-sampling highlight has to be Patricia and Thierry Verrat's Ribaudière, on the river at Bourg-Charente. The big dining room was buzzing the night we went there to eat a meltingly delicious tomato-and-goat-cheese tart, a perfectly cooked sole on the bone and glorious mashed Oléron potatoes, before getting down to the real task at hand—tasting a few of the 280 Cognacs tended by François Loretz, the sommelier.

One standout: the bronze, balanced, slightly spicy Grande Champagne Très Rare made by Paul Giraud in the minuscule village of Bouteville.

In the world of corporate Cognac, Delamain stands apart. Its office is in a stone house in Jarnac, built in 1741, with only a modest brass plaque on the door. Patrick Peyrelongue, whose mother was a Delamain, and Charles Braastad-Delamain, whose grandmother belonged to the family, run the business in Dickensian style, from antique desks facing each other (with computers on nearby tables).

Yet Delamain is considered by many experts the standard by which other, bigger brands should be measured.

What does it do differently? It buys only Grande Champagne Cognac, and it buys it only after tasting; there are long-term relationships with growers and distillers, but no contracts. It uses only old barrels, in the belief that new oak imparts undesirably harsh tannins. It ages its Cognacs not only before but for two more years after blending. Its bottles are washed and rinsed with Cognac before filling. And it sells only old Cognacs; the youngest, Pale and Dry XO (Extra Old), contains no Cognac less than 15 years old, and the two costlier blends contain none younger than 35 or 55 years old.

A third of the very limited output, which totals only 30,000 12-bottle cases a year, goes to Europe, a third to Asia, a third to the Americas.

As he led us into the riverside cellars beneath Jarnac that Delamain has used for 80 years, Mr. Braastad-Delamain, a lanky 33-year-old, said he tasted (or rather smelled) Cognacs every workday, except when traveling. Like a concert pianist, he needs a daily workout to maintain his form.

"The nose is the key," he said. "When I get back from a sales trip, it takes several days to get the nose back in shape. I get as much satisfaction from smell as from taste."

In the sweet- and woody-smelling cellars, I tasted Cognacs ranging from 2001 (71 percent alcohol, with a real sting at the end) through 1986 (60 percent, oaky and lacking in complexity) and 1977 (56 percent, with hints of vanilla, flowers and grapefruit), to 1949 (44 percent, no oak, minimal alcohol taste, notes of dry fruit, elegant—"Fred Astaire," our host said).

Delamain still sends a few casks most years to England, where years in wood in the damp climate changes the taste of the spirit, making it rounder and more mushroomy. This "early landed" Cognac can be matchless. I still hoard a few bottles of a fruity, gutsy, bright-tasting 1962 Exshaw, landed in 1963 and bottled in 1986 by my chum Bill Baker, an English wine merchant.

In addition, Delamain bottles unblended vintage Cognacs. It is one of the few houses willing to take the trouble of maintaining a special cellar, under lock and key, as required by law, to guarantee the authenticity of these rare stocks. It bottled a cask of 1971 last year and will bottle another in 2003—a total of 2,400 bottles.

Some other merchants, noticing the success of single-malt Scotches, have begun to release single-estate Cognacs, in which all the processes of Cognac-making—growing the grapes, making the wine and distilling it, aging the spirit and bottling it—must be carried out on one site. One of the pioneers in this field has been the Château de Lignières, a property of Renault Bisquit near Rouillac in the Fins Bois district, northeast of the town of Cognac.

Cognacs from the Fins Bois mature more rapidly and exhibit the aroma of freshly pressed grapes, as we discovered when Jacques Rouvière, the cellar master for Renault Bisquit, offered us glasses of his "baby," a supple, almond-scented blend of three vintages, each at least 10 years old. It occurred to me later that he looks like the great cellist Mstislav Rostropovich, and he has exactly the same charm and contagious enthusiasm as the Russian master.

Unhappily not everyone who makes, sells or drinks Cognac is as endearing a character as Mr. Rouvière.

For some reason, brandy evokes fakery and pomposity as few other drinks do. Unscrupulous dealers are always ready to haul out dusty bottles of "Napoleon"

Cognac that they claim was made in the year of the emperor's death or in 1815, the year he lost at Waterloo. Rest assured, it was not.

Then there are the rituals of consumption. Any balloon or tulip wineglass is just fine, wrote André Simon, the dean of the English wine and spirits trade, in a chapbook published 40 years ago. Only nouveaux riches demanding "the best," he said, would dream of using "a footed aquarium, without water and goldfish, of course, and making it hot over a spirit-lamp flame, before pouring in it a few drops of a priceless centenarian brandy, which will lose most of its bouquet the moment it comes into contact with the heated glass."

September 2002

In a Glass, a Swashbuckler Called Armagnac

By R. W. APPLE Jr.

To tell the truth, I don't remember when I had my first swig of Armagnac, but I know when I really fell for the stuff. It was a rainy day in the fall of 1971, or maybe 1972, at a restaurant in Villenueve-de-Marsan, a little crossroads town about halfway between Bordeaux and the Spanish border. The food was excellent (two stars in the Michelin guide, as I recall) and the wine copious. But it was the encyclopedic Armagnac list that bowled me over.

I was a semiretired war correspondent at the time, a two-fisted eater yet to learn the more recherché points of food and drink. I knew I was in the Armagnac-producing region, but I had no idea I was at the very heart of it, at the nexus, at the epicenter. It turned out that this place, called Darroze, was to Armagnac exactly as the Second Avenue Deli is to corned beef.

I was too green to choose intelligently among the 50-plus offerings, and too thirsty not to ask for help. So the kindly patron, Jean Darroze, picked an Armagnac for me that I found fascinating—bold, yet full of velvety finesse. When I said something subtle and worldly like "Zut alors!" he smiled, suggested I stay the night, and asked me to his cellar.

To Ali Baba's cave, you might well say. I eyed, sniffed and tasted Armagnacs both young and very old, some dating back 100 years. Mr. Darroze showed me how to shake the bottle and watch the foam that formed; if it lasted too long, that was a sure sign, he said, that the booze had been doctored. "Notice how the aroma lingers in the glass even after the liquid is gone," Mr. Darroze said after we had sampled one bottle. "C'est un vrai! It's a real one!"

Today, the Darroze clan is the first family of Armagnac. One of Jean Darroze's sons, Francis, an international rugby star in his youth, spent three decades building up unrivaled stocks of the best his region has to offer. Armagnacs bearing a plain tan Darroze label slowly found their way onto the drinks trolleys of the best restaurants in Europe, and a few in the United States.

Francis retired recently, and his son Marc, 33, took over the family business. One of Francis's brothers, Claude, owns a classic restaurant in Langon, south of Bordeaux, offering a vast array of wines and Armagnacs, and his daughter, Helene, owns a chic, innovative place on the Left Bank in Paris. Both have stars in the current Michelin guide.

Hooked by "le Roi Jean," as his friends called the patriarch, I have been happily tasting Armagnacs ever since. Almost without exception, I have found, the best ones come from the westernmost of the three Armagnac districts, known as Bas-Armagnac (the other two are called Haut-Armagnac and Ténarèze). The best of the best come mostly from a sandy area only 10 miles from east to west and 20 miles from north to south—from villages with evocative names like Labastide and Arthez, Hontanx and Le Houga, scattered along the border between the two most important Armagnac-producing départements, Gers and Landes.

Although Armagnac antedates Cognac by more than 200 years, having been introduced in the 16th century, it has had to play Avis to Cognac's Hertz for generations. The Cognac region, north of Bordeaux, is five times the size of the Armagnac region. Worldwide, Cognac sales are 25 times as large as those of Armagnac; in the United States, the ratio is 120 to 1. But in France competition is keener, with Cognac outselling its rival only three to one.

There are fundamental differences between the ways the two brandies are produced. For Cognac, wine is distilled twice, but for Armagnac, it is distilled only once, and at relatively low temperatures, which helps foster robustness of flavor. Cognac is aged in white oak, Armagnac in black oak with more pronounced tannins.

As a result, Armagnac is racier, rounder and fruitier than its cousin from the north, with an earthier, markedly more pungent aroma. Much of the best of it is sold unblended—the product of a single artisanal distiller in a single year, or vintage. Vintage Cognac is rare; skillful blends are the norm, usually produced by large négociants, or shippers. Armagnac, therefore, has more "goût de terroir," as the French say. It is more rustic, and thus more identifiable with a single piece of land.

If a sip of Cognac transports the drinker to the lounge of a London club, a sip of Armagnac evokes the swashbuckling aura of D'Artagnan and his fellow Musketeers, who, like foie gras, rugby and bullfights, hold a central place in the culture of this part of France, which is known as Gascony.

This is a profoundly rural area, isolated from the main highways and rail lines of France. Its people cling to the old ways, and its undulating landscape has been little touched by the modern world.

As Montesquieu said of his beloved estate, not far north of this area, "Here nature is in its nightgown, just getting out of bed."

But as we drove west from Condom to Villeneuve-de-Marsan this summer, my wife, Betsey, and I passed fewer fields planted with vines than on past visits.

More plots were planted with golden sunflowers, destined for the oil mill, and tall green corn, destined to fatten ducks and geese.

According to some estimates, as little as 15,000 acres are now devoted to growing the grapes used in distilling Armagnac. Thousands of acres, we were told by knowledgeable people, have been ripped out by small farmers in need of more reliable cash crops.

"People make Cognac for profit, but they make Armagnac for love," said Michel Guérard, the noted chef, as we sat in the garden of his Michelin three-star restaurant, Les Prés d'Eugénie at Eugénie-Les-Bains, just outside the Armagnac zone. "Like Champagne, Cognac is a corporate drink, with tremendous marketing resources behind it. There have been several efforts to assemble big combines in Armagnac, but no luck. Gascons just aren't joiners.

"More and more, sadly, Armagnac has become an esoteric drink, a drink for connoisseurs who have the patience to smell out good producers."

In fact, crisis grips the region. Sales of Armagnac are falling steadily.

"With the market in turmoil, Armagnac is becoming a depressing subject for many farmers to talk about," writes Charles Neal, a California importer of premium wines and spirits, in his excellent, privately printed 1999 study, "Armagnac: The Definitive Guide to France's Premier Brandy." "The financial compensations for products of the vine are extremely unpredictable."

The independent producers and their unblended, carefully aged spirits have been hardest hit; Armagnacs less than five years old now account for 85 percent of worldwide sales. The consumer, Mr. Neal asserts, "wants something that doesn't exhibit tremendous personality," so much Armagnac is reduced to 80 proof with water, rather than letting time and natural evaporation do their work, and sugar and other substances are added to "round off" the flavor.

But adulteration has undermined authenticity while helping sales only slightly. Social and political trends have hurt as well.

"For me, Armagnac is the bijou of brandies," said Michel Trama, who stocks a dozen Armagnacs, including a half-dozen of the very best, at his restaurant, L'Aubergade, in Puymirol, east of the Armagnac region. "Historically, it's our regional drink. But not many people order it here anymore. If they're driving, they're afraid of the cops. And if they're not, they may order a whiskey after dinner, because it's chic.

"I sell a Cognac once a night, an Armagnac twice. It's depressing, but it's true."

A few independents have managed to swim against the tide, finding means to distribute high-quality Armagnac reasonably widely and to earn consistent if modest profits.

Among these are the Domaine de Jouanda at Arthez, owned by the de Poyferré family, which once owned part of Château Léoville-Poyferré, a second growth in the commune of St.-Julien in the Médoc; the Domaine d'Ognoas, also at Arthez, owned by the Landes government, where distillation is done in a magnificent copper still, made in 1804; and the Château de Lacquy, in the hamlet of that name, which has been in the de Boisseson family since 1711.

Annual output is small—at the Domaine d'Ognoas, only about 30 barrels of amber liquid, with aromas of vanilla, prune, cinnamon and licorice.

One domaine is linked to another by roads no wider than the driveways in American suburbs, often shaded by plane trees, with their distinctive dappled, two-tone bark. Some villages have unusual pyramid-capped church towers; others have squares surrounded by medieval stone arcades.

We stopped in Labastide, a charming village built in 1291, for coffee with two of the more colorful figures in the Armagnac trade, Marguerite Lafitte and her daughter, Martine. In the jolliest way possible, they teased us with tales of inexplicable Anglo-Saxon behavior—for example, how Armagnac samples sent to the United States were held up on one occasion by customs but cleared the next time when the container was marked "Holy Water from Lourdes."

Naturally, Armagnac from the family's Domaine Boingnères was served with the coffee, though it was still early afternoon. One of the most intriguing was a rich, refined 1975 made wholly from colombard grapes, which Martine described as the grape of the future for Armagnac. It is more widely used for wines; ugni blanc, folle blanche and bacco are the more usual Armagnac grapes.

Bacco is the subject of considerable controversy. It is a hybrid, a cross between folle blanche and an American vinifera grape called Noah, developed by and named for a local schoolteacher in the 1930s. European Community officials, hostile to hybrid grapes, are trying to outlaw its use; some producers argue heatedly that bacco alone can give Armagnac the full-blown character they seek. Others have torn out all their vines, as the Lafittes did in 1991.

Although négociants, who buy and usually blend spirits produced by others, are less important here than in Cognac, there are several of consequence, including Samalens and Trépout. Some, like Janneau and Sempé, have undergone wrenching changes of ownership. But none can match Darroze, mostly because of the unusual way the firm does business.

Darroze does no distilling. It does no blending. Its trade consists of buying individual barrels from the finest artisan distillers when they become available, sometimes a barrel at a time, sometimes more—as in 1976, when Francis bought the entire stock, about 300 barrels, of the Domaine de St.-Aubin at Le Houga. That was the coup that made him famous.

Once the casks were kept in Francis Darroze's garage. Now 600 of them from 30 domaines, each chalked with the producer's name, lie on two levels in a modern chai, the older ones downstairs, where the atmosphere is humid, the younger ones upstairs, where it is drier.

As the Armagnacs are coaxed toward their prime, which he defines as roughly 25 years after distillation, Marc Darroze bottles that for which he receives orders, and no more. The producer's name goes on the label together with the vintage, as well as the firm's name. On a separate back label the date of bottling appears—a vital detail because spirits do not improve once they leave wood and enter glass.

"We get good stock," said Marc Darroze, who spent part of his apprenticeship in Sonoma County, Calif., "because we respect the little farmers who make it. We use their name, we never blend their stuff with someone else's, we use no water or additives. That's all very important to these guys."

Using up-to-date office systems, Mr. Darroze has brought the firm into the new century, strengthening sales in Britain, the United States and, recently, Russia. Two days a month, he drives into the backwoods, looking, as he said, "for barns with dark roofs," caused by the mold that grows as Armagnac evaporates. Sometimes he finds a widow who sells him a few barrels.

We tasted some old bottles together, including a 1965 from Eauze, which hinted delightfully of cacao and tobacco. That Armagnac, he said, "was the work of my father, and now I work for my son"—Clément, then just 20 months old.

September 2002

Grappa, Fiery Friend of Peasants, Now Glows With a Quieter Flame

By R. W. APPLE Jr.

Through uncounted decades, grappa was little more than a cheap, portable form of central heating for peasants in northern Italy.

A shot (or two, or three) after dinner helped ward off the damp, misty cold that often settles over the Alpine foothills and the flatlands just beneath them. And a shot in the breakfast espresso—yielding a "corretto," or corrected coffee—got the motor started in the morning gloom.

Grappa is made by distilling debris left in the press after grapes have yielded up their precious juice. The debris is called pomace and consists of skins, seeds and dry pulp. A fiery, rustic, usually colorless alcohol, grappa (the name derives from the Italian word for grape stalk) has an oily, earthy taste with something of the barnyard about it, and a marked alcoholic kick.

Even at its best, grappa is not subtle. The French writer J. K. Huysmans said, with some justice, that if Cognac's music resembled a violin's and gin and whisky "raised the roof of the mouth with the blare of their cornets and trombones," grappa's "deafening din" suggested the growl of the tuba.

But properly distilled and served cool (not cold), it has a beguilingly smoky taste, with hints of stone fruits like cherry and plum. Especially if made from the pomace of dessert wines, it can display a slight sweetness.

Grappa used to be made mostly by traveling distillers or by big industrial outfits like Stock, the Trieste brandy manufacturer. Too often it was a cheap, ill-made product, an Italian version of white lightning.

Fancier Italians, and most foreigners, disdained it.

But that was before the Noninos of Percoto came to prominence. Here in their native town, a furniture-making center about 75 miles northeast of Venice and only 10 miles from the Slovenian border, they tamed grappa, taught it table manners and gave it mass appeal, not only in Italy but overseas, too.

The United States has become the second-largest export market, trailing only Germany. At Felidia in New York, Obelisk in Washington, Spiaggia in Chicago, Valentino in Los Angeles and dozens of other fine restaurants across the country, grappas are prominently displayed and eagerly consumed after dinner instead of Cognac or some other digestif. Tony May, the owner of San Domenico in

Manhattan, said he had sold $50,000 worth this year, not to Italian visitors, but to Americans "who come to Italian restaurants determined to laugh like Italians, eat like Italians and drink like Italians."

You might say, with a bit of poetic license, that grappa runs in Benito Nonino's veins. For several generations, stretching back into the 19th century, his family has been distilling in Friuli, the northeastern corner of Italy. A questing, hawk-nosed man, he and his handsome, extroverted wife, Giannola, longed, as he often says, "to turn grappa from a Cinderella into a queen."

Together, the two of them did it. Instead of a single still, they installed a whole battery of discontinuous copper stills, which allowed them to interrupt the process in the middle of the run, when the spirit was at its peak, and discard the rest—a process known as "topping and tailing." The pomace could thus be processed faster, while it was fresher, which muted the barnyard taste. While continuous stills are cheaper, they boil the pomace nonstop.

Unlike Cognac and Armagnac, which are made by distilling acidic wines few would care to drink, the best grappa is a byproduct of the best wines. The Noninos contracted for pomace from the stars of Friulian winemaking, including Mario Schiopetto, Josko Gravner, Livio Felluga and Gianfranco Gallo.

But raw ingredients and technique would not have been enough. The Noninos had another idea: instead of lumping all the pomace together, the residue of common grapes mixed with that from the more noble varieties, they would distill each separately, starting with picolit, a variety that produces a sweet, delicate dessert wine. The result was a delicious, highly perfumed grappa.

The Noninos made their first batch in 1973 and bottled it in individually blown flasks with silver-plated caps. The labels, handwritten by Giannola, a budding marketing genius, were tied onto the bottles with red yarn.

If the idea was to call attention to the product and to themselves, it worked. Others soon copied them, but the Noninos demonstrated a rare gift for self-promotion. In their ads, they used a sunny family photograph of Benito, now 63, Giannola, 59, and their three stunning daughters—Cristina, 34, Antonella, 31, and Elisabetta, 29—which soon became familiar all over Italy. They commissioned special bottles from great glassmakers like Baccarat, Riedel and Venini, and even established an annual literary prize. Most important, they worked tirelessly to insure that the best Italian restaurants stocked their products.

"The picolit is still our best grappa," Mr. Nonino said with an eloquent shrug. "I know it, the customers know it. I'm satisfied. You can ask for one miracle in life and get it, but to ask for two is ridiculous."

Nardini, a big semi-industrial concern based in Bassano del Grappa, northwest of Venice, was the first to begin commercial production, in the 18th century. Now, more than 1,000 Italian vintners, including many of the very best, like Bruno Ceretto in Piedmont, Silvio Jermann in Friuli and Antonio Mastroberardino near Naples, either produce their own grappa or have a distiller produce it from their pomace and then send it to market under their own labels.

Although their products do not quite fill the mouth in the same way as the best of the Italian grappas do, American distillers like Clear Creek in Oregon and Germain-Robin in California have leaped aboard the grappa express, as have winemakers like Araujo in the Napa Valley. The French make a grappalike drink that they call marc, with special success in the Burgundy and Champagne regions, and the Spanish also produce a version of their own, called aguardiente.

But Nonino remains the marquee name, and this year, the Noninos will sell almost 1.3 million bottles of grappa. Giannola and Benito Nonino retain a remarkable zest for life and for work. One evening last fall, when my wife, Betsey, and I were visiting Percoto, he said his farewells after a long day at the office, jumped onto his bike and pedaled away, whistling "Sentimental Journey."

With the exception of a few grappas that are aged in wood, giving them an amber hue, one looks just like another. So how do I distinguish my colorless liquid from yours? Like vodka distillers, grappa makers quickly found an answer in packaging. In addition to Nonino's flasks, you now find grappa in colored bottles and hand-painted bottles, in containers shaped like a bunch of grapes or a perfume flagon, even in bottles topped with miniature Alpine fedoras.

Some people think that things have got out of hand, like George Lang, the New York author and restaurateur, who remarked tartly not long ago, "I'm afraid that grappa-making has turned into glass blowing."

But it would be a mistake to conclude that clever packaging is always a ruse to conceal an inferior product. A case in point is Jacopo Poli, who makes grappas with finesse and packages them in elegant, long-necked bottles. I especially like his Amoroso di Torcolato, which has an appealing floral bouquet. Should you ever find yourself in Bassano, you can taste it at his little grappa museum, filled with portraits of Louis Pasteur and Leonardo da Vinci and Catherine de' Medici, shelves of ancient tomes on distilling technique and old alembics, or stills.

"Distillation, daughter of alchemy, was born in remote antiquity," a placard announces gravely.

Bassano itself is a pretty, welcoming place, tucked beneath a pre-Alp called Monte Grappa. Some of the fiercest battles of World War I took place there, and it is now crowned with an ossuary holding the remains of 25,000 Italian and Austro-Hungarian soldiers. The neighborhood is dotted with Palladian villas, including Maser, where Veronese painted a delightful set of frescoes, and Palladio is also said to have designed the often-rebuilt covered wooden bridge that crosses the sparkling little River Brenta in the center of Bassano.

The Nardini company operates a smoky, atmospheric grappa bar at one end of the bridge, and one of the best artisan distillers in Italy, Vittorio Capovilla, a muscular man with an evangelical spirit, can be found at the end of a dusty lane just outside the village of Rosa, a half-hour's drive from Bassano. Armed with the latest in German technology, he makes not only grappa but also uva, which is distilled from the grapes themselves rather than from pomace, and which he considers much easier to digest. The seeds in the pomace used for grappa, he told me, contain essential oils that "stun the gastric juices," causing trouble.

Mr. Capovilla's masterpieces, however, are distillates made from cultivated fruits like Gravenstein apples and Saturno pears, as well as rare wild fruits like sour mountain cherries and honey pears that he finds on his hikes in the hills. His products bear comparison to the best in Europe, but they are all but impossible to find; he has yet to master the ropes of commerce.

And then there is Romano Levi, the one and only, the living national treasure, the uncrowned king of Piedmontese distilling. A minute, Hobbitlike figure in a Greek sailor's cap, he works in a ramshackle old structure in the village of Neive, tending a Rube Goldberg assemblage of antique copper boilers and tubes. It is the size of a one-car garage, this world-famous grappa factory, and every bit as cluttered.

But it works. The grappa is superb, if a bit aggressive.

Mr. Levi is a recycler. To fire his still this year, he uses bricks pressed from the residue of last year's distillation. After they have burned, he returns the ashes to the wine producer who originally supplied the pomace, to use as fertilizer in the vineyard. He calls this the Piedmont life cycle.

He is also an inspired improviser. He offers visitors tastes of his products not by pouring them into glasses from bottles or from a pipette, but by lowering a medicine jar on a string through the bunghole into a Slovenian oak cask, hauling some grappa out and handing it over. You drink from the jar.

"You have to go back to the Etruscans to find anything this rudimentary," said Burton Anderson, the wine writer, who was with us when we visited the operation. Black eyebrows arched, Mr. Levi professed not to understand how his gear operated; indeed, he told us, "I know nothing at all about grappa."

Maybe not, but he has the soul of a poet and an artist. Asked how long he had been in business, he replied that he used only one match a year, to fire up his alembic when it was time to begin distilling, and had used 53 matches so far. He makes 6,000 to 10,000 liters a year, using pomace from Angelo Gaja and other Piedmontese winemakers, and he writes all the labels himself—in colored inks on torn pieces of paper, or directly on the bottles with paint.

I am currently working on a bottle produced in 1988, decorated with pictures of flame-red hibiscus flowers. The label specifies that the liquid inside is 48 percent alcohol, and as ever there is a line of enigmatic verse.

"In a dream," it says, "I dreamt."

December 1997

A Fine Roughness:
On the Trail of a Spirit Called Marc

By R. W. APPLE Jr.

Hard to find outside the districts where it is produced, with a name that is often mispronounced, marc is a heady, earthy-tasting French relative of moonshine. It makes some people gag. A few nuts like me love it.

Marc (pronounced mahr, rhymes with car) is made by distilling the pips and skins left in the press after juice has been extracted from wine grapes. Some producers use the stalks, too, but they can add an off-putting strawlike flavor. Properly speaking, marc is the mass of pulpy leftovers; officially, the distillate is eau de vie de marc, but people call it marc for short.

It is identical to the grappa produced in Italy, except in one respect: unlike grappa, it is aged in wood, taking on a rich, tawny color. (This being France, there is an exception to the rule: marc de gewürztraminer, made in Alsace, is clear, like the clear fruit eaux de vie of the region. It is usually drunk ice-cold, again like fruit spirits and unlike other marcs.)

Twenty-five years ago, marc was better known and more widely sold in the United States than grappa. But then the grappa producers vastly improved their product and, probably more important, their packaging. In its distinctive (if sometimes silly) hand-blown bottles, grappa elbowed marc off American shelves.

"We used to have 8 or 10 terrific marcs in stock," said Michael Aaron, chairman of Sherry-Lehmann in New York. "Now we have one, sometimes two."

Which seems a shame.

In theory, marc can be made from the pomace, as the pips and skins are called in English, of any wine. But in fact, it is made almost entirely in eastern France (Alsace and Champagne, where the marc is often put up in a bottle shaped like a ten-pin) and along the axis running from Burgundy down through the Rhône Valley to Provence.

Marc de Bourgogne is the best and most expensive, a favorite of some redoubtable eaters and drinkers, including the British restaurateur Sir Terence Conran (and, I discover from an article he wrote in *The New York Times*, James Villas of *Town & Country*, who likes to end dinner with a marc, a coffee and a cigarette).

I myself like a splash of marc in my espresso some mornings. This is called corrected coffee, maybe because it corrects hangovers. I like the tang that marc gives to Époisses, one of the greatest and gutsiest of French cheeses, whose rind is washed with marc de Bourgogne every day or so during maturation. I like little game birds, like partridges and quail, flamed in marc. And of course I like to sip a fine old marc from a snifter late at night.

Not long ago, at Greuze, a venerable two-star restaurant next to the striking Romanesque cathedral in Tournus, north of Lyon, my wife, Betsey, and I injudiciously began a lunch with snails (with garlic) and frogs' legs (with garlic), with a roast chicken to follow (with lots of garlic). Before the bird, Jean Ducloux, the chef, sent out a sorbet made with marc and lemon that had magical properties, saving us from indigestion and the dreaded dinosaur breath.

This least-known of the great French digestifs, or unsweetened after-dinner drinks, is usually much coarser and more rustic than its sophisticated cousins, Cognac and Armagnac, which are distilled from wine, and Calvados, which is distilled from cider. But the stuff made by or for the producers of noble Burgundies is something else again—refined, aromatic, complex.

Seeking further enlightenment on the subject, I called one drizzly morning this July on Aubert de Villaine, the patrician manager of the Domaine de la Romanée-Conti, the greatest Burgundian estate, which has its headquarters here. He told me right off that he himself was not much of a fan of marc, which he described as "the fifth wheel of the winemaker's cart." But he nevertheless has strong views on what makes marc good; quality, he argued, depends largely upon the aging process.

At the domaine, the clear liquid that comes from the still after a single pass (Cognac gets two) goes into new oak for at least 12 years; right now, the marc from 1981–82 is on sale. After two years the barrels are racked, a process in which the liquid is drawn off the solids, or lees, and topped up, then left in a remote corner of the cool, damp cellars to mature.

Before bottling, the marc is fined, or clarified, in the old-fashioned way, with the addition of a small quantity of milk at 175 degrees. The result is pure elegance, but few ever taste it. Annual output is only 600 bottles, each marked with a vintage year, which is highly unusual among marcs. Fewer than 100 are sold in the United States, for $200 a bottle and up.

Why bother? I asked.

"It's a tradition," Mr. de Villaine said, "and Burgundy is a traditional place."

Up the road in Morey-St.-Denis is Domaine Dujac, run by Jacques Seysses and his son, Jeremy, 25, who recently finished his studies at Oxford. One of their wines was served in 1975 by President Valéry Giscard d'Estaing at the famous luncheon at Élysée Palace honoring the restaurateur Paul Bocuse, and they take as much trouble with their marc as with their wines.

Careful handling of the pomace, the elder Seysses said, is one essential, because it is vulnerable to spoilage. So is the quality of the distillation; Dujac uses a distiller with an elderly, wood-burning apparatus. And so are the temperature and the humidity in the cellar where the marc is kept.

"Too humid," he said, "and as it ages you lose alcohol but no volume, and the marc gets feeble. Too dry, and you lose volume but no alcohol, and the marc is overwhelmed by tannins."

The marc that I tasted with him suffered from neither of those maladies. Thirty years old, with an elegant, sherry-scented nose, it was a deep brown-red in color, as if it had been matured in mahogany rather than oak. There was not a stalky note in the flavor. Nothing aggressive. No alcohol "sting." Just an ample, round, fruity flavor.

"Not many people make it," Jeremy Seysses said. "Not many people make it well, and the market for it is shrinking."

Does the best wine always make the best marc? Not necessarily. Jacques Seysses thinks that poorer vintages sometimes produce better marc, perhaps because the winemaker exerts greater care in pressing the grapes in the first place. And although he is a maker of great red wines, he believes that the pomace from white-wine grapes tends to produce superior marc.

Steve McCarthy, an Oregon distiller who produces marc, also prefers to work with white-wine pomace. He explains: "Most red wines go through a long maceration process that extracts all the color, tannins and flavor from the skins, and there's not much left for the distiller to work with."

At his own wedding, Mr. Seysses told me, he served a marc made by the late Guy Roulot. Mr. Roulot's son, Jean-Marc, a former actor, now heads the family firm, which is based in Meursault, and still makes a light, bright marc, sometimes available in the United States for about $50.

On our trip through Burgundy and down the Rhône Valley last summer, we kept running into Guy Roulot's marc. When I asked Thierry Gazagnes, the proprietor of Le Montrachet, an excellent small hotel in the wine-producing village of Puligny-Montrachet, what he would suggest as a digestif, out came the Roulot. Marked "hors d'age" or "ageless," it was in fact a 1979. Mr. Gazagnes said of it, "I think that it's the best, or one of the best—no added coloring, no filtering, straight from the barrel." I detected notes of cedar and maple syrup in the nose, and the flavor was sumptuous.

A few days later, at Troisgros, the extraordinary three-star restaurant in Roanne, we were served a house-label marc de Bourgogne, but the small print said, "Domaine Guy Roulot."

Every sommelier has his favorite. Jean-Paul Despres, at Lameloise, a three-star landmark in the village of Chagny, on the edge of Burgundy, came up with one of the gems of the trip, a marc, vintage 1968, of remarkable clarity and subtlety, made by Michel Gaunoux, one of the top growers in Pommard. Like many of the very best marcs, it is produced in tiny quantities.

Marcs come in many styles and colors. They are rugged individualists.

In the Rhône Valley, we drank a marc from Château-Grillet, the 9.4-acre vineyard at the heart of Condrieu. Pale and gentle, it had the floral bouquet and ethereal flavor of the viognier grapes grown there. Farther south, at one of Alain Ducasse's delicious inns in Provence, the Auberge de la Celle, we drank its mirror image, a marc from Bandol, made from mourvèdre pomace, which was dark and powerful, producing a slight catch in the throat on the way down.

I still have, on my bar at home, a fabulous marc de Bugey, from the Savoie hills near Geneva. Somehow, it manages to taste both grapey and woody, both light and unusually full-bodied, in the most satisfying way. It was bottled for the superb restaurant of Georges Blanc, in the countryside north of Lyon, and he gave me a bottle several years ago. There is about an inch left.

When that is gone—and it soon will be, even if I drink only a few drops at a time—I plan to console myself with a little something I picked up in England in May, a marc distilled in 1935 from the pomace of the Marquis d'Angerville's Volnay Clos des Ducs and bottled for the American market. I took a very modest sip before I bought it. It was an absolute knockout.

But it is also a link between then and now, a kind of time capsule, and not just an old bottle of firewater. Molded into the bottle is the legend "Federal Law Forbids Sale or Re-Use of this Bottle," and typed onto the revenue label are the words "Leeds Imports Corp., Phila., Pa." Prohibition had been repealed a mere two years earlier.

One night recently, totally by chance, I ran into Daniel Haas of Vineyard Brands, an importer of French wines, at a Washington dinner party. I asked him whether he had ever heard of Leeds Imports.

"Sure," he said. "My grandfather, Sidney Haas, started it."

September 2001

Port Is a Welcome Guest at Cocktail Parties

By ERIC ASIMOV

Ask me about port and I'll tell you I love it. I have fond memories of the sumptuous flavors of a well-aged vintage port, and, even more so, the delicate, subtle pleasures of a 20-year-old tawny. Alas, these delights reside mostly in the past. I almost never drink port anymore.

The urge for a nice after-dinner glass of port or Cognac has largely faded, overcome by the diminished stamina of middle age and the desire to be not only awake and productive the following morning, but eager as well. Port is a fortified wine, after all. You may not taste the 20 percent alcohol in a well-balanced version, but it can quickly catch up with you.

Still, when I put my mind to it, the cinnamon-sweet, nutmeg-spice notes of a 20-year tawny come right back to life. It makes me think that I do need to reacquaint myself with the pleasures of port. Yet, how?

I wish port weren't consigned to the end of the meal. Other fortified wines are more versatile. Even the sweetest Madeira, with its jolt of acidity, seems much less sweet than port, and therefore more flexible with savory foods. Fino sherry is dry, with far less alcohol, and makes a glorious aperitif. It also works well supporting many dishes in the traditional Spanish canon.

But port? It's hard to see beyond cheese, especially blue cheeses and aged Cheddar, or chocolate, of course. As for savory dishes, Roy Hersh, who runs the Web site For the Love of Port, rhapsodizes about port with steak au poivre, ahi tuna and leg of lamb. And Fiona Beckett, a British writer who has a Web site called Matching Food and Wine, suggests that tawny makes a fine substitution for Sauternes in the classic pairing with foie gras. She told me she also suspected that it would pair well with caramelized pork, although she hadn't tried it herself.

Now that's an invitation I can't resist. So I tried it—actually sautéed medallions of Berkshire pork with a caramelized onion jam—and a bottle of Taylor's 20-year-old tawny. The pork-and-onions brought out enjoyable mineral flavors in the port, but the wine was simply too imposing to coexist comfortably throughout the meal. Cheese afterward, alas, was the better bet.

Maybe the impulse to drink port with dinner was wrong. I decided to call Jim Leff, the founder of the Chowhound Web site, who, back in the 1990s, I recalled, was a dedicated port lover.

"I'm still holding the torch for port, but everybody else has forgotten it," he said. Mr. Leff, who since selling Chowhound in 2006 has reverted to life as a professional trombonist, has a treasured cache of vintage ports, primarily 1983 and 1985, which he bought in the late 1990s.

"They're my go-to celebration wines," he said. "Everything since then is too young, and everything older is too expensive. Every time I have a sip, I say, 'That's just great,' and everyone I ever serve it to never fails to be impressed."

Mr. Leff is interested only in the vintage variety, but port is produced in many different styles. The grapes come from daunting terraces built into impossibly steep, rocky hillsides in the Douro region of Portugal, where they bake in dry, often unrelenting heat. Once picked, the best grapes are still trod by feet in stone lagars, or tanks, while the rest are crushed mechanically. The juice is then fermented about half way until the process is halted by the addition of brandy.

Vintage port, which is bottled after two years or so in barrels, and tawny, which is typically aged longer, are the two best-known styles, for good reason. They are by far the most magnificent expressions of port. Vintage ports are made only in very good years—maybe three every 10 years—and can require decades to soften their fiery, extravagantly fruity character. Tawnies mellow in the barrel, where they acquire their reddish brown color, and are generally a blend of vintages.

Good tawnies generally come with an age statement, indicating the average age in the blend. For me, 20-year tawny is ideal, showing the complexity of age at a still-affordable price. I find a 10-year tawny often to be too sharp and simple, while 30- or 40-year tawnies are too expensive and can lack the vivacity that still enlivens the 20-year-olds.

While I have fond memories of vintage ports, I would pretty much be buying them for my children to drink, so long do they need to age. But Mr. Leff makes a good case for enjoying vintage port—vicariously, at least—and he rejects the notion that they need to be paired with food.

"I'm the kind of guy who doesn't use soy and wasabi with sushi," he said. "So I serve it after dinner, on its own. And it needs a relaxed setting—it doesn't go well with anxiety."

What, me worry? What could be more calming than a glass of vintage port in the paneled confines of the cocktail lounge at the "21" Club, complete with club chairs and fireplace?

"Port by the glass is one of our more popular items," said Phil Pratt, the wine director at the restaurant. Still, he said, by-the-bottle sales are not what they once were.

"There was a precipitous drop-off when they changed the smoking laws," he said. "There's all this mystique around port, or baggage, if you want to look at it that way."

While Mr. Pratt says young women do order port, it still has the image of being an old man's drink. Mr. Hersh, of For the Love of Port, acknowledges this image problem and suggests a simple but direct method of appealing to younger generations: cocktails!

For some cocktail perspective, I checked in with David Wondrich, the mixed-drinks authority.

"It's one of my favorite cocktail ingredients, along with sherry," he said. "One of the easiest ways to come up with new cocktails is simple substitution, port for vermouth, for example. Equivalent proof, but new textures and flavors."

By port, Mr. Wondrich means ruby port, a simpler, fruity, more accessible cousin of vintage port, and a blend of several vintages. Years ago Mr. Wondrich invented the St. Valentine, a blend of ruby port, white rum, Grand Marnier and lime juice that has a wonderfully ripe, round, punchlike refreshing quality. He reserves tawny ports for things like variations on the manhattan.

"I'll stir it together with a good rye or Cognac, and a dash of bitters, but I wouldn't use it as much with the sours, because it's delicate," he said.

You rarely see port in cocktails, but in the past it was an important ingredient. In his book *Imbibe* (Perigee, 2007), Mr. Wondrich describes the St. Charles Punch, named for the St. Charles Hotel in New Orleans: a blend of port, Cognac, lemon and sugar.

Audrey Saunders has made another historic punch, the hot port sangaree, a popular cold weather offering at the Pegu Club, her New York cocktail lounge.

These excursions into cocktail history, though, don't do much for port's musty image. "The old view of port needs to be modernized," Mr. Hersh said. "I've even seen sushi paired with port wine."

As eager as I am to drink port more frequently, maybe I'm not that eager.

November 2010

EDITOR'S NOTE:
In conjunction with his column on port, Eric Asimov posted the commentary below on Diner's Journal, on NYTimes.com.

The Smoke Cleared, Leaving Port Behind

In my column on port, I talk about why I rarely drink port anymore. I'm not alone. Port consumption is way down, but not nearly as low as you might expect.

In 2009, 350,000 cases of port were shipped to the United States, according to the Port Wine Institute, a trade group. That's considerably down from a recent high of 469,000 cases in 2006, but still, 350,000 cases is nothing to dismiss.

To put that figure in perspective, let's look back 20 years, to 1990. That year, only 127,000 cases of port were shipped to the United States. The figure dipped down to 103,000 cases in 1991, and back up to 116,000 in 1992. Then, port consumption began a rocket trajectory: 143,000 cases in 1993, 192,000 in '94, 202,000 in '95, 311,000 in '96, 356,000 in '97 and upwards, with the occasional dip, to the high-port mark in 2006.

What caused the rapid increase? Well, in the mid-1990s three very highly rated vintages of port were released: the 1991, the 1992 and especially the 1994.

"The momentum was building simultaneously with the discovery of port by the affluent young, who were also discovering the pairing of port with cigars for the first time," Roy Hersh, who runs the web site For the Love of Port, told me in an e-mail.

Ah yes, remember cigars?

"That was the height of Wall Street with the tech boom and the economy was skyrocketing," Mr. Hersh continued. "The 25-to-45-year-olds were reading *Wine Spectator* to learn about wine and port was sizzling hot. *Cigar Aficionado* added fuel to the flames."

Prices for port shot up then as well. "I remember over an 18-month period, 1977 Fonseca went from a two-year plateau at $49 sailing upwards to $229 per bottle!" Mr. Hersh said.

Clearly, the excitement has worn off, both of port and of cigars. The association of the two was clear to Phil Pratt, the wine director at "21" Club, where port by the glass is still a popular after-dinner ritual. But he said bottle sales of port dropped precipitously after the 2003 ban in New York City of smoking in bars.

But certainly other issues worked against port, too. Jim Leff, the former proprietor of Chowhound.com, who is a confirmed lover of vintage port, has his own theory.

"The 1994 vintage, I think, killed port," he said. "It was one of the most stupendous port vintages of the century, and everybody went out and bought bottles and cracked them immediately and said, 'This isn't so good.' And of course it wasn't good—it needs 80 years of aging! You still can't drink it."

December 2010

Vintage Madeira's Enduring Charms

By ERIC ASIMOV

As the wine director of the River Café in Brooklyn for almost 30 years, Joseph DeLissio has gladly sold vintage Champagnes and old Bordeaux, California cult wines and rare Burgundies. But about five years ago a terrible thing happened: he put some rare old Madeiras on the wine list—and sold them, too.

"If you get to the level where you know Madeira and love Madeira, you hoard them," Mr. DeLissio said. "They are meant for very special, thoughtful moments, and when you see somebody just down a glass, it's hurtful."

Few wines stimulate the hoarding instinct like old vintage Madeira, the fortified wine produced on a jagged Portuguese island about 300 miles off the Atlantic coast of Africa. Because no other wines age as well as Madeira, it's not uncommon to find bottles from the 19th century, or even the 18th. Not only are they still drinkable, they are in their prime. But very little vintage Madeira is produced, and even less leaves the island that gave the wine its name.

Since those painful sales, Mr. DeLissio has stockpiled vintage Madeira, cases of it, from 1978 to 1863. He thinks he has invested $100,000 in old Madeira, $100,000, mind you, belonging to Buzzy O'Keeffe, the River Café's owner.

Though his instinct may be to lock the Madeira cellar, Mr. DeLissio has had to face the economic consequences of his obsession and must do what he most dreads. And so, starting the day after Thanksgiving, the River Café will offer 40 to 50 vintage Madeiras, a list outdone in this country only by Bern's Steak House, a wine lovers' destination in Tampa, Fla. A rotating selection of 10 to 15 of them will be available by the glass, and the rest by the bottle.

"Hopefully we won't sell any!" Mr. DeLissio said, half-jokingly.

What drives a Madeira fanatic? It's only partly the romance, knowing that a bottle of 1863 Barbeito bual was made the year Gettysburg was fought.

But when you pour a glass of the 1863 and it is stunningly fresh and refreshing, with aromas of spices and roasted nuts, caramels and chocolate, and the flavors ricochet through your mouth like beams of light off mirrors, then you want to have a lot more of that Madeira to savor.

The same is true of a youthful 1969 Blandy's, made from rare terrantez grapes, which tastes brightly of lemon, lime and brown sugar before fading to—get this—cream soda. Or of a dry, elegant, perfectly balanced 1929 Barbeito verdelho, smelling of grapefruit and walnuts, changing constantly in the glass.

"Madeira is almost like a conversation," Mr. DeLissio said. "It's the most thoughtful wine there is."

Contrarians must love Madeira, because it turns wine facts on their head. Everybody knows wines must be kept in cool, dark places free of excess vibrations. But Madeiras are purposely heated to more than 100 degrees and were once considered best when subjected to the pitching and rolling of ships on long ocean voyages. In fact, it was in the era of colonization when Madeira's greatness was first recognized, by accident, as legend has it.

In the early 17th century the island of Madeira was a port for those sailing to Africa, the West Indies and America. Ships would pick up casks of wine for the voyage. One time, the story goes, a cask was somehow misplaced and not discovered until the ship had returned. Amazingly, it was judged to be far better than when it had left. Producers began to send wine on voyages, just for the ride. The best were called vinhos da roda: round-trip wines.

Ocean voyages are no longer a part of Madeira production, but today barrels of the best wines are placed in the attics of warehouses to bake naturally under the island sun. The heat; the slow, controlled oxidation of long barrel aging; the high alcohol content, 17 or 18 percent, after fortification with grape spirits; and the searing acidity of the Madeira grapes render the wine practically invulnerable to the ravages of age. Even opened, a bottle can last months without noticeable deterioration.

Most Madeiras are blends of vintages and grapes. Some can be excellent and more affordable introductions to the pleasures of Madeira, particularly those aged for 5, 10 or 15 years and made with one of the leading noble grapes: sercial, verdelho, bual and malvasia. Sercial is the driest and the lightest of the wines, and malvasia, or malmsey, the richest and the sweetest, though even a malmsey, with its beam of bracing acidity, can sometimes seem dry because it is so refreshing.

But it is the vintage Madeiras, made in minute quantities, that are the most exciting. By law, these wines must be aged 20 years in barrels, although a new category, colheita, or harvest wines, can be released after five years in barrels. In practice, many vintage Madeiras are aged far more than 20 years.

Mannie Berk, head of the Rare Wine Company, a leading Madeira importer, says vintage Madeiras are becoming more expensive. "Between the dollar and its scarcity," Mr. Berk said, "there's a growing appreciation that these wines are very valuable."

While he hasn't completed his list yet, Mr. DeLissio thinks he will charge $40 to $100 for a one-and-a-half to two-ounce glass and $300 to $1,400 for a bottle. Among his treasures are three terrantez Madeiras and an anise-scented 1927 wine made from the bastardo grape, which is now practically extinct on Madeira.

Mr. DeLissio says he is still searching for old bottles. For the record, Mr. Berk has a few bottles of a 1720 Madeira, which he says is absolutely ethereal. Not surprisingly, he's not selling.

November 2007

Hidden in Hungary, Treasures on the Vine

By EVAN RAIL

The mold covered every surface of the cellar, coating the walls and ceilings in layers of loose black gauze. On one shelf, sheets of mold had grown so thick that it was nearly impossible to tell what was underneath, making the ancient wine bottles seem like ash-colored homunculi, an army of toy soldiers made from fungus.

Walking farther into the cellar, I ducked under a low ceiling and felt dangling fingers of mold touch my head.

"The mold is fed by the wine that evaporates," said my guide, Zsuzsanna Szobonya, leading me into a hexagonal tasting room where even the arabesque chandelier overhead was adorned with more black fluff. "Try this," she said.

Standing in the dim light, I sniffed, then tasted. Though the cellar air was damp and musty, the scent from the glass was richly aromatic and floral. The wine, a Tokaji aszu, was full of citrus blossoms and fruit in the nose. In the mouth, crisp flavors of apricot and orange burst forth, followed by an invigoratingly sharp finish that begged for another quick sip.

Lucky mold, I thought.

"Can you imagine?" Ms. Szobonya asked, taking a sip. "So light and fresh, and yet it's about 20 percent sugar."

Though not all wines from the region are quite so saccharine, the legendary aszu sweet wines were a large part of what had brought me to this corner of northeastern Hungary. Known by the name of the region's main winemaking town, Tokaj, the moist and moldy area at the confluence of two mysterious, slow-moving rivers is the oldest classified wine region in Europe—older than Bordeaux in France, older than Porto in Portugal, older than Chianti in Italy. In fact, many of the stone wine cellars here date to the mid-16th century.

And now, 20 years after the changes that brought democracy, market capitalism and wide-open borders to the former Eastern bloc, Tokaj is emerging as one of the most interesting wine regions in Europe, not just for its sweet aszus and distinctive dry whites, but also for its unusual blend of history and cultures—Jewish, Russian, Hungarian and Greek—and for the low-key experience of a less-traveled wine trail where the curious and enterprising can easily rub shoulders with working winemakers, often right in their homes and vineyards.

"You can taste the wines right where they're made," said Carolyn Banfalvi, the author of *Food Wine Budapest,* who also provides culinary tours of the Tokaj region. "There's a real range of wines in Tokaj. There are the sweet wines that everybody thinks about first, but there's also the excellent dry wines, which are becoming more and more well known."

That renown seems to have spread faster and farther than the wines themselves, which remain a relative rarity outside their homeland, making a trip to Tokaj a near necessity for travelers who want to taste the full range. So, armed with several tips from Ms. Banfalvi, I made a wine-tasting road trip to the region this spring, driving there in just over seven hours from my home in Prague.

Dusk was falling as I arrived, creating a mysterious twilight zone out of the rolling Carpathian foothills: with tractors often occupying the road and small farmhouses surrounded by vines and impressive oaks, the setting was a far cry from the overtouristed wine trails of Beaune or the Napa Valley. In fact, the wide horizons and tree-lined country roads felt closer to the place where I grew up in rural central California.

What we don't have a lot of in the long San Joaquin Valley, however, are luxury hotels run by European aristocrats, like the Grof Degenfeld Castle Hotel, a chateaulike property owned by a German-Hungarian family of counts and earls located in Tarcal, a traditional winemaking village on the western side of Kopasz-hegy, also known as Mount Tokaj.

After checking into a surprisingly large room and admiring the view over the well-tended grounds and vineyards, I went downstairs to the Degenfeld wine cellar, where the hotel manager, Pal Visztenvelt, had a selection of the estate's own bottles waiting for me as part of the wine-tasting package I'd booked.

Though the stately "castle" looks a lot like a chateau, he explained, it was built as a winemaking school in 1873, just 10 years after the Hungarian émigré Agoston Haraszthy founded the Buena Vista Viticultural Society in Northern California, helping to create the wine industry there. Now in the hands of the Degenfeld family, the former school operates as a combination hotel and winery, producing wine from its own vineyards. High-season occupancy at the hotel, he said, can be fairly busy, but the off-season—from October to May—is generally empty, because of the weather.

"In November this isn't a very nice place," he said. "We have so much fog you can't see anything."

With just a few noticeably elegant Continental couples booked in for wine tastings and vineyard tours during my midweek visit in mid-April, the airy, salonlike public areas of the hotel contributed to the languorous feeling that seemed endemic to the region. The damp was apparent, as well. Set at the meeting of the Tisza and the Bodrog Rivers, the Tokaj region's microclimate is a haven for fungus: both the black mold, *Cladosporium cellare*, which thrives in its wine cellars, and *Botrytis cinerea*, the so-called "noble rot" that attacks grapes in the vineyard, and one of the secrets to Tokaji aszu and some of the area's other sweet wines.

The majority of the region's vineyards are planted with furmint, Mr. Visztenvelt said, a varietal especially conducive to the fungus. When *botrytis* attacks, the grapes dry up, becoming nearly solid. This concentrates the sugars, creating a characteristic flavor. Although the result was delicious, I couldn't help wondering who first got the idea to produce wine from moldy grapes.

"One story is that it was because of the Turks," Mr. Visztenvelt said, referring to the era when the Ottoman Empire occupied a large portion of what is today Hungary. "The Turkish border was in the neighborhood, and they used to make raids across the border during which the winemakers had to hide. Afterwards, they came back and they tried to make wine out of the grapes that had rotted while they were gone."

That sounded as plausible as just about any other explanation. Whatever the cause, it clearly didn't happen recently: the Hungarian government's application for Unesco World Heritage status for the region, which it earned in 2002, notes that most of the area's wine cellars were built between the mid-1500s and the late 17th century.

Though all the samples were excellent, I was most struck by Degenfeld's 2008 Fortissimo, a sweet, late-harvest wine made from 80 percent yellow muscat, with the remainder coming from two other types of grapes: harslevelu and dried but not *botrytis*-infected furmint grapes. It had a nose of syrupy, overripe fruit, with lush spoonfuls of melon, apricot and cinnamon-spice in the mouth, followed by a honeyed finish with just a touch of dry minerality.

"The goal was to produce a wine at the same level and with a similar taste every year," Mr. Visztenvelt said. "With an aszu, that would be impossible."

For a wine that was supposedly easy to produce, it had a meditative complexity, and I soon found myself asking for another glass, which I carried outside. As the sun was setting, I walked through the parklike chateau grounds and considered my options for the next few days.

Given enough time, I hoped to visit the nearby village of Mad, partly to see the well-regarded Royal Tokaji Wine Company there, partly to see the town's restored Baroque synagogue from 1795—a focal point for the area's once vibrant Jewish community and another draw for cultural travelers. In warmer weather, I could hike or bike the many trails on Mount Tokaj or even rent a canoe and spend time on the river. But the dark clouds scudding in from the west made me think that I should get to know the area with an indoor approach: by drinking as well as I could.

The next morning the front desk arranged for a driver to take me to the village of Tolcsva, a 30-minute journey to the northeast made just slightly longer by a slow drizzle. Through the rain I watched vineyards and isolated hilltop farmhouses roll by before we came to the town and stopped in front of Oremus, one of the area's largest and most famous wineries.

That fame was earned in large part because of its dry white furmint, now called Mandolas after the vineyard where the grapes are grown, which once received a not-too-shabby 89 points from *Wine Enthusiast*. It was there that I met Ms. Szobonya, who, after giving me a tour of the spotless, laboratory-like winery, led me to the cellar's hexagonal mold-encrusted tasting room. There, we tried the winery's three-, five- and six-puttonyos aszu wines. Modern aszu wines are rated on a scale of three to six "puttonyos," or "baskets," an old measurement originally designating the amount of botrytised grapes in each barrel, now used to denote the amount of remaining sugar in the finished wine (six being the sweetest). We also tried two vintages of Mandolas from 2006 and 2004.

Tasting the wines in the near-dark, I thought the 2006 was stony and crisply dry, while the vintage from just two years earlier had more peach fruitiness in the mouth and far less minerality.

After a two-hour tasting, it was time to follow up the morning's liquids with lunch. But after tasting fine wines, where would I find a meal of the same quality?

About a block away, as it turned out, at Os Kajan, a restaurant that also functions as an art gallery and, with just one guest room, a hotel.

Despite the place's all-trades angle, the food was surprisingly good, merging local ingredients with French techniques courtesy of the Hungarian- and English-speaking French owner, Pascal Leeman, who seemed to have a knack for discovering and presenting the region's culinary ingredients at their best. As a member of the local mycological society, he explained, he had himself gathered the local truffles for his restaurant's fragrant ravioli, served just al dente with a large accompanying salad of fresh mâche and boiled quail eggs. The house specialty, sautéed Hungarian foie gras, arrived in a sweetly acidic sauce of honey and aszu wine, whose tartness formed a nice counterbalance to the rich goose liver. Aszu wine even showed up in a dessert, taking the role of the alcohol in what would have otherwise been a baba au rhum.

Floored by the cuisine, I resolved to find a way to stay in Os Kajan's guest room, if not move in permanently.

The town of Tokaj itself can also feel remarkably homey, provided your home is somewhat monomaniacally focused on wine. That afternoon, I wandered its narrow streets and lanes, stopping into small bottle shops and wine stores, bars and tasting cellars. With just over 5,000 residents, it has an intimate, neighborly feel, though it was hard to find anything not related to the grape. Cherry trees were blossoming next to the town's tall stone walls, while Mount Tokaj loomed to the west, creating a nestled, well-protected air that felt quite unlike anywhere else I knew in Central Europe.

It seemed as if the town had suddenly moved to the Mediterranean, though with even more neo-Classical architecture: restored masterpieces with tall Doric columns supported sturdy triangles; other, wonderfully decrepit buildings displayed ornate arches and facades that evoked Athens by way of Austria. It was Hungary, to be sure, but it somehow reminded me most of Vilia, my grandmother's hometown in Greece.

This turned out to be not too far off. As the town's small but colorful museum recounted, Greek merchants came to dominate the wine trade in Tokaj starting in the early 17th century. They were followed by groups of Jewish and Russian wine merchants who were subsequently supplanted by Communist-era state cooperatives, which were ultimately replaced by the international collectives that control much of the production today.

The two major players are Oremus, which is part of the Vega-Sicilia concern from Spain, and AXA Millésimes, a large French wine company, which owns the Disznoko winery. After seeing several larger wineries, I was especially curious about the smaller vintners in the region, so the next day I arranged to meet Judit Bodo, the owner of Bott Pince, a small winery in the town of Tokaj with a cultish following among connoisseurs in Budapest. One of Ms. Banfalvi's tips was to schedule meetings with winemakers well in advance, as the undercommercialized nature of the region means that very few wineries have visitors' centers with regular hours.

This can present challenges for the impetuous: if you don't plan, you might show up at a winery only to discover no one is there. But as I learned at Bott Pince the payoff is often a more intimate, less touristic experience. As Ms. Bodo set a pair of Riedel wineglasses down on a cask, it became apparent we would be tasting her wines directly atop the 16 oak barrels that contained the entirety of Bott Pince's current production, a vintage that had been especially limited because of the caprices of Mother Nature.

"Every year we get three barrels of wine from our Teleki vineyard," Ms. Bodo said. "But in 2009 the birds and the pheasants, they ate everything, and we got just one barrel."

With just one room and a very small amount of cellar space, Bott Pince gave the impression of a mom-and-pop operation. Most of the bottles I saw didn't yet have labels.

"I take them home, 100 bottles at a time," Ms. Bodo said, "and we put the labels on in the kitchen."

Born in a Hungarian-speaking part of Slovakia, Ms. Bodo recounted how she had arrived in Tokaj after first working for a winery in Austria. A bookish brunette, she could have come from just about anywhere in Europe, speaking a crystalline, slightly academic English inflected with words from various other languages, as when she began talking about her favorite varietal, harslevelu: "Sometimes the furmint is too harsh," she said, "too 'gerade' in German, too 'straight,' and harslevelu has more play. It's more layered, it has more nose, it has more nuance."

Tasting her winery's dry furmint-harslevelu cuvée, I thought I got a sense of the difference: while Bott Pince's 100 percent furmint wine had been stony and sharp, the blend brought out more cantaloupe and sweet melon with less acidity, finishing with just a touch of linden blossom.

The sell-it-now, small-scale nature of her business has meant that Ms. Bodo currently has no archival wine to speak of: she recalled that at a recent wine dinner in Budapest fans of her wine had brought bottles from their own cellars in order to taste and compare earlier vintages. Until this year, Bott Pince had never put out an aszu wine, though she noted that its first, a very sweet six-puttonyos version, was just about ready for release.

Pouring a small glass of aszu, she noted that the wine should age for many years, recounting that the very first aszu she tasted was more than 50 years old at the time.

I sniffed at the wine, then tasted. Despite a light color—Ms. Bodo assured me that it would get darker in time—it had complex layers of flavor, starting out with the taste of candied oranges before revealing notes of pineapple and brown sugar. With such wonderful flavors in the wine, it seemed a pity that the production was so limited: just 480 bottles would be available, she said.

After another sip, I noticed that the mold on the cellar walls was also small-scale; unlike the fluffy strata of fungi at Oremus, Bott Pince's more modern cellar had but a few flecks of black. But it also appeared to be growing, with bigger clumps visible on the stone arches, and I imagined that there would probably be a lot more of the fungus by the time her wine was also 50 years old.

"It'll happen naturally," Ms. Bodo said, pouring another glass. "It's nice to see what nature can do. That's why we're here."

July 2010

A Dessert Wine That's a Public Secret

By FLORENCE FABRICANT

The imposing Renaissance Château de Monbazillac, in southwestern France, has a lovely sweet wine to offer, but few Americans, even wine buffs, have tasted it.

Monbazillac (pronounced moh-bah-zee-YAK) is a wine the French have kept largely to themselves, exporting no more than 20 percent of it, mostly to Belgium and the Netherlands, with less than 5 percent going to the United States. Yet Monbazillac is France's largest late-harvest sweet wine district as gauged by acreage and production.

Though the soil differs from that of the Sauternes region, Monbazillac is made from the same grapes—sémillon, sauvignon blanc and muscadelle—as Sauternes, France's best-known late-harvest dessert wine, especially the illustrious, costly Château d'Yquem.

Monbazillacs are grown about 60 miles to the east of the Sauternes region, in five districts clustered around the town of Bergerac.

Like a good Sauternes, a fine Monbazillac can become a deep gold, concentrated wine, but it tends to be somewhat less voluptuous, with a spicier, less floral bouquet. Monbazillac delivers exotic touches of honeyed mango, quince, passion fruit and citrus, often with a distinctive nuttiness in the aftertaste.

There's a bigger difference: the price. "You'll get a terrific bottle of Monbazillac for what you'd pay for the most ordinary Sauternes," said Jean-Luc Le Dû, the wine director at Daniel. That's about $20 or so in a New York wine shop.

Considering the economic downturn, this may be the perfect time for Monbazillac. It has more complexity and character than muscat de Beaumes-de-Venise, from the southern Rhône, the usual French sweet wine for budget-minded Americans. The reasonable price also makes it a good candidate for cooking: for poaching pears or making a jelly to serve with a pâté.

In the Dordogne and Bergerac regions of France, a glass of Monbazillac is likely to accompany local foie gras. At Le Centenaire, a Michelin two-star restaurant in Les Eyzies-de-Tayac, there are 10 Monbazillacs on the list, many from La Domaine de l'Ancienne Cure. For Timothy Harrison, Le Centenaire's English-born sommelier, the sometimes smoky, nutty, quince-paste concentration of older vintages make them a perfect complement for foie gras.

To test the versatility of the wine, and to compare it with Sauternes, Daniel Boulud prepared a number of dishes for me to taste: ceviche of hamachi with clementines, slabs of foie gras both hot and cold, various cheeses and desserts. In general, the Monbazillacs complemented the food more agreeably, even the foie gras. The Sauternes were best only with blue-veined cheese and tarte Tatin.

"Sauternes are heavier in the mouth than Monbazillac," Mr. Boulud said. They're a bit higher in alcohol.

There's no Château d'Yquem equivalent to give luster to Monbazillac. But a number of Monbazillacs, especially the ones made by a new generation of producers like Tirecul la Gravière and Domaine de l'Ancienne Cure, are bound to satisfy a discerning palate, even one that appreciates Sauternes.

It still takes a bit of searching to find Monbazillacs like these on the shelves of New York's wine shops. Most of the better wine shops have one or two, and prices range from $15 to $50 a bottle. When buying, it's important to look for a chateau-bottled Monbazillac.

Monbazillacs are scarce in restaurants. Roger Dagorn, the sommelier at Chanterelle, who pours it by the glass with foie gras, said, "I don't find a huge difference between many Monbazillacs and Sauternes."

The rivalry between Monbazillac and Sauternes has gone on for more than a century, with Sauternes usually prevailing.

For decades, many Monbazillacs were badly made, from grapes harvested by machine. But since 1990, when machine picking was no longer allowed, the wine has been steadily improving, and it has been shedding its reputation as a poor man's Sauternes.

As with Sauternes, the overripe grapes, often infected with *Botrytis cinerea*, or noble rot, are picked by hand, with the harvesters going through the vineyards several times, selecting only the grapes that are ready. At Château d'Yquem there can be as many as 10 pickings.

Monbazillacs of varying quality are made by more than 200 growers and producers. About a third of the wines are made by a cooperative based at the Château de Monbazillac, for which two or three pickings are typical.

Christian Roche, whose grandfather helped found the cooperative in 1935, said that although the quality of the cooperative's wines has improved, he preferred to control his small production at the Domaine de l'Ancienne Cure every step of the way.

Monks from the Loire Valley first planted grapes around Monbazillac in the 11th century. By 1550, when construction started on the Château de Monbazillac, the production of white wine, notably sweet as tastes at the time insisted, was flourishing.

But Bordeaux, the nearest seaport, gave preferential treatment to its own wines, including Sauternes, a holdover from centuries of control by the English. So winemakers from Monbazillac found markets among the Dutch and Germans instead of the English.

Monbazillac is not made every year. For example, none was made in 1992 because the condition of the grapes was not good enough, and very little was made in 1991, 1993, 1994 and 1996. Wines made in those years could be declassified as Côtes de Bergerac and not labeled Monbazillac.

The wine must have 12.5 percent to 14.5 percent alcohol, but typically Monbazillac is 13 percent, slightly lower than Sauternes. Less sauvignon blanc and more muscadelle is often used in the blend, giving a trifle less acidity but a more exotic fruit flavor. Many, but not all, Monbazillacs are aged for up to two years in small oak barrels.

Like Sauternes, a good Monbazillac improves with age, deepening in color, often to amber, and releasing ever greater concentrations of flavor. Monbazillacs are not only worth discovering and buying, they're worth keeping.

April 2003

Frozen Vines (and Fingers)
Yield a Sweet Reward

By JULIA LAWLOR

It is 14 degrees above zero as a group of wine lovers converges in a vineyard on the Niagara Peninsula. Frosty bundles of riesling grapes hang on rows of vines in the pale, gathering daylight. A storm the night before has left behind six inches of fresh snow.

Perfect conditions, the winemaker Shiraz Mottiar declares, for picking the frozen grapes that he will soon transform into Canada's specialty, ice wine, for his employer, Malivoire Wine Company. By law, Canadian ice-winemakers cannot call their product by that name unless it is made from grapes picked off the vine at or below −8 degrees Celsius (17.6 degrees Fahrenheit). So far, so good. Mr. Mottiar is confident that the temperature will hold, at least for a few hours, and instructs the group to get to work. What is ideal for the harvest, though, is not so great for human extremities.

"My feet are very cold now," said Peter Scott, who woke up at 4:45 a.m. to make the hour-and-10-minute drive from Toronto with his wife, Jessica Dolman. This is the fourth year of picking for the couple, who, like the other 25 or so loyal Malivoire customers bending intently over their work, are not paid for their labor. They will, however, receive a free bottle of ice wine with their names listed among the workers on the 2010 vintage label. After the harvest they'll also be invited back inside the winery, where the proprietor, Martin Malivoire, has been preparing vats of hot chocolate and chili spiked with ice wine.

"The whole experience is very addictive," Ms. Dolman said.

Among devotees in North America, this stretch of flat farmland bordered by Lake Ontario to the north and Lake Erie to the south is ground zero for indulging a taste for ice wine, a sweet wine that is often paired with dessert, rich cheeses and foie gras.

Canada vies with Germany for the title of world's largest producer of ice wine—some years, because of inconsistent weather, Germany's crop is small or nonexistent. (Austria, Switzerland and New York's Finger Lakes are among the many areas that also make ice wine.)

More than 75 percent of all the ice wine in Canada comes from Ontario. (The remainder is made in regions like southern Quebec and the Okanagan

Valley in British Columbia.) Unlike more temperate parts of the world, Canada has consistently cold winters, which guarantee an annual crop of frozen grapes. Still, ice wine represents just a small percentage of wine being produced here. It's expensive to make: a ton of grapes yields only one-sixth the amount of ice wine as table wine—hence its nickname, liquid gold—and its prices start at $50 for a half-bottle. Leaving grapes on the vine long past normal fall harvest also is risky.

"There are all kinds of hazards," said Norman D. Beal, a former oil trader who in 2000 turned a decrepit barn into an opulent tasting room at his Peninsula Ridge Estates Winery on a hill in Beamsville. "There are the birds, mildew, all kinds of diseases." That's in addition to the vagaries of the weather, including rain, hail, ice storms and midwinter thaws.

Extreme winemaking, as some call ice-wine production, calls for extreme wine touring. In winter that means lots of layers, and maybe a face mask with an opening big enough for sipping. The trade-offs: there's plenty of room to belly up to the tasting bars, and it's easier to get a table at one of the region's many fine restaurants.

Each tasting inevitably leads to a game of identifying classic ice-wine flavors: lychee nut, caramel, toffee, strawberry jam, crème brûlée, burnt orange, citrus, tropical fruit. Then what follows is a discussion of the improbable alchemy that goes into producing a drink that is said to have been created by mistake in a German vineyard in 1794.

Ice-winemakers here like to leave the grapes on the vine through a series of mild freezes and thaws instead of picking at the first opportunity. That process produces the right balance of sweetness, acidity and the nuanced flavors that separate great ice wine from something that is cloyingly sweet.

"You're always watching the sugar and acid levels," Mr. Mottiar said. "Once they peak, then you pick and press." The ice-wine harvest usually doesn't occur until well into December, and in some years it has stretched into February.

When the frozen grapes are pressed at just the right temperature, usually immediately after picking, the water is crystallized, and the juice that remains consists of the most exquisitely concentrated sugars and flavors.

"It's like squeezing marbles," said Juan Miranda, the assistant winemaker at Peninsula Ridge. (Some wineries have broken their presses when trying to extract the juice from grapes at too low a temperature.) Most ice wine is aged about a year before it is bottled, though it can be aged much longer.

A key to this area's success in creating some of the world's best ice wine is its geography. Because Lake Ontario is so deep, the heat that it stores up during the summer months is released over the land as air begins to cool in the fall. During the winter, the constant flow of warm air moderates temperatures in the fields. The Niagara Escarpment, a ridge running through the peninsula close to the lake, plays a similar role. Winds coming off the lake hit the ridge, known here as the Beamsville Bench, then recirculate over the land, acting as natural antifreeze for the vines. Otherwise, typical Canadian winter temperatures of –20 degrees Celsius (–4 degrees Fahrenheit) or below could easily destroy the crops.

Like the wineries in the Finger Lakes, the 65 wineries operating in Niagara-on-the-Lake and farther west in the Niagara Escarpment have had to overcome a reputation for the sickeningly sweet wines made in the days when all that grew there were native labrusca grapes. Those grape vines were mostly replaced by European vinifera vines in the 1970s.

The Finger Lakes have adjusted to their fickle winters by making more sweet, late-harvest wines that don't require grapes to be frozen on the vine. They also produce "iced wines," which are made with grapes picked in the fall, then frozen later under artificial conditions. But Canadians tend to dismiss these wines as inferior. "We're one of the rare regions in the world that has the right soil and cold enough winters for the grapes to freeze," said Ben Nicks, a sales associate for Stratus Vineyards in Niagara-on-the-Lake.

Canadian winemakers also argue that their strict rules regulating ice wine—inspectors check each winery's harvest to measure sugar levels and ensure that grapes were picked at the proper temperature—have given them an advantage over other areas.

"We have the ice-wine cops," said Joseph DeMaria, president of Royal DeMaria in Beamsville, which says that it is the only winery in the world that exclusively makes ice wine. Mr. DeMaria, a Toronto hairdresser who started making ice wine in 1998 with no background in the industry, has earned close to 300 awards for his small winery.

To visit the original makers of ice wine on the peninsula, you must head 25 miles east of the Beamsville Bench to Niagara-on-the-Lake, a quaint tourist town surrounded by vineyards. Just outside the downtown along the Niagara River are Inniskillin Wines and Reif Estate Winery, which were the first to perfect and sell ice wine on the Niagara Peninsula in 1984.

Inniskillin, Canada's largest maker of ice wines, has seen a big jump in visitors during the cold months. About 40 percent of the 250,000 people who visit the winery each year arrive between November and March, said Deborah Pratt, a spokeswoman for Inniskillin, up from 15 percent a decade ago. Inniskillin has also been a pioneer in making sparkling ice wine.

Every January, as part of Niagara-on-the-Lake's ice-wine festival, Inniskillin puts up a giant tent and offers an ice-wine tasting at a bar created from—what else?—ice. Ms. Pratt says ice-winemakers are working to convince people that it is not just a drink for special occasions. "Our challenge is to get people to take out that bottle they have sitting in the cupboard, open it up and experiment," Ms. Pratt said.

Just down the road is Reif Estate Winery, whose president and chief executive, Klaus W. Reif, took over his uncle's winery here in 1987 after studying winemaking in his native Germany. Winemaking is in his blood—his German ancestors tended vineyards beginning in 1638—but ice wine has been in his heart since he took his first sip 23 years ago.

"There is so much effort and time that goes into it," he said as he stood in a room full of oak barrels that his grandfather once used to store wine. "The first time I had ice wine, I drank the whole bottle by myself. It took me three or four hours. It was so beautiful."

February 2010

CHAPTER SIX

A Magnum
of Miscellany

Natural Winemaking Stirs Debate

By ERIC ASIMOV

The world of wine is full of hornets' nests. The minute you step on one, whether you nudge it accidentally or boot it with malice aforethought, the angry buzzing begins, rising to a high-pitched howl that would send anybody in search of shelter and a beer.

Prime among these are natural wines. These wines, which barely make up a tiny slice of the marketplace, effortlessly polarize, not least because of the implied repudiation contained in the word "natural." If your wine is natural, what does that make mine? Unnatural? Artificial?

Even defining the term incites the sort of Talmudic bickering usually reserved for philosophers and sports talk-radio hosts. Generally speaking, though, it is intended to mean wines made of grapes grown organically, or in rough approximation, and then made into wine with a minimum of manipulation—nothing added, nothing taken away, the winemaker simply shepherding the grape juice along its natural path of fermentation into wine.

This would seem to be the kind of laudable idealism worth encouraging. Instead, in recent months natural wines and their adherents have been harshly criticized in newspaper and magazine articles, in conferences and on Internet bulletin boards. Some writers have warned of greenwashing, the practice of making false or exaggerated claims about ecologically virtuous practices in order to reap marketing gains. Others resent what they feel is a scolding, finger-wagging sanctimony inherent not only in the term "natural wines," but also in the admirers of the wines. Most damning is the assertion that many wines regarded as natural are unclean, impure and downright bad.

"Natural Isn't Perfect" was the headline in *The Washington Post* this spring for an article by the wine columnist Dave McIntyre, who wrote, "The minimalist approach of the natural-wine movement, taken to its extreme, can be an excuse for bad wine-making."

For fans of natural wines, and I am one, the criticism can be profoundly frustrating. Most people who make or like the wines feel as they do simply because they enjoy the way the wines taste, not because they follow a particular dogma. When successful, natural wines can be superb, seeming bold, vibrant and fresh, graceful and unforced.

"Do you like raw milk cheese and dry-aged beef, do you prefer real sourdough over white bread?" asked Lou Amdur, whose wine bar in Los Angeles, Lou on Vine, took part last month in a series of seminars and discussions of natural wines. "These wines are in the same constellation."

A lot is expected of natural wines, partly because of the term's connotations of purity. Yet to criticize the genre because not all the wines measure up holds them to an unfair standard. Bad winemaking is bad winemaking wherever you find it. Mr. McIntyre could just as easily criticize mainstream brands for using their popularity and financial success to excuse atrocious winemaking.

I've had natural wines from the Loire and Beaujolais, where the movement began, that are as clean and crystalline as anybody might ever want. Others have been murky and funky, yet nonetheless enchanting. And yes, some have been microbiological disasters, refermenting in the bottle or worse. The mistakes have been few, though, while the good examples have been among the most beautiful, intriguing wines I have ever tasted.

"These are often experimental wines, and I love that people are risking their livelihoods making their wines," Mr. Amdur said. "These people are not making a lot of money."

Nonetheless, some producers are trying to capitalize on the growing environmental awareness of consumers by touting their wines as biodynamic or organic. Partly, this parallels the organic-food movement, in which big corporations, not wanting to cede the business, have instead tried to co-opt it by weakening standards and employing their marketing might.

"There are producers who say they are farming organically, but when you dig a little deeper you find it's true only 85 percent of the time," said Scott Pactor, who owns Appellation, a wine shop in Manhattan that carries a loosely defined collection of organic, biodynamic and sustainably produced wines. "Greenwashing creates cynicism."

Indeed, some wine writers have used examples of this sort of greenwashing to batter the entire genre.

I'm not surprised to find exaggeration among those who claim to make natural wines, or any other kind of wine. The history of the wine trade is replete with fraud, adulteration and all manner of chiseling from antiquity to the present.

While the numbers of natural-winemakers and of restaurants, bars and shops that champion them is small, their influence is disproportionate. Like artists, musicians and writers in the avant-garde, the movement traffics in ideas that swirl far beyond the interests of the vast majority of ordinary fans. Nonetheless, their ideas may change the way people think of grape growing and winemaking.

Some of the winemakers might be primitive in their methods, but others are decidedly scientific in their craft. The fact is that making wine without benefit of chemicals or other technological shortcuts demands precision and exactitude. Far more so, perhaps, than in conventional winemaking. I find this passion and determination inspiring.

Not so long ago the organic and local food movements were condemned as the province of eccentrics and fanatics. Yet the proof was in quality and flavor, and many of their ideas have won out. The same may eventually be true in wine.

June 2010

New Wine in Really Old Bottles

By ERIC ASIMOV

Josko Gravner has thrown it all away, more than once. When he started making wine 30 years ago outside this small town in the Friuli–Venezia Giulia region of northeastern Italy, he produced crisp, aromatic white wines in a popular style, using the latest technology.

But he was not satisfied making wines like everybody else. He replaced his temperature-controlled steel tanks with small barrels of French oak, and he won acclaim for white wines of uncommon richness. But not even that was sufficient, and Mr. Gravner began to experiment with techniques considered radical by the winemaking establishment. The hazy, ciderish hue of the resulting white wines, so different from the usual clear yellow-gold, persuaded some that the wines were spoiled. But one taste showed they were fresh and alive, with a sheer, lip-smacking texture.

Was he happy? Please.

Rejecting the modern trappings of the cellar, Mr. Gravner has reached back 5,000 years. He now ferments his wines in huge terra-cotta amphorae that he lines with beeswax and buries in the earth up to their great, gaping lips. Ancient Greeks and Romans would be right at home with him, yet his 2001 wines, his first vintage from the amphorae, which he is planning to release in September, are more vivacious and idiosyncratic than ever.

"With every change, I had clients who lost faith in me," Mr. Gravner said. "The cantina was in a crisis. Now I'm out of crisis, but the rest of the world is in crisis."

Perhaps it's something in the air, or in the wine, but few places on earth have such a concentration of determined, individualistic winemakers as Friuli–Venezia Giulia, particularly in the low rolling hills that stretch across the border with Slovenia. To their fans they make deeply personal, almost artistic wines. To detractors they are fanatical eccentrics.

There's Edi Kante, who in the mid-1980s tunneled deep into the limestone in the Carso region near Trieste to create a spectacular cavernous cellar and then trucked in earth to construct a vineyard, layer by layer, right over the top. There's Stanislao Radikon, who, in the latest incarnation of his relentless experimentation, is determined to do without sulfur dioxide, a stabilizer considered essential by most winemakers for shipping wines.

And then there's Ales Kristancic of Movia, an estate just over the border in Slovenia with vineyards that straddle the line. Mr. Kristancic, whose family has farmed the estate since 1820, is so adamantly rational in his natural approach to grapegrowing and winemaking, so steeped in the wisdom of eight generations spent among the vines and in the cellar, that everyone else thinks he is insane. That is, of course, until they taste his wines, which are astoundingly fresh and soulful.

"Great winemaking is a risk," said Mr. Kristancic, a lean, charismatic man who seems to know the personality of every vine in his 50 acres of vineyard. "You have to walk on the border."

The border here is as important literally as it is figuratively. The vineyards surrounding Oslavia have been the sites of countless battles and savage violence. The Habsburg empire ruled the region for centuries, Napoleon for considerably less time. More than 100,000 people died on battlefields here in World War I. Then came World War II, and famine afterward. An earthquake leveled many towns in 1976. In the 1990s wars in the Balkans threatened to spill over into Slovenia, then a part of Yugoslavia but tied to this region by the vineyards that stretch across the border regardless of political lines.

Now the land is peaceful, the vineyards replanted, but the turmoil remains under the surface.

"At the core of all this is the fact that these people are all about identity and not about ideology," said Fred Plotkin, author of *La Terra Fortunata: The Splendid Food and Wine of Friuli-Venezia Giulia* (Broadway Books, 2001). "You find your identity in the soil, in what you produce from the soil and in what it says about you."

Few areas in Italy embody so many paradoxes. From its southern extreme, the regional capital of Trieste, on the Adriatic, Friuli–Venezia Giulia stretches north through snow-capped Alps to Austria. The region itself is actually the combination of two areas: Friuli, which accounts for much of the land, and Venezia Giulia, in the extreme southeast.

More than any other region, Friuli–Venezia Giulia continues to make wines from indigenous grapes, among them ribolla gialla, a beautifully floral white; tocai Friulano, which can be crisp, refreshing and minerally; and refosco, which produces dark, fruity reds. Yet many wines carry familiar names like merlot, cabernet franc, sauvignon blanc, pinot grigio and chardonnay, French grapes that were introduced 200 years ago by Napoleon's army.

"The French soldiers stayed here, married beautiful women and zak zak," said Mr. Kristancic, employing a phrase he uses frequently to indicate the natural order of events.

Today some of Italy's best white wines, clean, crisp and fragrant, come from Friuli–Venezia Giulia, from winemakers like Schiopetto in the Collio wine district, Lis Neris and Vie di Romans in Friuli Isonzo, Scarbolo in Friuli Grave, and Livio Felluga and Bastianich in Colli Orientali del Friuli. Reds, too, can be striking, although the aggressively herbal style of merlot, for example, that is favored in the region is far from the chocolate-covered-cherry style embraced by much of the world.

Yet it is the visionaries who give the region its special character, its touch of greatness. To hear Mr. Kristancic speak of why wine from a young vineyard cannot have the character of that from an old vineyard is to understand that making great wines is not something that can be done by hiring the right consultants or reading the right books. And to taste a bottle of 1963 Movia merlot, full of laserlike fruit flavors, is to understand that graceful yet intense merlot is not restricted to Pomerol.

Mr. Kristancic walks a path traveled by his ancestors, but Mr. Gravner is blazing his own trail. He seems the placid type, but when he speaks, it's with a quiet, philosophical intensity, the sort that attracts followers because of its idealism but can drive them away by its single-mindedness.

"The problem wasn't that the consumers didn't like the wine anymore," he said, explaining the quest that led him to the amphorae. "I didn't like the wine anymore."

Mr. Gravner began experimenting with amphorae in 1997 and made the leap with the 2001 vintage. "As soon as industry invents something new, the last thing isn't good anymore," he said. "I was looking for a way to make wine where I didn't have to change something all the time."

Of course you can't just drive down to the local supply house for 3,500-liter containers made in the ancient style. Mr. Gravner acquires them from the

Caucasus mountains in Georgia, where such traditional winemaking is still practiced, and has the fragile vessels carefully trucked to a special stone-walled cellar he constructed just for them.

Thirty-one of the amphorae are currently buried there. He ferments the wine in them and then, just as unconventionally, leaves it to macerate with the skins, seeds and pulp for six to seven months before transferring it to large barrels of close-grained Slovenian oak.

It's a technique that requires exquisite care in the vineyard. "You can't correct the wine once it's in the amphorae," Mr. Gravner said. "Whatever is good or bad will be amplified."

So far the results have been spectacular. A 2001 ribolla gialla, which will be released in September, is so vibrant it practically leaps out of the glass, while an '01 Breg, a blend of several white varietals, has a concentrated floral, honeyed flavor yet is profoundly dry.

Like all the Gravner wines, the amphora wines can be disconcertingly cloudy. Mr. Gravner shrugs.

"The color of a wine is like the color of a man," he said. "What matters is what's underneath."

Others have followed Mr. Gravner, but have not pushed the boundaries as far as he. Castello di Lispida in the Veneto makes an amphora wine, but not with the prolonged aging Mr. Gravner gives his. In the Collio Damijan Podversic, who began making wine in 1998, says he hopes to use amphorae but cannot yet afford them. Nicolò Bensa, who with his brother, Giorgio, owns La Castellada in Oslavia, has adopted some of Mr. Gravner's vineyard management techniques but has hesitated at adopting longer maceration times.

"The public resists the deep color," he said.

Perhaps none of Mr. Gravner's admirers have gone as far down an individual path as Stanislao Radikon. Like Mr. Gravner, Mr. Radikon has replanted vineyards and discarded chemical pesticides, steel tanks and small oak barrels, and though he has not adopted amphorae, he has his own radical notions. He wants to do away with conventional 750-milliliter bottles and instead sell the wines in half-liter bottles (for one person) and one-liter (for two). And he has stopped using sulfur dioxide as a stabilizer, which makes it risky to ship his wines unless they are very carefully handled.

Tasted at his small family winery, the Radikon wines are alive with fruit. An '03 ribolla gialla, aging in a large wooden barrel, had the flavor of ripe strawberries. "We're working on a very dangerous border," Mr. Radikon said. "But it's a maximum expression of nature."

As an experiment, a 2002 chardonnay had been left to sit in a demijohn for two years, as his great-grandfather might have done. Would it travel? Who knew, but it had the lovely fragrance of meadow flowers and lemon compote.

"Why shouldn't we discover these things?" he asked. "When you make wines like these, it's hard to like others."

May 2005

A Thinking Man's Wines

By ERIC ASIMOV

As with many small, utilitarian wineries in California, barrels and tanks practically spill out of Tenbrink, home of Scholium Project, here in the Suisun Valley, just east of Napa Valley. Yet to call Scholium Project a winery and its proprietor, Abe Schoener, a winemaker is a little like calling Salvador Dalí a painter. It's true, but it does not begin to capture his visionary character.

No winery in California is more unconventional, experimental or even radical than Scholium. Half the wines it makes in any given year are exquisite. The other half are shocking and sometimes undrinkable. All of them are fascinating, which is exactly the way Mr. Schoener wants it.

From his intuitive winemaking practices to the obscure names he gives each cuvée to his almost heretical approach to winery hygiene, Mr. Schoener marches to his own muse. In the winery, for example, he insists on using only cold water, no soap, to clean equipment and the plant itself.

"Maintaining a complex microbiology is the best way to make wine," he says.

He is a fount of such gnomic sayings. Perhaps not surprisingly, Mr. Schoener, 47, was a philosophy professor at St. John's College in Annapolis, Md., when he caught the winemaking bug. While on sabbatical in 1998 he took an internship at Stag's Leap Wine Cellars and never looked back. By 2000 he was making tiny lots of his own wine, and now, in 2008, Scholium (pronounced SKOH-lee-um) Project is a full-fledged cult wine, although surely the most idiosyncratic cult wine around, with sales driven by curiosity and word of mouth rather than critical approval.

By the dictionary, Scholium, derived from the Greek word "scholion" for school or scholar, refers to marginal notes or commentaries intended to illustrate a point in the text. On his Web site, Mr. Schoener, whose Ph.D. is in ancient Greek philosophy, describes it as "a modest project, not a pre-eminent one, undertaken for the sake of learning." In other words, winemaking by discovery.

My first encounter with a Scholium wine was, alas, an undrinkable one. It was a 2006 pinot grigio that went by the name Elsa's Vineyard School of the Plains, inspired, Mr. Schoener said, by an experience in the Collio, in Friuli-Venezia Giulia in northeastern Italy, one of his favorite wine regions.

This pinot grigio was like none I'd ever had. It was huge: 16.6 percent alcohol.

The aromas were piercing, almost painfully so, and while the wine was dry, it was excruciatingly powerful and overwhelming.

I said as much in my blog. The next day I received an e-mail message from Mr. Schoener, with whom I had never spoken.

"I am so sympathetic to your reaction to my wine," he wrote. "I don't think that you said anything unfair about it. It is a kind of behemoth." He suggested that a roast chicken and a minimum of four people would make such a big wine more bearable.

Most winemakers tend to rival politicians in their efforts to stay on message and spin catastrophe into triumph, but Mr. Schoener freely and cheerfully discusses his failures, which made me receptive to his invitation to try some of his other wines. He makes 10 or so different wines each year, and a total of about 1,500 cases.

So, on a trip to Northern California this summer, I spent a day with Mr. Schoener, visiting tiny vineyards in Sonoma and the Suisun Valley, where he buys grapes, and Tenbrink, where today, long after most of the 2007 whites in California are either finishing their aging or are on the market, his 2007 whites are still struggling to complete their fermentation. "I learn by accident, through inattention," he says.

The wines ranged from massive and far out to almost classically delicate. Another 2006 Collio-inspired pinot grigio, called Rocky Hill Vineyards San Floriano del Collio, was in a style completely different from the first one. It had a lovely cidery color, which came from macerating the wines with their skins, and a captivating tannic texture.

Even more impressive was a 2006 Farina Vineyards the Prince in His Caves, inspired by the eccentric Alberico Boncompagni Ludovisi, prince of Venosa, who made astonishing wines at his Fiorano estate outside of Rome before tearing his vines out in the 1990s. Mr. Schoener's wine, a sauvignon blanc, is serious, textured and complex, intense but not heavy, and, in contrast to his pinot grigios, only 13.3 percent alcohol.

While Mr. Schoener carries the tools of the modern California wine guy— pruning shears, iPhone and laptop—the resemblance to other winemakers ends there. After his internship at Stag's Leap, he was hired by John Kongsgaard, a prominent Napa winemaker who was then at Luna Vineyards, to home-school his son. In return, Mr. Kongsgaard taught Mr. Schoener about winemaking and great wines.

In 2002, with Mr. Kongsgaard gone to focus on his own wines, Mr. Schoener took over at Luna. "It was a radical choice—he was a real freshman," said Mr. Kongsgaard, who has remained Mr. Schoener's mentor. "But we did it because he's my favorite of my students, even though he's not a very respectful or obedient student."

Many of Mr. Schoener's techniques may seem eccentric in California. He prefers natural fermentations, using minimal amounts of sulfur dioxide as a preservative, and while most California producers exalt bountiful fruit flavors in their wine, Mr. Schoener does not. In the course of his cellar work, he said, "I do everything to banish fruit flavors."

Occasionally, his methods don't succeed, as with his 2005 cabernet from Margit's Vineyard.

"I blew it," he says. "I had made cabernet before and done it by the book, and it was very good. So I said, I'm going to make it even better now. But I blew it. In 2006 I got it right, though."

California is apparently not large enough to contain Mr. Schoener. He has another winemaking product in Maury, in the Roussillon region of France, and an unlikely consultant's job at a facility that is to make wine in Red Hook, Brooklyn, from New York grapes.

"That is it," he says. "Nothing in Ohio or Brazil yet."

September 2008

The Truth About "Suitcase Clones"

By ERIC ASIMOV

You heard the one about the suitcase clones, no?

It goes like this: In the black of night a guy sneaks into a famous Burgundy vineyard—let's say La Tâche, but it could just as easily be Le Musigny or Clos de Bèze. He takes some cuttings of pinot noir vines, wraps them in wet cloth and smuggles them back to California. He propagates the vines and, voilà! He's got grand cru pinot noir.

Dubious? It supposedly happens all the time—the smuggling part, at least—if we are to believe the marketing for dozens of American wineries. Their promotional materials tell the story of the suitcase clones, or the brand-name version, Samsonite clones. In some variations, it was a friend of a friend who obtained the clones. Either way, vineyards all over the West Coast associate themselves in their marketing with Burgundy's greatest.

Such stories may excite gullible consumers who are looking for something, anything, to distinguish one of the myriad pinot noirs from another.

But the truth is that the origin of a vine, whether from a clone boldly swiped from Domaine de la Romanée-Conti or meekly purchased from the local nursery, is at best meaningless. The grand cru association is a little like picking up a guitar like one Jimi Hendrix used and expecting "Purple Haze" to burst out. Fat chance.

And by the way, it is illegal to import agricultural material without proper quarantining.

Yet the continued fascination with suitcase clones, and with the arcane issue of grape clones in general, hints at the desperation of consumers to gain some sense of control over where their wine dollars are going. The more we know about the clonal selections, soil composition, rootstocks, trellising techniques, pruning methods and degree days, the better we can guess what's going to be in the bottle, right?

To an extent, yes, but even well-informed wine drinkers have a difficult time making sense of many of the technical details of winemaking, especially when it comes to clones. So let's take a closer look at clones and the actual role they play in what's in your glass, regardless of their origin.

Vines grow grapes because they want to reproduce the old-fashioned way, by enticing birds or other critters to eat the sweet fruit, a natural means of transporting the seeds to a new location for planting. Such methods prove inefficient to meet human needs.

The scourge of phylloxera, for one thing, makes it impossible for most vinifera grapevines to grow on their own roots. This makes growing from seeds cumbersome, so instead growers propagate vines from cuttings of parent plants.

The time-honored technique was a mass selection, in which growers would take cuttings from many different vines. The result was a diverse vineyard that produced grapes of many varied characteristics, particularly if that grape was pinot noir, which is somewhat genetically unstable and mutates far more easily and frequently than, say, cabernet sauvignon or syrah. This is why most suitcase clone tales are about Burgundy and pinot noir.

Many growers in Burgundy still believe a mass selection is the best way to plant a vineyard. Since many if not all of the great Burgundy vineyards are mass selections, the folly of filching a few dozen or even a few hundred cuttings is clear: it can't approach the diversity in the original site.

Meticulous growers used only particular vines for their cuttings. Perhaps these vines were the healthiest or produced the most flavorful grapes. Short-sighted growers might have singled out the most vigorous vines. Either way, by narrowing the clonal selection they were emphasizing their preferred characteristics.

By the late 20th century, scientists had grown expert at isolating clones that produced particular aromas and flavors, that were early ripening or slow to mature or were resistant to disease or produced wine dark in color.

In Dijon, France, a series of pinot noir clones became available with such designations as 113, 114 and 115, which were not only free of grape viruses but also emphasized the aromas and flavors of red fruits like cherry and raspberry, and 667, 777 and 828, which were reminiscent of darker fruits.

Regardless of the attention paid to suitcase clones, these Dijon clones have become the dominant selection among California pinot noir growers, particularly recently, when the number of acres of pinot noir planted in California has almost doubled, to 29,191 in 2007 from 15,514 in 1999.

An over-reliance on these clones has troubled some wine writers, like Matt Kramer of *Wine Spectator* and Allen Meadows of Burghound.com, who have singled them out as one reason that so many California pinot noirs taste the same and lack complexity. Both writers, in fact, used the same word: boring.

It stands to reason. In a vineyard with a wide array of pinot noir clones, some will ripen faster, some slower. Some will taste like red fruits, others like black fruits, and some, maybe, will have fresh herbal touches. Blended together, they would most likely produce a wine of more complexity than a wine made from a small number of clones.

Mr. Meadows, in his latest issue, argues that the Dijon clones in particular taste pretty much the same regardless of where they are grown, which further contributes to uniformity.

Both writers have urged growers to aim for a greater mix of clones, not just the numbered Dijons but also older clones that go by names like Swan, Pommard, Mount Eden and Calera. There are quite a few others, some of which, in fact, originally came to California as suitcase clones.

One of the best-known suitcase couriers is Gary Pisoni, who owns vineyards and a winery in the Santa Lucia Highlands. The story of his 1982 vineyard rifling has been told so often and in so many different ways that it's difficult to separate fact from myth. These days Mr. Pisoni prefers to play down the whole episode, insisting wisely that clones are just a small component of the larger picture, which includes rootstock, soils, trellising and all the rest.

"Don't forget, Burgundy's had hundreds and hundreds of years to find out which clones grow best in which area," he told me by phone. "We're just getting started here in America."

October 2008

Lack of Sex Among Grapes
Tangles a Family Vine

By NICHOLAS WADE

For the last 8,000 years, the wine grape has had very little sex. This unnatural abstinence threatens to sap the grape's genetic health and the future pleasure of millions of enophiles.

The lack of sex has been discovered by Sean Myles, a geneticist at Cornell University. He developed a gene chip that tests for the genetic variation commonly found in grapes. He then scanned the genomes of the thousand or so grape varieties in the Department of Agriculture's extensive collection.

Much to his surprise he found that 75 percent of the varieties were as closely related as parent and child or brother and sister. "Previously people thought there were several different families of grape," Dr. Myles said. "Now we've found that all those families are interconnected and in essence there's just one large family."

Thus merlot is intimately related to cabernet franc, which is a parent of cabernet sauvignon, whose other parent is sauvignon blanc, the daughter of traminer, which is also a progenitor of pinot noir, a parent of chardonnay.

This web of interrelatedness is evidence that the grape has undergone very little breeding since it was first domesticated, Dr. Myles and his co-authors report in the *Proceedings of the National Academy of Sciences*.

The reason is obvious in retrospect. Vines can be propagated by breaking off a shoot and sticking it in the ground, or onto existing rootstock. The method gives uniform crops, and most growers have evidently used it for thousands of years.

The result is that cultivated grapes remain closely related to wild grapes, apart from a few improvements in berry size and sugar content, and a bunch of new colors favored by plant breeders.

Cultivated grapes have almost as much genetic diversity as wild grapes. But because there has been very little sexual reproduction over the last eight millenniums, this diversity has not been shuffled nearly enough. The purpose of sex, though this is perhaps not widely appreciated, is recombination, the creation of novel genomes by taking some components from the father's and some from the mother's DNA. The new combinations of genes provide variation for evolution to work on, and in particular they let slow-growing things like plants and animals keep one step ahead of the microbes that prey on them.

The grapevine fell extinct through much of Europe in the phylloxera epidemic of the 19th century. The French wine industry recovered from this disaster only by grafting French scions, as the grape's shoots are called, onto sturdy American rootstock resistant to the phylloxera aphid.

Despite that close call, grape growers did not rush to breed disease resistance into their vines. One obstacle is that wine drinkers are attached to particular varieties, and if you cross a chardonnay grape with some other variety, it cannot be called chardonnay. In many winegrowing regions there are regulations that let only a specific variety be grown, lest the quality of the region's wine be degraded. More than 90 percent of French vineyards are now planted with clones—genetically identical plants—certified to possess the standard qualities of the variety.

The consequence of this genetic conservatism is that a host of pests have caught up with the grape, obliging growers to protect their vines with a deluge of insecticides, fungicides and other powerful chemicals.

This situation cannot be sustained indefinitely, in Dr. Myles's view. "Someday, regulatory agencies are going to say 'No more,'" he said. "Europeans are gearing up for the day, which will come earlier there than in the U.S., for laws that reduce the amount of spray you can put on grapes."

At that point growers will have three options. One is to add genes for pest resistance, risking consumer resistance to genetically modified crops. A second is to go organic, which may be difficult for a plant as vulnerable as the grape. A third is to breed sturdier varieties.

Breeding new grapes takes time and money. The grower has to plant a thousand seedlings, wait three years for them to mature, and then select the few progeny that have the desired traits. But a new kind of plant breeding now offers hopes of an efficient shortcut.

The new method depends on gene chips, like the one developed by Dr. Myles, that test young plants for the desired combination of traits. The breeder can thus discard 90 percent of seedlings from a cross, without waiting three years while they grow to maturity.

The new method, called marker-assisted breeding, or genomic selection, is already being used in breeding corn. "We can predict flowering within a couple of days by looking at the DNA," said Edward S. Buckler, a leading corn geneticist at the Agriculture Department's research lab at Cornell.

Dr. Buckler said he felt the government's large collections of crop plants could be used much more efficiently by analyzing the genomes of each species. He recruited Dr. Myles to work on the grape genome.

In major crops like corn, rice and wheat, "everyone is shifting to these new technologies," Dr. Buckler said. He expects grape growers to follow the trend. Wine drinkers' insistence on their favorite varieties need not necessarily be a problem, because with enough genetic markers the breeder could identify and maintain the genes responsible for the taste of varieties like chardonnay or merlot. Genomically selected grape varieties may be ready for market in about a decade, said Dr. Buckler, who is a co-author on Dr. Myles's report.

M. Andrew Walker, an expert grape breeder at the University of California, Davis, said that there are "ample pest- and disease-resistance genes" in the grapevine genus, which has about 60 species, but few in *Vitis vinifera*, the particular species to which wine and table grapes belong. He agreed that it will be necessary to introduce many of these genes from other Vitis species into vinifera. "Consumers and wine promoters will have to move beyond dependence on traditional vinifera varieties," Dr. Walker said.

So far Dr. Myles has only 6,000 useful genetic markers on his grape gene chip, and needs a larger chip to identify all the traits of interest to breeders. He started his scientific career working on human genetics at the Max Planck Institute for Evolutionary Anthropology in Leipzig, Germany. On a bicycle tour of German vineyards he decided the grape's genome might hold as many surprises as the human one. The pursuit fit in well with another aspect of his life—his wife is a winemaker in Nova Scotia.

Canada might seem too far north for vineyards to thrive, but the growing season is like that of Champagne in France, Dr. Myles said. "For high-acid grapes that don't fully ripen, which is the Champagne strategy, you can make fantastic sparkling wines in Nova Scotia and lots of good whites."

January 2011

The Earliest Wine:
Vintage 3500 B.C. and Robust

By JOHN NOBLE WILFORD

L ong before Noah supposedly planted his vineyard after the Flood or the first toast was drunk to Dionysus on the shores of Homer's wine-dark sea, the taste of the grape was one of life's pleasures. Indeed, archeologists have now found chemical evidence that people were making and drinking wine at least as long ago as the fourth millennium B.C., the earliest established occurrence of wine anywhere in the world.

And a robust vintage it must have been, to have left a trace at all. The bouquet was long gone, of course. But there inside an earthen jar from Sumerian ruins excavated at Godin Tepe in western Iran were red-colored deposits, a residue that chemists determined was rich in tartaric acid and so almost certainly was the lees of an ancient wine. Tartaric acid is found in nature almost exclusively in grapes.

"We're 95 percent sure," said Dr. Patrick E. McGovern, an archeological chemist who directed the analysis at the University Museum of Archeology and Anthropology at the University of Pennsylvania. The results, determined by a technique known as infrared spectroscopy, are reported in the current issue of a museum publication, *Research Papers in Science and Archeology*.

Anthropologists said the findings carried a further significance, yielding insights into the economy and stability of a society able to indulge in the production of a luxury item like wine. This should help fill out the cultural picture of the fourth millennium B.C. in the Middle East, a time of social innovation with the invention of writing, the introduction of copper metallurgy and irrigated agriculture and the rise of urban centers.

In fact, Dr. Solomon H. Katz, an anthropologist at the University of Pennsylvania and specialist on the early history of beverages, postulates that the dramatic cultural changes of the period encouraged not only production of wine but its consumption. People probably imbibed to relieve the stresses of living in an increasingly complex and urbanized society.

If the chemical analysis is correct, it confirms the existence of wine in the mid-fourth millennium, about 3500 B.C. "We've broken the Bronze Age barrier," Dr. Katz said, suggesting that the origins of winemaking probably extend back several thousand more years.

In *Vintage: The Story of Wine* (Simon & Schuster, 1989), Hugh Johnson, a wine expert, wrote, "We cannot point precisely to the place and time when wine was first made any more than we can give credit to the inventor of the wheel."

Grape pips from the seventh millennium B.C. have been found in the Caucasus, near the Caspian Sea in what is now the Soviet Union, but it is not certain that these were from domesticated plants. The earliest firm evidence for wine had been in Egyptian texts referring to wine at the beginning of the third millennium, the dawn of the Bronze Age. The Sumerian epic of Gilgamesh from the same millennium celebrated the enchanted vineyard whose wine was the source of immortality. Wine must have been common by the time of Hammurabi, the Babylonian king in the 1700s B.C., because his laws are explicit on the subject of when and how people could drink.

The new findings will be evaluated by anthropologists and historians at a symposium on wine's role in the cultural and economic development of earliest human societies. The participants, invited by the University Museum, will get into the spirit of their scholarship by meeting at the Robert Mondavi Winery in Oakville, Calif.

The telltale residues were discovered by Virginia R. Badler, a graduate student in archeology at the University of Toronto. In research on the Uruk period of Mesopotamia, she pieced together shards from pottery excavated at Godin Tepe in the Zagros Mountains of western Iran between the modern towns of Hamadan and Kermanshah. This was the site of a trading outpost or fortress on a trade route that later became known as the Silk Road. The outpost had economic links to the Sumerians who lived to the south in the valley of the Tigris and Euphrates Rivers.

Uruk, on the Euphrates, was one of the earliest urban centers of the Sumerians. They had a thriving agriculture in the river valleys of what is now southern Iraq, but had to look elsewhere for such raw materials as minerals, metals and timber, as well as wine. The Godin Tepe site was presumably one of their outposts in their trading for copper, semi-precious stones and other products in the eastern regions of present-day Iran and in Afghanistan.

Dr. Steven W. Cole, an assistant professor of Assyriology at Harvard University, said: "It's amazing how far flung the Sumerian trade was in the Uruk period of the fourth millenium. They had to reach out to fill their needs."

When Ms. Badler reconstructed one large jar from Godin Tepe, she noticed the red stain on the interior at the base and on one side, evidence that the vessel had contained a liquid and been stored on its side, presumably to keep the seal moist and tight and thus prevent wine from turning to vinegar. Other suggestive evidence included the shape of the jar, with its narrow mouth and tall neck that seemed suited for pouring out liquids, and the presence of earthenware stoppers and funnels.

Similar jars were found in one room that appeared to have been where the wine was made or at least stored. Across a courtyard, opened jars were excavated in what seemed to be the residence of people of some affluence, judging from the luxury items like a stone-bead necklace and a marble bowl fragment found there.

"Almost from the start, wine is a high-end item, a status symbol," Dr. Katz said.

In previous studies, Dr. Katz traced the origin of beer, brewed from barley, to the time soon after the introduction of agriculture in the Middle East about 10,000 years ago. Since grain could be grown more widely and be stored for long periods, beer became more readily available than the seasonal, more perishable grapes. These apparently grew only in northern regions like the Zagros and Caucasus Mountains and had to be traded for and shipped great distances.

Dr. Katz said in an interview that he was developing a hypothesis on the early history of wine. Even before modern agriculture, people could have discovered ripe wild grapes that had fallen to the ground and fermented. The yeast for fermentation comes naturally to grapes, as the waxy white stuff on the skin. People who tasted these grapes got a glow on, and figured out how to get more, first from wild grapes crushed in a bag and then by domesticating the vines for higher production.

With the introduction of agriculture, people became more settled and could produce more than they needed for subsistence. For the first time, Dr. Katz said, people "had enough security and stability and foresight to be willing to invest in the future." He noted that the olive tree is the classic example. "It is said, you grow olive trees for your grandchildren," he observed, "and it's much the same with vineyards."

In their report, Dr. McGovern, Ms. Badler and Dr. Rudolph H. Michel, also of the University Museum, concluded, "Godin Tepe during the Uruk period would appear to fit the model of a society that has evolved to a sufficient level of complexity to engage in horticulture, specifically that of the grapevine."

Dr. Lawrence Stager, an archeologist at Harvard, contends, however, that large-scale winemaking did not begin until the outset of the Bronze Age after 3000 B.C.

A similar chemical test on an amphora from the fourth century A.D., found at a tomb at Gebel Adda in southern Egypt, identifed tartaric acid in a vessel known to have once contained wine. This encouraged the scientists in their interpretation of the sediments from the Godin Tepe vessel.

Archeologists said many questions remained about the early history of wine. Were these local wines? Had viticulture advanced far enough to support an export trade with the urban centers to the south?

"For the time being," Dr. McGovern's group wrote, "the earliest wine ever found must remain a delicious foretaste of future archeological and chemical discoveries to be made."

April 1991

Cave Drops Hints to Earliest Glass of Red

By PAM BELLUCK

Scientists have reported finding the oldest known winemaking operation, about 6,100 years old, complete with a vat for fermenting, a press, storage jars, a clay bowl and a drinking cup made from an animal horn. Grape seeds, dried pressed grapes, stems, shriveled grapevines and residue were also found, and chemical analyses indicate red wine was produced there.

The discovery, published online in *The Journal of Archaeological Science*, occurred in a cave in Armenia where the team of American, Armenian and Irish archeologists recently found the oldest known leather shoe. The shoe, a laced cow-hide moccasin possibly worn by a woman with a size-7 foot, is about 5,500 years old.

These discoveries and other artifacts found in the cave provide a window into the Copper Age, or Late Chalcolithic period, when humans are believed to have invented the wheel and domesticated horses, among other innovations.

Relatively few objects have been found, but the cave, designated Areni-1 and discovered in 1997, is proving a perfect time capsule because prehistoric artifacts have been preserved under layers of sheep dung and a white crust on the cave's karst limestone walls.

"We keep finding more interesting things," said Gregory Areshian, assistant director of the Cotsen Institute of Archaeology at the University of California, Los Angeles, and the co-director of the excavation, which is financed by the National Geographic Society and other institutions. "Because of the conditions of the cave, things are wonderfully preserved."

Experts called the find a watershed.

"I see it as the earliest winemaking facility that's ever been found," said Patrick E. McGovern, an archeological chemist at the University of Pennsylvania Museum, which is not involved in the project. "It shows a fairly large-scale operation, and it fits very well with the evidence that we already have about the tradition of making wine."

Some of that evidence was identified by Dr. McGovern and colleagues, who determined that residue in jars found at a northwestern Iran site called Hajji Firuz suggested that wine was being made as early as 7,400 years ago.

But "that's just a number of wine jars that we identified," said Dr. McGovern, author of "Uncorking the Past."

"Just how elaborate this one is suggests that there was earlier production" of a more sophisticated nature.

Stefan K. Estreicher, a professor at Texas Tech University and author of *Wine: From Neolithic Times to the 21st Century* (Algora Publishing, 2006), said the Armenian discovery shows "how important it was to them" to make wine because "they spent a lot of time and effort to build a facility to use only once a year" when grapes were harvested.

The wine was probably used for ritual purposes, as burial sites were seen nearby in the cave. Dr. Areshian said at least eight bodies had been found so far, including a child, a woman, bones of elderly men and, in ceramic vessels, skulls of three adolescents (one still containing brain tissue).

Wine may have been drunk to honor or appease the dead, and was "maybe also sprinkled on these burials," he said.

The cave, with several chambers, appeared to be used for rituals by high-status people, although some people, possibly caretakers, lived up front, where the shoe was found. Researchers have also found two "dark holes, essentially jars filled with dried fruit, including dried grapes, prunes, walnuts and probably the oldest evidence of cultivating almonds," Dr. Areshian said.

And there is evidence of a 6,000-year-old "metallurgical operation," including smelted copper and a mold to cast copper ingots, he said.

Mitchell S. Rothman, an anthropologist and Chalcolithic expert at Widener University not involved in the expedition, said these discoveries show "the industry and technology developing," and "the very inklings of some kind of social differentiation."

It is "the sort of thing where ritual becomes not only part of the desire to appreciate the gods, but a way in which the people involved in that become somehow special," added Dr. Rothman, who has visited the cave.

The winemaking discovery began when graduate students found grape seeds in the cave's central chamber in 2007, and culminated last fall. A shallow, thick-rimmed, 3-by-3½-foot clay basin appears to be a wine press where people stomped grapes with their feet. The basin is positioned so juice would tip into a two-foot-deep vat.

Scientists verified the age and function with radiocarbon dating, botanical analysis to confirm the grapes were cultivated, and analysis of residue for malvidin, which gives red wine its color.

Dr. Areshian said scientists are undertaking "a very extensive DNA analysis of the grape seeds" from the cave and "our botanists want to plant some of the seeds."

January 2011

In Wine Country, Pruning Isn't Just a Part of the Job

By JESSE McKINLEY

It may be the world's most boggling spectator sport.

Each February and March, hundreds of farm-hands with razor-sharp shears take to the vineyards to battle for the ultimate prize in agricultural athletics: the county pruning championship. Once just a back-breaking, mind-numbing exercise in field management, pruning has become a sort of boutique sporting event across Northern California, complete with regional qualifiers, nail-biting finishes and strutting superstars.

"This is my sport," said Manuel Chavez, 34, a two-time county champion. "I want to be back. I'm ready."

But on Friday, a new top Sonoma County pruner was crowned, after a showdown of 10 finalists that drew 150 spectators to a sun-drenched farm here, about 50 miles north of San Francisco, in just one of several wine-rich California counties to hold the contests. Competitive pruning even has an international flavor, with a bigger contest held in France this weekend, drawing about 350 of Europe's finest vine-shapers.

Fans of the Sonoma competitions, which started eight years ago, say they shine a light on a little-respected but vital part of the horticultural—and economic—process. And, of course, they have also led to more than a little gamesmanship down on the farm.

"Pruning is really the first time you have to affect the quality of vintages," said Dana Grande, the president of the wine growers association in the Alexander Valley in northern Sonoma. "And we dominate at it."

And while pruning lacks the tourist-drawing glamour of the fall harvest, those on the front vines of California's $125 billion wine industry say it is one of the last skill sets that demand a human hand in an age of increasingly mechanized agriculture. Every winter, thousands of workers fan out to fields across California's wine country to prepare the vines for the coming year, usually working from just after Thanksgiving to early March.

"If harvest is the No. 1 job, then pruning is No. 2," said Joe Dutton, a fifth-generation Sonoma County farmer. "The money comes from the harvest, but you have to have that money to pay these guys to prune. It's a big circle."

It is a grueling process, with crews of a dozen or more men working each ranch eight hours a day, methodically going from plant to plant, on acre after acre, cutting back dead or dormant vines to allow new grapes to grow.

In competitive pruning, however, the game is accelerated: each contestant is given five vines to groom and is ranked on both speed and quality, with deductions for things like poor-quality cuts and "mummies," or desiccated grapes left on the vine. A good pruner can trim five vines into shape in about four minutes, or about the time it takes a world-class runner to finish a mile.

But judges at these competitions say the more important quality is precision and cleanliness, which can mean the difference between a vine stocked with healthy bunches of grapes and one rife with bunch rot. In general, each of the vines is expected to carry 11 "spurs"—essentially offshoots of the main vine—which are expected to produce two bunches each. But too many spurs can cause overcrowding on the vine, increasing the possibility of potentially devastating diseases spreading from grape to grape. Too few spurs, meanwhile, means not enough product.

"If you screw it up here, you're going to be paying for it all summer," said Nick Frey, the president of the Sonoma County Winegrape Commission, which has sponsored the competition for the last seven years.

Mr. Frey said the level of interest and number of competitors had been growing ever since the first competition in Sonoma in 1999. "This is the biggest pruning event we have ever had," he said. "The quality and speed of the pruning was exceptional."

Spectators say the events are oddly riveting, especially for anyone with a passing interest in how wine gets made. Like at most big games, the crowd in Sonoma was predominately male and occasionally rowdy, clapping and cheering as the pruners snipped, hacked and yanked a series of rugged chardonnay vines into shape. Unlike most athletic crowds, however, the spectators here could talk you into the ground about plant biology, soil acidity and the relative merits of cane versus spur pruning. (Don't even ask.)

One spectator, Rosa Brown, an office manager at the local Kendall-Jackson winery, said she had tried pruning once and was impressed by the men's skills and endurance. (For now, pruning seems to be a male-only sport.)

"It's amazing what they do," Ms. Brown said. "I went out there for an hour, and I came back and my arms were sore, my back was sore, my shoulder blades were sore. And they do it eight hours a day."

Considering the size of the American and French wine industries—and the long-standing rivalry between the two—it is not completely surprising that there are pruning competitions in both countries. The French held their national event this weekend in Charente-Maritime, on the country's Atlantic Coast.

And while the Americans value speed, the French, of course, have a much different focus, with a written exam, an oral exam and a slow-moving practical exam in the fields.

Stéphane Poggi, the director of marketing for Felco, a Swiss company that specializes in pruning equipment, said he attended championships in California in 2005 and was impressed by the pace of play.

"In terms of quality, however, it's another question," Mr. Poggi said. "French pruners are very good in quality, but they are not fast. I suppose it is a question of whether you are looking for quality or quantity."

A win at the county championships can mean instant fame on the farm. Mr. Chavez, for example, is well known on his ranch because of his win. "Everybody knew him," said Celene Torres, a co-worker who helped cheer him to victory in 2005. "Everybody knew about him winning."

It is also lucrative, with winners receiving prize money and bonuses from their employers. The winner at Friday's competition earned a little more than $2,200, or about a month's wages for an average farmworker.

But winners also speak of the pride of their hard work being recognized. "My whole body was vibrating," Mr. Chavez said about his county win in 2005. "It was very beautiful, and I was very happy." Alas, Mr. Chavez's chances for a third championship ended last month when he was eliminated during a regional qualifier after winning a preliminary round at his ranch.

Like many farmhands, all of the finalists on Friday were Mexican or of Mexican heritage. (The competition's rules were given only in Spanish.) They ranged from the young and brash—23-year-old Gustavo Rico, who wore torn jeans, a scruffy beard and a baseball cap cocked to one side—to Pedro Figuenoa, 61, who started pruning in Sonoma in 1971, before Mr. Rico was even alive.

Neither man, however, could keep up with Samuel Campos, a 34-year-old who finished his vines in four minutes flat and impressed judges with his clean cuts and mummyless vines. His winning score was one of the highest in competition history.

In addition to the prize money and a plaque, Mr. Campos received a bundle of agricultural swag, including gloves, T-shirts and, of course, shears.

"I'm happy," he said, moments after winning, as a mariachi band played in his honor. "I'm going to have fun with it."

March 2007

When Velvety Red Is Only Skin Deep

By ERIC ASIMOV

What color is your red wine? This is not a trick question, like asking about George Washington's white horse. For many wine professionals the color of a red wine is serious business.

Implicit in the varied hues are all sorts of clues about the quality and characteristics of the wine. You can tell, as a red wine arcs from bright and brilliant to dull and faded, whether it is young, aging gracefully or over the hill. You can sense whether it has matured in new or old barrels, and whether it's been filtered to the point of sterility.

Yet when producers today consider the colors of their red wines, they may think of them more as a marketing tool than anything else. Somewhere along the way consumers have come to equate darker red wines with better red wines.

"People are absolutely obsessed with color, and I think it's a mistake," said Neal Rosenthal, who imports wines, largely from France and Italy. "It has been said that the deeper the color, the more concentrated the wine. That's clearly inaccurate."

Anyone can confirm Mr. Rosenthal's point by tasting a traditionally made Burgundy or Barolo, wines of intensity and concentration that are from the paler side of the red spectrum.

To describe the myriad shades of red, you need a 64-crayon box of terms. Different hues can appear in varying degrees of intensity and luminosity, depending, of course, on the quality of the light and the background. Lighter red wines, like Beaujolais Villages or Valpolicella, can be pale ruby, not much darker than the darkest rosé. The darker reds, like young syrahs, petite sirahs and cabernet sauvignons, can be practically blue-black. In between are subtle, incrementally different shadings from copper to crimson.

But winemakers today seem to view deep, dark colors as paramount. Indeed, red wines of all sorts tend to be darker nowadays than they used to be. The brick red of a traditionally made Chianti, for one, is just a pale patch on the darker Chiantis that prevail today. California reds have also gotten noticeably darker than they were, say, 15 or 20 years ago.

"There's no question that winemakers in Italy are making darker reds," said

195

Burton Anderson, who has written about Italian wines for 30 years. "I've seen it everywhere in Italy over the last 15 years or so, from Barolo to Valpolicella to Brunello to Chianti to the deep south."

Mr. Anderson said he believes the darker wines are a byproduct of a trend toward stronger blockbuster styles, which so many critics seem to favor and so many consumers seem to want. To make these wines, many growers favor very low yields from densely planted vineyards. The competition among vines and the low yields produce grapes of great richness and concentration, as well as more intense pigmentation, which contributes to a darker color.

Modern winemakers have other ways to get dark colors: clones that produce more richly colored grapes, equipment that prolongs the juice's exposure to pigment-rich skins and limiting the use of sulfur as a preservative.

So while a darker color may signal a big wine, it doesn't guarantee one. The context is crucial. A pale garnet may signal a problem in a young cabernet, which is traditionally dark, but not in a Burgundy. "Côte de Beaunes tend to be this beautiful light cherry color, which I think is charming, but nowadays people say it's too light," Mr. Rosenthal said.

Like almost every characteristic of wine, color is subject to myth and misinterpretation. Though color may tell more about a wine than the legs that climb the inside of a glass, color offers far less information than a sniff and a taste.

As the winemaker for Turley Wine Cellars in California, Ehren Jordan makes zinfandels of rare intensity and power, yet they tend to be closer to cherry red than ultradark. Under his Failla label, he also makes subtle pinot noirs and syrahs.

"There's no doubt that people are fixated with color," Mr. Jordan said. "People seem to equate darker wines with better wines. For me it always seems odd, and it's maybe because I like Burgundy and I enjoy pinot noir, and pinot is not about color."

For a while, back in the 1980s and early '90s, pinot noir, the grape of red Burgundy, was about color. Many producers back then experimented with an unconventional technique that produced dark wines. They postponed fermentation, leaving grape skins to leach pigment into the juice for an unusually long period, producing a darker wine. But many winemakers turned away from this technique, feeling it dulled nuances in the wine rather than bringing them to life.

In California, the dark color of some pinot noirs has led some critics to question their makeup. Josh Jensen, the Calera Wine Company's winemaker, who makes intense, long-lived pinots, said he believes that some producers achieve dark colors by adding other grapes to their pinot noirs. It's legal in California, where a wine has to contain only 75 percent of a particular grape to be named for it, but for pinot noirs based on the Burgundy model of 100 percent pinot noir, this is close to heresy.

"I know of winemakers who have admitted adding 5 percent syrah," Mr. Jensen said, without naming names. "Of all the things you can do, that's an absolute no-no."

Blending grapes for color's sake is not without precedent. Mr. Jordan has found that in many of the oldest vineyards he uses for Turley, dating back 100 years or more, zinfandel is interplanted with small amounts of alicante bouchet or petite sirah, grapes that produce darker wines than zinfandel.

"Why else except for color?" Mr. Jordan asked, suggesting that this was a concern back when the vineyards were planted. "If somebody farmed it for that long, there must be some logic behind it."

May 2005

A Zin Oasis in Mexico's Dusty Hills

By ERIC ASIMOV

Nothing about the tan, boulder-strewn hills and the occasional cinderblock dwelling, deserted in the noonday sun, remotely suggests that grapes are growing nearby.

The prickly pear cactuses looming alongside a road instead inspire a thirst for Tecate, the namesake beer brewed in this city east of Tijuana in Baja California. But the brewery and the city seem a million miles away.

Crawling slowly up a dirt path in a four-wheel-drive Ford Explorer, with only the occasional ground squirrel and lizard for company, the brown expanse seems more desert than anything else.

Then the long, winding road leads to the top of the hill, and from there, like a mirage in a valley in the middle of nowhere, grape vines burst forth, lots of them, an oasis of green rows against a background of dry brown hills.

The trunks and canes are gnarled and contorted, characteristic of the head-training technique that is found in so many old vineyards. Twisting vines emerge, each bearing one or two tight bunches of grapes that are just ripening, turning from green to purple. These are zinfandel vines, and not just any zinfandel, but vines that are decades old, judging by the girth of the trunks.

How did this precious old zinfandel vineyard, the kind that California wine-makers spend years seeking out, come to be in this valley hidden from view in a place that nobody knows? Winemakers scour the back roads of Sonoma, of Paso Robles, of the Sierra Foothills, of Arroyo Grande, looking for old vineyards, peering into fields overgrown with blackberry vines and decrepit refrigerators, talking to old-timers, poring over county records, but why would anybody think of looking in Mexico, of looking here?

"You think you're just being led on a chase, and then you crown the hill, and, my God," said Ehren Jordan, the winemaker for Turley Wine Cellars, which makes burly, voluptuous much-in-demand zinfandels from old vineyards all over California, and now, from Mexico, too. Next month it will release its 2004 Rancho Escondido zinfandel, made from this vineyard, appropriately named Rancho Escondido, or hidden ranch.

The story of Rancho Escondido parallels the story of Mexican viticulture, which nowadays is thriving in Baja California but which practically didn't exist in 1930, when a farmer named Leonardo Reynoso first planted what would eventually become the 200-acre Rancho Escondido vineyard.

Why there? "Who knows," said Camillo P. Magoni, the chief enologist of L. A. Cetto, a big Mexican winery that purchased the vineyard in 1968. "Because it was cheap? Because he found a remote area for quiet living? Or he had the perception that this hidden valley had special conditions for zinfandel grapes?"

Whatever the reason, the old farmer made a fine choice. "The fact is, Escondido Ranch has a particular soil that I haven't found elsewhere in my 40-plus years in Baja," Mr. Magoni said. "I classified it as eolic, moved by winds through the millenniums, because of its fine texture. Of course, the base is mostly decomposed granite from the surrounding hills, but it is so deep that we found roots at 30 feet. That is the secret."

Indeed, the soil is sandy, with a crusty surface that helps to keep moisture from evaporating upward. The vines are not irrigated, and somewhere below ground is an ample water supply. Tiny sagelike plants grow between the rows, giving off a faint herbal aroma, and down the hill from the grapevines a grove of olive trees looks surprisingly Mediterranean in the Mexican sunshine. But while the sun is bright, the temperature is moderate. A cooling breeze consistently blows inland from the Pacific, bending the vines to the northeast, like coastal cypress contorted by the ocean wind.

In the 1940s and '50s, Tecate was an important grape-growing area, Mr. Magoni said, planted mostly with mission, alicante bouchet, carignan and other, lesser wine grapes. But as the city of Tecate expanded, almost all of those vineyards were torn up. Nowadays, the center of Mexican viticulture is the Guadalupe Valley, about an hour or so to the south. In the Tecate area, Rancho Escondido is one of the few survivors.

It was just by luck that Turley learned of the existence of this vineyard. Following in the tradition of California zinfandel pioneers like Ridge and Ravenswood, Turley seeks out old vineyards to make its zinfandels. Assuming a vineyard is well situated and well managed, most winemakers would agree that the older the vines, the better the potential for the wine. Young vines, under 20 years old, are like teenagers: gawky, unruly and unpredictable. But as the vines age, they seem to mature and become self-regulating. They are better able to deal with weather extremes, and they begin to yield fewer but more intense grapes.

As vines pass 50 years, the yields diminish further and the grapes become even more concentrated. The oldest known zinfandel vineyards, like Old Hill in Sonoma Valley and Grandpère in Amador County, are about 125 years old, which makes the 75-year-old Rancho Escondido middle-aged, perhaps, but old enough to draw Turley's attention.

Credit goes to three alert young Turley workers, Pat Stallcup, Brennen Stover and Karl Wicka, who were attending a zinfandel convention in early 2004 when they were approached by a man who represented several Mexican wineries. He asked them whether they would be interested in seeing some old Mexican zinfandel vineyards. It rang a bell with Mr. Stover, who recalled seeing some photographs of an old Mexican vineyard in a book, *A Zinfandel Odyssey* (Practical Winery & Vineyard, 2002), by Rhoda Stewart. They agreed to take a trip.

"We're always prospecting," Mr. Jordan said. "It never hurts to kick some dirt around."

So, in June 2004, the three took a day trip to Mexico. They first went to Guadalupe Valley, looking at one vineyard after another. All were disappointing. Finally, Mr. Stover said, they drove up to Rancho Escondido. "I thought it was just beautiful," he said.

"It was exactly what you want to see after searching all day and not finding anything." Mr. Stallcup added. "It looked just like what we do."

They immediately called Mr. Jordan and Larry Turley, the owner, who visited as soon as they could. They walked the vineyard, met Mr. Magoni, and Luis Agustín Cetto—Don Luis—the proprietor of L. A. Cetto, which was founded by his father, Angelo Cetto, an Italian immigrant. They had lunch at the Cetto winery in the Guadalupe Valley, maybe the only winery in the world with a bullfighting ring on the premises. They decided they definitely wanted grapes.

"You figure, three generations of people have gone to a lot of trouble to farm this vineyard," Mr. Jordan said. "I mean, it's not exactly convenient. Even just for curiosity's sake, we wanted to make wine from these grapes."

Turley specified that their grapes would come from the oldest section of the vineyard. Cetto, which generally blended the grapes into their light-bodied, inexpensive zinfandel, saw the deal as an opportunity to demonstrate the potential of Mexican wines when made by a top boutique producer like Turley.

"It's a good opportunity for us," said Marco Amador, a Cetto spokesman. "People get a little upset about Mexican wines. They believe in Turley. They don't believe in us, yet."

Turley did not get a lot of grapes, just about three and a half acres' worth, which translates to about three and a half tons, or about 225 cases of wine. That may be all the Rancho Escondido for a while; Turley plans to make the wine each year, but Cetto declined to sell them grapes in 2005, saying the vintage was poor.

It has been almost two years since the 2004 grapes were picked, and now the wine was ready to taste over lunch at La Diferencia, a fine Mexican restaurant in Tijuana. The zinfandel, labeled Rancho Escondido, Baja California, Mexico, is made in the typical Turley style, which means a huge wine, with plenty of alcohol. This one clocked in at a hefty 16.3 percent, yet it differs from the more typical fruit-bomb zin. This one has aromas of anise and sour cherry, but there is a definite herbal element, too, reminiscent of those sagelike plants in the vineyard. The flavors last in the mouth forever.

The wine doesn't really go with the first course, crunchy fried crickets on a blue corn sope, with cotija cheese and spicy salsa verde. The chili pepper clashes with the wine's soft tannins. But it is superb with the last course, tender steak with a light green squash sauce and huitlacoche, the Mexican corn fungus delicacy, which brings out the wine's cherry kirsch flavors.

But something else makes this wine compelling, something that cannot be measured by a score or a rating. Each sip casts the mind back to those brown, boulder-strewn hills and to the farmer who decided to plant right there. It's a wine that makes you wonder, that asks questions rather than answers them.

"You look around the vineyard and you say, who came here and decided it was a great place to grow grapes?" Mr. Jordan said. "I mean, it's not exactly welcoming terrain. I wish I could go back in a time capsule and see why they chose it. You have to wonder whether we lack that instinct today."

August 2006

Illegal Sale of Rice Wine Thrives in Chinese Enclaves

By KIRK SEMPLE and JEFFREY E. SINGER

The restaurant looks like so many others in the roiling heart of Chinatown, in Lower Manhattan: a garish sign in Chinese and English, slapdash photos of featured dishes taped to the windows, and extended Chinese families crowding around tables, digging into communal plates of steamed fish, fried tofu and sautéed watercress.

But ask a waitress the right question and she will disappear into the back, returning with shot glasses and something not on the menu: a suspiciously unmarked plastic container containing a reddish liquid.

It is homemade rice wine—"Chinatown's best," the restaurant owner asserts. It is also illegal.

In the city's Chinese enclaves, there is a booming black market for homemade rice wine, representing one of the more curious outbreaks of bootlegging in the city since Prohibition. The growth reflects a stark change in the longstanding pattern of immigration from China.

In recent years, as immigration from the coastal province of Fujian has surged, the Fujianese population has come to dominate the Chinatowns of Lower Manhattan and Sunset Park, Brooklyn, and has increased rapidly in other Chinese enclaves like the one in Flushing, Queens.

These newcomers have brought with them a robust tradition of making—and hawking—homemade rice wine. In these Fujianese neighborhoods, right under the noses of the authorities, restaurateurs brew rice wine in their kitchens and sell it proudly to customers. Vendors openly sell it on street corners, and quart-size containers of it are stacked in plain view in grocery store refrigerators, alongside other delicacies like jellyfish and duck eggs.

The sale of homemade rice wine—which is typically between 10 and 18 percent alcohol, about the same as wine from grapes—violates a host of local, state and federal laws that govern the commercial production and sale of alcohol, but the authorities have apparently not cracked down on it.

A spokesman for the New York State Liquor Authority said the agency had recently received complaints about illegal Chinese rice wine and was looking into them, though he offered no further details. New York police officials said the department had never investigated the trade.

The Fujianese wine sellers are reminiscent of an earlier group of immigrant entrepreneurs: During Prohibition, Jewish and Italian immigrants were among New York City's most active bootleggers. But several ethnologists and sociologists said that these days there did not seem to be an equivalent illegal brew—made and sold in New York—among any other immigrant population.

The rice wine, which is almost always a shade of red, is the result of a fairly simple fermentation process involving glutinous rice, red yeast rice and water. Its taste varies from producer to producer and, of course, from drinker to drinker. The best versions recall sherry or Japanese sake. The worst, vinegar.

"Don't underestimate this alcohol," cautioned a winemaker in Chinatown, who would give only his surname, Zhu. "You'll get drunk."

In Fujian Province, people make rice wine in their houses, drinking it themselves, serving it to guests or using it in cooking. In New York City, many Fujianese immigrants do the same—a legal practice as long as the product does not enter the stream of commerce.

There are about 317,000 Chinese immigrants in New York City, according to census data, but that figure is widely regarded as an undercount. Zai Liang, a sociology professor at the University at Albany who has studied the tightly knit Fujianese population in New York, estimated that as many as 40 percent of the Chinese who immigrated to New York in the past two decades were from Fujian Province.

The underground trade in rice wine is foreign even to many Chinese from other provinces.

Since rice wine can go bad after excessive exposure to heat, it is widely regarded as a winter beverage, and vendors flourish in Fujianese neighborhoods during the colder months. But even in the depth of summer, a glass of it is never hard to find.

Indeed, many Fujianese are more than happy to talk about rice wine, explaining how it is made, describing its delights and extolling its virtues as an all-around elixir.

"If you drink this, you'll stay young," explained Chen Dandan, a retired garment factory worker from Fujian Province. "It helps you with your circulation."

"If you drink this, you'll live to an old age," said Lin Yong, a long-distance bus driver who lives in Flushing. He said his grandfather, who died several years ago at the age of 99, lived by a simple dictum: It is all right to forgo a meal, but it is not all right to forgo a glass of rice wine.

Many said that even though legal rice wine is commercially available, they prefer homemade brews because they are said to have fewer additives.

But finding consumers is one thing. Tracking down moonshiners is another.

Over the past several weeks, interviews with dozens of Chinese store owners, restaurateurs and street vendors yielded prevarications, obfuscations and otherwise fraught conversations.

Nearly all said they were simply selling a product that others had made. Some spoke mysteriously of unnamed wholesalers who materialized once a week with supplies. Others seemed less concerned about the legality of the product and more concerned about the competition.

"What if you were to learn how to make it and set up shop across the street?" asked one restaurateur in Flushing.

In some places, it appears, anyone can buy bootlegged rice wine, as long as you know what to ask for and hand over money, usually between $3 and $5 a quart. But in other places, a non-Chinese person, even one fluent in Chinese, might not get far.

When the manager was asked for rice wine at a store on Market Street in Manhattan's Chinatown, fear swept over her face, and she said she did not have any. What about those unmarked containers sitting in a soft-drink refrigerator next to the Coca-Cola and Gatorade? "Not for sale!" she blurted.

At a store on Allen Street, a cashier first said she did not stock rice wine and went back to watching a video on a laptop. But when it was pointed out to her that several quarts of rice wine were stacked on the counter next to the cash register, she looked flustered and exclaimed: "It's for cooking, for sautéeing!" Then: "It's only for the Fujianese!"

A vendor below the overpass of the Manhattan Bridge on East Broadway said he did not know who had supplied him with the rice wine stacked on metal shelves on the sidewalk. But several containers were affixed with a small label for a Fujianese food supplier on Catherine Street.

At that address, a Fujianese man wearing an apron came to the unmarked door. Shown the label, he said it was the wrong address. Then he said that it was the right address, but that the business on the label had moved.

Finally, he admitted that the business on the label was his, but he insisted that he did not make rice wine. With that, he said he had to get back to work, and shut the door.

July 2011

Japanese Wineries Betting on a Reviled Grape

By CORIE BROWN

The Japanese have made wine for years; it is just that no one outside Japan wanted to drink it, particularly if it was sweet swill made from a native table grape called koshu.

But Ernest Singer thinks koshu deserves a place among the world's fine white-wine grapes.

Mr. Singer, a wine importer based in Tokyo, said koshu captured his imagination nearly a decade ago when he tasted an experimental dry white wine made from the grape. Light and crisp with subtle citrus flavors, it was a match for Japan's cuisine, he said, and could become the first Asian wine to draw international recognition.

With grapes from local growers and expertise from France, he began making his own wine, seeking to help koshu reach its potential. Now he and a clutch of family-owned Japanese wineries working under the banner Koshu of Japan are racing one another to be the first to produce koshu good enough to succeed in the world market.

"We have shown you can make real wine in Japan," Mr. Singer said. The question remains, he said, whether established vintners will change their wine-making practices or "continue to sell their schlock."

"The good news is that I've encouraged a small number of young winemakers," he said. Even his chief rival, Shigekazu Misawa, the owner of Grace Wine and a leader of Koshu of Japan, said that without Mr. Singer, it was unlikely that anyone would even think of exporting koshu.

"It was Ernie's idea to raise quality to improve the position of koshu in the world market," Mr. Misawa said. "He knew that koshu could become a wine that represents Japan to the world."

Ever since Japan discovered European and California wines during the 1970s economic boom, the country's homegrown wines have been losing ground to imports. In the mid-1990s, a few Japanese winemakers began trying to make better wine with koshu.

Japanese fine-wine drinkers, however, are haunted by what koshu has been for the past 150 years. Found almost exclusively in Yamanashi Prefecture at the base of Mount Fuji, koshu is a tart, gray grape. Growers would dispose of damaged and rotten fruit by making wine with heavy doses of sugar.

Yet, while Japan's climate, with rainstorms common throughout the summer and fall, conspires against most wine grapes, koshu is well suited to a wet world. It resists the rot that plagues vinifera grapes in Japan. Late ripening, it retains its natural acidity.

Mr. Misawa was one of the first Japanese vintners to reject the idea of sugary koshu.

"I am the fourth-generation owner of Grace Wine," Mr. Misawa says. "Koshu is two-thirds of all of the wine we make. And we needed to make it better."

Yet, while he and other vintners traveled to Europe and Australia to learn modern winemaking methods, progress was slow. Viticulture methods from dry regions did not translate. And no one outside Japan had ever heard of koshu, a hybrid of *Vitis vinifera*—the species responsible for the world's most popular wines—and an unidentifiable wild variety, according to DNA research at the University of California, Davis.

"I learned to make wine here," said Mr. Koki Oyamada, the winemaker at Château Lumière, affiliated with Koshu of Japan. A new generation is pioneering new methods, he said. "We support each other, discuss problems, find solutions. We are improving quality." After his first taste of dry koshu, Mr. Singer gambled big on it, flying in Denis Dubourdieu, professor of enology at the University of Bordeaux, to work on his first four vintages (2004 to 2007), which were made at Mr. Misawa's winery with grapes he helped provide. To secure a steady supply of high-quality fruit, Mr. Singer leased land in three central Japan prefectures and now has nine koshu vineyards, a huge land-holding for a nonfarmer in Japan.

Mr. Singer's confidence in koshu is due in no small part to the wine critic Robert M. Parker Jr. The two men have worked together since 1998 when Mr. Parker hired Mr. Singer to be his representative in Asia. Mr. Parker tasted Mr. Singer's 2004 koshu at the Grace winery in December 2004 and gave it a score of 87/88 on a scale of 100 in what Mr. Parker refers to as "an educational tasting."

That first vintage was produced with grapes grown on old-fashioned pergola trellises. The canopies of these vines can stretch 50 feet in all directions from a mother vine the size of a tree. Mr. Singer says that his new vineyards, which are planted with vines planted closely together in neat rows with new shoots trained up, a system common in Europe and America, are producing smaller grapes with more-concentrated flavors that will make even better wine.

In setting up the winemaking protocol for Mr. Singer's koshu, Mr. Dubourdieu eliminated what was once the only thing that made koshu drinkable: sugar. The wine is bone dry with a very low alcohol content. He accomplished this by getting rid of the grape's bitter skin early in the process.

"I tried to extract nothing from the skin," he said. "The bitterness of the koshu skin is extreme."

The wine is bottled in the spring to be sold fresh and young.

With such a simple wine, Mr. Dubourdieu said he was surprised that it pleased Mr. Parker, who is usually seen as a fan of full-bodied wines.

"I was afraid," he said. "I was not sure he could like a wine with 10.5 percent alcohol. That's not exactly the wine he ranks well. But he was enthusiastic."

Still, Mr. Dubourdieu is skeptical that koshu will prove to be a valuable wine.

"It is simple, clean, fresh, nice," he said. "That, and no more. It is a big mistake to think you can produce Montrachet in Japan. Koshu is more of a vinho verde."

The Bordeaux producer Bernard Magrez is distributing a small amount of the Katsunuma Jyozo winery's koshu in Europe and the United States. But the executive director of the winery, Youki Hirayama, said that beyond that, his company is focusing on Asian markets.

"This is Asian wine for Asian food," he said, noting that the subtle flavors do not overwhelm delicate dishes.

Mr. Parker remains upbeat about koshu. "Up until this year, it was the best one I've tasted," he wrote in an e-mail response to questions about Mr. Singer's wine. "Now Bernard Magrez has one that is dry, crisp and very tasty, and much in the style of the Dubourdieu koshu. I think the wine, if made in these styles, has a quasi-Muscadet character—light-bodied and very refreshing."

But there are wide variations in the new koshus, with some vintners experimenting with oak-barrel aging and each winery relying on a different level of chaptalization—adding sugar before fermentation—to increase alcohol levels along with adding weight and body to the wine. It is impossible, however, to be certain what Japanese wineries add to their wines. The country's wine labeling regulations require that only 5 percent of the wine in a bottle be from Japanese grapes. The rest can be from anywhere.

Mr. Singer, Katsunuma Jyozo and the wineries of Koshu of Japan insist that their wines are 100 percent koshu.

But jaded Japanese wine drinkers have been slow to believe that they are worth their price tags of $20 and up.

After their first shipment to Europe this summer, the Japanese vintners involved in Koshu of Japan are hoping to gain international appreciation that would give koshu cachet in Asia.

On a recent trip to Japan, Michael Cimarusti, the chef and owner of Providence in Los Angeles, tasted a koshu produced by Katsunuma Jyozo and was so impressed that he added it to the wine pairings on his tasting menu.

But in New York, Mr. Singer's importer, Robert Harmelin, said koshu had been a hard sell at $50 a bottle on restaurant wine lists. "No one knows the wine," he said.

Mr. Singer asks for more time. "I've been in Japan for 50 years," he said, "this movement is going to blossom."

October 2010

Wines Have Feelings, Too

By ERIC ASIMOV

Almost from the moment humans began putting goblets to lips, they have challenged themselves to describe the experience of consuming wine. It has not been easy.

What does a wine smell like, anyway, and how does it taste? Does it remind you of fruit or flowers, or mushrooms and brambles? Possibly those metaphors are too literal. Maybe the overall effect is of a symphony, or a string quartet, or a Jimi Hendrix solo, or crumpled sheets the morning after. You could, of course, just say, "It smells like grapes and tastes like wine," but you'd be laughed out of the tasting club. And to differentiate among wines, even if just for yourself, you at least have to make the effort.

Trouble is, most efforts focus solely on aromas and flavors, which seems to make sense because they are a wine's most immediately striking characteristics. But another important distinguishing feature is not detectable by eyes, nose or taste buds. That is texture, the tactile sense of wine on the mouth, tongue and throat. If it's difficult to find words for the aromas and flavors of wine, how much tougher it is to describe the feel.

Think about it too much, and you might find it embarrassing to describe a liquid as crisp, or steely. But that's really no sillier than calling wines harsh or smooth; most wine drinkers know those sensations, whether the components that produce them are apparent or not.

The idea of texture in a liquid is so difficult, in fact, that wine experts cannot even agree on what to call it. You won't find the word "texture" listed in the encyclopedic *Oxford Companion to Wine*, for example. Instead, you must settle for the unwieldy term "mouthfeel" and its constituents: body, density, weight and, for the truly geeky, viscosity. Joshua Wesson, chairman of Best Cellars, a chain of eight wine shops, uses the term "umami," a Japanese word for the elusive, indescribably delicious quality that goes beyond salty, sweet, sour and bitter.

Whatever you call it, great texture is a crucial though undervalued characteristic of the best wines. It's a crackling vivacity that insinuates itself in your mouth, almost demanding that you take another sip simply because it feels so good.

"It's the same seduction that one first feels when touching cashmere or fur,"

Mr. Wesson said. "Nobody touches fur once, or cashmere once. With wine, you want to keep it in your mouth, you want to play with it, you want to roll it around until you get it."

Almost all the most memorable wines I've tasted in the last year or so have had beautiful textures in common, wines as diverse as a '92 Puligny-Montrachet Les Pucelles from Domaine Leflaive and a '94 Hillside Select cabernet sauvignon from Shafer in the Napa Valley.

These are world-class bottles, with three-figure prices, but a wine doesn't have to be expensive to feel great in the mouth. I can think of a luscious '02 Austrian riesling from Hirsch in the Kamptal for $28, a minerally '02 Sancerre from Etienne Riffault for $20, and a smoky '98 Tuscan sangiovese from Montevertine for $27. All had a mouthwatering quality that, whatever the price, both refreshed and entranced.

It's a rare winemaker who, unbidden, actually speaks about texture, but recently Richard Geoffroy, the cellar master for Dom Pérignon Champagne, told me that for him the quest for the proper texture was the supreme goal in his winemaking.

"That feel, that chew, that third dimension: that's really what I'm working on," Mr. Geoffroy said, grasping for words in English, his second language, and coming up with some evocative ones.

For Mr. Geoffroy texture is sort of a conveyor belt that carries the aromatic and flavor components through the mouth from sip to swallow and beyond. Champagne's effervescence offers a different textural experience from that of most wines, of course. Some people, trying to explain why Champagne goes so well with fried or spicy foods, talk about the bubbles' "scrubbing" the mouth. I don't know about that, but I do know you can feel the difference between a lively, vibrant Champagne and one that fatigues the mouth. It's texture.

"I'm always amused that people are so interested in aromatics," Mr. Geoffroy said.

Obtaining a deeper understanding of texture is not easy. Wine books devote scant attention to it, and a research foray can easily lead to terms like "polysaccharides" and "anthocyanins," from which there is little hope of escape. In an effort to codify the textural experience of red wine, the Australian Wine Research Institute developed something it calls the mouthfeel wheel, with a vocabulary including words like "parching," "grippy," "watery" and "sappy." Frankly, consulting the mouthfeel wheel is about as appealing as contemplating a mouthful of polysaccharides.

A simpler way of thinking of texture is to keep in mind its integral components, which most often are acidity and, especially in red wines, tannins. Most wine drinkers are familiar with tannins. They are the astringent compounds that in a young, tannic red wine—a Barolo, say, or a Bordeaux—can seem to suck all the moisture out of your mouth. Ideally, the tannins soften over time, allowing other characteristics to emerge. Tannins come from the grapes' skins, seeds and stems, and, if the wines are aged in new oak barrels, they can come from the wood, too.

Acidity is the juicy, zingy quality. Too much acidity, and a wine can feel harsh and aggressive. Too little, and it feels flabby and shapeless. During the making of a wine, the acidity can evolve from the crispness of malic acids in the direction of softer lactic acids. Interestingly, lactic acids often provide a creamy texture to a wine. Aging a wine without removing its yeast remnants can also add silkiness.

While descriptions of texture will never replace those of aromas and flavors in the tasting notes so dear to the hearts of consumers, the feel of a wine is worthy of more attention. Yet most people bypass texture and go directly from smelling to tasting, even well-meaning wine lovers who violently agitate the wine in their mouths before swallowing.

"When people chew wine, you don't really get a sense of its texture because you're putting it through the wash-rinse cycle of the mouth," Mr. Wesson said. "On first sip, I just let it sit there. Then I push it around with my tongue. When you push it around slowly, you get a much better sense of texture."

Then, maybe, you can figure out what to call it.

June 2005

Too Broad a Stroke for Labeling Wines

By ERIC ASIMOV

A merican winemakers have learned an awful lot in the last 25 years. For example, many of them used to believe that given rich soils and plenty of sun, they could grow whatever kind of grapes they wanted, wherever they wanted, and turn them into wine. As a result, in Napa Valley, pinot noir was planted next to cabernet sauvignon next to zinfandel next to chenin blanc, and an awful lot of pretty bad wine was produced.

Now, most winemakers understand that each grape has its particular characteristics and does well only under certain conditions. Delicate pinot noir may do well in a foggy coastal vineyard, with warm days and cool nights, where cabernet sauvignon may not ripen. But cabernet might flourish in a warm valley vineyard that would bake pinot into jam. Only a fool, or a cynic, would nowadays plant cabernet next to pinot noir in the same vineyard. The same is true for turning the grapes into wine. The techniques are as different as playing the guitar and playing the violin.

Given the clear distinctions in growing conditions and winemaking techniques required for various grapes, you would think the governmental labeling rules would differ for each varietal. Yet, as it turns out, one set of rules governs almost every type of grape and wine, sometimes to the detriment of the wines themselves.

Consider the rules for calling wines by the names of grapes. In the United States since 1983, any wine named for a grape, whether merlot, chardonnay, zinfandel, or any other, has to be made from at least 75 percent of those grapes. The well-meaning intent of that federal law was to give consumers truth in advertising. Before 1983, wines needed to be only 51 percent chardonnay to be called chardonnay, even if the remainder was made from cheap French colombard or some other lower-quality grape.

While the solution may have given consumers more truth, it did not necessarily give them better wine, and today the rule is simply anachronistic. It affects different wines in different ways.

Take pinot noir. In Burgundy, where pinot noir is the historic red grape, the law requires almost all red Burgundies to be made of 100 percent pinot noir. Though unscrupulous producers have always tried to stretch production by tossing in some cheap red from Algeria or Campania, most Burgundy lovers, who assume a pinot noir wine is 100 percent pinot noir, regard such adulteration as sacrilege.

In California, it's a different story. Demand for pinot noir has increased significantly since the movie *Sideways*. With wine you cannot increase production on the fly. You plant vines, tend and nurture them, and maybe in five years you've got wine—not a timetable for capitalizing on quick consumer shifts. But can anyone doubt that producers, especially on the low end, are using other grapes—strictly legally—to meet the increased demand by blending some of those pinot noirs down to the 75 percent limit?

Blending may be taking place on the high end as well, for different reasons. Americans have come to equate darker red wines with better red wines, and pinot noir falls on the pale side of the spectrum. Josh Jensen of the Calera Wine Company and other winemakers have said they believe some pinot noir producers are adding syrah to darken their pinot noirs. Again, it's strictly legal, but in the world of pinot noir it's not ethical.

By contrast, grapes from the Bordeaux family, like cabernet sauvignon, merlot and cabernet franc, are traditionally blended, and they are affected by the 75 percent rule in a different way. In Bordeaux, producers adjust the blend of grapes each year, depending on the characteristics of the vintage. Most wines, it is fair to say, would never meet California's 75 percent threshold, but who cares? Consumers select Bordeaux wines not by the grape, but by the label. They buy a Clerc-Milon, for example, not a cabernet sauvignon, and the winemaker for Clerc-Milon can use whichever blend makes for the best wine.

In California, though, winemakers don't have that luxury, not if they want to be able to benefit from the powerful marketing advantage that comes with having a grape name on the label. California merlot in particular has suffered because of this rule. Even in Pomerol and Saint-Émilion, where merlot is the dominant grape, it rarely surpasses 75 percent of the composition. But a California winemaker may be forced to accept a weedy wine simply to call it merlot when it would have benefited from a higher percentage of cabernet sauvignon or cabernet franc.

California has created a category, Meritage, for Bordeaux-style wines that don't meet the varietal threshold, but the mere existence of this category does little to discourage winemakers from trying to achieve the limit.

Common sense dictates that the rules ought to be different for each grape. The rules should require that pinot noir and chardonnay be made of 100 percent pinot noir and chardonnay, or the wine should be called something else. Oregon has raised the threshold for all grapes to 90 percent, except for cabernet, which stays at 75 percent. But that seems too inflexible. For non-Burgundian varietals, every grape that makes up 5 percent or more of the blend ought to be listed in descending order of percentage. Rather than forcing a wine to meet the 75 percent threshold to be called merlot, it would be called merlot-cabernet sauvignon-petit verdot, or whatever the blend dictates.

Admittedly, this would take some getting used to. Perhaps, by the law of unintended consequences, winemakers would put together a 95 percent blend to maintain the single-varietal name, but I doubt it. Australia has a rule like this and consumers don't find its blends too complicated to understand. They might even learn something interesting, that some syrah producers blend their wines with viognier, a white grape, as they do in Côte-Rôtie. The point is to put the winemaker, not the law, in charge of the blend.

Many wineries would oppose such changes, thinking they would lose out on successful marketing tools. But they don't mind stretching the idea of truth in advertising anyway.

The Wine Institute, a trade group, wants the federal government to relax from 95 percent to 85 percent the proportion of wine that must come from a particular vintage in order to place a vintage date on labels.

The change would affect wines from general appellations like California or Napa County, but not those from more prestigious American Viticultural Areas, like Russian River Valley and Napa Valley. The wine institute says American rules, which also govern imported wines, cannot be enforced overseas, so foreign producers can stretch good vintages with wine from bad years.

Apparently, beating them to the punch is the institute's solution.

August 2005

The Rites of Vintage Assembly

By FRANK J. PRIAL

O n a chill, rainy day in early spring, seven men gathered in the refectory of Château Prieuré-Lichine, in the tiny village of Cantenac, 20 miles north of Bordeaux. They had come here at the invitation of the owner, Alexis Lichine, to help him make a wine.

Awaiting them on a huge oak table in what used to be the monks' dining room were some 200 glasses and 22 bottles of wine, samples from all the vineyards that are part of Prieuré-Lichine. Their task: to help Mr. Lichine fix the blend that would become his 1982 vintage.

The cycle of the vine—and the wine—begins with the budding in the spring, follows through the flowering of the vines in early summer, and goes on to the harvest and the grape crush in the fall. Each step is important, but none more than the assembly of the wine—the assemblage—some six months after the wine is made. It is the day when professional wine men bring all their skills to bear, the day they create a vintage.

The members of the group that morning were Émile Peynaud, director emeritus of the Enological Laboratory at the University of Bordeaux and probably the world's most prominent enologist; Jacques Boissenot, a professional enologist and a specialist in the wines of the Médoc region; Patrick Leon, president of the Enologists of Southwest France, and, in his youth, a student and employee of Mr. Lichine; Jean Delmas, the director of Château Haut-Brion; Hugues Lawton, a Bordeaux wine merchant; Sacha Lichine, a Boston wine importer and Mr. Lichine's son; Edmond Caubraque, the business manager of Prieuré-Lichine, and Mr. Lichine himself.

I had thought that a chateau's vines were all treated the same. I knew there were different kinds of grapes—cabernet sauvignon, cabernet franc, merlot, malbec, petit verdot—but I thought that each property's blend varied little from year to year. And I thought everything was mixed together at harvest time. Well, that's not the way it works.

Prieuré-Lichine was once actually the priory of the Benedictine church in Cantenac. When Alexis Lichine bought it in 1951, it had been a wine property for several hundred years and was known as Château Cantenac-Prieuré. It was a rundown, ragtag, has-been vineyard that had not been properly tended for half a century. This is not uncommon in the Médoc, where owners die and heirs are indifferent. Absentee ownership, inept management, incompetent advice— all contribute to the deterioration and sometimes the destruction of once-proud wine properties. Some Bordeaux vineyards, famous a century ago, exist today in name only, in old books.

Many Bordeaux properties were decimated by legacies. Heirs divided and sold their parcels until some vineyards were crazy quilts of divided ownership. When Mr. Lichine arrived at the Prieuré, he found himself the owner of a jumble of vineyard patches and strips: a few vines here, a few vines there, a small good vineyard here, a big poor one there. He has spent the ensuing three decades wheeling, dealing, begging, borrowing, threatening and cajoling in an unceasing effort to create the kind of vineyard he thinks the Prieuré should be.

His experience is not unique. Some years ago, Baron Philippe de Rothschild talked about the rebuilding of Château Clerc-Milon, a property he owns adjacent to his famous Château Mouton-Rothschild in Pauillac, 20 miles north of Cantenac.

Over the years, Clerc-Milon also had fallen into disrepair. A key portion of the vineyard—in the very center of the best vines—was owned by an elderly woman who had no interest in wine but no desire to sell her vines, either. "Every year, I would invite her to tea at Mouton," Baron Philippe said, "and every year I would ask her to sell. Every year she turned me down." Eventually, she relented, but it took decades of the legendary charm and financial clout of a Rothschild to overcome the inherent French reluctance to part with land. Mr. Lichine's resources are more meager than Baron Philippe's. "I've picked up some good vines here," he says, "traded a few of them for a less valuable piece of land there, then in turn sold that for a couple of very good vines somewhere else."

The key is this: The town of Cantenac is adjacent to the town of Margaux, one of the most famous of all the French wine communes. Cantenac actually shares the right to use the name, or appellation, Margaux on its wine. So do several other small villages. So long as Mr. Lichine buys within the confines of the wine area of Margaux, his vines are legitimately part of the vineyard of Prieuré-Lichine.

June 1983

CHAPTER SEVEN

Made in the U.S. of A.

Pickers to Vintners:
A Mexican-American Saga

By ERIC ASIMOV

When Amelia Morán Ceja and her brother-in-law Armando Ceja look out at the vineyards around her house, they can also see the past, when their fathers traveled from Mexico to harvest fruit in stifling heat for meager wages. Ms. Ceja can still feel the grape juice on her hands, made raw from helping her father tend the vines in fields just like these.

But now the Ceja family owns its own vineyards and produces critically praised wines, a global emblem of the good life.

Over the past few years the first fine wines made by former migrant workers, the children of those workers and other Mexican-Americans have been released, winning good reviews. All told, there are more than a dozen such labels. Fifteen years ago there were none. Mexican-Americans have also become managers or winemakers for important vineyards.

The California wine industry was built on the backbreaking labor of a largely Mexican seasonal work force. But the rise of the fine-wine business created a growing demand for year-round workers with special skills in Napa and other regions. Many former migrant workers settled down in wine country. They sent their children to school and taught them how to tend the vines. Some saved money and bought land, and soon began growing their own grapes.

Ceja Vineyards' first wines came out in 2001. The year before, the Robledo Family Winery, owned by Reynaldo Robledo Sr., a former migrant worker, offered its first bottles for sale. Also in 2000 Salvador Renteria, who came to the Napa Valley as a field worker in 1962, and his son, Oscar, offered their first bottle of Renteria Wines cabernet sauvignon. Alex Sotelo, who arrived in the Napa Valley as a field worker in 1991 and is now the winemaker at the Robert Pecota Winery, will begin selling his own wines this fall under the label Alex Sotelo Cellars.

Their tales are new versions of a familiar story, in which the children of immigrants, by working hard and celebrating the virtues of family, achieve the American dream of ownership. These immigrants, though, came with even less than, say, the Gallos or the Mondavis. And unlike those families, they did not come from a land with a great tradition of winemaking. Like the dishwashers in

218

a fancy restaurant, the Mexican field workers have long been invisible players in the history of the wine industry, hired to do the work that Americans would not or could not do themselves.

Today the wine industry uses far fewer seasonal workers than it did 25 years ago, said Karen Ross, president of the California Association of Winegrape Growers in Sacramento. Still, an overwhelming proportion of the field workers in the wine industry—98 percent by Mr. Sotelo's estimate—are Mexican.

It was not always that way. Until World War II the field workers were Americans, an image immortalized by John Steinbeck. But when the draft caused a shortage of agricultural workers, the Mexican and American governments collaborated on the bracero program, which brought Mexicans to the United States for field work.

Ms. Ceja's father, Felipe Morán, first came to the United States in 1947. Pablo Ceja, the father of her husband, Pedro Ceja, and her brother-in-law Armando, worked in the bracero program for many years. Mr. Robledo came to the Napa Valley in 1968 as a migrant worker, living in a transient labor camp set up at the Christian Brothers Winery. Typically the migrants would work their way up the West Coast, following the harvest of grapes, pears, plums, cherries and apples before returning to their families in Mexico.

Some liked California so much that they decided to stay. It helped if they had particular skills that were useful year-round. Mr. Morán was a mechanic, and Mr. Robledo became a specialist in grafting, a valued skill in the wine industry because vines are almost never grown on their own rootstock.

"I didn't speak a word of English when I arrived here," said Ms. Ceja, who was 12 when Mr. Morán relocated his family to the Napa Valley in 1967. "Neither did Armando or Pedro, but that wasn't an obstacle."

As a boy, Armando Ceja hung out with his brothers among the vines while his father worked.

"Growing up in the vineyards, you understand it from the ground up," he said. "It's second nature: plant, prune, grow, succor, harvest. When the fruit goes away, it leaves kind of a void." He is now the winemaker for the Ceja Vineyards.

As with many immigrant families, the Cejas, the Moráns and the Robledos had ambitions for their children and encouraged them to get an education. Amelia Ceja studied history and literature at the University of California, San Diego. Armando Ceja studied winemaking at the University of California, Davis, which has perhaps the nation's leading program. Mr. Robledo so much wanted his nine children to work in the wine industry that he decided to start his own business so that each would have a place.

He worked long hours on his own time, he said, to learn every aspect of the wine business: matching budding vine to rootstock, making thousands of grafts that will thrive, pruning so the vines get just the right amount of sun, determining the proper number of grape bunches per vine, and any number of other small but important skills.

In the 1970s he bought a house, which he sold in 1984 to pay for his first vineyard. The Robledos now own 200 acres, 160 of which are planted with vines.

"All seven of my brothers are involved in the farming," said Vanessa Robledo, a daughter, who is the president of the Robledo Family Winery. The ninth child, Lorena, has contributed in another way. Her husband, Rolando Herrera—himself the son of migrant workers—is the Robledo winemaker. Mr. Herrera, too, makes his own wine, which he bottles under the label Mi Sueño, which means "my dream."

In 1983 the Cejas—Amelia, Pedro and Armando—bought 15 acres in the Carneros, the gently rolling hills southwest of the city of Napa, with Pablo Ceja and his wife. They now own 113 acres of vineyard, including the 20 acres that surround the house Amelia and Pedro Ceja share with their three children. Through the 1990s Armando Ceja managed the vineyards, while Amelia worked in marketing and sales at the Rutherford Hill Winery. In 1998, when the Cejas decided they were ready to strike out on their own as winemakers, Ms. Ceja quit her job to devote herself to Ceja Vineyards.

"To give up everything and to start a wine production company is very scary," she said.

Making wine requires money for barrels and bottles, for labor and for a place to do the work. And starting up is tricky, especially for fine wines, because the product must be stored for a few years or more before it can be sold and start to offer a return on the investment.

"We're able to do it because our vineyards subsidize our wine production," Ms. Ceja said. Of their 113 acres, the Cejas keep only 10 to 15 percent of the grapes for their own use, selling the rest to other wineries. They produce about 4,500 cases a year. The Robledos produce about 5,200 cases of sauvignon blanc, chardonnay, pinot noir, cabernet sauvignon and syrah. They also run a well-regarded vineyard management company, as do the Renterias.

The Ceja wines include a creamy-textured, minerally chardonnay; an elegant and compact pinot noir; a very good cabernet sauvignon; and two exceptional blends, one red and one white, that they call Vino de Casa. The single varietals sell for $28 to $38 a bottle, the blends for $18.

"We're all making top-of-the-line wines, which I think is very interesting," Mr. Sotelo said. "I think because people looked at us as farmers for many years, and we're proud of it, but we wanted to prove that we're able to do much more than that."

Mr. Sotelo was 18 when he arrived in the United States in 1991. He got a job in the fields through an uncle who had been in the Napa Valley for 23 years. He fell in love with the place, he said, and then learned to speak English and got a job working in the cellar at the Robert Pecota Winery. With the encouragement of Mr. Pecota, he took classes at Napa Valley College in viticulture and learned the laboratory skills necessary for modern winemaking. He graduated in 2000. He says the formal education was crucial in gaining the confidence to become a successful winemaker, a position that, like executive chef at a restaurant, now requires some public image building.

"We've been making the wine for many years, although people don't notice this," he said, "but we have to learn to feel comfortable to step out and take charge."

Mr. Sotelo says the success of Mexican-American winemakers has encouraged him to pursue his dreams. In an effort to help others pursue their dreams, 15 Mexican-American winemakers and brand owners are to gather at the Robledo winery on Sunday to discuss forming an association that would coordinate marketing and help finance education programs.

"We're just getting started," he said. "The sons and daughters of the Robledos, they're going to get into the industry. They're going to get formal educations, going to Davis and Fresno State.

"I think we're limited to a certain point," he said of his generation, "but they're not going to have limitations."

Just as important as moving into winemaking, Vanessa Robledo says, is elevating the status of those who remain in the field.

"One of my main goals is to promote what the farmers do," she said, "because it's their labor that helps to produces these fine wines. A lot of times it's called unskilled labor, but it's very highly skilled labor, and that's why I'm proud to say that my father was a migrant worker."

October 2004

Gratification, but Not the Instant Kind

By ERIC ASIMOV

The California wine industry sometimes seems to exist in two parallel universes. In one, the air is heavy with a smug sense of self-congratulation. Billionaires buy pieces of Napa Valley, charge $150 a bottle for the first vintage and want you to understand, by the way, that they do it all for charity.

Earnest ideologues natter on about the terroir in their 16 cuvées of pinot noir, but the wines all taste the same. Hot young consultants notch more 95-point wines than Paris Hilton has boyfriends. It's the gospel written by publicists.

The other universe is a more modest one, where a respect for the past tempers the can-do certainty. It's a world where you realize that for all the accumulated knowledge of viticulture, winemaking and marketing, some forces are simply beyond control; where after 50 harvests or more it begins to dawn on you that, paradoxically, the less you think you know the more you begin to understand.

It's this sense of accumulated wisdom that characterizes many of California's visionary wineries like Ridge Vineyards and Mount Eden Vineyards in the Santa Cruz Mountains, the Calera Wine Company on Mount Harlan, Stony Hill Vineyard in the Napa Valley and Hanzell Vineyards here, on a winding dirt road that gently rises into the hills overlooking the city of Sonoma.

Though respected, Hanzell is rarely mentioned these days when people speak of California's greatest wines. Yet year after year, Hanzell's chardonnays have stood with California's best.

And while California wines are frequently condemned as fruit bombs that have little sense of place and will not age, Hanzell, approaching its 50th vintage, has produced wines of subtlety and power that age beautifully and, above all, speak clearly of the vineyards that crown this hill on the southern end of the Mayacamas ridge.

On a bright, cool August morning, I sat down at the winery to taste 10 older vintages of chardonnay and 8 of pinot noir with Bob Sessions, who was Hanzell's winemaker for 30 years, before he retired in 2002; Jean Arnold Sessions, the president; Michael Terrien, the general manager and current winemaker; and Alexander de Brye, the owner.

What makes these wines so distinctive? "Ageability is what we feel is the hallmark," Ms. Arnold Sessions said. "You just can't have a wine that is ready to drink now but will age for 20 years." Mr. Terrien added, "Burgundy is about potential, while most California wines are about delivering the potential right away." Indeed, young Hanzell chardonnays are clenched and coiled, but with, say, a decade, they start to open up.

A 1995, though still tightly wound, was beginning to exhibit a rich, tangy texture, while a 1991 was in its prime, full of citrus, apple, herbal and mineral aromas and flavors. A 1990 was rich and deep, more open than a 1986, which, though it showed floral and nutlike aromas, might have benefited from decanting.

A 1973, Mr. Sessions's first vintage at Hanzell, was vibrant with anise, apple and pineapple aromas, while a 1965 had aromas of wet earth, mushrooms and hazelnuts and continued to improve in the glass for a full two hours.

Each wine had a lively energy and freshness that kept me going back to the glass for more, and showed distinct mineral aromas and flavors, qualities often hard to detect in California wines.

"Minerality is often a characteristic of wines made with restraint," Mr. Terrien said. "I think a lot of minerality is covered up in wines by oak and other things."

While Hanzell is known more for its chardonnays than its pinot noirs, the pinots, too, are compelling for their unusual tannic power and the intense flavors that eventually evolve. Both a 1998 and a 1993 seemed too young, with piercing fruit aromas that were kicking like newborn foals.

But a 1981 had beautiful raspberry, strawberry, licorice and mineral aromas that were intense yet light, while a pale ruby 1974 was complex and harmonious. These pinot noirs demand patience to say the least.

Through his 30 years as winemaker, Mr. Sessions was determined to maintain Hanzell's stylistic legacy though the winemaking world around him was changing. Now Mr. Terrien has taken on the challenge, even as Hanzell's own world has changed.

In 2003 Hanzell's 2000 chardonnay and 1999 pinot noir were found to be tainted with 2,4,6-trichloroanisole, the compound that causes musty aromas and flavors in corked wines. The taint was traced to its old cellar, and the wines were taken off the market. The winery was then in the process of building a new facility and moved its operations to the new cellar later that year.

But while the equipment has changed the Hanzell winemaking has remained steadfast. Years back, Hanzell was one of the bigger California wines, with alcohol levels hovering above 14 percent. It's still in the range of 14 to 15 percent, even as many top California wines now surpass it.

Walking through the 42 acres of vineyards, where the gorgeous panorama can stretch all the way to the Golden Gate on a clear day, it's easy to see why James D. Zellerbach, an industrialist and later an American ambassador to Italy, chose this site back in 1953 to plant six acres of pinot noir and chardonnay.

Mr. Zellerbach was not without ambition. California then had less than 100 acres of chardonnay and even less of pinot noir. But he envisioned his winery, which he named Hanzell Vineyards after his wife, Hana, to be a piece of Burgundy in the Sonoma Valley. He even modeled the facade of his winery on an ancient structure at the Clos de Vougeot, the historic Burgundian vineyard.

With an innovative winemaker, Brad Webb, Hanzell helped to revolutionize winemaking in the late 1950s. It was the first winery to use stainless-steel temperature-controlled tanks for fermentation. Such tanks are now used all over the world. Hanzell also is credited with introducing French oak barrels to California, though only a third of the oak barrels it uses each year are new.

"We prefer a gentle oak pedestal rather than a slathering-on of flavor," Mr. Terrien said.

Mr. Zellerbach died in 1963, and the estate was sold to Douglas and Mary Day in 1965, then to Barbara and Jacques de Brye in 1975. Alexander de Brye, then a teenager, inherited the vineyard in 1991.

Perhaps in the face of change at the top, safeguarding the identity in the wines became that much more important. Or maybe it was simply a respect for tradition, an overused word that ought to be earned rather than seized.

"Now it's our legacy to protect," Mr. Terrien said.

September 2006

A Cult Winemaker Tinkers With Success

By ERIC ASIMOV

Out here in Sonoma County south of the Russian River, where a rolling ocean of vineyards surrounds a few surviving Gravenstein apple orchards, the growing season is typically long and warm. Grapes customarily bask in the ripening sun until they practically burst with sweetness. The challenge is to prevent the grapes from ripening too much.

Last year was different. Until the heat spiked at the last minute, 2010 had been one of the coolest seasons on record. Nobody knew if the grapes would mature enough. That meant trouble. Or maybe a lucky break.

"Everybody was worried about getting things ripe," said Jason Kesner, the assistant winemaker at Kistler Vineyards. "We had the acid, we had the color, we had the flavor, but we didn't have the typical California sugar to match up with it. We had the tremendous opportunity to make wines at lower alcohol levels. It was the holy grail we'd all been asking for."

Really? For more than 30 years, restraint was not a quality remotely associated with Kistler. In the 1980s and '90s, as Americans developed a ravenous thirst for chardonnay, Kistler set a standard of quality with its powerful, oaky, voluptuous wines. Using grapes from small lots in prime vineyards in Sonoma and the Carneros, it was among a handful of California wineries that pioneered the use of Burgundian techniques, like fermenting in small oak barrels.

American critics raved about the wines, placing them at the pinnacle of California chardonnay. More quietly, Kistler was also lauded for its pinot noirs.

As Kistler's lush, exuberant style was widely emulated, it became one of the first modern California cult wineries, its wines available only in restaurants or to long-term customers. It was a model for today's mailing-list avatars of the full-blown California chardonnay style, like Aubert and Peter Michael. Indeed, some producers began making even more powerful wines so overflowing with flavor they made Kistler's look almost sedate.

But with little fanfare, the Kistler style has changed in the last few years. Following the evolving tastes of Steve Kistler, one of its proprietors, rather than the pressure of economic necessity, Kistler has stepped back, striving for finesse and energy rather than power.

Kistler's departure from its extraordinarily successful style is a shock, and

225

perhaps even risky business. And yet the California wine industry has seen a stylistic evolution in the last decade, especially with chardonnays. More and more wines seek elegance and vivacity rather than sumptuous force.

Partly, this is a retreat from the overuse of oak, with many more producers marketing their wines as "unoaked" or "steel fermented." Similarly, more producers now tout their chardonnays as "Chablis-like," evoking the leaner, more minerally style of that region rather than the richer, more opulent chardonnays of the Côte de Beaune, the home of Meursault and Montrachet.

Even many chardonnay producers who continue to pursue the Côte de Beaune ideal, like Littorai, Peay, Rivers-Marie and Failla, are aiming more for grace than for power. As a result, the spectrum of California styles seems wider and less monochromatic today, with room for chardonnays in the leanest to the most luxuriant styles. Kistler's wines are still ample—certainly not on the Chablis end of the spectrum—but they now seem fresher, more focused and finely etched.

"Was there a time when we erred on the side of uniformity, of over-fine tuning, of picking later, only when every last cluster was ripe?" asked Mr. Kistler, who owns the company with his business partner, Mark Bixler. "Maybe so, but we've evolved, as I think others have, too."

While some customers say they miss the wines that made Kistler famous, he says the evolution has mostly been well received.

"We don't worry if the pinot noir isn't dark enough," he said. "Some people do ask us to return to the overblown, blowzy style of chardonnay, but no."

Indeed, the Kistler business has been affected more by the economy than by the stylistic change, but even the economy hasn't put a serious crimp into sales. The entire production, about 20,000 cases of chardonnay and 5,000 cases of pinot noir, used to be available only in restaurants or by the mailing list, where the single-vineyard chardonnays sell for around $75 and the pinot noirs range from $75 to $90. But now you can find the Kistler Noisetiers chardonnay, the lowest echelon, a blend of several vineyards but representative of the style, for around $60 in retail shops.

Mr. Kistler, 62, attributes the change inside the bottle to his own developing preferences. "My tastes now run toward more structured, lively wines that go with food, that have power and finesse at the same time," he said as we spoke outside his winery, looking out over the adjacent Vine Hill Vineyard, the source of some of his best chardonnays. Even there, change is visible. He and Mr. Kesner are replanting part of the vineyard, reorienting and tweaking the vines so the grapes can be picked earlier, when, as Mr. Kesner puts it, "the fruit is at a peak level of energy."

Even before the changes, Kistler chardonnays were pure and deep. Yet I'd had mixed experiences with them. Some I had found to be wonderfully ripe and laden with mineral flavors, rich yet tense. Others seemed flaccid, hot and oaky, without much staying power. The pinot noirs were commanding expressions of fruit, but somewhat chunky rather than elegant.

The move to harvest earlier began, almost serendipitously, with the 2006 vintage, when Mr. Kistler had to pick certain lots of chardonnay grapes earlier than usual to beat bad weather. In the resulting wines, which were not released until 2008, he found wonderful and surprising characteristics.

"That was a definite eye-opener," Mr. Kesner said.

It was a decisive element in a continuing effort, particularly with the pinot noirs, to make wines that were intense but not heavy, fresh rather than brawny. In their quest, they've committed themselves to indigenous rather than cultured yeasts, to using fewer new barrels and, over all, to letting go of overt control in the vineyard and cellar. Describing their approach, Mr. Kesner quoted the jazz great Charlie Parker: "Don't play the saxophone, let the saxophone play you," he said.

Mr. Kistler said, simply, "We've really worked hard on them the last 10 years, and we're making much better wines."

Tasting the wines, I can't help but agree with Mr. Kistler. The 2008 McCrea Vineyard chardonnay from Sonoma Mountain is lovely, light-bodied and energetic, with creamy mineral flavors. The '08 Vine Hill is more austere and tightly coiled than the McCrea, while the '08 Hudson is richer in texture, with an almost briny flavor, and the '08 Stone Flat is tangy, with a waxy, lanolin texture and beautiful mineral flavors.

What has not changed at Kistler is an underlying philosophy of meticulous attention to detail with an aim to express subtle differences in terroir. As it always has, Kistler tries to reduce variables so that vineyard characteristics will stand out. It uses only one clone of chardonnay, for example, a California heritage selection rather than something developed in France to meet Burgundian needs. That clone, in turn, mutates over time within each vineyard, becoming part of the terroir.

"We were unusual 30 years ago in that we planted vineyards and chose techniques to make wines of a certain style," Mr. Kistler said. "We never were interested in fruit-driven chardonnays. Our goal was wonderful mineral wines with a soil-driven character."

For the pinot noirs, Kistler has narrowed its focus to western Sonoma County and coastal sites east of Bodega Bay. The '08 Kistler Vineyard pinot noir, from a few miles south of the Vine Hill Vineyard, is surprisingly delicate and harmonious, with lingering floral, fruit and mineral flavors. The '08 Cuvée Natalie from the nearby Silver Belt Vineyard is more intense, not quite as well-knit, perhaps still a work in progress. By contrast, a barrel sample of a 2009 pinot noir from one of the coastal vineyards stands out for its freshness and energy.

"That's what makes us as excited as we were 30 years ago," Mr. Kistler said.

Changes have come not only to the wines, but also to the business. Since its founding in 1978, Kistler has largely been a two-man operation. Mr. Kistler oversaw vineyard and winemaking operations, while Mr. Bixler took charge of laboratory work and the business. In an era of uninhibited marketing in which winemakers have been propelled to superstar status, Mr. Kistler has shunned publicity and overt salesmanship.

"We've always been more comfortable letting the wines speak for themselves," said Mr. Kistler, a lean, private man with a quiet, almost hesitant manner.

In 2008, though, he expanded the roster, adding Mr. Kesner, who, as manager of Hudson Vineyards in Carneros, a prime source for Kistler chardonnays, had established a comfortable working relationship with Mr. Kistler.

"For all those years we got by without assistance," Mr. Kistler said. "But in order to take everything to the next level, there was only so much I could do."

The next level meant more than refining the vineyard and cellar work. It also meant thinking of the future. As with many family-run operations, generational succession is an issue. Just a few years ago, Warren Winiarski sold Stag's Leap Wine Cellars, the historic Napa estate, after it became clear that his daughter was not committed to carrying it on. Mr. Kistler has two daughters, but neither so far has become involved in the wine business. Instead of selling, Mr. Kistler hired Mr. Kesner, 42, who says he views his job as an Old World apprenticeship.

Mr. Kesner says he shares Mr. Kistler's inclination for privacy. But he also said he believes Mr. Kistler deserves more recognition, both for his wines and his dedicated approach, and prodded him to speak publicly.

"I feel very much like Charlie Bucket, and I've found the golden ticket," Mr. Kesner said. "I want everyone to know how wondrous it is inside the chocolate factory."

January 2011

Garages for Chardonnays, Not Camrys

By PATRICIA LEIGH BROWN

The fever comes on suddenly for Tom Clark, a lawyer with the Port of Oakland, when he spies his office phone blinking with an urgent message. The news on the voice mail will haunt him, cost him sleep, draw him from his bed into the garage in the middle of the night, where, giddy and nervous with anticipation, he will wait in musty seclusion illuminated by a single light bulb until sweet deliverance arrives: 550 pounds of freshly picked wine grapes.

"I couldn't go to bed," he would say the next evening as he punched down a Rubbermaid container of fermenting booty with a toilet-bowl plunger. "I wanted to play with those sangioveses."

In fact, the fever is rampant in northern California. At this time of year in neighborhoods like Mr. Clark's in Piedmont, a small bedroom community tucked into the Oakland hills, nondescript garages housing wet-vacs and lawn mowers are transformed into chateaus by "garagistes"—amateur home vintners—who obsess about malolactic fermentation and how to carpool 650 pounds of petit verdot grapes in the back seat during rush hour.

"When the crush is in, there is nothing better," said Mr. Clark, whose two-car garage, along with the three-car garage of his neighbor Mike Masero, has been transformed into a grease-stained Napa. In this inelegant tableau, the two are producing their ambitious 2004 vintages—about 2,000 bottles of 13 varieties—that began with muscat canelli grapes crushed in August and continued to the sangioveses that Mr. Masero, an information technology specialist for a webcasting company, recently raced to pick up late after work.

"Part about having a passion about something is, you're not in control," said Mr. Clark, a sophisticated winemaker who will drop everything for the right grapes. "You're having to accommodate yourself to some other force. There is also a kinetic energy to it. I sit in front of the computer all day, and it's a real relief. We're physical beings. So it's 'Let's go out there, get our hands all mucky and crush some grapes.'"

Spurred by the grape glut of recent years, do-it-yourselfism and, perhaps, the indefatigable baby boom desire for perfection, the garagiste scene is expanding throughout California, the Pacific Northwest, the Finger Lakes region of New York and other hubs of winemaking. Thanks to the increasing availability of cultured wine yeasts and wine-quality concentrated grape juice, home vintners are also flourishing in less likely places like Vermont and especially Canada, where, largely for economic reasons, one quarter of the wine consumed is now made by hobbyists, according to Brad Ring, publisher of *WineMaker*, a magazine geared to home winemakers founded six years ago in Manchester, Vt.

Across the country, there are an estimated 750,000 home winemakers and counting, Mr. Ring said, among them members of intensely serious wine clubs like Cellarmasters Home Wine Club in Los Angeles, the Sacramento Home Winemakers and the Contra Costa Wine Group outside San Francisco, who compete in amateur wine competitions at state and county fairs and at events like the International Amateur Wine Competition in Vermont. Unlike the landed gentry or old-time rural families, most garagistes do not have their own vineyards but buy grapes in bulk, sometimes doing the picking themselves. They produce wine for their own consumption and to share or trade with friends; the sale of wine is limited to bonded wineries.

"You get close to your inner Dionysus," said Jerry Miller, 56, an energy utility analyst, who has been making wine since 1979 and whose garage, filled with neighbors and friends with chronically wine-purple hands during crush season, has the festive quality of an Amish barn-raising. "I do it for the sensuality of it."

Around the San Francisco Bay area, arguably the hub of the garagiste movement, placid oak-lined streets are alive with the clickety-clack of hand-cranked wine presses, as home winemakers with a penchant for jazz and chèvre sit on milk crates in their driveways, buckets at the ready to catch the torrential "free run" of flowing juice—the wine equivalent of nirvana. Cars banished to curbsides, they speak of "brix" (sugar content), "hot" wine (too much alcohol) and "M.O.G." (material other than grapes, like spider webs and bees, that gets mixed in during picking).

Vacations are out, as internal clocks are reset to the rhythm of grapes. Weekends and wee hours are consumed with crushing, de-stemming, pressing and racing—particularly if, like Mr. Clark, you have your heart set on a certain row of petit verdot hanging provocatively in a grove of eucalyptus near Lodi, 75 miles away, and learn it is to be picked that day.

Many garagistes fantasize about going pro. "Home wines are some of the best wines in California," said Kent M. Rosenblum, a veterinarian turned vintner whose respected winery, Rosenblum Cellars, got started in his basement. "They're also some of the worst wines in California."

Since the repeal of Prohibition, government rules permit households to make up to 200 gallons—1,000 bottles—of wine a year. At Bissie and Jerry Miller's, six couples get together each harvest season to purchase a ton of grapes, which yields between nine and 11 cases for each family. Each couple's $500-a-year investment works out to about $5 a bottle.

Their wine, which is pumped through a siphon hose from the garage to the basement, is also liquid memory. Their Wedding Ring wine of 1991, a pinot noir, commemorated the year that Bevan Vinton, a high school social studies teacher, lost her wedding ring in the crush (it was retrieved during pressing a week later in the "cake" of smashed skins and seeds). The Fire zinfandel was named for the Oakland Hills fire, during which the Millers temporarily fled their home, leaving the grapes behind in the garage.

The Bay area's extreme garagistes "know they can buy Two-Buck Chuck," said Lisa Van de Water, a technical wine consultant and founder of the Wine Lab in Napa, which does scientific analyses for home winemakers and sells yeast nutrients and related products. "They're trying to make really good wine, something that's theirs."

It helps to be a geek. Bonneau Dickson, 60, who has christened his home elixirs Chateau Bonneau, for instance, is a sanitary engineer who lives in Berkeley. "Wine is an anaerobic process, like sludge digestion," he said, an observation not likely to be repeated in *The Wine Spectator.*

The ceiling of his 700-square-foot third-floor walk-up is dented from an errant stopper blown off a vigorously fermenting chardonnay. His kitchen is a welter of calibrated cylinders, acidity kits and pH meters. His décor consists of 65 wine-filled carboys, six-gallon glass containers, which have subsumed nearly every inch of his apartment. His preoccupation, however, does wonders for his social life. "As soon as I started making wine, I noticed I had more friends," he said.

Stephen and Susan Abbanat, who, like Mr. Dickson, are members of the Contra Costa Wine Group, spend their leisure time developing math-laden spreadsheets to monitor the parts-per-million of potassium metasulfite and the like, spurred by the yeasty smell of wine fermenting in their Oakland basement. "You start to build a taste for your own wine, and that's what you prefer," Mr. Abbanat said.

"There's a mystery to it, a random element," he said, turning philosophical as he drove home from a vineyard recently with 155 pounds of merlot grapes in his Lexus. "Making things is a survival trait, part of our genetic code. It's a piece of ourselves we're trying to connect with."

Nevertheless, romance can fade with panic, spurred, say, by pernicious *Brettanomyces*, a spoilage yeast, or, in the Abbanats' case, "Pepto-Bismol-colored bubbles coming off during fermentation that could have been a funky bacteria." Because he lives near wine country, Mr. Abbanat was able to drive a vial of the suspicious cabernet up to the Wine Lab in Napa, founded by Ms. Van de Water, who has earned the nickname "the bad wine lady" (everything was fine). Home winemakers, she noted, must function without microbiologists, state-of-the-art filtration systems and other resources available to commercial wineries. "Their expectation that everything will turn out O.K. leads to a lot of ruined wine," she said.

A big reason winemakers form groups, at least in California, is access to know-how and most important, good grapes. The grape glut, which peaked in 2000 with a staggering 90,000-plus tons of grapes, has opened up many once-exclusive vineyards to home winemakers, but many growers still regard them as the equivalent of telephone solicitors in the middle of dinner. "It is difficult to convince a grower to sell 300 to 500 pounds of grapes," said Dave Lustig, 48, a Pasadena computer programmer and secretary of the Cellarmasters, who admits to having driven 23 hours nonstop from the Willamette Valley in Oregon with five tons of pinot noir in a rented Ryder truck. "In a co-op you can buy a 1,000- or 2,000-pound quantity, so it's easier to be treated like a big boy than someone showing up with garbage pails and a cooler."

Mr. Clark and Mr. Masero said they have had great success obtaining grapes from stellar vineyards, first sampling commercial wines to decide on a growing region, then setting out on a field trip to meet growers. "You say, 'Man, whatever you're doing to that mourvèdre is so fine,'" Mr. Clark said. "You have to establish a rapport. It's about friendships. It also helps to pay cold hard cash."

His face was pure ecstasy one night recently as he sat with Mr. Masero at a TV table set up in front of his garage, drinking a 2003 mourvèdre while a pink cascade of sangiovese emanated from the basket press. In Mr. Masero's "annex," Big Bertha, a 110-gallon tank of petite sirah, was improving every day. "It's pure gold," Mr. Clark said. "You know they are going to give you pleasure for 15 years."

In Berkeley, Bonneau Dickson was euphoric, too, as he sat on his porch watching carbon dioxide bubbles percolate through the carboys' air locks. He keeps his windows open at night so he can hear them, the surround-sound of bubbles luring him to dreamland. "They're nice at night," he said. "They help me sleep. It's like a babbling brook."

October 2004

Growing in Napa:
Club, and Camp, for Wine Lovers

By PATRICIA LEIGH BROWN

At 5:30 a.m., the stars still in the sky, the pickers approached the fields. Wearing miner's lamps, they attacked vines heavy with cabernet grapes of the finest French stock. Occasionally, the sticky clusters of grapes would muck up the prongs of the women's Cartier jewelry.

It was harvest time at the Napa Valley Reserve, the nation's first wine "country club." Here, on Napa's choicest land, C.E.O.'s, venture capitalists, lawyers and other Type A's indulge their agrarian fantasies by playing farmworker for a day.

As Augusta National is to golf lovers, so the Reserve is to elite enophiles prone to using phrases like "depth of color." For a $140,000 initiation fee, each member gets several rows of picturesque grapes to harvest—a foolproof proposition, given the resident wine experts who supervise the operation, along with such guest "lecturers" as Robert Mondavi.

Dr. Orrin Devinsky, a professor of neurology at the N.Y.U. School of Medicine, had been making his own wine in a refrigerated garage in Short Hills, N.J. "It was perfectly drinkable," he said. "Though I loved having my fingers soaked in grape juice, the truth was I could buy a $25 bottle that exceeded it."

Now Dr. Devinsky has joined the Reserve because he cannot manage a vineyard cross-country on his own and does not want to make mediocre wine. "I love the visceral side—the land, the grapes, the biology," he said. "That whole thing is extremely appealing."

The Yoda of this good life is a millionaire businessman, H. William Harlan, the club's founder. Mr. Harlan is owner of the famed Harlan Estate winery, and his own cabernet sauvignons have thrice earned a rare 100 points from the wine kingmaker Robert Parker. His 2001 cabs now retail for around $475 a bottle, with a three- to five-year waiting list.

Though wine clubs have become common in many American cities and suburbs, the 80-acre Reserve is in a league all its own. Its grapes come from root stocks and clones on Harlan Estate, and its 244 members can cook with the author Patricia Wells, and confer with the superstar Bordeaux enologist Michel Rolland. A resident wine historian quotes Thucydides and other ancient Greeks.

Members—the club will cap its list at 375—pay monthly dues of $80 and commit to "personal wine production" ranging from a minimum of 150 bottles a year, for $7,500, up to three barrels, or 900 bottles, at a cost of $45,000. They pay for use of the vines, rather than ownership of them, and are strictly prohibited from selling wine, though they are free to impress friends and business associates with a label named for a ranch or yacht. Barrels are sequestered to age in a 35,000-square-foot steel-reinforced wine cave, which is under construction.

It is slow going. "I have a new appreciation for the difficulty of the work," said Cam Garner, a venture capitalist from Rancho Santa Fe, who was hacking young vines with a sickle-shaped knife as roosters crowed. "You spend that much for a bottle of wine, you might as well appreciate all the aspects."

At the harvest in mid-October Daryl Bristow of Houston, who helped George W. Bush secure the 2000 election in Florida as a senior law partner of former Secretary of State James A. Baker III, was huddled intently in the West Barrel Room of the East Fermentation Building. Before him was a conveyor belt ferrying thousands of berries—they are never called grapes—toward oak barrels, the scene a dead ringer for the famous chocolate-factory episode in *I Love Lucy*.

Mr. Bristow's mission was to ferret out teeny green unripe berries; mushy, bird-pecked berries; shriveled, raisin-y berries; and M.O.G., material other than grape. "Here I am throwing out spiders, leaves and little green berries, right there with the grapes that will make our wine," said a euphoric Mr. Bristow. "It's a very neat feeling."

Along with "fireside chats" by Mr. Mondavi, held in a chic pre-weathered barn, members get to personalize their vintages, select the amount of time their oak barrels will be toasted and steep themselves in the club's wine library, which is full of rare first editions.

Members will also have their own private wine storage lairs within the cave, which they may decorate. "Ooooh—can we store shoes, too?" asked Kathi Mallick of Rancho Santa Fe, who resembled Nancy Drew as she peered into the wine cave's inky blackness.

The club, which had its first harvest, a limited one, last fall, is a shrewd gesture to both wine's snob appeal and the seemingly limitless marketing of Napa Valley's gauzy Mediterranean allure, fueled by Greystone, the Western outpost of the Culinary Institute of America, and celebrity winemakers like Francis Ford Coppola. Two-thirds of its members come from outside Northern California.

Avid collectors like Mr. Garner may spend $100,000 a year on wine, but the frenzied apogee of American wine connoisseurship may be Auction Napa Valley, a premier charity event held at Meadowood, Mr. Harlan's luxury resort up the road. Last summer, ferocious bidders spent over $10.5 million, with Jay Leno auctioning off the first 15 lots; the high bid of $650,000 went for a rare Colgin Cellars quartet of double magnums, with a private dinner for eight by Thomas Keller of the French Laundry.

The Reserve redefines the notion of a cult wine, said Daphne Derven, the program director at the Stone Barns Center for Food and Agriculture on the Rockefeller estate in Pocantico Hills, N.Y. "He is creating an exclusive closed group," she said of Mr. Harlan.

Before he opened his first winery, Mr. Harlan, 65, made millions as a co-founder and chairman of Pacific Union, the real estate company.

The Reserve is a microcosm of Napa history, beginning as a ranch, then farmed by Swiss immigrants until Mr. Harlan and two partners purchased it in 2001. Today it is prime acreage of Cezanne-like beauty, holding—in addition to grapes—550 Tuscan olive trees and exotic plantings like shiso, a Japanese herb that is infused in oil and drizzled over tuna tartare in the club's demonstration kitchen.

Mr. Harlan, who has invested tens of millions in the Reserve—he would not divulge the exact amount—said he hoped to create a legacy for "people of discernment" and their families (though no one has yet tasted the club's wine, which takes two years to age).

"For 15 years I kept hearing, 'I'd love to have a little vineyard,'" he said of his customers. "Now they can have the good part without the responsibility and risk."

"It's not just a return on investment," he added, waxing philosophical. "It's a return on life."

Indeed, ownership of a Napa vineyard is becoming increasingly unattainable, even for the megarich. Sales of vineyard land now average $150,000 to $200,000 an acre, with a 40-acre zoning minimum, but there isn't much of it left. "The Napa Valley is pretty well planted out," said Sean Maher, a wine business consultant here.

County erosion control regulations and ordinances protecting scenic vistas keep much of the land off limits for winemaking, said Tom Jordan, a real estate appraiser in Napa. Most available land, he added, is located in marginal cooler reaches that would not produce a "high-end cab." Mr. Harlan estimated the cost of a serious vineyard at $15 million to $20 million.

"To own a vineyard is pretty stupid," said Kellie Seringer, 35, a Reserve member who runs a hedge fund focusing on health care in San Francisco. "So we're outsourcing the expertise." Ms. Seringer, who has a degree in biochemistry and genetics, tracks sugar levels and the sun on the Valley floor as meticulously as she does health care equities.

And investing millions of dollars in a B-team is a scary prospect. "I'd probably make bad wine, so this is a way to hedge," said Richard Helppie, a 49 year-old self-described "recovering workaholic" from Bloomfield Hills, Mich., who sold his company, Superior Consultant Holdings, last January for $122.2 million.

Mr. Helppie was eating breakfast on the stone patio with his fellow pickers, an impressive post-harvest spread with truffles and tartlettes and fresh berries laid out with silver tongs. The strains of jazz wafted through the air.

"There's a spiritual element to wine," he said. "You know you're producing something from the earth."

In the amber-lit perfection of the vineyard, the handsome club buildings stained silver-gray, the members of the Reserve were nevertheless dabblers, chasing after an authentic experience that by its nature remains elusive. When they finished their tasks, of course, the pros took over.

Real vineyard workers, noted Rosa Segura, chairwoman of the county's Migrant Farmworker Housing Committee, get paid by the ton, usually $90 to $140. They pack a bean or fried potato and egg burrito, taking a quick break under an oak tree. They go home to overcrowded apartments, she said, "or maybe somebody's garage, where they pay $100 a month to sleep on a sofa."

Real vineyard workers, she added, "pick with a needy passion." Club members, she suggested, "should pick with the real pickers. Then they would have the full experience."

October 2005

Too Sweet to Be Invited to Dinner

By ERIC ASIMOV

It's happened so many times that I've lost count. I'm having dinner with another person, trying to choose a wine that will complement the odd combination of dishes that we've ordered—meat, fowl, fish or whatever.

Back in the old days, 10 years or so ago, California pinot noir was one of my go-to wines. Its reputation was poor, and critics lambasted American pinot noir as a pale imitation of Burgundy, but I found it a great food wine, light-bodied enough to go with fish, yet intense enough to match up with meat. Not unlike Burgundy, in fact, but a lot cheaper.

Not anymore. California pinot noir has shot up in stature. Its popularity has skyrocketed, and the critics now love it. But on the dinner table? I rarely look at pinot noir nowadays. Not only because it's gotten so expensive but because many modern pinot noirs have lost the dry, lithe character that made the wine so fine a partner with food.

Why is this? Far too often now, pinot noir tastes sweet and has a heavy, almost syrupy character. And while pinot noir is the most glaring example, it's often true, too, of many other high-end, supposedly dry red American wines like cabernet sauvignon and zinfandel.

Now sweetness itself is not intrinsically a problem. Some of the greatest, most versatile food wines in the world are sweet, like German rieslings and demi-sec chenin blancs from the Loire. But those wines have more than sweetness going for them: they have balance. The sugar is balanced by acidity, which provides structure and liveliness, allowing the wine to be both sweet and refreshing.

The American red wines, on the other hand, are meant to be dry, like their French forebears Burgundy and Bordeaux, which are dry by definition.

Burly zinfandels have always flirted with a tinge of sweetness, but nowadays they too taste sweeter and sweeter. I've particularly noticed this problem in pinot noirs from the Santa Lucia Highlands and Santa Barbara County on the central coast of California, in Napa Valley cabernets and in zinfandels from all over.

I'm not the only one bothered by this. Dan Berger, a critic who publishes *Dan Berger's Vintage Experiences*, a weekly newsletter, called the rising sense of sweetness in American red wines "a sad and pernicious trend."

"They're impressive wines, but the word 'impressive' is not always a positive word," he said in a telephone interview. "There's lots to them, but maybe more flavor is less good. What you want is a harmony of flavors."

Dry wines that are not really dry are an American tradition. As the old saw in the wine industry has it, "Americans talk dry but drink sweet," and the history of American wine consumption bears that out.

Popular mass-market wines from California, like white zinfandel and Kendall-Jackson Vintner's Reserve chardonnay, have always had more than a subversive touch of sweetness, while the best-selling Champagne in the United States by far is Moët & Chandon's White Star, a cuvée made especially for the American market that is a step sweeter than the typical brut Champagne.

The rationale has always been that the American palate is shaped by the sugary soft drinks, ketchup and breakfast cereals of the childhood pantry.

Modestly sweet wines therefore help a wine-wary population make the transition to more classically dry wines, especially if that population believes it is drinking dry wines.

Sweet wines were associated with low-status fortified wines, like Thunderbird, or the sort of syrupy Concord grape wines that appear on many kosher tables.

But now, apparently, the sensation of sweetness has triumphed over the belief that fine red wines were dry bordering on tart and even somewhat austere. The changing character of the wines may even change the way people think of drinking wine. Justin Smith of Saxum Vineyards, a small but acclaimed producer in Paso Robles, Calif., calls them "social wines."

"These wines aren't meant to go with food," he said. "They're for when you get home from work: you open a bottle, pour a glass and sit with it out on the deck."

In other words, they're to be consumed like cocktails, which they resemble in another way, too. Most of these wines are high in alcohol, at least 14.5 percent and often above 15, which contributes to the impression of sweetness even if they are not actually sugary.

California red wines are made in a fruitier style than they used to be, which also contributes to an impression of sweetness, said Dr. Susan E. Ebeler, a flavor chemist in viticulture and enology at the University of California, Davis. Grapes nowadays are allowed to ripen on the vine much longer than 10 or 15 years ago, resulting in much higher concentrations of sugar at harvest.

More sugar requires longer fermentation, which produces more alcohol and more glycerol. Dr. Ebeler said glycerol, whose name is derived from the Greek word for sweet, also contributes to a perception of sweetness.

Let's see: fruitiness, high alcohol and higher glycerol. Add it up and what do you have? "It could be the sum of the parts," Dr. Ebeler said.

While wines made in this style may try to appeal to the American sweet tooth, they may also reflect the wine business's dependency on high ratings from critics who taste dozens of wines at a time.

"I think it's a real, conscious effort on the part of some winemakers to make the wine taste supple and soft and hedonistic," Mr. Berger said. "I think this style of wine is designed to be a home run. You don't see very many people bunting. I think the more flashy, expressive style tends to be the style that catches people's eye."

Of course, not all California red wines fall into this sweet category, not by a long shot. I've enjoyed many excellent reds in the last year, including, just last weekend, Etude's 2003 Heirloom Carneros pinot noir, which was full of complex sweet fruit aromas and flavors, held together by a firm structure.

But the Etude was in marked contrast to two sweet pinot noirs that I could not drink with dinner. One was the Loring Wine Company's 2004 Rosella's Vineyard in the Santa Lucia Highlands. The other was an '04 Cuyama River in the Santa Maria Valley from Taz Vineyards.

Whatever else wine is, ultimately it must be at home on the dinner table. Obviously Americans enjoy sweet beverages with food, whether Coca-Cola, white zinfandel or this year's top-ranked pinot noir or cabernet.

But for the long term, red wine that seems sweet runs the risk of becoming a marginalized beverage, served on the deck before dinner, yes, or maybe afterward with cheese or chocolate, like port. Then it will be time to stop and praise the winemaker's impressive achievement, and reach for something else to drink.

July 2006

Finessed and Light:
California Pinot Noirs With a Manifesto

By ERIC ASIMOV

As the rain slanted down onto the vineyard around Copain Wine Cellars, just outside this town in northern Sonoma County, Wells Guthrie, the proprietor, poured a glass of one of his 2006 pinot noirs.

The wine was fresh and light with aromas of flowers and red fruit. Even in the gray dimness of his tasting room I could see my fingers on the other side of the glass through the pale ruby wine.

It was vibrant and refreshing, nothing like the dark, plush, opulent wines that have made California pinot noir so popular. Mr. Guthrie used to make wines more along those heavier lines, but not anymore. After the vinous equivalent of a conversion experience, with his 2006 vintage he renounced the fruit-bomb style in favor of wines that emphasize freshness and delicacy.

"It got to the point where I didn't want the wine to be fatter than the food," he said. "Wine should make you think of what you want to eat."

From Mendocino and Sonoma through the Santa Cruz Mountains and Arroyo Grande south to the rolling hills of Santa Barbara County, a rebellion is brewing. The dominant style of California pinot noir remains round, ripe and extravagant, with sweet flavors of dark fruit and alcohol levels approaching and sometimes surpassing 15 percent.

But on a recent trip through these leading pinot noir areas I was thrilled to find a small but growing number of producers pulling in the opposite direction.

Instead of power, they strive for finesse. Instead of a rich, mouth-coating impression of sweetness, they seek a dry vitality meant to whet the appetite rather than squelch it. Instead of weight, they prize lightness and an almost transparent intensity.

Some of these producers are fairly new to the pinot noir game, like Anthill Farms in Healdsburg, a partnership of three young men who share a taste for balanced, elegant wines, or Peay Vineyards on the northern Sonoma Coast, which makes spicy yet polished pinot noirs, or Rhys Vineyards in the Santa Cruz Mountains, which after just five vintages is already producing brilliantly distinctive wines.

Others, like Ted Lemon of Littorai Wines, Josh Jensen of the Calera Wine

Company and Jim Clendenen of Au Bon Climat, have been preaching the virtues of finesse for more than a few years now.

"I wish somebody could explain to me how picking grapes when they're precisely in balance and making a wine in balance became unfashionable," Mr. Clendenen said as we stood in the middle of his utilitarian winery, in the middle of the Bien Nacido Vineyard in the Santa Maria Valley. On a big industrial stove Mr. Clendenen was preparing lunch, as he often does, for the winery staff and the occasional visitor. When it's ready, work at Au Bon Climat stops as everybody sits at a long, indoor picnic table to eat and drink a glass or two of wine, a reminder to all of the place and intent for their beverage.

"The ultimate use for wine is pairing with food," said Rick Longoria, who makes intense yet balanced pinot noirs in Santa Barbara County. "There is no greater experience than the beautiful synergy between wine and food that elevates both."

Food and wine's role at the table is seemingly what divides these stylistic camps. Is wine a supporting player at a meal, intended to harmonize with food? Or is it meant to be, figuratively speaking, a meal in itself, best consumed on its own?

The answers can sometimes seem paradoxical. Leslie Mead of Talley Vineyards in Arroyo Grande, north of Santa Barbara County, makes fresh, earthy pinot noirs that would do well on any table. Yet for herself, she appreciates the other approach.

"I think there's a place for every style," she said. "Sometimes I like water with dinner and wine on its own."

I can respect that point of view, but I can't understand it. For me, wine's place is with food, and that's why I had begun to despair of so many California pinot noirs. Their power and sense of sweetness were overwhelming at the table. But it turns out that more than a few California producers share my feeling, like Ehren Jordan of Failla and Thomas Brown of Rivers-Marie, Joe Davis of Arcadian and Alex Davis of Porter Creek. Almost to a person, they make no secret of being inspired by the wines of Burgundy.

"It's not that we're trying to make Burgundy in California," said Adam Tolmach of the Ojai Vineyard, which makes lively, savory Central Coast pinot noirs. "But the world loves Burgundy because of its sense of style, that's a style that we'd like to emulate, and it's hard to do that at 17 percent alcohol."

It's fashionable among the makers of bigger, heavier pinot noirs to reject any comparison with Burgundy. We don't make Gevrey-Chambertin, they will say. We make wines representative of the Russian River Valley, Santa Rita Hills or Santa Lucia Highlands—take your pick. This stance implies that California conditions dictate wines of extravagance and power. In fact, this style of wine is more often determined by winemakers' decision making. And no decision is more important to the ultimate style of a wine than when to harvest the grapes.

In Burgundy, a cooler climate prevails. Grapes historically struggle to ripen, and the dilemma is whether to play it safe and harvest before the autumn rains arrive or take a chance and wait a little bit longer to achieve proper ripeness. In California, with ample sun and warmth and little chance of autumn rains, growers can allow the grapes to hang for as long as they want.

As a result of this option, and with the help of improved vineyard techniques and new vine clones unburdened by viruses and other plant diseases, California growers in the last 10 or 15 years gained the ability to ripen grapes almost to the point of shriveling, well past what was once considered desirable. Where grapes 20 years ago were considered ripe if they achieved 23 or 24 on the Brix scale for measuring sugar content, producers of ripe pinot noirs today aim for a minimum of 28, 29 or even 30 Brix.

In fact, Mr. Guthrie of Copain doesn't even use the grapes from the 13-acre vineyard around his Healdsburg winery because he feels the weather gets too warm and the fruit too ripe.

Instead he gets grapes from cooler sites, largely in the Anderson Valley of Mendocino County. He sells the Healdsburg fruit to producers like Kosta Browne, who have won widespread plaudits for their dark, plush, opulent Russian River Valley wines.

Such extravagantly ripe—some would say overripe—grapes have their own set of problems. Sugar in fruit accumulates at the cost of acidity, which balances out sweetness with a zingy liveliness. This is especially true of the pinot noir grape. When all that sugar ferments into alcohol, little zing is left.

"With pinot noir, at a higher alcohol level, you don't get the acidity that you do with, say, zinfandel," said Mr. Jordan of Failla, who, in his day job as winemaker at Turley Wine Cellars, has ample experience making big zinfandels.

To compensate, many producers of big pinot noirs will add tartaric acid to their wine, which is permitted, and also add water to cut down on the alcohol, which is a murkier legal area that producers rationalize as simply adding back water lost as the grapes began to dehydrate in the final stage of ripening on the vine.

Yet when the pieces are assembled, what results is not necessarily a seamlessly integrated wine. "To me, pinot noir is a house of cards, and each manipulation adds more cards," said Joe Davis of Arcadian, a steadfast believer in early picking. His wines are slow to develop but are meant to age. While many producers are about to release their 2007s, his graceful, fresh 2005s have only recently hit the market.

Before Mr. Guthrie saw the light, he said, he, too, was adding water and acid to his wines. When he sampled those wines after several years, all he could taste was the water and acid.

"In 2006, I made the decision to pick earlier to retain freshness and vibrancy rather than play the game of picking ripe and adding water and acidity later on," he said. "It was the first year I made pinot where I didn't have to add acid or water, and it felt good."

The differences in well-made examples of early picked and late picked pinot noirs are striking. The earlier picked wines smell of flowers and red fruits rather than black fruits and jam. They are vivacious rather than dense and concentrated. They are dry, not cloying, and offer nuance rather than impact.

"I do not like pruney wines," said Kathleen Inman of Inman Family Wines, which makes small amounts of lively yet delicate pinot noirs in the Russian River Valley. "I'm kind of the bellwether. People say, 'Kathleen's picking—that means harvest is in two weeks.'"

Well, honestly, nobody is going to 'fess up to liking pruney wines. Nonetheless, these ultra-ripe pinot noirs are highly popular. Partly that's because they've received such critical acclaim. In the current issue of *Wine Spectator*, the highest-scoring pinot noir from California is described as "superrich, bordering on syrupy." Those are apparently compliments.

Now, I haven't tried that wine, but I can't say those qualities are what I desire in a pinot noir. I prefer words like elegant and energetic, which I used to describe Anthill Farms' 2007 pinot noir from the Comptche Ridge Vineyard in Mendocino County, or restrained and mineral, as in the 2007 Rivers-Marie Summa Vineyard pinot noir from the Sonoma Coast.

Clearly, not everybody agrees with me. Of course, wines that soar for one person thud to the ground for the next. Accounting for divergences in taste can be a thorny subject, especially for those who on some level may feel they haven't received proper respect for their achievements.

"I think it's been whacked into a naïve public's head that these big wines are the wines that people are supposed to like," said Lane Tanner, who has been issuing pinot noirs under her own name from Santa Barbara County since 1989. Her wines are light-bodied, fragrant and floral—"feminine," she calls them, in contrast to the hulking masculine wines that some critics favor.

It takes determination to stick to a style that is less popular.

"There is a lot of pressure in California to make wines in that other style, and you can understand why," said Alex Davis, whose 2006 Porter Creek Fiona Hill pinot noir from the Russian River Valley has a freshness that will wake up the most tired palate. "People have a lot of bills to pay."

Still, none of these producers is suffering, and many are encouraged by the growing demand for their wines.

"The palate in Europe, like the wines, has had a thousand years to develop," said Ted Lemon of Littorai, whose wines beautifully combine structure and intensity with restraint. "We're only starting."

On the Lighter Side

The following are among the California pinot noirs made in a lighter style, emphasizing finesse over power. Some wines are widely available; others are sold by mailing list. Prices can range from around $20 for entry-level bottles up to about $75 for some single-vineyard wines.

ANTHILL FARMS Sonoma/Mendocino; lovely, fresh and floral.
ARCADIAN South Central Coast; lively, pure and age-worthy.
AU BON CLIMAT Santa Barbara; well-balanced and complex.
CALERA WINE COMPANY Mount Harlan; intense
     single-vineyard wines.
COPAIN Mendocino; delicate and nuanced.
FAILLA Sonoma Coast; elegant and focused.
INMAN FAMILY WINES Russian River Valley; bright and pretty.
JOSEPH SWAN VINEYARDS Russian River Valley;
     restrained and delicate.
LANE TANNER Santa Barbara; light-bodied and fragrant.
LITTORAI Mendocino/Sonoma Coast; structured and energetic.
LONGORIA Santa Barbara; earthy and intense.
THE OJAI VINEYARD Santa Barbara; light and savory.

PEAY VINEYARDS Sonoma Coast; spicy and polished.
PORTER CREEK VINEYARDS Russian River Valley;
    fresh and elegant.
RHYS VINEYARDS Santa Cruz Mountains; graceful and complex.
RIVERS-MARIE Sonoma Coast; intense, lively and balanced.
TALLEY VINEYARDS Arroyo Grande; earthy yet fresh.

March 2009

Letting a Grape Be a Grape

By ERIC ASIMOV

Here at the rustic wooden headquarters of Ridge Vineyards, nestled 2,400 feet up in the Santa Cruz Mountains overlooking Silicon Valley, the winery is celebrating its 50th anniversary this week, practically an eternity in the California wine business. Most wineries seize anniversaries as an opportunity for marketing and promotion, and Ridge is not immune, assembling a small group of wine writers and sommeliers for an in-depth, historical tasting of its top wines.

Ordinarily, I pay little attention to such events. But for a half century Ridge has made one of California's greatest cabernet sauvignons, Monte Bello, in a remarkably consistent style independent of the twists and turns of fashion. Ridge has also been the leading standard-bearer for zinfandel, which has likewise followed a serpentine path of styles.

Perhaps because of its longevity and its consistency, and because its wines are actually available to consumers, Ridge tends to be taken for granted, its achievements noted dutifully even as attention shifts to the new, the expensive and the scarce. That seemed reason enough to spend an afternoon visiting Ridge before the celebration.

Over the last few years I've had the opportunity to drink Monte Bellos covering a range of 40 vintages. The 1970 is one of the greatest California cabernets I've ever drunk, beautifully balanced and graceful with a pronounced minerality and the sort of herbal accents that are routinely denounced in California but which I think are integral to good cabernet.

Meanwhile, the latest release, the 2006, offers all of these qualities, along with the gentle fruit and violet flavors and aromas that you would expect to find in a young wine. In an era when cabernet growers pick grapes ever riper for wines of great power, fruit magnitude and impact, Monte Bellos remain focused and intense yet, above all, balanced.

Not that Monte Bello hasn't evolved at all. The first vintage, 1962, cost $3.50 a bottle. It's now up to $145, though it is still cheap next to other elite wines. (The vineyard-designated zinfandels are more approachably priced, from $25 to $35.)

Over time, Ridge has refined its approach in the cellar, treating the youthful wine more gently so the tannins are softer and less imposing. One thing that hasn't changed: Ridge's reliance on American oak for its barrels, rather than the French oak that is standard for almost all leading California cabernets. In its style and the methods by which it is made, Monte Bello manages to bridge Old World and New.

In many ways this is a testament to Paul Draper, Ridge's chief executive and winemaker, who is marking the 40th anniversary of his affiliation with the winery. For as much as Ridge wines display the greatness of place—Monte Bello as well as its two primary zinfandel vineyards in Sonoma, Geyserville and Lytton Springs—Ridge's success also affirms the greatness of Mr. Draper's vision of applying traditional European techniques to wines that demonstrate the potential of California.

Indeed, it may seem odd to celebrate Mr. Draper, who attributes his success to what he calls "nonaction."

"Our main thing is to allow grapes to show their character rather than imposing our will on them," he told me as we looked out over the dormant cabernet vines awaiting their winter pruning.

Noninterventionist winemaking has become one of the great modern marketing clichés. But Mr. Draper's beliefs are grounded in preindustrial techniques practiced by Europeans for centuries: rely on natural yeasts for fermentation, use minimal amounts of sulfur dioxide as a stabilizer and otherwise do as little as possible beyond gently guiding the transformation of grape juice into wine.

Crucially, he also believes that wine's place is on the table with food, which explains why, year in and year out, Monte Bello's alcohol content hovers around 13 percent, even as other top California cabernets break the 15 percent level. Its zinfandels are higher in alcohol, naturally, but not as high as the full-bore, high-octane zins that top most critics' charts.

Here in the Santa Cruz Mountains, cabernet and the other Bordeaux grapes in the vineyard cannot achieve the high levels of ripeness typical of grapes grown in the warmer parts of Napa Valley. Warm air wafts over from the San Francisco Bay, fending off the fog and cold that blow in from the Pacific and moderating the temperatures just enough to ripen the grapes.

Apparently not enough for some critics. In his blog last fall, James Laube, who covers California for *Wine Spectator*, suggested that the cool climate made for reds that were too green and herbal to suit his taste. It was an opinion that stung Mr. Draper.

"We've always made wines that we loved to drink," he said. "We've never made for the market. Luckily, people have always bought our wines."

Mr. Draper has always contended that he knew nothing about making wine when he joined Ridge in 1969. The winery was founded in 1959, which makes both anniversaries a bit approximate. Four scientists from Stanford Research Institute bought 80 acres on Monte Bello Ridge, including an abandoned winery and a mature vineyard. Without training, they made wine and liked the results so much that they went into business.

Mr. Draper, born in the Midwest and educated at Choate and Stanford, had served in Army intelligence in Italy, where he developed his taste for fine wine and food. After his discharge and further work for the government, Mr. Draper and two partners began an economic development project in Chile. Among other things, they had the idea of creating a model winery, making first-class wine that could be exported for hard currency.

When the partners determined that the political climate in Chile would not support a profitable enterprise, Mr. Draper returned to California with the cabernet he had made. The Ridge partners, impressed by its quality, invited Mr. Draper to join them.

Mr. Draper had no formal training, either, so he took as his guiding light an 1883 manual written by E. H. Rixford, who coincidentally planted a cabernet vineyard in the Santa Cruz Mountains that became legendary as La Questa. Cuttings from La Questa were the basis of the original Monte Bello vineyard, planted in 1886 by Osea Perrone, an Italian doctor from San Francisco.

Even today, getting to Monte Bello requires a harrowing 4.4-mile drive of narrow hairpin turns around which one can only pray a truck is not barreling. Whatever possessed somebody, I asked Mr. Draper, to plant a vineyard up here?

"They were Europeans," he said. "You grew grapes where nothing else would grow."

Mr. Draper, who will turn 74 next week, has made few concessions to age. He still moves easily up and down the old steps of the restored three-level winery, where the original 19th-century redwood joists and limestone walls are covered in the sort of black mold common in ancient European cellars but rare in California. His new Acura is equipped with a five-speed manual transmission, and he doesn't plan to rest on his laurels.

"Every year we're trying to learn something that will push us 1 percent or 5 percent forwards," he said, "and it's gone on for 40 years."

March 2010

Is There Still Hope for Syrah?

By ERIC ASIMOV

There's a joke going around West Coast wine circles: What's the difference between a case of syrah and a case of pneumonia? You can get rid of the pneumonia.

It would be funnier if it weren't so sad. In the last few years, beginning even before the economic downturn, sales of American syrah essentially dropped off a cliff. While precise numbers are not available—for tracking purposes, syrah is often lumped in with Australian shiraz, or consigned to "other red wines"— American syrah producers all tell the same story.

"It appears to have crashed and burned in this country," said Randall Grahm of Bonny Doon Vineyards, who 20 years ago was one of the early proponents of planting California with grapes from the Rhône Valley, like syrah, grenache and mourvèdre. Or, as Ehren Jordan, proprietor of Failla Vineyards, put it: "There has been a collective running into a brick wall by people who make syrah."

Such an impact is hard to fathom with a glass of a Failla syrah in front of you. The aroma—of herbs, olives and flowers—stimulates the appetite. The question is not, what's wrong with syrah, but, where's dinner? Back in the mid-1990s, syrah was thought to be the next great hope for American red wine. Growers and winemakers, looking for an alternative to cabernet sauvignon and merlot, pinned their hopes on syrah, known for making savory wines in Rhône appellations like Hermitage, Côte-Rôtie, Cornas, St.-Joseph and Crozes-Hermitage.

How syrah went so horribly wrong may be a cautionary tale for anybody looking to capitalize on the next great trend.

It's fair to say that much of the syrah produced in California is dreadfully generic red wine of little character. But perhaps more important to recognize is that quite a few producers like Failla are making superb California syrah, a fact that should not be lost in any analysis of the moribund market.

Some producers have made good syrah for years. Others are fairly new to the field and are plunging resolutely ahead, even as the market shrinks. Crucially, though, they are succeeding by staying true to the northern Rhône ideal of making balanced, pungently aromatic wines that belong on the table.

Here in Forestville, a small crossroads town in western Sonoma County, two childhood friends, Duncan Arnot Meyers and Nathan Lee Roberts, are making beautifully aromatic, elegant syrahs under the label Arnot-Roberts. Rather than emphasizing power, concentration and heavy fruit flavors, the Arnot-Roberts wines are graceful and relatively low in alcohol.

"We're California kids," said Mr. Meyers, standing in front of barrels holding the previous year's vintage. "We believe that we can make really good wines here, but our reference points are the northern Rhône."

He and Mr. Roberts teamed up in 2002 on a shoestring budget. With little financial pressure to cater to the marketplace, they have enjoyed the luxury of stubborn idealism, making wines aimed at achieving the classic northern Rhône aromas and flavors of olives and herbs, bacon and minerals, flowers and spices, blood and earth.

"We don't want to make really fruity wines," Mr. Roberts said. "It's those non-fruit aromas that we're really focused on."

One sniff of the Arnot-Roberts 2006 Clary Ranch syrah, made from grapes grown on the Sonoma Coast near Freestone, leaves no doubt of their ideals. With captivating aromas of black olives, laurel and minerals, the direct connection to the northern Rhône is clear.

In the beginning, that was the idea. Back in the 1970s and '80s, the early efforts of American syrah pioneers like Mr. Grahm, Joseph Phelps, Bob Lindquist of Qupé and Steve Edmunds of Edmunds St. John were all intended to emulate Rhône wines.

Later entrants to the game had different ideas. Syrah was barely on the radar screen in 1990 when, according to the California Department of Food and Agriculture, only 164 acres of the grape were planted in the state. Then came an explosion. By the end of that Rhône-mad decade, more than 10,000 acres were planted, and since then even that number has doubled—less perhaps than other red grapes like cabernet sauvignon, merlot, zinfandel and pinot noir, but significant nonetheless.

"People were looking for something that would not be too tannic or challenging, and syrah was poised to be that go-to drink," said Patrick Comiskey, who is writing a book about the American Rhône movement.

What happened? Partly, Mr. Comiskey said, pinot noir with its cinematic *Sideways* boost stole syrah's thunder. More damning, though, was a confusion of styles that robbed American syrah of any sense of identity.

As syrah production was beginning to take off, some American wine critics were starting to award their highest scores to big, broad, powerfully fruity wines that displayed richness and opulence. Prominent among them was Barossa Valley shiraz, as syrah is known in Australia. The desire for critical approval, Mr. Comiskey suggested, caused many American syrah producers to emulate this intensely ripe, jammy style.

"Syrah tends to lose its character at higher ripeness levels," he said. "The thing that makes syrah beguiling, beautiful and feral is all lost, and you end up with a much more generic, fruity experience."

Pax Mahle can attest to that personally. Back in 2000 he founded Pax Wine Cellars, making rich, powerful single-vineyard syrahs that were acclaimed by critics like Robert M. Parker Jr. and *Wine Spectator*. Some of these wines reached alcohol levels above 16 percent. But after a dispute with a financial backer, Mr. Mahle left Pax. He and his wife, Pamela, now make wines of a completely different style under the Wind Gap label, right here in Forestville.

"The Pax wines were good of their kind," he said. "But I found on a Tuesday or Wednesday night they were the wines I least wanted to drink."

So he recalibrated his approach, and now aims for lower alcohol, subtler, more savory wines.

"I want the wines to show more earth than fruit, more savor and spice than sweetness," he said. "I want them above all to be bright and fresh."

His 2006 Sonoma Coast syrah is full of the herbal, meaty, bacon and olive flavors craved by lovers of northern Rhône wines. It weighs in at 13.1 percent alcohol, but even his biggest wine, at 14.9 percent, from the Castelli-Knight vineyard in the Russian River Valley, is discernibly Rhônish.

Contributing to the confusion is the fact that a good deal of California syrah is simply planted in inappropriate places.

"If you want it to actually have character, it needs to be grown in a very cool climate," said Mr. Grahm of Bonny Doon Vineyards, and most top syrah producers would agree.

The Peay brothers, Nick and Andy, along with Nick's wife, Vanessa Wong, grow syrah on their vineyard near Annapolis, in the extreme northwestern corner of Sonoma County just four miles from the Pacific Ocean. There, the fruit struggles to ripen each year, but retains a freshness that comes from sufficient acidity in the grapes.

"Syrahs from warm areas lack the syrah signature of pepper, olive, meatiness, iron and mineral," Nick Peay said. "From warm areas they just have this monochromatic blueberry and oak quality."

His brother chimed in: "There is no better wine for lamb, game and meats, but people are making wines with too much alcohol, too much fruit, no elegance and too much oak."

The Peay syrahs are elegant and polished, not quite as savory as the Wind Gap or Arnot-Roberts wines, perhaps, yet still dripping with the pepper, olive, meat and animal character of syrah.

Cool climates, at least in Northern California, are not without risk. Arnot-Roberts made a delectable wine from the grapes from Clary Ranch on the Sonoma Coast in 2006. In 2009, they didn't ripen enough to make a single-vineyard wine.

As with any grape there is no single correct way of making a syrah. It mostly comes down to the personal preference of the growers and winemakers.

"The single most important thing is making a good decision about when to pick the grapes," said Mr. Edmunds of Edmunds St. John, who makes gentle, graceful syrahs with grapes purchased from a variety of sites in California. His preference is for freshness, so he tends to favor those picked on the early side. Other producers, including many in Paso Robles and Santa Barbara County, prefer riper grapes and bigger wines.

"Just because you can get it riper doesn't mean you should get it riper," said Mr. Lindquist of Qupé, who has never strayed from his original ideal of balanced, Rhône-influenced wines.

While the finest syrah producers still manage to sell their wines, it is not without a struggle. Wells Guthrie of Copain Wine Cellars makes excellent single-vineyard syrahs with enthralling mineral, saline, briny flavors. His loyal customers buy direct from the winery. Nonetheless, from the 3,000 cases of single-vineyard syrah that he made in 2006 he reduced his production to 1,200 cases in 2009.

"Without the good portion that we sell direct, I don't know how you would sell any syrah," he said.

Still, producers are keeping their hopes up. Mr. Jordan of Failla points out how young California's syrah vineyards are, and how much the grapes will improve as the vines age.

"People are already making dynamic wines, and are increasingly conscious of where things should be," he said.

Mr. Grahm, Mr. Edmunds and Mr. Lindquist, who've seen consumer interest in California syrah rise from nowhere only to crash and burn, likewise continue to focus on the potential.

"It's a great grape, obviously," Mr. Lindquist said. "And great grapes always rise to the top."

10 That Defy the Trend

Here are 10 of the best California syrah producers (which make wines that emphasize balance and savory aromas and flavors rather than power, concentration and fruitiness), along with some suggested bottles to seek out:

ARNOT-ROBERTS Clary Ranch and Griffin's Lair, both from
   Sonoma Coast.
BONNY DOON VINEYARD Le Pousseur.
COPAIN WINE CELLARS Baker Ranch, Brosseau and Hawks Butte.
A DONKEY AND GOAT Mendocino and Sierra Foothills.
EDMUNDS ST. JOHN Cuvée Fairbairn and Wylie-Fenaughty.
FAILLA Estate, Phoenix Ranch.
THE OJAI VINEYARD Melville.
PEAY VINEYARDS La Bruma and Les Titans.
QUPÉ Bien Nacido and Stolpman.
WIND GAP Sonoma Coast, Griffin's Lair.

June 2010

The Hard Stuff Now Includes Wine

By ERIC ASIMOV

Not so many years ago, back when Americans sought out compact cars and calculated their gas mileage, most California wines clocked in at an economical 12 to 13 percent alcohol. It was perhaps a shade higher than what their European colleagues achieved, but California was blessed with generous sunshine that made ripening grapes an easier proposition than in the cooler climates of Bordeaux and Burgundy.

Twenty-five years later, the 12 percent California wine seems as quaint as the gas-saving hatchback. Today, it's the rare bottle from California, red or white, that doesn't reach 14 percent alcohol. Many now hit 15, even 16 percent, a difference that may seem insignificant until you realize that a 15 percent bottle contains 25 percent more alcohol than one labeled 12 percent.

Casual consumers seem to pay little attention to the small print on the label that indicates the approximate alcohol content. And while these extreme wines do not hide their alcohol levels, few winemakers trumpet them, either.

In fact, many of these wines come from some of California's most critically acclaimed producers, who charge from $25 to $100 or more a bottle. Clearly, consumers intent on intoxication can find far cheaper pathways, like a bottle of bourbon with 40 percent alcohol.

But among California producers and those who follow wine closely, the wines have provoked sharp debate.

Opponents have called them wines on steroids, and insist that the qualities of elegance and subtlety, and the ability to evolve gracefully with age, so prized in traditional wines, are completely lost. Wine's place on the dinner table, they say, is in danger, too. These wines, they argue, overwhelm food instead of enhancing it. High alcohol can create the impression of sweetness, which can clash with food. And then there's the headache factor, not to mention the issue of driving.

"You raise the alcohol just a couple percent in wine, and you change people's experience," said Andrew Murray, a winemaker in Santa Barbara County, who says he has tried taming the alcohol in his wines. "The old concept, my wife and I can split a bottle of wine with dinner, is no longer true."

Proponents say the alcohol level is irrelevant, as long as the wines are balanced and taste good. They complain that opponents are judging them by Old

255

World benchmarks. These producers assert that they are carving out an identity for California in the most traditional fashion, by allowing the wines to reflect the characteristics of the soil and climate in which the grapes are grown. They contend that higher alcohol levels are not a flaw as long as other factors, like acidity, which gives a wine zing, and tannins, which give it structure, do their part.

"We're not trying to be Burgundy, we're not trying to be California pinot," said Greg Brewer, who, with his partner, Steve Clifton, makes pinot noir and chardonnay in the Santa Rita Hills of western Santa Barbara County. "We're only interested in the two grapes that grow best in the area in which we live." The Brewer-Clifton wines are often above 15 percent alcohol. They are intense, but unlike many of the high-alcohol wines they can be balanced and graceful as well.

"It's a number," Mr. Brewer said, dismissing the focus on alcohol. "Are people checking the B.T.U.'s on a chef's burner?"

At the Adega Restaurant and Wine Bar in Denver, where the higher-alcohol wines are popular, the issue of percentages almost never comes up, said Aaron Foster, the wine director. "Their popularity is due to the name recognition," he said. "To a certain degree, most people assume that wines are all the same, and they're looking at taste."

High alcohol levels are not completely new in California. Zinfandels have a long history of surpassing 15 and 16 percent. What's different are the wines from grapes not known for producing blockbuster alcohol levels. The Heavyweight 2003, a blend of cabernet sauvignon, merlot and two other grapes from Behrens & Hitchcock in the Napa Valley, weighs in at 15.6 percent. A 2001 roussanne from Sine Qua Non is at 15.5 percent. The 2002 Hard Core, a blended red wine from Core in eastern Santa Barbara County, hit 15.7 percent. Syrahs from Pax Wine Cellars in northern California regularly approach 16 percent, while the Bulladóir, a 2002 syrah from the Garretson Wine Company in Paso Robles, reached nearly 17 percent. Each of these wines has received scores of 90 points or higher from Robert M. Parker Jr., the influential wine critic.

"It used to be anything above 14 percent was really up there," said Bob Lindquist of Qupé Wine Cellars, who has been making wine in Santa Barbara County since the 1970s. "Now, 15 is the new 14."

Around the world, a few wines, like Amarone in northeast Italy, are typically above 15 percent. Australia has had many high-alcohol wines, and in hot years, like 2003 in France, some producers may achieve elevated alcohol levels. But nowhere else can match California's concentration of extreme wines.

In the state, the alcohol watershed came roughly around 1990. Previously, grape growers judged the ripeness of their grapes simply by gauging the sugar content. When the grapes hit a certain point on the Brix scale, which measures sugar content, they were picked. In the last 15 years, though, the buzz phrase has been "physiological ripeness." This takes into account the ripeness of other parts of the grape, like the seeds and the skins. A physiologically ripe grape, in which the seeds have turned from green to brown, yields softer, more supple tannins with less astringency, making traditionally long-lived wines easier to drink at an earlier age.

In most California vineyards, the seeds and skins lag behind sugar in reaching their ideal level of ripeness. As the seeds and skins ripen, the grapes get sweeter and sweeter. Growers using the standard of physiological ripeness are picking grapes at a much higher sugar level than they had previously.

That's only part of it. Many winemakers say that scientific advances in viti-culture have turned grapevines from plow horses into thoroughbreds, able to photosynthesize sunshine into sugar far more efficiently than a couple of decades ago. Scientists have sharply reduced the viruses that used to afflict leaves and turn them a brilliant red late in the growing season. Now those leaves are green and absorbing far more light than before. In the modern nursery, growers are able to select their rootstocks, graft them to any number of grapevine clones, and in a sense custom-design their own grape-producing factories.

"Because we've done such a great job in the selection of budwood and elimi-nated the viruses, photosynthesis is working far more efficiently," said R. Michael Mondavi, the former chief executive of the Robert Mondavi Corporation, who is now a consultant. "It's forcing people to have much higher sugar levels before the skin and seeds become mature."

In order to deal with ultra-sweet grape juice, scientists have developed vora-cious strains of yeast that are far more efficient in transforming sugar into alcohol than wimpier yeasts of old.

"These are Schwarzenegger kinds of yeasts," said Bruno D'Alfonso, the wine-maker at Sanford Winery in the Santa Rita Hills. "They would ferment a building if given a chance."

Mr. Mondavi does not favor the higher-alcohol wines.

"To me a wine is a beverage to be enjoyed with a meal," he said. "These wines remind me of what my grandfather used to do with a big, heavy wine. He would add water, then drink it with his meal."

In fact, Mr. Mondavi's grandfather used a technique not that different from what some winemakers do to avoid having wines too high in alcohol. They add water to their grape juice before fermenting it into wine, resulting in less alcohol by volume.

"I pick ripe and water back," said Mr. D'Alfonso, saying out loud what many winemakers would prefer not to admit. "I shoot for between 14.2 and 14.5. But I've had wines that were above 14.8 and they were balanced."

Other winemakers employ more advanced methods, like reverse osmosis or spinning cone columns, which can remove alcohol from wines after they are made. "Pick at 16 percent, spin a third of it down to 12, then blend it together under 15 percent," said Jim Clendenen, owner of Au Bon Climat Winery in Santa Barbara County.

Mr. Clendenen continues to make wines under 14 percent, and occasionally under 13 percent. So does Randy Dunn, owner of Dunn Vineyards in the Napa Valley, who makes powerful cabernet sauvignons that are always long lived. His 2001 weighed in under 13.8 percent, and he tries to keep his wines in that range, even if he has to resort to techniques like reverse osmosis. Figures like 13.8 percent, by the way, are not as accurate as they seem. A wine below 14 percent, according to federal regulations, has a margin of error of plus or minus 1.5 percent. Above 14 percent, the margin of error is reduced to 1 percent. And for reasons that are more arcane than scientific, the federal government taxes wines above 14 percent at a higher rate ($1.57 a gallon) than those 14 percent or lower ($1.07). Winemakers seem not to care.

"I go with, the numbers be damned if you're picking the fruit when it's really ripe," said Mat Garretson of the Garretson Wine Company, whose wines typically run from 15 to 17 percent alcohol. He acknowledges that his wines may be a little much at a dinner party.

"To do more than two or three of those at a meal is kind of scary," Mr. Garretson said. "I know that does present a problem for some people, but I'm just trying to make the best wines I can from the area. There's a lot more pain to be had from people who pick too early or pick too late."

April 2005

The Day California Shook the World

By FRANK J. PRIAL

O
n May 24, 1976, six weeks before America's bicentennial celebration, there occurred in Paris a tasting that American winemakers and cultural historians have come to characterize as the defining moment in the evolution of fine wine in this country.

The effects on the California wine industry, as well as its distributors and, indeed, their customers, were profound. The winemakers had known they could make great wine; wineries like Beaulieu and Inglenook had been doing it for at least 30 years. What the Paris tasting did was bolster their self-esteem. It encouraged many who had been content making mediocre wine to go for the very best.

More important, it showed American consumers that they no longer had to look abroad for fine wine. Little more than a decade earlier, a general American embarrassment had greeted President Lyndon B. Johnson's decree that American embassies serve only American wines.

At that tasting 25 years ago, nine judges, all prominent French food and wine people, gathered in the enclosed courtyard of the Paris Inter-Continental Hotel and tasted 20 wines, red and white, French and American. The tasting was blind; all the bottles were covered; no one was told which were French, which were American.

When the bottles were unwrapped, the tasters were astonished to discover that the highest scorers were American: a 1973 cabernet sauvignon from Stag's Leap Wine Cellars and a 1973 chardonnay from Chateau Montalena, both from the Napa Valley. Under the headline "Judgment of Paris," *Time* magazine said that the "unthinkable" had happened: "California defeated all Gaul."

The tasting had been staged by Steven Spurrier, a 34-year-old Englishman who ran a wine shop and wine school just off the Place de la Madeleine. It grew from the influence of many of his customers and students, most of whom were American. I.B.M.'s French headquarters, with its cadre of upwardly mobile young Yankee executives, was just across the street.

In 1975, intrigued by their talk of American wines, he sent his American partner, Patricia Gallagher, to California. She was so impressed that Mr. Spurrier made his own voyage of discovery.

He returned to France excited by what he had found and determined to arrange a tasting event. He hoped to twit the xenophobic French, publicize the fine California wines he had found and, understandably, win some publicity for himself.

He succeeded on all three counts. The French tasters, who included the chief inspector of the Institut National des Appellations d'Origine Contrôlée, the owners of two famous Paris restaurants and the sommelier of a third, were true to form. They lavished praise on what they thought were French wines and derided those they thought were American.

The California reds were all cabernet sauvignon; the French reds all cabernet-based Bordeaux. The California whites were chardonnay, the French whites Burgundy chardonnay. Here is how the judges ranked the wines.

The reds, in order of finish: Stag's Leap Wine Cellars, 1973; Mouton-Rothschild, 1970; Haut-Brion, 1970; Montrose, 1970; Ridge Vineyards Monte Bello, 1971; Léoville-Las-Cases, 1971; Mayacamas Vineyards, 1971; Clos du Val, 1972; Heitz Cellars, Martha's Vineyard, 1970; Freemark Abbey, 1969.

White: Chateau Montelena, 1973; Domaine Roulot, Meursault-Charmes, 1973; Chalone Vineyard, 1974; Spring Mountain Vineyards, 1973; Joseph Drouhin, Beaune Clos des Mouches, 1973; Freemark Abbey, 1972; Ramonet-Prudhon, Bâtard-Montrachet, 1973; Domaine Leflaive, Puligny-Montrachet, Les Pucelles, 1972; Veedercrest Vineyards, 1972; David Bruce, 1973.

"The egg on the judges' collective faces," wrote Paul Lukacs in his *American Vintage* (Houghton Mifflin, 2000), "came from their inability to discern what until then everyone had assumed was obvious—namely, that great French wines tasted better than other wines because they tasted, well, French."

Still, there is one notion that the tasting should have dispelled, and that is that California wines do not last. I don't know why the doubt persisted, but perhaps because it did, Mr. Spurrier decided to recreate the red-wine tasting in 1986.

By then, the wines were 13 to 16 years old. The French ones were in perfect condition, but so were the Americans. And a California wine again placed first—this time, Clos du Val—and the Ridge Monte Bello was second. The Stag's Leap 1973 was sixth, after three French wines, but hardly because of age. Warren Winiarski, who owns Stag's Leap Wine Cellars, served it at a dinner I attended at Stag's Leap six weeks ago. It was in beautiful condition.

For the French, the impact of all the comparisons, starting with the first tasting, has been subdued. One early result was that it became easier for French and

American winemakers to overcome their mutual suspicion and begin to exchange visits and information. It is a rare California winery these days that doesn't employ a French apprentice or two, while young Americans can be found pulling hoses and scrubbing tanks in wineries in France.

But the overall effect on the French has become more evident over the years: American wines may still be rare in the French market, but then many French wines, particularly Bordeaux, now taste like American wines. Bordeaux producers have always prided themselves on their wines' restraint, elegance and subtlety. But anyone who tastes them regularly can attest to how much more fruity, full-bodied and forward many have become.

Once, chateau owners were proud to say their wines took three decades to mature. Now there are Bordeaux winemakers who, like many Californians, insist that their wines are ready to drink after a few years.

One major change, both in France and California, is price. In its June 7, 1976, issue, Time magazine said of the Paris tasting: "The U.S. winners are little known to wine lovers, since they are in short supply even in California and rather expensive."

Time's definition of expensive? "$6 plus."

May 2001

A Dissenter's View of California Wines

By FRANK J. PRIAL

I used to be among those who were constantly trying to write something perceptive and flattering about California wines. "The California miracle . . . 30 years ago an industry in ruins . . . up from the ashes of Prohibition . . . new wineries every week . . . better and better . . . more and more"—not original, but heartfelt.

Not surprisingly, a couple of years in Europe, away from that charged atmosphere, effects a few changes. Actually it started fairly early in my tour. Lonely travelers would appear bearing California wines in their kits. They—the wines, not the travelers—seemed to have lost some of their charm, the reds in particular. Was it some kind of latent snobbism? Was it possible to become the Henry James of wine, eager to embrace the Old World and shuck off the New?

Then there were a couple of trips home and the concomitant access to plenty of California wine. Same results. I found myself asking, reluctantly, what all the fuss was about? The wines were good, some of them, and often delightful to drink. But the unremitting enthusiasm of their fans and promoters, the breathlessness, seemed excessive. The miracle seemed a bit more commonplace; it appeared that, having expressed our amazement that the dog could talk, it was time to determine what it might have to say.

Ask a professional marketing man about wine statistics and he will dazzle you with charts: huge increases in purchases, in per capita consumption; America becoming a wine-drinking nation. Then ask him about what America drinks. Wine dwindles into relative insignificance. Another batch of charts will show that while it is true that consumption has gone up, it is also true that the number of people who drink wine has not.

In America wine has its own newsletters, its own stars, its own clubs, even its own vocabulary. Where else in the world would someone sip a little wine and then, with a straight face, remark, "I understand they brought these grapes in at 24 Brix."

What is or are "Brix"? Sorry, you are not a member. Cultists flourish not so much on shared joys as on imagined enemies. American wine enthusiasts dearly love the image of the French expert, white-faced and with fists clenched because he has just identified a California cabernet as a Château Mouton-Rothschild 1945.

Indeed, the French wine world—the people who make it, the people who sell it and, to a lesser degree, the people who drink it—are intensely interested in the American wine scene. They love to visit our wineries and vineyards, they love to welcome American winemakers here and, given the problem of the language barrier, they are happy to receive touring American wine drinkers. They just do not consider American wines particularly good. They do believe that American wines will one day be very good—but not for a long time and probably not from the vineyards we now consider among the best. I am inclined to agree.

This is no blinding Archimedian revelation. There were, for me, those years at the Los Angeles County Fair, judging literally hundreds of California wines— judging them with California vintners—and in many categories finding it difficult to come up with something drinkable. And these were wines their producers thought worthy of honors.

Recently a reformed newspaperman turned California wine fan appeared in Paris. Here is one of the stories he told: It seems that there is a small winery "up in the valley" whose output is highly prized by the cognoscenti, so much so that the winemaker-proprietor can sell everything he makes with his mailing list. My friend was ecstatic because he had been able to take over a place on the list from a friend who preferred drugs.

This particular winery does produce good wines, but not all are worth getting in line for. The notion that one winery will turn out consistently superior wines, year in year out, the way Cartier does watches, is absurd. This is not wine drinking; it is a kind of bush league elitism, like clothes with someone else's name on them.

Not that elitism is confined to the customers. An astute Frenchwoman with years in the wine trade said recently: "I adore the California chardonnays, but I don't know what to do with them. They certainly don't go with meals." She was half right. They are meant to go with meals, but many of them do not. Like overbred dogs, they have gone beyond their original purpose. They are too aggressive, too alcoholic. They are showoff wines made by vintners who seem to be saying, "I can out-chardonnay any kid on this block."

We took one of those macho white wines from a famous North Coast winery to a dinner at a three-star restaurant in the French countryside. We matched it with a famous Burgundy. Both were chardonnays, from optimum vintages and in the same price range. At first the California wine was impressive and the French wine seemed weak and bland. Twenty minutes into the meal, however, the American wine was clumsy and overpowering while the charm and subtlety of the French wine was only beginning to emerge.

If I mentioned the name of the California wine, a host of its devotees—well, two or three—would leap forward growling. "Why, that wine took top honors in my last 15 tastings!" an opthalmologist would cry. Exactly. There should be a special label warning that says: "This wine was designed for competition and is not to be used for family dining."

What is this frantic tasting business all about, anyway? Is it not possible to enjoy wine without having won the equivalent of a black belt?

The point is this: The drinking of wine in America, particularly American wine, is on the brink of becoming inbred and precious. Wine enthusiasts, including we writers, who should know better, ape the jargon of the trade and feel special when we exchange arcane trivia about grape crushers, red spiders and who is opening next week's winery. A continuing hyperbole competition distorts wines, places and people beyond recognition.

One day the rest of the country, bemused and probably irritated by all this, might just shrug and walk away. Thousands of people wake up every day, smile and say: "I don't have to play tennis anymore or listen to people who do." One day the same people might wake up and say: "I don't have to drink wine either, or listen to—or read—people who do."

September 1981

An Actress's Presence Is Still Felt

By TERRY ROBARDS

A plume of yellowish dust rises from a distant field, signaling a plow at work, as Butts Canyon Road snakes through the farmland of northern California en route to a patch of vineyard and an old house that once was the country home of Lillie Langtry, star of the British and American stage, who summered here before the turn of the century.

The road is a strip of macadam that soon turns to hardpan and gravel as it runs past cattle and horses grazing beneath shade trees near a creek, past a young woman in a white cotton dress hitchhiking with two small children in the bright summer sun, past the Circle D Ranch before dipping into a canyon where the Guenoc Valley begins.

Now the road twists and turns as it passes Dedert Reservoir, and the land is a little greener. Suddenly vines are growing as we make a turn up an unmarked road along Bucksnort Creek and then through an open gate and on to the house that Miss Langtry bought in 1887 for $82,000. The price seems modest, for it included 4,200 acres of Lake County, an area that is emerging as a producer of fine California wines.

The house stands in the vineyard, a wooden structure with an outside staircase leading to the second-floor veranda that opens into Lillie's bedroom, with its westward view into the setting sun across the chardonnay vines. A canopied four-poster bed stands near a closet with a window so that her gowns could be aired in the cool night breezes.

A Victorian chaise is positioned across a corner on the plank flooring, and there is a sense that time is standing still here in this remote and rugged part of the West. Lillie Langtry, once the mistress of Prince Albert, who became King Edward VII, used this house as her country home from 1888 to 1906, a retreat far from her public, a place to come to between American tours.

Now we are downstairs at dinner at a great round table beneath an ornate chandelier, and Orville Magoon is saying: "Just think, Lillie and all those folks were sitting right here just like us. I've read so much about her, I've fallen in love with Lillie Langtry."

Orville Magoon and his brother Eaton Magoon Jr. are the principal owners of the Guenoc Ranch and the Guenoc Winery. They are Hawaiians by birth who, in a tax deal, exchanged land in Honolulu for 23,000 acres of northern California, equal to some 36 square miles. Their great-grandfather, John Henry Magoon, a Scotsman, sailed to Hawaii in the 1880s, married a Hawaiian princess and developed cattle ranches and plantations in the islands.

Now a portion of that fortune has been converted to cattle land and vineyards here, and the Langtry house is the centerpiece. Wild boars, coyotes, deer, bears and occasional mountain lions roam the ranch. Its lakes are filled with large-mouth bass, and quail and wild turkeys nest in the brush.

"This was the best swap we ever made," says Orville Magoon in a reference to his family's acquisition of the Guenoc Valley in 1963. The purchase was facilitated by a provision of the law that enables land in one area to be sold on a tax-free basis under certain circumstances if the proceeds are reinvested in land elsewhere.

The winery and vineyards established here by the Magoons are among the most extraordinary in the nation. The federal government has granted them the right to a new viticultural appellation, Guenoc Valley, and it is the only one in the United States entirely under one ownership. It is almost as if the Napa Valley, some 50 miles to the south, where 135 wineries now operate, were owned and operated by only one, although the Guenoc Valley is somewhat smaller.

The Guenoc winery is an enormous structure ingeniously hidden by a ridge from Butts Canyon Road and from the Langtry house. It is a redwood structure containing 55,000 square feet of floor space, the largest building of any kind in Lake County and probably the largest winery built in California in recent years.

"It was kind of fun designing it, knowing you're going to go first-cabin," says Walter Raymond, the winemaker, who also is one of the proprietors of Raymond Vineyards in the Napa Valley. He and his brother Roy, the vineyardist, are responsible for the wines that the Guenoc Winery will be marketing within the next few months.

The first planting of vines under the Magoon proprietorship took place in 1972, involving a dozen grape varieties to determine which would yield the best wines in the Lake County climate. Now the choice has narrowed down to sauvignon blanc, chardonnay, chenin blanc, cabernet sauvignon, merlot and small amounts of malbec and petit verdot for blending. There are also plots of zinfandel and petite sirah.

Eleven years of experimentation so far, and the first commercial crop, the 1980 vintage, has not even been marketed yet. "One of the questions you ask yourself," says Orville Magoon, "is whether you want to take 11 years of your life and do this. The answer is yes."

The 1981 chenin blanc—a crisp, dry white—goes on the market next month. It will be the first wine to carry the Guenoc Valley appellation. Later will come a 1981 chardonnay and 1980 cabernet sauvignon and petite sirah. The cabernet, initially bearing a North Coast appellation because only half the grapes came from the Guenoc Valley, is a balanced, intensely fruity red that was already charming when tasted in May.

A 1981 zinfandel, also sampled in May, displayed a spicy aroma and was full-bodied, rich, highly textured and peppery in flavor. Experimental bottlings of the cabernet and merlot from the 1977 vintage were superb, providing a clue as to how the more recent, commercial vintages will mature.

The winery was opened officially last spring with a feast at the Langtry house. Four wild boars were trapped, slaughtered and barbecued over an open-pit fire. A cast of actors and actresses reenacted some of the scenes from Miss Langtry's performances, and the first Guenoc wines were served.

The cooler for the whites was the old cast-iron bathtub removed from Lillie's quarters when the house was renovated. It was almost as if she were still here after nearly a century, parasol in hand, bonnet on her head, overseeing the festivities.

July 1982

A Farewell to the Baron of Bully Hill

By FRANK J. PRIAL

Dinner was supposed to be at 8. At 9 and again at 10, the guest of honor called, hopelessly lost in our New Jersey suburbs. We talked him in, so to speak, and close to 11 he appeared, in boots and cowboy hat, swearing mightily and with a case of wine under each arm. He was Walter S. Taylor, and he had arrived.

Walter, the self-styled Baron of Bully Hill, his winery in the Finger Lakes region, had invited himself. It would be the perfect way to show off his wines, he had said. He ended up presiding over a cold dinner and a tasting that, perfect or not, lasted until almost 5 a.m. Then he raced off to another engagement.

That was years ago. Walter Taylor—outrageous, flamboyant, single-minded, immature, irritating, charming—died April 20 at his home in Hammondsport, N.Y., at 69. He had been a quadriplegic since a 1990 minivan accident in Florida.

He was the scion of an old upstate New York family. His great-grandfather had been a cooper. His grandfather, the first Walter Taylor, founded the Taylor Wine Company in 1880 and built a business making wine from native labrusca grapes like the Concord. Labruscas withstand harsh upstate winters but produce a harsh-tasting wine. To make labrusca wines more palatable, they are often cut with water, California wine or grape juice concentrate.

In the 1950s, most winemakers thought that delicate European vines like chardonnay and merlot could not survive the bitter winters of the Finger Lakes. But a few farmers were experimenting with French-American hybrids, crosses between rugged American varieties and the European vines. Walter believed that the wines produced from these hybrids were vastly superior to what his family and the rest of the New York State industry had been making for 70 years, and he began saying so, loudly and often.

In 1970, fed up with his criticism, the family banished him from the Taylor Wine Company, which in 1977 it sold to the Coca-Cola Company. But he and his father, Greyton, had meanwhile bought back the first Walter Taylor's original vineyard, just outside Hammondsport, on the high hills overlooking Keuka Lake. It was called Bully Hill, and it was planted with hybrids.

Using only hybrids, Walter produced a large selection of wines with names like Old Trawler White, Meat Market Red, Space Shuttle Rosé and Le Goat

Blush. The names, along with his unflagging self-promotion and the labels he designed, made Bully Hill the best-known winery in New York State. But he continued his attacks on the New York State wine industry, particularly the Taylor Wine Company.

He once had a railroad tank car hauled up to his vineyard to show visitors how many local winemakers, rather than using hybrid grapes, shipped in California wine and blended it with their product.

After it bought Taylor, the Coca-Cola Company wasted no time in going after Walter. In short order, a federal court judge enjoined him from just about everything but wearing his farmer's overalls. Most serious of all: he could no longer use the Taylor name on any of his wines.

Undaunted, he gathered 200 fans and, at a highly publicized tasting, had them ink his name off hundreds of bottles of Bully Hill wine. He designed a label bearing a picture of a goat and the slogan: "They Have My Name and My Heritage, but They Didn't Get My Goat." Decanter, a British wine magazine, declared it the ugliest label of the year.

Other labels depicted him as the Lone Ranger, with the inevitable caption: "Who Was That Masked Man?" He distributed bumper stickers that said, "Enjoy Bully Hill, the Un-Taylor." Another label showed an owl and was inscribed "Walter S. Who?"

All this humor earned him a further citation for contempt; he was ordered to turn over to the Taylor Wine Company all the offending material he had produced. "We brought it down to them in a manure spreader," he said at the time.

"I have been thrown out of the New York State wine industry," he once told me, "out of my local club, even the Hammondsport Episcopal church. Everybody in my family, except my father, my 10-year-old son and my winemaker, deserted me. The community completely rejected me and treated me like a dog. Why? Because I wanted honesty and integrity in the wine business."

It was a well-rehearsed speech; one he clearly relished. It was also irrelevant, because Walter Taylor was a transitional figure in the industry. He was right about labrusca grapes; they had had their day. But the hybrid grapes he championed were transitional, too.

Hermann J. Wiemer, whose family had made wine in Germany for generations, joined Bully Hill as winemaker in 1968, producing only hybrid wines. But he rejected the idea that vinifera grapes could not survive the Finger

Lakes climate. Another winemaker, Konstantin Frank, had grown them near Hammondsport in the '50s.

In 1973, while continuing to work for Bully Hill, Mr. Wiemer started a small winery of his own on nearby Seneca Lake, making vinifera wines, especially riesling. On Christmas Eve 1979, while Mr. Wiemer was with his family in Germany, Walter Taylor fired him, presumably for his disloyalty to hybrids.

Bully Hill offers some vinifera wines now, but it is still firmly rooted in the hybrid culture. And for Bully Hill, that works. Under the direction of Walter's widow, Lillian Taylor, the winery turns out around 200,000 cases a year and, in its museum and in its restaurant, entertains some 150,000 visitors annually. "On weekends you can't get in the parking lot," a friend told me. The Baron may be gone, but Bully Hill is booming. Not a bad legacy for a gadfly.

May 2001

CHAPTER EIGHT

You're Feeling Continental? This Is for You.

In the World of Fine Wine, There'll Always Be a France

By ERIC ASIMOV

Permit me to speak briefly in praise of France.

Yes, France, the greatest wine-producing nation in the world.

Don't look so shocked. I've heard about the Judgment of Paris, the famous blind tasting in which French and American wines went glass-to-glass in 1976, and the French lost. I know all about the greatness of California cabernets and shiraz from Australia, and I understand that the French lag in the clever global marketing of instantly recognizable brands of wine.

Nonetheless, no country comes close to matching France, either in setting demanding standards for its wine industry or in producing such a variety of consistently excellent wine. Bordeaux, Burgundy, Champagne and the Rhône go without saying, but those famous regions are simply the most visible. From Jurançon in the southwest to Jura in the east, from Nantes on the Atlantic to Alsace on the German border, France makes wines that are endlessly compelling and should be endlessly inspiring.

Why is it necessary for me to state what should be obvious? Because a prevailing attitude toward France and its wines, in the New World at least, seems stuck somewhere between pity and glee for an industry supposedly rotting from within.

New World producers and journalists like to jeer at the sacred French notion of terroir as a myth constructed to preserve French status in the industry, and they laugh at the rigidity of the French appellation rules, which dictate what French growers can plant, where they can plant it, and how they should tend the vines. The European Union's recent decision to spend millions of dollars in an effort to diminish a European wine glut by digging up vineyards and turning excess wine into ethanol contributed to a confused perception of industry-wide crisis. The perception springs from an oversimplification of the French wine business, and no doubt a bit of wishful thinking.

The latest chorus of American gloating was heard around the time of the 30th anniversary celebration of the Paris tasting, even as many of these same gloaters were lining up to pay record prices for the heralded 2005 vintage of Bordeaux. When French winemakers were understandably reluctant to participate in yet another re-enactment in May, American wine writers were quick to play the cowardice card. And when the event feebly played out, and the Americans won again, writers exulted.

"Sacré bleu! Make that red, white and blue," Linda Murphy wrote in *The San Francisco Chronicle,* which can perhaps be forgiven for boosterish support of an industry in its backyard. In maybe the unkindest blow of all, Hollywood is apparently considering a movie version of the original event, based on the book *Judgment of Paris: California vs. France and the Historic 1976 Paris Tasting That Revolutionized Wine* (Scribner, 2005), by George M. Taber.

Maybe it's payback for years of supercilious French sneering at the American wine industry. Or maybe Americans just need to lash out to pump themselves up with competitive energy, like football players pounding their lockers in an adrenalin-fueled frenzy. Any way you look at it, American wine partisans have got themselves a punching bag and they call it France.

Business-oriented types look at the French wine industry as old and tired. Through rigidity, bureaucracy and lack of creativity, they say, once-dominant France clings to old and outdated ways, and can no longer compete with modern wine powers like Australia, the United States, Chile and South Africa.

Those sympathetic to France heave a sigh, shrug their shoulders and say, What can you do? Meanwhile, some of the harshest critics are among the French themselves, particularly growers and winemakers in less prestigious areas, or entrepreneurs who feel hamstrung by French wine laws.

Make no mistake. France's troubles, as far as the wine business goes, are many. Consumption at home has dropped precipitously as the culture that once prized the long lunch and the arduous construction of a meal has taken a route toward convenience foods, quickly gobbled. The quest for productivity in a globalized economy, no doubt, has also taken its toll on daytime consumption, while stricter drunken-driving laws have also had an effect. Troubled fortunes in the wine economies of Bordeaux and the Languedoc are well known, if not well understood. And France's share of the wine export market has tumbled as well.

What's crucial to understand is that France has two entirely different wine economies, and one should not be confused with the other. The first produces oceans of cheap, occasionally palatable wine, sold for immediate consumption under lowly appellations, like plain Bordeaux or Beaujolais, for example, rather than the more prestigious and more specific St.-Julien or Juliénas. This industry is indeed in a deep crisis, with many growers hurting badly. Historically, much of this wine was for domestic consumption, and this segment has taken the biggest hit as the market has shrunk. Producers who would like to sell these wines overseas say they feel hampered because they cannot compete against the cleverly branded bottles of New World producers, who often use winemaking techniques unavailable to French producers.

The other industry makes the middle to high-end wines, those sold around the world, consumed in restaurants and reviewed in publications like *Wine Spectator*. Producers like Sylvain Pitiot, who makes the seductive, voluptuous Clos de Tart, a grand cru Burgundy, are doing exceptionally well, regardless of how many gallons of French wine the European Union wishes to convert to fuel. Like Clos de Tart, much of the high-quality end of the business is prospering.

In many ways, the French A.O.C. laws, for appellation d'origine contrôlée, which protect quality at the top, are simultaneously responsible for the demise of the low end. In other words, the law that insures the meaning of St.-Julien by dictating what the wine is made of and how it is labeled can stifle the producer of ordinary Bordeaux, who might want to legally blend some syrah into the cabernet sauvignon, or call the wine by a cute, memorable brand name—not Yellow Tail, but maybe Red Head. But while a producer in the Languedoc might wish he could pull out all his grenache and replace it with syrah, a Burgundy producer like Mr. Pitiot would be appalled at the idea of somebody wasting precious pinot noir territory by replacing it with merlot.

It may be that both ends of the French wine industry can only work at cross purposes, with the Old World tradition of exalting specific place names struggling against the New World merchandising power of the brand name. For France to try to accommodate the low end by compromising the standards that have insured its high-end dominance might in the end be catastrophic for the whole industry.

"Europeans should realize they can't play that New World game," said Neal Rosenthal, an American wine importer who is devoted to the concept of terroir. "They're better off protecting what they have and making sure people better understand the reasons behind it."

Not that the standards can't be beneficially modified. In a recent column in *Decanter*, a British consumer magazine, Michel Bettane, the French wine critic, suggested that St.-Émilion would be a fine place to plant chardonnay, which is currently not permitted under A.O.C. rules. Maybe so. And as in any bureaucracy, a stultifying rigidity often makes rational decision making difficult. But on the whole, the A.O.C. rules do far more to protect greatness than to prevent it.

While a further decline on the bottom end of the industry will have a tremendous social and human cost in France, it won't undermine the greatness of French wines. It's possible to imagine that France will be joined at the top by countries like Italy and Spain, which produce distinguished, singular wines like Barolo and Rioja, and are working hard to improve the quality in distinctive regions that have long been ignored.

It's harder to imagine New World countries like the United States and Australia reaching the same pinnacle. Their leading wines, whether made of cabernet, chardonnay, shiraz or pinot noir, will always be measured against the French, and regardless of the blind tasting here or there, few people really take seriously the notion that the New World wines will surpass the French reference points on a large scale. What's more important about New World wines is how they have improved their quality on the low-to-middle ranks, to the point where today it is possible to say that very few bad wines are produced.

No, France will always set a standard, barring some sort of colossal, self-destructive move, like gutting its appellation rules. Should that happen, Americans and the rest of the world would then have great cause to jeer.

July 2006

The Paler Shade of Bordeaux

By ERIC ASIMOV

I f you prefer a manual transmission, a vacuum tube amplifier or a phone that is just a phone and not a media center, then you understand how it feels to be a fan of good dry white Bordeaux. It's not at all easy to find what you want.

Almost any fine restaurant will offer a wine list with enough white Burgundies and chardonnays to float an aircraft carrier. But white Bordeaux? It has an archaic ring to it, reminiscent of the days of the British Empire, when the Bordeaux region seemed like one more of the king's dominions. Back then, fine wines from Graves, historically the most prestigious region for dry white Bordeaux, preceded the claret as surely as the fish course came before the mutton.

Red wine might have always dominated perceptions about Bordeaux, but white Bordeaux was once much more of a presence. A century ago more white grapes than red grapes were planted in Bordeaux, producing wines that included the sweet whites of Sauternes and Barsac as well as the ocean of dry to semidry vin ordinaire that was usually labeled Bordeaux blanc, Entre-Deux-Mers or Graves. Much of it was dreadful stuff, and after World War II growers began shifting to red. Clive Coates, an authority on French wine, estimates that the amount of red Bordeaux produced went from about a third of the harvest in the mid-20th century to more than 85 percent by the end.

Nowadays, white Burgundies outnumber white Bordeaux by roughly 30 to 1 at Cru, which has one of the finest wine lists in New York City. The proportion is slightly lower at Veritas, another wine-oriented restaurant. On lesser lists, you'll find scarcely any Bordeaux in the white section, which is full of wines from Burgundy, the Loire and California, along with Alsace, Germany, New Zealand and Austria. Even allowing that the producers of fine white Burgundy vastly outnumber the producers of fine white Bordeaux, there's no denying the fact that Bordeaux is an afterthought for lovers of white wine.

"It is one of my regrets that white Graves in stately maturity is almost unknown today," Hugh Johnson, the British wine writer, recently rued.

He might mourn as well the appellation Graves, the area south of the city of Bordeaux, which suffers from greatly diminished status. In 1987 the Graves region, the only one of Bordeaux's top appellations where most leading producers make both white and red wines, was cut in two. The northern end, encompassing the Bordeaux suburbs where many historic Graves vineyards like Haut-Brion and La Mission Haut-Brion are situated, was redesignated Pessac-Léognan, and now Bordeaux's best whites bear that appellation, although they can still be spoken of as Graves and bear the name Graves on the label as well. Bottles simply labeled Graves tend to be a lower order of wine.

Even when Graves was simply Graves, great white Bordeaux was always rare, yet whites from producers like Haut-Brion, Laville-Haut-Brion and Domaine de Chevalier make indelible impressions. These whites, made of varying blends of the sémillon and sauvignon blanc grapes, can evolve and improve for several decades.

I recently had a 20-year-old Laville-Haut-Brion, the white sibling of La Mission Haut-Brion, that was light-bodied yet dazzling in its intensity, with almost extravagant flavors of anise, buttered hazelnuts, coconut and beeswax. Its former rival, Haut-Brion Blanc (Haut-Brion and La Mission are now owned by Domaine Clarence Dillon), is perhaps a little more finely etched and elegant, yet cut from a similar cloth. And then there is Domaine de Chevalier, a different sort of wine yet profoundly compelling as well, with a rich, almost viscous texture, tightly coiled with great complexity and subtlety, too.

If you can find them in retail shops, Domaine de Chevalier runs about $50 to $60 a bottle, Laville $80 to $100 or so, while Haut-Brion blanc, which is much more scarce, can cost three times as much. Still, it's much less than white Burgundy of comparable quality.

But you don't have to spend that much to get a taste of what good white Bordeaux can offer. Producers like Château Carbonnieux, Château de Fieuzal, Château Haut-Nouchet and Château Smith Haut Lafitte make fine, less expensive whites that, if they don't have the depth of the top echelon, still give a sense of its texture and intensity. Outside Pessac-Léognan, very good Graves whites come from Château du Seuil and Clos Floridène. Even a few chateaus in the Médoc, like Margaux and Talbot, make good white wines, though they lack the grace of the best Graves whites.

What accounts for the absence of white Bordeaux from the American wine consciousness today? Partly, it's because the wine industry reared a nation of chardonnay drinkers who find it easy to transfer their allegiance to white Burgundy once they understand that it, too, is made from chardonnay. While it is true that Americans, and the world, have grown quite fond of sauvignon blanc, it is a different sort of sauvignon blanc than is produced, for the most part, in Bordeaux.

The sauvignon blanc from the Loire and New Zealand, and, increasingly now, from California and South Africa, is fresh, racy and lip-smacking, vinified in steel tanks and made to be drunk young.

You can find producers that aspire to make this sort of sauvignon blanc in the Entre-Deux-Mers region, that swath of flat vineyard area between the Garonne and the Dordogne Rivers that is the source of so much of Bordeaux's inexpensive white wine. But what stamps an identity on the best Bordeaux whites is the inclusion in the blend of sémillon, a grape that is little understood outside of Bordeaux, where it is also the crucial component in Sauternes and Barsac, and Australia, where it has always had a following. Sémillon adds richness to the texture and a honeyed, nutlike note that is sometimes described as lanolin.

In most top white Bordeaux, sémillon makes up 30 percent to 70 percent of the blend. Along with sauvignon blanc, which must be at least 25 percent of the blend, a tiny bit of muscadelle and sauvignon gris may be included, too. Of all the top Graves whites, Smith Haut Lafitte uses the smallest amount of sémillon, about 5 percent, and it's easy to sense the difference. Despite the wine's aromatic complexity, it lacks the textural presence that comes from sémillon.

The other crucial component of white Bordeaux is fermentation and aging in oak barrels. This, too, contributes a sense of controlled voluptuousness to the wine, though it makes it necessary to wait a few years—or a decade, perhaps, in the case of Domaine de Chevalier—for the wines to become accessible.

Winemakers around the world have followed Burgundy's lead with chardonnay and Sancerre's with sauvignon blanc, but very few have sought to make a fine Bordeaux-style white. In the United States I can think of only Clos du Val in Napa Valley, which makes Ariadne, an excellent barrel-aged white of 70 percent sémillon and 30 percent sauvignon blanc with fine mineral flavors and the potential to age. It's fitting, since Bernard Portal, the longtime winemaker at Clos du Val, is from Bordeaux.

Meanwhile, the rest of us—Luddites of the wine world who still prize those great whites of the Graves—will cling to the hope that fashion will once more swing our way.

March 2006

The Soulful Side of Bordeaux

By ERIC ASIMOV

Compared with the grand chateaus of the Médoc, the tiny Domaine du Jaugaret may seem irrelevant. The critics don't score its wines, it's barely mentioned in guides, it doesn't play in the futures game. The winemaking facility is no more than a series of stone sheds with floors of dirt and gravel and walls covered in a mushroomlike mold. Calling it rustic would be putting it kindly.

Yet for me, the importance of a place like Domaine du Jaugaret in St.-Julien cannot be overstated. In globalized, commercial Châteaux Bordeaux, a world of brand-name products sold like luxury goods, where too many wines seem polished and lustrous yet lacking in character, Jaugaret brims with soul. Its proprietor, Jean-François Fillastre, epitomizes the French vigneron, one who tends the vines and makes the wines.

Vignerons like Mr. Fillastre make up the backbone of wine regions all over France, from Burgundy to Languedoc to the Loire, embodying the essential truth that wine is both agriculture and culture, a centuries-old expression of French character. (Indeed, Jaugaret has been in Mr. Fillastre's family for more than 350 years.) But in the famous terroirs of the Médoc like St.-Julien, Margaux, Pauillac and Sauternes, such vignerons are the rare exception.

You can still find a few, like Bruno and Pascaline Rey of Moulin de Tricot in Margaux or Francis Daney of Cru d'Arche-Pugneau in Sauternes. They are slightly more common in areas of lesser status, like Canon-Fronsac, where Bénédicte and Grégoire Hubau operate Château Moulin Pey-Labrie, or in Bordeaux Supérieur, where Pascal and Chrystel Collotte make delicious straightforward claret and an excellent rosé at Château Jean Faux.

In the wines of vignerons like these, and none more so than Mr. Fillastre's, you can taste another side of Bordeaux, one grounded in the fields and the cellars, in cultural tradition rather than in commerce. Yet because of the way the Bordeaux business works, the odds are stacked squarely against small family estates like Jaugaret, which work outside the established mode of commerce.

"I use the methods of my father, natural, no manipulation, no chemicals," Mr. Fillastre said, as we stood in a room where three vintages sat aging in old oak barrels, illuminated by lamps wreathed in cobwebs. Using a pipette made of glass that he blew himself, he pulled samples from the barrels, wines that were fresh, alive and aromatic.

"I'm not making wines for consumers," said Mr. Fillastre, who, at 67, still shows in his shoulders and forearms a hint of the decathlete he was in his youth. "I'm making wines for my own pleasure."

These words might well have been spoken elsewhere by other idiosyncratic winemakers who have gone their own way, like Gianfranco Soldera of Brunello di Montalcino, Bartolo Mascarello of Barolo, Anselme Selosse of Champagneor Henri Bonneau of Châteauneuf-du-Pape. While they are celebrated for their very personal expressions, Mr. Fillastre is lost within a region that many younger American wine lovers perceive as stodgy, dull and lacking authenticity.

If only they could try a bottle of Jaugaret, even from an unacclaimed vintage like 2002, they might feel very different. The 2002 Jaugaret St.-Julien is classically structured yet graceful and elegant, with gorgeous aromas of violets and minerals. These wines have haunted me since I first drank them a little more than two years ago. They recall an era when, as Jaugaret's American importer, Neal Rosenthal, has said, the Bordelais were modest and the wines were grand.

Even as many estates in the Médoc have planted more merlot to make softer, fruitier and easier wines for drinking young, Jaugaret's blend is dominated by cabernet sauvignon, which gives the wine structure and freshness but demands aging before it will show at its best. Mr. Fillastre keeps his wines in barrels for 30 months, far longer than most, and he primarily uses older barrels, which won't add oaky flavors but allow subtle aeration over time.

"I don't demand of the wine, it demands of me," he said, dismissing the culture of enologists and consultants who employ the latest in technology to achieve the wines they desire.

What makes the estate so compelling does not end with what's in the glass. In a land of vast scale and tremendous output, where a great chateau like Mouton-Rothschild farms 280 acres of vines and produces maybe 170,000 bottles of its top wine each year, Jaugaret is a mere 3.1 acres, divided into a half-dozen parcels, making no more than 6,000 bottles of St.-Julien a year.

Setting it further apart, Jaugaret operates outside the négociant structure that dominates Bordeaux commerce. In almost every other region, producers sell their wines directly to importers, who then market the wines in their home countries. Bordeaux still depends on middlemen, négociants, who buy wine from the chateaus and market it worldwide. They sell much of the top Bordeaux as futures, to which importers must commit money as far as two years in advance of delivery.

The system works great for the big chateaus, and for the négociants. But the large upfront expense means that much of the Bordeaux in the United States has been imported by big, wealthy companies.

Small, groundbreaking importers like Mr. Rosenthal, Kermit Lynch and Louis/Dressner Selections don't have access to the classified growths or, with a few exceptions like Jaugaret, to producers in the most famous terroirs. They confine themselves to a few small estates in satellite appellations of Bordeaux that meet their quality standards and will deal directly with importers.

Instead, they have focused on building intense followings for wines from Burgundy, the Rhône, the Loire Valley and other, more obscure areas. An entire generation of Americans has learned about Old World wines by examining the importer's label, looking for names they trust enough to take chances on obscure producers. For the most part, Bordeaux has been omitted from this educational process.

This is one reason that the region, particularly among younger drinkers, has become something of an afterthought. Is this a crisis for Bordeaux? Hardly, at least not for its upper echelon. A worldwide audience seems ever-ready to pay whatever rates are required to accumulate bottles.

And to be fair, many people buy Bordeaux because they love it. But many wine fanatics, especially those of a contrarian bent, have turned on Bordeaux as representing all the pomp and pretension they dislike in the wine world.

Sadly, they would miss the wines of Bruno and Pascaline Rey, the fourth generation of their family to operate Moulin de Tricot, which has about nine acres in Margaux and four in Haut-Médoc. Their 2009 Margaux, still in barrels, is rich, pure and light in texture. The 2005 is beautifully perfumed and intense with fresh acidity, while the 2005 Haut-Médoc has great purity but is a bit rougher, befitting the different terroir.

They do most of the work themselves. "It's a very hard life, working seven days a week with no vacations," Mr. Rey said.

What's the motivation? "Once you start to care about the vines, you don't think about doing anything else," he said. "It's not feasible for a small vigneron not to have passion."

The Reys have two children, 25 and 21, but they don't want to push them into the business. The lack of a plan for secession threatens vignerons, particularly in top terroirs like Margaux.

"Grand chateaus are looking for estates to snap up, for people who have nobody to leave it to," Mr. Rey said. "In 10 or 15 years there may not be any more small producers in the Médoc."

The sweet wines of Sauternes are no longer fashionable, short of the big names like Château d'Yquem, but to taste the Sauternes of Cru D'Arche-Pugneau is exhilarating. A 2001 is honeyed by botrytis and is complex, balanced and perfectly refreshing rather than cloying.

The 2009, still in barrels, is lovely, delicate and alive. Mr. Daney, the vigneron, is the third generation of his family to run the estate. He is a former rugby player, and with his old comrades still gathers to sing folk songs.

Standing behind his small winery, he looks across fields of vines and points at neighboring chateaus.

"That one is owned by LVMH, that one by AXA, that one by Rothschild, that one by Crédit Agricole and that one by Credit Suisse," he said. "Corporations seek to buy more and more. They have all the money."

That's not so much the issue in the area southeast of Libourne, the so-called Right Bank, where the wines are labeled Bordeaux or Bordeaux Supérieur. Many vignerons in these areas of lesser status are struggling, and corporations are not so interested in buying, which leaves openings for couples like Pascal and Chrystel Collotte, who bought and restored the chateau after success in the barrelmaking business.

Now, at Jean Faux, the Collottes live what seems to be a fantasy of the winemaking life. They fill closets with preserved fruits and vegetables, and raise pigs to make hams, sausages and charcuterie, served with their own good red wine and rosé. Mr. Collotte farms his 15 acres, largely of merlot, organically. Asked why, he looked incredulous and said, "Because I drink my wine."

His commitment drew the attention of Daniel Johnnes, the wine director for Daniel Boulud's restaurants and an importer known for educating Americans about the joys of Burgundy. Now, he has decided to add a collection of Bordeaux estates to his import portfolio. He wants to work directly with vignerons, which has put him in conflict with the négociant culture.

"All this talk in Bordeaux of classified growths and the futures market and the commerce of wine, that's not what wine's all about," he said. "But I believed there were winemakers who were connected to the traditions and the culture."

Eventually, he put together what he calls "honest wines" from about a dozen producers like Mr. Collotte, who he believes represents the vigneron culture of Bordeaux. Most will sell for $15 to $30 a bottle beginning this fall.

These are good wines, but it's safe to say few have the potential of offering the thrills of a Domaine du Jaugaret, which sells for $60 to $100 a bottle. That's a lot of money, but little compared with Jaugaret's illustrious neighbors, and perhaps a pittance given all that Jaugaret represents, and all that may one day be lost.

Mr. Fillastre is a bachelor with no children. His younger brother, Pierre, has two daughters, but Mr. Fillastre said they are not inclined to be vignerons. The future is a concern.

"If I'm sick, I could lose everything," he said. "I worry about that."

When I mentioned my visit to people in the Bordeaux establishment, not one had ever heard of Domaine du Jaugaret. Mr. Fillastre's neighbors, though, are fiercely protective. One woman, who had cross-examined me about my intentions when I arrived, accosted me again as I left.

"It's a domaine, not a chateau," she said, making sure I got it right. "Very few people do as he does. He's extraordinary."

Think Bordeaux Is Stodgy? These 10 Could Change That.

While many estates in Bordeaux are huge operations with enormous staffs, there are also small, family-run places like these 10, all of which I've found particularly enjoyable.

CRU D'ARCHE-PUGNEAU Exquisite Sauternes, $50 to $75.
  (Rosenthal Wine Merchant, New York)
CHÂTEAU ANEY Classically shaped Haut-Médoc, $25.
  (Kermit Lynch Wine Merchants, Berkeley, Calif.)
CHÂTEAU BEAUSÉJOUR Fruity, earthy Montagne-St.-Émilion,
  $15 to $30. (Daniel Johnnes Selections/Michael Skurnik Wines,
  Syosset, N.Y.)
CHÂTEAU DE BELLEVUE Plush, mineral-laden Lussac-St.-Émilion,
  $25. (Kermit Lynch Wine Merchants)
DOMAINE DU JAUGARET Profound, old-school St.-Julien,
  $55 to $100. (Rosenthal Wine Merchant)

CHÂTEAU JEAN FAUX Gulpable red and rosé Bordeaux Supérieur, $15 to $30. (Daniel Johnnes Selections/Michael Skurnik Wines)

CHÂTEAU LANESSAN Classic bistro Haut-Médoc, $20. (Fruit of the Vines, Long Island City, N.Y.)

CHÂTEAU MOULIN DE TRICOT Pleasingly raspy Haut-Médoc; perfumed, intense yet graceful Margaux, $30 to $45. (Rosenthal Wine Merchant)

CHÂTEAU MOULIN PEY-LABRIE Plush, earthy merlot from Canon-Fronsac, $25. (Louis/Dressner Selections, New York)

CHÂTEAU LA PEYRE Fresh, minerally St.-Éstèphe, $40. (Rosenthal Wine Merchants)

August 2010

The 1855 Ratings, Etched in Stone (Almost)

By FRANK J. PRIAL

The 1855 classification of the wines of Bordeaux is probably the most important wine list ever written. Yet, few people, even many knowledgeable wine drinkers, know why it is important or even why it was made in the first place.

In 1851, Britain mounted a spectacular exhibition at the Crystal Palace in London to show off its industrial might. Not to be outdone, the French decided that they, too, would show the world what they could do.

In March 1853, barely three months into France's Second Empire, a great Universal Exposition was decreed. To be held in Paris two years hence, it would celebrate a return to French grandeur, the wonders of modern industry and, not least, the glorious—if faintly illegitimate—apotheosis of Louis Napoleon, citizen, into Napoleon III, Emperor of France.

It was a time not unlike our own. Money was plentiful, peace reigned and thousands of workmen, driven by Baron Haussmann, the Robert Moses of his day, were carving Paris into an urban jewel.

With chefs as popular as courtesans and the Rothschilds eyeing wine chateaus in Bordeaux, it was decided early on that food and drink would play important roles in the 1855 exposition. The Bordeaux Chamber of Commerce was given the task of choosing the wines and seeing that they got to Paris and were displayed properly.

The chamber invested licensed wine brokers in Bordeaux with the task of selecting and classifying the wines to be shown in Paris. They selected 61, divided into five categories called growths.

The brokers, known as courtiers, were (and still are) go-betweens, working for both the wine producers and the wine merchants, or shippers. Truly expert tasters, the brokers advise the merchants what to buy and how much to pay. For the chateau owners, the brokers find merchants who will buy their wines. Many 19th-century brokers grew wealthy on their commissions, becoming chateau owners and shippers themselves.

In seeking wines for the show in Paris, the brokers did some blind tasting, but, for the most part, classifying the wines had little to do with tasting skills and almost everything to do with past prices. Some wines—many, in fact—had over the years consistently fetched higher prices than others. Thus, chateau owners, by plotting the sales of their wines and others through five or 10 vintages, could easily see which wines were consistently the best or, at least, had been judged best by the market. The 61 that had done the best over the years made it to the honors list.

The emphasis on price helps to explain why no wines from the St.-Émilion-Pomerol region ever made the list. Good as they were (and are), they never commanded the high prices Médoc and Graves did.

Of course, classifications were nothing new, even in the 19th century. One of the earliest classifications had been made more than two centuries earlier, in October 1647. It rated not wines but wine-producing communities within the Bordeaux region. The results showed that the best wines—the wines that fetched the highest prices—were not that different from what they were in 1855 or, for that matter, what they still are in 1998.

The highest ratings went to the Graves and the Médoc for the reds, and to Sauternes, Barsac, Preignac and Langon for whites. A survey done in 1745 showed Château Margaux, Lafite and Haut-Brion selling for up to 1,800 francs a ton, while chateaus like Gruaud Larose and Beychevelle brought only 400 to 600 francs.

Four decades later, in 1787, Thomas Jefferson, the Ambassador to France, made his own classification, selecting Latour, Haut-Brion, Lafite and Margaux his favorite Bordeaux. Today, as they were in Jefferson's time, these four, plus Mouton-Rothschild, are still the top five, or so-called first growths.

In the 19th century, before the classification was generally accepted, owners often lobbied the local agricultural authorities for a boost into a higher category. But the only elevation of a wine since the creation of the 1855 classification happened in this century, due to Baron Philippe de Rothschild's long campaign to have Mouton-Rothschild moved up from a second growth to a first growth. In 1973, after 20 years of lobbying legislators, he was successful. Baron Philippe celebrated by putting a Picasso from his collection on the new label.

Why has the 1855 list never been modified? No one knows. It certainly needs it now: chateau owners die, managers move on, vineyards are neglected. In spite of the amazing consistency of many of the Bordeaux wineries over the decades—even centuries—ratings need to be updated regularly.

The engaging history of the 1855 classification is presented in lively form in a new book, *1855: A History of the Bordeaux Classification,* by Dewey Markham Jr., published by John Wiley & Sons. Working in the musty libraries of Bordeaux for almost four years, Mr. Markham has unearthed a storehouse of wine history and folklore, including the saga of Monplaisir Goudal.

Mr. Goudal was the manager of Lafite at the time of the 1855 classification, and he worked unendingly to enhance the chateau's reputation—and his own. To give the 1846 Lafite, one of the wines exhibited at the fair, a bit of age, Mr. Goudal had 50 bottles of the wine sent around the world to, as Mr. Markham said, "subject the wine to the accelerated aging that such sea voyages provoked." Accelerated aging? Clearly, the man had his own classification.

April 1998

Bordeaux Family Values

By FRANK J. PRIAL

One day in 1992, Lucien Lurton, then the owner of Château Brane-Cantenac, a major estate in the village of Margaux, France, called together his 10 children. Over the previous 40 years, Lurton had become one of the largest and wealthiest landowners in Bordeaux, and now, he told his family, he was going to divide his holdings—11 wine chateaus and their vineyards—among them.

A dramatic gesture, yes, but not for the Lurtons. Little known outside the French wine community, they are perhaps Bordeaux's last great dynasty. With some 3,000 acres in the region, they are collectively Bordeaux's largest holder of wine-producing land. They own more than 20 chateaus and manage several of the world's most famous properties. They also claim thousands of acres of vineyards in Latin America and the South of France. Lucien, 79, and his brother André, 81, are the family's patriarchs. The majority of Lucien's estates, now in the hands of his children, are in the Médoc, north of the city of Bordeaux; André's holdings, about as large, lie mostly south of the city, in the Graves region and in the little-known Entre-Deux-Mers, where the family's ascendancy began.

Lucien, who still lives at Brane-Cantenac, is quiet, religious and conservative. "History stopped for Lucien in 1789," said a neighboring chateau owner. André—vigorous, assertive, egotistical—resembles Martin Sheen's Jed Bartlet on the early episodes of *The West Wing*.

If Lucien represents old France, conservative and discreet, André embodies a different paradigm: outgoing, charming, often despotic. He bounds up stairs, opens doors for others and, most un-French, says, "Call me André."

"André defines himself as a peasant," Jean-François Werner, a journalist, wrote in the wine magazine *L'amateur de Bordeaux*. "He loves to count the hours he spent driving a tractor more than he loves to count the chateaus he owns."

The brothers do not get along—more exasperation than enmity. It's a subject they love to change. "We don't see much of one another," Lucien told me, smiling. "We work better that way." And then he began to show me his wine-book collection (André collects military vehicles). Mention Lucien to André, and the response is likely to be a grimace and a shrug that says, "What can you do with him?" It's a schism that has done wonders for the family's holdings and has poised them for even greater success when Bordeaux rebounds from its present downturn.

The Lurtons' founding father was, in fact, not a Lurton. Léonce Récapet was a prosperous distiller and vineyard owner in Branne, a village in the Entre-Deux-Mers, where he was born in 1858. In 1922, Récapet ventured north into the Médoc, Bordeaux's gold coast, where he bought a major share of the legendary Château Margaux, one of Bordeaux's famous first growths (the best vineyards), as well as Château Brane-Cantenac. He later traded the Margaux shares for Château Clos Fourtet in St.-Émilion. Léonce's daughter Denise married François Lurton, whose ancestors had been recruited to the area by the Catholic Church to help offset what was said to be a serious shortage of the faithful in the Bordeaux region. "They were farmers and skilled workers," Denis Lurton, one of Lucien's sons, said of his ancestors. "And they were hard workers long before they grew grapes and made wine." When Récapet died in 1943, he left his properties to François Lurton (Denise had died nine years earlier) and their four children: André and Lucien, along with another son, Dominique, and a daughter, Simone. Lucien inherited Brane-Cantenac and André, Château Bonnet, the family seat at Grézillac, in the Entre-Deux-Mers. Simone inherited vineyards, and Dominique took the Chateaux Martouret and Reynier, also in the Entre-Deux-Mers.

Lucien and André, working together at first and later separately, began to acquire chateaus at a time when the Bordeaux wine trade was in a deep slump. The Depression years had been catastrophic for the vintners, and the post–World War II years offered little redress. Social and political problems, along with the weather, combined to bring Bordeaux to the brink of ruin. A killer frost in 1956 devastated vineyards throughout the region. Then a succession of miserable vintages in the 1960s drove hundreds of growers and winemakers from the land. Chateaus were shuttered or abandoned, and vineyards were left to rot. "The experts said Bordeaux might never recover," André told me recently, "but we proved them wrong a hundred times over."

Thanks to their grandfather's foresight and their own acumen, Lucien and André profited from those lean years. They moved in, as one Bordeaux chronicler wrote in the newspaper *Sud Ouest*, "with a little money, large bank loans and a lot of hard work." They were risk takers. Lucien bought Château Durfort-Vivens in 1962, when the Médoc most resembled a wasteland. He bought Château Climens in Barsac in 1971, just after the market for sweet wines had collapsed. André bought one rundown property after another, mostly in the Graves, which had been virtually forsaken as a wine-producing region. One of them, Château La Louvière, is the gem in his diadem. He picked it up in 1965, when, he told me, "there was no roof and four inches of water in the hard dirt basement—it was love at first sight." Nine years later, he bought the dilapidated 14th-century Château de Rochemorin, and he has spent the last 30 years restoring its vineyards. The chateau, now a ruin, still waits for its makeover. First the vineyard, then the history.

When the 1956 frost wiped out the vineyards at Château Bonnet, André's original inheritance, he leased fields and, for 10 years, raised corn and alfalfa to recover. "When I could, I bought land and raised grapes," he said. "In Bordeaux, people use money to grow grapes. I grew grapes to make money." In due time, Bonnet's vineyards came back and helped underwrite André's relentless expansion throughout Bordeaux.

In 2005, Bordeaux is in trouble once again. But it's not the 1960s revisited. The top chateaus—perhaps I should say the best-marketed chateaus—are doing extremely well, their wines selling from Moscow to Las Vegas at prices unimaginable 40 years ago. It's the thousands of working-class growers and winemakers who annually produce millions of gallons of cheap Bordeaux who are in trouble. Wine consumption in France has dropped more than 50 percent since the '60s, while overseas markets, especially the United Kingdom, have been captured by cheaper (and often better) wine from Australia, Spain, Latin America and even the United States.

Twenty years ago, the Lurtons would have been caught up in the present difficulties. Then, they produced large quantities of mostly commercial wine. Now, at every property they own or manage, they work to produce wines that can compete with Bordeaux's best. At chateaus like Brane-Cantenac, La Louvière, Rochemorin, Bouscaut and Durfort-Vivens, they already do.

For Lucien, turning over his estates to his children struck him as routine. Inheritance, with its complications, is the ghost at every Bordeaux dinner table. Family battles over even small plots of vines can go on for generations, while, these days, newly rich outsiders, eager to buy their way into the chateau aristocracy, stand ready to snap up old properties whose inheritors cannot agree how to run them.

Which is where the Lurtons stand apart. The brothers long ago agreed not to agree—and developed two empires separately. "I had to go my own way," Lucien said. "It's worked out reasonably well."

Unlike his brother, André has kept his holdings intact. "André is afraid to die," said a chateau owner who insisted on anonymity because he is a competitor. "He clings to his properties. Giving one away would be to acknowledge that he might actually be running out of time." André has seven children: five daughters who are shareholders in his estates, and two sons (also shareholders) who are hardly waiting around for him to pass on. With their father's blessing, Jacques and François Lurton have gone global. In 1988 they founded Jacques & François Lurton, S.A., to acquire vineyards outside Bordeaux. Today they produce wine in Argentina, Uruguay, Chile, Spain and the South of France.

But perhaps the most visible Lurton is Dominique's son, Pierre. Starting at 24, he spent 11 years running Château Clos Fourtet, in St.-Émilion, for his fractious uncles. In the early '90s, he moved to Château Cheval Blanc, St.-Émilion's most prestigious wine estate, as assistant manager. In 1998, when Bernard Arnault, the billionaire head of LVMH Moët Hennessy Louis Vuitton, bought Cheval Blanc with the investor Albert Frère, he made Pierre general manager. In 1999, Arnault gained the majority stake in Château d'Yquem, the famous Sauternes estate, from the Lur Saluces family, which had owned it since 1785. Last year, he installed Pierre as chief executive.

Did Arnault give him specific instructions on running two of the most famous wine properties in the world? "He said: 'Wine is not my field. Do your best,'" Pierre told me.

Like all Lurtons, Pierre is proud of the family name. When he started at Cheval Blanc, the owners at the time, the Fourcaud-Laussac family, expressed some concern about associating the famous name of Cheval Blanc with the Lurtons, who were—and in some quarters still are—considered upstarts. Could he change his name, for business purposes? Perhaps use his mother's name?

"If you wish," he told them. "You understand, of course, that my mother's name is Lafite."

November 2005

Stealing From Thieves

By FRANK J. PRIAL

Tourists driving through wine country invariably are overcome by an urge to stop the car, get out and pluck a few grapes.

It's difficult to do in California because most vineyards are fenced in. So are most of the vineyards in Burgundy. But in Bordeaux, in the Médoc, the vines grow right down to the edge of the roadway and there are almost never any fences.

A century ago, there were very few tourists in the Médoc; in fact, there were none. But there were grape thieves, who came in the night in the weeks just before harvest. Unintentionally, those thieves contributed to one of the most important scientific advances in the history of viticulture.

The last half of the 19th century was a troubled time for European winegrowers. Three times in the course of about 30 years they were beset with devastating epidemics of disease and insect damage. The first was oidium, a mushroomlike growth that attacks young vine wood, leaves and grapes. Discovered in England in 1845 on plants that had been shipped from the tropics, it first appeared in Bordeaux in 1851. Sulfur was found to be the best treatment, but not until half a dozen vintages were decimated by it.

Phylloxera was found in the Rhône vineyards in the early 1860s. By 1882, some 80 percent of all the vineyards of the Gironde area had been affected. An aphid native to the eastern United States, phylloxera arrived in Europe on American vines that had been imported for experiments.

The French growers had just begun to control it by grafting their vines on the phylloxera-resistant American roots—a practice they still follow—when the third plague struck: mildew. Mildew first appeared in the southwest of France in the 1870s. By the end of the decade, it had become almost as serious a problem as phylloxera. It affects the leaves of the vine only but causes an imbalance in the plant that in turn affects the quality of the grapes and, ultimately, the wine. Many compounds to combat the problem were tried without success.

One day in late October 1882, Pierre Millardet, a professor of botany at the University of Bordeaux, was driving his carriage along the road in St.-Julien, not far from Château Ducru-Beaucaillou. Later, he wrote: "I was not a little surprised to observe that all along the edge of the road which I was following, the vines all still possessed their leaves, whereas everywhere else in the vineyard they had long since fallen. That was the year of the mildew outbreak and my first thought was that this persistence of the leaves on the roadside was due to some treatment or other. On examination I saw that they were covered almost entirely by a thin layer of a powdery blue substance."

When he arrived at Ducru-Beaucaillou, then known simply as Beaucaillou, he asked the régisseur, or manager, Ernest David, about the blue substance. "He told me," Millardet wrote, "that it was the custom in St.-Julien to cover the vine leaves with 'verdigris' along the roadside at the time when the grapes were turning purple in order to keep grape thieves away, for these people, seeing the leaves covered with coppery spots, would not dare to taste nor steal the fruit underneath."

In fact, it was not the first time Professor Millardet had come across this sort of empirical evidence that copper was an enemy of plant disease. Earlier, he had noticed that spores of the mildew fungus would not germinate in water from his well. When he had his well water analyzed by the university's chemistry department, he found it contained about 5 milligrams of copper per liter. Investigating, he discovered that the water was pulled from his well by an old copper pump.

Millardet and David began experimenting with copper sulfate at Château Beaucaillou and at Château Dauzac, both owned by the famous Bordeaux shipper Nathaniel Johnston and both managed by David. Tests were made in 1883 and 1884. In April 1885, Millardet published the results in the *Agricultural and Horticultural Journal of the Gironde*. Almost immediately, the other proprietors of the Médoc began treatments with what became known as bouilli bordelaise, the "Bordeaux mixture." In October 1885, Millardet and David invited the public to witness the benefits of their experiments on the vineyards at Dauzac and Beaucaillou. The crisis was over, or so everyone thought. For two decades, mildew presented no problems. Then, in 1910 and again in 1915, it struck again. It turned out that the growers had simply been too sparing in their application of copper sulfate. They were applying it by hand, sending workers into the vineyards with pails and whisk brooms. The treatment was applied three or four times a year. Today, with mildew still a problem, the copper sulfate solution may be applied 30 times in a particularly wet summer, such as 1977, but it will be done by tractors and, sometimes, helicopters.

While it really didn't take too many years to figure out how to use the solution to save the vines, no one has yet discovered who first used the mixture to fend off thieves. It may have been a certain Mr. Lacassagne, the régisseur at Château St. Pierre, also in St.-Julien. He was, in fact, given credit by Ernest David for having first made an effective Bordeaux mixture in the Médoc. According to historians, some chateaus did set up temporary fences when the grapes became ripe and at least one, Château Latour, paid two workmen armed with shotguns to guard the grapes for two weeks before and during the harvest. And the old-time cellar master at Château Beychevelle, who knew the Lacassagne family, said a few years ago that he had always heard that the Bordeaux mixture was used by people too lazy to put up a fence or too poor to hire armed guards.

March 1987

Bordeaux Loses Prestige
Among Younger Wine Lovers

By ERIC ASIMOV

The hyperbole over 2009 Bordeaux began building even before the harvest last fall. Ripples of praise grew into waves this spring as critics and the trade descended on Bordeaux for the annual ritual of tasting the most recent vintage from barrels. Their ecstatic reviews reverberated through Britain, which takes its claret extremely seriously. They rang out in Hong Kong, the leading edge of what Bordeaux hopes will be a huge Asian market.

In the United States, the huzzahs resonated with collectors and wine investors, and with high-end restaurants whose clients don't mind spending hundreds or even thousands of dollars on renowned bottles. These people paid attention when Robert M. Parker Jr., the wine critic whose opinions most influence Bordeaux prices, wrote, "For some Médocs and Graves, 2009 may turn out to be the finest vintage I have tasted in 32 years of covering Bordeaux."

But for a significant segment of the wine-drinking population in the United States, the raves heard around the world were not enough to elicit a response beyond, perhaps, a yawn. For these people, Bordeaux, once the world's most hallowed region and the standard-bearer for all fine wines, is now largely irrelevant.

What happened? Plenty of Bordeaux is still consumed in the United States. In 2009, 1.29 million cases of Bordeaux wine were imported, accounting for 0.46 percent of all still wines, domestic and foreign, distributed in the country. While this percentage rises and falls year to year, it is still a far cry from its highs in the mid-1980s. Bordeaux shipments accounted for 1.69 percent of all still wines distributed in the United States in 1985, for example.

While the drop stems from far more competition in the lower-priced market, it also reflects a shift in the demographic of Bordeaux aficionados. For young Americans in particular, Bordeaux has become downright unfashionable.

Not so long ago, young wine-loving Americans were practically weaned on Bordeaux, just as would-be connoisseurs had been for generations. It was the gateway to all that is wonderful about wine. Now that excitement has gone elsewhere, to Burgundy and the Loire, to Italy and Spain. Bordeaux, some young wine enthusiasts say, is stodgy and unattractive. They see it as an expensive wine for wealthy collectors, investors and point-chasers, people who seek critically approved wines for the luxury and status they convey rather than for excitement in a glass.

"The perception of Bordeaux for my generation, it's very Rolex, very Rolls-Royce," said Cory Cartwright, 30, who is a partner in Selection Massale, a new company in San Jose, Calif., that imports natural and traditional wines made by small producers, and who writes the Saignée wine blog. "I don't know many people who like or drink Bordeaux."

But the lack of interest is not just a question of perception. Nor is it solely a reflection of the weak economy, which drove down sales of most higher-priced wines in the last two years.

The more troubling sign for Bordeaux is that it has largely lost the loyalty of people like sommeliers and neighborhood wine shop proprietors, who can help build an audience for wines. The high-end, big-name wines will always have a market, but the less expensive, less familiar names, the natural points of embarkation for young wine explorers, may not fare as well without the support of those crucial intermediaries.

"I don't know any young sommelier who I've encountered in the last 15 years who is a Bordeaux hound," said Paul Grieco, an owner of the restaurant Hearth as well as two innovative wine bars, Terroir and Terroir Tribeca, all in Manhattan. Mr. Grieco has been a mentor for many young sommeliers. He himself learned about fine wine by drinking Bordeaux. Nonetheless, at his wine bars, he serves 50 wines by the glass, and not one is a Bordeaux. His shift has left him with mixed feelings.

"I think, 'I'm a history guy, how can I not revere Bordeaux?'" he said. "If even one person came in and said, 'I want a glass of Bordeaux,' I might think I really have to serve a Bordeaux. But not one person has said that. Not one! That's pretty sad."

For many younger sommeliers and wine lovers, the new standard of excellence is Burgundy.

Unlike Bordeaux, where many of the best-known chateaus are run by corporations or wealthy absentee owners, Burgundy is full of estates, including many of the leading ones, that are essentially small businesses. Dealing with Bordeaux often requires working with middle management and marketing specialists. It's much easier to visit a Burgundian estate and find the one person who has dirt on the boots, wine on the hands and a name on the bottle.

"For people of my generation, 30 to 50, I don't think we've had the same magical Bordeaux moments, not in the same way we've connected to Burgundy or even the Rhône," said Laura Maniec, who runs the wine programs for more than 15 restaurants in the B. R. Guest group.

She still buys a lot of Bordeaux for restaurants like Primehouse, a Manhattan steakhouse, and Blue Water Grill, a Manhattan seafood restaurant that hosts plenty of corporate parties where Bordeaux is nearly obligatory. "But there's a passion and a spark and a personal connection that are missing," she said.

For restaurants 30 years ago, having a serious wine list meant offering a lot of Bordeaux. That's no longer the case, except for steakhouses and very high-end restaurants. Nowadays, people in the wine trade say, Bordeaux is sold largely through retail establishments like Sherry-Lehmann in New York, Zachys in Westchester and K & L Wine Merchants in California.

"Young people are not exposed to Bordeaux in restaurants as much," said Clyde Beffa Jr., vice president of K & L, one of the country's leading sellers of Bordeaux. "Sommeliers, they want to find their own little thing, it drives me crazy. They can have five grüner veltliners or rieslings because they're discovering these things, and they're not recommending Bordeaux as much. And, it's the price thing."

Good Bordeaux might start at $35 to $50 retail, and $85 to $100 in a restaurant, and soar from there—far more than, say, reds from the Loire, Beaujolais or Alto Adige, darlings of the sommeliers and neighborhood wine shops.

Another significant barrier between young wine drinkers and Bordeaux is the absence of a charismatic advocate for the wines. The audience for Mr. Parker and the other leading wine critics tends to be older and more established. Meanwhile, boutique wine importers and distributors like Kermit Lynch, Neal Rosenthal and Louis/Dressner, who have won passionate followings, do very little business in Bordeaux, which has long been the domain of big companies.

For younger startup importers like Mr. Cartwright, the size and complexity of the business is the reason he is not searching for Bordeaux wines to bring in.

"Everything is too commerce-driven," he said. "You're never sure who is making the wine. I think for me and people my age, we're going back to grower-producers—people who are there the whole way—and Bordeaux seems the opposite of that."

While Bordeaux may have lost much of its mystique and allure, it still has its defenders, even among the sommelier crowd. Belinda Chang, the wine director at the Modern in Midtown Manhattan, acknowledges that Bordeaux has become a brand name, and that it's often too expensive, but argues that its intrinsic high quality and classic appeal make it irreplaceable.

"I'm a fan and I'm not afraid to say it," Ms. Chang said. "Who would not be excited to have a glass of Château Pétrus, if you're not footing the bill?"

Exactly right.

May 2010

Burgundy Learns to Bottle Consistency

By ERIC ASIMOV

The black clouds gathered last week over the Côte d'Or, the slender 30-mile-long swath that comprises the great vineyards of Burgundy. And for at least the fifth day in a row they burst forth, drenching the vineyards shortly before the critical period of flowering, when the grape bunches begin to form on the spindly vines.

Rain is the farmer's blessing, when it comes at the right time and in the right amount. But when the ground is saturated and the air is warm, the resulting moisture and humidity is a curse that can threaten the grapes with mildew and rot.

In past decades such weather might have spelled doom for the year's vintage. But nowadays it means something else entirely. "It means more work for us," said Benjamin Leroux, 33, the manager of Comte Armand, one of the best producers in Pommard in the Côte de Beaune, the southern half of the Côte d'Or. "All the things we're doing in the vineyard right now, we're insuring the vintage."

Twenty years ago nobody could have predicted that Burgundy could be trusted to produce reliably good wines in tricky vintages. As captivating as the great wines of Burgundy could be at their heights, too often they revealed their depths—diluted, overly acidic wines that seemed to vary not just vintage to vintage but almost bottle to bottle. The only thing consistent about the region was its inconsistency.

Just last month Robert M. Parker Jr., the wine critic, repeated the old saw when he wrote in his column in *Business Week*, "Red Burgundy is the ultimate minefield of the wine world—notoriously unreliable, often disappointing, and rarely living up to its illustrious reputation."

In fact, the quality of Burgundy—red Burgundy in particular—has risen strikingly over the last two decades. From the smallest growers to the biggest houses, the standards of grapegrowing and winemaking have surpassed anybody's expectations. These days, Burgundy has very few bad vintages, and among good producers, surprisingly few bad wines.

The best producers, like Domaine de la Romanée-Conti and Armand Rousseau, always managed to achieve a high standard, but nowadays the bar has been raised for everybody. And it's not just the Côte d'Or, the heart of Burgundy, that has shown such improvement. Surrounding areas like the Côte Chalonnaise and the Mâconnais, still part of Burgundy, are producing better wine than ever, at not unreasonable prices. Sure, you can still find bad Burgundy. But really, it's not hard to find bad wines from any fine wine region.

"It's not so much an improvement as a blooming," said Becky Wasserman, an American wine broker who has lived in Burgundy since 1968. "It's a realization of potential."

I spent five days in Burgundy last week to get a first-hand look at the reasons for the surge in quality. In traveling the Côte d'Or from Marsannay in the north to Santenay in the south, visiting two dozen producers, tasting hundreds of wines and drinking not quite that many, it was easy to see that this leap upward has been 25 years in the making, an eternity in the Internet world but a split second at the rhythmic agricultural pace of viticulture.

Most striking of all was the number of young producers making superb wines, whether they have taken charge of their family domains or started out new. In Marsannay, perhaps the least-esteemed commune in the Côtes de Nuits, the northern half of the Côte d'Or, Sylvain Pataille, 33, is turning out excellent reds, whites and rosés. In the Hautes-Côtes de Nuits, once a backwater in the hills, David Duband, 37, is producing light, fresh regional wines from his ancestral vineyards, along with a series of more ambitious, elegant reds from grand cru vineyards like Échezeaux and Charmes-Chambertin. Louis-Michel Liger-Belair, 35, in Vosnes-Romanée has reclaimed some of the greatest vineyard property in the north, which his family had leased out for years, and is making wines of purity and depth.

Meanwhile, in Meursault in the south, Arnaud Ente, who took over his father-in-law's vineyards in the 1990s, is turning out small amounts of whites of focus and clarity that show tremendous minerality. Pierre-Yves Colin-Morey, 36, left his father's domain, Marc Colin et Fils, and set up shop in Chassagne-Montrachet, where he is making light yet intense, mouthwatering whites.

"Half the superstar domains today didn't exist 20 years ago," Clive Coates, author of *The Wines of Burgundy* (University of California Press, 2008), told me in a recent interview. Few could have envisioned such a level of quality back in the early 1980s, a time when Claude Bourguignon, a French soil scientist who, with his wife, Lydia, works with numerous wine estates, famously said that the soil of the Sahara had more life in it than the soil of Burgundy.

"It was a shocking wake-up call," Ms. Wasserman said, and it was heard by the first wave in the vanguard of the new Burgundy, young vignerons like Dominique Lafon in Meursault, Christophe Roumier in Chambolle-Musigny and Étienne Grivot in Vosne-Romanée.

Their first order of business was to wean the soil off two decades worth of chemical fertilizers, herbicides and pesticides. The postwar dependency on science and industry had dealt a severe blow to Burgundy, which more than most wine regions prided itself on its soil. The nuances of terroir, the semi-mystical French term that encompasses earth, atmosphere, climate and humanity, were said to be transmitted to the wines by the qualities of the differing soils throughout the Côte d'Or.

Over the next 20 years a great many producers turned to organic farming, and others adopted biodynamic viticulture, a particularly demanding system that takes a sort of homeopathic approach to farming. These days it's the rare farmer who still uses chemical herbicides in the vineyard.

"The soils are alive again," Mr. Bourguignon said by telephone last week. "They've really changed, and it's one of the reasons the wine has changed."

Burgundy vignerons take pains, however, to make clear that they are not doing anything new. As Mr. Leroux pointed out, organic viticulture is simply a return to the pre–World War II methods.

"We can now understand what our grandparents were doing," said Jean-Marie Fourrier of Domaine Fourrier in Gevrey-Chambertin. "We're rediscovering the logic of the past."

Domaine Fourrier was moribund, with no market for its wine, when Mr. Fourrier took over from his father, Jean-Claude. Fourteen years later he exports wine to 27 countries and has just finished construction on a new fermentation room. His wines are pure and light-bodied, embodying the grace and finesse for which Burgundy's best wines were always known.

Prosperity is evident all over Burgundy, and every domain seems to be adding on, building a new cellar or a new winery, buying a tractor, or hiring workers. It's a far cry from 20 years ago when domains were going out of business and sales of Burgundy in the United States were plummeting.

Now, despite the plunge of the dollar, American thirst for Burgundy has never been higher, and the opening in the last few years of new markets like eastern Europe and Asia, along with demand for the widely acclaimed 2005 vintage, has sent prices for Burgundy soaring higher than ever. Much of the profit seems to be going back into the wine.

"It's a virtuous cycle," said Jeremy Seysses, who has joined his father, Jacques Seysses, at the helm of Domaine Dujac in Morey-St.-Denis, one of the best producers in the Côte de Nuits. "Our wines have never sold so well or for so much money, which is bad for the consumer, I guess, but we can now afford to invest in the extra worker, the new equipment, in taking the time necessary to make great wine."

A decade ago you might still find cellars in Burgundy without the equipment to control the temperature in vats of fermenting wine, by then standard in the rest of the winemaking world. Nowadays that's unthinkable. With increased knowledge has come a premium on hygiene in the cellar and precision in the vineyard. Where once farmers who sold their grapes to négociants were paid by quantity, winemakers who bottle their own production today know that they are judged and paid on quality.

"Everybody is aware that Burgundy has a lot of competition and people don't buy it because it says on the label, 'Bourgogne,'" said Véronique Drouhin, who, with her three brothers, has taken over from their father leadership of Joseph Drouhin, one of the biggest and best producers in Burgundy.

Profits and the willingness to put them back into the business have helped to save vintages like 2007, which was marked by rain and hail. Twenty years ago, said Mr. Leroux of Comte Armand, the domain would have played it safe in a vintage like 2007. It would have picked the grapes quickly over the course of a week even though ripening was uneven, both to protect itself against further bad weather and so that the part-time pickers would not have to be paid for so long. "This year it took us 21 days," Mr. Leroux said. "We stopped for seven days and I had to pay the pickers to do nothing, but the payoff in quality was great."

Back in the '80s, a year like 2007 could have been a disaster along the lines of the notoriously poor 1984 and 1975 vintages. Instead, tasted from the barrel, where the '07s are currently aging, the Comte Armand reds were fresh and minerally, the various crus in Pommard and Auxey-Duresses differing markedly in density and nuance according to where the grapes were grown, yet all lithe and agile. When they are released next year, the '07s may not be judged among Burgundy's best, but they certainly will be enjoyable, at least.

Mr. Leroux is typical of younger vignerons in Burgundy today. Unlike previous generations, who often began working in the fields as teenagers and never got far from their homes, they were trained in viticulture and enology. They've traveled the world, working in places like California, New Zealand, South Africa and even Bordeaux. Perhaps most importantly, they are not afraid to share knowledge.

"They all know how to taste," said Dominique Lafon, the Meursault superstar whose domain, Comtes Lafon, is one of Burgundy's leading estates. "The older generation was only tasting their own wines and were not sharing as much as now."

As consistently good as red Burgundy has become, white Burgundy still has a thorny issue to solve. The wines, when young, can be delicious and show every indication of being capable of ripe old age. But beginning with the 1996 vintage, some of the best white Burgundies began oxidizing in the bottle after seven or nine years.

Responding first with denial, then consternation, all of Burgundy now concedes the problem, which seems to have waned since the 1999 vintage. Its source has been elusive, although most people seem to blame corks treated with peroxide. Some vignerons are taking the time to hand-wax the tops of their bottles to keep oxygen out.

Regardless of the stability that Burgundy is able to achieve, absolute consistency will never be possible. It's antithetical to the nature of the pinot noir grape, which is proverbially fickle and troublesome to grow, and to the nature of artisanal winemaking, which takes as a matter of romantic faith that greatness only comes with risks.

"Burgundy is and will always remain the anti-product," Ms. Wasserman said. "Burgundies react differently according to their age, according to the weather, according to the ambiance. It's nice to have natural things that react."

June 2008

An American Hears the Call of Burgundy

By ERIC ASIMOV

Before his 29th birthday, Ray Walker became the first American ever to make Le Chambertin, the grand cru red Burgundy that is one of the most revered names in wine. How Mr. Walker came to make this wine is a story of passion and perseverance, family support and great good fortune, naïveté and surprises, not least of which is that Mr. Walker had never drunk a Chambertin before he made his own.

Happily-ever-after tales are rare in the wine business, which generally operates on the more down-to-earth plane of crafty marketing and cut-throat competition. But Mr. Walker's entry into the famously insular world of Burgundy, with little money, no connections and virtually no experience in winemaking, seems straight from the annals of fairy godmothers and Prince Charmings.

Today, Mr. Walker—tall and lean with sculptured good looks—and his wife, Christian, are the proud proprietors of Maison Ilan, a small négociant business here in the heart of the Côte de Nuits. It is named after their young daughter, Isabella Ilan Walker.

Up to now, they have made only a little bit of red wine, including two grand crus, Le Chambertin and Charmes-Chambertin. The wines are elegant, fresh, structured and graceful—astoundingly so, given they were made by a novice.

As a younger man, Mr. Walker, who grew up in the Bay Area and worked there in his family's real estate business, was decidedly not a wine drinker. It was not until he met his future wife, who liked wine, that the subject came up.

"We'd get into heated arguments," Mr. Walker, now 30, recalled during a recent visit to his small, spotless winery underneath his house here. "She'd say, 'Adults drink wine with food,' and I'd say, 'Only alcoholics do.' "

Not until they traveled to Italy, where Mr. Walker proposed marriage, did he see the light. It shined so brightly that he became obsessed with wine.

At first he studied Bordeaux. But early in 2005 he sampled a 2002 Meursault Clos de la Barre from Comtes Lafon, a white Burgundy. Another bright light went off.

"Oh my God, this is nature!" he recalled saying after tasting the wine, his excitement of the moment still palpable. "From that moment on, I was certain I was going to explore Burgundy. And then we got into the reds, and I couldn't believe it."

For two years, Mr. Walker carried around *Côte d'Or*, Clive Coates's magnum opus on Burgundy. Finally, in 2008, as he was training for a new job at Merrill Lynch, with his wife six months pregnant, he realized he was not happy. With her support, he quit to learn about the wine business.

Before long he was hired at Freeman Winery in Sebastopol, in Sonoma County, to wash barrels and help with bottling and the harvest.

"He's a really bright guy, and he gets it right away," said Ed Kurtzman, the winemaker at Freeman. "He was driven and knew exactly what he wanted to do, though I don't think he knew where he was going to end up."

At Freeman, Mr. Walker learned the basics of making wine. The ambition was growing to do it himself, but when he was offered some petite sirah grapes to turn into wine, he could not muster enthusiasm.

"My wife said: 'Don't do that. We don't drink wines like that,'" he recalled. She asked him what he was most passionate about, and the answer, Burgundy, was obvious. So were the obstacles.

In the real world, people do not leave their jobs, their wives, their new babies because they fantasize about making wine in Burgundy. If the all-too-real logistical and financial difficulties are not enough to swat down such ambitions, certainly the dubious prospects of acquiring grapes and equipment and enough money would do the trick. Yet here was Mr. Walker's wife and parents urging him to follow his heart. What else was he to do?

Mr. Walker hatched a plan. He would try to buy village-level grapes: good, but not as good as premier cru, and certainly not grand cru, which is exceptionally rare. Working the Internet, he drew up a list of grape brokers.

Meanwhile, Mr. Walker was trying to teach himself French by reading 19th-century wine texts, like Jules Lavalle's seminal 1855 work, *Histoire et Statistique de la Vigne des Grands Vin de la Côte d'Or*, which placed the vineyards of Burgundy in five classes. Finally, in 2009, armed with little more than a firm handshake and $20,000 contributed by a supporter who prefers to remain anonymous, he headed to Burgundy to seek grapes.

Over the course of months, Mr. Walker was rebuffed in his quest for village-level grapes. It wasn't that he was a nobody; they simply weren't available.

To his astonishment, though, he was offered some grand cru grapes, from Charmes-Chambertin, adjacent to Le Chambertin. This, in the year following the economic meltdown, was beyond his wildest dreams.

"I learned later that many producers were thinking they'd make their money on village wines because of the economy, and they were dropping grand cru," he said.

If so, Mr. Walker was ready to catch them. Having read Lavalle's text, he understood what most novices would not: that the grapes from the upper part of Charmes were considered superior to those from the lower part. He made sure that his grapes were from the upper part, which he thought proved his seriousness to the broker. Not long after he was also offered grapes from Le Chambertin, as well as from three premier cru vineyards.

Two weeks before the harvest of 2009, Mr. Walker had grapes but no place to live, no place to make the wine and no tools. So he called his anonymous investor.

"I think I can put together something that's never been done," Mr. Walker told him. "No American has ever vinified Chambertin."

"How much do you need?" the investor asked.

"$130,000."

"Is that all?"

Call it what you will, but Mr. Walker has his wine as evidence that it really happened. With funds in hand, he found a producer who was willing to share space and equipment. Now came the actual winemaking, and a feeling that for Mr. Walker, entering the hallowed realm of Burgundy came with a responsibility.

"You're awed by it," he said. "You're kind of stepping into a church."

Suffice it to say that Mr. Walker made his wine quite successfully, but obsessively, with the driven determination of an innocent purist.

Of necessity, he stuck to the minimalist methods of the past, influenced partly by the pure throwback wines of the legendary vigneron Jacky Truchot, now retired. Using the 19th-century texts (http://blog.maison-ilan.com/burgundy -library/), Mr. Walker employed methods that required few tools and minimal technology: for example, fermenting in big barrels rather than temperature-controlled steel tanks. He didn't really know what he was doing, yet he thought what he was doing was right.

"I guess being ignorant has its benefits," he said. "When you think you control things you have more of a chance of messing up. When you have to pay attention, you learn."

His first vintage, 11½ barrels of wine, was sold out shortly after he finished making it, mostly to 1,000 people on a mailing list who took a chance at least a year before they would ever taste the wine. His wife, he said, was especially impressed.

In 2010, he solidified his success, finding the winery here in Nuit-St.-Georges, where he brought his wife and daughter to join him. Burgundians are a reticent lot, not known for embracing outsiders, but Mr. Walker stepped right into their world as if he were re-entering a past life.

A Who's Who of Burgundy producers, he said, have gone out of their way to help him, including Mr. Truchot, with whom he has become good friends.

"I've felt more at home in Burgundy than I ever felt in California," he said.

Those in the region attribute his appeal partly to his modesty, to his obvious appreciation and love for Burgundy, and his commitment to the Burgundian notion of terroir, clear to those who have tasted his wines.

"What moves me the most is his respect for Burgundy, and his astonishment at walking in the footsteps of men and women who worked the vineyards for so many centuries," said Becky Wasserman, another American who found a home in Burgundy, where she has been a wine broker for 40 years, and is helping to export the Maison Ilan wines.

Sadly, few people have tasted the wines, which are made in tiny quantities and sold mostly through the mailing list. For his 2011 vintage, though, Mr. Walker is expanding production, having contracted for more grapes from both grand cru vineyards, as well as two new premier cru vineyards in Chambolle-Musigny and Volnay.

He is looking for a larger production facility, and a new house, as he and his wife are also expecting another child.

"Anybody can do it," he said, about the winemaking. "You just have to care enough."

July 2011

For Chablis Fanatics, Ah, 2007

By ERIC ASIMOV

For a wine of great character and long history, Chablis is all too easy to abuse. Often its own producers treat it with colossal disrespect, planting the vines in the wrong places, choosing to harvest quantity over quality and making the wine with broad, careless brushstrokes rather than the meticulous pointillism a pure, transparent wine like Chablis requires.

Then comes the issue of vintage and climate, which greatly and sometimes counterintuitively influences the Chablis you taste in the glass. While Chablis is considered part of Burgundy, it is northwest of the rest of the region. In fact, it's closer to Champagne than to the Côte d'Or, the heart of Burgundy, and so the vintage judgments for most red and white Burgundies don't necessarily apply to Chablis.

The best recent vintage of Chablis was 2004, which coincidentally was also very good for white Burgundy but not necessarily for reds. Neither 2005 nor 2006 was exactly bad for Chablis, but the wines they produced were plusher and more sumptuously fruity than classically austere, focused and precise. The '06 Chablis are fine wines for the most part, but less distinctive, lacking for me the singular qualities that make Chablis stand out among the seven seas of white wines.

The 2007 vintage is another story. If you are a fanatic, as I am, for the purer, clearer style of Chablis, 2007 is a year to get excited about. No, I haven't spent a week visiting Chablis cellars and tromping through vineyards. But in my scattered tastings of 2007 Chablis here at home, mostly straightforward village-level Chablis at that, I've found the sort of beautifully etched wines that can send even the most unimpressionable Chablis lover floating up among aromas and images of oyster shells, crushed rocks, limestone and chalk.

Odd things to find in a wine, to be sure. But Chablis is a remarkable wine. Like so many other white wines around the world, Chablis is made entirely of the chardonnay grape, but no chardonnay tastes like Chablis. The flavors in a glass of Chablis rarely suggest tropical fruits; often they don't suggest any fruit at all. Flavors of oak are thankfully infrequent. Instead, to an extent beyond other white Burgundies, a good Chablis calls to mind the myriad aromas and flavors often lumped together under the vague-but-useful term "mineral."

A bottle like the 2007 Première Cuvée Les Pargues from Domaine Servin

($27) epitomizes a classic village Chablis. With its pale yellow color, bordering on green, and its chalky aromas, the Servin brings to mind images of earth—white earth—the sort of limestone soils and fossilized oyster beds found in the best Chablis plots. It is bone dry and has an aroma more savory than sweet.

While all good Chablis share these characteristics, they can be subtly different stylistically, even at the village level, which, in the Chablis totem pole, is near the base, just above Petit Chablis and under the mid-level premier crus and the top-of-the-heap grand crus. A 2007 Chablis from Jean-Paul & Benoît Droin ($28) is likewise dry and minerally, but seems riper and richer on the palate than the Servin.

Then you have the 2007 Chablis of Alice and Olivier De Moor, who make two cuvées of village-level wine. The Bel Air et Clardy ($28), made with grapes from two different plots, exudes flowers, lemon and honey, though wrapped in that chalky Chablis minerality. It is pretty and delicious, and maybe a little exotic, but still precise. The other cuvée, Rosette ($33), tastes of flowers, minerals and anise and is ripe and rich, though not heavy by any means. Each of these wines is distinct, yet each is clearly a Chablis.

William Fèvre is one of the Chablis elite. While I haven't tasted the top-level Fèvre 2007 wines, its '07 Champs Royaux, made from purchased grapes, is a delicious Chablis for about $25, with mineral flavors that I could think of only as limestone scrapings, along with a bit of lemon, honey and herbs. Joseph Drouhin made a good basic négociant Chablis in 2007, for $22. Domaine Dampt and Gilbert Picq also make fine village Chablis for about $20 a bottle, as well as specializing in the silent final consonant.

As you ascend to the premier cru and grand cru levels, the wines get richer and more detailed, though always with their distinctive chalky minerality.

I found an '07 premier cru Vaillons from Vincent Dauvissat, maybe my favorite Chablis producer, and though it was really too young to drink now, it gave a hint of what it would taste like in a few years with its aromas of seashells and flowers. Right now, the wine's great acidity, which makes Chablis seem so lively and at times a bit stern, is very firm, but will soften with time. For comparison's sake, top Chablis from 2004 are delicious right now, and may well improve for another 10 to 15 years.

Because good Chablis is subtle, it is crucial not to serve it too cold, which will mask the flavors. Barely cool is just about right.

Despite the historical inclusion of Chablis with Burgundy, the wines often remind me more of blanc de blancs Champagne and even Sancerre. The best sites in all three regions share the same chalky Kimmeridgean soil, as do the white cliffs of Dover, for that matter. Despite what sets the wines apart—Sancerre made from the sauvignon blanc grape, and blanc de blancs a chardonnay with fizz—the best versions all seem to display the characteristics of their shared soil more so than their differences.

It occurs to me that I've made it this far without the obligatory cautionary note that real Chablis has nothing to do with the cheap jug wines that to this day in the United States are marketed as "chablis." Somehow, I doubt you need me to tell you that anymore.

May 2009

What's New in Beaujolais Is Not Nouveau

By ERIC ASIMOV

In the small courtyard cellar of the Morgon producer Marcel Lapierre, the barrels are talking. It's the gentle but insistent murmur of the juice of gamay grapes fermenting into Beaujolais wine, the yeast transforming sugar into alcohol and carbon dioxide, which, with no role to play in the finished product, can only hiss its protest at being left behind.

It is not the only hissing in the Beaujolais, a region long venerated for its bistro wines and now apparently withering on the vine. From the Terres des Pierres Dorées in the south, where the rocks seem to glow a soft gold, to the granite hills of Juliénas, Fleurie and the other crus to the north, the talk is of crisis: of rising costs and diminishing returns, of a public that has turned its back on a gentle wine it once embraced, and of a reputation damaged by decades of mediocrity and symbolized by the yawning response to the annual November announcement, "Le Beaujolais nouveau est arrivé."

But a different, equally insistent message is also emerging from Beaujolais, and it is a sign of hope for a region that has borne more than its share of condescension and scorn. It comes from the best, most serious producers in Beaujolais, who are making superb wines that bear as much resemblance to mass-market Beaujolais nouveau as a fine, dry-aged steak does to a fast-food burger. In a region known for jolly little knock-back wines to be drunk and forgotten, these are memorable wines of depth and class, thoughtful wines that nonetheless retain the joyous nature imbued in Beaujolais.

Few wines can induce joy the way Beaujolais does, and I would argue that that is an undervalued quality. When you add in the perfume and the nuance of the best Beaujolais wines, and combine them with a little bit of structure, you have a wine that deserves far more credit than it gets.

"People think, 'Oh, Beaujolais, it's light, it's fruity,'" said Jacques Lardière, technical director of Maison Louis Jadot. "But in Moulin-à-Vent you can produce a great wine, a great, great wine."

The idea that Beaujolais can produce great wine is antithetical not only to the image of Beaujolais but also to the notion of what constitutes great wine. Greatness among red wines is generally equated with power, profundity and aging ability.

Although Beaujolais can sometimes age well—I recently had a delicious 1929 Moulin-à-Vent—it is best enjoyed fairly young. It will never be profound the way Burgundy, Barolo or Bordeaux can be, and notwithstanding young Morgons, which can be tough on tender mouths, Beaujolais tends more toward elegance than power.

Just consider, for example, the purity of those whispering Lapierre Morgons, surprisingly light-bodied and elegant, or the density and balance of a Fleurie from Clos de la Roilette. To taste the fresh yet complex Moulin-à-Vent and Fleurie of Domaine du Vissoux, the pretty, floral Côte de Brouilly of Jean-Paul Brun or the powerful, structured Morgons of Louis-Claude Desvignes is to realize that there is a world of Beaujolais beyond the fatiguingly sappy, candied wines that by comparison taste like tutti-frutti gamay juice.

Great Beaujolais comes in many shapes and sizes. Domaine Cheysson in Chiroubles makes pretty, seductive wines, enticing for their lithe, floral grace. A Juliénas from Michel Tête is completely different, spicy, structured and laden with mineral and raspberry flavors. And then there are the dynamic, finely detailed Moulin-à-Vents of Louis Jadot's Château des Jacques, like La Roche 2005, smelling of violets and dark fruit, a wine of clarity and finesse.

Even among these fine crus, though, it is hard to find a producer who will not talk about what they all call the image problem. And for that they blame Beaujolais nouveau.

"The nouveau has destroyed our image," said Jean-Pierre Large, director of Domaine Cheysson in Chiroubles, as we tasted the fresh, fruity 2007 vintage now resting in cement tanks. He winced as I joked that I was the first to taste his nouveau, which Cheysson does not produce. "All of Beaujolais is confused with nouveau," he said.

The man most responsible for this confusion, of course, is Georges Duboeuf, author of many Beaujolais triumphs. Mr. Duboeuf, who grew up in a farm family just outside the Beaujolais region, was already a successful négociant when he began to mass-market the quaint regional autumn custom of celebrating the arrival of the primeur, the year's first wine. The Beaujolais nouveau fashion took off in the 1970s and '80s. By 1988, some estimates assert, 60 percent of the basic Beaujolais appellation went into primeur.

The wine itself may have been a harmless fruity concoction, but its lack of consequence created lasting problems. Growers picked early at minimal ripeness to avoid risks, and compensated by chaptalizing, a legal process of adding sugar to the grape juice to increase the alcohol content, which can result in the impression of artificiality. They would maximize yields, which can dilute the wines, and they would make the wines according to the standardized recipes of the négociants, who bought most of the wine from the growers to be sold under their own labels.

When times were good, nobody much cared. But now that the nouveau fashion has diminished—nouveau is now about 30 percent of Beaujolais production—growers in the lesser regions of Beaujolais are stuck with an over-supply of poor wine. And the public is stuck with an image of insipid wine meant to be drunk immediately.

"Nouveau really contributed to the problems here," said Mathieu Lapierre, who works here with his father, Marcel, farming about 30 acres of grapes in Morgon. "People overproduced and made really bad wine."

Mr. Duboeuf does not see it that way. He says the problems in Beaujolais are similar to those faced all over France, where inexpensive wines have been losing international market share to branded New World wines. Increasing production worldwide combined with a stable level of consumption is the reason, he said, that abandoned vineyards can be seen in the southern Beaujolais, still thick with rotting grapes because troubled farmers decided it was less expensive to ignore their fields than to harvest the crops and make wine.

Yet Mr. Duboeuf is optimistic, and feels the region has taken major steps to right itself, reducing the legal maximum for yields and slowing growth. From 1957, he said, when Beaujolais produced 600,000 hectoliters of wine, to 2000, output had more than doubled to 1.3 million hectoliters, but in two years output will be down to one million.

"Growers are making great efforts, and already this year we should be in a more balanced situation," said Mr. Duboeuf, still slender and ramrod straight at 74, his hair combed back into a white pompadour, blue cashmere sweater draped over his shoulders. "In two years demand will exceed supply, so prices will go up."

Mr. Duboeuf still believes in nouveau. "Japan today is the biggest market for Beaujolais nouveau," he said. "Ten years ago it was nothing. It shows you how things can change in just a few years. There is always potential."

At the spotless Duboeuf headquarters in Romanèche-Thorins, amid the ultramodern bottling lines, pallets of wine stand ready for shipping. Much is not Beaujolais at all, but pinot noir or syrah (labeled "shiraz") from the Languedoc, in brightly adorned bottles. One line of wines is even encased in blue denim.

"It's easy to drink for a new generation," said Franck Duboeuf, Georges's son.

For a mass-market operation, Duboeuf serves up pretty good wine. But it is a world apart from the vignerons making wine from their own fields, in their own cellars, who are not cutting cloth to fit the fashions but are making the wines that they believe in. Most growers are reluctant to criticize Mr. Duboeuf, who seems to be held in high esteem, but they do not like to be lumped in with his methods.

"Duboeuf is producing a marketing product to give the people what they want," said Serge Condemine of Domaine des Souchons, who makes dense, balanced Morgons. "We still have honest winemakers who don't care for marketing or fashion. One day this foolishness will end and we'll still have the honest, authentic product."

By contrast, Pierre-Marie and Martine Chermette of Domaine du Vissoux are based in St.-Vérand in the southern end of the appellation, but they also own plots in the higher-status crus of Fleurie and Moulin-à-Vent. Doggedly, they keep yields low and scrupulously sort the grapes. They do not chaptalize, they use only the natural yeasts on the grapes rather than specialized yeasts that emphasize particular flavors and aromas, and they use very little sulfur as a stabilizer.

"You can't say we don't have problems," Ms. Chermette said, "but we've been at this since 1982 and we've got regular customers and good contacts."

Indeed, the best producers are not the ones who are hurting. Those with a history of making and bottling their own wine, like the Chermettes or like Michel Tête in Juliénas, are holding their own. But for those who have depended on supermarket sales and négociants to move their wine, prospects are dimmer.

Growers everywhere like to talk about their old vines and their sustainable agricultural practices, but in the Beaujolais it is not always easy to know how to interpret this talk. Do they have old vines because they have guarded a precious holding? Or is it because they cannot afford to replace ones that have deteriorated? Do they practice sustainable agriculture for philosophical reasons? Or is it because they cannot afford to spray against weeds five times a year?

Against the background of crisis, those who have dedicated themselves to making top-quality wines offer a model for the future. They are the ones who, like Jean-Paul Brun, have taken risks and demonstrated that the public will notice. Mr. Brun's estate, Domaine des Terres Dorées, makes wine as naturally as possible, a process that requires great attention.

"You have to select grapes very carefully," he said. "You have to smell, smell, smell and taste, taste, taste. There's always more risk."

The payoffs are wines of character and depth, and perhaps a public willing to listen to the wines.

"We're selling more and more," he said. "I think people are much more interested in Beaujolais, in the good people, at least."

October 2007

A Potion From a Town Named for Love

By FRANK J. PRIAL

I f there was no St. Amour, somebody would have had to make him up. Someone probably did. But I'm getting ahead of myself.

A good part of the world celebrates St. Valentine's Day tomorrow. Couples exchange greeting cards and gifts, and, if the timing is right, protestations of undying love. There apparently was a St. Valentine. In fact, there were probably three of them, and no one, least of all the Roman Catholic Church, is sure which was which.

Confirming its uncertainties, the church quietly dropped Valentine from its calendar of saints in 1969, leaving him—or them—more in the realm of legend than verifiable church history.

One story about Valentine goes like this: In the third century A.D., the Roman emperor Claudius II banned marriages because he wanted single men for his armies. Valentine, a priest, was caught performing marriages secretly and was condemned to die. On death row, he miraculously cured the jailer's daughter of some ailment and, as he was led off to be stoned, left her a note signed "Your Valentine." This was said to have happened on Feb. 14, 270.

In fact, Feb. 15 had long been a Roman festival, called the Lupercalia, during which men and women drew partners by lots, then paired off for sexual games. The church tried to counter the Roman event by asking the faithful to pick a saint and follow the saint's example for a year. The anniversary of Valentine's martyrdom, Feb. 14, was chosen for the counterfestival. In medieval times, these games, spiritual and erotic, morphed into what became St. Valentine's Day.

This is where St. Amour comes in. All we know about him is that he may have been a Roman soldier who may have quit the army in Gaul and settled down. His name may have been Amor, or Amore (just as in the old Dean Martin song). He was a decent sort, so the story goes, and the town where he lived, in what is now the northern part of Beaujolais, was named after him.

If you don't believe any of this, there is a statue of him near a church in St.-Amour that shows exactly what he may have looked like, if in fact he existed.

Let's jump ahead many centuries. It's 1940, and Louis Dailly, who was born in St.-Amour, has returned from Paris after 15 years working in his brother's bar. With him is his wife, Thérèse, a Beaujolais girl he met in Paris. Each comes from a winemaking family, so they invest their savings in vineyards.

Convinced that St.-Amour wines were equal to, or better than, many of the more famous Beaujolais wines like Moulin-à-Vent and Chiroubles, Mr. Dailly set out to have their rating changed from simple Beaujolais and Beaujolais-Villages to one of the famous "cru" wines that bear the name of the town where they are produced.

In 1946 he succeeded, and St.-Amour was raised to the same level as Morgon, Moulin-à-Vent, Chiroubles, Fleurie, Chénas, Brouilly, Côtes de Brouilly and Juliénas. Not until 1988 was another cru Beaujolais created: Régnié.

Cru status meant more prestige for St.-Amour—and more money for its producers—but it took some years before anyone realized the natural affinity of St.-Amour and St. Valentine. If St. Valentine's Day originally was for disaffected lovers, what better way for them to spend the day than drinking a wine named both for love and a saint, albeit an elusive one?

St.-Amour is among the least well known of the 10 Beaujolais crus. It's from the northernmost Beaujolais region, almost touching the Mâconnais, the mostly white wine region just to the north.

St.-Amour's total production is about 200,000 cases a year, less than half that of some medium-size California wineries.

The soil is principally crushed pink granite, and the wine is soft but well-structured, mirroring the qualities of the great Moulin-à-Vent wines produced a few miles to the south. In fact, a St.-Amour will probably age better than a Fleurie or a Brouilly because it has better acid levels than either of those wines.

Not unexpectedly, Georges Duboeuf, the famous Beaujolais négociant, has a strong presence in St.-Amour and usually bottles at least one wine with a label noting its connection with St. Valentine's Day. Other prominent négociants, like Joseph Drouhin in Burgundy, also offer wines from St.-Amour.

But I digress from the spirit of the day, however questionable its provenance. Here in Paris, the sky is gray and the rain never far off. But it's warm, and early bulbs are sprouting in every secret courtyard, daring the sun to appear.

Parisian florists, artists in their own right, have splashed every other street corner with great washes of spring color.

Could Valentine's Day have anything to do with all this? Let's give the old boy credit, if only for sentiment's sake. And if he has had a little help from St.-Amour, so much the better.

February 2002

Surprises From the Jura,
Jagged in a Velvet-Smooth Universe

By ERIC ASIMOV

Towns don't come much tinier than this quiet hamlet, population 86, north-west of Arbois in the heart of the Jura wine region. You can pass the church, the graveyard and a few farmhouses in about the time it takes one of the dozing dogs to roll over. And yet, within sniffing distance of this thriving metropolis is an even smaller suburb, Petit-Molamboz, which indeed does justice to its diminutive name.

The Jura defies many expectations, nowhere more so than in its wines. The leading whites have a nutty, sherry-like aroma that many people regard as hope-lessly oxidized, but they are actually tangy, complex, pure and delicious. The best reds barely have enough color to be called red. They are delicate and graceful, yet with an earthy intensity that can stand up to the smelliest of cheeses. Almost singularly among wine regions, the reds are usually served before the whites in the Jura because they are lighter in texture.

The region's most profound wine, vin jaune, or yellow wine, is hard to find in the United States. It is traditionally sold in squat clavelin, 62-centiliter bottles, a size that is not sanctioned by the American government, a pity since the saline, mineral force of this wine is extraordinary.

Even in France, the wines of the Jura are little-known, but they are as dis-tinctive as any in the world. The Jura is a bucolic green bowl between Burgundy and Switzerland, where the patchwork of vineyards and hayfields is occasionally interrupted by a village of tile-roofed houses or a herd of cows. Roads came fairly late to the region; canals never did. So the Jura evolved, like the marsupials of Australia, in relative isolation, which permitted the planting of grapes like savagnin, ploussard and trousseau that are grown almost nowhere else, made into wines with techniques that in most places would be regarded as downright peculiar.

The wines are surely not for everyone. Even lovers of vin jaune sometimes describe its flavor as "rancid walnut," yet this wine is an unmatched partner of regional specialties like chicken with cream sauce and morels, and of course Comté, the famous cheese of the Jura. In a world of smooth, rounded, velvet-lined wines, they stand out as jagged and resolute, like many of the most interesting winemakers.

Jean-Marc Brignot, 37, grew up in Normandy and learned about winemaking working in Beaujolais and Champagne, but when it came time to make his own wine, he chose the Jura, which he had first visited on a holiday as a teenager.

"I really love this area and I love the wine," said Mr. Brignot, a tall, dark man whose browned arms and permanent squint indicate many hours spent in the sun in his 13.5 acres of vines. After training with Pierre Overnoy, an elder statesman in the nearby town of Pupillin—"Capitale Mondiale du Ploussard," it says in the town square—Mr. Brignot and his partner, Matilde Vergeau, purchased an ancient stone farmhouse here in Molamboz. They added a concrete floor to the barn, and electricity, and with a budget the size of Petit-Molamboz they jury-rigged a winery.

In 2004, their first vintage, they made 17 different wines in minute quantities. Last year they made 15 wines, all without sulfur dioxide, a preservative that has been used since antiquity, except by iconoclasts like Mr. Brignot, Mr. Overnoy and Emmanuel Houillon, who took over for Mr. Overnoy after he retired. At their best, the Brignot and the Overnoy wines have an unusual freshness and purity, with deep, rich, tangy mineral flavors.

"We make natural wines just with grapes," Mr. Brignot said. "They are better for people, and they taste better, too."

By all rights, Mr. Brignot's wines should be completely unknown outside of the Jura. But at a conference on natural wines last year he met Arnaud Erhart, the owner of 360 restaurant in Red Hook, Brooklyn, who introduced him to Joe Dressner of Louis/Dressner Selections, an importer who brings in the Overnoy wines. Now you can find a little Brignot in the United States, though 360 seems to be the primary recipient.

While Jura wines are never easy to find, more restaurants in New York seem to be carrying them. In addition to 360, Jura wines are sold at Bette, Cookshop and Trestle on Tenth, all in Chelsea, and Balthazar in SoHo. Bottles from Jacques Puffeney, one of the best producers in Arbois, the central city in the region, turn up fairly regularly. Mr. Puffeney, formidably taciturn, bearded and portly, makes wines that have the incisive power of a hard stare combined with the grace of a smile.

He makes a pretty poulsard (as ploussard is known outside of Pupillin), with a delicate fragrance of raspberries, strawberries and earth. He makes a spicy pinot noir, and a tangy chardonnay. Fifty percent of the grapes planted in the Jura are chardonnay, more or less, and they can be very good. But by far Mr. Puffeney's and the region's most distinctive wines come from the savagnin grape. His 2002 savagnin is strong and cutting, yet with a light-bodied delicacy, while his 1996 vin jaune is rich and briny with razor-sharp focus.

What makes these savagnin wines so different? When most wines are placed in barrels to age, winemakers assiduously top off the barrels, replacing whatever wine is lost to evaporation and thereby preventing oxidation. But with their best lots of savagnin, Jura winemakers permit evaporation, and as room develops in the barrel a film of beneficial yeast forms over the surface of the wine. In Jerez, where sherry is made, a similar yeast forms called flor. Here in the Jura, the yeast is called la voile, the veil, and the wines are said to be made sous-voile, under the veil. The yeast, along with the oxygen and a forceful acidity, impart the characteristic tangy, salty, nutty flavor. The evaporation gave rise to the 62-centiliter clavelin bottles, which supposedly accommodate all that remains of a liter if it has been left in a barrel for six years.

Jura winemakers tend to bridle at the comparison with sherry. They point out that sherry is fortified, unlike their wines, and prefer to compare savagnin to furmint, the grape of the Hungarian tokay wines, or traminer, a paler-skinned version of gewürztraminer. "Furmint, chenin blanc, traminer, savagnin, we think they are all somehow cousins," Mr. Brignot said.

Not everybody falls for this sort of wine. Kermit Lynch, a seminal American importer who brought many unusual French country wines to the United States in the 1970s and '80s, passed on the opportunity to bring in wines from the Jura. "That purposeful oxidation wasn't to my taste, and I sure didn't think it was going to be to the taste of Americans back then," he said.

But Neal Rosenthal, another importer, is a big fan. He brings in the Puffeney wines as well as those from Nicole Dériaux of Domaine de Montbourgeau in L'Étoile, south of Arbois, who makes subtle, elegant chardonnays using the oxidative method. And Jeffrey Alpert, an American who began to import wine just a few years ago, has enthusiastically embraced the Jura, bringing in wines from Jean-François Ganevat with an unusual floral complexity.

"We don't all eat the same food, we don't watch the same movies every night, but we're programmed to drink the same wine," Mr. Alpert said. "It's ridiculous, because there are so many great wines out there."

Edward Behr, who publishes *The Art of Eating*, a quarterly journal, discovered the Jura wines recently while researching a piece on Comté cheese. He was so fascinated with them that he returned almost immediately to write about the wines.

"There are all these places in France that will never take off, the Jura perhaps being the extreme," Mr. Behr said, "but they're such good food wines."

Not everybody in the Jura is as enthusiastic about the oxidized wines as their American fans. Jean Rijckaert, a Burgundy producer, now makes very clean, Burgundy-style chardonnay and savagnin wines that are increasingly seen in the United States.

And Stéphane Tissot in Arbois, one of the region's most innovative winemakers, questions whether the oxidation-style chardonnays, at least, are traditional at all.

"I think it is a recent style of the last 50 years," Mr. Tissot said. "I'm not sure that a century ago that was how chardonnay was made."

Mr. Tissot, whose label bears his parents' names, André and Mireille Tissot, makes an excellent, pure, slightly tannic ploussard, and a handful of dry, minerally chardonnays that are Burgundian in spirit if not exactly in flavor. But his vin jaune, with its dense, oxidized, minerally aroma, is his most glorious wine.

Any sommelier or merchant in New York who sells wines from the Jura has a story to tell about customers who had no idea what they were getting. Some were astounded by how good the wines were, while others were befuddled, thinking the wines were flawed.

Mr. Behr recalled how one winemaker explained to him what made the Jura so different.

"He said, 'The thing about these wines is that they don't belong to the Old World and they don't belong to the New World, they are a world apart,'" Mr. Behr said. "What fascinates me is that they don't refer to anything but themselves."

August 2006

The Rewards of the Pampered Grape

By ERIC ASIMOV

From a chalky slope high above this little hillside town, a patchwork of vine-yards stretches as far as the eye can see, dotted occasionally with a thatch of trees or a cluster of buildings. Only the occasional rush of a high-speed TGV train interrupts the pastoral spell of this bowl-shaped valley in the Mâconnais region of southern Burgundy. Lacking the drama of the impossibly steep vineyards of the Côte Rôtie to the south or the allure of the exalted grand cru vineyards in the Côte d'Or to the north, the Mâconnais has had to get by on the sort of quiet beauty that you see only when you look closely.

For years, the Mâconnais has been known as the land of cheap white wine—innocuous stuff to be chilled for a picnic or dragged behind a boat while fishing. The Mâconnais is in Burgundy and uses the same white grape, chardonnay. But it is apart, joined awkwardly to the southern tip along with Beaujolais, its red wine counterpart. It is an unlikely union. The people here speak of the Côte d'Or as Burgundy, the way people from Queens or Brooklyn call Manhattan "the city."

But with humility and stealth perhaps typical of this modest region, white wines of the Mâconnais are slowly inserting themselves into the world of fine Burgundies. More precisely, they are drawing attention southward. No, there are no Montrachets or Meursaults in the Mâconnais—not yet, anyway, and that is a blessing, financially speaking.

What you have may be something better: a growing selection of distinctive wines that taste specifically and recognizably of their vineyards—vins des ter-roirs, as the French say. This sense of place is the precise quality that wine lovers covet in good white Burgundy, but for far less money.

Many of these bottles come from a new wave of Mâconnais winemakers, who have turned their backs on the way the other 90 percent of Mâcon's wine is pro-duced. Some are recent arrivals, like Jean Rijckaert in Leynes, who came here from Belgium in 1994 and whose wines are beautifully precise and well shaped.

Others, like Daniel Barraud, carry on the winemaking work that has been in their families for generations but combine the wisdom of their ancestors with the latest understanding of winemaking and viticultural techniques. Mr. Barraud produces razor-sharp wines of elegance and grace.

The young Bret brothers, Jean-Guillaume and Jean-Philippe, have brought energy and idealism to their new venture, Domaine de la Soufrandière, which since its first vintage in 1999 has turned out wines of great purity. Olivier Merlin, who acquired a vineyard in 1987, makes wines of concentration and depth. Jean Thévenet, a longtime producer, makes wines of rare richness and body.

Looming above the other Mâconnais winemakers, though, is an idiosyncratic Belgian named Jean-Marie Guffens, who with record-industry chutzpah and an infectious Keith Richards wheeze of a laugh, has barged into the top ranks of Burgundy winemakers. For 20 years he has been producing tiny quantities of exquisite wine from his own vineyards under the label Guffens-Heynen. In 1990, he founded Maison Verget, a small négociant house that offers a collection of stunning wines from the Mâconnais, as well as from Chablis and the Côte d'Or.

Over dinner one night in the town of Chaintré, Mr. Guffens poured a 1994 Guffens-Heynen Mâcon-Pierreclos En Chavigne that was still fresh and lively, coiled with acidity yet offering plenty of depth. He followed that with a '91 Guffens-Heynen Pouilly-Fuissé Clos des Petits-Croux that was both rich and youthful, with many years ahead of it, ample evidence demonstrating that when made with attention to detail, Mâcon wines can indeed age.

"Mâcon has to be good, because it's not expensive enough to be bad," Mr. Guffens said, repeating a well-practiced line that is nonetheless full of perception. The wine-buying public is all too willing to suspend its judgment with expensive wines like Meursaults or Montrachets. The pressure of the investment practically requires people to like them or feel as if they have wasted money. Spend less, and the critical faculties improve remarkably.

Buoyed by the evidence of how successful Mâcon wines could be, the region has drawn some unlikely investors. In 1999 Dominique Lafon, who heads Comtes Lafon, the renowned Meursault estate, bought around 20 acres of vineyard in Milly-Lamartine near La Roche-Vineuse. Last year he bought another 18, in the northern Mâcon near the towns of Uchizy and Chardonnay (where legend has it the grape received its name). Last year, too, Anne-Claude Leflaive of Domaine Leflaive, another celebrated white Burgundy producer, purchased around 20 acres in the Mâconnais.

For Mr. Lafon, the move to the Mâconnais was a natural. "There are no vineyards to buy in Meursault, not that anybody can afford," he said. "The clay and limestone soil in the Mâcon is the same class as in Meursault, and I already knew and understood the grapes."

Mr. Lafon's Mâconnais wines, sold as Les Héretiers du Comtes Lafon, include a simple, inexpensive Mâcon that is fermented in steel tanks and tastes fresh and pure, as well as more complex wines that he ferments in puncheons and foudres, oak barrels that are bigger than those typically used in Burgundy and California. Like many in the Mâconnais, he avoids new barrels, which impart the oaky flavor that dominates so many American chardonnays.

In his fifth year of making wine in the Mâconnais, Mr. Lafon said, he is finally figuring it out. More important, he feels he has gotten control of his vineyards, which when he purchased them, he said, were over-fertilized and under-pampered.

In the past, the grapes from Mr. Lafon's vineyards, as with 80 to 90 percent or so of the grapes throughout the Mâconnais, were sold to cooperatives, which turned the grapes into indifferent wine. Farmers sold their grapes by weight, a powerful incentive for quantity over quality. They used fertilizers and herbicides to encourage grape production, and they picked the grapes, with mechanical harvesters, before optimum ripeness, because to wait would be too risky.

Grapes from all over the region were pressed together, the standard formula for cheap assembly-line wine all over the world.

"Co-ops led to tractors and machines, and for a long time the word 'terroir' was forgotten," Jean-Philippe Bret said.

The new wave in Mâcon takes an artisanal approach. They plow the vineyards and abhor chemical herbicides, which along with the weeds can kill a multitude of organisms that are beneficial to the soil. Yields are kept low, which concentrates the juice in each grape. Grapes are picked by hand at ideal ripeness and gently pressed in the winery to preserve delicacy and purity. Grapes from different regions, and even from different parts of the same vineyard, are processed separately to preserve their specific character.

These expensive, labor-intensive practices are rare in the region, and the wines are still only a trickle in the vast flow from the Mâconnais. "I am alone in the town of La Roche-Vineuse to pick by hand," said Mr. Merlin, who supplements his own vineyards by buying grapes from like-minded growers. "When I started, we were maybe three or four winemakers. Now we are 20. It's not a lot, but it's a start."

One possibly daunting obstacle to improvement in the Mâcon is a lack of a vineyard hierarchy. In the Côte d'Or, vineyards are ranked in a pyramid. At the bottom are regional wines, simply labeled Bourgogne rouge or Bourgogne blanc (in fact, a lot of this mediocre white wine comes from the Mâconnais).

Wines from better vineyards might have a village name on the label, like Meursault or St.-Aubin. Even better vineyards might be designated premier cru, while the best are the grands crus.

Mâcon's system has no such precision. Plain Mâcon and Mâcon-Supérieur form the generally insipid base. A step up are the Mâcon-Villages, wines made in any of 40 or so villages in the region. If all the grapes come from one of these villages, the name can be used on the label, as in Mâcon-La Roche-Vineuse or Mâcon-Vergisson.

Three appellations around the town of Pouilly—Pouilly-Fuissé, Pouilly-Loché and Pouilly-Vinzelles—are often considered superior, but a river of bad, over-priced Pouilly-Fuissé that washed into the United States in the 1970s caused an image problem that persists. Finally, there is Saint-Véran, a collection of villages that border the Pouilly area. And that's it.

In the hands of good winemakers, though, it's astounding how specific the aromas and flavors of the Mâconnais can be. Regardless of stylistic differences from one winemaker to the next, and across vintages, the characters of various terroirs emerge. Wines from Vergisson or Milly-Lamartine tend to be minerally, while wines from Bussières or Davayé have a more pronounced fruitiness.

In a tasting of four vintages of Maison Verget's Saint-Véran Terre Noires, the characters of each were consistent, full of depth and complexity with persistent mineral and fruit flavors. Yet each was distinctly different from Verget's other bottlings.

"When people think of the Mâcon, they think of this nice little white wine that's all the same," Mr. Lafon said. "But there's as much diversity of wines and types as in the Côte d'Or."

To Mr. Guffens, the problem is one of attitude. He senses a modesty in the region that keeps winemakers from reaching their potential. Fifteen years ago, Mr. Guffens said, he took issue against the local trade organization, which used the motto, "Le Mâcon, C'est Bon."

"I didn't want people saying I made good wine," Mr. Guffens said. "My Mâcon, c'est grand!"

June 2004

Modern Love for Ancient Vines in Southern Italy

By ERIC ASIMOV

Rolling hills carpeted with vineyards surround this tiny village in the Irpinia region of Campania here in southern Italy, where the landscape has hardly changed for centuries. Then it hits your eye, a sleek structure of glass, brushed steel and concrete, Feudi di San Gregorio's new $25 million winery and hospitality center, as likely a feature of this countryside as an alien spaceship.

Huge diesel buses, miles from the tourist centers of Naples and the Amalfi coast, idle in the parking lot, awaiting the scores of German and Dutch visitors who are touring the building, which was designed by the Japanese architect Hikaru Mori, who lives in Milan. Perhaps the tourists have descended into the chaste white earthquake-resistant cellar, where thousands of barrels are soothed around the clock by 16th-century madrigals written by Carlo Gesualdo, an Irpinian composer infamous for having murdered his wife. Maybe they are sitting in the glass-enclosed tasting room, in sculptured chairs of soft leather. Or maybe they have descended on Marennà, a modern restaurant that has already won wide acclaim for its refined dining.

It's a huge change for Campania, which for centuries has been a viticultural backwater in a country that is an ocean of wine. While the world discovered the great wines of northern Italy, the Barolos and Barbarescos of Piedmont, and the Brunellos and modern blends of Tuscany, Campania and the rest of the south was given little thought. The prosperous, industrialized northern Italians have always dismissed the southerners' rustic wines, made from unknown indigenous grapes.

But Campania and the south have never accepted the north's version of the truth. And in the last decade the rapid pace of progress has transformed Campania and its neighboring province of Basilicata into the most exciting winemaking areas in Italy. And unlike the north, which initially attracted attention with wines made from French varietals like cabernet sauvignon and merlot, Campania is doing it with grapes that were growing in the region even before Vesuvius buried Pompeii.

Crisp, mineral-laden whites, made from grapes that can be traced back to ancient Greece, belie the image of Italian white wines as mere thirst quenchers. Fascinating reds are being produced from grapes so obscure they cannot be found in even the latest wine guides. Most important, though, are the fine red wines made from aglianico (pronounced ah-lee-ahn-EE-co), another grape with origins in ancient Greece.

Like nebbiolo, the grape of Barolo, aglianico can be tough and tannic, with flavors reminiscent of tar and tobacco. But it softens faster and, like pinot noir, the aromas and flavors of aglianico differ markedly depending on the soil and climate in which it grows. North of Naples in the Falerno area near the Tyrrhenian coast, aglianico has a full, earthy, almost floral character. To the south, around the ancient Greek settlement of Paestum, the wines seem tighter, with a light smokiness and herbal quality. Inland in the Taurasi zone, where aglianico is planted on the foothills of the Apennine mountains, and in Basilicata, where vines grow on the slopes of Mount Vulture (pronounced vul-TOUR-ay), the wines are structured and complex, with minerality that comes from volcanic soil.

"I consider aglianico with nebbiolo probably the most important Italian indigenous varietals," said Riccardo Cotarella, an enologist who has worked with some of Campania's most important winemakers.

Feudi di San Gregorio, one of Mr. Cotarella's clients, is the best financed and perhaps the most innovative of the south's newer winemakers. But while its new facility is a striking addition to the Campanian countryside, Feudi's high-spending approach is far from ordinary. The most exciting new producers in Campania and Basilicata characteristically come from farm families that have grown grapes for centuries. These families typically sold their grapes for meager prices to big producers, to be made into cheap wine. In tough economic times, when grape prices went down, these families struggled even more than usual.

"We had to try something else," said Salvatore Fucci, whose vineyard is in the heart of the Vulture area in Basilicata. "Growing grapes, we couldn't live. Necessity forced us to do this." With barely enough financing, Mr. Fucci and his family went into the winemaking business. The estate's first commercial vintage, 2000, was released under the label Elena Fucci, named for Mr. Fucci's daughter, who is studying winemaking in Pisa. He has received good reviews, though not good enough for Mr. Fucci to feel comfortable in his new life.

"We're not Tuscan," he said. "Here, things assume another dimension. We worry about bad things. The weather. We used to have to pay people to take our grapes."

The litany of landowners turned winemakers seemed endless: Fattoria Galardi, whose austere, complex Terra di Lavoro wines have been rapturously praised by Robert M. Parker Jr., the influential wine critic; De Conciliis and Luigi Maffini along the southern coast; Antonio Caggiano in Taurasi and Villa Raiano in Avellino; Salvatore Molettieri in Irpinia; Masseria Felicia near Caserta. They all began making wine in the 1990s after decades if not centuries of growing grapes.

"In Caserta 10 years ago there were 5 estates; now there are 28," said Nicola Trabucco, an agronomist who counts 15 properties in northern Campania among his clients. "In Benevento there are 50 new estates in the last five years."

Before the avalanche of new producers, one winemaker, Mastroberardino, held the torch high for Campania. Since 1878 Mastroberardino has been producing fine red wines from aglianico and whites from grapes like greco, fiano and falanghina. Almost alone it carefully tended the traditions, asserting a place for the wines that the rest of the world seemed to spurn.

"There is a strong conviction that we have an extraordinary patrimony," said Piero Mastroberardino, who runs the winery with his father, Antonio. "Twenty years ago maybe one or two wineries were making Taurasi. Now there are 30 or 40."

For elegance and complexity, few wines in Campania can match Mastroberardino's Taurasi Radici, a tar- and mineral-flavored wine that, like Barolo or Burgundy, can take on the aroma of truffles as it ages and can last for decades. Because Campania was ignored for so long, it is still catching up with the scientific advances that are taken for granted in most of the modern winemaking world. Grapes like chardonnay, pinot noir and cabernet have been thoroughly analyzed, allowing farmers to select clones and rootstocks best suited for particular combinations of soil and climate. But scientists have barely scratched the surface on the grapes of Campania.

"Research on aglianico has been going on for a few years," Mr. Mastroberardino said, "but for greco, fiano and the others, it is just beginning."

The transition from small grower to grower-producer has occurred all over the wine-producing world as farmers have figured out where the money is. But it's happening in Campania and Basilicata decades after regions like Piedmont, which went through its own shakeout in the 1960s and '70s. In Campania growers saw what happened in the mid-1990s, when Mr. Parker raved about new estates like Galardi and Montevetrano, which have since become the equivalent of cult wineries. But government loans and subsidies, available in the 1990s for existing farms, also encouraged growers to improve vineyards and cellars with new vines and new equipment, and to start bottling their own wine.

Typically for this land of contrasts, where the undulating pastoral beauty of olive groves and tobacco fields is defiled by slag heaps alongside mountains that have been gouged to make cement, the loans that helped so many in the last decade are squeezing these new producers, who must now repay the money they borrowed. With the slower economy, many of these wineries are facing frightening choices.

"Many new estates, with good potential, don't have the resources to wait out a bad market," Mr. Trabucco, the agronomist, said. "You need two or three years' investment to carry you through. They don't have it, so they look for an immediate return."

By that they mean high scores from influential critics who can cause a run on a particular wine. Many producers, believing that Mr. Parker's publication, *The Wine Advocate*, favors inky, powerful, concentrated wines with plenty of new oak flavor, try to make wines in that style, often at the expense of aglianico's characteristic medium body and earthy flavors.

Many winemakers were inspired by the success of Montevetrano, in southern Campania, which was started by Silvia Imparato, a photographer who caught the wine bug in the mid-1980s. With the help of Mr. Cotarella and his brother, Renzo, a winemaker for Antinori in Tuscany, she made 1,000 bottles of her first vintage, 1991. She had wanted to make a wine purely of aglianico, she said, but Mr. Cotarella, who is from Umbria, refused. Instead, Mr. Cotarella, who had made his reputation working with Bordeaux varietals, insisted on 60 percent cabernet sauvignon, 30 percent merlot and 10 percent aglianico.

"In the beginning I didn't trust this region, because there weren't any important wines," Mr. Cotarella says now. Ms. Imparato's wines, plummy yet light-bodied, with scents of cedar and tobacco, are now sought all over the world.

Several years after he began with Montevetrano, Mr. Cotarella began working with Galardi and with Feudi di San Gregorio. With Galardi, he makes one of Campania's most profound wines, Terra di Lavoro, out of aglianico and piedirosso, an indigenous grape that is often blended with aglianico.

"Montevetrano showed me the potential of the region, and Galardi showed me the potential of the indigenous grapes," he said. "Both represent what it can mean to work in the region with the right philosophy, the right terroir and the right varietals."

Montevetrano, with its use of familiar international grapes like cabernet and merlot, is practically unique in Campania. Recently Mr. Cotarella recommended to another client, Alois, that it rip out its small plot of cabernet and instead plant casavecchia, an obscure, ancient red grape that is only now being studied.

Alois, near Caserta, complied and now makes a silky, minerally 100 percent casavecchia, which it calls Trebulanum. Another producer, Vestini Campagnano, specializes in little-known indigenous grapes like casavecchia and pallagrello, which in its bianco form makes soft, supple white, and in its nero form makes powerhouse reds. By many estimates the older vineyards of Campania and Basilicata hold dozens of grape varieties waiting to be rediscovered.

Back at Feudi di San Gregorio, Mr. Cotarella is working on a new project, sparkling wine. Almost every region of Italy produces spumante, though Campania has yet to create a market for its own. Mr. Cotarella has enlisted as an adviser Anselme Selosse, winemaker of Jacques Selosse, a small but important Champagne house, but Mr. Selosse will not be coming to teach the Italians about chardonnay and pinot noir. Instead they will be making sparkling wine with greco, falanghina and fiano.

"The French people," Mr. Cotarella said with relish, "they are very jealous!"

January 2005

A Rare Tasting of Conterno Barolos

By ERIC ASIMOV

The Barolos of Giacomo Conterno are among the most beautiful wines in the world: gorgeously pure and packed with flavors that feel almost three-dimensional. Despite the intensity, the texture is sheer, almost delicate, like silken threads that can suspend bridges.

And yet, with wines like this, the flavors and aromas are really only the start.

Great wines pack history into a glass. Mostly, it's a natural tale—of calamitous weather or blue skies and sunshine. But the human element pours forth, too—weddings, births and deaths, war, prosperity and depression. Even that is only the beginning, especially if you are Roberto Conterno, the proprietor of Giacomo Conterno.

Mr. Conterno was in New York last month for a dinner at Eleven Madison Park to raise money for rebuilding Haiti. He brought with him seven vintages of both his Cascina Francia Barolo, the normal bottling, and the magnificent Monfortino riserva, plus one older Barolo, from 1937.

For Barolo lovers, this was a rare opportunity to compare the two Conternos in multiple vintages. For Mr. Conterno, this was an occasion to commune with his past, to hear once again the unmistakable voices of his father, Giovanni, and his grandfather, Giacomo, through the medium of the wine.

The voices tell not only the story of the Conterno estate but of the evolution of Barolo from a little-known wine sold largely in barrels and demi-johns in the early 20th century to one of the most prized wines in the world today. Giacomo Conterno, Roberto's grandfather, was one of the first small Barolo producers to bottle his own wine, beginning in the 1920s. His sons, Giovanni and Aldo, took over the estate in 1961.

Giovanni, who was Roberto's father, adhered closely to the traditional methods of his father. The just-fermented wine was kept with the skins for a prolonged maceration, imparting structure and texture. The wine then was aged in large, old oak casks—four years for the Cascina Francia and at least seven years for the Monfortino. The estate has never deviated from these methods, even as others turned to small French oak barrels, or barriques, to soften the wines.

Aldo, the younger brother, wanted to establish his own business. In 1969, he established Poderi Aldo Conterno, where he and his family continue to make superb Barolos. Giovanni remained, making wines on his own until Roberto, who was born in 1968, began to make the wine in 1988. Father and son worked side by side until Giovanni died in 2004.

"Whenever I enter the cellar, I feel my father and my grandfather with me," Roberto Conterno said before the dinner started. "We have them to thank for the wines we drink tonight."

And what wines. The youngest pair were from the fine 1999 vintage, 11 years old now but, in traditional Barolo terms, still too young to drink. The tight structure of the Cascina Francia restrained the aromas from bursting forth, while the Monfortino was lusher and richer—still better to wait another five years.

I was particularly interested in the next pair, from the superb 1996 vintage. Like other '96 Barolos I've had, it wasn't ready to drink. But the Monfortino was absolutely delicious, with classic Barolo flavors of tar and roses, plush yet graceful and elegant. It's still a baby, and will last a long, long time.

All of the Conterno grapes come from the Cascina Francia vineyard, in Serralunga d'Alba, an area of the Barolo region known for its powerful, structured wines. In exceptional vintages, a selection of the best grapes is used to make Monfortino. These grapes are fermented separately, with no effort to control the temperature of the fermentation, no matter how high it gets, and are macerated longer. While the Monfortino's extended aging results in an even more structured wine than the Cascina Francia, when compared directly, the Monfortinos seem lusher and more generous.

The pair from 1990, another great Barolo vintage, were beautiful in very different ways. The Cascina Francia was the first wine of the evening to show the secondary aromas that come from aging, in this case an earthy, truffly quality. It was also the first wine to show the high-toned flavors of a mature Conterno, which I always experience as skyrockets and colors. The Monfortino seemed younger, and yet was so invitingly graceful I couldn't put it down.

Now we were moving on to older vintages. For each vintage, Mr. Conterno had brought two bottles of each wine. But for the 1985 vintage, Conterno produced three Barolos: Cascina Francia, a rare Cascina Francia riserva and the Monfortino. Mr. Conterno, who had not intended to bring the riserva, was momentarily perplexed to discover after the wines had been decanted that one of the Cascina Francias was a riserva. Trouble was, he didn't know which decanter it was in.

So we tasted three wines of this vintage, though we would not know which of the Cascina Francias was the riserva. All three wines had the truffly aroma, while the Monfortino seemed characteristically richer. One of the Cascina Francias seemed a little more structured. Was it the riserva? We'll never know.

The Conterno wines did not always come from the Cascina Francia vineyard. Before Barolo became well known in the 1970s, the family purchased grapes each year to make their wines. Mr. Conterno said that it was easy for his father to buy the best possible Serralunga grapes until the demand began to rise.

"My father understood how things were changing in the 1970s, and he bought Cascina Francia in 1974," Mr. Conterno said. The first vintage made from the vineyard was 1978.

Whatever the source of the grapes, the 1971 vintage was a highlight. The Cascina Francia was lovely and subtle. The Monfortino, by contrast, was complex and elegant, powerful and long-lasting, yet still lively and agile, everything a great Barolo, a great Monfortino, could be.

For many of the tasters, the 1971 Monfortino was their favorite wine of the night. Yet the next pair, from 1961, was breathtaking.

The Cascina Francia was unbelievably fresh and graceful, elegant and complete. This is what Barolo strives for, I thought. But somehow, the Monfortino outdid it, absolutely gorgeous, harmonious, long-lasting and complex. This was my wine of the night, while Mr. Conterno said the freshness of the '61 Cascina Francia made it his favorite.

That was a lot for him to concede, because next up were a pair from 1958, which Mr. Conterno had cited as one of his favorite vintages of all time.

"Some people ask me, 'Why don't you use barriques?'" Mr. Conterno said. "I say, I drank 1958, the best wine of my life. Why use barriques?"

This night, however, the 1958s seemed a little past their prime and disjointed. A last Barolo, a 1937, seemed a bit caramelized, yet identifiable as a Barolo. Lovely, considering.

One last voice was to be heard. "I like to remember another person behind the scenes, a sort of shadow, and that is my mother," Mr. Conterno said.

He told the story of how his father bought Cascina Francia, and of how, the morning the sale was to go through, he had felt doubts.

"He said to my mother, 'They are going to raise the price at the last minute, what should I do?'" Mr. Conterno recalled. "My mother said, 'Just go, and come back with the land.'"

"They did raise the price, but he came back with the land."

Fertile ground for future memories in a glass.

April 2010

An Italian Prince and His Magic Cellar

By ERIC ASIMOV

In a secluded back room of a hotel not far from the Trevi Fountain, a dozen glasses of Italian white wine sat before each of a small group of tasters. All were used to this sort of thing and, really, how exciting are most Italian white wines? Six were made from malvasia di Candia, ordinarily a workman-like grape not known for producing great table wines, yet these were astonishing.

The oldest, a 1978, was dry and fresh, with aromas of flowers, honey and minerals. The flavors seemed to linger in the mouth forever. The wine in the other glasses was sémillon, the backbone of great white Bordeaux but practically nonexistent in Italy. Yet these wines were even more astounding than the malvasias. The oldest, a 1971, had the lively mineral flavor of a fine Puligny-Montrachet.

The older the wines got, the younger they tasted. They seemed almost magical, and indeed the story of these wines has a fairy tale quality to it.

Once upon a time there was a prince. By most accounts he was not so much charming as eccentric. His name was Alberico Boncompagni Ludovisi, prince of Venosa, and his family, which can be traced back at least 1,000 years, includes two popes.

The prince lived on an estate, Fiorano, on the outskirts of Rome near the Via Appia Antica, the ancient Appian Way. There he grew wheat, raised dairy cows and made three wines, one red and two whites, from a small vineyard. The vineyard had been planted with the local grapes that make the sort of nondescript wines typical of Latium, the region centered on Rome.

But in 1946, when the prince inherited Fiorano, he replanted the vineyard with cabernet sauvignon and merlot, long before these Bordeaux grapes became familiar in Italy, and malvasia and sémillon. The prince practiced organic agri-culture in an era when others embraced chemical sprays. He kept his yields ridic-ulously low, resulting in minute quantities of intense, concentrated wines, and he did not filter them. He aged the wine in large numbered barrels, which he reused year after year. A fine white mold grew naturally in his cellar, covering the barrels and the bottles that he stored in neat stacks. The prince did nothing to remove it; he believed it was beneficial.

Few people knew of the wines, but their reputation was excellent.

"The greatness of Fiorano is a secret shared by a few," wrote Burton Anderson in *Vino*, his 1980 guide to Italian wine.

The red made the most profound impression. Italian white wines were thought to be inconsequential, and few paid attention to the prince's whites, though Mr. Anderson called the sémillon "the most refined wine of its type and a rarity in Italy."

One who was in on the Fiorano secret was Luigi Veronelli, a leading Italian wine writer who regularly rhapsodized about the wines. He liked the reds well enough, comparing them to Sassicaia, the Tuscan Bordeaux blend that became famous in the 1970s. But he loved the whites. He was among the first to note their potential for aging, and he bemoaned their scarcity. "To obtain his cru is practically impossible," Mr. Veronelli once wrote. "If I lived in Rome, I would beg for them at the prince's door every morning."

By all reports the prince was strong-willed and stubborn. He was elusive and rarely spoke to business associates. Mr. Anderson said he never met him. Neil Empson, who exported Fiorano wines to the United States in the 1970s, also never met him or saw the winery. He dealt only with a secretary.

"He was a rather strange person to do business with," Mr. Empson said in a telephone interview. "You had to pay him when you made the order, and he would ship whatever he wanted to ship, not what you ordered."

Mr. Empson said this caused him to stop doing business with the prince, and eventually he lost track of the wines.

The aging prince continued to make his wines until 1995, although he had stopped selling the bottles. After the '95 harvest he pulled out all the vines in his vineyard, except for a small plot of cabernet and merlot. He offered no explanation, and at the time none was asked.

The prince is now 86 years old, in ill health and living in a hotel in Rome. He had one child, Francesca, who married Piero Antinori, the eminent Tuscan winemaker, at the Fiorano estate in 1966. Mr. Antinori suggests today that the prince was unable to bear the thought of anybody else making his wines when he could no longer do it himself.

"He is so in love with this estate, and when you are very much in love, you are also a bit jealous," Mr. Antinori said by phone. "When he was not able to do it himself in the old way, probably he preferred to give up."

And so the vineyards lie fallow. And 14,000 bottles remained in the prince's cellar, slowly becoming engulfed by the white mold, until 2000, when Mr. Veronelli, seeking to publicize some Roman wines in connection with a bicycle race, sought an audience with the prince. It was then, Mr. Veronelli said, that he learned of the destruction of the vines.

Mr. Veronelli requested a sample of one of the remaining bottles and sent an emissary, Filippo Polidori, a restaurateur and television personality, to pick it up. After being kept waiting for 90 minutes, Mr. Polidori said at the tasting in Rome, a secretary told him that Mr. Veronelli could not have one bottle, but he could have all 14,000—9,500 of the malvasia and 4,500 of the sémillon—if he could disperse them properly.

Mr. Polidori said the prince wanted the bottles to be treated as a legacy, and not consumed right away. But first the bottles, mostly from the 1985 to '95 vintages, which had lain untended in the cellar for years, needed to be cleaned and cataloged. It took two people almost a year to complete the task.

Mr. Veronelli and Mr. Polidori then held a series of tastings, looking for the right people to disperse the wines. They eventually settled on three: Andrea Carelli, an Italian wine broker, who would handle the European and Asian markets; Paolo Domeneghetti, an importer in New York, who will handle American restaurant sales; and Sergio Esposito, managing partner of Italian Wine Merchants near Union Square, who will handle American retail sales.

Mr. Esposito, who was invited to a tasting, said he had never heard of the wines, and could only find vague references in old catalogs. "At the tasting I was completely overtaken by the wines and fell in love with them," he said. "To me, they are treasures. They're wines made from grapes that nobody knew could make wines like that. They had no history. It was one person's devotion."

Highlights from the Rome tasting stand out: a 1982 malvasia with flavors of apples, minerals and pears; a 1980 sémillon that tasted of hazelnuts and wax and seemed impossibly young. As the wines aged, the youthful acidity seemed to give way to mineral, earthy flavors. Yet unaccountably, in contrast to most white wines, which get darker with age, the golden colors of the young wines turned pale as they got older. How to explain this?

Mr. Esposito suggests that the prince was correct about the white mold. "He was so in tune with his surroundings that he had confidence the mold was O.K.," he said. "I think it was much like how blue cheese was discovered. It's blue and you're eating it and it's O.K."

Mr. Esposito said he plans to sell his allocation slowly over the course of five years, aiming for collectors who allow them to age. He is also planning to hold back bottles from each vintage for charity tastings. "I want to participate in these tastings for the next 20 or 30 years and see how they develop," he said.

As much as these wines are a legacy of the prince, they are too a legacy of Mr. Veronelli, who died in November at 78. Of these wines, which will never be produced again, he wrote, "They enchant you with the first taste, burrow in your memory and make you forever better."

December 2004

Some See a Wine Loved Not Wisely, but Too Well

By ERIC ASIMOV

You need to have your museum legs for a visit to Il Greppo, the historic estate just south of this hillside town, where the Biondi Santi family virtually invented the wine now prized around the world as Brunello di Montalcino. Within minutes of my arrival, Franco Biondi Santi, the family's 84-year-old patriarch, was opening a glass display case and showing me a rifle carried by his grandfather, Ferruccio, when fighting under Garibaldi against Austria in 1866.

It was Ferruccio who, at a time in the 1880s when his fellow Tuscans preferred light, fizzy, semisweet wines, experimented with different strains of the sangiovese grape, locally called the Brunello, and created a dry, forceful red wine with the intensity to age and improve for decades. As he has with many visitors before, Franco Biondi Santi took me into his cellar to show me his three remaining bottles of the 1888 Biondi Santi, the first great vintage of Brunello. He pointed out the huge fermentation and aging barrels, or botti, made of Slavonian oak, some of which have been in continuous use since the late 19th century. After a lunch that included three vintages of Biondi Santi Brunello, he poured out glasses of 1969 moscatello di Montalcino, a delicate, gloriously fragrant and fresh sweet wine that was among the last produced by his father, Tancredi, himself a celebrated viticulturist, before he died in 1970.

"This is the original wine of Montalcino," he said, citing references that go back to the 1500s.

With such a family legacy, it is no wonder that Mr. Biondi Santi is troubled with the state of Brunello di Montalcino. Though the 2001 vintage of Brunello, which has just been released, may be one of the best ever, questions abound in Montalcino over what kind of wine Brunello ought to be, how the wine should be made and where the grapes should be planted.

Since the first half of the 20th century, when Il Greppo's hillside vineyard, 1,600 feet above sea level, was the sole source of Brunello di Montalcino, the appellation has grown explosively. Nowadays, vineyards cover hillsides and flatlands all over the Montalcino zone, in all sorts of soils and at many different altitudes, and producers employ almost as many different techniques for making the wine as there are sausages in a salumeria.

Strict traditionalists like Mr. Biondi Santi and his ally, Gianfranco Soldera, whose Case Basse di Soldera wines may be the greatest Brunellos of all, scorn much of what passes for Brunello di Montalcino today. They say the wine too often is fruity, round and rich, without any semblance of the classic angular, austere sangiovese character of old. Brunellos aged in barriques, or small barrels of new French oak, rather than in botti, they say, might as well be coming from California or Australia for all the distinctiveness they possess.

"If a producer puts wines in barriques, it's because he has bad wine, without tannins," Mr. Soldera said. "He must replace the tannins and aromas with what is gained from the barriques."

Others, however, assert that Brunello di Montalcino has never been better, and point to the high demand around the world as evidence of Brunello's success. They applauded the relaxing of rules that used to require that wines be aged in barrels for four years before being released. Now, although Montalcino still has the longest aging requirement in Italy, only two of those four years must be in wood, unless it is a riserva, which must be aged for five years, half the time in wood.

"As new producers came on the scene, I would say the average quality has stayed pretty high, and the changes they have made to the laws have been quite beneficial," said Leonardo Lo Cascio, president of Winebow, an Italian wine importer for more than 25 years.

Many traditionally minded producers accuse others of wanting an even more drastic change: eliminating the rule requiring that Brunello be made only from the sangiovese grape. Indeed, they insist that some producers are already adding wine made from grapes other than sangiovese to darken the color and to make the wine easier to drink at an early age. They point to recent allegations of fraud in the neighboring Chianti Classico region and say it is only a matter of time before such cases surface in Montalcino.

"I think what has happened in the last few months in Chianti is only the tip of the iceberg," said Francesco Cinzano, chairman of Col d'Orcia, which makes Poggio al Vento, a fine, traditional style riserva Brunello.

Filippo Fanti, a Brunello producer and head of the Consorzio del Vino Brunello di Montalcino, the local trade association, said most producers supported the sangiovese rule and that any discussion of changing it was "theoretical."

Stylistic conflict, of course, is as much a part of winemaking as corks and barrels. Whether in California, Bordeaux, Burgundy or Barolo, those who adhere to winemaking tradition are always scandalized by those who do not feel bound by it. But the conflict has special resonance in Montalcino, a rare wine region where the origin of the style is still fresh in memory and where the inventor has a direct line to the present in the Biondi Santis. Indeed, the Biondi Santi family might have been quite content back in the 1960s if nobody but themselves had been permitted to call their wine Brunello di Montalcino, and they continue to feel a special sense of guardianship for the wine.

Contrary to the popular perception that European winemaking traditions have been honed over centuries of trial and error, Brunello di Montalcino is a relatively recent phenomenon. Through the first half of the 20th century, only the Biondi Santis made Brunello di Montalcino, and in 1960 only 11 producers were bottling their wine, with about 157 acres planted with sangiovese grosso, the Brunello grape.

But by 1990 more than 3,000 acres were planted, with 87 producers making Brunello, and today, according to the Consorzio del Vino Brunello di Montalcino, the trade association, nearly 4,700 acres are planted, with 183 producers.

With such growth, the Brunello style evolved in different directions. While it is hazardous to speak too generally about styles, wines in the more traditional mode are usually characterized by a ruby color and a lean, spare texture, with good acidity, structure that comes from tannins in the grapes rather than from tannins imparted by oak barrels, and flavors of bitter cherry and smoke. Producers include Il Poggione, Cerbaiona, Poggio di Sotto, Il Palazzone, Col d'Orcia and Lisini.

Wines in the more modern mode tend to be darker, plusher and less acidic, with tannins derived from oak barrels and opulent flavors of fruit and chocolate. Producers in this style include Uccelliera, Camigliano, Fanti, Casanova di Neri and La Poderina. And many producers, like Caparzo, Castelgiocondo, Mastrojanni and Ciacci Piccolomini d'Aragona, toe a middle line.

To taste a traditionally made Brunello like Biondi Santi or Soldera is to wonder why anybody would ever want to make a different sort of wine. The Biondi Santis today are often criticized as too lean and austere and are said to require too much aging, but to my taste they are like precisely cut gems, offering clearly delineated flavors that, even in a relatively young 1999, are simultaneously graceful and intense rather than lush and rich.

Mr. Soldera takes just as extreme an approach to winemaking as the Biondi Santis, perhaps even more so. He keeps his wine in large botti well beyond the required two years. While most producers are releasing their 2001 Brunellos, his 2000 is still in wood—"whatever the wine needs," he said. He is a decidedly opinionated man who recently constructed a new cellar with walls of crushed rock rather than cement, which he says destroys wine. On a visit to his cellar he laid down the ground rules: "I don't allow spitting."

Not that I would want to spit this wine. Even in barrels, it has an unusual purity and grace, tannic perhaps, but with a lacy delicacy as well. Though you may drain a glass, you can't say the glass is empty. The aroma lingers.

Mr. Soldera points to the wine, the color of polished rubies, and assails those who assess a wine by the depth of color. "Judging wine by a dark color is for stupid people," he said. "This is the color of sangiovese. You should be able to look through the wine and see your fingernail on the other side."

Unlike Biondi Santi, Soldera wines have maintained their critical reputation and can command up to $200 or $300 a bottle. But traditional Brunellos are still available at more modest prices, though they are hardly inexpensive. A subtle, stylish Brunello from a producer like Il Poggione can run $50, while a more intense, though equally elegant, riserva might be $75.

Fabrizio Bindocci, the director of Il Poggione, is suspicious of those who stray from traditional methods. He believes that Brunello ought to be a long-aged wine and says that proposals to relax the aging requirements even further come from producers with deficient wine.

"Some Brunellos on the market should age only two years because they're so thin," he said. "But ours have such structure they need the time."

Iano de Grazia, a partner with his brother in Marc de Grazia Selections, a wine brokerage in Florence, counts himself as favoring traditional Brunello, but says the aging rules are too restrictive, and are especially harmful in weak vintages.

"Maybe there should be some limit, but each vintage will tell you," he said. "It shouldn't be a stone recipe. That's crazy."

Not all changes have been so controversial. Few would dispute that viticulture has improved dramatically in the last 35 years, or that replacing rustic chestnut barrels with oak has been a good thing.

For his part, Mr. Biondi Santi has a proposal of his own. He would like to see the Montalcino zone divided into a series of subzones, each with its own character, rather than having so many contrasting styles lumped together as Montalcino. He points to the communes that make up the Côte d'Or in

Burgundy as the perfect example, but acknowledges that this is unlikely to happen as it would not be in most producers' interests.

What else would he like to see happen? He answers quickly.

"No more vineyards in clay soil, or below 1,000 feet. Return to Slavonian oak. Return to three years in wood. Abolish barriques.

"That would be sufficient."

February 2006

In Apulia, Emancipation for the Grapes

By R. W. APPLE Jr.

In 1997, Mark Shannon, a California wine consultant, flew to Sicily to help a client trying to complete a bulk wine deal. Traveling around the island by car, he met Elvezia Sbalchiero, another consultant, who comes from Friuli, in the far northeastern corner of Italy. One thing led to another, as it often does, and eventually the two formed a personal and professional partnership.

Now they own a company called Fusione—guess why?—based here in Apulia, in the heel of the Italian boot. Drawing on grapes grown by up to 1,600 small farmers in the area, he makes and she markets wines that have scored an astonishing success all around the globe, with projected sales this year 15 times as big as those in the winery's first year, 1998. The wines are called A-Mano, meaning handmade, and by far the best-known is a robust red made from a once-obscure grape named primitivo.

"We created or played a large part in creating a clean, modern-style primitivo and taking it around the world," Mr. Shannon told my wife, Betsey, and me when we stopped at the couple's whitewashed farmhouse in the ambling hills about 45 minutes south of Bari. "We work with third- and fourth-generation growers, who tend tiny plots of very old, low-yielding vines."

Ms. Sbalchiero, 41, interjected: "We started a bit of a social revolution here. At first the farmers didn't get it, but eventually they came to understand and trust us. We paid them cash, and we paid promptly, which no one had ever done before."

These days, said Mr. Shannon, 46, "all the growers know my car, and they stop me on the road and say, 'Come to see my grapes—they're as good as the ones you're buying.'"

DNA testing by Carole Meredith, a plant geneticist at the University of California, Davis, established a few years ago that primitivo is a descendant of a grape called crljenak kastelanski, widely grown in the 18th and 19th centuries on the Dalmatian coast of Croatia. (A crljenak cross with dobricic, plavac mali, is grown in that area today.) California's zinfandel, she showed, is genetically the same as primitivo, though how it crossed the ocean remains a subject of considerable dispute.

Apulian primitivo and zin are not twins, of course; climate, soil and vinification all help to shape a wine's look, aroma and flavor, along with the grape variety. But the two share several characteristics: both are fruit-rich, chewy, sometimes lush wines, a deep violet-red in color, often too high in alcoholic content for comfort (a ferocious 15.5 percent in some extreme cases), but much more subtle if carefully handled.

For years, tank trucks of rough, raisiny primitivo headed north every fall, destined for use, unacknowledged, to add heft to Chianti, Barbaresco and even red Burgundy. But now, tamed into "a gentle giant," as the wine writer Burton Anderson puts it, primitivo can stand on its own sturdy feet.

Mr. Shannon's winery, in the nearby town of Laterza, is absolutely immaculate. He uses plastic corks to further minimize the possibilities of contamination. And he uses refrigeration at every step of the way to maintain control, chilling the grapes from the minute they arrive from the fields, chilling the fermenting tanks and shipping the bottled wine in chilled containers. When A-Mano's huge compressors are fired up, he joked, "the lights flicker all over Apulia."

The partnership's big break came when Neil Empson, one of the leading exporters of Italian wines to the United States, tasted A-Mano primitivo and added it to his range. Other A-Mano labels have been added since, including a reserve bottling, Prima Mano, produced only in extraordinary years from two exceptionally old vineyards.

"We take pride," Mr. Shannon said, "at a time when the American market is awash in mediocre $35 wines, in making a food-friendly bottle that can retail for $10 or $11."

Fusione is not the only producer of high-quality primitivo. Several of the others are grouped in an unusual organization called the Accademia dei Racemi, not a true cooperative but an association in which each member makes his own wine and joins with the others for marketing support and technical advice. Based in Manduria, between the old cities of Taranto, founded by the ancient Greeks, and Lecce, which dates from Roman times, the group includes value-for-money labels like Masseria Pepe, Pervini and the stylish Felline, made by Gregory Perrucci, son of a bulk-wine producer.

Elsewhere, other changes are afoot, and some of them involve not red but white wines. Traditionally, Apulian whites have been regarded as second-class citizens, although at their best, the vegetal, slightly astringent wines produced around the town of Locorotondo and elsewhere from the little-known verdeca grape can be the kind of partners Apulia's enticing swordfish, turbot, sea bass and mullet deserve.

Lifting a leaf from the book of Planeta, the Sicilian winery that has demonstrated in recent years that southern Italy is not too hot to make superior chardonnay, several Apulian producers have succeeded lately with that cool-climate grape. One that Betsey and I enjoyed at Il Melograno, a quietly luxurious hotel near Monopoli on the Adriatic coast, was Laureato, a round, beautifully balanced product of the relatively young Vetrere winery, which is run by the sisters Annamaria and Francesca Bruni. Like many good New World chardonnays, it has luscious overtones of banana and pineapple.

Bonny Doon, the California operation of the pun-prone Randall Grahm, markets an Apulian red based on the Uva di Troia variety, called Il Circo "La Violetta." Its vivid label shows a liberally tattooed woman, and Mr. Grahm has promoted it as a creamy, quaffable yet complex wine that avoids "the indignities of internationalism and the ravages of the new wood order."

Piero Antinori, the eminent Tuscan producer, has taken the plunge into Apulia as well, under the Tormaresca label, and one of his first big winners is a refined, lightly oaked chardonnay called Pietrabianca. This is produced from grapes grown in the northern part of the region, near Frederick II's extraordinary eight-sided Castel del Monte, but the Antinori interests stretch farther south as well, with extensive holdings around San Pietro Vernotico, a village near the Crusader port of Brindisi.

Experimenting with varieties relatively little grown in Apulia, like merlot and cabernet sauvignon, Tormaresca has made a major splash. I especially enjoyed the Bocca di Lupo red from the Castel del Monte area, made with cabernet and aglianico, which is used for aristocratic, long-lived Taurasi in Campania. It stood up well to Il Falcone, Rivera's more traditional longtime leader in Castel del Monte.

"Land is terribly cheap here," said Matthew Watkins, the wine-loving Canadian husband of Roberta Guerra, who manages Il Melograno. "Antinori will show the way, and other big guys will come in after him. He's very big and very powerful, and he is making superb wines. I only hope that he doesn't displace the little guys."

One morning during our time in Apulia I headed north from lovely Lecce, Apulia's Baroque marvel, with Giuseppe Malazzini, who works for Agricole Vallone, to learn something about Graticciaia, one of Apulia's wine treasures. It is made from negroamaro grapes (the name means "black bitter" in Italian) harvested in good vintages from a small plot of 60-year-old vines, unsupported by trellises, that are allowed to grow into bushy, five-foot-high shapes called alberelli, or little trees, with trunks as thick as a grown man's forearm. Only 10,000 to 20,000 bottles a year are produced.

The key to Graticciaia is a process in which the grapes are dried on reed mats for three or four weeks in the open air, concentrating their aroma and flavor, before they are made into a soft, dark, well-focused red wine, with just a hint of vanilla.

Over lunch at an old bougainvillea-clad masseria, or farmhouse, where the Vallone sisters live, Donato Lazzari, the company manager, told me that the idea for the Amarone-like wine had come to him and to Severino Garofano, the wine consultant who has probably done more than anyone to lift the level of Apulian wine, on a flight south from Milan. Their inspiration, he said, came from a wine made in days of yore for the marriage of a daughter.

Vallone also makes more conventional wines from negroamaro, the most basic of which are designated as Salice Salentino, after the area where they are produced, far down the Apulian "heel." Francesco Candido is another player in this mass market, as is Leone de Castris, but the dominant Salice Salentino producer, so far as sales in the United States go, has long been Cosimo Taurino, a firm founded by a former pharmacist and carried forward since his death a few years ago by his son Francesco.

Taurino makes two highly acclaimed blends of negroamaro (85 percent) and malvasia nera (15 percent), Patriglione and Notarpanaro—each from a single vineyard. Both are dense, intensely garnet-colored and slow to open in decanter or glass. Although Patriglione costs more and wins higher marks from critics, I find Notarpanaro much less cumbersome with food.

Three more recent introductions compete in the super-premium negroamaro sweepstakes. These are the arrestingly labeled Nero, made by Conti Zecca; Le Braci, produced by Mr. Garofano, the consultant, who works on several of the others, too; and Masseria Maime from Tormaresco.

Some experts see unlimited possibilities for Apulian wines, across the board from the less expensive ones, perhaps best suited to simple trattoria meals, to the top-of-the-line bottlings that aim to stand eventually among Italy's best. Others are much more skeptical, like Joseph Bastianich, a partner in the restaurant Babbo in New York, a grower and a wine author. He praises Apulian reds as "terrific value, terrific with food," but doubts that even the best of them will ever loom large in the global market.

New Yorkers and visitors to the city can judge for themselves at I Trulli, a restaurant at 122 East 27th Street, owned by Nicola Marzovilla, an Apulian, which usually has at least a dozen wines from the region on its list. Vino, an all-Italian wine shop across the street, stocks most of them.

July 2004

In Spain, These Hills Are Alive (Again!)

By ERIC ASIMOV

The stone terraces, thick with green vines, rise up the face of a mountain from the River Sil at the impossibly steep angle of a rocket ascending toward space. The only way down, or up, is by foot, and even thinking about the climb in the brilliant heat of the summer sun is enough to make the legs throb, the back protest and the mind boil in rebellion against such seeming insanity.

Yet outside this small town in the heart of the Ribeira Sacra, in the Galicia region of northwest Spain, grape growers have been making that crazy climb day after day for 2,000 years. The Romans first carved these terraces to supply wine for their march to the Atlantic. Over the centuries the locals joined in, led by monks, who cut vineyards into canyons and precipitous gorges of the Sil and two other rivers: the Miño and the Bibei.

For millennia, terraced vineyards have been the face of this land. Farmers tended animals, grew grain and raised grapes—another subsistence crop.

But the 20th century proved disastrous. First phylloxera, a scourge of root-devouring aphids, devastated the vines. Then the Spanish Civil War ravaged the economy. Young people left in droves, escaping agricultural life. Farmers abandoned the terraces, and forests reclaimed them, the crumbling stones ghostly shadows of an older way of life.

Yet alongside these abandonados, as the old terraces are called, new energy has come to Ribeira Sacra. Old terraces are being rebuilt, vineyards are being renewed and wine is being made again—sometimes stunningly good wine—which, to the astonishment of some older Galicians, is earning raves half a world away.

It is the potential for making great wine that is bringing the 21st century to a region that has barely come to terms with entering the 20th, and has brought Ribeira Sacra to a winemaking crossroads. Here in this isolated region, so obscure it is little known even in the rest of Galicia, the potential for distinction comes from the combination of indigenous grapes, the slate and granite soils, the peculiar microclimates of the rivers and terraces, and the human determination to make singular wines.

But there is pressure against making such wines as well. The local wine bureaucracy prefers squeaky clean, inexpensive wine for high-volume sales. Others argue for planting grapes with proven international popularity, like tempranillo, the grape of Rioja. Dedicated winemakers scoff at that view, calling it "Rioj-itis."

"There are two types of winemakers: those who want to make money and those who want to make wine," said Pedro Rodríguez, who makes small amounts of juicy, earthy, exotically-scented red wine under the Guímaro label. "The tradition here is to make your own wine, for yourself to drink. A lot of people say, 'Make more, make more,' but why?"

As long as anyone can remember, mencía has been the dominant red grape, as it is in the neighboring region of Bierzo to the east. But where Bierzo produces dark, dense wines, Ribeira Sacra's are lighter-bodied with a silky balance of fruit and minerality that can sometimes be reminiscent of Burgundy.

"If you look at the great wine regions of the world—Burgundy, Champagne, Bordeaux—it's very difficult to find similar conditions in the south of Spain, but you can find those conditions here," said Raúl Pérez, who makes wine from several Spanish regions, including Ribeira Sacra since 2002.

His 2005 El Pecado, made from grapes grown in those terraced vineyards overlooking the Sil, is astoundingly good—graceful and elegant with polished fruit and decidedly mineral flavors. "If I didn't think that I could make wines that could age, I wouldn't be here," he said.

If Dominio do Bibei didn't think it could make great wines, it would not have come to Ribeira Sacra, either. Dominio is an ambitious, well-financed project that is restoring terraces and vineyards on ridiculously perilous hillsides in the Bibei Valley. On the top of a hill it has built a sleek, minimalist winery, four stark white separate buildings that descend like stair steps, mimicking the terraced hillside.

"Imagine 10 years ago, the entire mountain was abandoned," said David Bustos, the commercial manager of Dominio do Bibei. "When we arrived in 1999 only a little bit was planted and maintained. The work is very hard, and preparing the soil as well as the terraces, it can take three or four years before a terrace is ready for planting."

Dotting the old vineyards are lagares, crumbling stone structures that once provided shelter and a place to ferment grapes right in the vineyard. Every family would have a lagar, to which they would carry the grapes at harvest. Sometimes families would sleep there for the duration. Dominio is restoring lagares to use for storage and a place for vineyard workers to eat a meal away from the grueling heat of the sun.

Dominio grows mencía, and a host of other grapes, too, indigenous varieties like brancellao, mouratón, garnacha and sousón that in the old days were interplanted with mencía. The old-timers would ferment the grapes together, but Dominio has adopted modern methods, growing and fermenting the grapes separately. The reds include a light, spicy Lalama, meant for early consumption, and the more serious Lacima, dense yet not heavy, with beautifully balanced spice, fruit and mineral flavors.

"Lacima expresses the Atlantic character of our wines," Mr. Bustos said. "It's 100 percent mencía, but we have no rules. If we have something that we think will taste good, we'll add it."

Dominio also makes whites, including a fresh, lively Lapola, made of four different white grapes, and the extraordinary creamy, waxy Lapena, made entirely of the godello grape. Godello is little known compared with albariño, the most familiar Galician grape in the United States, but it has the potential to make even more distinctive wines.

If Dominio do Bibei and Mr. Pérez represent a future of wine professionals recognizing the world-class potential of Ribeira Sacra, Ramón Losada exemplifies the centuries-old traditions of the region coming to terms with the present.

For centuries Mr. Losada's family farmed the terraces and made wine for themselves. If they made extra, they sold it by the barrel to restaurants and bars in Lugo, a city to the north. With no roads until surprisingly recently, the barrels were shipped by river.

Like so many other Galicians in the 1940s and '50s, Mr. Losada's grandfather decided the agricultural work was too much. He emigrated to Venezuela. But unlike many others, he returned to Ribeira Sacra and got serious about making wine. With the help of young Ramón, he bought up plots near the family's vines and set about restoring terraces and vineyards. By the 1990s Mr. Losada was in charge, and he began selling his wine commercially, calling it D. Ventura, after his grandfather.

Today, three red wines, made from three distinct vineyard sites, are exported to the United States. Viña Caneiro, made from a 3.7-acre plot of slate soil on terraces rising steeply from the edge of the Sil, is the most impressive, a beautifully balanced, graceful wine of 100 percent mencía that tastes of exotic red fruit, spices and minerals.

Still, Mr. Losada considers winemaking a hobby. He is a veterinarian, confining his vineyard work to weekends. Indeed, during the workweek, the vineyards are largely empty. But on a Saturday, driving the narrow roads that separate the terraces nearer the river from those higher up the mountain can be hazardous, with cars arrayed willy-nilly on the sides as weekend farmers tend their vines.

"I make money on the wine, but not enough to live on, which gives me the freedom to make wine however I want," Mr. Losada said. "Some urge me to change, but I won't."

He said he has been told his wine might sell better if he aged it in new barrels of French oak, adding a touch of vanilla flavor, rather than in the steel tanks he uses. Some denser wines, like those of Mr. Pérez or Dominio do Bibei, take well to the barrels. But Mr. Losada's more delicate wine would be overwhelmed.

In the Caneiro vineyard, stepping gingerly from terrace to terrace, chunks of slate underfoot, the River Sil is just below. Breezes coming from the water cool the vines in the heat of the day.

Here in the Amandi Valley, unlike the Bibei Valley, there were no lagares for fermenting the grapes on site. People instead used to carry the grapes on their backs twice a day uphill to the wineries. Now they just carry the heavy loads to the road above, which, incidentally, was paved just last year. Not surprisingly, many growers and winemakers here seem to have back trouble.

Some of the lowest of the original Roman terraces have been swallowed up by the river, since hydroelectric dams raised the water level. Across the river, on another steep hillside, the terraces are empty and overgrown. "The mountain used to be full," Mr. Losada said.

One can't help sensing the timeless nature of Ribeira Sacra, of how a bottle of Viña Caneiro can taste of 2,000 years of history. But Mr. Losada said if you really want to understand the wine and the people, you have to visit a small church.

He drives the narrow country roads of this district, known disconcertingly as Sober, passing first an old woman with a stick, guiding a flock of sheep, and then a meadow with a herd of grazing Rubia Gallega, the red cows of Galicia.

"Demographically, this is the oldest province in Spain," he said. "Young people just left—they didn't want to farm, and the wine work scared them to death."

In the tiny village of Pantón he stops at a 12th-century church, San Miguel de Eiré, which is still used for Mass and baptisms. Mr. Losada explained that Ribeira Sacra, translated as "sacred banks," is derived not from a veneration of the terraced vineyards, as is often suggested, but from the region's concentration of churches, monasteries and convents. "Monks made the wine, maintained the church and reconstructed all the terraces," he said. "They kept the tradition alive."

Mr. Rodríguez of Guímaro, who is 35, is one of those rare young people who returned to the region, after leaving to try law school. His love of the country drew him back. Painstakingly, he has been renewing his family's terraces, reconstructing the rock walls by hand.

High over the Sil, the heat is intense by day, though the nights are cool. His vines are spread over 15 different sites. The grapes, all mencía, seem to react differently to each bend in the row, each angle of exposure to the sun. "Same grapes, different flavors," he said.

The Galicians are known throughout Spain for their stubborn determination to go their own way, and for a somewhat gloomy perspective. Mr. Rodríguez sees hope for realizing the potential of Ribeira Sacra, but he also sees obstacles. He estimates that only 10 percent of the winemakers are serious about what they do.

For those who are serious, like Mr. Pérez, Dominio do Bibei, D. Ventura and Guímaro, which by the way means nonconformist, the wines do all the talking.

"What's missing," Mr. Rodríguez said, "is for people to believe in what they have."

Tastes of Galicia

The best wines from the Ribeira Sacra region are made in small quantities and may be difficult to find. Here are some producers worth seeking out.

ALGUEIRA Polished, substantial reds.

ALODIO Fresh, light, minerally reds.

DOMINIO DO BIBEI Superb wines, both red and white, especially the high-end Lacima and Lapena.

D. VENTURA Three different cuvées, each distinct and delicious, with Viña Caneiro the best.

GUÍMARO Light-bodied, juicy, inexpensive wines with a welcome earthy touch.

RAÚL PÉREZ Ambitious, elegant wines, both El Pecado from the Sil and Socrata from the Bibei.

PEZA DO REI Delicate, distinctive whites and reds.

July 2009

Rooted in Rioja, Traditions Gain New Respect

By ERIC ASIMOV

Abundant wreaths of ghostly mold hang from the ceiling like sentinels, guarding thousands of bottles of gran reserva wine deep in the cellars of the R. López de Heredia winery here in the heart of Rioja. More mold and copious cobwebs are draped over the bottles, some of which have been aging in their bins for decades.

Perhaps no winery in the world guards its traditions as proudly and steadfastly as López de Heredia does, especially in a region like Rioja, which has been swept by profound changes in the last 25 years. And yet, as fusty and as backward-looking as López de Heredia may seem, it is paradoxically a winery in the vanguard, its viticulture and winemaking a shining, visionary example for young, forward-thinking producers all over the world.

How is this possible? As López de Heredia has stayed true to its time-honored techniques in the 132 years since its inception, the rest of the wine-producing world has spent decades doggedly trying to improve what it does, only to come practically full circle, ending up where López de Heredia has been all along.

I don't mean that anybody the world over is making wine in the style of López de Heredia. Almost alone, the winery clings to the notion that it must age its wines until they are ready to drink. Rioja requires gran reserva wines to receive a minimum of six years of aging before they can be released. The current vintage for many gran reserva producers is 2001. López de Heredia has just released gran reservas from 1991 and 1987, exquisitely graceful wines that show the lightness of texture and finesse that comes of long aging.

And these are just the red wines. López de Heredia makes white Riojas that age just as well, achieving a beautifully complex, mellow nuttiness that is a special delight. Nobody makes white Riojas like López de Heredia anymore.

Red or white, the wines are great values, starting at $25 to $50 for crianzas and reservas, which can be 10 to 20 years old. Even 20-year-old gran reservas will be under $100, a steal compared to French or Italian wines of similar age and quality.

But while López de Heredia's wines are almost singular, its ideas about growing grapes and making wines have become increasingly influential, regardless of stylistic concerns.

For more than 50 years after World War II, the great wine regions of the world sought to modernize. Where once backbreaking labor was the only method to grow grapes, science and technology began to offer shortcuts. Growers and producers everywhere seized the chance to mechanize; to deploy chemical pesticides, herbicides and fungicides; to adopt the latest technological recommendations.

Increased knowledge was welcome, and some technology was useful. But, too late, many learned that chemicals were killing the soil and that techniques to increase vineyard yields also diminished the quality of the grapes, just as too much technology in wineries could harm the quality of the wine. All over the wine-producing world, the brightest winemakers have set out to relearn the wisdom and techniques of their grandparents. All, except for one Rioja producer right here in Haro.

"We don't need to, we never lost it," said Maria José López de Heredia, who today, with her sister, Mercedes; brother, Julio César; and father, Pedro, runs the winery founded by her great-grandfather. "New technology is fine, but you can't forget the logic of history."

But what many in the wine-producing world have seen clearly from afar is coming more slowly to the rest of Rioja, a region in transition, where many producers are debating stylistic and viticultural issues that have long been resolved in other parts of the world.

For decades, Rioja has emphasized brand over terroir. Many of the biggest names bought grapes from different parts of the region, blending them like the big Champagne producers to make wines—often delicious wines—that fit a house style but revealed little sense of place beyond a generic sense of Rioja.

But López de Heredia, and very few others in the old guard, like Marqués de Murrieta, have always owned their own vineyards and grown their own grapes. The López wines, which come from four distinct vineyards, almost always show characteristics of their site. The reds from the Tondonia vineyard, for example, tend to be lighter and silkier than reds from the Bosconia vineyard, which are sturdier and a bit more powerful.

Today, a growing number of smaller and younger producers are, like López de Heredia, trying to show a sense of place in their wines, by gaining control of vineyards, improving their viticulture and becoming more conscious of the ideals of terroir that have long been accepted in other wine regions.

"The old producers wanted to show a brand, not a place," said Telmo

Rodríguez, who produces wine all over Spain and has recently, with a partner, opened a small, sleek winery, made of earth and old barrel staves, in the village of Lanciego, east of Haro. "I want to make a wine that could show a village."

In some ways, Mr. Rodríguez seems the antithesis of López. He prefers French oak to the traditional American oak found in the López de Heredia cellars, and he no longer uses the traditional terms "crianza," "reserva" and "gran reserva" to indicate, in ascending order, the aging a wine has received before it has been released. Instead, he uses Burgundian terms—village, premier cru and grand cru—to describe his Riojas: LZ, Lanzaga and Altos de Lanzaga.

His wines are very different, too, fruity, floral and progressively dense moving up the quality scale. The Altos de Lanzaga is marked by the vanilla scent of new French oak.

Yet Mr. Rodríguez clearly respects and venerates López de Heredia. "For me, the only winery that works in an authentic way is López," he said. "Their vineyards are still worked in a traditional way with direct links to the past."

Driving through the gently rolling Rioja terrain, where grapes are often planted right up to the edge of the road, it is becoming harder to find vineyards planted in the older bush-vine style, their scraggly canes trained upward from thick, free-standing trunks in the shape of goblets. With the encouragement of agricultural authorities, more and more of the vines are now trained on neat rows of wire trellises, which make vineyards easier to negotiate with tractors and to harvest mechanically. Mr. Rodríguez abhors the changes, and has sought to buy old fields of bush vines, which he says are crucial to good Rioja. "We are more obsessed with authenticity than beauty," he said.

All the grapes in the López de Heredia vineyards are grown on bush vines, even though, climbing the hill on which Tondonia is planted, one can see occasional rows of grapes on trellises. When asked about them, Ms. López de Heredia explains that tiny parcels of Viña Tondonia are owned by small growers who, over the years, have refused to sell their land to López de Heredia.

"Everything on wires is not owned by us," she said.

Since the winery was founded 132 years ago by Don Rafael López de Heredia y Landeta, she said, each succeeding generation has adhered to the founder's guiding principles: "old vines, low yields and careful, gentle handling." It's a litany that today can be heard all over the wine-producing world.

While wine has been made in the Rioja region for centuries, Rioja wine as we know it is a relatively recent phenomenon, dating from the mid-19th century.

Back then, French vignerons, victimized by phylloxera, the voracious aphid that destroyed vineyards all over Europe, came to Rioja prospecting for new places to make wine.

The Bordelais taught the Spanish how to make wines in the style of Bordeaux, which emphasized long aging in barrels before release.

Today, López de Heredia may be the last Rioja winery still taking those lessons literally. Even venerable Rioja producers like Marqués de Murrieta and La Rioja Alta, which once stood with López de Heredia as bastions of tradition, have tweaked and tinkered in an effort to add a touch of modernity to their wines, hoping that rounding off the edges might make them more appealing to the critics who dispense the scores.

At Marqués de Murrieta's 741-acre Ygay estate, just outside the city of Logroño, the grapes are planted in a mixture of bush and trellised vines. Today, V. Dalmau Cebrián-Sagarriga, who took over the estate when his father died in 1996, is on a campaign to update his wines stylistically. "We refused to change the identity," he said. "But we added more fruit to the wine, we release the wines sooner, we use newer oak and we leave the wine in oak less time."

The reds clearly have become darker and fruitier. Yet the 2001 Castillo Ygay gran reserva remains true to the style, graceful, light-bodied and balanced. It will be a lovely wine in 20 years.

The same cannot be said with certainty about the white Rioja. Only a few years ago, Murrieta made a white Rioja in the traditional style, like López, the wine aged in American oak from which it gained an almost coconut-like character. Now the white is aged in toasty French oak, and while it may be delicious, it is no longer distinctive.

Like many Rioja wineries, Murrieta also makes a red wine in a modern style—darker, richer, with tannins imparted by French oak. It's called Dalmau, which Mr. Cebrián-Sagarriga calls "a modern concept of Murrieta." It, too, is balanced and not overripe, like other versions of what many in Rioja call "alta expression" wines. With Castillo de Ygay and Dalmau, Marqués de Murrieta manages to have it both ways.

Not every producer is as careful as Murrieta to stay tethered to its traditions. With its Frank Gehry–designed hotel on its grounds, Marqués de Riscal is the new face of Rioja in many tourist brochures and guides. The winery is a huge industrial operation, making 4.5 million bottles a year. A 1958 Riscal gran reserva today is a beautiful wine, delicate and harmonious. But Riscal doesn't make these sorts of wines anymore, opting even in its gran reservas for dark colors and big mouthfuls of fruit.

"Our technical director is very keen to protect the Marqués de Riscal identity, which I understand, but business is business," the commercial director, Javier Ybañez Creus, told me.

At López de Heredia, there is a serenity that comes with adherence to core principles. For many years, the winery was criticized at home for being backward and old-fashioned. Appreciation came instead from its export markets.

"Acceptance overseas has people here in Spain reconsidering our wines," Ms. López de Heredia said. "There are people who want to go back again, and we are happy to teach."

Classic, Spicy or Delicate

Here are some of my favorite Riojas. Younger wines, often labeled crianza or reserva, can cost $15 to $25. Gran reservas can rise above $100, but more often can be found for $50 or less.

BODEGAS RIOJANAS Mellow old-school Riojas.
FAUSTINO Look for Faustino I gran reservas.
HERMANOS PECIÑA Fresh, expressive wines.
LA RIOJA ALTA Look for rare Viña Arana reservas.
LÓPEZ DE HEREDIA Classic Riojas in white, red and rosé.
LUBERRI Delicate, pure wines.
MARQUÉS DE MURRIETA Graceful gran reservas.
MIGUEL MERINO Spicy, harmonious wines.
MUGA Prado Enea is spicy; Torre Muga is richer.
TELMO RODRÍGUEZ Exotic Riojas.

August 2009

Txakolina, a Tongue-Twisting Name for Simple Pleasure

By ERIC ASIMOV

In the terraced vineyards on a steep hillside overlooking this Basque town on the southern edge of the Bay of Biscay, it's hard not to feel a powerful thirst. With a salty breeze blowing in off the Atlantic, bright sunshine pouring down and a panoramic view that stretches along the twisting shoreline all the way to Biarritz, the mouth begins to tingle in anticipation of fresh seafood and cold white wine.

This is the land of Txakolina, the bracing, refreshing, often fizzy white wine that is enjoyed throughout Basque country. In restaurants and pintxos bars, on terraces overlooking the ocean or in dark, rustic wood-and-stone cellars, you can't help but notice Txakolina everywhere, especially as it is often poured in an exuberant arc from a bottle held high above the shoulder into tumblers to create a burst of bubbles in the glass.

"In San Sebastián, you wouldn't believe how much Txakolina is drunk in the month of August alone," said Ignacio Ameztoi Aranguren, whose family's winery, Ameztoi, is a leading Txakolina producer. "Here in Basque country, they drink it year-round. They drink it with meat, too. That's the culture."

The vast proportion of Txakolina is consumed in Basque country. You find it virtually nowhere else in Spain, except in Basque restaurants, and very little is exported around the world, with one major exception: the United States.

Surprisingly, given its tongue-twisting name, this wine—made from virtually unknown grapes in a light, simple, low-alcohol style—is becoming more and more popular in the United States. As recently as 2001, barely 1,000 cases, or 12,000 bottles, of Txakolina were exported to the United States, according to Wines From Spain, a trade organization. By 2006, that figure had shot up to 76,000 bottles, and by 2009, it was more than 111,000 bottles. Almost all of it is drunk in the summer months, mostly in restaurants where enthusiastic sommeliers preach the culinary benefits of zesty, high-acid whites.

"They're simple, they're fresh, they're easy, and I think that people are starved for something like that," said André Tamers of De Maison Selections, the leading American importer of Txakolina.

Yet, as with so many things Basque, Txakolina is nowhere near as simple as it may seem, beginning with the identity of the wine itself. In Basque it is mostly rendered as Txakolina (pronounced chock-oh-LEE-nah), but almost as often it shows up as Txakoli (CHOCK-oh-lee). Sometimes you'll see both words on the same wine label. You might even see it referred to by its Castilian guise, Chacolí.

The fresh, lightly fizzy wine made in the Getaria region of northern Spain—the appellation is Getariako Txakolina—is the most familiar expression, but other Txakolinas are made as well, all worth exploring. In the neighboring appellation of Bizkaiko Txakolina, centered on Bilbao, the wines are less fizzy and a bit fuller and rounder. Bizkaiko Txakolina has many variations, even a little bit of delicious red, made by Doniene Gorrondona, from vines more than 100 years old in the town of Bakio. A third, tiny appellation, Arabako Txakolina, was established in 2003 in the inland region around Álava.

But it is the lightly carbonated Getariako Txakolina that forms the impression many people have of the wine. Txomin Etxaniz, officially established in 1930, but with records dating to 1649, is the granddaddy of Txakolina producers. With nearly 100 acres of vines, it is also the biggest.

Ninety percent of its vines are hondarrabi zuri, a white grape grown virtually nowhere else but in Basque country. The rest are hondarrabi beltza, a red grape that is blended into the wine. The grapes that are grown on terraces overlooking the ocean benefit from the sea breeze, a natural ventilation that helps to prevent mildew and disease in this humid, rainy environment. The vines on flatter areas are trained high on overhead pergolas, and workers constantly trim the vigorous foliage so the grapes will be exposed to the air.

"The grapes have to see the vista," said Ernesto Txueka, whose family has run Txomin for generations.

Txomin and Ameztoi, and most Txakolina producers, for that matter, are surprisingly high-tech operations. At Txomin, the grapes are hand-harvested and delivered to the winery, where they are immediately chilled down nearly to freezing and blanketed with nitrogen, an inert gas that prevents oxidation, a process that preserves freshness, juiciness and tangy acidity.

The wines are then fermented with native yeasts in steel tanks, also kept cold and blanketed to capture carbon dioxide, which accounts for the fizziness. The carbonation is entirely natural, though it is widely suspected that less scrupulous Txakolina producers illegally inject their wines with carbon dioxide.

Standing on a catwalk in the spotless Txomin winery, one person can monitor the progress of the wines by way of a computer screen. A visitor in July, though, had to use the imagination. After the fall harvest, the first wines are ready to ship by December, and by June, the entire production of 300,000 bottles is sold out. For wine tourists accustomed to seeing last year's production aging in barrels and the previous year's settling in bottles, it's a remarkably swift process, and profitable as well.

The 2009 Txomin Etxaniz is fresh and tangy, with a slightly chalky mineral and lemon flavor. It goes beautifully with the ubiquitous Basque snacks of anchovies and preserved tuna.

If it's not exactly the image of Old World artisanal craftsmanship, that's because the Txakolina industry is a relatively recent phenomenon. Wine production was a way of life for centuries in Basque country through the end of the 19th century. Much of the wine back then was red, with some rosés. But phylloxera wiped out the vines around the turn of the 20th century, and the industry was slow to recover.

Not until the 1960s did winemaking stage a comeback, said Andoni Sarratea, one of the principals at Doniene Gorrondona.

"The Basque government encouraged planting vineyards as a way of keeping people from leaving for the cities," he said. "They pushed for white wines so as not to compete with Rioja."

While the vast majority of Txakolina today is white, some producers are experimenting with reds and rosés. Gorrondona's old-vine red, Mr. Sarratea said, was inspired by his study of history. "The real Txakolina of the region is red," he said. "The old people drink it because it's what they remember."

Perhaps. But almost all of the deliciously spicy, herbal, raspberry-scented red goes to the United States, where Mr. Tamers, of De Maison, parcels it out in small quantities around the country.

Similarly, Ameztoi revived the tradition of making a Txakolina rosé a few years ago. This gorgeously zingy, fruity wine was met with indifference in Basque country.

"This is a town that doesn't like rosé," Mr. Ameztoi said. "We sell it all to New York." Mr. Tamers got 14,000 bottles this year, yet the crushing demand for it means he can allocate only a few bottles to a customer.

Despite the output at places like Ameztoi and Txomin, Txakolina has a few artisanal producers as well, like Roberto Ibarretxe Zorriketa of Uriondo, which made about 15,000 bottles of Bizkaiko Txakolina last year in a valley south of Bilbao. Here, on an idyllic south-facing slope amid apple trees and conifers, Mr.

Ibarretxe grows not only hondarrabi zuri but txori mahatsa and mune mahatsa, the local names for sauvignon blanc and folle blanche respectively.

The apples distract the wild pigs from the grapes, but do little to dissuade foxes from threatening the vines, said Mr. Ibarretxe, a gentle, precise man dressed in a pale blue shirt and dark blue pants. He wears a Panama hat and has a blue cheesecloth scarf around his neck. A pair of white leather gloves poke out just so from a rear pocket.

"Even if I lose a few vines, I have to let the magic of the forest happen," he said, speaking quietly but intently. "You can't treat a vineyard for tomorrow, you have to treat it for the day after tomorrow."

In his winemaking facility, really just an expanded garage next to his house, he chills the grapes just a bit, not nearly as much as at Txomin or Ameztoi, and he handles them "tranquilo, tranquilo," as gently as possible.

The wine itself is smooth and mellow—fresh, of course, as Txakolina must be—but tranquilo, like the man, lovely and dry with tangy, long-lasting citrus and mineral flavors.

Txakolina has come a long way in the United States since 1989, when the importer Jorge Ordóñez introduced the wine, bringing in 200 cases of Txomin Etxaniz. Even four years ago, Ron Miller, general manager of Solera, a Spanish restaurant on the East Side of Manhattan, spelled the wine phonetically on his list so people could order it.

Mr. Tamers occasionally fears that American demand for the wine will have to wane. Mr. Ameztoi, however, has no such doubts.

"We're confident that anybody who tries this will enjoy it," he said. "A lot of white wines use the same grapes and the same style, and they're all the same. This is distinctive."

August 2010

German Rieslings, Light and Dry

By ERIC ASIMOV

The tulips on Park Avenue are blooming in gorgeous yellows, pinks and reds, confirmation that spring has finally arrived in New York City. My own seasonal signpost is an annual thirst for German rieslings.

Usually in spring I find myself drawn to the filigreed, finely etched rieslings of the Mosel, as delicate as the petals of those Park Avenue tulips. Unlike almost any other riesling-producing region, Germany has made a specialty of rieslings with a touch of sweetness.

I'm not talking about the thrilling dessert wines that riesling so famously lends itself to, which are great in their own right. I mean the wines from the Mosel and their bigger brothers from the Rhine that have some residual sugar but are so beautifully balanced that the overall impression is of exhilarating refreshment.

As much as I love these styles of riesling, this year is different. This year I'm craving dry German rieslings.

Dry? Many Americans assume all rieslings are sweet. In fact, most rieslings, whether from Austria, Alsace, Australia or the United States, are dry. Even more surprising is the fact that many German rieslings are dry, too, and that the preference in Germany today and for the last 20 years has overwhelmingly been for dry rieslings. But the most surprising thing to me is how delicious dry German rieslings have become.

When I first encountered the German dry riesling phenomenon on a trip to the Mosel and Rhine wine regions a decade ago I was appalled. So many of the dry wines were tart and shrill, parching the mouth and creating thirst rather than quenching it.

Now, I'm enchanted with dry rieslings like a 2006 Von der Fels from Keller in Rheinhessen, a wine that reveals and frames the great mineral soul of the riesling grape, exalting it yet doing so gently without any of the sharp edges of the dry rieslings I so ruefully remember.

The Von der Fels, which means "from the rocks," is not even Keller's top dry riesling. Those include the G-Max, a special old-vine cuvée, and the single-vineyard wines labeled grosses gewächs, a newly devised term that ought to be the equivalent of the French grand cru. If only! Trust the Germans to take simple terminology and render it not only complex but indecipherable. More on that another time. In any case, those Keller wines are hard to find, but I was more than happy with the Von der Fels.

Then there was the light and racy 2006 Grey Slate Kabinett Trocken from Dönnhoff in the Nahe, which had all the wonderful delicacy of a focused, pure kabinett-level riesling while offering a surprising noseful of mineral aromas. And most surprising of all were the dry rieslings from the Mosel-Saar-Ruwer, like the extraordinary—stay with me here—2005 Eitelsbacher Karthäuserhofberg Auslese Trocken "S" from Karthäuserhof, a mineral-laden wine that seemed impossibly light and delicate, rounded and perfectly balanced.

In fact, drinking through almost two dozen dry German rieslings over the last few weeks I was struck by the high quality. How did they get so good?

Terry Theise, a leading importer of German wines, casts something of a gimlet eye over the whole phenomenon, suggesting that the quest for dry German rieslings in the United States owes much to the sacrifices of the few. "Over here, you have importers screening out the many nasty ones," he said.

Still, he did allow that the wines were greatly improved.

"Ten years ago I'd have said a great dry German riesling was a four-leaf clover," he told me. "Five years ago I'd have said they were somewhere between sporadic and routine. Now, I'm happy to feel there's a true community of fine dry German rieslings, but this community is still rather small, and there's a large chasm between them and the general run of grim, shrill wines."

Among the first American importers to bring in dry German rieslings was Stephen Metzler of Classical Wines, who began working with Georg Breuer of the Rheingau in 1996. Even back then Breuer was making great dry rieslings, and for years Breuer, along with a few other producers like Dr. Bürklin-Wolf and Koehler-Ruprecht in the Pfalz were the lonely vanguard, carrying the torch in America for dry German rieslings.

Back then, Mr. Metzler suggested, when the German thirst for dry wine was more fad than anything else, many producers simply fermented the sweetness out of their wines and forgot about the importance of low yields, balance and careful winemaking.

Now, a new generation of German winemakers reared on dry wines is pursuing the style with thought and care. Oh, and global warming, which has made it possible to ripen grapes more fully in this extreme northern grape-growing region, hasn't hurt.

The producers making top-flight dry rieslings are legion these days. They would also include Knebel, von Kesselstatt and A. J. Adam in the Mosel; Schäfer-Fröhlich in Nahe; Wagner-Stempels in Rheinhessen; Ratzenberger in the Mittelrhein; and Rudolf Fürst in Franken.

So strong is the preference for dry wines in Germany these days that Mr. Theise, for one, is concerned that the rieslings with residual sugar will be crowded out.

"Why, when there are other sources for world-class dry riesling," he asked, "should Germany focus on being a member of an ensemble when with her table wines with residual sugar she is not only a soloist but an all-time great one?"

It's a good question, and the prospect of losing those wines should be cause for great concern. Still, I can't help but think that dry German rieslings are singular in their own way, combining grace, delicacy and power in a way that nobody else's dry rieslings can do. One can only hope that the world's taste for German rieslings with residual sugar will keep those styles in business, even if Germany itself no longer cares.

April 2008

Austrian Wines Have a Voice, and It's Excited

By R. W. APPLE Jr.

More than once in the last two decades, Terry Theise confesses, he has felt like Sisyphus as he traveled the country, trying to sell the German wines, especially rieslings, that captivate critics but leave many American consumers cold.

"That was hard enough," he said recently. "A labor of love, really, pushing that rock up the hill. So about 10 years ago I proposed to strap a grand piano on my back while I did it, and start promoting Austrian wines at the same time."

They turned out to be an easier sell than he expected. Americans searching for food-friendly alternatives to oak-bomb California chardonnays began discovering grüner veltliners, the peppery white wines, made only in Austria, that can be paired even with legendarily wine-hostile foods like asparagus and artichokes. From them it was a hop and a skip to full-bodied Austrian rieslings and honeyed dessert wines.

To be sure, Austrian wines remain a minority enthusiasm in the United States. According to the Department of Commerce, Austria ranked 13th among sources of American wine imports in 2005, just behind Greece and Israel; Austrian imports totaled 250,000 gallons worth about $7.1 million, compared with 14.8 million gallons from Chile, for example. Still, Austrian imports have increased fourfold since 1998.

As recently as 1985 the Austrian wine industry was back on its heels, after a scandal in which some winemakers gave their wines added sweetness by adulterating them with diethylene glycol, a toxic chemical. Four-fifths of the country's exports dried up overnight. But then passage of rigorous new laws halted the rot, and a long comeback began.

Mr. Theise, 52, has played a leading role in that comeback, at least in this country. He lives in the Washington suburbs with his wife, Odessa Piper, who for many years ran L'Etoile, a much-esteemed restaurant in Madison, Wis. The gems he ferrets out in central Europe are actually imported and distributed by Michael Skurnik Wines in Syosset, N.Y., freeing Mr. Theise to taste, sell and write. And, boy, does he write!

Every year he produces catalogs for each of his specialties, small books packed with anecdotes, opinions, tasting notes and love letters to his growers. An excerpt:

"The kinds of people I choose to work closely with are restless truth seekers, viti-culturally speaking." He has no qualms about singing the praises of their products. Austria, he writes, offers "the best values on earth for monumentally structured dry white wines." It produces "the world's best pinot blancs." Grüner veltliner is "the last of the great European white wine grapes"—and do not call it "grüner" for short, as some critics and merchants do, Mr. Theise says; he considers that an ignorant vulgarism.

A fierce foe of the American passion for scoring wines numerically, Mr. Theise also crusades (as you might expect a salesman of off-dry wines to do) against "the idea that sugar is evil." His argument: "A dash of salt in your soup isn't to make it taste salty; it is to awaken flavor, to make it taste more like itself. A similar dash of sweetness in a wine both enhances flavor, extends fruit, provides another voice to the dialogue of nuances, reduces alcohol and in many cases makes for a more elegant finish."

Sometimes, straining to convey his encyclopedic knowledge of his products lures him into prose as overripe as a starlet's lips, like this description of Nikolaihof wines from the Wachau: "These wines don't so much meet you halfway as show you a third place that's neither You nor Them, but somewhere you meet in truth only by dissolving your respective walls. Each of them is like a slow centering breath, a quiet breath, the breath of the world, unheard almost always beneath the clamor."

Bada-bing! Bring on Doc Gibbs and the *Emeril Live* band!

Mr. Theise (pronounced theece; rhymes with fleece) is not the only champion of Austrian wines, of course. While he handles big names like Nigl and Brundlmayer, competitors like Weygandt-Metzler of Unionville, Pa., bring in F. X. Pichler's wines, and Vin Divino of Chicago represents others, like Alois Kracher, king of Austrian sweet wines.

Austrian restaurateurs have played a role as well. David Bouley and Kurt Gutenbrunner in New York promote Austrian wines at Danube and Wallsé. Wolfgang Puck himself once materialized at Chinois, one of his Southern California restaurants, carrying a bottle of Nigl Privat riesling after I complained of the dearth of Austrian drink on the list. And Manfred Krankl, who now makes Mr. K sweet wines near Santa Barbara in California in partnership with Mr. Kracher, was an advocate of all things Austrian during his years as a partner at Campanile in Los Angeles.

The floral, herbal qualities of grüner veltliner—some taste sorrel, others smell mimosa—have endeared the wines to fans of Asian food; the noted San Francisco Vietnamese restaurant, Slanted Door, included a half-dozen of them on a recent list.

But by writing about it, talking about it, selling it and proselytizing for it in every way he can Mr. Theise has established himself as the voice of Austrian wine, its most knowledgeable and articulate (if occasionally overexcited) champion. Who can fail to appreciate a man who says of his favorite wine (grüner veltliner, of course) with perfect concision, "It can be as sleek as a mink or as big as Babe the Blue Ox."

Another of the great virtues of grüner veltliners, he said over lunch at Vidalia, a Washington restaurant that features several Theise selections, is their availability across a broad price spectrum. Those selling for $50 to $55—top-of-the-line aristocrats from growers like Brundlmayer, which are still much less expensive than blue-ribbon white Burgundies—will always outshine their more proletarian rivals priced from $9 to $13. (Many of the "introductory" grüner veltliners are now produced with screw-top caps.)

But the common lineage is almost always obvious. "The main difference in production is the ripeness of the grapes when picked and the level of cropping," Mr. Theise said. "The main difference in the glass is richness, complexity and concentration."

As an example of the bang-for-the-buck species, we tasted a 2005 Grüner Veltliner Renner from Gobelsburg, designed to sell at retail for $27 or $28. With lemony and peppery notes on the nose, medium-ripe, it had plenty of power— "fine-grained," as Mr. Theise remarked. It reminded me of something he said earlier: "For me, utility and charm are more important virtues than simply blowing your socks off."

In general, grüner veltliners from the Wachau are the costliest (and some think the best). A steep, almost indecently scenic valley through which the Danube flows with undeniable majesty, about 70 miles west of Vienna, it has two crowning glories: the great clifftop Baroque abbey at Melk and the castle above Durnstein, where Richard the Lion-Hearted was imprisoned after the Third Crusade in the 12th century.

I have a soft spot for the Wachau; decades ago I tasted Austrian wines for the first time at Jamek, a riverside restaurant now almost a century old. The warmhearted Landhaus Bacher in Mautern, where the Italian-inflected food lives up to the spectacular cave, came as a thrilling discovery to my wife, Betsey, and me on a cold, dark night not too many years after that.

But Mr. Theise finds all but the wines at the very pinnacle of quality over-priced, victims of supply and demand; only about 3,500 acres are planted to vines in the entire Wachau, and not all of that is grüner veltliner. So Mr. Theise looks downriver, toward Vienna, to the adjacent districts, the Kremstal and the Kamptal, where the falloff in quality is slight and the prices gentler, and to growers like Hirsch and Nigl.

I'm a Champagne man when it comes to bubbly; with few exceptions, other sparkling wines leave me flat. Mr. Theise added a new item to my list of exceptions with his Gobelsburg nonvintage reserve, a silky blend with a soft mousse, made from grüner veltliner (70 percent), riesling (15) and pinot noir (15). Without prompting, I would have had no clue what I was drinking.

Austrian rieslings are another matter. They are instantly recognizable as riesling but drier than their Alsatian cousins, with a somewhat more refrained floweriness, as Mr. Theise put it, than most of their German relatives. Juicier, too, I would add, with the aroma of yellow mirabelle plums in some cases and of tropical limes in others.

Once again, many of the best rieslings come from the Wachau (Jamek, Prager), which has its own system of nomenclature, just to live up to the Germanic tradition of confusing labels. Wines marked "federspiel" must by law contain between 10.7 percent and 11.9 percent alcohol, for example; higher than that, they command a premium price and are designated with the word "smaragd," which is the name of a small green lizard that likes to sun itself on the steep vineyard hillsides.

Austrian rieslings can be bargains. The other night, at a Legal Sea Foods outlet, Betsey and I drank a nicely aged federspiel (2001) from Franz Hirtzberger at Spitz in the Wachau, imported by Vin Divino, which cost only $39. With forward fruit flavors, round and clean, it was dry but not bonedry. Perfect with shrimp, clams and scallops, or grilled fish, almost anything from the sea, but not a very good match for oysters.

As always, a sturdy minerality underpins and focuses these wines.

Dry Austrian whites do not stop with riesling and grüner veltliner, the ever-enthusiastic Mr. Theise wanted me to know, so he brought out several bottles produced by Heidi Schrock in Burgenland, south of Vienna. Her furmint, made from the grape famous as the basis of Hungarian tokay, reminded me a lot of chenin blanc from the Loire Valley; her grauburgunder (pinot gris), gently oaked, struck me as a little too alcoholic (more than 14 percent); her muscat is a creamy, spicy delight.

If Ms. Schrock's whites constitute one kind of novelty, Austrian reds must represent the height of obscurity, medium-weight wines that are made from grapes few have ever heard of. Zweigelt, anyone? Mr. Theise touts it as a "lush, fine, useful" alternative to syrah. St. Laurent? A bit like an old-time Nuits-St.-Georges, he told me. Blaufränkisch? A hint of Chianti Classico, perhaps, or even of malbec.

Most of the best reds come from the sun trap that is Burgenland, hard by the Hungarian border and the large, shallow, reedy lake called the Neusiedlersee (which is also the region where Mr. Kracher and Willi Opitz make their world-class sweet wines, aided by the mist that rises in the autumn from the three-feet-deep lake).

Here Mr. Theise introduces an uncharacteristic note of caution. "Austrian red wine is to be taken seriously, that much is beyond dispute," he writes in his 2006 Austrian list. "Yet for every truly grown-up wine there are many others that are silly, show-offy, insipid, even flawed."

So leave the final word to Doug Mohr, Vidalia's sommelier, who is bold enough to list 13 Austrian reds with twice that many whites. The reds, he said with a smile, "do not yet have the following of grüner veltliner," but he still manages to sell them, often a glass at a time, to skeptics.

July 2006

An Honest Day's Work From Vienna

By ERIC ASIMOV

As a child growing up in Vienna, Carlo Huber would sometimes accompany his father, Rupert E. Huber, to wine bars and heurigen, informal little buffets where Viennese wine estates sold their own produce. When his father had an especially pleasing glass, Mr. Huber recalled, he would exclaim, "Das ist ein ehrlicher wein!"—That is an honest wine.

Mr. Huber never forgot the sentiment, and as he grew up he came to enjoy those delicate, graceful Viennese wines himself. When his work in marketing took him to New York City in 1993, he was disappointed to see that as Austrian wines gained popularity in the United States, wines from Vienna were virtually unknown.

A little more than a year ago, Mr. Huber met another Viennese ex-pat, Paul Darcy, who works in the electrical department of the Metropolitan Opera. Mr. Darcy, too, grew up in Vienna in a wine-loving family and was particularly nostalgic for Viennese wines and wine culture. Though they had no experience in the wine business, they teamed up and made it their mission to supply the United States with some of Vienna's best wines, and so created their wine import company, Darcy and Huber Selections.

That any wine comes from Vienna seems absurd on the face of it. Great urban centers are not known for their vineyards, beyond a novelty acre here and there. But Vienna is different. Around 1,700 acres of vines are planted within the city limits. Of the great metropolises in winegrowing countries, Vienna alone has its own appellation.

Viennese viticulture stretches back centuries if not millenniums to early Celtic and Roman settlements. But modern Viennese vineyards owe their existence to an environmentally far-sighted mayor, Karl Lueger, who a century ago prohibited development on the green hills that girdle the inner city. Through wars, depressions and shifts in fashions and taste, Viennese farmers and winemakers have continued to toil in their vineyards.

Most of their production was destined for Vienna itself, and most of it, Mr. Huber and Mr. Darcy say, was not very good—too thin, and often heavily manipulated to compensate for poor grapes and poor winemaking. But the memories of those wines were strong and, just as in the rest of the wine-producing world over the last 25 years, a revolution in quality was coming to Vienna, too. In the years since Mr. Huber, 39, and Mr. Darcy, 43, came to New York, a new generation of winemakers in Vienna has committed itself to making wines that can represent Vienna on the world stage.

Of particular interest to the younger winemakers, and to Mr. Huber and Mr. Darcy, were wines made of a mixed array of white grapes. Those are not blended wines, as in Bordeaux, where different grapes are planted and vinified separately, later to be mixed by a winemaker. Instead, these gemischter satz wines are made of grapes that are planted and vinified together, anywhere from three or four different grapes to maybe two dozen, as with field blends in California.

Such blends can sometimes create wines of unusual complexity. Modern winemakers, who tend to prize uniformity in ripening, usually plant different grapes separately because they may ripen at different rates. That way, they can all be harvested at a similar point of ripeness. But when they are planted and harvested together, some can be perfectly ripe, while others can be a little under- or over-ripe.

"The resulting wines are a melting pot of character, not unlike Vienna itself," Mr. Darcy said.

Let's not get bogged down in the morass of bureaucratic licensing and the intricacies of container ships and warehouse bonding that are part and parcel of importing wines. That is the price Darcy and Huber Selections must pay for deciding to go into the business. Suffice it to say that by virtue of hard work and the ability to withstand the effects of repeatedly banging one's head against a wall, Darcy and Huber Selections are now importing small quantities of exquisite Viennese wines.

The gemischter satz wines are particularly noteworthy. Rainer Christ makes two different versions. One is a fresh, light floral wine made of four grapes, with a peppery component that lets you know grüner veltliner is part of the blend. The second gemischter satz is altogether riper and richer, made from a dozen grapes from vines 60 years old or more.

Jutta Ambrositsch makes a dry, earthy gemischter satz from almost 20 different grapes. Richard Zahel's Nussberg gemischter satz, made from nine different grapes, is rich and almost oily in texture, yet still with light flowery aromas. My favorite gemischter satz, though, is the 2007 Weissleiten from Stefan Hajszan, a gorgeous wine that is both delicate and intense. Perhaps I'm being fanciful, but drinking this wine—and feeling the lacy lightness of its flavors—I could not help imagining myself at a Viennese café, watching the city go by.

The gemischter satz wines may be the most unusual that Vienna has to offer, but most Viennese producers make single varietal wines as well. I also tried a crisp and aromatic gelber muskateller from Christ, which would make a lovely aperitif wine. Hajszan makes a minerally grüner veltliner, while Ambrositsch produces a very floral riesling. Some Viennese producers also make red wines, but the few I have tried seem less compelling—good wines, but not as distinctive as the whites.

While Darcy and Huber Selections is drawing attention to Viennese wines, the producer who many consider the most important in Vienna, Wieninger, is imported by another company, Winebow. I haven't found those wines in New York yet, but I am going to seek them out.

As for the gemischter satz wines I have tasted, they can run from around $15 or $20 a bottle up to $40 or so. They aren't cheap, but they are indeed ehrliche wines.

November 2009

Meanwhile, Back in Alsace

By FRANK J. PRIAL

It had been raining for days. The low gray clouds scudded in over the Vosges Mountains, to the west, and dumped their sodden contents on the vineyards, then pushed eastward over the Rhine and the Black Forest. It was a typical winter day in Alsace.

But at Domaine Weinbach, a handsome but understated chateau—more a lived-in country house, actually—just outside this picture-book medieval town, all was warm and inviting. Here in the paneled front parlor, with its heavy, dark furniture and fading family photographs, Laurence Faller was pouring wine. For the last seven years, she has been the winemaker at the domaine, one of best-known wine estates in Alsace.

Disappearing regularly into the kitchen, she would reappear with yet more bottles of her latest handiwork, the 1998 vintage. For comparison purposes, there were a few 1997s, too, along with a couple of 1999s, which were still mostly fermenting juice.

Domaine Weinbach is famous not only for its wines, but also for the fact that it is run entirely by women. Ms. Faller, 32, is studying enology at Beaune, in Burgundy, and has an M.B.A. and a degree in chemical engineering. Her sister, Catherine, who popped in and out during our two-hour tasting, is 43 and handles sales and marketing. Their mother, Colette, nominally the president and chief executive, is better described as the dowager queen. Her age? "Do you have to publish that?" Well, no, probably not.

In the best tradition of French wine widows (Clicquot, Pommery, Bollinger), she took charge on the death of her husband, Theo, in 1979, and transformed Domaine Weinbach into one of northeastern France's most prominent wine names.

Theo Faller was the winemaker; when he died, Colette took over with the aid of a family friend, Jean Mercky. Photos show her in boots and old sweaters, hard at work in the damp cellars. Laurence joined the business in 1993; Catherine has always been in the business.

Fallers have owned the property here since 1898, but in Alsace they are relative newcomers. Families like the Trimbachs and Hugels had been making wine in Alsace for 300 years when the Fallers, tanners in Kaysersberg, got into the business.

Domaine Weinbach was once part of church-owned vineyards. Augustinian monks acquired the land in the ninth century. In 1612, the Augustinians donated a part of their estates to Capuchin Franciscan friars, who built a convent and church on the land and continued to develop its vineyards and farms. The "home" vineyard, surrounding the house and winery, is known as the Clos des Capucins. Weinbach, in the Alsatian dialect, means "wine stream" and is in fact the name of the small stream that flows past the domaine on its way to the Rhine.

An inventory made by the Capuchin friars in the 17th century listed 14,000 to 15,000 vines, including muscat, "riesselin" (riesling) and "chaselin" (chasselas). The friars also raised snails, and once a year gave a banquet for the local notables, at which one of the important dishes was escargots au riesling. The friars were ousted at the time of the French Revolution, and the property passed through several hands before the Fallers acquired it.

Originally, the estate consisted of the chateau and the 12-acre vineyard within the estate walls, or clos. In the years since World War II, the property has been expanded to about 150 acres, some of it leased vineyards. As an owner-harvester, under French wine regulations, the Domaine Weinbach is not allowed to buy grapes from other growers. But the Fallers can and do rent vineyard property, so long as they grow and harvest the grapes themselves.

Like other French vineyard regions, the best Alsatian vineyards are classified as grand cru, which translates—badly—into "great growth," and as premier cru, or "first growth." Domaine Weinbach owns two grand cru parcels, about 40 acres on the Schlossberg, a hilly slope just north of the domaine, and a piece of an adjoining vineyard called the Furstentum. The Schlossberg vines produce the domaine's best riesling; the Furstentum is the source of its best gewürztraminer. Other vineyards, including the Altenbourg, which is unclassified, turn out pinot blanc, pinot gris and muscat.

The best grape in Alsace is the riesling; the best-known grape is the Gewürztraminer. Gewürztraminer produces a pungent, flowery wine with a taste that some experts compare to litchi nuts. Even when fermented completely dry, it can seem to be sweet, because of the flowery bouquet. Riesling is Alsace's finest grape. It produces wines that, at their best, display layers of complexity and nuance. A good Alsatian riesling can last 15 years, and late-harvest versions can live in superb condition for 30 to 50 years.

Alsace produces a lot of wine, most of it indifferent stuff that, fortunately, rarely makes it across the Atlantic. Michel Bettane, the French critic, who tasted with me at Domaine Weinbach, contends that in Paris even some of the grand cru wines are watery and sugary. "Less than 10 percent of Alsatian wines are excellent," he said. "The other 90 percent are sugar water."

"Michel," Laurence Faller said, "tends to get carried away."

At the other end of the spectrum, too many of the best Alsatian wines are being made in the sweet style. Some of the finest producers are turning out wines that make fine aperitifs but very poor companions for most meals. Even Ms. Faller acknowledged that all of her 1998 gewürztraminer could have qualified for the vendange tardive, or late-harvest, designation. Late-harvest wines are invariably much higher in sugar content than dry table wines.

The total Domaine Weinbach production is about 15,000 cases, about half of them exported to 23 countries. The United States is the biggest customer. The domaine sells about a quarter of what it makes to tourists, mostly German.

My favorite Faller wines include the Riesling Schlossberg and the Riesling Schlossberg Cuvée Sainte Catherine Cuvée du Centenaire, both from 1997 and both in the $45-to-$65 price range. Perhaps the best introduction to the Weinbach rieslings is the less subtle Reserve Personnelle, which sells for around $24. The 1998 Riesling CuvéeSainte Catherine is a big, powerful wine that will last and last. It hasn't been shipped yet, and it will be expensive.

The real gems in the Faller collection are the late-harvest wines. The 1995 Pinot Gris Quintessence des Grains NoblesCuvée du Centenaire, for example, is made from individually picked late-harvest grapes and sells for around $300 a half bottle.

One of the best ways to enjoy good Alsatian wine is with the local cheese, Muenster. After our tasting, Colette Faller, elegant in jewels and eyeliner, swept in to announce lunch. It was simple fare, chicken and noodles and Muenster, accompanied by some of the best Faller wines. Anyone who says no meal is complete without red wine has never sat down to lunch in the big, warm kitchen at Domaine Weinbach.

January 2000

Hungarian Dry Whites? Forge Ahead

By ERIC ASIMOV

Comfort zone? Believe me, I understand. At restaurants, I'm always fighting the impulse to order a beloved dish again and again. I have to struggle against sticking to customary territory in music, books and, especially, in wine.

Habit partly explains the appeal of the familiar. The desire to drink nothing but Burgundy, for example—assuming you can afford such a desire—stems certainly from the titillating satisfaction derived from the wine. Like a laboratory rat touching a button wired to the pleasure center of the brain, you want to repeat the experience endlessly. With time, the quest broadens to the point where you want to learn as much as possible about this complex, nuanced region.

People who are just beginning to grasp wine naturally want to dive deeply into the pantheon regions. They have read such ardent descriptions of the thrills of these wines that they are no longer willing to settle for vicarious enjoyment. Again, with experience, comes the desire to focus and learn. Who can argue with the notion that one can lose oneself forever in the wines of Italy?

Yet no matter how alluring the desire to fixate on a particular set of wines, experimentation has great virtues. Practically speaking, wines from lesser-known regions are often cheaper. But more to the point, drinking wine with blinders on can deprive you of unexpected, deeply satisfying, even thrilling bottles.

Case in point: the dry white wines of Hungary. Who even knew Hungary made dry white wines? The country is best known for Tokaji aszu, gorgeously honeyed, lavishly sweet wines of such balance and precision that they can accompany savory meals. The history of this legendary wine stretches back centuries, and most likely, near the beginning, the wines were more dry than sweet. Now, in the post-Communist age, Hungary is making dry whites again, and some of the wines are stunningly distinctive and delicious.

It was by chance last year, at Terroir, the wine bar and merchant in San Francisco, that I first tried the 2006 dry white from Kiralyudvar, a winery that I knew made wonderful sweet wine. The '06 was only the second vintage of this dry white, made mostly of furmint, the region's leading grape, yet it was extraordinary, with a gorgeous aroma of herbs and flowers, and the luscious texture that comes from fermentation in oak barrels.

The wine was absolutely dry and balanced, with the waxy, lanolin quality that

I find so alluring in good white Bordeaux. Yet it had an indelible stamp of sweet richness to it, as if botrytis, the fungus that so beautifully intensifies the flavors of Tokaji aszu—and Sauternes, for that matter—had somehow insinuated its way into this wine as well, though I knew it hadn't.

I've had this wine several times since, and have not been let down. Moreover, it has spurred a fascination with dry whites from Hungary that has led to a few highly satisfying bottles, a number that is small because production of dry whites is still in its infancy in Tokaj, and few make it to the United States.

Still, in an Indian restaurant I managed to find a 10-year-old bottle of dry furmint from Tokaj Classic, and its delicate floral flavors complemented the spicy food beautifully. I also found a 2007 furmint from Royal Tokaji, with beguiling aromas of exotic fruit, Asian spices and anise. It, too, had that waxy quality, as did a 2005 from Dobogo, which had gorgeous fruit aromas and an attractive, almost savory mineral flavor.

All these wines come from the Tokaj region, about 130 miles northeast of Budapest in the foothills of the Carpathians. But I also found a bottle of 2006 Szent Ilona Borhaz from Somlo, in the western part of Hungary near the Austrian border. This wine, which had a floral aroma and a tangy apple and mineral flavor to it, was a blend of 30 percent furmint, 60 percent harslevelu and 10 percent juhfark. Talk about leaving a comfort zone!

At least I can pronounce Kiralyudvar—it's KEE-rye-oohd-var, which means king's court. Although the estate is historic, with records dating back to the 11th century, it was reconstituted in 1997 when it was bought by Anthony Hwang.

Mr. Hwang, an American businessman, is also the majority shareholder of Huet, the iconic Vouvray producer. His co-owner at Huet, Noël Pinguet, who oversees the winemaking, has worked closely with Kiralyudvar. Fittingly, chenin blanc, the grape of Vouvray, shares with furmint the capacity for making complex dry wines of elegance and finesse, and the versatility to make a range of long-lived sweet wines.

Because dry wine is relatively new to the region, Mr. Hwang wrote in an e-mail conversation, Tokaj producers are still working out the kinks. But he is optimistic about the future.

"Sweet winemaking mind-sets and techniques are at times practiced too often when making dry wines in Tokaj," he said. "The results are high-alcohol, tannic wines where the wonderful terroirs are obscured. As more producers find their own voices, more precisely made, terroir-expressive dry furmints will be produced."

Mr. Hwang suggested that most producers consider dry wine to be vital to the region's future growth, and that the region's greatest challenge is overcoming the public perception that Tokaj makes only sweet wines.

"The challenge is to get people to taste well-made dry Tokaj furmint," he said. "Once tasted, the wine speaks for itself."

That was certainly my experience. I've had a few other good dry furmints, like the Oremus Mandolas, refreshing with well-integrated oak flavors—oak and furmint take to each other very well. I'm still looking for a dry white from Disznoko.

Interestingly, Oremus is owned by Vega-Sicilia, the great Spanish producer, and Disznoko is owned by AXA, the French insurance giant, which owns a number of top-flight wineries. Foreign ownership certainly recognizes the potential of Tokaj. It's up to the rest of us to have a look.

February 2010

CHAPTER NINE

South of the Equator

New Heights for Andean Wine

By R. W. APPLE Jr.

The awesome crags of the Andes glitter like icebergs in the early morning sunlight as the plane lets down here in western Argentina, across the grassy Pampas from Buenos Aires.

Runoff from the melting Andes snows, diverted into canals built by the Tehuelche Indians as early as the 16th century and improved by the Incas and the Spanish, makes Mendoza bloom. Although located at the edge of the Cuyo desert, this is a city of plane trees and sycamores, shady parks and broad plazas, fountains and rose gardens.

That same water nourishes the vineyards surrounding the city. Mendoza wines have helped to make Argentina the world's fifth-largest producer, a reliable source of inexpensive red for the country's thirsty population, much of which traces its origins to Italy. But until recently they have never counted for much in world markets.

Dr. Nicolás Catena is changing things; not single-handedly, exactly, any more than Michael Jordan single-handedly won pro basketball championships for the Chicago Bulls. But he has shown customers in North America, as well as friendly rivals here, what Mendoza can do at every price level. At 61, slight, soft-spoken and studious-looking in rimless glasses, he is the acknowledged star, the pace-maker, the public face of the Argentine wine industry.

It is an industry in rapid ascendancy. More first-class wines appear with each vintage, and critics and consumers around the world have taken notice. On the shelves of shops in the United States, labels like Balbi, Flichman, Norton, Santa Ana and Terrazas have won space, along with Catena, of course.

Despite the country's debilitating economic troubles recently, foreign millions continue to pour in to finance new vineyards and wineries.

Beginning with Dr. Catena's grandfather in 1902, the Catena family established a local reputation for red wines. These wines, made largely from the criolla grape, were too sweet and too often oxidized.

"We never imagined," Dr. Catena said, that "anyone here could compete with the Europeans—perhaps 10 percent as good, no more."

Dr. Catena's great awakening came when he went to the United States. Already armed with a Ph.D., he studied economics and mathematics at Columbia

University during the turbulent late 1960s and then, in 1982, found himself at Berkeley as a visiting professor. Inevitably, he visited the Napa Valley. Almost as inevitably, he fell under the spell of Robert Mondavi, whose winery was at that time helping to establish lofty new standards for American wines.

"I discovered what investment, research and enthusiasm could achieve," Dr. Catena told me and my wife, Betsey, over a candle-lit dinner under the maple trees at 1884, the restaurant that he has set up in his century-old Bodega Escorihuela. "I saw that the Americans had done in 10 years what the Europeans took over 300 years to do.

"I decided that I had to do something similar. I thought we needed to make cabernet and chardonnay, even though we didn't use those grapes much in Argentina at the time. They were the best, obviously, and I wanted them."

After a time, Dr. Catena got to know the peripatetic Mr. Mondavi, and they discovered that their families had come from the same part of Italy—the Marche, on the Adriatic coast.

Top Catena cabernets and chardonnays have been exported to the United States for a decade now, and they have received enthusiastic notices from the world's wine critics—easily the equal of the reviews accorded to the much better-known vintages of Argentina's neighbor to the west, Chile.

Unlike some Chilean producers, Dr. Catena has been careful not to price himself out of the North American market. The number of wine drinkers in New York or Los Angeles willing to pay $50 a bottle and more for his top-of-the-line Zapata reds may be limited, but for those who are not, there are Catena wines at more modest prices, sold under Catena Alta, Catena and Alamos Ridge labels.

"In the end," said my English friend Bill Baker, one of his country's most respected wine merchants, "Argentine wines will be better and better priced than their Chilean competitors."

I tasted Catena Alta cabernets, merlots and malbecs from 1997 and 1999 with Dr. Catena, and they were only slightly less aristocratic than their Zapata counterparts, which had not yet been released. They had just as much fruit, just as much robustness of flavor, perhaps a little less opulence and complexity. The Alamos Ridge wines, tasted in the United States, made a less vivid impression, of course, but they struck me as good values at around $10 a bottle.

The Argentine wines that interest me most are the ones made almost nowhere else, including the chunky, chewy, spicy malbec among the reds and the tangy torrontés among the whites.

Malbec, which is also called Auxerrois by the French, was once an important grape in Bordeaux, used extensively in the days before the great phylloxera epidemic of the 19th century in wines like Château Latour. Now it is used only in Cahors in southwestern France, where it traditionally produced heavy, intensely tannic wines, almost black in color, which were often not ready to drink until they had spent two decades in the bottle. Modern Cahors is a bit gentler.

Argentine malbec is different. The deep violet glints in the glass are similar, as are the jammy flavors of ripe berries. But where the tannins in Cahors can be quite harsh, those in the best Argentine malbecs are sweet and silky, and the wines give no impression of heaviness at all despite their power. They make perfect companions to Argentina's great beef or to our own.

In 1960, Argentina had 120,000 acres of malbec, but then came the stampede to "international" grape varieties like cabernet. Now there are only 25,000 acres left, but the best of those vines, including several owned by Catena and by the Austrian-controlled Bodegas Norton, are 70 to 100 years old. At the moment, Pedro Marchevsky, the Catena vineyard manager, is conducting experiments with 135 malbec clones in the company's Tikal vineyard.

The torrontés vineyards are some of the world's highest, many more than a mile up, near the village of Cafayate in the northwestern corner of the country, not far from the Bolivian border. No movie theater or bright lights there, "just work," laughed Susana Balbo, a highly regarded Argentine winemaker who toiled for a time in Cafayate. Two of the best examples are made by Etchart and Michel Torino, both reminiscent of albariño and viognier in their jasmine-scented bouquets and fresh tropical-fruit flavors (mango? pineapple?).

Another, only slightly less appealing torrontés, easier to find in the United States and irresistibly priced at about $7, is made by Santa Julia.

At the moment, the light of Dr. Catena's life is a striking new winery near here, built of cream-colored local stone and pale, indigenous hardwoods in the shape of a Mayan pyramid. It opened earlier this year. His daughter Laura Catena, the company's export director, a Harvard- and Stanford-educated physician who somehow combines the practice of medicine in San Francisco with her work in the wine trade in Argentina, commented recently that the $12 million building "shows our pride in our own culture."

So does 1884, the Catena restaurant. The family recruited Argentina's premier chef, Francis Mallmann, to create a menu that celebrates the Incan influence in the region, with dishes incorporating corn and pumpkin, as well as the beef of the Pampas—not to mention, of course, the wines of Mendoza.

Much of the cooking is done in the courtyard in traditional igloo-shaped mud ovens, or hornos. We sampled bitter, palate-cleansing chicory, seared at 600 degrees, with almonds and sun-dried tomatoes; empanadas made the old-fashioned way with hand-chopped instead of ground beef; a tart of onions and leeks, and magnificently juicy goat, scented with lemon and oregano, roasted in an iron box—all the while talking politics, monetary policy, Machiavelli and wine prices with Nicolás Catena.

On the latter subject, he said, "I have known from the start that if I charged $40 a bottle, the wine had to be comparable with a French wine selling for $60 or $80, because people are not used to costly wines from here." And he acknowledged that like Mr. Mondavi and his Italian friend Piero Antinori, he makes far more money on his cheaper wines than on his prestige products.

But he pours his passion into the top of the line. He has raised the quality bar in Argentina by limiting production through the pioneering use of controlled irrigation and by rigorous thinning of his grapes. He has planted vineyards at altitudes as high as 4,900 feet, which provide the cooler temperatures and lower humidity that help to produce premium grapes. He has imported French barrels and computerized European winemaking gear, installing them in immaculate wineries that contrast starkly with the unhygienic facilities and poor barrels that plagued wine production in Argentina for decades.

Others have joined him here in the pursuit of modern excellence. Hiram Walker, Moët & Chandon, Pernod Ricard, Kendall-Jackson, Allied Domecq, Sogrape of Portugal and several Chilean companies have made huge investments. Exports have grown to about $140 million from $40 million in the last five years.

Norton, which was founded in 1895 by a British engineer who had worked on the railway across the Andes, now belongs to the family that controls Swarovski crystal. Carlos Tizio Mayer, the technical manager, described its strategy: to keep prices down—no more than $15 for the top blend, marketed as Norton Privada—"so we can earn a little money and a lot of customer loyalty."

"It's easy to produce very expensive wine here, but it's not so easy to produce good value," he told us as we toured the winery, which is surrounded by spectacular rose gardens. "We want to make our name and attract our customers now, because in the next few years only three or four Argentine names will loom large in the international market, and we intend to be one of them."

I was taken with Norton's 2000 sauvignon blanc, a crisp yet fruity wine with just the right sharpness, but there, too, it was the malbec that turned my head. The 1999 exhibited had a nose like a magnet that drew you right into the glass, and a typical big-shouldered, almost rowdy style on the palate.

Never contaminated by phylloxera, the Argentine malbec, as Mr. Tizio said, "is a natural treasure in its genetic purity." It can make great wine.

August 2001

South African Goes From
Never a Sip to Vineyard Fame

By BARRY BEARAK

When Ntsiki Biyela won a winemaking scholarship in 1998, she was certainly a curious choice. She had grown up in the undulating hills of Zululand, living in a small village of huts and shacks. People tended their patches of pumpkins and corn. The only alcohol they drank was homemade beer, a malt-fed brew that bubbled in old pots.

Indeed, Ms. Biyela had never even tasted wine, nor had anyone she knew. Her choice of study was a fluke. Though she had been a good student, none of her grant applications for college were approved until an airline, hoping to promote diversity, offered to pay her way to study viticulture and enology: grapes and wine. What was wine? the young woman wondered, guessing it was another name for cider.

She had never been outside the eastern province of KwaZulu Natal, but she boarded a bus and traveled across South Africa to the wine country of the Western Cape. She gazed at the immense mountains. She puzzled over the short, thin trees planted in perfect rows. She had no idea what they were.

Finally, Ms. Biyela tasted the beverage she had come such a distance to study. She and a handful of other black scholarship students met with a wine connoisseur, Jabulani Ntshangase. He opened a superb red, raised the moist cork to his nose and talked rapturously about the wine's fruitiness and color and fragrance. She was expecting to sip something sublime when handed the elegant, long-stemmed glass. *Instead, she was stunned. It was disgusting.*

Ms. Biyela, having definitely adapted her tastes, is now one of this nation's few black winemakers in an occupation that has been dominated by white people for 350 years. Her blends of merlot, cabernet sauvignon and pinotage have won gold medals and four-star ratings. She was named South Africa's Woman Winemaker of the Year in 2009. Last month, she was busy judging the country's entries for the International Wine and Spirit Competition.

"Somehow I fell in love with the ever-changing content of wine," she said as if still surprised by her own journey. "Wine is never the same today as it is tomorrow. It even depends on where you drink it and who you are with and what mood you are in. It's a very, very nice thing."

Though apartheid has been swept away, this country is still a racially divided society. Ms. Biyela is a pioneer in its transformation, not someone elevated through political connections, but a rural woman who made it on grit.

"I live in two worlds," she said recently. "I'm still able to fit in the village, speaking Zulu and eating pap. I also fit in the European-style world."

She pondered the difference. "In the European style it's about striving, the 'me life,' everything about me. In the village, it's all about the community."

South Africa regularly ranks among the world's top 10 wine producers, and while the climate and soils are welcoming to the grape, the industry's history has dismal chapters. Vineyards were long tended by slaves, and even after emancipation, working conditions remained both horrendous and insidious. In the so-called dop system, laborers were paid partly with a daily quotient of cheap wine. Dependence on alcohol was the boss's method of control.

Things have improved, though hardly by enough in one of South Africa's showcase industries. Just this week, Human Rights Watch issued a report severely criticizing the working and living conditions in the vineyards.

The country has far more wine than wine drinkers. More than half the production is exported, and even if everything were shipped away, most of the population would barely notice. A large majority of South Africans are black and poor. Beer is their drink, and they are not interested in a lot of conversation about bouquet. No one sniffs the bottle cap.

The wine industry has a few mentoring programs for nonwhites, but there are still only about 20 black winemakers. "You have to respect Ntsiki; she comes from a culture that is so thoroughly alien to wine," said Tim James, a leading wine critic. "She's actually incredibly brave."

Ntsiki (pronounced n-SEE-kee) is short for Nontsikelelo. Her mother was a maid in Durban who saw her daughter maybe once a year. Ms. Biyela, now 33, was raised by her grandmother in the village of Kwa Nondlovu. Like other young girls, she fetched water each day from a river. She walked seven miles to a forest to gather firewood. She studied in a poorly equipped rural school.

Her scholarship was to Stellenbosch University, in wine country. Most everyone on campus spoke a language heavy with "cch" sounds as if they were clearing their throats. This was Afrikaans, the main tongue of the region and the language in which her instructors taught. She did not understand a word of it.

During the first year, the courses were basic: mathematics, physics, biology, botany. To her relief, the same subjects were taught to forestry students in English, and she attended classes with them. But the rest of the four-year program was mostly in Afrikaans. She kept up with notes prepared in English.

Tariro Masayiti, a black Zimbabwean, was one of her classmates. He did not speak Afrikaans either, but he had already been trained in winemaking and excelled from the start. "Ntsiki was a typical village girl, in the way she looked, in the way she talked," Mr. Masayiti said. "I don't think she even knew how to turn on a computer. But then she changed. I say this with admiration."

While still a student, Ms. Biyela was given a part-time job at Delheim, a large winery, and this led to her enological conversion. She not only worked in the vineyards and the cellar but also served wine to visitors in the tasting room and was consequently obliged to discuss what she poured. So she too tasted. She developed her palate.

After graduation, Stellekaya, a boutique winery in Stellenbosch, hired her as its winemaker. It was a big leap, and the winery was taking a big chance on someone so inexperienced. A consultant helped her in the beginning, but soon she was on her own. Her very first red blend won a gold medal at the country's prestigious Michelangelo awards. Most other blacks at the awards ceremony were waiters. They erupted in cheers at the announcement.

Ms. Biyela is a short, energetic woman with freckled cheeks. Braided strands of hair swing from her head. She discusses her craft without pretention. "Very nice" is her favorite superlative. She hopes more of her black compatriots will warm up to wine and says, "It won't happen until people think of it as part of their food and not something that needs to be smelled and talked about."

The vocabulary of the wine world sometimes amuses her. At one tasting, she listened to the connoisseurs as they detected the intricate flavors.

"One is saying, 'I am picking up hints of cassis,' and another is saying, 'I can smell truffles,'" she recalled. "I probably shouldn't have done this, but I said what I was smelling was cow dung."

She did not use those words to be mean, she said. In one of her two worlds, cow dung is used to make floors and walls. "It's a smell I grew up with. I didn't grow up with truffles."

August 2011

A Winemaker, Transplanted

By R. W. APPLE Jr.

Zelma Long has cut a broad swath through the California wine world for a quarter-century and more. Soon she will see whether her widely acknowledged expertise as a winemaker will enable her to do the same thing in this country's heart-stoppingly beautiful Cape vineyards, more than 10,000 miles from the Napa Valley.

"This place is made for fine wines," Ms. Long told me over a lunch of calamari and shredded oxtails in saffron cream sauce at Tokara, the winery where her new wines will be made for the next few years. "It has all the advantages of soil and climate you could want, plus a viticultural tradition stretching back many centuries."

Ms. Long and her husband, Phil Freese, a leading authority on the planting and cultivation of vines, will introduce two cutting-edge blends bearing the Vilafonté label to the South African and American markets later this year: an "M" series, mainly merlot and malbec, and a "C" series, mostly cabernet sauvignon. The prices will be hefty: $50 and $70 a bottle respectively, on a level with California's classic reds.

With the globalization of the wine trade, French and Australian and a few Italian winemakers have taken on consulting jobs around the world. "Flying winemakers," they are called, because they flit from country to country. But Ms. Long and Mr. Freese intend to play a role more sustained than that. She said that she planned "to be as hands-on as I can possibly be," spending three to four months here every year.

Although some local growers privately expressed skepticism that Ms. Long would find her American experience quickly applicable in this country, and others predicted that her prices would prove too high, John Platter, a prominent South African wine writer, said that so far Ms. Long and Mr. Freese had been warmly welcomed by their peers.

"There's no sense at all that they're interlopers," he added, "because they've been coming here for such a long time."

Now 61, Ms. Long was one of the first women to study for a master's degree in enology at the University of California, Davis, the top wine school in the United States. She honed her craft under Mike Grgich at Robert Mondavi's vineyards, later serving there as chief winemaker for almost a decade. In 1979, she shifted to the Sonoma Valley, scoring a notable triumph at Simi Winery, which she restored to its former eminence before stepping down as president and chief executive in 1999.

For the last 28 years, she has also owned Long Vineyards in the hills east of the Napa Valley with her first husband, Bob Long, turning out rich and very long-lived chardonnays in the European style, as well as several other superb wines. That, too, helped to establish her as the most important woman in American wine, a trailblazer who helped open the door for later stars like Helen Turley and Cathy Corison.

A rangy woman who looks a lot taller than her 5 feet 8½ inches, Ms. Long is a bluejeans-and-khakis, plain-talking type who seems equally at home in the vineyard, the boardroom and the barrel room.

She and Mr. Freese own 50 percent of Vilafonté; the other 50 percent belongs to Michael Ratcliffe, scion of the family that has operated the highly regarded Warwick Estate in nearby Stellenbosch for more than four decades. The founder of a group of young and progressive winemakers called Rootstock, he will oversee Vilafonté's operations when Ms. Long is out of the country.

A fourth major player at Vilafonté, the San Francisco–based wine merchant Bartholomew Broadbent, has an equally impressive pedigree: he is the son of Michael Broadbent, the celebrated London wine auctioneer and commentator. He will import Vilafonté wines to North America.

Vilafonté's initial production, the 2001 and 2002 vintages, was privately bottled; now comes the big test, the 2003, which was bottled last January at Tokara, a showplace hillside winery outside Stellenbosch. It will reach stores sometime this autumn. An initial tasting of both the "M" and "C" series showed great promise, the "M" suppler and fruitier, the "C" more commanding.

The two demonstrate what modern techniques and liberation from bureau-cratic shackles have done for the best new South African wines. Stale, musty flavors and ham-handed heaviness have been supplanted by clarity, subtlety and finesse.

Attracted first to South Africa by Gyles Webb, the Indiana-educated pioneer who made some of this country's first and best modern wines at Thelema, Ms. Long paid her initial visit in 1990 and returned in 2001 to make a speech "defining the unique position that I believe South Africa can build for itself" in world wine markets.

It came at an apt time. The country and its winemakers were just emerging from the long, dark tunnel called apartheid, which not only stunted the sales of South African wines in many foreign markets but also blocked the importation of virus-free clones. Ms. Long gave her audience every reason to be confident about the future.

She noted the country's "enormously old and diverse soils," which support more than 8,000 species of often vividly flowering plants, including the magnificent proteas. As a result, she continued, "along with California, South Africa has more potential for varietal diversity in a relatively small area than any wine-growing country in the world." It also benefits from coastal fogs rolling in from the Indian and Atlantic Oceans, which converge at South Africa's southwestern tip, near the main winefields.

A relatively cool climate, low rainfall and moderate humidity, Ms. Long argued, "give wines that have personality and flavor length" without the aggressive tannins that mar reds in some growing zones.

Since then, dozens of South African wines have achieved world-class quality, and many others stand on the verge of excellence. Far-flung new wine areas like Swartland and Walker Bay are thriving. My friend Anthony Hamilton Russell's pioneering Hamilton Russell vineyard, situated above Walker Bay in the well-named Hemel-en-Aarde ("Heaven on Earth") valley, makes superlative pinot noir, as does Bouchard Finlayson. New varietals like mourvèdre, shiraz, viognier, riesling and sémillon (new to South Africa, that is) have been more extensively planted, and chenin blanc is staging a comeback.

In addition, a few black South Africans are slowly moving into ownership and management positions in the wine industry—far too slowly, many complain, but at least the transformation is under way.

Vilafonté was laid out in 1998 and 1999 in a shallow bowl on the northern slope of the Simonsberg, one of the stark peaks that lend the Cape region such drama. It was planted with classic Bordeaux varietals, including cabernet sauvignon, malbec, cabernet franc and merlot, using global positioning satellite data to establish vine rows in harmony with sun and drainage patterns.

Mr. Freese, who holds advanced degrees from Davis, also uses a technique that he developed while working at Mondavi, called the Normalized Differentiated Vegetative Index, to monitor the plants' vigor. With the aid of aerial photos taken by a special camera at particular wavelengths, the index helps to pinpoint weaker vines and to detect any early symptoms of the infestation by phylloxera lice that is fatal to vines.

Ms. Long told me there were no plans to build a winery for now. By 2007, she and her husband hope to have found and converted a building for such use, with a built-to-order facility to follow later if the economic climate makes it practical.

About 30 acres have been planted so far, with a potential for 50 more on the same property. The present 30 produced 1,700 cases of "M" and 1,300 cases of "C" in the 2003 vintage. When fully planted, the vineyard will produce 15,000 to 18,000 cases, which is a fair-to-middling total, certainly well outside the boutique range.

Ms. Long grew up in the Pacific Northwest and graduated from Oregon State University. She is especially attracted to the wines from the Walla Walla district in southeastern Washington, a few miles north of the Oregon border, most of all the merlots made there, which she said she considers some of the best in the world.

Those merlots—powerful, well-structured wines with big, soft tannins rather than the lightweights often made elsewhere—bear a strong resemblance to those being produced by some South African wineries. Vilafonté intends to join them.

A bit later, Ms. Long said, she and Mr. Freese also plan to "take another look at pinotage." That grape, uniquely South African, resulted from a crossing in the 1920s of cinsaut and pinot noir. Wines made from it are sometimes coarse, with an unpleasant aftertaste, but winemakers at vineyards like Kanonkop and other estates near Vilafonté's property have been producing well-oaked pinotage with a fruity aroma.

Under the umbrella of Zelphi, their new company, Ms. Long and Mr. Freese have kept busy as consultants, working with clients in South Africa, Washington State (Abeja), California (Gundlach-Bundschu) and Israel (Golan Heights Winery).

But they have been less successful in their own small-scale projects abroad. Simunye, their initial South African effort, a joint venture with Michael Back of Backsberg, also in Paarl, foundered because of disagreements among the partners. It was discontinued a few years ago.

In Germany's Nahe Valley, through which flows a small tributary of the Rhine, the two teamed with Monika Christmann, a leading German wine educator and writer, to produce a riesling that they called Sibyl. From the first vintage in 1998 it attracted highly favorable comment, but with Germany's depressed wine prices, Sibyl was not big enough (four and a half acres, 450 to 900 cases a year, depending on the harvest) to prosper.

"It cost much too much to market the wine," Ms. Long said, "so we have just closed the whole operation down."

All of which serves as a reminder that even for people as obviously talented and widely experienced as Ms. Long and Mr. Freese, there are plenty of pitfalls in starting new ventures in far-off winelands.

June 2005

Meals in the Bush, Now With Fine Wines

By R. W. APPLE Jr.

Guess what? Some of South Africa's choicest wines and most satisfying food are served far from the bright lights of Cape Town, right in the midst of the wilderness, along a shimmering stream called the N'wanetsi, where hippopotamuses frolic, crocodiles slither and vivid birds of several hundred species fill the air with their trills.

At Singita Lebombo Lodge in Kruger National Park, hard by the Mozambique border, a few privileged clients live for a few magical days in suites hung like eagles' nests on the face of basaltic cliffs, amid cactus-like, candelabra-shaped euphorbia plants.

Buffalo heads and zebra rugs have been banished from these airy quarters, which blend natural fabrics, eucalyptus floorboards and outdoor showers with plate-glass walls, high-tech chrome fixtures and furniture designed by Arne Jacobsen.

Nothing had prepared me for such marvelous digs or for the terrific meals that came with them. When I lived in Kenya in the 1960s, the food in the game reserves was pretty rudimentary, just a notch or two above mess-hall chow.

Things are different now, and not only in the culinary department. This is the new South Africa—worldly, eco-friendly and postmodern.

The day starts just after dawn with a three-hour drive by open Land Rover through a private, 33,000-acre concession accessible only to the lodge's guests. Lions and giraffes, buffaloes and elephants and rhinoceroses, impalas and zebras, waterbucks and kudus with majestic corkscrew horns all remain unfazed by human visitors.

Back at the ranch, a bountiful breakfast awaits to deal with appetites whetted by the fresh, unpolluted air, featuring fresh orange and litchi juice, luscious passion fruit yogurt, and a cornucopia of local fruit. My wife, Betsey, a connoisseur in these matters, pronounced her eggs Benedict (three days running) the best she had ever eaten, and I was equally pleased with a zesty potato, sautéed onion and chili omelet I concocted from a long list of potential ingredients.

Boerewors (beef sausage)? Bacon? House-cured salmon? Grilled portobellos or tomatoes? Homemade muffins? Toast made from freshly baked bread? Tea?

Faultless espresso or cappuccino? Merely ask and it shall be given, delivered by a corps of waiters more competent than those in some of New York's more pretentious restaurants. Ours was named "Secret."

Midday heat is for resting or swimming, and perhaps a light lunch—salade niçoise with hard-boiled quail eggs, or chilled strawberry soup, or a well-made B.L.T. (no commonplace thing). We mostly passed, already amply fed for the moment.

But on our first day, we indulged, and in the process we got an inkling of the wonders hidden in the lodge's air-conditioned 4,600-bottle wine cellar (a silo-shaped tower, actually, between the hotel bar and a baobab tree). The Singita group buys the very best South African vintages available, matures them in Cape Town, then dispatches them in refrigerated containers to the four lodges it operates, including Lebombo. The much more traditional Boulders Lodge, outside Kruger, stocks as many as 6,000 bottles.

Gerry Terblanche, the Lebombo sommelier, led me proudly through his carefully annotated list of 200-odd wines, with winemakers duly credited. He conducts tastings for interested guests and recommends wines for each day's menus. But anyone can order anything at all from the full list, including rarities like the honeyed, lime-accented 1999 Vergelegen Semillon Show Reserve, which is available in no other restaurant. It made an ideal partner later for our Asian-inspired spring rolls.

On a visit to the tower, Mr. Terblanche pointed out some of the delightfully fresh viogniers that South African winemakers have recently begun producing, as well as two of his favorite reds—the supple, well-balanced 1999 Rubicon, a Bordeaux-style blend from the Meerlust estate, and the intense, ruby-red, prize-winning 1999 Peter Barlow 100 percent cabernet from the Rustenberg estate, which was established in 1682, not long after Château Latour.

It all costs a pretty penny—$1,000 a day per person, including room, meals, cocktails, wines and game tours. Only Champagne costs extra.

"I think of us as missionaries for South African wine," Mr. Terblanche said. "I hope our visitors leave us with a vastly improved impression of our wares."

Dinner each day is preceded by a second game drive. We hit the jackpot with Derek Boshard, peerless ranger-driver, and Dudu Mabunda, tireless tracker and dispenser of good cheer, spotting superb beasts and birds (like the awesome bateleur eagle, the carmine bee-eater and the spectacular lilac-breasted roller) and learning a lot about local botany, geology and geography as well as animal feeding and mating habits.

The chef Rachel Buchner's simple yet sophisticated food—"wholesome and uncomplicated," the lodge's brochure calls it, with reason—lived up to the wonders of the bush and the riches of the cellar.

In the open-sided dining room overlooking the pool one night, we ate those delicate, phyllo-wrapped chicken spring rolls with a mango and coriander relish, followed by a juicy steak and rich house-made fresh fig ice cream. South African beef, generally grass-fed and additive-free, is famously tender and universally popular, and we couldn't resist. But a well-spiced Moroccan chicken casserole was on offer as well.

Another night, Ms. Buchner and her team mounted a luxury version of South Africa's favorite meal, a barbecue or braai (rhymes with eye), in an amphitheater of boulders, lighted by campfires burning in braziers. No paper-plate picnic, this: a full bar had been set up, three red and three white wines had been readied and tables had been set with proper china, wineglasses and modern cutlery, with chrome-and-canvas directors' chairs drawn up around them.

After serving a bracing corn and lemongrass soup, a battalion of cooks wearing white toques took their posts behind a battery of charcoal-filled oil drums to grill giant Indian Ocean prawns from Mozambique; coils of boerewors; venisonlike kudu steaks, medium-rare—the equal of any hoofed game I have eaten—and lean, dark ostrich fillets. There were lots of veg to go with them, including glazed baby carrots, herbed new potatoes and butternut squash. Most of the British clients chose cauliflower with cheese sauce from the buffet line, and Betsey, ever the Anglophile, joined them.

We had heard a lot about a new wine called De Toren Fusion V, so we tried the 2000 vintage. It nicely symbolizes the newfound democratic spirit that animates both the political and viticultural worlds in South Africa, in that its makers actively seek feedback not only from experts but also from rank-and-file enthusiasts. A blend of the five classic Bordeaux grapes, it proved just the ripe, lusty ticket with our grilled meats.

No one could argue with a tart-sweet sorbet made with local passion fruit, and we ended contentedly with that.

I couldn't help thinking how astounded Ernest Hemingway and his sometime hunting partner, the columnist and novelist Robert C. Ruark, would have been by this spread. Both Africa-lovers with big bucks to spend, they had to settle on safari for francolin, a duck-size bird as tough as an elderly owl, cooked on a campfire.

But they would have recognized the sights and sounds we encountered later that night. A crocodile lazily crossed our path and long-eared bush hares hopped down the road as we drove home, thoroughly enchanted by the whole place, beneath a sky filled with stars of incredible intensity.

June 2005

An Australian Sibling Comes Into Its Own

By ERIC ASIMOV

Half a century ago, two wines were born at Penfolds in South Australia. They were like brothers, really. Both were made largely of shiraz, with a little cabernet sauvignon occasionally thrown in, yet they offered completely different expressions of the same grapes. As with so many siblings, each seemed to represent all that the other was not, the apparent differences concealing their shared pedigree.

One of these wines is now justly celebrated around the world. It is prized by collectors and commands $200 to $300 a bottle for recent vintages and far more for bottles with a little age. This wine, christened Grange Hermitage and now known simply and grandly as Grange, is today the most famous of all Australian wines.

Its brother has lived a considerably more obscure life. It goes by the modest name St. Henri, which sounds especially self-effacing if you pronounce it with an Australian accent. As you might guess, it is a quieter wine than Grange. Yet its elegance and purity, for those who take the time to know it, are undeniable.

Back in the 1950s, Grange and St. Henri cost essentially the same. Today, you can find St. Henri for around $50 a bottle, not cheap by any means, but a relative steal for a wine of this quality.

The history of St. Henri and Grange is a story of the importance of preserving choices among wines. It is a reminder of how different styles can best be understood and appreciated in contrast to one another, and a cautionary tale about how fragile this diversity can be. As Grange and its stylistic adherents became wildly popular, Penfolds considered doing away with the St. Henri approach.

"Marketing types kept urging us to keep the name, keep the label, but change the style," said Peter Gago, the chief winemaker at Penfolds, who visited with me in New York last week. "But we resisted, and it's never changed."

Mr. Gago came to New York with 13 different vintages of St. Henri, ranging from a 1958, which offered a quick impression of its youthful allure before slowly fading in the glass, to a robust-yet-juvenile 2002, which will be released this spring. As he and I tasted through the wines, it was fascinating to compare the St. Henri style with the better-known Grange, and to see how beautifully St. Henri stands up for itself.

Grange, which was first produced as an experiment in 1951, was at first considered shockingly modern. Max Schubert, its creator, was consciously trying to produce a shiraz with the aging potential of top Bordeaux, and he made a big, powerful wine that was aged in small barrels of American oak.

The initial reception was lukewarm.

"Knife and fork stuff," one journalist said at the time, referring to the young wine's almost impenetrable concentration, a style that many have since come to prize.

By contrast, St. Henri was considered an old-fashioned wine, even in the 1950s. Unlike Schubert, John Davoren, a Penfolds winemaker who created St. Henri, looked backward for inspiration. He wanted to make a wine that demonstrated the pure character of the shiraz grape rather than framing it with the flavors of new oak. Yet he was not making a small wine; younger St. Henris have a sort of raw-boned power, while grape tannins offer a structure that can last for years.

Instead of using small barrels of new oak, which can impart powerful flavors, he chose to age the wine in huge oak vats that were at least 50 years old, which have minimal impact on the flavor of the wine.

The battle of styles characterized by the use of small new barrels or big, old, neutral containers has been fought all over the wine-producing world, from Barolo and Montalcino to the Rhône and Burgundy to California. Those who have favored the lusher, rounder flavors imparted by new oak have held sway for the last 20 years, but tastes may slowly be moving back toward the center as a small but significant portion of the public has been registering its vote in favor of less oak influence.

Mr. Gago said he has noticed an increased interest in St. Henri in the last few years.

"Everything is about fashion, isn't it?" he said. "What's old is new again."

From the almost joyously grapey 2002 back to the still-dignified 1958, each decade offered different insights into St. Henri. A 1962 had a eucalyptus quality, while a 1966 had a sense of power and a caramel-like flavor that Mr. Gago called "praline."

A 1971, from one of South Australia's best vintages, was rich and complex, with smoky, meaty flavors that lingered in the mouth, while a 1974—a poor vintage—was pleasing, though without the concentration of the '71. A 1976 was inky black, with a pronounced licorice flavor. I loved two vintages from the 1980s, the '83 and the '86, but my two favorites in the tasting were the 1990 and the 1991, both excellent wines that kept changing in the glass. The '90 was pure, with sweet fruit aromas and a high-toned brightness, while the '91 seemed to have darker licorice and plum flavors.

What was striking about the wines was their transparency, each offering clear insights into the peculiar characteristics of different vintages.

"It's much harder to make this style," Mr. Gago said. "The fruit quality has to be that much better because it's not just a component, it's the structure, too. So much more effort is put into the fruit, the vineyard and the grapes, because you don't have the other support."

The grapes for St. Henri, like those for Grange, come from a variety of sources in South Australia. Each year, Mr. Gago and his team of winemakers do numerous blind tastings to select what will go into the St. Henri blend. For St. Henri, he said, he is looking for fleshy, succulent flavors, as opposed to the assertive, darker, chunky Grange flavors. Neither wine offers the pleasure of tracking the flavors of a single vineyard over time. For that, there are other shirazes, like Henschke Hill of Grace or Penfolds's own Magill Estate. Nonetheless, both Grange and St. Henri have their important place.

"Too many people, they don't even look sideways at St. Henri because they don't get the style," Mr. Gago said. "But there are so many different variations on a theme. Why not offer them?"

February 2006

CHAPTER TEN

The Night (and Day) They Invented Champagne (and Sparkling Wine)

Taking Champagne Back to Its Roots

By ERIC ASIMOV

With rough, work-thickened hands, unruly hair and a steady gaze, Anselme Selosse looks the image of the French vigneron, a man more comfortable tending vines and working in his cellar than he is in a New York restaurant talking to sommeliers and wine writers.

But there he was last week, at Eleven Madison Park, leading a tasting of his wines, speaking smoothly in French, gesturing with long arms that seemed as if they would be a lot more comfortable sprung from the confines of his rumpled blazer.

Mr. Selosse, 54, is not the usual emissary from Champagne, a smooth guy in a suit, talking about product positioning, luxury brands and lifestyles. To hear them tell it, Champagne pops into this world like a genie from a lamp, ready to make magic.

But to Mr. Selosse, the magic occurs long before there is a wine. It takes place deep underneath Champagne's chalky soil, where the roots of the vines take hold of what Mr. Selosse calls the essence of the earth.

Jacques Selosse Champagne, named for Anselme's father, is not something found at the corner wine shop. In fact, for five years, from 2002 to 2007, it wasn't sent to the United States at all, not after Mr. Selosse severed ties with a previous American importer. But last year another importer, the Rare Wine Company, made a deal with Mr. Selosse and began to bring it in again—though in minute quantities at high prices.

Suffice it to say that most of us probably can't afford Selosse Champagne and may never drink it. Well, then, why should anybody care about it, especially now when $20 for a bottle of wine seems like a lot of money, much less the $250 you might pay for Selosse's top-of-the-line Substance cuvée?

Because, as superb, striking and idiosyncratic as the Selosse Champagnes can be, what Mr. Selosse represents is equally important, if not more so. Yes, he and his wife, Corinne, had taken this rare trip to New York to reintroduce their Champagnes to the wine trade, but what he had to say about Champagne was possibly more meaningful than the wines themselves.

The key word is wines. In almost every possible way, the corporate line from Champagne is the antithesis of what consumers are taught about every other important wine region in the world. Great wines, almost everyone can agree, are distinctive. They ideally reflect their terroirs and the conditions of their vintages. In short, as the rest of the wine world preaches with varying degrees of honesty, great wines are made in the vineyard.

But the dominant Champagne houses have divorced what's in the bottle from what comes from the earth. Their story of Champagne, told through decades of marketing, associates bubbles with elegance, luxury and festivity, achieved through master blenders in the cellar. Champagne does not celebrate the land and the vigneron, but the house and the event. Too often, Champagne is a commodity, not a wine.

Mr. Selosse, by his example and his Champagnes, is intent on restoring the ideas of vineyard, terroir and wine to the perception of Champagne. He is not alone by any means. He is one of a growing number of Champagne vignerons—grape growers who also make the wine and bottle it themselves—who are intent on changing the nature of Champagne. Some of the big houses make great Champagne, and not all of the small growers are successful. But their influence has increased, and the big houses are paying attention.

Any restaurant in New York with a decent wine list will have at least one of these small Champagne houses among the big names. Grower-producers like Larmandier-Bernier, Egly-Ouriet, Pierre Gimonnet, Pierre Moncuit and Pierre Peters are making Champagnes that are distinctive if not profound, reflecting the terroir in which the grapes are born, and forcing people to rethink their ideas about Champagne. In this company, no Champagne producer has been more influential or more original than Mr. Selosse.

Not that Mr. Selosse heads any organized group. He leads more by inspiration. He won't criticize his colleagues big or small, though he was more impolitic as a younger man after he took over from his father in 1980. His Champagnes are not adored unanimously, although you can count me among the adorers. He has been criticized for making Champagnes that are too oaky—perhaps a fault once but no longer. That said, his Champagnes—his wines—are distinctive, and distinctive wines will always be at least somewhat divisive.

Mr. Selosse was trained in Burgundy, and his ideas about grape growing are indeed Burgundian. He has likened himself to the Cistercian monks who planted many of Burgundy's great vineyards in an effort to make the most of their terroir. "They were motivated by religion," Mr. Selosse told me once. "My religion is the vineyard."

Mr. Selosse does not adhere to biodynamic viticulture, but he thinks of the vineyard in biodynamic terms, seeing it as a harmonious eco-system of plants, animals and micro-organisms. "The greatest danger is man, who can upset the balance," he said. His job, he said, is to observe and guide with a gentle hand, but to stay out of the way.

"Essentially, we're of the countryside, and our goal is to give expression to the countryside," he said. It's not an unusual thing to hear from a vigneron, but revolutionary in Champagne, which strives for a decidedly urban image.

Mr. Selosse is determined to emphasize what is singular in his wines, rather than the Champagne norm of seeking house consistency year after year. Yet he is not so Burgundian that he believes only in vintage wines. Of the eight cuvées he poured at the New York tasting and at a dinner later that evening, only one was a vintage wine, a 1999 blanc de blancs extra brut. The others, including a floral, chalky rosé, a rich yet energetic blanc de noirs and a beautifully subtle and textured extra brut blanc de blancs called Version Originale, are all made from multiple vintages.

Perhaps the most unusual of his Champagnes is Substance, made from a single chardonnay vineyard in Avize. It uses a solera system, similar to what is used to make sherry, in which successive vintages, back to 1987, are blended. The result is an almost ethereal Champagne, with aromas of flowers and seashells.

Rather than obscuring the terroir, Mr. Selosse asserts, the blending of his solera Champagne emphasizes the qualities of the vineyard by eliminating variables like weather.

"It takes all the different years—the good, the bad, the wet, the dry, the sunny—and neutralizes the elements to bring out the terroir," he said.

I asked him whether he would ever suggest this method to his friends in Burgundy, where it would be looked on as heretical.

"No," he said. "In Burgundy they already understand the terroir—it rises above the vintage." He looked thoughtful for a moment. "Maybe in Bordeaux," he said.

November 2008

In Small Houses, Champagne Finds Its Soul

By ERIC ASIMOV

Like any bottle of Champagne, Larmandier-Bernier's Terre de Vertus, with its tapered, graceful curves, can ignite the imagination. Simply glancing at it transports you to a world of tuxedos and gowns, where the music is soft, the dancing close, and elegance as near as a pop and a pour and a sigh. A more careful examination of the bottle, though, reveals a label completely at odds with the bubbly, urbane notion of Champagne. Its central image?

Dirt.

More precisely, it's a photograph of the gravelly, gloriously chalky soil of a vineyard here in the heart of the Côte des Blancs in the southern part of the Champagne region. For Larmandier-Bernier and other small producers that, unlike the famous houses, make their Champagne almost entirely from grapes they have grown themselves, this image of dirt conveys a truth that is often overlooked amid the elegant imagery: Champagne, above all, is a wine, made from grapes that grow in the ground. It should be thought of, like other great wines, as having a provenance—a terroir, as the French say—and a home on the dinner table.

"We make wine before bubbles," said Laurent Champs, the young head of Vilmart & Cie in Rilly.

These grower-producers account for no more than a trickle of foam in the river of sparkling wine that flows out of Champagne. But their significance far out-weighs their numbers. Tiny Champagne houses like René Geoffroy in Cumières, Chartogne-Taillet in Merfy, Jean Milan in Oger, Pierre Gimonnet et Fils in Cuis and Godmé Père et Fils in Verzenay produce excellent wines that demonstrate more than just another side of Champagne. Rather than the smoothly consistent blends that dominate the production of the biggest Champagne makers like Moët & Chandon and Veuve Clicquot, these winemakers produce Champagnes with clear, pronounced personalities that bubble up through the wine, expressing the quirky nuances of each particular combination of soil, climate and producer.

In the hands of the best of these winemakers, the Champagnes are utterly distinct. The intense, almost austere minerality of the Terre de Vertus, or the equally lean and stony Champagne from José Dhondt in neighboring Oger, offers a marked contrast to the creamy fruit of a bottle of Michel Genet from Chouilly.

Each of these wines is a blanc de blancs, made entirely of chardonnay from the Côte des Blancs, which is known as chardonnay territory. They are completely different from, say, the rich, round power of an Egly-Ouriet from Ambonnay, a pinot noir-based Champagne, which in turn bears little resemblance to another pinot noir-based Champagne, like one from Godmé, with its clear, precise raspberry flavors.

"Each village has a different style of wine, and within each village different locations have different styles," said Paul Couvreur, who, with his wife, Françoise, has joined forces with Becky Wasserman, a wine broker in Burgundy, to market grower-produced Champagnes. "These Champagnes are much more on the wine side. We sell to people who think that Champagne is not only bubbles and fizz, but chardonnay and pinot noir. It's wine you can think about."

Champagne is wine? This is news? Indeed, if you travel the narrow, back roads winding through towns like Rilly and Ambonnay south across the Marne River to Oger and Vertus, Champagne looks pretty much like any other wine region. Vineyards dominate the hillsides and flatlands, where the underlying chalk pushes up through the soil here and there in crumbly patches of white. In a chilly early November drizzle, the vines hang with resignation, seemingly counting the days until the arrival of the pruner's shears, a last few bunches of unpicked grapes waiting to be plucked by the birds.

In the small towns of this northernmost fine wine region of the world, where buildings seem to cluster for warmth, signs point in almost every direction to Champagne producers. Most are tiny. Aside from the several dozen big houses that account for more than 70 percent of the Champagne produced, only 5,000 or so of the 20,000 grape growers in Champagne also sell wine. Around 3,000 simply take their grapes to a cooperative, where it is made into basic Champagne for them, bottled and returned to the grower with a label slapped on. The remaining 2,000 make their own Champagne, often achieving something special.

Most of the growers sell to weekenders from Paris who back their Peugeots to the door and load up with bottles. A mere handful of these grower-producers make enough of their own wine to export bottles to the United States, though their number is growing. Last year, grower-producer Champagnes accounted for 1.9 percent of all Champagne imported into the United States, said Terry Theise, the leading importer of such Champagnes, more than triple the 0.62 percent of 1997, when Mr. Theise put together his portfolio.

To most of the world, wine is wine, and then there's Champagne. No other wine has been so brilliantly defined by its marketing, which places Champagne at the center of weddings, ship launchings and other cultivated, congratulatory affairs, but never at the center of a meal, where you would put any other wine.

"These are food wines, intended to go with food," Mr. Couvreur said. The combinations practically suggest themselves. The more mineral-laden Champagnes would be exceptional matches for oysters, or for scallops in a sauce flavored with citrus and herbs. A more robust bottle would go exceptionally well with roast chicken, veal or rabbit. Almost any dry Champagne will go well with sushi, not to mention fried chicken.

Champagne and wine are perceived differently in other ways, too. Almost everywhere else, wine lovers want to know where the grapes were grown. In Burgundy, connoisseurs fancy they can taste the difference between wines from the Meursault-Perrières vineyard and its neighbor, Meursault-Charmes. Barolo fans know that wines from La Morra are distinguished by their elegant perfume, and wines from Serralunga d'Alba by their power. In Germany, Mosels are known for delicacy, Rheingaus for their voluptuous richness.

What's more, in almost every other winegrowing region, the best wine producers grow their own grapes, or wish they could. It's become a sometimes disingenuous cliché for winemakers to proclaim their desire simply to allow the grapes to express their terroir in the glass.

But not in Champagne. Few of the big houses own more than 30 percent of their vineyards. Even connoisseurs would have trouble naming the three key zones in the region, Montagne de Reims, Côte des Blancs to the south, and Vallée de la Marne in between, much less a fourth region, Côte des Bar to the southeast. And while the communes of the Côte d'Or might roll easily off the tongue of any Burgundy hound, few Champagne lovers could name any of the 17 villages ranked as grands crus, the highest classification. In fact, it's fair to assume that most people have no idea that Champagne vineyards even have a ranking system. What the public does know are brand names, especially prestigious ones like Cristal and Dom Pérignon. Although the big houses reserve their best vineyards for their high-end bottles, it will strike few people as odd that they see no need to even mention the provenance of the grapes.

"It's only at the grower level that a person can luck into a nonvintage Champagne that's 100 percent grand cru," Mr. Theise said.

To a far greater extent than any other wine, Champagne has celebrated the art of blending. Most Champagnes are a mixture of wine from three grapes—pinot noir, chardonnay and pinot meunier—and a blend of different vintages. Nonvintage Champagne (or multivintage, as the big producers like to say), accounts for around 90 percent of all Champagne sold.

There are sound reasons for the development of this system. The grapes, grown in these northern vineyards, have historically battled each year simply to ripen. The annual struggle of the grapes gives Champagne the blend of fruit, intensity and acidity that distinguishes it from all other sparkling wines, but it also makes the Champagne business a risky proposition.

Some years the grapes didn't ripen enough, or at all, so for producers to depend only on the annual crop would have been highly dicey. Some years the pinot meunier, which provides perfume and fruitiness but little structure, does best. Some years it's chardonnay, and some years it's pinot noir. It might be a different combination each year, so by necessity in Champagne the winemakers blend what they have.

Over time the big Champagne makers turned this necessity into a virtue, so much so that the exalted image of the blender's art long ago overtook any notion of terroir in Champagne. "The names of the wine villages, for example, need hardly concern the wine drinker, for the essence of Champagne is that it is a blended wine, known in all but a handful of cases by the name of the maker, not the vineyard," wrote Hugh Johnson and Jancis Robinson, in the 2001 edition of the *World Atlas of Wine* (Mitchell Beazley).

In fact, blending really can be as high an art as the Champagne producers assert. One need only taste a bottle of Krug Grande Cuvée, a blend of up to 50 different wines from six to 10 different years, to appreciate the level of complexity a blend can achieve. In the neat, laboratory-clean tasting room at Krug headquarters in Reims, Rémi Krug, who runs Krug, possibly the most prestigious Champagne producer, demonstrated the art of the blend.

With seven still wines in carafes in front of him, he poured into a tall beaker first a little 2003 chardonnay from Le Mesnil-sur-Oger, newly made yet already intense. He added some supple '03 pinot noir from Ay, rich with a light raspberry edge; a leaner '03 pinot from Verzenay; and some seductively perfumed '03 pinot meunier from Ste. Gemme. Then he reached for some older wines. First a 2000 pinot noir from Ay, with aromas of wet earth; then some crisp, beautifully fruity pinot noir from Verzenay, from the great vintage of '96; and finally, some '90 chardonnay from Mesnil, already aging like a good white Burgundy, crisp and acidic yet with aromas of hazelnut and honeysuckle.

After sniffing and tasting, he added a few dashes of this and a dollop of that, and voilà. His blend was indisputably more complex and remarkable than any of the individual wines.

"Blending is not destroying individuality, it's creating a cuvée," Mr. Krug said. "We're not blending to correct, we're blending to enhance. If you would transform Champagne into Burgundy you would destroy it."

Of course, few big producers and no small producers can hope to match the elegance of Mr. Krug's blend. Krug Champagnes begin at more than $100 a bottle and surely fit into the artisanal category. Most growers might produce 3,000 to 10,000 cases of Champagne a year, as against Krug's 40,000, which in itself is a drop in the ocean compared with Moët's two million cases a year. While the growers, too, blend their nonvintage wines, it is a far more limited composition, with wines taken from different parcels in the same general area, and covering far fewer vintages.

"We want to express the style of the village," said Pierre Larmandier, who, with his wife, Sophie, runs Larmandier-Bernier. "We can't make the sophisticated blends of the big houses. This is what we can do."

Slowly but clearly, consumers are gaining awareness of these small Champagne houses. As with heirloom vegetables and microbrews, their success depends on developing a small but select public for whom connoisseurship is as important as the wallet.

"What the big houses are seeing is that connoisseurs are looking for specificity and individuality, notwithstanding that we've spent the last 40 years saying great Champagne can only be blended," Mr. Theise said. "You definitely see the impact of this kind of thinking in that no less than Moët & Chandon is releasing single-vineyard Champagnes."

Moët first offered limited quantities of its three single-vineyard Champagnes, each demonstrating one of the three grapes of the region, in 2001, with the intention of promoting its own vineyards. These are intense, powerful wines, thoroughly unlike other Moëts, which are typically more balanced. "The way we present this trilogy has a bit to do with the world of still wines, rather than what is typical of Moët & Chandon," said Georges Blanck, Moët's head winemaker. "It's something completely new."

In fact, some of the greatest and most expensive Champagnes of all are terroir wines, produced in tiny quantities, like Bollinger's Vieilles Vignes Françaises, an all-pinot-noir Champagne from ancient vines in Ay and Bouzy; Salon's Le Mesnil from the Côte des Blancs; and Krug's Clos du Mesnil, which comes from a single walled vineyard in the town of Mesnil. For Krug, the apostle of blending, this single-vineyard Champagne, which it started producing in the 1970s, was a complete departure. Mr. Krug calls it a "contradiction wine."

"So what," he said. "We're not selling concepts. We're selling pleasure."

These days, many of the grower-producers are selling all the Champagne they can make. Jean-Baptiste Geoffroy, who has about 32 acres in the Vallée de la Marne, is the fifth generation in his family to grow grapes in the region. While his family always made a little wine, they began to emphasize Champagne production in the bad years after World War II, when they were unable to sell their grapes to the big houses. In the 1970s, Mr. Geoffroy's father decided to keep all the grapes and turn them into Champagne.

As you walk through a hillside vineyard in Cumières overlooking the Marne, Mr. Geoffroy's parcels are easy to distinguish from the others. The lush green grass growing between his rows of bare vines is evidence of his distaste for chemical pesticides and herbicides.

"If you don't have the passion, you won't make a very good Champagne," he said as he strolled the vineyard, waving at local hunters who also walked the rows, shotguns in hand, searching for rabbits and pheasants.

Passion can be expensive to maintain. Mr. Geoffroy said good vineyard land was going for 800,000 to 1 million euros per hectare, around $400,000 an acre, enough to set up the Geoffroy family for several generations.

But that would mean sacrificing the graceful, lightly smoky Cuvée Sélectionée that Mr. Geoffroy says expresses the personality of Cumières, and the wine-making facility underneath his grandmother's house. And that would mean more of what Mr. Geoffroy calls "normal Champagne."

"To me," he said, "that's not to my taste."

November 2003

Champagne's Servants Join the Masters

By ERIC ASIMOV

U nlike Reims and Épernay, the Marne cities to the north that are rivaled only by caviar in their close association with Champagne, this pleasant medieval city in the Aube, with its cobblestone streets and timbered architecture, is rarely considered the hub of a thriving Champagne region.

Perhaps that's because for years the Aube has served anonymously as the workaday supplier of grapes to the production areas to the north, a sort of scullery in the elegant house of bubbly, essential to the smooth operation of Champagne, but best ignored.

Yet today, the spotlight is unexpectedly shining on the Aube, and its primary growing area, the Côte des Bar. Now, the region is coming to be known for its independent vignerons, whose distinctive, highly sought wines have caught the attention of Champagne lovers the world over.

The grandes marques of the Marne made Champagne one of the world's leading luxury brands by marketing it as an urbane beverage for special occasions. They emphasized the art of blending, in which the distinctions of terroir, grape and vintage are absorbed into a house style.

By contrast, many Aube producers are taking their cues instead from Burgundy, with its emphasis on farming and on being able to trace terroir through the wines. Rather than the hushed pop of the cork and the silken rush of bubbles, these Champagnes suggest soil on the boots and dirt under the fingernails.

Even so, Champagnes from producers like Cédric Bouchard and Vouette & Sorbée, Marie-Courtin and Dosnon & Lepage, Jacques Lassaigne and Drappier, the closest thing to a grande marque in the Aube, can be as ethereal as their siblings to the north, if a trifle idiosyncratic.

"The identity of Champagne has been as a beverage for celebrations, and there's nothing wrong with that," said Davy Dosnon, who, with his business partner, Simon-Charles Lepage, issued his first wines in 2007. "But it's also a wine of terroir, of place, and should be thought of that way as well. And why not in the Côte des Bar?"

The focus on terroir in the Aube reflects a larger discussion throughout the entire region, in which small producers making distinctive, terroir-specific Champagnes from grapes they farm themselves have seized initiative from the big houses. These small grower-producers account for barely an eyedropper's worth of the Champagne that flows from the region, but they now lay claim to an outsize portion of the fascination among Champagne lovers.

"Before, it was Champagne, singular," said Michel Drappier of Drappier, the largest and best-known producer in the Aube, which was founded in 1808 but didn't begin to bottle its own wines until the early 20th century. "Now it is Champagnes, plural, as sophisticated and complex as Burgundy, with as many villages, winemakers and styles as any place."

Mr. Dosnon studied viticulture and enology in Beaune, the heart of Burgundy, and he brings a Burgundian passion for the land to his work. Strolling through a hillside vineyard in the hamlet of Avirey-Lingey, about 25 miles southeast of Troyes, one parcel among 17 acres or so that they farm, I noticed another similarity to Burgundy, tiny fossilized seashells in the earth, like those often seen in the vineyards of Chablis.

Indeed, the Côte des Bar is closer to Chablis than to Épernay, and its limestone and clay soils are more like those of Chablis than the chalky soils to the north. Yet, despite the geological resemblance to Chablis, which makes the most distinctive chardonnay wines in the world, the vast majority of the grapes in the Côte des Bar are pinot noir.

"The soil is also interesting for pinot noir," Mr. Dosnon said. "There's a lot of volume and complexity."

The Dosnon & Lepage Champagnes are superb, especially the 100 percent pinot noir Récolte Noire, powerful yet graceful, wonderfully fresh and aromatic, and a blanc de blancs, Récolte Blanche, a wine of finesse and nuance, with savory, focused floral and mineral flavors.

If the evolution of the Aube seems a bit of a Cinderella story, it's with good reason. A century ago, in 1911, riots tore through Champagne as, among other issues, the big houses in the Marne tried to exclude the Aube from the Champagne appellation. Eventually, a compromise was reached in which the Aube was granted second-class Champagne status. Even after the Marne finally, if gingerly, embraced the Aube as a full part of Champagne in 1927, none of its vineyards were designated grand cru or even premier cru, marks of quality reserved only for the Marne.

And so the Aube served primarily as a faceless source of grapes. While a small amount of Champagne has always been made here, the grapes mostly traveled 80 miles or so north, through the flat farmland that separates the Côte des Bar from the production areas of the Marne.

In Épernay, I met with an executive at one of the grand marques and told him I was heading to the Côte des Bar the next day. "Oh?" he asked. "They make Champagne there?" Well-worn mockery, perhaps, but an indication that grudging appreciation from the Champagne establishment is not so easy to come by.

Many producers in the south still feel the sting of northern scorn, and it is a driving force.

"Always, we were second class," said Emmanuel Lassaigne, whose Champagne house, Jacques Lassaigne, is in Montgueux, a small village west of Troyes. "People in the Marne will still say, 'The Aube is no good.'"

The vineyards of Montgueux, largely on an imposing south-facing hillside, are distinct from the Côte des Bar, and are one of the few places in the Aube that emphasize chardonnay. In Montgueux, achieving sufficient ripeness is rarely a problem. Indeed, the exotic, tropical-fruit flavors of Montgueux chardonnay are highly unusual for Champagne. Mr. Lassaigne's aim is to capture the aromas and flavors of this singular terroir.

"My job is to say, 'Montgueux is good,'" he said. "It's not better, but it's absolutely not worse."

His nonvintage blanc de blancs Les Vignes de Montgueux is very much its own Champagne, with light aromas of tropical fruit and flowers. It feels broad yet is dry and refreshing. His vintage blanc de blancs are a step up in elegance, with more mineral flavors yet still with the distinctive Montgueux fruit.

Foremost, perhaps, among the region's new stars is Cédric Bouchard, whose single-vineyard Champagnes are exquisitely delicate and subtle, gently expressive of their terroir. His dark, tussled hair and piercing olive green eyes give him the brooding look of a young philosopher. Indeed, his uncompromising winemaking might be called highly philosophical.

"I'm only interested in the wine, the grape, the parcel and the terroir," he said. "It's got to have emotion to it; otherwise, it's going to the négociants."

Mr. Bouchard's father grew grapes and made a small amount of his own Champagne, but as a young man Mr. Bouchard left for Paris, where he worked in a wine shop. There, he said, he discovered the wines of vignerons he described as working naturally, and decided that he, too, wanted to make wine. He returned to the Aube only because his father offered him land.

Right away, he proved himself independent. "Whatever my father did, I did the opposite," he said. "Spiritually, I'm the first generation because it's my own style and philosophy. I think my father is proud of the wines, but he would never admit it directly."

Mr. Bouchard tries to be as natural in his approach as possible, even rejecting the use of horses in his vineyards, which he now plows by hand. In that sense, he said, he is lucky to have only small parcels.

Another rising star in the Côte des Bar, Bertrand Gautherot, named his label Vouette & Sorbée, after the two vineyards he farms biodynamically. His family grew grains and grapes and raised animals around the town of Buxières-sur-Arce. As a young man he left, to design lipsticks, but the call of agriculture was great, and he soon returned.

"We were not in the business of Champagne," he said. "We were more farmers than winemakers."

Mr. Gautherot, too, focused on farming, selling off all his grapes to cooperatives or the big houses. Among his good friends were superb grower-producers from the north, like Anselme Selosse and Jérôme Prévost, who he said urged him to begin making his own wines.

"But I understood I had to learn the terroir of my village," he said. "A big problem in Champagne is that wines are easy to make by recipe. It's much harder to learn the taste of your vineyards. That's why it's called Vouette & Sorbée rather than Bertrand Gautherot."

His first vintage was 2001—only 2,000 bottles, he said, in case he had to drink it all himself. He's now up to around 30,000 bottles, which all seem as if they are fine wines that just happen to be effervescent rather than simply celebratory bubbly. Perhaps his most unusual Champagne is the Saignée de Sorbée, a rosé that emphasizes the lovely spicy fruit of the pinot noir grape and its exuberant aromas. It's a beautifully fragrant, exuberant Champagne, with spicy, smoky flavors.

The Côte des Bar seems rife with small producers waiting for discovery. Some, frankly, are rustic, not yet ready for prime time. Others, like Dominique Moreau, whose label, Marie-Courtin, is named for her grandmother, make breathtakingly gorgeous, elegant Champagnes in such minute quantities that they can be frustrating to try to find.

While the bubbling up of talent in the Aube is clear, Mr. Drappier prefers a historical perspective. With an annual production of 1.6 million bottles, Drappier is the size of a small grande marque, like Pol Roger or Billecart-Salmon. Its facility in Urville sits over an original cellar that traces back to 1152.

"The Aube was the wealthiest of the Champagne regions in the Middle Ages, and Troyes was the capital," said Mr. Drappier, who is the seventh-generation Drappier to lead the house.

"Before phylloxera," he said, referring to the pest that destroyed European grapevines in the late 19th century, "there were many more vineyards in the Aube than in the Marne."

Today, Drappier's Champagnes are discernibly more mainstream than those of the smaller producers, dry and refreshing with full-bodied, sometimes smoky flavors.

Mr. Drappier suggests that the rise of the Aube is due partly to the new prosperity in the entire Champagne region, which allowed growers to start making their own wine; to better education, which contributed to the arrival of dynamic young winemakers in the region; and to the changing tastes of consumers, who now understand that Champagne is more than simply a luxury good.

"Terroir used to be considered rude in Champagne," he said. "It was all about blending and dosage. Now we say we are from the Côte des Bar, and we are proud of it."

July 2011

Buried Treasure in Baltic Has Vintage Taste

By JOHN TAGLIABUE

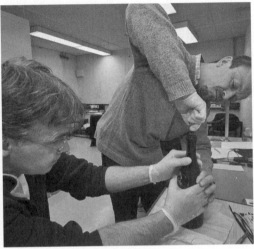

When Christian Ekstrom, a local diver, finally got to explore a sunken two-masted schooner he had known about for years, he found bottles, lots of bottles, so he brought one to the surface.

"I said, 'Let's taste some sea water,'" he said with a laugh, over coffee recently. "So I tasted it straight from the bottle. It was then that I noticed, 'This is not sea water.'"

Mr. Ekstrom, 31, a compact man with a shock of blond hair, brought the bottle to experts in this town of 11,000 on Aland Island, which lies midway between Finland and Sweden, then to others in Sweden and finally in France.

Though the bottle had no label, burned into the cork were markings that made clear it was a bottle of Juglar, a premium French Champagne that ceased to be sold under that name after 1830, when it was renamed Jacquesson, for another of the winery's owners. It remains one of the smaller but finer producers of French Champagnes.

"You could still see the bubbles, and see how clear it was," Mr. Ekstrom said.

The 75-foot wreck, in 160 feet of water, contained other cargo as well: crates filled with grapes, long withered; carpets; coffee beans; spices including white and black pepper and coriander; and four bottles of beer.

Not including the bottle Mr. Ekstrom swigged from, the divers soon discovered a cargo that numbered 172 bottles of Champagne.

Four were broken, but 168 others were intact, and in early August they were hoisted to dry land and stored in Mariehamn. The Baltic Sea floor proved an ideal wine cellar, with 40 degree temperatures, total darkness and enough pressure to keep the corks in.

Getting help in recognizing the find was not easy. "It was quite tricky to get someone to listen," Mr. Ekstrom said. When he contacted Veuve Clicquot, one of the largest French Champagne houses, in search of expertise, a voice on the phone said, "It's a fantastic story, but I have to ask you, 'Where is Aland?'"

Gradually, word got out to the Champagne world, and this November experts from abroad, including from Jacquesson and Veuve Clicquot, were invited to Aland (pronounced AH-lahnd) to replace the crumbling corks in 10 bottles and for a tasting. In the meantime, the Champagne had become the property of the local government, which lays legal claim to anything found in undersea wrecks that is more than 100 years old.

The first three bottles recorked were Juglar, but on the bottom of the fourth cork were the star and anchor of Veuve Clicquot. The star represents a comet that crossed the skies of Champagne in 1811 and supposedly caused fabulous vintages. "I thought, 'Madame Clicquot is watching us,'" Mr. Ekstrom said.

At another recorking, further bottles of Veuve Clicquot appeared. François Hautekeur, a Veuve Clicquot winemaker who attended, pointed to the name Werle branded into the bottom of the cork, referring to Édouard Werle, the man who in 1830 assumed much of the business from the Widow Clicquot, actually Barbe Nicole Clicquot, née Ponsardin, who inherited the company from her husband in 1805 and ran it until her death. "So it is later than 1831," Mr. Hautekeur said.

Jean-Hervé Chiquet, whose family now owns and operates Jacquesson, the winery that absorbed Juglar, said that the shape of the bottles and the use of the name Juglar indicated the Champagne was from the late 1820s, and may have been stored for some time before it was shipped.

He was "overcome with emotion," he said, when he first tasted the Champagne at the recorking in November.

"There was a powerful but agreeable aroma, notes of dried fruit and tobacco, and a striking acidity," Mr. Chiquet said by telephone. The oldest Champagne in Jacquesson's inventory is from 1915, he said.

The Champagne was probably en route to the court of Czar Alexander II in

St. Petersburg when the wooden cargo vessel sank. Though the exact age of the Champagne is not yet known, it goes up against tough competition in the oldest Champagne category.

The Champagne house Perrier-Jouët claims that its vintage of 1825 is the oldest recorded Champagne in existence. Mr. Hautekeur said Veuve Clicquot's oldest drinkable bottle was from 1904.

Richard Juhlin, a Swedish author of numerous books about Champagne, said he noted "great variations" in the first 10 bottles tasted, "from seawater to great stuff." After overseeing the recorking, he said both Juglar and Veuve Clicquot "had in common a mature aroma, almost of cow cheese, Brie or Vacherin, almost too strong," combined with a "liqueur-like sweetness." Of the two Champagnes, he found the Juglar, "a little more intense, bigger, the French would say, 'rustique,'" but said they both compared favorably to some of the best Champagnes today.

Not much goes on in this collection of islands that belongs to Finland but whose inhabitants speak Swedish, so the residents are understandably hoping the Champagne will put Mariehamn on the map. The government wants to auction the bottles over time; there are also, somewhat inexplicably, plans to blend some of it with modern Champagne and sell it in local restaurants and liquor stores.

"We see events and different possibilities with Champagne for small companies and restaurants," said Britt Lundberg, responsible for culture, and hence for Champagne, in the local government. Asked whether Veuve Clicquot and Jacquesson would get some of the antique bubbly, Ms. Lundberg replied, "Not get, but they'll have the possibility to buy."

Some experts, like Mr. Juhlin, have suggested that the bottles could fetch as much as $70,000 each at auction. The previous record price was $21,200 paid for a 1928 Krug auctioned last year in Hong Kong.

"There is obviously a market and collectors," said Bjorn Haggblom, the government spokesman. "You have London, New York, Hong Kong—why not Mariehamn."

Some islanders, like Mr. Ekstrom, wish less were auctioned and more kept on the island. "There's too much business in it, you're losing the history," he said. "You could create a food event, serve it with a meal and tell the story of the Baltic Sea. Even if you got 3 million euros," about $4 million, from an auction, "that's nothing." As part-owner of the island's only beer brewery, he would like to brew a special beer if the yeast in the beer bottles proves to be alive, as experts expect.

Others approve of an auction. "I think it's a waste to keep it on the island, people drink it maybe at New Year's," said Patrik Helander, 34, a salesman in a hunting and fishing store. Beer, he added, was "more my cup."

Some said the auction proceeds should go to clean up the notoriously polluted Baltic. "The Baltic Sea preserved the Champagne," said Henri Pettersson, 18, a high school student. "That would say thank you."

December 2010

A Greener Champagne Bottle

By LIZ ALDERMAN

Deep below a lush landscape of ripening Champagne grapes, Thierry Gasco, the master vintner for Pommery, ran his finger over the shoulders of a dark green bottle that looked just like the thousands of others reposing in his chilly subterranean cellars.

But to the practiced hand and eye, there is a subtle, if potentially significant, difference.

"This is how we're remaking the future of Champagne," he said, pointing to the area just below the neck. "We're slimming the shoulders to make the bottle lighter, so our carbon footprint will be reduced to help keep Champagne here for future generations."

The Champagne industry has embarked on a drive to cut the 200,000 metric tons of carbon dioxide it emits every year transporting billions of tiny bubbles around the world. Producing and shipping accounts for nearly a third of Champagne's carbon emissions, with the hefty bottle the biggest offender.

Yet while many other industries might plaster their marketing with eco-friendly claims, changes to Champagne, as with so much else in France, are being made discreetly. Producers in this secretive business are tight-lipped about the costs and occasionally enigmatic about how much their carbon emissions will really be cut.

"Champagne is sometimes more humble than it should be," said Philippe Wibrotte of the Comité Interprofessionnel du Vin de Champagne, the region's trade organization. "Much is done for the promotion of the environment, but it's kept quiet because we want to make sure each step is perfect."

The industry speaks in hushed tones, too, in deference to the luxurious image and ritualistic traditions of Champagne, as symbolized for centuries by the bottle. It was Dom Pérignon, a Benedictine monk, who first thickened the glass in the mid-1600s to contain what was often referred to as "the devil's wine" because its vessels exploded so often. Over time, the bottle was gradually recalibrated until 900 grams, or about two pounds, became the standard weight in the early 1970s.

The current retooling, which uses 65 fewer grams (2.3 ounces) of glass, is in response to a 2003 study of Champagne's carbon footprint, which the industry wants to cut 25 percent by 2020, and 75 percent by 2050.

The move comes as efforts to reduce carbon output and improve vineyard ecology are accelerating worldwide, as wine houses reduce packaging, pesticides, water use and transportation. In California, for example, winegrowers are promoting what their trade group, the Wine Institute, says are nearly 230 "green practices," including methods to cut carbon emissions.

Champagne accounts for only 10 percent of the three billion bottles of sparkling wine produced globally each year. But the bottle stands out for its heft. Italian prosecco, for instance, uses a 750-gram bottle. But it and its various fizzy cousins have only about half the pressure of Champagne—which generates three times the air pressure of a typical car tire.

Although some of Pommery's restyled bottles are already on the market, the C.I.V.C. expects all Champagne houses to start using the new 835-gram vessel next April for bottling this month's grape harvest; the new wave of bottles will hit stores after three years of fermentation. The effort, the group says, will trim carbon emissions by 8,000 metric tons annually—the equivalent of taking 4,000 small cars off the road.

"For Champagne producers to reduce the weight of their packaging is definitely a step in the right direction," said Tyler Colman, an author of environmental studies on the wine industry, "because there's less mass to transport around the world."

Vranken-Pommery Monopole, which in addition to Pommery owns Heidsieck & Company Monopole and other labels, got a head start by adopting the lighter bottle in 2003. Consumers around the world may have already uncorked some specimens without noticing the new bottle. Moët & Chandon, Veuve Cliquot and a few others quietly switched this year, with those bottles still under fermentation.

The rest of the Champagne producers are deciding whether to embrace the C.I.V.C.'s mandate, which is voluntary but carries special force in this clannish community.

Designing a new bottle was no small feat. The container still had to withstand Champagne's extreme pressure. It would also need to survive the four-year obstacle course from the factory floor to the cellars to the dining table, and fit in existing machinery at all Champagne houses. And it had to be molded so that consumers would barely detect the difference in the bottle's classic shape.

"The bottle is part of Champagne's image, and we don't want to affect it," said Daniel Lorson, a spokesman for the trade group.

Mr. Gasco said Vranken-Pommery, one of the largest houses, has spent 500,000 to one million euros ($635,000 to about $1.3 million) each year since 1994 on environmental initiatives, including research and testing of the lighter bottle.

But the bottle, he said, is not about money, which has become tighter since the financial crisis. Industrywide sales for Champagne last year were 3.7 billion euros ($4.7 billion), down from nearly 5 billion euros in 2007.

"Reducing their carbon footprint and energy use is also a great way to make their operations more financially viable, especially with the economy the way it is," said Euan Murray, an official at the Carbon Trust, a nonprofit group that advises businesses and government on global warming issues.

Sipping a glass of Pommery during an interview, Mr. Gasco eventually disclosed that the new bottles cost around 32 euro cents (41 United States cents) each, not much cheaper than the classic. But Mr. Gasco, who sits on the C.I.V.C.'s bottling panel, said "if everyone starts to use it, the price will come down." Any savings, however, would be too slight to pass on to consumers, he said.

Most of the new Champagne bottles are made at the St. Gobain plant near here, where molten red glass is dropped from a 20-foot-high chute into molds at a rate of 160 a minute. The glass is cooled from more than 1,000 degrees Celsius for over an hour, scanned for imperfections and stacked on pallets for shipping.

A worker on Pommery's assembly line, who declined to be named, said he noticed that a few more of the new bottles were exploding, and that they made a higher-pitched sound when they clinked together. Mr. Gasco denied there were more explosions, and said any damage more likely came from using heat to inject the cork.

Bruno Delhorbe, the director at the St. Gobain factory, said that using less glass lowered the carbon emissions necessary to make each bottle by 7 percent, and allowed about 2,400 more to be placed inside delivery trucks, reducing the number of trucks on the road.

Slimming the shoulders while thinning the glass, he noted, also allowed his clients to avoid giving their customers more Champagne for the same price.

Of course, there are even lighter alternatives: Many of the world's producers of still wines are employing plastic bottles and box containers to reduce their carbon footprint.

But it may be a long time before Champagne goes that route. Most houses take pains to cultivate an image of luxury through packaging and pricing—and intimations that other sparkling wines are inferior because they simply are not Champagne.

Still, many producers insist that while tradition has its place, the environmentally motivated changes are about the future. Patrick LeBrun, an independent producer, said he started going green "for personal reasons." He has not used herbicides for five years, and this year, he is putting all of his product into the lighter bottle.

"There's about a 2-cent price difference but that's not what decided me," he said. Trying to improve the environment "is my contribution to the next generation."

August 2010

Spring Comes for a Prince of Champagne

By FRANK J. PRIAL

Winemakers come in most shapes, sizes, sexes and political persuasions, and I thought I'd pretty much come across all of them. Until someone mentioned that the chief enologist for Pommery Champagne was a prince.

An authentic prince?

I was skeptical. As a result of mergers upon mergers, most of the old-line Champagne houses are run by bean counters these days. But some of them are clever enough to keep a title or two around to convey the image of privileged elegance that Champagne has always tried for.

Would Alain de Polignac turn out to be just another titled front man, tanned from the Côte d'Azur and eager to gossip about polo and the price of a new Aston-Martin? I called from Paris, and Prince Alain, as everyone at Pommery calls him, from the forklift drivers up, agreed to spend time talking about Champagne and, I hoped, the Polignacs.

"Good morning, good morning," he called, striding across the parking area. "Thank you so much for coming to see us." Sixtyish, trim and with a striking resemblance to Noël Coward, Alain de Polignac was a model of a successful businessman, down to what had to be Savile Row tailoring. Around his neck and tossed insouciantly over his left shoulder was a vivid yellow cashmere scarf. I later learned that it is his trademark.

"Isn't it lovely here?" he asked as we headed toward his office. It was in fact a beautiful morning. In the distance was Rheims, dominated by its immense cathedral where so many kings of France had been crowned, and all around us were the buildings of Pommery Champagne, looking much as they must have when Mme. Louise Pommery had them built more than a century ago. Prince Alain laughed when I voiced my egalitarian suspicions about him. "I am a chemical engineer," he said. "I am also an enologist and have been the chief enologist at Pommery for 10 years. I also happen to be a prince."

Pommery was founded in 1836 by Alexandre-Louis Pommery, a Rheims textile merchant, and Narcisse Greno, a wine merchant who eventually left the business. When Pommery died in 1858, his widow, then 39, took charge. Over 30 years, she built a modest little business specializing in red wines into one of the largest and most prosperous of all Champagne houses. Today, it produces seven million bottles a year.

The Polignacs, who trace their history back to 809, came to Pommery in 1879, when Louise Pommery married Count Guy de Polignac, later a marquis. A son of that marriage, Melchior, also a marquis, ran the company from 1907 to 1947. In 1952, one of his nephews, another Guy de Polignac, took over and ran Pommery until 1979, when it was sold to the Gardinier family, owners of Lanson Champagne. Since 1991, Pommery has been owned by LVMH, Louis Vuitton Moët Hennessy, which owns Moët & Chandon, Dom Ruinart, Veuve Clicquot, Krug and other Champagne producers. The second Guy de Polignac ran Pommery with his two brothers, Louis and Edmond, all of them princes. Alain de Polignac is Edmond's son.

"My title was awarded to us by the King of Bavaria," Prince Alain said. As if that would clear things up.

In 1972, when Patrick Forbes wrote about Pommery and the Polignacs in *Champagne* (Victor Gollancz), he noted that the family seat was the Château de Polignac, in the Loire Valley, but that there were "no less than 15 Polignac ancestral homes scattered about France." Prince Alain is proud of his family background but proud, too, of his winemaking heritage at Pommery. "In almost two centuries, there have been only eight winemakers," he said. "Each of us has held the job for 20 to 30 years. Each of us has spent his last 10 years training his successor." He has been working for five years with Thierry Gasco, now the Pommery cellar master.

"There is no father-to-son line," Prince Alain said. "The only link is taste. It takes years to understand the house style, what is Pommery and, more important, what is not. Actually, there are two lines at Pommery, the family line and the taste line. In me, for the first time, the two are joined." And what is Pommery?

"Ah, a light Champagne, yes, but full-bodied. And fresh, always fresh and lively on the palate." Over lunch we sampled "Louise," Pommery's tête de cuvée, or top-of-the-line bottling, and the vintage brut. Mme. Pommery was the first to introduce the brut, or very dry-style Champagne, in the 1870s. It became the basic style of almost all the Champagne houses.

Architecture is also an interest of Prince Alain. "I would have loved to be an architect," he said, adding quickly, "Of course, I am an architect: each year I build my wines."

The buildings that interest him most are those of the Pommery winery on the outskirts of Rheims. Built over 10 years, mostly in the 1870s, the domaine, with its warehouses and parks, covers 200 acres on what was a city dump. Below ground are spectacular chalk caves from the Gallo-Roman era, 2,000 years ago. Some 20 million bottles of Champagne are stored in them now.

The main buildings, often derided by modern critics, are in a neo-Elizabethan style, popular in England in the late 19th century, and were partly meant to symbolize Pommery's strong ties to the English Champagne market. "The buildings give a face to Pommery," Prince Alain said. "The style is in the Champagne. Architecture connects the look of Pommery and the style."

Alain de Polignac may look like a businessman, but the yellow scarf says he is a sensualist. As we walked out of the winery, he paused. "Listen," he said, dropping his voice dramatically. "Hear that? Dring, dring, dring—the bottles bumping along the bottling line? For me, each year, it means the beginning of spring.

"Then, in fall, it's the smell of the new wine. Sight, sound, smell—all come together right here. Ah, I adore it."

March 2001

They Make the Champagne of Champagnes

By FRANK J. PRIAL

"I would like to see people drinking Krug at picnics," said Rémi Krug, the man who makes Krug Champagne. "The wine is too revered, overworshipped. How often have I heard someone say: 'I've had a bottle of Krug for years. I'm saving it for something special'?"

We were sitting in an austere reception room at the Krug winery here one January day, Rémi, 62, and his less voluble brother, Henri, 65, and before us on the table, like some precious icon, a bottle of Krug's 1990 vintage, which is just now being released.

As a chill winter rain rattled the windows, Rémi Krug described a cricket match he attended in England not long ago when the players refreshed themselves between wickets with Krug 1961. "I loved it," he said, "and I'd love to see more of it. People enjoying Krug, not just praising it."

Yes, yes, of course. But Mr. Krug is a romantic. His least expensive Champagne, at something like $100 a bottle, is more costly than the top of the line at other houses. Krug at a picnic? Why not caviar at a Knicks game or pheasant for breakfast? Occasional reverence is a small price to pay for Krug's extraordinary reputation, one the Krugs themselves have nurtured carefully for five generations.

I had long wondered about the Krug reputation. Was it justified? The wines are magnificent, but there are other great Champagnes: Bollinger, Salon, Moët's Dom Pérignon, Roederer's Cristal. Even so, critics with far more experience than I invariably place Krug ahead of all of them.

So I came out from Paris to learn the secret, and finally, in that studiously dull tasting room, listening to Rémi Krug talk about commitment and passion, I began to understand. For one thing, there before us and in our glasses was the 1990 vintage, a Champagne made 13 years earlier, in the days of the elder George Bush, just now being released. There has to be something special about a business that makes a product, then waits 13 years before selling it. In fact, all Krug Champagnes are aged at least six years before they are released.

And then there is the 1988 vintage, held back until well after the 1989 was released. "We just didn't feel it was ready," Henri said, "and the 1989 was." What's more, "ready," in Krug parlance, means ready to sell.

A Krug Champagne can be drunk as soon as it is released, but Krug fanatics

425

insist the wines should be held a decade or more before opening. Actually, part of Krug's vintage production is always held back for long aging in the cellars here in the Rue Coquebert. The wines are eventually sold to the most loyal of all Krug fans, known as Krugistes, who eagerly pay $350 or more a bottle for 30-year-old wines. Krug Champagnes seem to last forever. The family's own favorites include 1928 and 1959, both, they maintain, still lively and fresh. I can vouch for the 1959, a wonderful wine 10 years ago, but not yet for the 1928.

Despite all the talk of vintages, the star of the Krug cellars is the Grande Cuvée, a nonvintage blend, which may include wines from 20 crus and 10 vintages. It is a dry Champagne of great depth and power with immensely complex flavors. To one commentator the Grande Cuvée is as detailed and textured as a Gobelin tapestry. There is a nonvintage Rosé Brut and, for true Champagne connoisseurs, the legendary Clos du Mesnil, a vintage Champagne that first appeared in 1979. All Krug Champagne is fermented in oak barrels, a practice begun when the company was new. "But we don't do it because our grandfather did," Rémi Krug said. "We do it because wood brings out the Krug taste."

Wine purists complain that Champagne, being invariably a blend of wines from all over the Champagne region, cannot possibly express the native soil from which it springs, as in Burgundy and, more and more, in California, too. There are exceptions in Champagne, and the Clos du Mesnil is one of them.

Its 4.5-acre walled vineyard in the center of the town of Mesnil-sur-Oger was once part of a Benedictine monastery. It is entirely planted in chardonnay, making it one of the most exclusive of all blanc-de-blancs Champagnes. Only a few thousand cases are made in years when a vintage is declared. Most of it is reserved for restaurants and special customers, and what is left usually sells for $250 to $300 a bottle.

Krug was founded in 1843 by Joseph Krug, who came from Mainz in what is now Germany and worked for other Champagne houses before setting up his own business. He was said to have exceptional skills as a blender and for many years made Champagne cuvées for other houses. Evidently, he passed his blending skills on to his descendants.

Neither Rémi nor Henri is an enologist, but they alone are responsible for the Krug style. Remarkably, Krug has maintained its individuality even though it has been owned by others for almost 30 years. In the mid-1970s, the house was sold to Rémy-Martin, later Rémy-Cointreau, the Cognac producers. In 1999, Rémy-Cointreau sold its interest in Krug to LVMH Moët Hennessy Louis Vuitton, which also owns Veuve Clicquot, Ruinart, Mercier, Pommery and Canard-Duchêne.

The outside owners, whatever their influence on Krug's business practices, appear to have had no impact at all on the Krug style. The Krugs themselves rarely refer to their corporate masters, preferring to concentrate on their share-holders. The only visible sign of outside corporate policy may be Henri's mandatory retirement this year. He will continue to be a consultant while his son Olivier, who has joined the company, hones his own blending and tasting skills.

Henri's career marks a change from the days when his grandfather Joseph Krug II was running the company. He took over in 1910, but in 1915, as an artillery captain in World War I, he was severely wounded in the Ardennes and taken prisoner. After the war, his health was so poor that a nephew took over the business. He recovered, however, and remained head of the firm until 1959, when he was 90. Even then, he remained as a technical adviser until 1965, when he was 96. Paul Krug, the father of Henri and Rémi, continued to join final-blend tastings until his death at 85 in 1997.

Nor was Joseph II the only strong-willed Krug to head the firm. When he was taken prisoner, his wife took over. She made several vintages of Krug in her own style, which apparently leaned toward more red grapes than her husband liked. In fact, according to Patrick Forbes's *Champagne: The Wine, the Land and the People* (Gollancz, 1977), she used mostly red grapes because it was difficult to get white grapes from outlying vineyards in the middle of the war. She ran a dispensary for wounded soldiers in the Krug cellars and was gassed twice. In World War II, she hid downed British airmen here until the Gestapo caught on and jailed her.

Krug is a small Champagne house, producing less than 50,000 cases of wine a year. The Krugs would like to grow, "particularly in America, which was the biggest Krug market before Prohibition—but not at the expense of quality," Rémi Krug said.

"We could double our American sales," he added, "but not at the expense of quality."

"Often people say to us, 'I remember the first time I had Krug.' I never want to hear anyone say, 'Krug was not what I expected.' Our clients expect so much of us. We feel we have a commitment. This is very personal with us."

January 2004

A Drink With Drama

By FRANK J. PRIAL

At this time of year, the question most often asked of anyone in the wine world is: "What kind of Champagne do I buy for (a) my daughter's wedding, (b) my son's graduation, (c) the launching of my new aircraft carrier?"

The aircraft carrier presents no problem. Almost any Champagne bottle will smash nicely on the prow of your average warship. If the vessel is American, of course, it might be politic to use an American wine. The wedding and the graduation are something else. Champagne was never more reasonably priced than it is right now, thanks to the strong dollar and a string of good years in the Champagne vineyards. Even so, Champagne is not cheap, and when one is buying for a crowd it can become very expensive indeed.

If money is truly no object, then by all means serve genuine French Champagne. Even routine parties take on unexpected elegance—or seem to—when Champagne is served. But for most special events, when a sparkling wine is appropriate, there are dozens of excellent substitutes for Champagne that will keep the guests happy and the host out of bankruptcy.

The remarkable Spanish sparkling wines, such as Codorníu and Freixenet, are made in the classic Champagne method and still manage to sell for under $6 a bottle. If it must be French, there are dozens of excellent vins mousseux at a third less than the cheapest genuine Champagne.

I guess what I'm saying here is this: Be serious about Champagne for a moment. We think of it in terms of lawn parties, summer weddings, diplomatic receptions and such memorable cultural events as the locker-room fete that ends the World Series.

But that's not really what Champagne is about. Champagne is not supposed to be incidental music for someone else's drama. It is, or should be, a superb sensual experience to be enjoyed for its own sake. It has color and drama in the glass, it has a bouquet like no other wine in the world, and—if it is a true Champagne—it has a taste like no other wine in the world.

But these are qualities to be experienced in quiet moments, alone or with a friend or two; not after the ambassador's speech nor just as the band swings into "From this moment on. . . ."

The people who make Champagne, and their publicists, will tell anyone who pauses long enough to listen that in fact Champagne goes with almost anything.

To prove their point, they promote dinners among gourmet societies and at certain restaurants at which Champagne is the only wine served.

Accordingly, there are big, robust Champagnes such as Krug to accompany the heavy dishes, and lighter, more delicate Champagnes such as Piper-Heidsieck with the fish and the desserts.

Do such dinners work? Whether anyone goes home from them inspired to create his own all-Champagne dinners is unlikely. But in fact there is a tradition of all-Champagne dinners in France.

The food and wine writer Robert J. Courtine, who uses the nom de cuisine La Reynière in the newspaper *Le Monde*, recently unearthed a menu for the 1899 Christmas Eve dinner at Maxim's. It included Marenne oysters from Ostend, consommé, fillet of sole Maxim's, white and red blood sausage (boudin), potato purée, chaud-froid of chicken, glazed oranges and the traditional Christmas cake Bûche de Noël. What Champagnes were served was not recorded. But the prices were. The dinner cost 25 francs a person; the Champagne, 18 francs a bottle. Courtine goes on to list menus for all-Champagne dinners prepared by Raymond Oliver, late of Le Grand Vefour, Claude Terrail of La Tour d'Argent and René Lasserre of Lasserre. And he offers his own menu: fresh foie gras, écrevisses, wild duck and floating island. In each case he leaves the Champagne choices up to the reader.

Courtine believes that there are some dishes that almost demand Champagne. We all know that connoisseurs love Champagne with oysters. Ah, says Courtine, but what Champagne with what oysters? He does not hesitate: nature, or totally dry, with the Marennes; crémant, which is less fizzy and usually lighter in taste, with the Belons. Now that is refinement.

A famous restaurateur once maintained to him that Champagne was the only possible wine to serve with pot-au-feu. Courtine said he tried it and liked it. Champagne with a red-meat stew? Well, why not, so long as it is a good hearty Champagne, a Bollinger, perhaps.

He is equally enthusiastic about Champagne with game birds, suggesting an older vintage blanc de noirs, "just on the edge of maderization." When wine, Champagne or any other, maderizes, or oxidizes, it takes on a nutty flavor and a darker, slightly brownish tinge. It acquires a more pronounced taste, one capable of standing up to the strong taste of a pheasant or quail.

Courtine suggests Champagne with goat cheese and pink Champagne with some of the cheeses of the Champagne region, such as Riceys, which I've never seen in this country. Certainly it will go well with the new goat cheeses being made here.

Or, perhaps, it would be better to say that the cheeses go with Champagne. If Champagne is being served alone, as an aperitif, some thought should be given to what goes with it, and appetizers made with light, preferably white, cheeses will fill the bill.

In the last three or four years, there has been a growing awareness of the fact that so-called Champagne glasses are not the best way to serve such an elegant wine. The flat Champagne glass, which also serves for shrimp cocktail and fruit cup, lets all the bubbles escape and allows the wine to become warm quickly.

Most Champagne enthusiasts prefer the flute-style glass, which is tall and narrow. It's harder to clean, but it highlights the color of the wine and the flow of the bubbles from bottom to top. Courtine, ever the iconoclast, criticizes both the classic coupe de Champagne and the flute; the coupe for the reasons cited above, the flute because it traps the bouquet. He opts for a regular red or white wine glass. He's probably right, but there is supposed to be something celebratory about Champagne, and special glasses always add a bit to the occasion—even if you're commissioning a dinghy and not an aircraft carrier.

May 1985

Royal Wedding Wine
May Be Bubbly and English

By ERIC ASIMOV

In January, Michel Roux Jr., a London chef who is on the tasting committee that recommends wines to be served by the royal family, made a suggestion that would have been unthinkable not long ago. Wouldn't it be nice, Mr. Roux asked a reporter for *The Telegraph*, if at the wedding reception for Prince William and Kate Middleton the glasses were filled not with Champagne but with English sparkling wine?

"It might be a bit controversial, but I think it would be great to see, and it would say a lot about Britishness," he said.

Nobody is saying whether English sparkling wine will be poured at any of the events related to the royal wedding on April 29. Yet those who follow these issues note that when Queen Elizabeth II turned 80 in 2006 the wine poured at her reception was an elegant blanc de blancs produced by Ridgeview Estate outside this little village in East Sussex. Indeed, last year the 2006 vintage of the same wine was voted the best sparkling wine over more than 700 other wines from around the world, including Champagne, in a competition put on by Decanter, a British wine publication.

The notion of fine English wine may seem as absurd as the thought of fine English food once did. Yet, just as London has become a dining destination, southern England has become a source of excellent sparkling wines, made in the illustrious mode of Champagne. From Kent, where the white cliffs of Dover face across the English Channel toward France, stretching westward along the southern coast through East and West Sussex, Hampshire, Dorset, even as far west as Devon and Cornwall, hundreds of acres of new vineyards have been planted in the last 10 years, with far more projected.

The same geology visible in those famous white cliffs also plays a role in the rise of winemaking here. In Champagne, the best vineyards often lie in chalky limestone soils, sometimes mixed with clay. A line of this limestone stretches up from Sancerre and Chablis, through Champagne and across the Channel to England, past Dover and across southern England. The vineyards along this chalk belt are mainly growing chardonnay, pinot noir and pinot meunier, the three grapes that go into Champagne.

Christian Seely, who owns Coates & Seely vineyards in Hampshire with his partner, Nick Coates, has high hopes for their 30 acres of vines, planted on south-facing slopes of chalk and flint, and their two vintages of sparkling wine, 2009 and 2010, aging in bottles.

"I believe that there is the potential to make something really great, if one finds the right place," he said.

"Above all, it's the existence of terroirs that bear striking geological resemblance to what exists in Champagne," said Mr. Seely, the managing director of AXA Millésimes, the arm of the French AXA insurance group that runs a portfolio of top wineries in France and elsewhere.

If few people in history ever thought to plant Champagne grapes in southern England, it was not without reason. Champagne itself, 49.5 degrees latitude at its northernmost point, pushed the climatic boundaries for making fine wine. In fact, the perennial problem of ripening grapes sufficiently in Champagne made sparkling wine the perfect solution: to achieve a crisp, refreshing quality in sparkling wine the grapes must ripen enough to no longer be stridently acidic, yet they must retain sufficient acidity to be brisk. Hence, grapes destined for sparkling wine are harvested at lower degrees of ripeness than grapes for still wine.

Here in Ditchling, Ridgeview Estate is 88 miles northwest of Champagne, approaching 51 degrees latitude. For centuries Sussex and the surrounding counties were considered too cold to grow grapes for fine wine. Yet climate change has warmed things up just enough to make that possible.

"I don't know that I buy into climate change, or at least that the cause is human rather than cyclical, but it's there and has certainly had an effect," said Andrew Weeber, a South African orthopedist who in 2004 began planting Gusbourne Estate in Appledore, Kent. He now has 50 acres on a slope facing south, looking down toward the flat Romney Marsh and the sea.

The pace of planting has accelerated in the last few years. In 1990, two years after an American couple, Stuart and Sandy Moss, planted Nyetimber in West Sussex, the first major vineyard for sparkling wine, England had about 140 acres of chardonnay, pinot noir and pinot meunier, according to Stephen Skelton, the author of *UK Vineyards Guide 2010*. By 2007, more than 660 acres had been planted, and by 2010 that figure had doubled, to about 1,360 acres.

Among the newer plantings is Bride Valley Vineyard in western Dorset, a natural amphitheater of chalk soils facing south, owned by Steven Spurrier, a columnist for *Decanter,* and his wife, Bella. Just after buying the property in 1987, Mr. Spurrier said, he noticed the chalk soil and sent it to Chablis for analysis. It was pronounced auspicious for chardonnay.

April 2011

In Albuquerque, French-Style Wines That Sparkle

By SARAH KERSHAW

It would be really easy to whiz past the demure sign and stately entrance of the Gruet Winery on the Pan American Freeway here, not far from Target and almost subsumed by an R.V. dealership on one side and Tuff Shed on the other.

Inside, though, a sister and brother who moved here from the Champagne region of France 27 years ago and took the risk of planting grapes in this high desert climate are producing what have become phenomenally successful domestic sparkling wines. While the recession has pummeled wine producers in Champagne, Napa and elsewhere, Gruet has held its own, and even made headway in some markets, with only some minor wholesale losses.

Credit for this goes to budget-minded pricing: most of Gruet's sparkling wines sell for well under $20. Customers wanting Champagne or sparkling wine have been moved to taste less-expensive products, wine buyers and restaurateurs say, giving these French expatriates in New Mexico a timely edge. Their sparkling wines are especially popular in New York and California, and have, in the last 10 years, appeared on the wine lists of high-end restaurants, including Craft, Del Frisco's and Bar Americain in Manhattan.

The siblings, Nathalie and Laurent Gruet, were pioneers when the family planted an experimental vineyard in 1983, in Lordsburg, N.M., and then settled a year later on land near Truth or Consequences, a small town about 150 miles south of here known among local tourists and retirees for its natural hot springs and mild climate. As it turned out, the climate was an advantage for winemaking, with cool evening temperatures that slow the ripening to produce a pleasantly sharp acidity.

Some critics say that despite its high quality-to-price ratio, Gruet pales beside unquestionably superior sparkling wines made in France and even in California.

But many wine buyers and reviewers see Gruet as a source of affordable domestic gems that hold up to—or can even outdo—more expensive domestic products.

"You can get decent things from the Finger Lakes, and Virginia is doing some nice sparkling wines, but there are very few that are classics, and I think Gruet is a classic now," said Tracy Wilson, general manager of the cafes at the Museum of Modern Art in Manhattan, where the Gruet blanc de noirs is served at Terrace 5 for $12 a glass, or $44 a bottle. "Its profile is beautiful, it drinks like a French wine, but it's got this twist on it, so it's not as minerally. It's crisp. It's just a pleasant drink."

It makes sense that Gruet drinks like a French wine, because the family behind it has deep roots in France. Gruet et Fils was established in Champagne in 1952 by the family patriarch, Gilbert Gruet, in Béthon. Mr. Gruet, who died in 1999, was an architect who agreed to help build a winery in Champagne in exchange for lessons in making the region's sparkling wine.

He founded the first wine cooperative in Béthon in 1967, persuading the villagers to rip out the sugar beets in the fields and plant grapes instead, family members said.

In the early 1980s, like other winemakers in the region, Mr. Gruet decided that with a change in the French government and impending tax increases, it was time to start a winery in another country. With two of his four children, Nathalie and Laurent, he toured California, Texas, New York and finally, on the suggestion of some European winemakers he knew there, New Mexico.

"We were pretty charmed by the rugged beauty of New Mexico, and to see these lush vineyards in the middle of the desert was very intriguing to my father," said Ms. Gruet, 47. The land was also less expensive than other options they considered, she said.

New Mexico had a centuries-long history as a leading producer of American wine. But in the early 20th century, flooding and groundwater in the state's wine country, near the banks of the Rio Grande, became a crippling obstacle, turning fertile land into swamps. By 1920, there were no wineries left. It was not until the early '80s that a government-sponsored study meant to attract European vignerons, some of whom were beginning to set their sights on California and other states, reported improved growing conditions.

But the early years were not easy for the Gruets. At the first vineyard in Lordsburg, the brother and sister, together with Ms. Gruet's husband and their 5-month-old baby boy, lived in a trailer on a small plot of land. They soon discovered the area was too hot for chardonnay and pinot noir grapes, sold the land and planted a new vineyard 100 miles east, in an area called Engle, about 10 miles outside Truth or Consequences.

"We didn't speak a word of English and we were in the middle of nowhere," Ms. Gruet said. "That was pretty strange. But when you're in your 20s, you take a challenge better. You have a bit more adventure in your soul."

They wanted to try the Champagne method of making sparkling wines in New Mexico, so they had samples of the sandy and earthy soil sent to France for testing, to make sure the vines could grow the deep roots they needed to thrive. Encouraged by the results, they imported their first press and other machinery from France and rented a small production space in Albuquerque, as their father financed an operation that grew in small increments over 20 years.

"We started very small, we didn't know if it was going to work," Ms. Gruet said. "I think my father was living his dream through his children. He had a pioneer spirit, a spirit to start something totally oddball in the middle of nowhere."

They went from producing 2,000 cases of wine in 1989, to 100,000 cases a year now, doing everything but the growing in a 45,000-square-foot plant in Albuquerque. The French and New Mexican wineries now produce about the same amount of wine, the Gruets said. (Their other two siblings, twin sisters, stayed in Champagne and now run the operation there.)

The New Mexican branch of the family said that they have found the climate here even better for grapes than in Champagne; the days can be very hot, but the nights, as much as 30 degrees cooler, slow the maturation process in what would otherwise be a short growing season. The arid air that wards off rot also helps with the wine's consistency, Laurent Gruet said, adding that they use no pesticides on the vines.

Before they hired a distributor, Mr. Gruet and his brother-in-law carted cases of wine across the state to restaurants, liquor stores and tasting events, aggressively marketing it any chance they got.

"We started with one state, then two states, then we were adding states and it took over 20 years of labor," said Mr. Gruet, 45. "We would tell the distributors, 'We're from New Mexico, open the bottle and taste it.' Sometimes it would be a long time between when they received it and getting them to taste it."

Within a few years, mentions in newspapers and wine magazines helped the Gruets capture the attention of wine buyers and distributors far beyond New Mexico. Their wines are now sold in 49 states—60 percent of it at about 5,000 restaurants and the other 40 percent at retail stores, Mr. Gruet said. The winery produces seven sparkling wines, four that retail for an average of $15 a bottle, as well as three more-expensive vintage sparklers, which range in price from $17 to $46. They also produce a small amount of still chardonnay and pinot noir.

Robert Lemberger, the wine buyer for the Artichoke Cafe in Albuquerque, one of the first restaurants to serve Gruet, was working at a bistro in Florida 10 years ago when he first heard of Gruet, which was on the wine list there.

Gruet is produced "in such high-quality fashion that the flavors just layer in their wines," he said. "Their grand reserve is beautiful, with the taste of caramel and apples, citrus and a little bit of vanilla, as good as a reserve should be, and the blanc de noirs is wonderfully complex."

The region around Truth or Consequences also produces chilies and other crops, but all of them are grown closer to the Rio Grande than the Gruet grapes are. Water for irrigation has to be pumped about 15 miles to the vineyard, which proved to be too cumbersome and expensive for the other wineries in the area. Gruet is the only one left, according to Olivia DeCamp, executive director of the New Mexico Wine Growers Association. Ms. Gruet said that the winery was doing well enough to sustain the extra cost and that the family decided it was not worth uprooting a vineyard that was consistently producing quality grapes.

As to whether the Gruets would consider striking out again, adding another Champagne house or American winery, Ms. Gruet laughed and sounded a bit weary.

"That's for the next generation," she said.

June 2010

Produced in Champagne,
but What Do You Call It?

By JOHN TAGLIABUE

Makers of sparkling wine in the United States, Russia and Ukraine can appropriate the Champagne name for their products, but an innocent biscuit maker in this tiny Swiss town is out of luck.

Marc-André Cornu was salmon fishing in Norway when he got word. His secretary was on the line, saying that lawyers for the Swiss distributors of French Champagne had written to say he could no longer use the brand name his family had used since the 1930s. Three generations, beginning with his grandfather, had labeled their baked goods "de Champagne," after their Swiss village, nestled among the vineyards that creep north from the shores of Lake Neuchâtel.

The lawyers' letters were only the first twist in a legal tangle as intricate as the gnarled and knotty grape vines hereabouts.

In 1998, Switzerland reached an accord with the European Union that allowed its former national airline, Swissair, to make stopovers in European Union cities. In return, Switzerland, which is not a member of the union, agreed to forbid the people of Champagne, population 710, to use the town's name on their products.

In demanding the quid pro quo, the Europeans were doing the bidding of France, ever vigilant about defending the integrity and identity of Champagne. But that vigilance has not extended to threats from the United States and other big countries. In 2001, Swissair went bankrupt, and its successor, Swiss International Air Lines, is owned by Lufthansa. Yet now, Mr. Cornu, 46, and his baked goods company, which employs about 80 people, including his children, risk a fine if they invoke the name of their town. So, too, do the winemakers here, who in the best of years before the ban sold about 110,000 bottles of their light, nonsparkling wine, but now, without the Champagne label, are down 70 percent.

"Our village is first mentioned in a document from Feb. 15, 885, in a transaction between the Emperor Charles the Fat and a local governor," said Albert Banderet, the former mayor, who grew grapes until he entered public administration, leaving the vineyards to his son.

Recently, the local people have organized demonstrations to draw attention to their plight. Earlier this month, they used a forklift to rip up a road sign bearing the name Champagne at the village entrance, to which they affixed a French flag and a bottle of French Champagne. Swiss-style, they carefully replanted the sign after the demonstration.

"Our goal is not to be the bin Ladens of wine, to be terrorists or ideologues," Mr. Banderet, 59, said, "but wine is a reality here." His son cultivates 70 acres of grapes, compared with 79,000 acres given over to the production of Champagne in France.

The French say they are struggling to protect an Appellation d'Origine Contrôlée, or A.O.C., a convoluted certification that authenticates the content, method and origin of a French agricultural product.

"Yves Saint Laurent came along in 1993 or 1994 and wanted to introduce a Champagne perfume, and before that a tobacco company wanted a cigarette called Champagne," said Daniel Lorson, spokesman for the Interprofessional Committee of the Wines of Champagne, a trade group in Épernay, France.

Harrods, the London department store, sold a mineral water called Champagne a few years ago, at $20 a bottle, Mr. Lorson said by telephone. "You put our name on it, and it's worth $20."

"Why is it worth so much to us?" Mr. Lorson asked. "To prevent it from becoming a generic name, on yogurt or toothpaste, and lose its authenticity. That's why we carry the fight daily."

Mr. Lorson says it was not his committee that began the scrap. A few years ago, a Swiss vintner sold about 3,000 bottles of wine under the name Champagne to a French supermarket chain. An anti-fraud agency, which inspects food stores, reported them.

The Swiss villagers admit there have been bad apples in the basket. After World War II, a farmer came here and made sparkling wine that he sold as Champagne, though only in Switzerland, said Mr. Banderet, seated in the dining room of his family's sprawling 17th-century home.

More recently, a stranger from La Côte, along Lake Geneva, tried the same trick. "That triggered the issue," said Thomas K. Bindschedler, spokesman for a committee established to protect the village's name. "Everybody was upset about it, not only the French."

Mr. Bindschedler, whose father was Swiss and mother Norwegian, was fishing with Mr. Cornu when the fateful phone call came. He runs salmon farms in Norway but lives in Champagne, where he is turning centuries-old farmhouses into deluxe apartments.

"I am not a winemaker, and I'm not a biscuit maker, so I'm not defending my own interests," he said. "But I sincerely think that this is illogical."

Mr. Bindschedler called the French action "arrogant and shocking," and added, sarcastically, "They produce something very high class, and we produce rubbish."

In 2004, the last year the villagers could use "Champagne" on their wine labels, they sold 110,000 bottles. By last year, sales had plummeted to 32,000. The vintners have tried using names like Libre Champ, Champagnoux and C-Ampagne. "Those were really artificial names," Mr. Bindschedler said. "It's deadly not to be able to use your own name."

Mr. Cornu said French Champagne makers obtained a court order in Paris in 2005 barring him from making and selling products with the brand name "de Champagne," and from using his company's Web site. The decision is a delicate matter because he has a factory in Besançon, France, and is appealing the rulings. Mr. Cornu accuses the French of bullying tiny Switzerland. "They are less aggressive toward Russia, Ukraine or the United States," he said, where the French allow the use of the name Champagne as a semi-generic term for sparkling wine. "We have a problem understanding this."

The villagers also mock France's recent decision to increase the number of officially designated plots of land where grapes may be used to make Champagne with a capital C, as global demand soars. "On the level of credibility," said Mr. Banderet, "if you're going to enlarge the Champagne country, why not enlarge it all the way to here?"

Mr. Bindschedler said no one here expected a full victory. "On the legal side, we don't expect to break the legal decision," he said. Under a compromise, the villagers might keep the right to use their name, he said, but would be obliged to police possible violations.

"If some Korean came over here and started making sparkling wine for the French market," he said, "we would be responsible."

April 2008

A Second Life in Champagne

By ROGER COHEN

Jérôme Philipon, the managing director of Bollinger, the venerable house that makes perhaps the world's finest Champagne, grew up on a Picardy farm. As a boy, he would find scraps from World War I battles: belt buckles, helmets, shell fragments.

These relics fascinated him. They summoned a remote world of Franco-German carnage. But never did he expect to see with his own eyes a triage of the dead.

"I suddenly found myself in a world I'd only imagined," he tells me. "Bodies covered in mud and blood arriving on pick-ups and being sorted in front of me and my wife, piles of dead to the left, survivors to the right."

As Philipon recalls this post-tsunami scene, we are seated at a wooden table in a handsome room in the heart of Champagne. Below us run cellars that stretch for miles and contain 14 million bottles. Around us are hills of fine pinot noir vines.

Everything speaks of a rooted place: the 2007 vintage won't go on sale until 2016. Almost a decade is needed to usher fruit and acidity to perfect balance.

Tumult and equilibrium: it is not easy to marry these images of devastation and death on the one hand, patient purpose on the other. But if I were to try, I would say that after unimaginable loss, we strip away the superfluous and, guided by a kind of homing instinct, return to the essential.

Modern existence scatters us. It can take tragedy to gather us in. Modernity is about me. Loss can be an awakening to service.

On Dec. 24, 2004, Philipon, then a Bangkok-based executive with the Coca-Cola Company, checked into the Sofitel Hotel at the Thai beach resort of Khao Lak with his wife, Florence. With them were their four young children: 8-year-old Mathilde; Charles, aged 7; Auguste, 4; and 1-year-old Octave.

The children had been born across Asia—in the Philippines, South Korea and Thailand—as Philipon, working first for Nestlé and then Coke, moved across a region that inspired him.

He felt unshackled from heavy French habits. New products prospered in expanding markets. Even on a Christmas Day far from home, there was a feeling of "plenitude."

Then the tsunami struck. After breakfast together on Dec. 26, the family had scattered: Florence and Mathilde to their room, the three younger children with a nanny to the "Kids' Club" on the beach, Philipon to an adjacent gym.

He was on a treadmill when he saw people running. A post-Christmas prank, he thought, until he saw the wall of water. He jumped from the machine as the gym windows exploded. The wave flipped him as if he were "in a huge washing machine."

Wedged under a pick-up truck, he thought: this is how it ends. But the debris-filled tide dragged him onward. Breathless, he clung to a palmtree. When the water rushed back out, he cleaved to a plastic cooking oil container.

On the first floor of the hotel, he found his wife and daughter, who had scrambled to safety on the roof. They looked down at the Kids' Club, a flattened ruin among corpses.

Philipon scrambled onto the beach but could not find his kids. Evacuated to a hospital, he witnessed the triage of the dead, before returning. Charles, his oldest son, had been a champion swimmer. Might he?

But there, under the ruins, was the boy's corpse.

It took six months to identify the other boys—Octave on April 1, 2005, and Auguste on July 3. "It was impossible for me to think of the future until I had found their bodies," Philipon says.

Three children gone: the hardest thing still is considering what they might have been. "But we had to start again and knowing that life can be very short, really knowing that, we knew you must do what you love."

Philipon, 45, has brown eyes of a boyish candor. He is bereft of self-pity, a man who's come home. The stoical are discreet.

Coca-Cola brought him back to Paris to a great job, but when the offer from Bollinger came, he had no hesitation. The very French history he had fled now provided ballast. Here was a family business offering the top job for the first time to an outsider: tradition and innovation.

Philipon and his wife found strength—in their Catholic faith and their roots. In October, 2006, they had a son, Constantin, and late last year, a daughter, Penelope. "We now have three on earth and three in the sky," he says.

This Wednesday, he tells me, Constantin will be exactly the age Octave was when he died. As in the Bollinger cellars, past is woven into present and future. Balance is all; and bravery at once the most silent and eloquent of virtues.

March 2008

CHAPTER ELEVEN

Wherein Contrarianism Bursts Forth

Taking a Closer Look
at Wine's Conventional Wisdom

By ERIC ASIMOV

It doesn't take a lot of knowledge to be considered a wine expert. Sadly but surely the key to earning respect for your wine aptitude—or more accurately for intimidating others—is simply to hold forth loudly and repeatedly.

This is one reason that what is undeniable one year is laughable the next. Here are some widely repeated assertions, and some explanations suggesting that nothing is that simple.

ASSERTION No-oak chardonnay is better than oaked chardonnay.

TRUTH Oaky may be bad, but oak is good.

Back in the 1990s, when the fashion for big, bombastic, oaky chardonnays was at its height, nobody would have taken this belief seriously. Fashion has changed and oak barrels have now been branded the villain for previous excesses. The fact is, for aging wine, no better vessel than oak barrels has yet been discovered. How those barrels are used is another question.

New oak can imbue a wine with all sorts of flavors, including vanilla, chocolate, coffee and just plain woody. But many people tired of over-oakiness, and so came chardonnays, mainly from Australia and California, called "No Oak," "Metallico" (for the steel tanks in which no-oak chardonnays are made), "Inox" (a French term for steel) and the like.

The no-oak method can produce wines that are lively, pure and delicious. It's also much cheaper for winemakers than buying new barrels every year. But wines made in this style lack some of the crucial benefits of barrel aging, namely a very slight exposure to the oxygen that passes through the wood, which can enhance a wine's texture and complexity. One way to retain the benefits of barrel aging while avoiding its excesses is to use older barrels, which impart fewer or no flavors to wine. Many great chardonnays in California and in Burgundy are made this way.

The bottom line: No-oak is an alternative style, but not necessarily a better one.

ASSERTION Red wine with meat, white with fish is an archaic rule.

TRUTH It's really not such a bad guideline.

In the last 20 years the matching of foods with wines has become an exercise in wizardlike precision. Seemingly every aspect of ingredients, cooking methods, seasonings and the position of the moon must be figured into selecting the one wine that will marry, as they used to say, with the food. This exercise has been carried to absurd lengths.

Many guidelines in books and periodicals make sense, but they require esoteric knowledge of wine regions, producers and vintages well beyond what most people might be expected to have. That's why simple generalizations are made. Most people don't want to work at wine-and-food pairing, they just want something that will taste good.

For red meat, red wine is a no-brainer. Might you find a white wine that will go with steak or lamb? Sure, but it's likely to be a very unusual wine. Will there be differences if you choose a Chianti or a Washington cabernet? Yes, but they'll both be enjoyable.

For fish, dry white wine is the odds-on choice. Exceptions and nuances? Indeed. California chardonnay is better with lobster or scallops than with oysters or sole. Sauvignon blanc, Muscadet and Champagne are versatile, and light-bodied reds will go beautifully with salmon, tuna and more assertive fish. But so will many whites.

Then there's the great in between—poultry, pork and the rest. White's fine. So's red. So are semi-sweet wines like Mosel rieslings. In this area you can truly drink what you like.

The bottom line: Matching food and wine is not sweat-worthy.

ASSERTION The lower the grape yield the better the wine.

TRUTH Most vines have an ideal yield below which the quality of the grapes does not improve.

While the issue of grape yields has moved from a subject for wine geeks to a vehicle for marketing, it is based on a crucial truth: The quality of the grapes is inversely proportional to the yield of those grapes. Roughly speaking, the more grapes you harvest from a vine, the more dilute those grapes will be. Conversely, farmers who reduce their yield will harvest grapes with juice of greater intensity.

The truth, naturally, is never so simple. Yields depend on many variables, including the type of grape, the age of the vines, the soil in which they are planted, the type of rootstock, the trellising system and the climate. Overly high yields may never produce very good wines, but lowering yields won't improve grapes planted in the wrong places, while unnaturally low yields can result in unbalanced wines.

The bottom line: Yields should be based on sound viticulture, not marketing.

ASSERTION It doesn't matter how big a wine is if it's balanced.

TRUTH Good whiskey is balanced, but you wouldn't want to drink a bottle with dinner.

Of all the current wine shibboleths, this is the one I hear most frequently. It generally comes from producers who want to rationalize their high-alcohol wines, and it is guaranteed to set off a heated debate over the importance of a wine's alcohol content.

High-alcohol wines have always existed, like Amarone and certain cuvées of Châteauneuf-du-Pape, and alcohol levels have been rising all over the world, but only in California and Australia do so many wines come in at 15 percent or more in alcohol. These wines can be complex, well-made, even balanced, so the heat of the alcohol does not stand out. But these wines almost always feel huge, seem sweet, and tend to dominate food. You cannot drink as much of them.

The bottom line: Big is fine if you drink wine as a cocktail; not so good with food.

October 2007

Berkeley's Wine Radical, 35 Years Later

By ERIC ASIMOV

The 1980s were a dark time for French wine, as Kermit Lynch told it in his 1988 book *Adventures on the Wine Route: A Wine Buyer's Tour of France*. Much of it was plain bad. What was good was made by hand, with traditional methods passed on through the generations.

But the young were turning away from their fathers to embrace technology like mechanical harvesters, sterile filterers and chemical pesticides and herbicides. They were sacrificing their heritage and turning over wines to what he called "men in white lab coats." Mr. Lynch was appalled, and said so.

People apparently listened. While *Adventures* was a lament for a disappearing world, Mr. Lynch now is confident that the wines he loves, made naturally and expressively, are here to stay.

"Am I optimistic?" he said as we stood in his unprepossessing wine shop, tasting some of the myriad wines he imports, almost entirely French with a smattering of Italian. "Absolutely. Look at all the importers who do now what I was doing back then."

Thirty-five years have passed since Mr. Lynch first hung up his shingle as a wine merchant here in the cradle of radical youth. While he is the first to say he was not much for politics back then—naïvely selling South African wine until his customers brought up the issue of apartheid—his efforts as a wine importer and merchant shook up the world of wine in the best Berkeley tradition. It is no exaggeration to say that a significant segment of the fine wine industry today is stamped in Mr. Lynch's image.

His influence can be seen almost any time you go into a good wine shop and spot people looking at the labels of wines to check the importer. Instead of memorizing esoterica about producers, regions and vineyards, these canny consumers learned that finding an importer they can trust is a reliable navigational tool. Nowadays, many names they follow are those of the spiritual descendants of Mr. Lynch.

If he had been only an importer, Mr. Lynch would have left a significant legacy. With little company, he traveled the back roads of France, seeking esoteric producers whose wines were fresh, delicious and unaffected by the industrialization shaping the post–World War II wine industry.

The little-known names he turned up are now a pantheon of French country wines: Henri Jayer, Raveneau, Coche-Dury and Hubert de Montille in Burgundy; J. L. Chave, Auguste Clape, Thierry Allemand and Vieux Télégraphe in the Rhône; Didier Dagueneau in Pouilly-Fumé; Charles Joguet in Chinon; and Domaine Tempier in Bandol.

But like Frank Schoonmaker, another significant figure in American wine history, Mr. Lynch was not merely a merchant and an importer but an author as well. He began in the 1970s by writing descriptions of his inventory and sending them out to customers—"little propaganda pieces," he called them.

They were really much more than that, for Mr. Lynch never engaged in the sort of contrived tasting notes that often pass for wine writing today. Instead, he wrote of the joy and pleasures of consuming good wine, of the winemakers he met and the places he visited. He provided characters, context and travelogue, and even recipes.

In 2004, many of these pieces were gathered into a book, appropriately called *Inspiring Thirst* (Ten Speed Press). It's the commercial companion piece to *Adventures on the Wine Route*, which, even after 20 years, remains one of the finest American books on wine.

Today, Mr. Lynch still travels the back roads, though he has more company. Once, he struggled to persuade his discoveries to sell their wines in the United States. "These days it's more about finding who doesn't already have an importer," he said.

That has taken him beyond the more familiar regions, into Languedoc and Cahors, to Irouléguy in the French Basque country and to Corsica. The wines are distinctive, fresh and alive, all with a clear sense of place.

We tasted several dozen of his offerings, standing in the middle of his cluttered store, which sells only wines that he imports, most in cardboard cartons with minimal display. Many of the most interesting wines were under $20, like a 2005 Cahors from Clos la Coutale, which smelled of wild berries and flowers, and an elegant yet chug-worthy 2006 Vin de Pays de la Vallée du Paradis from Maxime Magnon.

"How can anybody say that French wines are all expensive?" he asked. "I've never seen the dollar this low, but French wines are still the best values."

Mr. Lynch is notorious in northern California for not selling any California wines. He shrugs. "I promised in my first brochure, I won't sell you anything I haven't tasted," he said. "I didn't have room for anything else."

These days, Mr. Lynch spends half his time in Provence, where he and his wife, the photographer Gail Skoff, and their two children have a house not far from Domaine Tempier, the Bandol estate where he spent many formative hours with the Peyraud family. He counts the late Lucien Peyraud, the guiding spirit of Tempier, along with Richard Olney, the late food writer who introduced him to the Peyrauds, as his two primary influences.

"There was a guy on each of my shoulders when I went around looking for wines," he said. "One was Lucien, and one was Richard, and I asked myself: 'Would I serve this to Lucien? Would I serve this to Richard?'"

Mr. Lynch is also now a winemaker himself. In 1998 he joined with the Brunier family of Vieux Télégraphe to buy Domaine les Pallières in Gigondas, which makes big, chunky reds scented with black olives and herbs. "They say, 'Oh, he only likes light wines,' but sometimes you want big wines," he said. "Finesse does not mean little."

At 65, Mr. Lynch is by no means stepping back, although he leaves more time for other pursuits, like playing guitar and writing songs. But he takes great satisfaction in the thought that the wines he loves are still here.

"They can never be mainstream, but they're out there," he said. "I feel like I won."

November 2007

A Rosé Can Bloom in Winter, Too

By ERIC ASIMOV

If you look really hard, you will find them condemned to a dusty back shelf underneath a few cobwebs, or perhaps looking forlorn on the half-price rack, their once brilliant colors dulled by neglect.

They are the rosés of winter, remnants of last summer's lighthearted cheer. Now, they are disregarded, disdained or, at best, a benign recollection, like a poolside flirtation, pleasant but inconsequential. Next June, when the bottles pop up again like pink flowers in the prime selling soil of every wine shop, the enthusiasm will return. But for now, forget it.

More than any other wine, rosés suffer from a sort of seasonal affective disorder. Near the end of summer, sales begin to slow. By winter they are depressed, if not dead. It really makes no sense. For most wines, the old seasonal guidelines are largely passé. We drink reds all summer, whites all winter. But rosé? Because it is marketed as a summer accessory, its relevance evaporates at all other times of the year.

But what if we consider rosé as a wine, rather than as a prop? Who wouldn't want a rosé like a 2009 Domaine Ilarria any time of the year? This $17 wine, a shimmering, translucent garnet in summer sun or winter snow, comes from Irouléguy in the Basque country, about as far southwest as you can go in France without crossing into Spain. As fierce as rosés ever get, it's made of tannat and cabernet franc, and it tastes like liquid rock, combined with iron and blood. I love this wine, and it was terrific recently with roasted duck and wild rice.

Sadly, most rosés shrivel up next to a wine like the Ilarria. The unfortunate truth is that many rosé producers have little ambition beyond the palatable. They've seen crisp, innocuous rosés sell wildly in springtime, destined for poolside sipping and no more. So they are content to produce inoffensive, assembly-line wines, made quickly to accentuate immediate fruitiness, but that, like hothouse vegetables, have little or no character.

Now, I have nothing against carefree wines. I love them, in fact. But I have no interest in banal wines that are rushed into fermentation, hustled out of the winery and dead by the end of summer. Those rosés in the dusty sale bins? Many deserve to be there because they're not worth drinking. They weren't worth drinking in the summer either. Good rosés are another matter entirely.

"It's the terror that lives in the hearts of retailers and distributors, of having leftover rosés that they have to close out," said David Lillie, an owner of Chambers Street Wines in TriBeCa. Chambers Street is that rare retailer that keeps an active supply of rosés throughout the year, up to two dozen in the spring and summer, and nine or 10 through the winter.

"We feel like they're beautiful food wines, at least the ones made in a real, serious style," Mr. Lillie said. He concedes that 95 percent of his rosé business is in the spring and summer, but nonetheless he believes in them year-round. "It's a very small segment, but we just happen to like to do it."

That segment would never deprive itself of a wine like the 2009 rosé, or rosato, from La Porta di Vertine, a small producer in Chianti territory. This wine is made of a mixture of the red sangiovese and canaiolo grapes and the white trebbiano and malvasia. The fermentation is allowed to proceed at its own pace—the 2009 took six months, rather than the matter of days for industrial rosés. The result is a richly hued, textured, juicy yet substantial wine that smells like pressed flowers and would go beautifully with a good ham.

Yet the prejudice—what else can one call it?—endures. In a Twitter post, Lockhart Steele, the founder of Eater.com and other Web sites, suggested that few excuses were acceptable for drinking rosé in January. Well, excuse me, Mr. Steele, you've obviously never tried a wine like Jean-Paul Brun's 2009 Rosé d' Folie, a minerally pink Beaujolais that I would drink any time of the year, especially if I had a plate of chicken roasted with garlic, rosemary and thyme.

You want Bordeaux? How about a Bordeaux rosé like Château Jean Faux's '09, clean and refreshing yet sumptuous, with a pleasant heft to it? Or a Burgundy rosé, like Domaine Bart's Marsannay '09, its color a little darker than salmon, light textured with flavors of flowers and licorice that cling to the mouth after you swallow. All of these wines are priced at less than $20, great values at any time of the year.

I haven't even mentioned the greatest rosés of the world, like the deep, complex Bandols from Tempier and Pradeaux, or the cerasuolo d'Abbruzzo from Valentini, wines that can age and improve for years. And speaking of aging, what about the great Viña Tondonia rosado from López de Heredia, the venerable Rioja producer? These wines are not even released until a decade or more after the vintage. The current rosado is the 2000, a pale, coppery, complex wine that compels you to smack your lips at the tactile pleasure of rolling it around your mouth. Jamón ibérico, please!

We've been talking about dry rosés, but another category exists as well, good, sweet rosés. It's small, to be sure, epitomized by the once-famous rosé d'Anjou, and unlikely to grow given the aversion of former white zinfandel drinkers to residual sugar.

I confess, I can't say I'm thrilled by rosés with residual sugar, either. Yet when an exciting producer like Éric Nicolas of Domaine de Bellivière issues a ripe, rich, balanced, lightly sweet rosé like Les Giroflées, I am willing to fly my rosé flag high, even in January. Residual sugar? Bring on the Indian food.

January 2011

So Who Needs Vintage Charts?

By FRANK J. PRIAL

About a decade ago, Bruno Prats, then the owner of Château Cos d'Estournel, in St.- Estèphe, declared that there would be no more bad vintages of wine. At the time I considered his remarks the height of arrogance, a characteristic not unknown among the Bordelais.

I was wrong.

His was a bit of an overstatement, perhaps, but essentially, Mr. Prats was right on the mark. Great wine may still be elusive, but rarely now does a year go by that doesn't produce good wine, even in marginal regions like Bordeaux, where the weather is as risky as a dot-com stock.

The fact of the matter is that in the cellar and the vineyard the winemakers of the world have rendered the vintage chart obsolete.

For the uninitiated, a vintage chart tracks various categories of wine over a period of years. Most vintage charts use numerical ratings; some add a code indicating whether the wines are too young to drink, ready to drink or seriously past their prime.

Over the years I have produced vintage chart after chart, always adding enough qualifications and caveats to make the reader wonder why I bothered in the first place. I am not alone. Each year, Robert M. Parker Jr. publishes a vintage chart of daunting thoroughness. This year's has 28 separate wine categories. Even so, he warns: "This vintage chart should be regarded as a very general overall rating slanted in favor of what the finest producers were capable of producing in a particular viticultural region. Such charts are filled with exceptions to the rule. Astonishingly good wines from skillful or lucky vintners in years rated mediocre, and thin, diluted, characterless wines from incompetent or greedy producers in great years."

Vintage charts assume a high degree of homogeneity: Northern California, the Central Coast, the South Central Coast. But can a single rating for Northern California adequately cover the northern reaches of Mendocino, the furnacelike valley floor of Calistoga and the fog-shrouded hills of Carneros? And what about the Amador County vineyards, far to the east? In Sonoma County, the wines of Dry Creek are different from those of the Alexander Valley, which are not the same as those from the Russian River or the Sonoma Coast.

The first vintage charts came from France and were compact cards with listings for Bordeaux, Burgundy, Beaujolais, the Rhône, Champagne and the Loire. Today, superior wines are made in Alsace, the Languedoc, in Roussillon and the Southwest, often when wines from more traditional regions are less than exciting.

Can any single vintage chart do justice to Italy, where there are a hundred different wine regions, where remarkable wines might be made in the foothills of the Alps and in Sicily in the same year that mediocre or poor wines come from Tuscany and Umbria?

A chart might report conscientiously that, say, 1997 was a good year in Spain. Where in Spain: Penedès? Rioja? Navarre? Priorat? Rueda? Ribera del Duero? And what of the newest wine sources—Chile, Argentina, Australia, New Zealand and South Africa? Don't they deserve space on the charts? And even if they got it, what chart could show their growing diversity?

Both Chile and Argentina are developing new wine regions far to the south of their traditional vineyards; Australia's Margaret River region is 2,000 miles from its Hunter Valley; South Africa makes different wines in Hermanus from what it does in Stellenbosch.

A vintage chart will advise, say, that the 1998 Bordeaux will need several years of bottle aging after they arrive here in 2001. But a consumer finds the shops already filled with 1998s that are, he is told, ready now. Of course, the chart concerns itself only with the classified growths, the finest of the Bordeaux wines, and ignores the hundreds of lesser wines, many of which, these days, are startlingly close to their better-known siblings in quality.

The vintage chart speaks to wine regions at a time when winemakers—and consumers—are increasingly concerned with terroir, the uniqueness of small plots of land. Some vintners now produce five or six separate wines from half a dozen small contiguous vineyards, while others make two or three different wines from the same vineyard.

There are highs, like 1945, 1961 and 1982 in Bordeaux and 1994 in the Napa Valley, and lows, like 1991 or 1992 in Bordeaux and Tuscany, but not one year when some decent Bordeaux wine was not produced. But it's unlikely that we will ever see vintages like 1963 and 1965, dreadful years in Bordeaux that resulted in dreadful wine. There will always be years when nature doesn't cooperate, like 1991 and 1992 in Bordeaux, but even in those years, pleasant, drinkable if not age-worthy wines were made.

Everywhere, hardier rootstocks, better grapes, limited yields and severe grape selection at harvest time have increased quality. So, too, have new organic methods of pest and disease control and new planting techniques. In the 1960s, wine was made much as it had been made in the 1860s. Now, NASA satellites tell growers where to plant and which efforts have been the most successful.

This is not quite a golden age of wine; in spite of everything there will always be dull or poorly made wines around. But those are not problems of the vintage. And competition, which is keener than ever, makes it difficult for plonk to survive in the market.

Vintage charts are not entirely passé. Wine can be confusing, and the chart does offer some general information, as Mr. Parker, the critic, suggests. And of course, in the auction rooms, where collectors haggle over the 1982 Pétrus and the 1994 Romanée-Conti, vintage charts can serve as a handy reference tool. Elsewhere, though, vintages are increasingly irrelevant.

And I don't think I'm alone in that point of view. In the past, letters would begin to come in about a year after the last vintage chart appeared here. When, they asked, would the next chart appear? No longer. A lot of people must be deciding for themselves.

In the final frames of *Little Caesar,* Edward G. Robinson snarls, "Is this the end of Rico?"

To my way of thinking, that sacred talisman of the wine buff, the vintage chart, is just as dead as Rico was when the screen went to black.

February 2000

Three Cheers for the Also-Rans

By ERIC ASIMOV

The quest for greatness is the stuff of myth and romance. Americans revere the star-bound strivers, whether Lincoln or Edison, Babe Ruth or Muhammad Ali, Bill Gates or Warren Buffett, who aimed to be the toppermost of the poppermost, as the Beatles used to say, and made it. Few remember the good, the competent, the runner-up.

When it comes to wine, though, the focus on greatness comes at a significant cost in both pleasure and money. This is most obvious in terms of wine ratings, where consumers irrationally (at least from a wine lover's perspective) chase after bottles that critics have awarded 90 points or more, but shun those in the 85 to 89 range, even though the lower-rated wines may be cheaper, more flexible with food and readier to drink.

Less obviously, this fixation on greatness plays out with vintages. Each spring the wine-drinking world waits breathlessly as critics descend on Bordeaux for the first tastings of the previous year's vintage, which is unfinished and still in barrels. Raves for the vintage can stampede the herd and send prices skyrocketing, as happened with the 2000, 2003 and 2005 vintages. More measured responses can provoke yawns and ho-hums, as happened with 2001, 2002 and 2004. Yet none of those three vintages was badly received. Each was considered very good. They just weren't great.

That's fine with me. In the latest catalog from Sherry-Lehmann, you can buy a 2003 Saint-Julien from Léoville Barton (a vintage rated 95 by Robert M. Parker Jr.) for $160. No thank you. But I would consider the 2001 Léoville Barton for $75. Why the discrepancy? Mr. Parker awarded 2001 only 88 points, even though he gave the individual bottles 95 for the '03 and 92 for the '01. In this case, I prefer the '01 vintage to the '03.

The tyranny of the great vintage is not restricted to Bordeaux. Wherever vintages matter in the wine-producing world, consumers are infatuated with the great ones while paying little attention to wines from good vintages, even when they are significantly less expensive.

Sometimes lesser vintages can offer better experiences. In restaurants I look for red Burgundies from the 2000 vintage. Most critics would rate that vintage as among the weaker ones of the last 10 years, not bad but certainly not as good as '99 or '02, and the wines are generally less expensive.

But they are delicious right now, at a time when the higher-rated '02s and the '99s tend to be in sullen adolescent phases. Ten years from now, those denser wines will most likely be in top form while the lighter 2000s will be on their way out.

If you buy wine with long-term aging in mind, the overall quality of the vintage might be more important to you. But for current drinking, you have to approach things differently.

As with the 2000s, the very decent 2004 Burgundy vintage is destined to be overshadowed, in its case by the 2005s. I don't dispute the greatness of 2005, but those wines are going to be very expensive and will require aging. Meanwhile the '04s are more affordable and the reds from good producers have been charming at an early age. I expect I'll be enjoying them as the 2005s begin their slow march toward drinkability.

Not so long ago I bought some 2004 Morey-St.-Denis from Fourrier, a producer I like a lot, for about $40 a bottle. You can be sure the '05s, when they go on sale, will be a lot more expensive.

Vintage tyranny is alive and well in Italy, too. In Tuscany, Brunellos di Montalcino are more valued from the 1997, 1999 and 2001 vintages than they are from 1998 and 2000.

The critics aren't wrong about the vintages, but the '98s and '00s are pretty good, too, and should not be sneered at. Similarly the Piedmont region had excellent vintages from 1996 to 2001.

These wines are still very young in Barolo terms, but in restaurants they are generally priced higher than bottles from, say, 1993, which was a very good year. A 1993 Monprivato from Giuseppe Mascarello is selling for $135 at Del Posto in Chelsea, while the '96 is $175. I have no doubt the '96 is ultimately the greater wine, but right now I'd prefer to drink the '93.

Northern California hasn't had a bad year in a while, according to the critics, but I remember winemakers complaining bitterly that they couldn't sell their 2000 or their 1998 vintages because they were rated badly.

Let's be clear about winemakers: they have no bad vintages. If they're not great, they're "classic style" or, at worst, "difficult." Nonetheless, I loved the light-bodied, elegant 2000 Insignia from Joseph Phelps Vineyards, even if it wasn't as big and rich as the 1999 or the 2001, both considered superior years. This is not to say 2000 was a better vintage, only that vintage is not necessarily destiny.

Vintage ratings, like wine ratings in general, have a powerful psychological effect on consumers. The higher the number, the greater the desirability of the wine, which feeds into the myriad reasons people make their buying decisions. It should be no surprise that, as with cars, clothes, handbags and other consumer goods, status seeking, showing off and fear of embarrassment all play important roles.

If there were any doubt that beliefs influence judgment in wine, researchers at the California Institute of Technology showed in a recent study that people enjoyed wine more if they thought it was more expensive.

As 20 volunteers were given sips of cabernet sauvignon, scientists scanned their brains, measuring neural activity in areas thought to register pleasure. They were told they were tasting five different wines, and they were given the price of each.

In reality, only three wines were used, and each volunteer had two duplicates at different prices. The experiment showed that the pleasure response increased when the volunteers believed they were drinking a more expensive wine.

I don't think we need a study to say this applies as well to wine ratings and vintage ratings. For now, value hunters can thank the rules of mass psychology.

February 2008

Screw Tops Gain Acceptance Worldwide

By FRANK J. PRIAL

Two years ago, the announcement that a well-known winery, or a little-known winery for that matter, was switching to screw caps for its bottles was news. Winemakers were divided on the subject. "Right on," said the younger vintners. "Waste of time," said older and presumably wiser types. Or "Money down the drain." Or, more often, "The consumer will never accept it."

No longer. Acceptance of screw-on tops for wine bottles—by both winemakers and consumers—has been astonishing. From Burgundy to Beaujolais, from Spain to South Africa, winemakers are switching from corks. No one seems to have an accurate count of how many wineries are using aluminum tops, but people in the industry agree that the number is in the hundreds.

Corked wine—wine that has been spoiled because of a bad cork—is a serious problem in the wine business. It affects even the fine old chateaus. Many years ago, I spent a weekend at Château Lafite-Rothschild, tasting very old wines from its cellar. Later, the staff acknowledged that it had had to open many more of the priceless bottles than we tasted, mostly because of faulty corks.

James Laube, an editor of *Wine Spectator* magazine, reported two years ago on a tasting of elite 1991 California cabernets in which nearly 15 percent of the wines were spoiled by bad corks.

Some of the problem is physical: as corks age, some dry out and crumble. Others were poor fits to begin with and allowed too much air into the bottle, oxidizing the wine. But the contamination derives principally from trichloranisole, or TCA, a substance formed by the action of chlorine on cork bark or wood.

Traditionally, corks were bleached in a chlorine solution as part of the manufacturing. Other substances have been used but, despite major efforts by the cork industry and regular announcements that the problem had been eliminated, it persists. Winemakers estimate that up to 5 percent of all bottled wine is contaminated by TCA. Cork producers say the figure is much lower.

The industry was hardly unfamiliar with screw tops. For years, jug wines and cheap fortified wines had been closed with them. Some years ago, when the E.&J. Gallo Winery switched from screw tops to corks for its famous Hearty Burgundy, it was an unmistakable sign that the wine had increased in stature.

Most objections to screw-top wine bottles appear to be directed at restaurants, where their presence has more to do with image and prestige than in the home. This is certainly true of expensive wines. But restaurateurs who have used screw tops on moderate-price wines say they have encountered little objection from customers. And anyone who has used the bottles at home—or who has taken screw-top wines on a picnic—quickly sees how convenient they are.

A small Napa Valley winery called PlumpJack broke the ice, so to speak, in 1997, offering a $135 cabernet with a screw top. Bonny Doon Vineyard in Santa Cruz followed, first putting screw tops on 80,000 cases of its moderate-price wines and later moving to bottle all of its wines, including its top-of-the-line Cigare Volant, with screw tops.

Among the other California wineries that have switched wholly or in part to screw caps are Beringer Blass, Calera, Sonoma-Cutrer, Murphy-Goode, the Napa Wine Company, Whitehall Lane, Robert Pepi, R. H. Phillips and E.&J. Gallo, which is using metal caps for its huge Turning Leaf line. Fetzer Vineyards uses screw caps on wines it exports to Europe. In Oregon, WillaKenzie and the Argyle winery in Dundee are using screw caps.

Hogue Cellars in Washington is to switch to screw caps next year for its 450,000 case annual production. Hogue and R. H. Phillips are owned by Vincor International, a Canadian company. Vincor also owns Kim Crawford Wines in New Zealand, which has been using screw caps exclusively since 2001. In both New Zealand and Australia, it is estimated that 40 percent of all wineries—about 200—use screw tops.

Specially treated corks and plastic corks have met with little enthusiasm in the wine business. The best-known screw cap, with a long seal covering the bottle's opening, is the Stelvin, made by Pechiney Capsules of France. Pechiney has a factory in California.

The Stelvin was first developed in the 1970s for Swiss wines, which are said to be sensitive to TCA. Since then, the market for Stelvins has expanded to include Australia, New Zealand, Argentina and Chile, as well as the United States.

Customers in France include Michel Laroche, who bottles a premier cru Chablis under screw caps, Yvon Mau in Bordeaux, Domaine Blanck and Georges Lorentz in Alsace and the Domaine de la Baume in the Languedoc. Fortant de France, one of the best-known Languedoc wines, is now bottled with screw caps. Even Bodegas Torres in Spain, a major cork-producing country, uses Stelvins on some of its white wines.

Tesco, the largest wine retailer in Britain, has more than 100 screw-capped wines in its stores and expects more. Georges Duboeuf, the largest of the Beaujolais producers, ships some of his wines to Tesco in screw tops. Switzerland, too, sells Duboeuf Beaujolais in screw tops, but Mr. Duboeuf said last week that he produces only about 30,000 cases with screw tops. While the market for his screw tops is increasing, he said, he is also using plastic corks. They are, he said, entirely satisfactory and will probably be a more important replacement for cork than the metal caps.

Most producers have been hesitant to use screw caps on wines destined to age. Ironically, they are the wines that probably need them most because even corks not tainted with TCA dry out over time and fail to keep delicate old wines safe from air.

But 98 percent of all wine is drunk within six months after its purchase. I am willing to predict that within a decade, 75 percent or more of these wines will be sold with metal caps.

April 2004

A Musty Myth

By FRANK J. PRIAL

The only thing harder than getting people to accept a good idea is getting them to abandon a bad one. A relevant example: the almost universal reverence for old wines.

Let's suppose for a moment that we're eavesdropping on a small gathering of wine connoisseurs. A lot of good food has been eaten and good wine drunk, and now it is time for the high point of the evening, the opening and tasting of a rare old bottle. For sake of argument, we'll say it's a 1945 Château Mouton-Rothschild. It could as well have been a 1958 Beaulieu Vineyards Private Reserve or some Burgundy of equally impressive age and lineage.

The wine is opened. Tension mounts. There is sniffing, swirling and, finally, tasting. Affirmative nods follow; also appreciative murmurs and ecstatic sighs. The wine, we conclude, is terrific. But wait; listen to what these sages have to say: "Fantastic; tastes like a young wine!" or "It's still full of life," and "It's got the color of a wine bottled last year!"

What they are saying, what they are exclaiming over, in effect, is that the wine, in spite of its great age, still displays some of the charm of its youth. The inescapable conclusion: If youthfulness is such an asset, why all the fuss over age?

It is a bit more complicated than that, of course. A truly great old wine combines the subtlety of age with the freshness of youth, taking care to see that the latter does not overwhelm the former. But a lot of old wines are not truly great. They are just old. Which means they are brown in color and musty in the nose, and taste like dried leaves. To a dedicated expert, perhaps, these wines have some information, some arcane pleasure to impart. Like listening to a French tenor on a 1910 wax cylinder. For most of us, old wines are just something to be able to say we've had.

The wine trade, unfortunately, works hard to foster the old-wine myth. Even inexpensive bottles are often pictured in beautiful wine cellars, surrounded by other wines hoary with age. Novelists and screenwriters dote on them. Thomas Mann wrote about the '28 Veuve Clicquot; James Bond said, "Ah, the '69 Bollinger." Demimondaines order by vintage with not a clue as to what the wine is like. In fact, we all pull that trick once in a while. It's easier to memorize a few vintage numbers than to learn about the wine.

I'd hate to know how much money is spent by anxious hosts of a Saturday afternoon, buying a few bottles at the last minute and hoping some impressive-looking label dating from the Johnson administration will complement the lamb and wow the guests. And guests rarely know any more about wine than their host. Those who do know that a simple, fairly inexpensive wine is often more fun to drink. Nothing is more irritating than having to praise a wine because the label is impressive. To people not well versed in wine, old wines rarely taste great.

There was a time when wines achieved great old age because it took them many years to become drinkable. A century ago, the winemaking process was still basically empirical. Vintners knew what was happening but not why. So, little could be done about controlling tannin and alcohol in wine. Tannins, which can take years to soften, more than anything determine the age of a wine. Today, wines are made to mature much more quickly and, consequently, to be drunk much younger.

The most famous red wines of Bordeaux, the Lafites and Latours and Margaux and Moutons, are made to last, and there is no doubt that they get better as they get older. But even these rare and expensive wines usually reach their peak at around 10 years of age. Hundreds of lesser wines of the Bordeaux region are usually ready to drink in two or three years.

Some of the greatest Bordeaux wines, those from St.-Émilion and Pomerol, rarely mature as well as the best of the Médoc and Graves wines. Thirty-year-old Château Pétrus, for example, the most famous of the Pomerols, is rarely the equal of a great Médoc of the same age. Some fine Burgundies will last for decades, but few of them will improve after 10 years in the bottle. Most good Burgundy is ready to drink, is at its peak, after five years.

California wines age, too; some of them quite well. Probably only a handful will achieve great old age and remain drinkable. It's too early to tell. There aren't that many wineries more than 15 years old and most winemakers make modest claims for their first three or four vintages.

Perhaps the collecting and drinking of old wines should be seen as a pastime apart from the fundamental enjoyment of wine. But no one who seeks to enjoy wine as part of everyday life should be too concerned with antiquity. There is too much good wine around, from last year's Beaujolais to the year before's zinfandel to the Burgundies of two years before that.

These are the wines that are available now, that are meant to be enjoyed now and replaced by other wines tomorrow. Rare old wines have their place, but probably not at the dinner table tonight. Rare old books are beautiful to behold; but they don't have much to do with reading.

January 1987

A Sommelier's Little Secret: The Microwave

By WILLIAM GRIMES

A new question is creeping into wine service in New York: How do you want that cooked?

For many years, Americans have confounded the rest of the world by drinking their white wines too cold and their red wines too warm. Sommeliers no longer hesitate when diners ask that a luscious Corton-Charlemagne be plunged into an ice bucket. They just do it. It's easy.

Red wine poses a different problem, since it often arrives at the table with a slight chill. If the diners want their wine the temperature of a blood transfusion, and fast, the sommelier must resort to wiles, and the wiliest wile of all, it turns out, is the microwave oven.

Sometimes it's the customer who wants his wine 'waved. Sometimes it's the hard-pressed sommelier who makes the decision to go nuclear. But it happens. There really are wines that go into that silent chamber at 58 degrees and come out, like a client at a tanning salon, flush with radiation and 7 to 10 degrees warmer.

"There is no way any sommelier is going to admit to doing it," said Dan Perlman, the wine director at Veritas. "They'll say, 'I've heard of it,' like I just did. I'm in the clear, though, because we don't have a microwave."

The practice is by no means widespread, or even widely known, but it is something that happens at even the top restaurants. Alexis Ganter, the wine director at City Wine and Cigar, reacted with stunned silence when informed about the microwave trick. Then he let out a long, shuddering sigh and moaned, "Oh my God."

Like other members of the "wine is a living thing" school, Mr. Ganter expressed deep fear of this new technological breakthrough. Others showed a native American willingness to at least experiment. "It makes sense," said Ralph Hersom, the wine director at Le Cirque 2000. "I don't see that it would harm a wine, but I'd recommend doing it with a younger wine."

Still others fessed up, some expressing shame but others not. "I did it once when I was working at a wine bar in Madison, Wis.," said Eric Zillier, the wine director at the Hudson River Club. "It was an '85 Burgundy from Verget, one of my favorites, but I made the customer, who was very insistent, swear he would never tell anyone I did it."

Christopher Cannon, at the Judson Grill, has used the microwave and doesn't mind saying so. It's a method of last resort, but it is a method that works, and he will use it. "I zap it for 5 to 10 seconds," he said. It seems more reasonable than the customer who wanted his Gaja Barbaresco served with ice cubes.

And why not? Most Champagne houses turn their bottles by machine, not hand. The plastic cork and the screw top work just as well, if not better, than a cork. So why resist the microwave?

"The microwaves are heating the water, which is the main constituent of wine," said Christian E. Butzke, an enologist at the University of California at Davis. "If you do that for a very brief period—10 seconds maximum—no other chemical reactions are going to take place, and nothing will be destroyed."

The phenolic structure of the wine, Mr. Butzke said, should not be disturbed by the microwaves. "It is awkward," he admitted, "because you associate a microwave with TV dinners."

Winemakers, somewhat surprisingly, do not run screaming from the room at the idea. "It's not something I'd do with a fine wine," said Richard Draper, the winemaker at Ridge Vineyards, "but if it's an industrial product, which 90 percent of wine is, it's been through a lot worse already." As for fine wines, Mr. Draper said that his objection to microwaving was philosophical rather than rational.

Some wine lovers even see magical powers in the microwave. Richard Dean, the sommelier at the Mark Hotel, used to serve a wine club that gathered once a month at the Honolulu hotel where he worked. The members were convinced that warming a red wine in the microwave for five seconds put an extra five years of age on the wine.

A professional to the tips of his fingers, Mr. Dean did not laugh. He did not argue. Nor did he tell his customers that the hotel had no microwave. He simply disappeared with the wine, reappeared after a decent interval, served it, and everyone was happy—until a rival hotel snitched on him. "That was embarrassing," he said.

The same sommeliers who shrink before the microwave do not mind employing all sorts of nontechnological tricks, like running a decanter under warm water before pouring the wine in it, replacing glasses on the table with glasses that have just come out of the dishwasher, or even putting the bottle in the dishwasher. Joseph Funghini, the wine director at the Post House, said that he has wrapped a bottle in a warm towel. Others plunge the bottle into a bucket of warm water.

Nearly every restaurant, bending to American preferences, has raised the storage temperature from classic cellar temperature, which is 55 degrees, to about 60 degrees. (Wines in long-term storage remain at 53 degrees to 55 degrees, with a humidity of 70 percent.) "Ninety-five percent of customers will object to 55 degrees," Mr. Hersom of Le Cirque said.

Some object to 75 degrees. "I had a customer, very sophisticated, who simply liked to drink red wine at body temperature," said Mr. Perlman of Veritas. "He asked that it be decanted and then placed on a shelf above the stove." Mr. Perlman has a lot of stories like that. There's the customer who wanted the Champagne decanted, to get rid of those annoying bubbles, and the one who wanted to add fruit juice to his Mouton-Rothschild to make a sangria. Mr. Perlman suggested a more modest red. The customer said no. He wanted a good sangria.

The microwave, however, seems to be the philosophical point of no return. Some sommeliers simply cannot cross the threshold.

"You're destroying everything in the wine that makes it wine," Mr. Zillier of the Hudson River Club said. "It's catastrophic." When informed of Mr. Butzke's line of argument, he dug in his heels. "Instinct tells me the fragile biochemical ingredients are going to be affected by the highly excited water molecules," he said. "You're cooking it. If you put wine in a sautépan to bring the temperature up, people would laugh at you. What's the difference?"

Convenience, for one thing. Efficiency for another. And one thing more.

"You get a sick feeling in the pit of your stomach, but you do these things," Mr. Perlman said. "After all, the customer is paying for the bottle of wine."

Now for the gory details: how to nuke a wine

There is a very simple way to bring a chilled wine up a few degrees in temperature. Let it sit at room temperature for 15 minutes. This technique, known to the ancients, produces spectacular results with minimal effort. But there are times when the harried host does not have 15 minutes. That's where the microwave comes in, for those with the nerve to put a cherished bottle on the hot seat.

The microwave moment presents itself more frequently than one might think. True, most people do not have wine cellars, and therefore their wine is more likely to need chilling than warming. They do, however, have refrigerators. The red wine that was left to cool off a bit can come out cold, and white wine is almost certainly well below cellar temperature after several hours on the shelf. This is not a good thing. Cold helps mask the deficiencies of a white wine, accentuating its crispness and thirst-quenching properties, but it kills the taste of a complex white. Enter, to boos and hisses, the microwave oven.

Before enlisting its help, remove the metal cap from the top of the bottle and discard. It is not necessary to remove the cork, since warming the wine a few degrees will not significantly expand the volume of air between the cork and the wine. Set the microwave on high power. Every five seconds of microwaving will elevate the wine's temperature by two degrees. Five degrees is probably the most extreme variation anyone would want to shoot for. A big-bodied red wine should be served at 60 to 65 degrees, a complex white wine from 55 to 60 degrees, and a light, fruity red at 50 to 55 degrees. Rosés and simpler whites can be served at 45 degrees or even a little cooler. A digital thermometer inserted in the bottle neck will provide an instant progress report.

March 1999

For a Tastier Wine, the Next Trick Involves . . .

By HAROLD McGEE

I have used my carbon steel knife to cut up all kinds of meats and vegetables, but I had never thought of using it to prepare wine. Not until a couple of weeks ago, when I dunked the tip of it into glasses of several reds and whites, sometimes alone, sometimes with a sterling silver spoon, a gold ring or a well-scrubbed penny. My electrical multimeter showed that these metals were stimulating the wines with a good tenth of a volt. I tingled with anticipation every time I took a sip.

My foray into altering wine flavor with knives and pennies ended in failure. But it was one small part of a fruitful inquiry in which I learned new ways to get rid of unwanted aromas, including the taint of corked wine, and what aeration can really do for wine flavor.

It all began when a colleague sent me the Wine Wand, a glass device that is said to speed the aeration of a freshly opened wine and bring it to its "peak flavor" in minutes. During his blind tasting, my colleague found that the wand seemed to soften the flavor of several wines almost as well as an hour's decanting.

The Wine Wand is a hollow glass tube that has a large cut-glass knob at one end and contains a rattling handful of pierced faceted balls that look like costume jewelry beads. A small wand for use in a wineglass sells for $325, with a travel case. A larger version that fits in a bottle is $525, with case.

The promotional literature explains that the wand speeds aeration by means of "permanently embedded frequencies, one of them being oxygen."

This sounds like pseudoscience, and I couldn't imagine how a glass tube could alter the aeration of wine, apart from dragging in some air as it is inserted into the bottle or glass. Yet when I and two dinner companions compared glasses of a red and a white wine with and without the Wine Wand, we found some differences.

I soon discovered that the wand is one of several wine-enhancement devices marketed to drinkers who can't wait for their wines to taste their best. But it doesn't come with the weirdest explanation. That distinction belongs to a bottle collar that claims to modify a wine's tannins. With magnets.

A couple of wine-enhancement devices simply aerate wine, just as sloshing it around in the bottle or glass would. There is a battery-powered frother, and a small glass channel that adds turbulence and air bubbles as the wine flows through it from the bottle into the glass.

More intriguing was something called the Clef du Vin, or "key to wine," a patented French product sold in several sizes, starting with a pocket size that costs about $100. It consists of a quarter-inch disc of copper alloyed with small amounts of silver and gold, embedded in a thin stainless-steel plate. The user is directed to dip the disc briefly into a glass of wine. A dip lasting one second is said to have the same effect as one year of cellar aging.

Copper, silver and gold are all known to react directly with the sulfur compounds found in wine. Copper (and the iron in my knife) also catalyzes the reaction of oxygen with many molecules. Slow oxidation in the bottle is known to cause the tannins in aged red wines to become less astringent, and it's widely believed that aerating a young red, for example by decanting it, promotes rapid oxidation and softens its tannins.

Maybe this Clef was something more than a gimmick.

To help me evaluate the Wand, the Clef and the whole idea of enhancing freshly opened wine, I called on two friends, Andrew Waterhouse and Darrell Corti. Mr. Waterhouse is a professor of wine chemistry at the University of California, Davis, and a specialist in oxidation reactions and phenolic substances, including tannins. Mr. Corti is the proprietor of Corti Brothers grocery in Sacramento, one of the most influential wine retailers in California, and a recent inductee into the Vintners Hall of Fame.

We met at Mr. Corti's house for an afternoon of taste tests, lunch and discussion. Some tests were blind, others open-eyed. By the end, we had indeed detected some differences between carafes and glasses of wine that were treated with the Wand or the Clef, and the wines that were left alone. The differences were not great, and not always in favor of the treated wine, which usually seemed to be missing something.

Mr. Corti said: "There do seem to be differences. The question is, are they important differences? You could buy a lot of good wine for the price of that wand."

He also pointed out that the Clef is a very expensive version of the copper pennies that home vintners have long dipped into wine to remove the cooked-egg smell of excess hydrogen sulfide.

Mr. Waterhouse thought the elimination of sulfur aromas is all that these accessories—or, for that matter, aeration—had to offer.

"A number of sulfur compounds are present in wine in traces and have an impact on flavor because they're very potent," he said. "Some are unpleasant and some contribute to a wine's complexity. You can certainly dispose of these in five minutes with a little oxygen and a small area of metal catalyst to speed the reactions up, and change your impression of the wine."

But Mr. Waterhouse maintained that no brief treatment could convert the tannins to less astringent, softer forms, not even an hour in a decanter.

"You can saturate a wine with oxygen by sloshing it into a decanter, but then the oxygen just sits there," he said. "It reacts very slowly. To change the tannins perceptibly in an hour, you would have to hit the wine with pure oxygen, high pressure and temperature, and powdered iron with a huge catalytic surface area."

So why do people think decanting softens a wine's astringency?

"I think that this impression of softening comes from the loss of the unpleasant sulfur compounds, which reduces our overall perception of harshness," Mr. Waterhouse said.

With devices debunked and aeration unmasked as simple subtraction, the conversation turned to genuinely useful tips for handling wine.

Mr. Waterhouse said that the obnoxious, dank flavor of a "corked" wine, which usually renders it unusable even in cooking, can be removed by pouring the wine into a bowl with a sheet of plastic wrap.

"It's kind of messy, but very effective in just a few minutes," he said. The culprit molecule in infected corks, 2,4,6-trichloroanisole, is chemically similar to polyethylene and sticks to the plastic.

He also counseled a relaxed approach to wine storage, which he adopted in the 1980s after moving from California to Louisiana and back.

Mr. Waterhouse had a small collection of fine wines that he kept for a few years in a New Orleans closet with no temperature control. When it came time to return to California, he thought there was no point in shipping wines that had probably been spoiled in the southern heat. So he started opening them.

"There was one bottle, I think a Concannon cabernet, that was absolutely spectacular," he recalled. "A lot of that wine had sat in our accelerated aging system and reached perfection.

"So there's no single optimal temperature for aging wines. I'd tell people who don't keep wine for decades to forget about cellar temperatures. Take those big reds and put them on top of the refrigerator, the most heat-abusive place you can find, and in three years they'll probably be at their peak."

Mr. Corti agreed.

"Wine is like a baby," he said. "It's a lot hardier than people give it credit for."

January 2009

CHAPTER TWELVE

They Don't Make 'Em Like That Anymore

His Big Idea Is to Get Small

By ERIC ASIMOV

Randall Grahm is a changed man, again. But this time he thinks he means it.

Those who have followed him on his 25-odd-year journey as winemaker, jester and all-around philosopher king of Bonny Doon Vineyard have gotten used to the periodic pivots that twist his vinous trajectory like one of Escher's Moebius bands. But then, straight lines never really fit the Bonny Doon aesthetic.

Since its inception in 1983, Bonny Doon often seemed one step ahead of the rest of the California wine industry, yet incapable of prolonged focus. Mr. Grahm began with a fascination with pinot noir. He became a leading voice in California promoting Rhône grapes, and then, just as vigorously, touted Italian grapes, the obscurer the better. There was riesling, too, and delicious sweet wines. At its peak, in 2006, Bonny Doon sold some 450,000 cases of wine, more than 5 million bottles.

But, as anyone so philosophically inclined might wonder, what did it all mean? Mr. Grahm, 56, indeed asked himself that question, just a few years ago, and the answer was not satisfying.

"I took stock of my situation," he said, as we sat down recently in the new tasting room of his winery, which, not surprisingly, occupies an old granola factory here in this free-spirited university town. "My wines were O.K., but was I really doing anything distinctive or special? The world doesn't need these wines—I was writing and talking about terroir but I wasn't doing what I was saying. I wanted to be congruent with myself."

What followed was a paring back. Mr. Grahm sold off moneymaking labels like Big House and spun off Pacific Rim, under which he sold a lot of riesling. Gone were popular Bonny Doon wines like Old Telegram and, my personal favorite, Clos de Gilroy, a lively, fresh grenache that was as good on a hot summer's day as it was at Thanksgiving. Production has dropped to 35,000 cases.

As Mr. Grahm saw it, these may have been profitable wines, but not original wines. All told, the lineup of 35 different wines has been reduced to around 10, still a fair number.

"I know, I know, but what can I do?" Mr. Grahm said, throwing up his hands. "Honestly, it doesn't matter whether we make a few wines or a lot of wines. What matters is that we make wines of originality that have a reason for being.

"The question is, how do you create the conditions for originality?"

For Mr. Grahm, that means owning a vineyard, embracing biodynamic viticulture and farming without irrigation, as the best Old World vineyards are farmed. "Dry farming is absolutely crucial," he said. "It's more important than anything—biodynamics, schmiodynamics."

The last requirement rules out Bonny Doon's Ca' del Solo vineyard outside Soledad in Monterey County, where it is so dry Mr. Grahm is obliged to irrigate. "In retrospect, I shouldn't have planted a vineyard in Soledad, but I did," he said.

Seeking land that could be dry-farmed and that was in driving distance of his base in Santa Cruz ("It's my 'hood, and these are my peeps!") brought Mr. Grahm to some unusual sites for a new vineyard. He settled on 280 acres on a northeast-facing hillside outside San Juan Bautista, a mission town about 35 miles east of Santa Cruz.

It has not been a smooth process, but barring worldwide catastrophe, as Mr. Grahm put it, he is due to close on the parcel within a few weeks. He already has goats grazing the land, while a geomancer has helped ease his fear that the site will not have enough water.

"You could say it's just a real estate deal, but it's really been an existential struggle," he said.

With his frizzy, graying hair tied back in a ponytail, his black-rimmed glasses perched slightly askew on his nose, one tip of his shirt collar lapping over the lapel of a rumpled jacket, Mr. Grahm looks the part of an aging hippie who found a way to prolong graduate school indefinitely, at someone else's expense.

That's always been part of his roguish appeal—the ability to entertain, to charm, to fascinate and ultimately to get by, with comic wine labels, cosmic puns, rococo satires and elaborately staged publicity stunts. He was the philosopher as ringmaster. He was also contradictory, or perhaps refreshingly honest, speaking reverentially of terroir, yet rarely finding terroir expressed in his own wines, even if they were usually pretty good. Why original wines? Why now?

In the course of the last six years, since he and his partner, Chinshu Huang, had a daughter, Amélie, their first child, Mr. Grahm has had something of a conversion experience. First he had a health crisis, a bout with osteomyelitis, that left him in a haze of IV drugs and wearing a halo brace for three months.

"It was like getting hit by a meteor," he said. "You realize you take your body for granted and everything else for granted."

Taking stock of what he had been doing did not leave him feeling particularly proud.

"I actively resorted to all manner of marketing tricks," he said, as if standing before the congregation to confess.

"I don't want to rely on winemaking tricks anymore," he said, enumerating aroma-enhancing yeasts, enzymes and spinning cones among the modern techniques he's used to change the composition of a wine. "You can't make an original wine that way. You can make something clever or artful, but not great."

In a sense, Mr. Grahm had been on one big business bender since 1994, when his original Bonny Doon Vineyard in the Santa Cruz Mountains succumbed to Pierce's disease, an incurable bacterial disorder.

"It was definitely a loss of mojo at that point," he said. "I decided I'll just sit on the sidelines and buy grapes and think a while."

Instead, he became a phenomenal negotiant, buying grapes not only from all over California, but from Oregon, and even from France and Germany.

"I think Randall Grahm is the smartest winemaker I've ever met," said Jim Clendenen, a fellow larger-than-life California winemaker who owns Au Bon Climat in Santa Barbara County. "The decisions I've made based on advice he gave me back in the '80s have served me very well indeed."

He recalled in particular Mr. Grahm's observation in the mid-'80s that Americans were so obsessed with chardonnay that a winery could make a lot of money if it produced 80 percent chardonnay and less red wine. It was advice Mr. Clendenen followed, even as Mr. Grahm himself never acted on the thought.

"It was the smartest thing I'd ever done," Mr. Clendenen said. "He didn't always take his prognosticating as seriously as I did."

This time, Mr. Grahm seems determined to follow his own muse. Standing on the hillside of his prospective vineyard on a crisp, clear afternoon, he gazed off at the lettuce groves in the valley. "I think this place can make something really distinctive and unusual," he said. "You have to put your money where your mouth is. Purchased grapes are less risky, but you're never going to make a vin de terroir."

Assuming the purchase goes through, it may be six or seven years before Mr. Grahm can make wine from the site, leaving him the challenge of making the intervening time feel vital. Still, he has a winery to run. Cash must flow to finance the plan. And in the meantime, he's got no shortage of fascinations.

He dreams of growing vines from seeds, unheard of in this post-phylloxera era of rootstocks and cuttings and grafts. He is intrigued by wines made in amphorae, as cutting-edge producers are doing in northeastern Italy. There is the ongoing challenge of screwcaps, used on all his wines since 2002. Changing over from cork has presented a different set of unforeseen problems.

"We're still mastering the screwcap," he said. "It's like the sorcerer's apprentice. It's extremely powerful technology and you want to channel it in the proper direction."

Back at the old granola factory, the winery is divided into two segments. In one are wooden puncheons and tanks—conventional looking, at least. In the other cellar, dozens of glass carboys line one wall. Inspired by Emidio Pepe, a producer in Abruzzo who ages his wines in glass for years, Mr. Grahm is using the carboys to age a portion of his 2008 Cigare Volant, his southern Rhône blend, to be compared with a similar lot aging in wood.

"This is either going to revolutionize everything we do, or not," he said. "But I think it will."

Mr. Grahm likes to say that wine is a reflection of the human psyche. No doubt 25 years of whimsical, mercurial wines have been a reflection of his own. Now he is hoping his next adventure will reflect his newfound dedication.

"I'm taking a risk, but it's a rational risk," he said. "Maybe it'll turn out great, maybe not. But I'll have made a sincere effort to create something new and strange and different, which may be the best you can hope for in the New World."

April 2009

The Tastes of a Century

By FRANK J. PRIAL

André Tchelistcheff was a teenager when the Russian Revolution began, living on his family's estate east of Moscow and planning to become a physician. Today, approaching 90, he lives in a modest house here on the edge of California's wine country.

He never became a physician. He became one of America's—and the world's—most prominent enologists, an honor that, by the way, he has no immediate plans to relinquish.

From 1938 to 1972, he was the chief winemaker at Beaulieu Vineyards, where his name became permanently linked with one of America's greatest wines, Georges de Latour Private Reserve. As a consultant to countless other wineries and mentor to several generations of winemakers over more than 60 years, he had a hand in creating the modern California wine industry.

He spends more time in airplanes and on the road than men who are a third his age. His wife, Dorothy, drives him now; he stopped driving last year after he destroyed his Nissan sports car in an accident near here. He emerged virtually unscathed.

Until recently he had 13 major winery clients in California, Washington State and Italy. Last week, he gave up most of them to return to a job he held 53 years ago, working with Beaulieu Vineyards here in the Napa Valley. Mr. Tchelistcheff (pronounced CHEL-a-chev) was the company's principal winemaker from 1938 to 1972. Now he will be a consulting enologist.

"I am not looking for a new career, my dear sir," he tells a visitor; "I am not going back to compete. But I still have work I want to do." And his remarkable face crinkles into a smile.

Meeting Mr. Tchelistcheff for the first time can be a mild cultural shock. He is a compact man, barely 5 feet tall. His manner is courtly, his dress elegant. Even when he relaxes at home, his sweater is draped modishly around his slight shoulders.

His voice is heavily accented, easier to understand in French than English. "Well, when I think of wine, I think in French," he says. His long Slavic face recalls portraits of Nijinsky or perhaps an icon of some forgotten Orthodox saint. Slanted eyes seem to close entirely when he smiles, which is often.

After the Bolshevik victory, he fled to Western Europe. "I saw Communism as a brief cycle in Russian history," he said the other day. "I knew the country would need agricultural specialists one day so, in exile, I studied agronomy."

It was as an agronomist that he settled in France, and it was in France that he became interested in wine and the vines that produce it. Georges de Latour, a native of the Dordogne and the founder of Beaulieu Vineyards, returned to France in 1938 to find a new winemaker. Someone suggested the young Russian émigré André Tchelistcheff, and the rest is California wine history.

Mr. Tchelistcheff is quick to dispel myths about his career at Beaulieu and to credit his mentor for the creation of Georges de Latour Private Reserve, California's first great collectible wine. "I did not create the Private Reserve," he said; "Monsieur de Latour did. I was not the one who first aged the wine in small oak barrels; he was."

The first vintage was produced in 1936, two years before Mr. Tchelistcheff's arrival. The winery recently celebrated the wine's 50th anniversary by releasing the 1986 vintage.

Just what a winemaker does is unclear to most wine enthusiasts, but they lionize their favorite winemakers, much as experts on food anointed favorite chefs. Mr. Tchelistcheff detests the phenomenon of wine-maker-as-media-star, though he may have been its earliest example. "It means that the winemaker must go out and sell the wine," he said. "And that is not his or her job."

Winemakers are chemists and microbiologists who spend most of their time in laboratories, removed from any glamour in the wine business: the harvest, the crush, the fermentation and, of course, the parties.

In fact, to call Mr. Tchelistcheff an enologist is not entirely accurate, even if he has spent much of his life in a laboratory. He believes wine is born in the vineyard, which has long been the most neglected part of winemaking.

"We begin in the vineyard," he said, "and, always, we must come back to the vineyard. Finally, finally, after so many years, the California winemakers are beginning to come back to the soil.

"I think," he continued, "that it was a question of prestige. The winemaker wore a white coat; he was a scientist; he knew the secrets. The grower was a dirt farmer. What did he know of fine wines?"

Beginning with the 1930s and '40s, when scientists were identifying particular climates in California, the weather has always been the primary concern of California winemakers. But in recent years, more and more winemakers have come to appreciate European's emphasis on soil and plant culture.

The singular qualities of the B. V. Private Reserve have always been born in the soil, Mr. Tchelistcheff said—the special soil of the famous Rutherford Bench region, where the best Beaulieu grapes are grown.

The current phylloxera epidemic, which is ravaging California vineyards, would never have come if the industry had paid more attention to vine selection 20 years ago, he believes. "Commercial interests prevailed," he said. "There are vines that are completely resistant to the phylloxera, but they don't produce as well. So now the good producers are being pulled out at enormous cost. It is a real tragedy."

Mr. Tchelistcheff's reputation is founded on cabernet sauvignon. Beaulieu Vineyards Private Reserve is 100 percent cabernet sauvignon, a product that he might change now for a more Bordeaux-styled blend.

He may have made great wines from cabernet, the grape of Bordeaux, but he confesses that his own weakness is for pinot noir, the grape of Burgundy. "I don't drink much wine anymore," he said. "After tasting 30 or 40 wines in a day, I'm too tired. But when we do drink, my wife and I prefer a good Burgundy."

Which may help to explain why his own favorites among the many wines he has made over 60 harvests were two pinots noirs, the 1946 and 1947 vintages. He admits he has no idea why those two were so good and subsequent ones were not. But now, at the age of 89, he hopes to find out. "I want to work on pinot noir," he said. "I would like once again to make a truly fine pinot noir."

As with the 100 percent cabernet, Mr. Tchelistcheff's ideas have changed over the years. "So much has happened in the laboratory, in the cellar and in the vineyard," he said. "I would never take today some of the advice I gave to people 50 years ago.

"For example," he said, "the first Private Reserves, the two made by my predecessor Leon Bonnet, were aged in French oak, barrels Monsieur Latour had bought in France in the 1920s. I changed over to American oak because I wanted more flavor, a more aggressive wine. Today I dislike the American oak and would go back to French."

Mr. Tchelistcheff has always had other clients. Over the years, he did work for Robert Mondavi, Louis M. Martini, Franciscan Vineyards, Conn Creek, Clos Pegase, Swanson, Firestone, Jordan, Buena Vista, Villa Mt. Eden and Atlas Peak, in California; Chateau Ste. Michelle, in Washington, Antinori, in Italy.

Why, over the long span of his career, was there never a Tchelistcheff winery?

"Because I never had the courage," he said, with a touch of irony. "There were plenty of offers. People with money who wanted to be my partners. But remember, I am a child of revolution. I know what it means to lose everything overnight.

"No, I am not a rich man, but I enjoy my life this way: independent."

Few people become rich in the wine business, but some become famous, at least in the industry. Many worked for Mr. Tchelistcheff. Among them: Theo Rosenbrand, who worked at Sterling Vineyards and is now consulting; Joe Heitz of Heitz Cellars, whose Martha's Vineyard cabernet has long rivaled B. V. Private Reserve; Richard Peterson, who headed Monterey Vineyards and later Atlas Peak; Mary Ann Graf, former winemaker at Simi and now also a consultant; and Jill Davis, the winemaker at Buena Vista.

"There is still another generation of winemakers coming along," Mr. Tchelistcheff said, "and they will lead California in directions we don't even think of now." He predicts that chardonnay and cabernet will fade as the dominant varieties—"I do not believe in the duration of the American market" is the way he puts it—and that there will be more and more interest in other varieties, particularly those of the Rhône Valley in France and of Northern Italy that are now grown in California.

"Ah, but to create a great Hermitage—that will take time. It took many centuries in France. And, too, the soils are so specific in the Rhône. I don't think there is any way we will ever duplicate a great Côte Rotie here.

"Now the Sangiovese, from Italy, that's another story. I have tasted the '86s and '87s in barrel and they are beautiful, beautiful, beautiful!"

But it takes time to create a great wine, and time is money.

André Tchelistcheff is well aware that he will not be around to see many of the changes he predicts. "I don't have much time left," he says, but not in sorrow or anger. He knows he has lived a long life and accomplished most of his goals.

One goal may be beyond his reach: to see his native Russia one last time. "Some friends went," he said. "They told me the estate is gone but that in the graveyard they found the cross of my grandfather's tomb. Oh, I would like to see that."

Once, years ago, he was invited to come to the Soviet Union as a wine consultant but, as an old White Russian, he was denied a visa. Now he is free to go but he worries about his diet. "Perhaps," he says, smiling. "It may happen. One never knows."

January 1991

A Twilight Nightcap With Alistair Cooke

By FRANK J. PRIAL

Not so many years ago, but before e-mail, I received a letter, obviously produced on a well-worn typewriter, from Alistair Cooke, the renowned broadcaster and newsman who died last week at 95. How was it, he wanted to know, that *The New York Times* so rarely devoted any space to German wines? Was it a question of personal distaste, some commercial consideration or just an unfortunate oversight?

I responded promptly, noting that none of his suggestions applied. I suggested a lunch at which this thorny problem could be discussed at length. It's what reporters do: open the door an inch to them and they insinuate—I hesitate to say "force"—themselves in the rest of the way.

Mr. Cooke was notoriously reluctant to grant interviews, probably because after conducting so many himself, he knew how easily things could go awry. I had no intention of pushing for anything beyond the lunch, but still, one never knew.

We met at the Carlyle, not far from his home at Fifth Avenue and 96th Street, and we did, indeed, share a good riesling. Alas, I can no longer recall its name. Mr. Cooke was well known at the hotel and was treated with the deference due to a legendary figure then in his 80s. I knew it was going to be an interesting day when a Babbitt-like fellow approached the table and, addressing himself to Mr. Cooke, said, "I know you, but I can't remember your name."

"Bob Hope," Mr. Cooke said. He chuckled softly as the interloper backed off in confusion. "I do that all the time. They know I'm not Hope, but they don't know what to say, and they leave."

We talked about the old Ambassador liquor store on East 86th Street, which specialized in German wines. We talked about trips through the German wine country, touching on Wagner and Siegfried's Rhine journey. I explained that enthusiasts like him were as rare as old trockenbeerenausleses. So rare, in fact, that growers in the Rheingau were then desperately planting chardonnay in vineyards where riesling had ruled since the time of Charlemagne.

Of course, some good German wines were around, and we shared a few at subsequent lunches. Alistair—we were on a first-name basis by then—may not have been a willing interviewee, but he was a brilliant raconteur. Imperceptibly, he warmed to the idea of some kind of profile, even supplying the kind of anecdotes that would make it work. He recalled, for example, that H. L. Mencken, an early mentor and lover of all things Germanic, knew a thing or two about the riesling grape as well. But while Mencken, the Sage of Baltimore, enjoyed a good hock when the occasion called for it, he was essentially a beer drinker. Mr. Cooke soon surpassed him in wine sophistication.

Mr. Cooke said that during his middle years, at the height of his popularity, he drank whatever was fashionable in wines and spirits, returning to his early love, riesling, only later in life. After the profile appeared in *The Times,* in 1999, we saw each other less frequently until two or three years ago, when he called to say he was trapped, so to speak, in his apartment, at his doctors' insistence. His heart couldn't take the effort necessary to get out of the house and back. No more lunches, no more riesling—which incidentally, had regained much of its popularity. Would I come by for a drink? I did, and we had Scotch.

One night, with some family members there, he brought out a bottle of a California wine favored by his stepson, Stephen Hawkes, who grows wine grapes in Sonoma County. Everyone had a glass but Mr. Cooke. "Better not," he said. "I'll stick with my Scotch." A single Scotch, not too strong.

Early last month, he called to say that his long career was reaching its end, that his doctors had advised him to stop doing his weekly "Letter From America" for the BBC. The news would be kept secret for several days, but, he said, he wanted to give me time to put something together in advance.

Of course the secret didn't keep. Secrets never do. Someone leaked the story in London, and I had to write something quickly.

I went uptown to see him. We had our Scotch—"the wine of Scotland," he called it—and chatted for a while, and I left. His health was far more precarious than he had let on over the phone. His doctors had given him three to six months to live. He didn't want that mentioned.

The article appeared several days later. Mr. Cooke was on the phone that morning, his voice as strong and elegant as it had ever been on television or radio. "I have some problems with your article," he said sternly. He had in fact identified a minor grammatical glitch, and he objected to having been characterized as "proud" of his accomplishments. He would have preferred "satisfied." But he was furious about a quotation—"the wine of Scotland."

"No, no," he said. "It should be 'the twilight wine of Scotland,' a much more beautiful phrase." As indeed it is. "You must get it right if you use it again," he ordered. And so, today, I have gotten it right.

It was our last conversation. We began with wine; we ended with whiskey. A good friendship.

April 2004

A Wine Man Who Vowed to Drain the Cup

By FRANK J. PRIAL

Back in the early 1990s Len Evans, the Australian wine man and legend in his own lifetime, gave me some advice.

"I'd say you're about 60," he said, "and from the looks of you, you'll be lucky to make 75. You've got about 15 years ahead of you, and it's time for you to learn my Theory of Capacity.

"You've got to make the most of the time you've got left, man. You've got to calculate your future capacity. A bottle of wine a day is 365 bottles a year. Which means you've probably only got 5,000 bottles ahead of you.

"People who say you can't drink good stuff all the time are fools. You must drink good stuff all the time. Every bottle of inferior wine you drink is like smashing a superior bottle against a wall: the pleasure is lost forever. You can't get that bottle back."

Leonard Paul Evans, who died on Aug. 17 at 75, practiced what he preached. For years he made no decision, held no meeting, started no venture without first opening a bottle of Krug Champagne. He switched to Bollinger when that house invested in one of his wineries.

One day in 1984, or perhaps 1985, a winemaker from Burgundy and his wife stopped by Len's home in Pokolbin, about 75 miles north of Sydney, for lunch. After a meal with some good Australian wines, he took them to his winery, Rothbury Estates, for a tour and tasting. They finished off the afternoon with two or three bottles of Champagne.

Back at the house, just before the guests were to leave, a friend turned up with an enormous fish. A skilled cook, Len prevailed upon the French couple to stay and help eat the fish. More wine was consumed, games were played and, Len recalled for his biographer, Jeremy Oliver, "someone sang all the arias from an opera, doing all four parts and most of the duets and quartets."

Lunch finished around midnight. The next day, it was determined that the party of 10 had downed 37 bottles of wine and, Len insisted, "none were ever drunk—perhaps a little happy and intoxicated."

As a boy in England Len was introduced to wine by his father, but it made little impression on him. He was set on becoming a professional golfer. When that did not happen, he moved to New Zealand, where he worked as a forester.

Two years later, he moved to Australia, where he ran a duck farm, made auto mufflers, wrote scripts for radio and television and gave golf lessons on weekends.

From washing glasses in a bar in Sydney, he graduated to a job as food and beverage manager of a large hotel there. In 1968 he opened his own restaurant in Sydney, Bulletin Place, which included a retail wine shop and tasting rooms. Soon he formed a Friday Lunch Club, a Monday Lunch Club and, in 1977, the Single Bottle Club, dedicated to drinking very old wines.

The menu of the first Single Bottle dinner was graced with wines like a dry oloroso sherry from 1796, a Clos de la Roche Burgundy from 1921 and, with the beef, a 1928 Château Haut-Brion. After dinner, the guests partook of a tasting that included an 1898 Château Ausone, an 1893 and a 1987 Lafite-Rothschild, an 1825 Château Gruaud Larose and, from Germany, a Rüdesheimer Apostelwein from 1727.

I first met Len in the early 1970s at a lunch Robert Mondavi gave for him at the Mondavi winery in the Napa Valley. A short, compact fellow with an easy grin and a boxer's athletic grace, he had James Cagney's pugnacious charm.

Len had brought with him a bottle of Grange Hermitage, long reputed to be Australia's best wine but still unknown to the winemakers around the table. After tasting it, one guest, André Tchelistcheff, then with Beaulieu Vineyard, bowed deeply before Len as a way to express his feeling about the wine.

Len eventually bought a vineyard in the Napa Valley, along with two chateaus in Bordeaux, only to lose them, and a lot more, when his friend and financial backer, Peter Fox, rammed his Ferrari into a tree and was killed. It took years, but Len paid his debts and prospered once again.

Len was far more than a Rabelaisian show-off, even if he reveled in that role. An indefatigable traveler and promoter, he took his message, and Australian wines, all over the world. He lived to see an Australian wine, Yellow Tail, reach sales in this country of over eight million cases a year in less than five years, and he saw Australian wines, once the target of jokes in Britain, surpass French wines in sales there.

To hear it, Len's recounting of his Theory of Capacity was a comedic masterpiece. (He estimated in 1976 that he probably had only 8,000 bottles left to him—along with about 2,500 "succulent steaks." What's more, he said ruefully, "I might make love only another 5,000 times.")

But there was a somber side to his merriment. His frantic pace and gargantuan appetites for food, wine and life served to mask the fact that he was beset with, if not particularly hampered by, heart trouble. He had an angina attack in 1976 and a bypass operation in 1988. "If there is a key to me," he once told Mr. Oliver, "it is my energy. Never ambition; always energy."

He seemed barely to sleep. He wrote, he painted, he worked with ceramics and tiles. He designed his home and had it built using old ironwood pilings pulled from the Sydney Harbor site where the famous opera house was being built. He sculptured massive pieces resembling the heads on Easter Island. He boasted that he had a collection of the world's dullest books. (I contributed one of my favorites, *The Speeches of Enver Hoxha*.) He often said he had no time to lose.

Len died suddenly while parking his car at a hospital where he had gone to pick up a relative who had had surgery.

When he spoke of the end of life, he liked to quote Byron, who once observed that all farewells should be sudden, when forever. His was just that.

August 2006

Remembrances of a
Champion of the Champagne World

By FRANK J. PRIAL

Christian Bizot was a Parisian by birth but a true Champenois by nature. Warm and generous when you came to know him, he was outwardly formal and even a bit austere, like the Champagne country itself.

That's only fitting, as Mr. Bizot had a long career at Champagne Bollinger, one of France's foremost Champagne makers. He retired as its chairman in 1998. Mr. Bizot died on July 7 at age 73 at his summer home near Grenoble, France, not long after playing a round of golf.

Mr. Bizot was more than a premier winemaker: he was one of the strongest advocates of ethical standards in the wine industry. Originally destined to be a banker, he was needed elsewhere, specifically at Aÿ, a little wine village near Épernay in the Champagne region. There, when he was a young man, the famous house of Bollinger was presided over by his aunt Elizabeth, widow of Jacques Bollinger, grandson of the founder of the company.

Known as Lily to her family and Madame Jacques to the workers in the vineyards and cellars, she presided over the firm until she retired in 1971. One of her nephews, Claude d'Hautefeuille, ran the company until 1978, when Mr. Bizot took over as president.

Christian Bizot's mother was Guillemette Law de Lauriston-Boubers, Lily Bollinger's younger sister. His father was Henri Bizot, president of the Banque National de Paris. Christian attended Jesuit schools in Paris, served in the French Army in Saumur and Morocco, and apprenticed in a Paris bank before switching to the wine business. He worked in the cellars at Veuve Clicquot in Rheims, spent some time in the British wine trade with the wine merchants Corney & Barrow, then went to New York to work for Julius Wile Sons & Company. There, he recounted in later years, he drove 25,000 miles though the United States, selling wine.

He joined Bollinger in 1952, at age 24, and in 1994 became chairman of Jacques Bollinger & Company, a holding company he created to fend off possible takeovers. Bollinger remains one of the few family-owned major Champagne houses.

But perhaps his greatest contribution was serving as standard-bearer for the industry. In the 1980s, the Champagne business was faltering. Its impeccable reputation, which had taken several centuries to create, was suffering from a pro-liferation of mediocre or poor wine. To many it recalled the time just before World War I when workers rioted because the Champagne houses were importing cheap wine from other parts of France and selling it as their own. Devoted Champagne drinkers were turning to other wines, and importers in London and New York were complaining bitterly.

In 1988, Mr. Bizot created the Madame Bollinger Foundation to promote ethical and professional standards in the industry. The foundation's first grant was $45,000 to the Institute of Masters of Wine in London, an educational orga-nization supported by the English wine trade.

In 1992, Mr. Bizot released the Bollinger Charter of Ethics and Quality. It was a statement of principle in which the firm committed itself to following the highest winemaking standards and, by implication, challenged its competitors to do the same.

Some winemakers in Champagne derided the charter as a bit of grand-standing, but there was no doubt that too many of them were declaring vintages when the wines didn't deserve it, and too many were releasing nonvintage wines that were thin and acidic. It may be coincidental, but Champagne quality has improved markedly since the Bollinger Charter was promulgated. Ghislain de Montgolfier, who now runs Bollinger, has said that the charter will stand as a major event in Champagne history.

Champagne is often judged in terms of its strength and power. Some Champagnes are light and delicate (Taittinger), most are medium bodied (Pol Roger) and some are big and robust (Bollinger, Krug, Veuve Clicquot). That is not surprising, considering that the Champagne region encompasses 79,000 acres, about 300 wine villages and five separate subappellations, and produces 200 million bottles a year.

Bollinger's line includes its nonvintage Special Cuvée, the vintage Grande Année, the vintage Vieilles Vignes Françaises (Old French Vines) and the vintage Bollinger R. D. (Récemment Dégorgé, or recently disgorged). The R. D. is Champagne in which the lees or residue of the original yeast are left in the bottle for many years to add strength to the wine. In most Champagnes, disgorgement takes place about two years after bottling. The 1979 Bollinger R. D. was disgorged in 1999.

Bollinger wines last. On separate years at the Bizot table in Aÿ, I tasted the 1911 and 1914 vintages, both still alive and well. In 2000, Tom Stevenson, a British writer, described the 1990 Vieilles Vignes as "the beast of Bollinger," a "hulking great blanc de noirs" and "a massive mouthful of fabulously rich, mind-bogglingly complex fruit." A bit over the top, perhaps, but you get the idea.

Mr. Bizot is survived by his wife, Marie-Hélène, and five sons, all of them, like their father was, over six feet tall: Henry, Charles, Étienne, Guy and Xavier.

My most vivid recollection of Christian and Marie-Hélène was a day about 10 years ago when my wife and I had driven out to Aÿ from Paris for lunch. They received us warmly, excusing their casual dress and distracted air and only reluctantly explaining that we were a day early. In later years, he would slyly imply that it wasn't inept scheduling that had got us out of town that day, but rather an intense love of Bollinger Grande Année.

July 2002

The Greatest Vintages of Alfred Knopf, 90

By TERRY ROBARDS

A lfred A. Knopf, enophile, closely resembles Alfred A. Knopf, bibliophile. He is a collector of exquisite works, surrounding himself with the best, indulging a passion for the rare and exceptional, expressing intolerance for the mediocre and, at age 90, still keen about the differences.

"I rarely bought one case of any wine and never bought more than two," the publisher says, preparing to decant an old bottle here in the Tudor-style house where he has lived since 1928. In the small but exquisite cellar below, behind an oak door that is eight inches thick, lies the evidence of his passion.

In racks and bins are quantities of Château Lafite-Rothschild 1945 and 1959, Château Haut-Brion 1945, Château Latour 1945, 1953, 1959 and 1961, Château Canon 1929, Château Cheval Blanc 1929, 1949 and 1959, Château Pétrus 1959, Romanée-Conti 1964, Richebourg 1961, Clos Vougeot 1961 and other collector's items.

With one exception, the cellar contains no off-vintages or oddities. It holds only the best, reflecting the same devotion to quality and ability to recognize it that enabled Mr. Knopf to become perhaps the foremost book publisher of his time. Rarely acknowledged in all the accolades he has won over the years is that he was the dominant influence in gastronomic publishing in this country.

He had the temerity to publish P. Morton Shand's classic *Book of French Wines* in 1928, during Prohibition, and to come out with Julian Street's *Wines* in 1933, the year Prohibition ended, when the public's interest in wines was sharply curtailed by the Depression.

"We did it anyway," he says. "I was devoted to Street. We were all set to do that when Prohibition was repealed. The idea that anybody would get in the way of it or that it wouldn't sell had no bearing."

The roster of food and wine authors published by Alfred A. Knopf Inc. includes James Beard, Julia Child, M.F.K. Fisher, Marcella Hazan, Maida Heatter, Alexis Lichine and Michael Broadbent. Mr. Knopf himself has belonged to most of the leading gastronomic societies, including the Chevaliers du Tastevin, the Commanderie de Bordeaux, the Lucullus Circle and the Wine and Food Society of New York.

"I find wine is a drink that simply doesn't work if you sit down and drink a bottle all by yourself," he says, bemoaning the lack of mobility that has come with advancing age and the paucity of friends and acquaintances sufficiently sophisticated to appreciate what he has in his cellar.

"I always liked good food," he says. "I had a father who was terribly fussy." But he says his taste for wine came later: "Remember, you had to go through Prohibition, a very strange period. The only people that gave me a taste for wine were the Berrys and Lichine." The former was a reference to Berry Bros. & Rudd in London, a wine dealer famous among connoisseurs.

The one oddity in Mr. Knopf's cellar is a five-bottle cache of Château Lynch-Pontac 1893 given him one at a time by a friend who was unable to come any closer to his birth year. It seems that 1892 was a better vintage for publishers than for Bordeaux. Mr. Knopf has yet to find an appropriate moment to sample any of the wine that is only a year younger than he is.

"It's amazing," he says. "I would say that nine out of 10 people who come here don't want a drink of any kind. This is a big problem. They don't want a soft drink, they don't want a drink of water, they don't want anything." The impression is strong that the Knopf cellar has remained mostly untapped in recent years.

Within the last month, Mr. Knopf says, he shared a bottle of Pétrus 1959 with his doctor. "It was great," he says. But somehow he resists the temptation that all of those spectacular wines present. He is comfortable with the knowledge that they are there, waiting for just the right moment.

At the same time, Mr. Knopf has a reputation for responding with disdain when a guest asks for anything stronger than sherry as a cocktail. According to one story that has circulated for decades, a group of dinner guests, knowing of their host's disapproval of spirits, partook of a ration of martinis prior to their arrival.

The publisher, irked at what he regarded as the prematurely jovial state of his guests, told his butler, Alphonse, to refrain from serving wine with dinner that evening on the grounds that his guests had destroyed their palates.

According to another often-repeated story, a neighbor and close friend in Purchase became frustrated with years of drinking dry sherries at the Knopfs' in place of the martinis that he preferred. So he bribed Alphonse to lay in a supply of gin and vermouth and became the only guest regularly to receive the cocktail he wanted.

When asked if he still holds the same view about the consumption of spirits in his home, Mr. Knopf throws open the door of a buffet to disclose an array of liqueurs and spirits. He then ambles slowly into the pantry, where he opens a cupboard to disclose a further array of bottles. But they look dusty and unused, and the display does not represent a direct answer to the question.

"He gives them a glass and stares," says Helen Knopf, his wife. And both cite the example of the neighbor with the predilection for martinis as proof that hard liquor is in fact served in their household. Mr. Knopf himself says rum is an exception to his general aversion to spirits.

He likes to reminisce about his first wine trip to France with Alexis Lichine in 1950, just before he published *Wines of France,* and about visiting the Burgundy country with Mr. Lichine and Claude Philippe, the late chef of the Waldorf-Astoria. He recalls running out of gasoline en route to the Hotel de la Cote d'Or in Saulieu and having to buy some from a farmer.

He speaks of parties in the Hotel de Crillon in Paris, of drinking Champagne with Lily Bollinger and of sojourns at Château de Saran, the country house of Moët et Chandon that was built for Napoleon. He has kept diaries of his travels, recording the foods, the wines and the people he met during his visits to famous restaurants and vineyards all over the world.

One entry records lunch at the Hotel Bergerand in Chablis, where he ate sole in Chablis sauce, ham cooked in Chablis and an orange souffle. The wines were Chablis Les Preuses 1947, Chablis Blanchots 1947, Chablis Vaudesir 1947, 1948 and 1949, and Chablis Montée de Tonnerre in the same vintages.

Another luncheon, in Beaune, included many of the best-known Burgundy producers of the period, their names carefully recorded in Mr. Knopf's diary: Baron Thenard, Louis Gros, Henri Gouges, Pierre Damoy, Charles Noellat, René Engel and Claude Ramonet—a blue-ribbon roster.

Each evening Mr. Knopf meticulously wrote down the foods and wines and people encountered, the time dinner was served and often the number of hours at table, frequently adding notations about the weather or the automobile in which he was traveling.

His last trip to Europe was in 1968 ("I can't go again," he says). But the trips are all here, on lined paper in notebooks with covers of blue imitation leather, and in calling up those occasions from memory he frequently consults the words he recorded decades ago. His pronunciation of French is flawless as he runs through page after page, relishing the memories.

On this day, Mr. Knopf has an array of bottles on an oak sideboard in the dining room of his house. He is planning to demonstrate how he uses a basket or cradle and a funnel when decanting old red wines that contain sediment, a natural byproduct of aging. He has decided to decant and share a bottle with some guests, under the watchful eye of his wife.

On the sideboard are mostly younger wines, a Château Ducru-Beaucaillou 1971, a Nuits-Saint-Georges Les Perdrix 1971, a Clos de la Roche 1976, a Chateau Montelena 1978 from California and a Volnay-Santenot 1961 produced by René Roy. The Volnay, curiously lacking the final "s" that normally appears on Santenots, is the oldest and clearly the most likely to have sediment, so it is chosen.

It is lying on its side in a basket. As Mr. Knopf peels off the lead capsule covering the cork, he gestures toward a pewter funnel nearly a foot tall and says: "This is my secret. It's just a funnel, a piece of English pewter." Then he wields a plastic corkscrew, a Screwpull, which he calls "the best invention after the electric razor."

Inserting the corkscrew, he gently turns it and the cork begins to emerge. Then suddenly it splits in two, although it is mostly out of the bottle. "Well, not a very beautiful job," he observes, expertly inserting his little finger into the bottle to make sure no cork remains.

Now he puts the funnel into one of a pair of crystal decanters bearing the emblem of Château Lafite-Rothschild. He grasps the bottle, simultaneously wrapping his fingers around the basket, and pours the wine into the funnel.

"I believe in decanting any red wine," he says. "You can see when the wine ceases to be clear, and you just stop pouring." The wine is illuminated by a bulb in a wall sconce and by the wintry afternoon light coming through a nearby window overlooking the macadam driveway.

"It's got a nice color," he says and stops pouring. He sets the decanter in an ornate silver wine coaster on an antique harvest table and carefully seats himself on a bench. The aroma of mature Burgundy fills the air. Four of the glasses that Burgundians call "ballons" stand nearby.

"Somebody ought to pour the wine," he says to one of his guests. "I think you ought to do it." The Volnay is firm and full and rich, perhaps just a bit past its peak at age 21 but superb. A toast is proposed to a healthier, more prosperous 1983. "I'll drink to that," says Alfred Knopf, hoisting his glass.

January 1983

By Wine Besotted: A Fantasy Fulfilled

By ERIC ASIMOV

All wine collectors, no matter how small their hoards, have cellar fantasies. Whether they keep wines in hall closets, in special coolers, at their parents' houses or spilling out of basement corners, they harbor the dream of a cellar of their own. For the true believer, a collection is no mere cache of bottles but, even more than the eyes, a window into the soul. In the imagination a cellar is a sanctuary where the tactile act of communing with one's bottles can border on the religious.

For most people, of course, the wine cellar remains a fantasy. A select few maybe have achieved some portion of their dream, carving out a room to serve as their vinous retreat. But perhaps nobody has realized the vision in details so glorious as Park B. Smith, a textile entrepreneur who is also one of the world's great wine collectors.

In the limestone and shale beneath the weekend house that he and his wife, Linda, share in this little New England town in northwestern Connecticut, Mr. Smith has constructed a cellar of thousands of fantasies, covering almost 8,000 square feet and holding more than 65,000 bottles. As if that weren't enough, more than half of Mr. Smith's collection is in magnums, twice the size of normal bottles, and the count doesn't include the 14,000 bottles auctioned off by Sotheby's last November, which raised almost $5.33 million for his alma mater, the College of the Holy Cross in Worcester, Mass.

A cellar that size is no simple room. Mr. Smith's is actually seven cellars built over 25 years or so and joined together, each more elaborate than the last. What began in 1978 as a small, claustrophobic root cellar has evolved into rooms with double-height ceilings and columns, filled with Asian art accumulated during his business travels. To fulfill the kid-in-a-candy store fantasy, Mr. Smith added to his domain a full kitchen and bath, and a comfortable dining room with a sound system, all enclosed in smoky glass to protect his guests from the 53-degree chill of the cellar.

"If I've had a crummy week, I just come down here for a few hours and talk to my bottles," Mr. Smith said, giving voice to the desires of frustrated wine lovers everywhere. "Linda said, 'That's all right, as long as they don't start talking back to you.'"

Mr. Smith, 75, is so passionate about wine that he practically pulses with ardor. Still lean with a head of straight white hair and surprisingly white teeth for a man devoted to red wine, Mr. Smith bears a passing resemblance to the actor Jason Robards, especially in his assertive, slightly raspy voice and no-nonsense diction. He's a Jersey guy, born in Madison, a beer drinker who discovered wine while in the Marine Corps stationed at Camp Lejeune, N.C.

"I went to buy a six-pack and the store had a promotion, Beaujolais for 99 cents a bottle," he remembered. "So I bought one and tried it, and said, 'This isn't bad.'"

Soon he was a civilian again, in the textile business, flying regularly to Asia and enjoying wine. By the early 1970s he was stopping on his way back in California, visiting wineries and befriending talented winemakers like Warren Winiarski of Stag's Leap Wine Cellars and Dexter Ahlgren of Ahlgren Vineyard. The relationships he made seemed almost as important as the wines.

"Something happens to people who love wine," he said. "You really discover a camaraderie. It's not like coin collecting or something cynical. It's like sharing love in a glass."

The wines that Mr. Smith essentially gave away in the Sotheby's auction represent themselves a mind-boggling world-class collection: cases of La Tâche 1990 and 1985, Richebourg 1990 and Montrachet 1985 from Domaine de la Romanée-Conti; cases upon cases of first-growth Bordeaux, including one extraordinary lot of 50 cases of 1982 Mouton-Rothschild, which sold for $1,051,600; vertical collections of Harlan Estate and Araujo; and hundreds of bottles of Mr. Smith's beloved Châteauneuf-du-Pape, especially those from superstar producers like Château Rayas, Henri Bonneau, Domaine du Pegau and Château de Beaucastel.

But don't cry for Mr. Smith. It's true that six cases of Château Margaux 1982 went in the auction, but he still has 12 cases left.

Is it possible that Mr. Smith is a little excessive in his devotion?

"When I like something, I get a little carried away," he concedes.

No more so than after he discovered Châteauneuf-du-Pape, a wine that transfixes him to this day.

"I don't know any other wine that is so drinkable early on and ages so well," he said. "The first I had was a 1978. It was a magnificent year, and those wines are beautiful now."

Early on, he realized the importance of getting to know the winemakers, and he has established close relationships with even the most reclusive of them, like Mr. Bonneau. As a result, Mr. Smith is able to buy in quantity wines that border on cult objects, like the 2000 vintage of Pegau's Cuvée Capo, a wine that the critic

Robert M. Parker Jr., who Mr. Smith calls "my closest friend in life," awarded 100 points. Mr. Smith has 135 magnums of the Capo, the equivalent of 22 cases, in addition to myriad regular bottles.

It's a good thing Mr. Smith is a generous soul with an enthusiasm for opening bottles. A visit to his cellar rarely ends without him opening at least a handful of rare treasures—the count reached 14 over the course of a long lunch for five people late in January.

"Wine to me is an emotional thing—I've tried drinking alone but haven't done too well," he said. "A bottle of wine and a conversation with someone you like—wow!" He waved his hand over the glossy black dining table, littered with dozens of crystal glasses and the 14 bottles, including one Champagne; two 2003 Chave Hermitages, white and red; and 11 Châteauneufs including Cuvée Capo '03, '00 and '98; Bonneau Réserve des Célestins '90 and '89; Rayas '90, '89 and '78; and Beaucastel '66. "This is what I'm all about," he said.

Like even the smallest wine collector, Mr. Smith has had a problem outgrowing his storage space. By the time his fourth cellar was done, his first wife, Carol, who died in 2002, asked him a question.

"She said, 'If you never buy another bottle of wine in your life, and you drink a bottle each night with dinner, how long would it take you to drink up all you have?'" he recalled. "I said, 'I don't know, 25 or 30 years?' She said, 'Nope, 119 years!' I said, 'I got a problem.' We decided to open a restaurant."

That restaurant, Veritas, opened in 1998 with an extravagant wine list largely based on the collections of Mr. Smith and another partner, Steve Verlin, whose holdings of Burgundy and Champagne dovetailed with Mr. Smith's Châteauneufs, Bordeaux and California wines. But opening his collection to the Veritas clientele has by no means alleviated his storage challenge.

"We've added three more cellars since Veritas, so it wasn't quite the panacea we expected," Mr. Smith said.

February 2007

A Wine Spree Worth Savoring

By FRANK J. PRIAL

I was sitting at my desk in Paris one day in 1988 when the phone rang. It was Jean-Claude Vrinat, the owner and director of Taillevent, the famed Paris restaurant, who died of cancer last week at the age of 71.

Mr. Vrinat was beginning his summer vacation shortly, he said, and perhaps I might enjoy a day or two tasting wines with him in Burgundy. It was an offer no one interested in wine could refuse.

Mr. Vrinat was no ordinary restaurateur. Not only did he own perhaps the finest restaurant in Paris, but he also was a wine expert of long standing.

Most restaurants in France, then as now, were run by chefs, like Paul Bocuse and Georges Blanc. Most chefs started as poor boys hired to chop onions. They knew little about wine when they started, and after years in the kitchens, most still knew little about wine. In many restaurants, the wine stewards were there for the boss's benefit as much as the customers'.

Taillevent was started in 1946 by Mr. Vrinat's father, André, who had already won two Michelin stars when his son joined him in 1962. The elder Vrinat was not a chef, nor was his son. As François Simon, the food critic at *Le Figaro*, said of the younger Vrinat last week, "He didn't cook, but he knew exactly what good cooking should be."

Before he took over Taillevent in 1972, Mr. Vrinat served as the restaurant's wine steward and buyer. His wine knowledge was as vast as his patience with my questions.

I love Burgundy and after his invitation I envisioned two leisurely days in the country, sipping samples here, sharing a bottle or two there, our rustic idyll punctuated by at least one classic Burgundian feed, at Lameloise in Chagny, perhaps, or with Bernard Loiseau at La Côte d'Or in Saulieu. It would be unforgettable.

It was, but not as I had envisioned. We would stay at a motel in Beaune, he said, "and meet the next morning in the lobby at 7 a.m." Seven a.m.? Yes; there he was in the deserted lobby when I came down at 7:05. "Let's go," he said by way of greeting. "We'll be late." He had, I discovered, already been tasting for two days in southern Burgundy.

By 7:30 we were tasting in the bone-chilling cellars of François Jobard, a great white winemaker in Meursault, five miles south of Beaune. Mr. Jobard, a Harry Dean Stanton sort of guy, stood by nervous and silent while Mr. Vrinat and I tasted. By 8 a.m. we had been through his 1987 vintage, still in barrels; his '86s, some bottled, some in barrels, and some of his '85s, all bottled.

We thanked Mr. Jobard and were back on the road. By lunch time, we had done the Domaines Michelot and Sauzet, both also in Beaune, and, for our first red wine, the estate of the Marquis d' Angerville, one of the great old men of Burgundy, in Volnay.

In this country a wine tasting is often a social event. In fact, professional wine tasting can be exhausting, sampling small glasses of raw unfinished wine and trying to determine which will be the best two, three or perhaps 10 years hence. Reputations and a lot of money are at stake as the men and women who taste for a living are well aware. The concentration required is immense.

Finally, it was time for lunch. Where, I wondered as we drove north out of Beaune, does the owner of one of the great restaurants of the world stop for lunch? I didn't have to ask. "We'll get something to eat at the Rotisserie du Chambertin," Mr. Vrinat said. I knew the place, in the town of Gevrey-Chambertin, just south of Dijon, near the northern end of the main Burgundian vineyards. Mark Mennevaux and his wife, Céline, who did the cooking, were the owners. She was a great cook and I anticipated a couple of restful hours with good food and wine—out of a bottle, no sips.

It was not to be. The Mennevauxes were excited to see him. Not often does one get to cook for the owner of Taillevent. "Ah, M. Vrinat," they said. "Welcome, welcome."

Mr. Vrinat held up his hand, like a cop stopping traffic. "Thirty minutes," he said. "That's all we have." Their disappointment was obvious. Mine, too.

Mme. Mennevaux took up the challenge. In 15 minutes we had before us a delicious poached chicken breast with vegetables probably right out of their garden. With a glass of wine, a bit of cheese and good bread, we were back on the road in the time it would have taken to unfold a starched Taillevent napkin.

That afternoon we took in five red wine producers: Jacky Confuron in Vosne-Romanée; the Domaine Pernin-Rossin in Flagey-Echézaux; the Domaine Boillot in Nuits-Saint-Georges; Barthold-Noëllat in Chambolle-Musigny, and Robert Jayer-Gilles in Magny-les-Villiers in the hills north of Aloxe Corton.

By the end of the day, I was, as the French say, "épuisé"—wiped out. Mr.

Vrinat was as energetic as he had been at 7 a.m., already deciding, but not disclosing, which of the dozens of wines we had tasted might eventually show up on Taillevent's list and at his Paris wine shop, Les Caves Taillevent.

Taillevent offers 3,000 different wines and Mr. Vrinat boasted that he had chosen every one. With his death, the job falls to his daughter, Valerie, who worked for him for 20 years.

January 2008

A Restaurateur Who Bought for Himself

By FRANK J. PRIAL

When Harry Poulakakos locked the door of his restaurant in Hanover Square for the last time on Friday, he left behind a lot of memories and by his estimate about 60,000 bottles of wine. It was one of New York's best cellars.

Bordeaux? Yes, there was Bordeaux, including 16 vintages of Château Latour; 13 of Margaux; 13 of Haut-Brion, beginning with 1961; 11 of Pétrus, of which the youngest listed was 1988; and 8 of d'Yquem.

California? There were magnums of Beaulieu Vineyards' Georges de Latour Private Reserve, Shafer Vineyards Hillside Select and Silver Oak Alexander Valley cabernet.

There were hundreds of cases of younger wines, not listed, because in Mr. Poulakakos's severe judgment, they were not ready to drink.

Five years ago, when the Zagat Survey published its first and, alas, only comparative listing of wine prices in New York City, the top wines at Harry's at Hanover Square were often half or a third of what they were in luxury Midtown restaurants. And Harry's, while never inexpensive, was never a luxury place, either. It was a casual, clublike mecca for Wall Streeters who came for the camaraderie, good drinks, no-nonsense food and excellent cigars of unspoken provenance.

It should come as no surprise that few among this extroverted mob—in its prime, in the '80s, Harry's served 900 lunches—burst through the doors demanding 1997 Chambolle-Musigny from Domaine Dujac. Nor, quite honestly, did the owner expect them to. Truth be told, he bought his wine for himself.

Few restaurateurs know about wine other than as a profit center. Most came up through the kitchen, hardly a trajectory leading to knowledge of the grape. Arriving from Greece in 1956, Harry Poulakakos did time in greasy spoons but was lucky enough to hook on with Oscar Tucci at Oscar's Delmonico, a hangout of traders. "He was my boss and mentor," Mr. Poulakakos said, "and he introduced me to wine."

As he moved up to bartender and to manager at Oscar's, Mr. Poulakakos began buying wine, for the restaurant and himself. "I started in the early '60s—'61 and '62," he said. "I fell in love with Bordeaux."

When he opened at 1 Hanover Square in 1972, he began buying in earnest. "I bought 25 cases of 1971 Pétrus," he said. Then he smiled and added: "And I drank most of it myself. I still have six bottles left."

He became obsessed. "It was the '66 Gruaud Larose," he said. "I'd never tasted anything that good." A Second Growth in the Bordeaux rating system, Gruaud Larose is a famous old property in the commune of St.-Julien. The 1966 Gruaud was highly rated. Harry Poulakakos bought 100 cases of it and, again, drank most of it himself.

"At one point, I was up to three, four bottles a day," he said. "It was good, but it wasn't good for me. My liver was distended, and the doctor said I had to cut back. I asked him, 'To what?'"

"He said, 'Two or three glasses a day.'"

"I said: 'Three glasses is almost a bottle. How about a bottle?'"

"He said, 'O.K., O.K., a bottle.'"

"I stuck with that, my liver got better, and I've never had any trouble since."

Unkind friends claim to have seen Mr. Poulakakos push the envelope, so to speak, but only on special occasions. "Like maybe it's Friday night," he said with a grin.

It's tempting to criticize Midtown restaurants for charging twice Harry's wine prices, or more. Greed is always a factor, but there are special circumstances. If a restaurateur runs out of tomato soup, he can make more or buy more. If he runs out of 1982 Mouton-Rothschild and customers will pay anything for it, he has a problem: there isn't any more.

His distributor may find a few bottles. The négociant, or exporter, in Bordeaux, may help, or the restaurateur can go to auctions and bid against his competitors. Staggering prices are the result. Because Harry Poulakakos bought his 1982 Mouton in 1984, and didn't face the demand imposed on Midtown places, he could charge $1,500 for the wine, not $5,000.

The problem is particularly acute for new restaurants. The cellar at Harry's was stocked with wines bought before some new young owners and chefs were born. Hot new places start with no wine and are expected to have well-stocked cellars the day they open. They cross their fingers and push the pinot grigio.

It's sad that Harry's has closed. Mr. Poulakakos said he didn't want to continue after his wife and partner, Adrienne, died of cancer in August. But in a way it lives on. Harry's was in the basement of the famous old India House, a private club open during the day to members and before that the Cotton Exchange.

Today, the upper floors of the landmark 1851 building are occupied by Bayard's, named for the man who lived on the property in the 17th century. Bayard's, whose chef is the estimable Eberhard Müller, formerly of Lutèce, is owned and run by Peter Poulakakos, Harry's son. Harry (wink, wink) serves as consultant. Bayard's serves meals to club members during the day and is a restaurant at night.

Not entirely by chance, Bayard's has a pretty good wine list of its own, including—quelle coincidence!—most of the same rare Bordeaux in the basement. What's more, Harry says, with a straight face, he's thinking of selling a lot of his stock to his son. Well, you can't just give the stuff away, for heaven's sake, even to your kid. Family ties don't count for much with the State Liquor Authority.

Meanwhile, no law says Harry cannot tap into his liquid assets for his own pleasure. Professional boniface no more, he is free to contemplate a life of leisurely dinners with good friends and good wine. Strangely enough—ah, the inconsistency of man after a lifetime of devotion to Bordeaux—he thinks more and more of Burgundy these days. Some of us, of course, recognize this as merely the wisdom of maturity. And we wait anxiously for an invitation.

November 2003

Naked Came the Vintner

By WARREN St. JOHN

When the typical Savanna Samson fan hears her name, the first thing that comes to mind is probably not wine. In fact, wine is probably not even the fourth or fifth thing that comes to mind when fans contemplate Savanna Samson. It's even possible that no fan of Savanna Samson has ever had the thought, "Savanna Samson: wine," at any time, ever.

Savanna Samson—her real name is Natalie Oliveros—is a porn star, and a noted one at that. As a Vivid girl, one of the actors whose work is produced and marketed by the goliath Vivid Video, Savanna Samson is a porn celebrity.

She is the star of 25 sexually explicit films, a two-time winner of the Adult Video News Award for best actress, and her work with Jenna Jameson in *The New Devil in Miss Jones*, a remake of a classic, won last year's award for the best all-girl sex scene.

But Ms. Oliveros is also an aspiring winemaker. Her first production, a 2004 vintage of an Italian red wine that she calls Sogno Uno (Dream One), makes its debut this week at wine stores and restaurants in Manhattan.

A porn star making wine, Ms. Oliveros readily admits, is a gimmick. But what sets her effort apart from the vanity wines of other celebrities like Madonna and the Rolling Stones is that it is good—extremely good if the wine expert Robert M. Parker Jr. is to be believed.

After tasting a young bottle of Sogno Uno at a Paris bistro last fall, Mr. Parker gave Ms. Oliveros's wine a rating of 90 to 91 or outstanding, a judgment that quickly became the talk of the wine world.

"It's a very fine wine—awfully good," Mr. Parker said by telephone. "It was really opulent and luscious and it had a personality."

Sipping a glass of Sogno Uno last week at La Masseria, an Italian restaurant in Midtown, Ms. Oliveros said she put the same passion into her wine that she puts into her sex scenes, even as she expected the wine world to turn up its nose.

"People have to be laughing when they hear about it," she said. "But I didn't want it to be a joke." As for the Parker rating, Ms. Oliveros said, "He should've given it a 93."

Peppe Luele, the owner of La Masseria, said he plans to serve Sogno Uno at his restaurant, where it will sell for $70 to $80 a bottle. He said he is also a fan of Ms. Oliveros's other work.

"Have you seen the movies?" he asked. He shook his head in astonishment. "Incredible."

Ms. Oliveros insists her winemaking venture is more than just a lark. As a porn star of a certain age—Ms. Oliveros won't say exactly how old she is—she said she knows she's running out of runway on her film career. In her relatively short time in the porn industry—Ms. Oliveros shot her first movie in 2000—she said she has seen many in the industry falter when their time in front of the camera is up. She said she sees the wine business as her career parachute.

"I've seen so many fallen stars," Ms. Oliveros said. "I don't plan to be one of them."

If there is a such a thing as the "average porn star," it's a safe bet that Ms. Oliveros does not fit into that category. For one thing, she lives on the East Side, with her husband and son. She began her career in pornography when her son was 8 months old.

"I worked out all through my pregnancy," she said.

Ms. Oliveros said she happened into her pornography career. She grew up in upstate New York, one of five daughters, and came to the city at 17 to pursue a career in ballet. That didn't happen, she said, "because I wasn't good enough," so she took a job dancing at the strip club Scores "to make killer money." From there it was a short distance to making her first porn movie, which came about when she wrote a letter to Rocco Siffredi, a European porn star, asking if she could work with him.

"I figured I could go to Europe, get this fantasy out of the way, and no one would ever hear about it," she said. Instead the movie was nominated for best foreign movie at the Adult Video News film awards, and pretty soon Ms. Oliveros was invited to be a guest on *The Howard Stern Show*.

"So much for that secret," she said.

News of her career didn't go over well with family and friends back home, Ms. Oliveros said.

"My parents are devastated by my career choices," she said. "What really troubles me about what I do is the pain I've caused them."

Ms. Oliveros said that her chief talent is her passion for her work. She said she genuinely enjoys having sex with strangers.

"For those few minutes that I'm working with someone, I love that person," she said. "For that reason it makes me good at what I do."

Ms. Oliveros kept dancing at Scores, where she had a strict policy of not dating customers, she said. That rule fell by the wayside when she met Daniel Oliveros, a Manhattan wine merchant who was there with his girlfriend at the time.

"I had to kick her out of the picture," Ms. Oliveros said.

On their first date Mr. Oliveros invited his future wife to a wine-soaked dinner with friends and colleagues in the wine business. That began their relationship as well as her education about wine.

"I was impressed," she said.

Ms. Oliveros said her husband is a "very strange breed" who supports her porn career. She makes six sexually explicit movies a year, and can earn anywhere from $20,000 to upward of $100,000 per film, depending on sales. All are shot in California, and each one takes three days to two weeks to make. She said her husband is her toughest critic.

"I know that he'll be watching, so I just put that much more into what I'm doing," she said. "If I can just spark a little jealousy out of him, then I would be so happy. But that never happens."

Mr. Oliveros said: "I was aware she had a skeleton in the closet. But as long as she looks me in the eye and says she loves me, I'm not a jealous person."

As much as she enjoyed making pornographic movies, Ms. Oliveros said there was something about them that left her unfulfilled. On a vacation in Tuscany last year, she said, she was struck by something akin to an existential crisis. "How can I leave a mark on this world?" she asked herself. "And I thought, 'Wine.'"

Ms. Oliveros has had some help with her first winemaking venture. Through her husband, she met Roberto Cipresso, a noted Italian winemaker and consultant. She asked Mr. Cipresso to experiment with blends of local grapes to achieve her ideal flavor. She tasted the blends along the way, she said, dismissing merlot and cabernet grapes as boring, and eventually falling for cesanese, an ancient and little heralded grape found mainly in the Lazio region that has a light, but spicy taste.

Ms. Oliveros said she wanted something slightly sweeter, so Mr. Cipresso added sangiovese to the mix. For backbone they added montepulciano, the aromatic grape from the Tuscan hills. Ms. Oliveros said she made her preferences known, even if the language of wine tasting eluded her.

"When they say, 'leather,' I think 'old boots,'" she said. "And when they say, 'vanilla,' I think 'ice cream.'"

Eventually they settled on a blend of 70 percent cesanese grapes, 20 percent sangiovese and 10 percent montepulciano to create a complex wine with hints of pepper, earth and cotton candy.

"This wine will make you think," Ms. Oliveros said.

Ms. Oliveros ordered 409 cases—"more than I could really afford," she said—and began working on a label, settling eventually on a design that plays on her notoriety as a Vivid girl. It's an image of Ms. Oliveros's naked profile beneath a sheer gown, wearing the type of heels you might expect to see on, say, a dancer at Scores. She plans to introduce the wine with a Venetian-theme mask party tomorrow night at La Masseria.

Ms. Oliveros plans to sell Sogno Uno for $38 a bottle.

She said that the success or failure of her wine venture will be determined in the coming weeks by wine distributors and critics. She said she is optimistic, enough so that she just went to Italy to taste potential blends for a white wine, which she would call Sogno Due. She suggested that potential customers approach her wine the way she approaches some newfangled sexual position on the set of one of her movies.

"Don't knock it till you try it," she said.

February 2006

He Can Bring the Wine and the Music

By ERIC ASIMOV

For music and for wine, David Chan says, language has its limitations. He should know.

Mr. Chan is a concertmaster of the Metropolitan Opera Orchestra, the position traditionally held by the leader of the violin section, and he is also a wine lover and Burgundy fanatic. He is a Harvard graduate who was named concertmaster in 2000, at the ripe old age of 27, and he sees a crucial similarity between his twin passions.

"Talking about wine is like talking about music," he told me over dinner recently at Bar Boulud, across Broadway from Lincoln Center. "If I could tell you in words, then there wouldn't be any point in playing it. A great piece of music, and a great wine, holds your attention and has more than you can say in words."

It's a piece of wisdom that seems obvious, especially when I find myself trying to describe the sensation of a wonderful 15-year-old Puligny-Montrachet with phrases like "sluicing a mouthful of pebbles." Yikes! I'm sure describing the effect of a telling passage of music is no easier.

Perhaps it's the necessity of embracing the nonverbal that so often binds music and wine. Mr. Chan says that almost any orchestra or group of musicians will include a significant minority who are involved in tasting groups or who gather regularly to have dinner and share wines. It was one such group that got him interested in wine in the first place.

Mr. Chan grew up in San Diego. His parents, who came from Taiwan and met as graduate students at Stanford, were not wine drinkers. They had heard that children who studied music did better in math and reading, so they enrolled him in a violin class at age 3. He never stopped playing.

He was first exposed to great wines at a summer music festival in La Jolla, Calif., where a few patrons with extensive cellars were opening bottles for the visiting musicians. But he began to develop his interest when he got to the Met and fell in with a crowd of wine-loving musicians.

At first, it was slow going. "They would talk about wine with all this jargon, and mostly I was kind of lost," he said. The turning point came in 2002, after he married Catherine Ro, also a violinist in the Met orchestra. His father-in-law, a wine lover, had to give up drinking for health reasons and gave Mr. Chan two dozen special bottles, mostly top Bordeaux and cabernet sauvignons.

While he understood the greatness of those wines, it wasn't until he started to drink Burgundy that he fell head over heels into wine fanaticism. So began an obsession to get to know the Côte d'Or, the heart of Burgundy, almost vineyard by vineyard.

"As a teenager, if I discovered one Mahler symphony I had to know all of them—one Wagner opera, I had to know them all," Mr. Chan said. "You can imagine how Burgundy hit me like a ton of bricks. If I had one producer's Meursault Genevrières one night, I had to have the Perrières the next night. Whatever would advance the knowledge."

Burgundy, particularly the haunting perfume of red Burgundy, is often thought of as a wine that bypasses the brain to grab the soul. But Mr. Chan is captivated above all by the intellectual appeal of Burgundy, of linking great wines to the earth from which they originated. "It's not that they're not hedonistic, but wines of terroir clearly offer an additional level beyond all that," he said. "Over time you get to know a terroir signature when you encounter it again and again in blind tastings or whatever. I definitely love that analytical element. It's irresistible to a certain nerdy personality that I have."

Ah, terroir, that French word with no real English equivalent, pointing to the qualities of a place: the soil, climate, exposure to the sun, the human touch. While some scientists and winemakers outside of France dispute the notion of terroir, Burgundy lovers embrace it religiously.

Mr. Chan sees parallels between music and terroir: "Music that has lasted 100, 200, 300 years, there's a reason for it. Mostly, we've weeded out the music that isn't worthy. But there's more: they bring pleasure, they make you think about it, and they bear the stamp of the composer."

Great composers are like great vineyards, he says. Both require a particular sort of selflessness to bring them to life. "If you seek to only be yourself, that's what you get, but if you seek to faithfully bring the composer to life, that will happen, and your personality will enter the picture because you're performing the task," he said. "I think the same thing happens in wine. If you try to faithfully capture the terroir, inevitably you enter the picture, whereas if you're not careful, it results in a house style."

A consequence of Burgundy fanaticism is that one tends to spend a lot of money on wine, and as a new family man (his second child was born a few weeks ago), Mr. Chan sensed his limits. While his wife objected to his traveling to Burgundy solely to buy wine, she acknowledged that if he had a good reason for visiting Burgundy it might make a difference.

So motivated, and feeling as if he wanted to give something back to the wine producers who had embraced him, he came up with an idea for giving a concert in Burgundy. In 2007 he approached Bernard Hervet, a music lover who is the chief executive at Maison Faiveley, a longtime grower and négociant in Burgundy. One thing led to another. Aubert de Villaine, head of Domaine de la Romanée-Conti, got involved, and a music and wine festival was born.

A first concert was held in 2007 at the historic Château du Clos de Vougeot, and in 2008 Mr. Chan gave three concerts. "Music and wine are two arts that are able to destroy the language barrier," Mr. Hervet told me in an e-mail message.

Needless to say, Mr. Chan's future Burgundy visits are assured.

November 2008

Alois Kracher, Austrian Winemaker and Advocate, Is Dead at 48

By ERIC ASIMOV

Alois Kracher Jr., a visionary winemaker whose luscious sweet wines and forceful personality were instrumental in restoring the Austrian wine industry's international reputation after a scandal in 1985, died at his home in Illmitz, in the Burgenland region of Austria. He was 48.

The cause was pancreatic cancer, said Seth Allen, president of Vin Divino, Mr. Kracher's American importer.

Mr. Kracher's wines are coveted throughout the world, admired as much for their silky finesse and balance as for the intensity of their sweet, honeyed fruit flavors.

Before turning to wine, Mr. Kracher (pronounced KRAHK-er) was trained as a chemist, and he brought the systematic skills of a scientist to his work, with the imaginative reach of an artist and a thorough understanding of the traditions of Burgenland.

"He transformed a beautiful but coarse and rustic style with his technical know-how," Mr. Allen said. He described Mr. Kracher's wines as casting "a wave of adolescent vitality upon the reticent and formal domain of world-class wine."

At least as important as Mr. Kracher's winemaking was his fierce and determined advocacy for Austrian wines. Not content with the success of his own label, he tirelessly promoted other Austrian winemakers while advising younger colleagues in the industry on techniques and on marketing their wines internationally.

"He was one of the godfathers of Austrian wine without a doubt," said Aldo Sohm, the chef sommelier at Le Bernardin restaurant in New York, who is originally from Austria.

Today, Austria, one of the world's oldest wine regions, is much admired for its peppery grüner veltliners; dry, pure, intensely minerally rieslings; and dense, nectarlike sweet wines enhanced by botrytis, the famous noble rot, which concentrates flavors and sugars.

But back in the 1980s it was a different story. Austria's wine industry, which had been plodding along in relative obscurity, captured attention in 1985 when unscrupulous merchants were caught adding diethylene glycol, a component of antifreeze, to their wines to increase body and sweetness.

The scandal resulted in Austria's withdrawing from the world market, revamping its wine laws and tightening controls over the wine industry.

In 1981, Mr. Kracher started working with his father, Alois Sr., at the family estate in Illmitz, in the wetland region east of Lake Neusiedl, near the border with Hungary.

While continuing to work as a chemist in the pharmaceutical industry by day, young Alois took over the winemaking in 1986 while his father oversaw the vineyards.

Mr. Kracher was determined that Austria would rejoin the international winemaking community, yet it was not until 1991 that he quit his job as a chemist to devote himself fully to the winery.

"He desperately wanted to communicate the potential of his zone and his country to the outside world," Mr. Allen said.

Mr. Kracher is survived by his parents; his wife, Michaela; and his son, Gerhard, 26, who had worked closely with his father. The family announced that Gerhard would take charge of the winery.

Mr. Kracher was known for his enormous energy, which was not restricted to his winery. He had joined forces with Manfred Krankl, the Austrian-born founder of the Sine Qua Non winery in California, to make a small quantity of extraordinary sweet California wines, called Mr. K.

He also found time to make sweet wines in Spain with Jorge Ordóñez, a wine importer based in the United States, and to make his own blue cheese soaked in sweet wine, Kracher Grand Cru.

"The guy was always going full speed, very passionate and eager," said Mr. Sohm, the sommelier. "I never saw him calm."

December 2007

Nelson Shaulis, 86, Is Dead; Toiled to Improve Vineyards

By HOWARD G. GOLDBERG

D r. Nelson Shaulis, whose grape-growing experiments in the Finger Lakes region of New York State revolutionized vineyard practices worldwide, died on Saturday in Newark, N.Y. He was 86 and lived in Geneva, N.Y.

Before Dr. Shaulis retired in 1978 as professor of viticulture—the science and methods of grape growing—at Cornell University's New York State Agricultural Experiment Station in Geneva, he developed a vine-training system known as the Geneva Double Curtain. He also worked at Cornell's Vineyard Laboratory, a station branch in Fredonia, N.Y.

Dr. Shaulis's trellising concepts "have been applied in every major grape-producing region in the world, and served as the knowledge base that allowed New World winegrowing to emerge as a major factor in international trade in the last 20 years," said Prof. Robert Pool, who succeeded him as chief viticulturist at the experimental station.

The concepts have been most widely applied in the United States—especially California—Australia and New Zealand.

Dr. Shaulis also worked with Cornell's department of agricultural engineering to develop the mechanical grape harvester, especially for use with the Double Curtain. Today, harvesters modeled after the Cornell machine bring in grapes everywhere.

Experts in modern viticulture consider Dr. Shaulis the father of canopy management, a term used in the industry for a spectrum of techniques to control vine diseases and improve grape yields and wine quality. The canopy consists of all vine growth above the soil, including trunks, canes, stems, leaves and fruit. The core principle of leading-edge management is to broaden the exposure of leaves and grapes on trellises to the sunshine.

While working with vines that produce Concord grapes, a red variety that once dominated upstate winegrowing and is still most familiar to consumers in sweet kosher wines, Dr. Shaulis observed that excessive shade inside canopies reduced grape yield and ripeness.

He discovered that by separating one thick canopy into two less thick ones, more sunlight (and thus more photosynthesis) could be introduced on leaf surfaces, improving vine maturation and increasing not only grape yields, sometimes by 90 percent, but also quality.

The Double Curtain technique was first tried at Geneva in 1960, and four years later field trials with growers began. Although Concord belongs to a species of native North American grape known as labrusca, Dr. Shaulis's discovery was quickly applied to vinifera grapes, the classical European variety that produces today's premium wines. Bordeaux was quick to see its merits.

Late-summer visitors to grape farms who look straight down a Geneva Double Curtain row will see that the vine wood and luxuriant vegetation are trained both to the left and right over wires, supported by cross arms that are four feet apart and five or six feet above the ground.

Seemingly nothing escaped Dr. Shaulis's investigations. He looked, too, into proper siting of vineyards, the physiology of grapevines, mineral nutrition, root stocks and microclimates.

Virtually every properly educated and trained winegrower in the English-speaking world has a copy of *Sunlight Into Wine: A Handbook of Wine Grape Canopy Management*, a 1991 book whose principal author is Dr. Richard E. Smart, a renowned Australian viticulturist. Dr. Smart was a student of Dr. Shaulis, and the book's content owes a significant debt to Dr. Shaulis's findings.

Dr. Shaulis received a bachelor's degree in horticulture in 1935 and a master's degree in agronomy in 1937, both from Pennsylvania State University. He received his doctorate in soils from Cornell in 1941.

Dr. Shaulis's wife of 55 years, Lillian, died in 1996. He is survived by two daughters, Catherine Shaulis-Santomartino of Scotia, N.Y., and Margaret Harty of Sodus, N.Y.; three grandchildren; and three great-grandchildren.

January 2000

Joe Dressner, an Importer
With No Use for Pretense, Dies at 60

By ERIC ASIMOV

Joe Dressner once made one of my best friends cry. Joe, an iconoclastic importer of naturally made wines, died on Saturday at the age of 60 after a three-year battle with brain cancer. Even if he did make my friend cry, I'll miss him sorely.

He would regularly bring a crew of his vignerons from France to the United States, where they would meet members of the trade, offer consumer tastings and raise hell after hours. These visits were important to him. They helped sell wine, of course, but he also believed that it was crucial for the public and the trade to see for themselves that wine—good wine—was made by people who had a vision and philosophy as well as warts and flaws and sometimes bizarre hairstyles.

The problem was that among Joe's own flaws, he lacked tact and a sense of diplomacy. Or maybe his brusque irascibility was part of a conscious shtick, the same way he was a sentimentalist but pretended to abhor sentiment. I was never sure. In any case, the vignerons were at the Crush Wine Company in Midtown Manhattan when my friend, a doctor, made an innocent jest to Joe that drew such a harsh bark in response that her tears flowed.

But that was Joe, in part: blunt, acerbic, uncompromising and provocative, and not necessarily in control of his ridicule. Yet Joe was also principled, honest, articulate, outrageously funny, and man, did he know wine.

How did Joe know wine? To my knowledge, he never went to a class to learn how to deconstruct a wine into esoteric aromas and flavors. I never saw him try to identify a wine blind, as if that were ever a sign of useful knowledge. He had no formal training. He simply drank a lot of wine. With time he learned to distinguish between what he liked and what he didn't, and he was sufficiently curious and resolute to work out the reasons for those differences.

It turned out that the wines he liked had much in common. They were generally made by small producers who worked their own plots, who did not use chemicals in the vineyard and kept their yields small, who harvested by hand rather than by machine and who used no additives in the cellar but merely shepherded the grape juice along its journey into wine.

These were the wines he grew to love and sell, made by people whose personal histories often involved generations of dedicated grape growing. Even as these wines came to be known as "natural wines," a term he occasionally used and often disdained, and wines like these came to be a hot-button topic among the wine lovers of the world, Joe would scorn the notion that he was involved in some sort of movement.

"The natural wine movement is not a movement with a leader, credo and principles," he wrote just last year. "If you think there is a natural wine movement sweeping the world, triumphantly slaying industrial wineries and taking no hostages, then you are one delusional wine drinker. The natural wine movement thinks that you might want to lessen your alcohol consumption for a few months."

Wine for Joe was not about movements or dogma. Despite his predilections, he liked the wines he liked not because they were made according to a certain philosophy, but because he thought the wines tasted better. One of the core beliefs of his company, Louis/Dressner Selections, was that wines should be made with indigenous yeasts that were present on the grapes and in the winery, rather than inoculated with yeasts selected by the winemaker. Yet the wines of Didier Dagueneau, one of the shining domains in his portfolio, are inoculated. Well, you can't argue with these wines.

Joe represented far more than simply a preferred way of making wines. Whether he would admit to it or not, he represented a culture that does not exalt wine into something overly complicated or turn it into a fetishistic object. His way of thinking did not reduce wine to scores and tasting notes, either, or strain to demystify it. To Joe, wine was a pleasure and a joy, to be shared with friends and family with great food, and, as he once said, if you wanted to drink wretched wine with awful food, who was he to object? That was his way, and everybody else could do as he wanted, so long as it did not intrude on Joe or on his business.

Of course, Joe made such intrusions easy. It was not so much his enemies who disturbed him as his friends, people he thought should know better, and yet who persisted in straying into the realm of the self-important or pretentious. Out came the ridicule, the satire, the absurdities, and if he were on your tail he would pursue with an unholy tenacity. He could make people cry. Now, he's done it again, by dying.

September 2011

CHAPTER THIRTEEN

So, There You Are
in a Restaurant

Postcard From Paris: We Drank! We Ate!

By FRANK J. PRIAL

My friend Daniel Johnnes was on the line. A New York importer and sometime sommelier, he was lunching with some other wine enthusiasts at La Tour d'Argent, the Michelin two-star restaurant. Someone had not shown up. Would my wife and I be interested in filling in? There would be some great wines. I hesitated. I had just managed to get a table for the following night at Taillevent, three stars. Five stars in two days? Yes, indeed.

I grabbed a tie—needlessly. Standards had relaxed at the Tour since my last visit seven years ago. We hailed a taxi. The Tour d'Argent is a 15-minute walk from our apartment, but I did not want to hold things up. Or miss any of the wines. Mr. Johnnes and his party had come directly from the airport.

Here are some of the wines we drank from the Tour d'Argent cellar. Among the whites: Meursault-Perriers, 1990 and 1989, from Coche-Dury, and Bâtard-Montrachet, 1983 and 1982, from the Domaine Leflaive. Among the reds were: Chambolle-Musigny Les Amoureuses, 1990 and 1985, from the Domaine Georges Roumier, and Échezeaux 1980, in magnums, from Henri Jayer. The only non-Burgundian wines were Château Rayas, 1990 and 1989, from Châteauneuf-du-Pape.

This was not some wimpy tasting, with sips, sniffs, frowns and scribbling of notes. The wines were for drinking, and there was a full meal to set them off: quenelles de brochet, baked St. Pierre and of course the famous Tour d'Argent duck with its companion postcard to send home to inform the folks you were served duck No. 1,102,506, or parts thereof.

The travelers then hastened to the Gare de Lyon for their train to Dijon and two days of Burgundian excess. I ambled over to Notre Dame for the Sunday organ concert, counting on César Franck to aid my digestion.

Taillevent, in the Rue Lamennais, was once a duke's residence. It still has a regal feel, even when, as was the case that Monday, the owner and director, Jean-Claude Vrinat, is not around. He was off at the 50th anniversary dinner of a restaurant owners group that his father helped found. "If you write anything about Taillevent," he said in a note he left for me, "I hope you don't say it was better when I was not there."

No way, Jean-Claude. My wife and I were in the hands of the affable Jean-Marie Ancher, a solidly built, easygoing captain who can make guests feel at home in half a dozen languages and recall what they ordered 10 years ago. Like his boss, Jean-Marie has been at Taillevent all his professional life. As we left, he pulled out a slightly tattered old photo of an awkward 16-year-old in a white jacket. "Me, when I started here," he said. "Thirty years ago."

No need to study the menu; we ordered the spit-roasted Bresse chicken for two. It is delicious, and watching M. Ancher carve it is, as the Michelin Guide says, vaut le voyage, worth the trip.

For the wines I chose the red, a 1998 Vosne-Romanée Les Suchots, from the Domaine L'Arlot, a great wine from a not-so-great vintage. The opener I left up to the young sommelier, Manuel Peyrondet, asking only for something reasonable (under $50) in a white. His choice: a 2000 Meursault from François Jobard, a winemaker I first met many years ago while tasting with Mr. Vrinat in Burgundy, a trip I thought would be laid-back fun. But I will never forget finding myself at 7:30 a.m. on a cold autumn day, stomping my feet and trying to concentrate on a little glass of new wine in Mr. Jobard's freezing cellar.

Four days after that dinner, I had lunch with another old friend, Christian Pol-Roger, who heads up the Champagne company that bears his name. Pol Roger is in Epernay, about 90 miles east of Paris. My wife had fled back to New York, so I took along a companion of many a memorable feed, a retired music critic.

Christian picked us up at the Epernay station in the mild rain that seems always to be falling in Champagne country. There was a nip in the air that justified the crackling fire in the Pol-Rogers' hearth and made the first, welcoming bottle that much more appealing. It was the 1982 Blanc de Chardonnay Vintage Brut, 22 years old, medium-bodied and as fresh as if it had been bottled last spring. But it was just a harbinger of what was to come. With a delicious steamed bar as a backdrop—it was Friday after all—we moved to the star of the Pol Roger lineup, the Cuvée Sir Winston Churchill, named after the wine's most famous fan. Churchill, who preferred older vintages bottled in imperial pints, named a race horse Odette Pol-Roger after one of the most glamorous of the Pol-Roger women. When Churchill died, a black border was added to Pol Roger labels in his memory. We drank the 1990, a powerful wine similar to a big Bollinger.

The pièce de résistance of the Champagnes we drank that afternoon was the 1921 Vintage Brut. It was astonishingly light for a Pol Roger but perfectly balanced with not a hint of oxidization. It could easily have passed for an 8- or 10-year-old wine. Later we dipped into the 1988 Réserve Spéciale, another limited production Pol Roger, close to the Churchill in elegance but not as powerful. Before that, with the cheese, Mr. Pol-Roger produced a truly dramatic surprise, a 1911 La Tâche. My friend the music critic pronounced it the finest Burgundy he had ever experienced. I would be hard put to disagree. Mr. Pol-Roger suggested that its remarkable condition may be due partly to conditions in the Pol Roger cellars. "Our temperatures are lower than Burgundy's," he said.

Like the final notes of a great symphony, that exquisite 1911 was the perfect way to end an extraordinary and probably never-to-be duplicated week of great wine.

December 2004

If the Wine Is Off . . .

By FRANK J. PRIAL

E verything up until now has been amateur night. All the training, all the sweat were nothing but preparation for this moment. It's Randolph Scott climbing out of the back cockpit and saying: "Take her up, kid. She's all yours."

You're about to send back your first bottle of wine. Don't expect much help. No one can go with you into this no man's land. Your guests don't know Lambrusco from Château Léoville-Poyferré. And your wife thinks it's all nonsense anyway.

The waiter will think you are trying to impress your guests. And the wine steward, if it's that kind of a place, may take it as a personal affront. But you think the wine is bad and you're going to say so. So do. At best you will meet your trial with steadfastness and courage facing down your adversary like El Cordobés. At worst you can console yourself that you've come a long way from the days when you were afraid to order the bottle in the first place.

I still recall with shame and humiliation trying many years ago to overwhelm a young woman with savoir faire by ordering the right bottle—and coming up with Sauternes as a dinner wine. Alas, there are some things that can be learned only the hard way.

Have you ever been out with people who ordered wine, then made no fuss when it turned out to be bad? Rest assured, there is a lot of bad wine consumed by people who actually know it is poor but are afraid to say anything.

There is a way to do it, of course. It is a little ploy that seeks to involve the waiter in the painful process of rejection. Once you've made your fateful decision, call him over and say: "I think this wine is off." Don't use the word "bad." It's an angry word and gets people angry. On the other hand, "off" sounds slightly technical, so he might think you know something. Then quickly add: "What do you think?"

If you're lucky, he will agree—only because he doesn't know much more than you do. If he calls over the maître d'hôtel, you are in deeper water, but you still have some momentum on your side. In the best of all possible worlds both of them will bow deferentially, saying, "Of course sir, forgive us, we will replace it immediately."

If they stonewall it and declare, "Seems O.K. to us," well, there is nothing you can do but get tough. One gambit, albeit a dangerous one, is to announce loftily, "I think it's off and I want it replaced, even if I have to pay for it."

No place will let you pay for the first bottle, no matter how many dark looks they may direct your way. Some years ago, after three days of tasting several hundred red wines at the Los Angeles County Fair, I drove north to San Francisco where, among other places, I lunched at a dramatic but awful restaurant in the Embarcadero Center. I was served a perfectly rotten zinfandel from a highly respected winery. It was just bad.

The young woman took it away. Ten minutes later she returned to say, "The manager is a wine expert and he says the bottle is good. You don't have to drink it but you have to pay for it." I allowed as how I had yet another choice: to walk out. Which I did.

Of course there is another side to this coin. There are people who really do send bottles back to impress their guests, and there are people who send bottles back simply because they don't know what a good Bordeaux tastes like.

These people are a problem for restaurateurs. The late Henri Soulé, maître d'hôtel of Le Pavillon, had a technique for the showoffs who announced their 1959 Lafite was no good. First the captain tasted the wine, then the sommelier, then the maître d'hôtel, then the great Soulé himself. By then everyone in the restaurant was watching and the Hollywood mogul or captain of industry was squirming in his seat.

Inevitably all the staff would agree that the wine was perfect. Just as inevitably, Mr. Soulé would agree to replace it, of course. It cost him money but it tamed or got rid of another obnoxious guest.

A guest who thinks a bottle is bad because he or she simply doesn't know the taste of Bordeaux or Hermitage or Barolo is usually handled in much the same way, but less theatrically. Again, a good place will offer something else, counting on having made a friend.

The ultimate solution is, of course, to lay the whole problem on the restaurant. This is what I am eating—what should I drink with it? Let the restaurant decide.

But suppose it's still a bad bottle? Then what? Then refer to paragraph six above. Or switch to beer.

October 1981

Just Pour, He Said, and Put a Cork in It

By FRANK J. PRIAL

In contemporary mythology, the sommelier is an unsmiling, self-important type whose role in life is to embarrass and anger as many restaurant customers as possible in the course of an evening. He—or she—rides roughshod over customer's requests, brooks no queries and pouts when anyone questions his selections.

Then, when the put-down is done, he lurks close by to better extract a tip from another flustered diner.

It's only a myth, of course. There may be a sommelier from hell out there somewhere, but it's unlikely. In any case, modern restaurant clients are more worldly than their forebears and far more at home in restaurant surroundings. And the sommeliers have changed. More of them are known as wine stewards now or by some other nonthreatening title. Most of them have impressive knowledge of their métier and are eager to impart some of what they know to their clients. Many now are wine directors; they select and buy the wines they sell. They are profit centers and well aware that profits come from happy patrons.

That being said, wine service, even in the best of restaurants, is not always perfect. I find several practices rather irritating. In fact, like the Lord High Executioner, I have a little list.

First up is the "excellent choice" exchange. "I'll have the 1982 Mouton-Rothschild," the customer says. "Excellent choice, sir," the sommelier replies.

"I'll have the pooly-foosie," a man at the next table says. "Excellent choice, sir," the sommelier says.

I would like one day to say to him, "Dr. Pepper, please, shaken, not stirred," just to hear, "Excellent choice" once again.

Then there is the kidnapper. I order a dozen bluepoints and a bottle of Chablis. They arrive more or less together. I taste the wine, find it acceptable and am about to go for the first oyster when the wine man says, "Let me put this in some ice for you, sir," and disappears with my bottle. The ice bucket is either in the basement or out the kitchen door. I nurse my ounce of wine and down two more oysters before I spot my man across the room. No eye contact. He disappears again.

When half the oysters are gone, he returns with my bottle. "May I refill your glass, sir?" he asks. Before I can swallow another wineless oyster and tell him to leave the bottle, he—and it—are gone off to the ice bucket. I finish the oysters. On his next pass-by, I grab the bottle and drink it with the bread.

A variation of this outrage occurs daily in the business-class seats on airplanes. The attendant half-fills your minuscule glass with wine then disappears into the galley. The chances of a refill before touchdown are remote. The folks back in steerage probably fare better with the 15 cents worth of wine they get in the little $4 bottle.

Then there is the compulsive pourer. He or she is usually not a sommelier but a waiter, and is more nervous than compulsive. The restaurant is half empty, the manager is on the prowl and the staff wants to look busy. So this person runs up every three minutes, gives you a frozen smile and pours. Again. I like to pour my own. I've tried hiding my glass behind the menu. I've tried putting my hand over the glass. Absent lightning reflexes, I get expensive wine on the back of my hand. The server and I both pray the manager will knock off early.

The raconteur is another irritant. You're dining tête-à-tête with a lawyer, a lover, maybe an accountant. Serious stuff. The sommelier brings the Mondavi cab you ordered. You taste distractedly and wave him off.

"You know," he says, "I met Bob Mondavi once." You stare at him in horror.

"Yes," he says, "Lurleen and I—that's my wife—we were driving up Route 29 in the Valley—that's the Napa Valley—and we were stuck in traffic. And there was the Mondavi winery, right alongside of us. So I said to Lurleen, I said. . . ."

Your dinner partner's fingers begin to drum. The evening is sliding downhill, gathering momentum.

"He was really a friendly guy, Bob was. . . ."

One of my favorites is the man who primes the glasses. This involves taking a bit of wine from the bottle you ordered and swirling it around in each of the glasses you will be using. It kills off errant aromas and it probably makes the rest of the wine feel at home when it hits the glass.

The first time I had this trick explained to me my comment was: "You're kidding." It was not well received.

Some of these antics are management-inspired and not necessarily the fault of the perpetrator. There are places where the server is not allowed to place the bottle on the table—any table—while pulling the cork. I've seen sommeliers wrestle with uncooperative bottles for several tense minutes and still come off with a broken cork. Many restaurants demand that the server present the customer with the cork, who has no idea what to do with it, either.

Some people smell it, some gaze at it reverently, some pass it around to their friends, some take it home, perhaps to make a bulletin board or place mats.

More and more restaurants are making wine service as casual as their dress codes. Some like Joe Allen here in New York open your bottle at the bar, plunk it down on your table and let you do the rest. The growing acceptance of screw caps in place of corks, even on premium-quality wines, will make wine service simpler and more relaxed. As more people begin to enjoy wine, they will understand that it is what's in the bottle that counts, not how it's served.

The days of wine rituals are coming to an end. And as Ko-Ko says in *The Mikado*: "And they'll none of 'em be missed; they'll none of 'em be missed."

August 2003

Americans Prefer It by the Glass

By FRANK J. PRIAL

Two young women sit down at a bar. "I'll have a cosmopolitan," says one. "And I'll have a glass of chardonnay," says her friend. The second woman is doing something peculiarly American: drinking wine as a cocktail.

At bars, at parties, at receptions and family gatherings, more and more people are drinking wine the way they used to drink spirits and beer, as a social gesture. It is an American phenomenon because so few of us have ever shared the Old World tradition of wine with meals. Wine by the glass probably represents 10 percent to 12 percent of all table wine sales volume in the United States, said Jon Fredrikson, a California wine industry consultant.

There is much to be said for wine by the glass. It represents less alcohol than spirit-based drinks, and it presents the consumer with a wider variety, two or even three different wines at the same meal, if the glasses are small enough. And it can be profitable.

Even so, not everyone approves, not even in the wine trade. "It's O.K. at the bar, I guess," said Joe Delissio, the wine director at the River Café in Brooklyn, "but I love having a bottle of wine on the table. I'm not sure why, but I guess I like to see people sharing the wine, talking about it, not drinking it because it's the thing to do. It just adds something to the dining experience."

Daniel Johnnes, the wine director at Montrachet in New York and for the Myriad Restaurant Group, is not a fan of wine by the glass either. "We use fairly large glasses," he said, "and when I pour from a bottle, I usually fill about a third of the glass. We offer a little over six ounces when we serve by the glass, or about half a glass of wine."

"I've had people say, 'Hey, fill it up; I paid for a full glass,'" he added. "That would be almost half a bottle."

Mr. Johnnes also wondered about restaurants with extensive lists of wines by the glass. "What happens to the wine that sits around for a week because no one ordered it?" he asked. Charles Scicolone has one answer for that. He is the wine director at I Trulli, a popular Italian restaurant in Manhattan that has a separate wine bar with its own menu and a variety of wine programs. I Trulli offers eight wines by the glass in the restaurant and an impressive 50 by the glass in the wine bar.

"Most of our wines are sold in the wine bar," he said, "where we specialize in tastings of flights of three wines." Mr. Scicolone said a customer can order three wines from the same vintage, one wine from three different vintages, three wines from the same grape or three from the same region. "We have no problem using up all our wines," he said.

A standard 75-centiliter wine bottle holds just over 25 ounces. At Montrachet, the Four Seasons and other top restaurants in Manhattan, that usually breaks down to about four, six-ounce glasses of wine per bottle. Four glasses of a wine usually cost a dollar or two more than a bottle of the same wine, to cover the cost of the extra service and the glassware, restaurateurs say. Which means that two people drinking two glasses each with dinner are better off ordering a bottle.

At the Four Seasons, prices for wine by the glass start at about $13 and can reach $30 or more. At Gramercy Tavern, prices start at about $6 for a Minervois from the South of France and climb to $20 for Billecart-Salmon Rosé Champagne. Gramercy Tavern also offers a three-ounce taste of each of its by-the-glass wines. A taste of the Minervois is $3.25; of the Billecart-Salmon, $10.25.

Some restaurants offer variations on the theme. Orso in Midtown, which specializes in Italian wines, offers its by-the-glass wines in little quarter-liter pitchers. A quarter of a liter is about the same as eight and a half ounces. Orso allows its patrons to sidestep the glass-versus-bottle quandary by ordering its house wine by the carafe. There are liter, half-liter and quarter-liter carafes, the last apparently the most popular. The price for a liter is usually just under the lowest-priced bottled wine, which makes the liter something of a bargain. The wine is anonymous, but the waiter can usually tell you what it is, and it will be a Rosso di Montalcino or something similar.

Lesser restaurants tend to squeeze more wine—and more profit—from each bottle of by-the-glass wine. "We generally go for five five-ounce glasses," admitted an East Side bartender who asked not to be identified, adding, "I've never had any complaints."

Most casual, bistro-style restaurants use a cheaper, smaller glass meant to hold just five or six ounces to begin with. The customer gets less wine and cheaper wine but invariably a full, or almost full glass. Customers like the woman at the bar ordering her chardonnay rarely specify a brand or label. Which means the bar or restaurant is free to offer relatively modest stuff.

Major wine producers offer wines specifically meant to be sold by the glass. E.&J. Gallo, for example, offers 18-liter casks—really, bags of wine in boxes—under the William Wycliff, Burlwood and Copper Ridge labels. Constellation, formerly known as Canandaigua, sells 18-liter casks under their Paul Masson, Almaden and Inglenook labels. Other brands are Pebble Creek, Three Oaks, Cutler Creek and Summerfield. An 18-liter cask, the equivalent of two cases of wine, costs a restaurant about $35. Sold at $6 for a five-ounce glass, casks can be immensely profitable.

Even wine poured from traditional bottles can return respectable profits when sold by the glass. The rule of thumb in the trade is that the first glass pays for the bottle. In other words, whatever the customer pays for the glass of wine is roughly what the restaurateur paid for the bottle. When a restaurateur is being particularly thrifty, eking out five glasses from a bottle of very inexpensive wine, the return on the first bottle will probably pay for the case.

There are deals for the customer, too. Many restaurants built up danger-ously high wine inventories during the economic downturn. Some of them have been working off their stocks by offering exceptional wines, by the glass, at bargain prices. This is usually done quietly, and to profit from it, it helps to know something—not too much, but something—about wine.

February 2004

On Tap? How About Chardonnay or Pinot Noir?

By ERIC ASIMOV

The bartender pulls the handle and the liquid pours forth from keg to glass with the distinctive gushing sound that has launched a zillion thirsts. Ah, yes, that fresh draft flavor—nothing like wine on tap.

Wine? On tap? Is this another attack by the same philistines who insist on screw caps, stemless glasses and other means of depriving wine lovers of their pretensions?

On the contrary, wine, stored in kegs and served through a method similar to a draft-beer line, may be the glorious future of by-the-glass pours in bars and restaurants.

It's just a trickle right now, but the keg and tap system has successfully taken hold in restaurants in Los Angeles and San Francisco, and in wine bars in the city of Napa, Calif.; in Atlanta; and in Traverse City, the heart of Michigan wine country. And it's coming soon to New York City, to no less a place than Daniel Boulud's downtown outpost, DBGB, tentatively scheduled to open on the Bowery in May.

"It's the wave of the future," said Colin Alevras, DBGB's beverage manager, who will have 24 taps at his disposal, 22 for beer and one each for a house red and a house white. The number of wine lines may increase there, he said, if the public is receptive.

What makes wine on tap not merely good but brilliant? It's not the tap, it's the keg.

Taps themselves have been used for many years as part of complex preservation systems intended to protect open bottles against the demon slayer of wine, oxygen. Perhaps you've seen such a system, bottles in a refrigerated glass cabinet, taps on the outside, a Medusa's tangle of hoses extending upward in an effort to rebuff the oxygen with inert gases like argon. Systems like these are an improvement over the half-empty bottle recorked behind the bar, but they are imperfect, complicated and expensive.

The bottles are a problem. Even with the best preservation system the wines don't always stay perfectly fresh. A lot of wine is thrown away, or served in poor condition, resulting in a lesser experience at a greater price for consumers and a lot of waste for the restaurant.

"You have to calculate in your pricing the wine you didn't sell, the wine you had to throw away," said Sang Yoon, the chef and owner of two Father's Office restaurants in the Los Angeles area, and a true believer in the keg and tap method. "The wine is 20 percent cheaper right off the bat."

Mr. Yoon served wines by the glass the conventional way at his first Father's Office in Santa Monica, where his fanatical pursuit of top-quality ingredients and superb craft beers, along with an autocratic style ("no substitutions, modifications, alterations or deletions," the menu reads) turned his little bar into a cult restaurant. But he wanted something better for the wine when he opened his second restaurant, in Culver City.

"I can't remember having had a positive wine-by-the-glass experience unless the bottle was freshly opened," he said. "As an owner, you also come to realize how wasteful wine by the glass becomes. As a result your pricing has to reflect that waste, so most places serve cheap wine with big markups for glass pours, which equals bad value for consumers."

Then it hit him. "Why can't we just serve good wine out of a keg like we do with beer?" he said. In kegs, which keep out the air, wine could stay perfectly fresh for months, he reasoned. Mr. Yoon found a restaurant in Atlanta that was serving wine from modified beer kegs, and, with an energy born of obsession, he set out to perfect the system.

He found a treasure-trove of five-gallon soda kegs, big enough to hold about 25 bottles of wine each, no longer used by the bottlers, who had turned to bag-in-box containers. He worked to persuade wineries to fill the stainless steel kegs for him. And he custom-designed coolers for the wine kegs, separate from the cooling system he used for the 36 beers he offers on tap.

"Whites are kept at 46 degrees, and reds 55 degrees," he said. "Once the wines hit the glass, the temperature rises about two degrees, thus bringing the actual service temperature to 48 and 57 respectively. I did a lot of testing."

Mr. Yoon now offers eight wines on tap, including wines from Brewer-Clifton, Melville, Stephen Ross and Flowers, and with the reusable kegs he estimates he saves having to dispose of 10,000 bottles and related packaging a year.

It was on a scouting trip to Los Angeles last year that Mr. Alevras of DBGB visited Father's Office to look at Mr. Yoon's beer system. He came away fascinated by wines in kegs.

"It's beautiful in its simplicity," he said. "Gas goes in as wine goes out."

Gas? Well, of course. That's how a beer keg works. Except beer systems generally use a high-pressure carbon dioxide system, which carbonates the beer. Wine simply needs a low-pressure system in which gas pushes the wine from keg to tap and occupies the empty space in the keg, preventing oxidation. Mr. Yoon uses nitrogen, which the restaurant produces itself with a reverse osmosis generator.

While Mr. Yoon may have improved the system, he by no means invented it. For centuries in the ancient wine-producing regions of the world, a barrel and a tap method was the low-tech way to dispense wines in countless bars and taverns. Even today, you see wine on tap frequently in Europe, even if it doesn't have the sleek 21st-century perfectionism of Mr. Yoon's system.

Europe was the inspiration for Craig and Anne Stoll, the owners of Delfina in San Francisco. In their new pizzeria, which opened in October, they serve vino alla spina, as wine on tap is called in Italy.

At Oxbow Wine Merchant, a retail shop and wine bar in Napa, Peter Granoff is going through two 15-gallon kegs of white wine a month.

"We can pour a very nice glass of wine, five ounces, for $4 or $5," said Mr. Granoff, an owner. "There are no packaging costs, the kegs get used over and over. No corks, no capsules. I would guess the consumer savings is 25 or 30 percent, depending on the wine."

Gillian Ballance, the wine director at the Carneros Inn in the Napa Valley, was intrigued enough by what she saw at Oxbow to put in a tap at Farm, one of the inn's restaurants, about three months ago. She's now serving verdelho from Scholium Project for $6 a glass.

Is wine by the keg a novelty? Or is this just the beginning of a trend that will benefit purveyors and consumers? It makes too much economic sense, I think, for it not to take hold.

But it won't happen overnight. While the technology is not new or experimental, existing beer lines cannot simply be converted for wine. It's far easier, restaurateurs say, to install wine lines to begin with, preferably during construction. "You can retrofit almost anything," Mr. Granoff said, "but it gets really expensive."

So far the public seems to be embracing wines on tap, although Mr. Granoff isn't taking chances. He likes to offer customers a glass to taste, and tells them only after they try it how the wine was dispensed.

"Their jaws kind of drop," he said. "You've gotten past their perception, by giving them the wine without telling them where it's coming from."

April 2009

Sometimes, Half a Bottle Is Better Than One

By WILLIAM GRIMES

S he's ordered oysters. He's ordered foie gras. The sommelier approaches. Tension mounts. What wine?

This question haunts the thinking portion of humankind. The lone diner searches futilely for a wine that will split the difference between a delicate shellfish appetizer, hard-wired for Chablis, and a lusty, truffly main course that has red Burgundy written all over it. For two diners, a bottle each of red and white is too much to drink. In most restaurants, the wines served by the glass are too humble to make a serious contribution to the meal.

Unlike the mind-body problem, the meat-fish problem has a solution. It's the half bottle, and against the odds it seems to be making a comeback in New York restaurants, for common-sense reasons. At a time when Americans are drinking less, the half-bottle format allows diners to get quality without quantity. It allows customers who yearn for adventure to experiment without going into debt, and because wine ages more quickly in half bottles, younger wines show better.

"I am always looking for half bottles," said Dr. William Schlansky, a dentist from Brooklyn who eats out four nights a week. He likes wine. His wife drinks very little. "We find a full bottle is a little much, but I don't like wine by the glass," he said. "I feel you're drinking what they pick for you."

Veritas, a new wine-theme restaurant, carries 30 half bottles now and is adding to the list daily, with about 100 as the goal. John Gilman, the new sommelier at Picholine, is expanding the restaurant's selection of half bottles. "I looked at the list here and said, 'We've got to get more,'" he said. "We have a specific need with our cheese course." At Gotham Bar and Grill, his previous employer, Mr. Gilman worked with a list of 60 half bottles, one of the biggest in New York.

Half bottles also dovetail nicely with tasting menus, making it possible for a table to match four or five different wines with a multicourse meal. "On any given evening, we may have as many as five tasting menus circulating on the floor," said Joseph Nase, the wine director at Lespinasse. "That's a golden opportunity to pair wines and establish themes for the meal."

Mr. Nase usually carries 100 to 150 half bottles. He is currently reworking his wine list so that he can offer 200 to 250 half bottles, a monster list.

French restaurants like La Côte Basque, La Caravelle and La Grenouille have always carried well-chosen half-bottle lists of perhaps 15 or 20 wines. Peacock Alley at the Waldorf-Astoria Hotel offers 30. But the half-bottle habit is being picked up by more modest restaurants, like Cafe Centro, the Tonic, and Chelsea Bistro and Bar, which all have about 20 half bottles on their lists. Coup, a restaurant in the East Village, maintains a carefully pruned list of only 25 wines in bottle. Eight are half bottles.

"Things are on the upswing of late," said Mr. Gilman of Picholine. "Producers and importers are making an effort to get better wines into half bottles."

Even so, the diner in the market for a good half bottle often seaches in vain, because most winemakers hate the format, with some reason. Glassmakers charge a premium for the bottles, and filling them often requires a separate bottling line. As a result, supplies tend to be very limited.

There are virtually no wines from Australia, New Zealand or South America in half bottles. Almost all half-bottle lists are made up of French, Italian and American wines, with a few German and Spanish wines. Within France, the winemakers of Burgundy have traditionally been reluctant to use half bottles, while their counterparts in Bordeaux have not.

When half-bottle cases are available, they sell for as much as 20 percent more than the equivalent amount of wine in full bottles, which gives a restaurant owner two choices: accept a lower profit or invite customer complaints about half bottles that cost more than half the amount of a full bottle.

Another reason for winemakers' reluctance to use half bottles has to do with the way wine ages. Because all bottles have the same amount of air between the cork and the surface of the wine, the ratio of air to wine is quite different for a half bottle, a full bottle and a magnum. Half bottles age more quickly, and some winemakers are nervous about putting their best stuff into an inferior vehicle.

They may be worrying needlessly. When Eberhard Müller took over as the executive chef at Lutèce, he searched the cellar and came across several half-bottle cases of top Bordeaux dating from the 1930s and 1940s, about 400 bottles in all. "I was worried about their well-being, but to my surprise every single one was in perfect condition," Mr. Muller said.

Alas, only one bottle remains, a 1949 Lafite-Rothschild priced at $400. The restaurant does have a startling lineup of 11 Mouton-Rothschilds from 1979 to 1989, however, priced from $110 for the 1981 to $775 for the 1982.

A half-bottle list does not need a first-growth Bordeaux, or lofty prices, to command interest. Le Cirque 2000 has a Mâcon-Lugny for $11, only $3 more than a bottle of sparkling water. Windows on the World and Gotham Bar and Grill have both given their lists a distinctly American accent, while restaurants like Montrachet, Daniel, the Tonic and Patroon have created distinctive personalities for their lists by searching out unusual selections.

"With a number of producers you can reserve and get half bottles, or you can ask the importer to put in a request," said Daniel Johnnes, the wine director at Montrachet. "It does take some more effort, but to have a good list, you have to work."

The diner jaded by overexposure to half bottles from big producers like Sonoma-Cutrer, Trefethen or Robert Mondavi can get a new lease on life at the Tonic, where the 21-bottle list includes a Sancerre from Lucien Crochet, a Bandol rosé from Domaine Tempier and a merlot from Georis in Monterey County.

Jean-Luc Le Dû, the sommelier at Daniel, has introduced quirks that match the cooking of Daniel Boulud, the restaurant's owner and executive chef, demoting Bordeaux and promoting wines from Burgundy and the Rhône. "I think his flavors require something more assertive than the cabernet grape," Mr. Le Dû said.

In the ideal meal, as conceived by Mr. Le Dû, a guest might start with a shellfish course paired with a half bottle of Savennières, move on to fish and a more substantial St.-Aubin from Burgundy, ease into a red Burgundy like Morey-St.-Denis when the meat makes an appearance, and finish strong with a big Côte Rôtie from the Rhône.

"It's a little more work for us than if someone simply orders a bottle of white and a bottle of red, but that way doesn't fit as well with the philosophy of the restaurant," Mr. Le Dû said.

One meal. Four wines. It's true: less really is more.

February 1999

Of Wine, Haste and Religion

By ROGER COHEN

I was dining the other night with a colleague, enjoying a respectable Russian River pinot noir, when he said with a steely firmness: "We'll pour our own wine, thank you."

This declaration of independence was prompted by that quintessential New York restaurant phenomenon: a server reducing a bottle of wine to a seven-minute, four-glass experience through overfilling and topping-up of a fanaticism found rarely outside the Middle East.

I know I'm being elitist here, a terrible thing in this political season, and quite possibly nobody in small-town Pennsylvania gives a damn how wine is poured. But I don't care and, come to think of it, last time I was in small-town Pennsylvania—at Gettysburg—I drank rather well.

Acceptable cappuccino was also available throughout the commonwealth at Dunkin' Donuts outlets, which makes one wonder if liberal elitism really begins and ends in Cambridge, Hyde Park and Berkeley these days. I even saw a Volvo somewhere west of Harrisburg.

But that's another story, albeit important, of seeping American sophistication-cum-Europeanization.

The liberation I felt at my colleague's I'll-pour boldness was intoxicating. That's right, I thought, we need to take our lives back. Drinking at your own pace is the best revenge.

It's humiliating to pay through the nose and suffer at affronts to good taste. Wine should glide, not glug, from a tilted, not tipped, bottle. The time that goes into the making of it should be reflected in the time it takes to drink.

That's so obvious that I got to wondering why wine glasses, even at fine New York tables, get filled almost to the brim, and refilled to that unseemly level, every time you're distracted from Second Amendment–authorized armed guard of your receptacle.

As with many things, there's a generous view and a mean one.

The kind interpretation would be that, through a gross misunderstanding of the nature of pleasure, servers and the restaurant managers behind them are convinced that solicitude is measured by the regularity with which a glass is topped up.

The uncharitable view would be that, guided by an acute understanding of the nature of commerce, servers are told by restaurant managers to hustle

531

clients through a meal and as many bottles of wine as possible.

After long reflection, of at least 12 seconds, as measured on my elitist Rolex, I've decided the second theory is more convincing.

It's more plausible partly because it tracks with another unhappy New York dining phenomenon at some remove from the languorous pleasures of Manet's *Déjeuner Sur L'Herbe*. I refer to the vacuuming away of your plate, at about the speed of light, the second you are deemed to have consumed the last mouthful.

Just as you prepare to dab bread into the unctuous leftover sauce from those slide-from-the-bone short ribs, the plate vanishes. The fact that others around the table may still be eating—and to be without a plate is to feel naked in such circumstances—does not trouble the stealthy masters of this Houdini routine.

As usual, in such matters, the French have it right. If you deconstruct the leftover, you find something that's yours, a little messy, even mucky, but yours. No wonder there's pleasure in poking around in it a little. Manet's revelers are surrounded by their picnic leftovers. Nobody's whisked them away.

In the same way, that mix of soil, hearth and tradition the French call "terroir" is personal. You poke around in it and discover that some ineffable mix of the land, its particular characteristics, and a unique human bond has found expression in a wine—not a "cabernet" or a "pinot" or a "merlot" but, say, a Chambolle-Musigny Derrière La Grange.

That's because "derrière la grange"—behind the barn—a small parcel of land produces a Burgundy distinct from another 50 yards away. Discovering this takes time, just as it takes time after bottling—perhaps a decade—for fruit, tannin and acidity to attain their full harmony.

American wine is rushed onto the table, as well as into the glass. Most is drunk five to 10 years too early. But, hey, this is a country in a hurry: Google's founders made a couple of billion dollars overnight last week, an un-French achievement. This is a great nation.

Perhaps it's so great I should wear an American flag lapel pin. Perhaps it's so great I should put myself in a duck blind this weekend. Perhaps it's so great I should join the great U.S. blood sport of anti-intellectualism. Perhaps it's so great I should go bowling more often. Perhaps it's so great I should stop praising France and conceal the fact I speak French.

But I don't want to grow bitter. Maybe I'll just cling—yes, cling—to my glass and the religion that's in it.

April 2008

A Stroll Through the "21" List, Circa 1945

By FRANK J. PRIAL

The restaurant consultant Roger Martin began a long career in New York restaurants by checking coats at the "21" Club in the early 1950s while still a New York University student. Mr. Martin, who died on Dec. 4, went on to work for Restaurant Associates and Windows on the World, and for a time he ran his own place in the Hamptons.

Last spring, when Food Arts magazine ran an excerpt from his memoirs, about his "21" days, it reminded me that somewhere I had my own "21" memento, a copy of the club's wine list from 1945, when it was known as Jack & Charlie's "21." I pulled it out.

Today, greasy spoons have wine lists. Fifty years ago, New York was a steak-and-potatoes town for the most part and wine sophistication, such as it was, was confined to a handful of restaurants and a couple of European-style hotels. The "21" Club was one of those places. Its celebrity-laden clientele may have consisted largely of whiskey drinkers and martini addicts, but the club was proud of its wine cellar.

In 1945, any wine list was bound to be mostly French. The "21" list was no exception. But long before anyone else did it, "21" also offered wines from Italy, Spain, Germany, Hungary, Chile and Switzerland. And, yes, the United States.

Nowadays, recent vintages will predominate. Anything more than eight years old is special. In 1945, just the opposite was true. The youngest Bordeaux on the "21" list were nine years old—from 1936—and many dated from the 1920s. In fact, it could hardly have been otherwise. World War II had ended earlier that year. Some of the best vineyards in Europe had been devastated, and wine shipments had virtually come to a halt.

California and New York, which might have been expected to fill the void, had only begun to make fine wine in the 1930s and '40s, and very few people in watering holes like "21" were inclined to drink it.

So "21" was selling its old wines, and what wines they were. Château Lafite-Rothschild 1934 was $11; so were the 1933 and the 1928. The 1924 was $9.50 and the 1920, a 25-year-old wine, was $14. The 1934 Haut-Brion was $10. The 1920 was $12.50 and the 1916 a dollar less.

A magnum of Château Latour from the memorable 1929 vintage was $23 and a magnum of Château Margaux was $21, but a magnum of Mouton-Rothschild, listed among the Second Growths because it would not become a First Growth for another 28 years, was $25.

The depth of the restaurant's Bordeaux cellar was exceptional: five vintages of Château Brane-Cantenac, the youngest being 1929; six of Gruaud Larose; five of Pichon-Longueville; six of Château Margaux going back to 1904 ($17.50); and eight vintages of the famous Sauternes Château d'Yquem, from 1936 back to 1919, ranging in price from $8 for the 1936 to $18 for the 1920.

A separate cellar held truly old Bordeaux, including the 1865 Lafite, made three years before Baron James Rothschild bought the estate, and Mouton-Rothschild 1869, made 16 years after Mouton had become Rothschild property.

The Burgundy list was long and distinguished, with great wines like a 1934 Chambertin from Liger-Belair and a 1929 Clos de Vougeot 1929 from Mugnier priced at $8 and $11 respectively. The most expensive of the Burgundies was a 1929 Romanée-Conti from the Domaine de la Romanée-Conti for $18. Surprisingly, Beaujolais was not much cheaper than Burgundy. A 1933 Beaujolais was $7, a 1926 Fleurie $7.50, the same price as a 1928 Beaune or a 1934 Pommard Rugiens.

Wine drinkers who are just now beginning to discover German wines would be fascinated by the six pages of German rieslings "21" offered 58 years ago. On average, they were priced two to three dollars more per bottle than the Bordeaux. True, there were 15 Liebfraumilch, but there were dozens of fine estate wines under $15 and a priceless spätlese Moselle, a 1934 Bernkasteler Doktor, Dr. Thanisch, for $18.

Bear in mind that a full dinner at "21" might cost as little as $15 in 1945, and working men and women paid 35 or 50 cents for an adequate lunch at the Automat. Inflation would bring all of these fantasy prices more in line with what we must pay for these wines today. The Bernkasteler Doktor from a current vintage would sell for close to $100 in a restaurant, while contemporary versions of many of those $10 and $11 Bordeaux sell for $200 and more.

Most intriguing to me were the listings in the American wine section part of the old "21" list. Inglenook, Beaulieu Vineyards, Louis M. Martini and Wente Brothers are all represented. There is a nonvintage B.V. cabernet, four different cabernets from Martini and a sauvignon blanc from Wente. Inglenook is repre-sented by a white wine and not by one of its memorable prewar cabernets. New

York is represented by American grapes like Niagara, Delaware and Elvira, from Widmer's Wine Cellars in what the list spells as the "Canadaigua District."

The restaurant must have been nervous about offering American wines. Napa rieslings were described as "Alsatian type," a Wente chardonnay as a "Burgundy type" and a Martini cabernet from Santa Clara as a "Château Latour type." The Beaulieu Vineyards B.V. cabernet (Bordeaux type) sold for $3; most of the other American wines for about $4.

These days at "21," $4 might get you a big smile from the coat checker, but not much more.

January 2003

With Your Kids
at the Table

Can Sips at Home Prevent Binges?

By ERIC ASIMOV

Parents always want to share their passions with their children. Whether you're a fan of baseball or the blues, sailing or tinkering with old cars, few things are as rewarding as seeing a spark of receptivity in the eyes of the next generation.

It usually doesn't take. Most of the time kids—teenagers, anyway—would as soon snicker at their old man's obsessions as indulge him. Even so, I can't help hoping that my sons might share my taste in music and food, books and movies, ball teams and politics. Why should wine be any different?

It's the alcohol, of course, which makes wine not just tricky but potentially hazardous. Nonetheless, I would like to teach my sons—16 and 17—that wine is a wonderful part of a meal. I want to teach them to enjoy it while also drumming it into them that when abused, wine, like any other alcoholic beverage, can be a grave danger.

As they were growing up I occasionally gave them tastes from my glass—an unusual wine, perhaps, or a taste of Champagne on New Year's Eve. They've had sips at seders and they see wine nightly at our dinner table. With both boys now in high school, I thought it was time to offer them the option of small tastes at dinner.

In European wine regions, a new parent might dip a finger in the local pride and wipe it lovingly across an infant's lips—"just to give the taste." A child at the family table might have a spoonful of wine added to the water, because it says, "You are one of us." A teenager might have a small glass of wine, introducing an adult pleasure in a safe and supervised manner. This is how I imagined it in my house.

But about a year ago, my wife attended a gathering on the Upper East Side sponsored by several high schools addressing the topic of teenagers and alcohol.

The highly charged discussion centered on the real dangers of binge drinking and peer pressure, of brain damage and parental over-permissiveness, and of the law.

One authority disparaged the European model, saying that teenage drinking in Europe—never mind which part—is much worse than it is in the United States. The underlying message was that nothing good comes from mixing alcohol and teenagers.

My wife was shaken. We agreed to hold off on the tasting plan. But I decided to try to get some answers myself.

I found ample evidence of the dangers of abusive drinking. Recent studies have shown that heavy drinking does more damage to the teenage brain than previously suspected, while the part of the brain responsible for judgment is not even fully formed until the age of 25.

"If we were to argue that responsible drinking requires a responsible brain, theoretically we wouldn't introduce alcohol until 25," said Dr. Ralph I. Lopez, a clinical professor of pediatrics at Weill Cornell Medical College who specializes in adolescents.

The law specifies 21 as the age when people can buy and drink alcohol. Bill Crowley, a spokesman for the New York State Liquor Authority, confirmed that it was illegal to give anyone underage a taste of an alcoholic beverage in a restaurant, cafe or bar. But in the home?

"We don't have any jurisdiction over what happens in the home," Mr. Crowley said. Of course, each state's laws differ, and lack of jurisdiction doesn't mean immunity. The police or social service agencies could intervene if underage bingeing were encouraged in the home. And when driving is a factor, everything changes. But inside the home, the law, at least, seems to permit the small tastes that I had in mind.

Even so, are small tastes justified? Abundant research shows the dangers of heavy drinking and the necessity of getting help with teenage alcohol abuse. But little guidance is offered on teaching teenagers about the pleasures of wine with a meal.

It would be easy to preach abstinence to children until they're 21, but is it naïve and even irresponsible to think that teenagers won't experiment? Might forbidding even a taste of wine with a meal actually encourage secrecy and recklessness?

Some experts think so. Dr. Lopez began to offer his daughter a little wine at dinner when she was 13.

"You have to look at a family and decide where alcohol fits," he said. "If you demonstrate the beauty of wine, just as you would Grandma's special pie, then it augments a meal. However, if there is an issue about drinking within a family then it's a different situation."

If a family member had an alcohol problem, or if cocktails were served regularly for relaxation, he said, "That's a different message than wine at the table."

I called Dr. Paul Steinberg, a psychiatrist in Washington, who is the former director of counseling at Georgetown University.

"The best evidence shows that teaching kids to drink responsibly is better than shutting them off entirely from it," he told me. "You want to introduce your kids to it, and get across the point that this is to be enjoyed but not abused."

He said that the most dangerous day of a young person's life is the 21st birthday, when legality is celebrated all too fervently. Introducing wine as a part of a meal, he said, was a significant protection against bingeing behavior.

What is the evidence? In 1983, Dr. George E. Vaillant, a professor of psychiatry at Harvard University, published *The Natural History of Alcoholism*, a landmark work that drew on a 40-year survey of hundreds of men in Boston and Cambridge.

Dr. Vaillant compared 136 men who were alcoholics with men who were not. Those who grew up in families where alcohol was forbidden at the table, but was consumed away from the home, apart from food, were seven times more likely to be alcoholics that those who came from families where wine was served with meals but drunkenness was not tolerated.

He concluded that teenagers should be taught to enjoy wine with family meals, and 25 years later Dr. Vaillant stands by his recommendation. "The theoretical position is: driving a car, shooting a rifle, using alcohol are all dangerous activities," he told me, "and the way you teach responsibility is to let parents teach appropriate use."

"If you are taught to drink in a ceremonial way with food, then the purpose of alcohol is taste and celebration, not inebriation," he added. "If you are forbidden to use it until college then you drink to get drunk."

In a more recent study of 80 teenagers and 80 young adults in Italy, Lee Strunin, a professor at the Boston University School of Public Health, found that drinking wine in a family setting offered some protection against bingeing and may encourage moderate drinking. But she cautioned against extrapolating from Italy to the United States.

Her colleague, David Rosenbloom, director of the School of Public Health's Youth Alcohol Prevention Center, emphasized that family context was crucial. "Does the kid see the parents drunk?" he asked. "Does the kid understand expectations? Is there violence in the family setting?"

"It is certainly possible that in some family contexts the introduction of wine at family dinners could have a mild protective factor," he said, adding that he believes that expecting abstinence is a perfectly reasonable parental position.

In the best of all possible worlds, I suppose, young adults would not touch alcohol until they turn 25 and then would instantly understand the pleasures of moderate consumption. It seems to me as silly to imagine that as it is to expect the same at 21.

Although the issue is not settled in my household, my cautious opinion now is that my teenage sons have more to gain than to lose by having a taste of wine now and then with dinner. By taste, I mean just that: a couple of sips, perhaps, not a full glass, and decidedly not for any of their friends, whose own parents must make their own decisions.

The years between ages 15 and 25 are dangerous straits, and it doesn't help to know that alcohol is associated with many of the hazards young adults face. Finding that sweet spot between sanctimony and self-centered frivolity is a parent's job. I think I'm there, but it's not quite comfortable.

March 2008

The Last Drops

The Driest Wines (and the Drollest) Are in the Museum

By HOWARD G. GOLDBERG

Intoxicating dry wine in open bottles, stoppered decanters and goblets lies within easy grasp throughout the Metropolitan Museum of Art. This wine, mainly European and American, never spills or ages. It is a blend of the painter's palate and palette.

The canvases in many galleries reward a wine lover's single-minded search for wine themes in the Met. Literal and symbolic, these motifs are central and incidental to depictions of life and the afterlife. Some take on fuller dimensions in marble, bronze, lead, earthenware and plaster.

No surprise. From the birth of civilization, wine has stimulated personal and cultural highs, as the fevered revels (chaperoned by Eros) on the Met's ancient Greek pottery illustrate. Lows, too: Take wine coolers, the pop-top refresher concocted from chintzy grapes and fizz in the '80s. Wine words and meanings, like wine styles and preferences, change with the times. The Met shows us the original coolers, one in mahogany (attributed to Duncan Phyfe, in the Luce Center), which speak of nights at table, not under it.

Had servants named Bartles and Jaymes poured wine at dinners given by Sir Robert Walpole, England's first prime minister, they might have fetched the bottles from water in the hexagonal silver cooler embossed with his coat of arms, which is housed near the English period rooms. A silver monteith, perhaps like the one in the Landsdowne House dining room, would have chilled the glasses.

Wine artifacts, secular and sacred, prosaic and ethereal, are so profuse in the permanent collections that they need no structured tour, just a taste for serendipity and a patient, selective eye. The best visiting times are Fridays, Saturdays and Sundays, when every gallery is open. Once attuned to the miniature and the splashed grape clusters, leaves and tendrils that are engraved, raised and carved in gold, glass, stone and clay, romantic visitors can imagine themselves in mini-arbors.

The Vine, a Beaux-Arts bronze by Harriet Whitney Frishmuth gracing the Engelhard Court of the American Wing, personifies the Met's commitment to viticulture. Several Fokine Ballet dancers posed for the figure of a nude bacchante who, the label redundantly says, is "shown stretching upward and outward in imitation of a living vine." There is no evidence of pruning.

Nearby, nurtured by the court's Rhine-like sunlight and humidity, the ripe fat blue, purple and green fruit in two tall stained-glass Tiffany panels of trellised grapevines taste juicy and sweet to the imagination. On the balcony, a 19th-century pressed-glass wine urn that resembles an oversize decanter with a spigot, probably made in New England, awakens envy in sideboard owners.

One aperitif is *Prudence,* a 15th-century glazed terra-cotta roundel by Andrea della Robbia, near the door of the Lehman Collection, which in part depicts meaty bunches of dark grapes resembling ripe cabernet sauvignon.

In the Wallace Wing, the bottle and grapes, a voluptuary's delight, in Bonnard's *Terrace at Vernon* leave the impression that life is wine and roses, but other oils have different ideas. *Vanitas,* a Pieter Claesz still life in a European gallery, is explained this way: "Here a skull, an overturned glass roemer with its fleeting reflections, an expired lamp . . . suggest that worldly efforts are ultimately in vain."

Maybe so, but you won't get far telling it to the overwrought wine-driven satyrs and maenads negotiating eternity on Greek and Roman pottery (discreetly placed far from the Met's delicately wrought chalices). And if the origin of "enophile" remains a mystery to wine snobs who affect that title, innocence is lost among the labels' Greek prefixes: "oinochoe," for wine jug.

The modern Greeks' practice of putting a resinous flavor into wine, now fortunately dying, perhaps originated in their ancestors' habit of mixing two parts of water to one of wine in immense vessels. Many such kraters are shown, along with an enough cups, bottles, bowls and storage jars to have stocked an Attic branch of Macy's Cellar.

The Greeks diluted wine, an everyday beverage, to keep it from turning into vinegar and because there was a cultural taboo against intoxication. Taboo? Who, surrounded by these orgies, would ever dream of such a thing? The Met ought to offer a leaflet written, say, by Robert W. Wallace, professor of classics and ancient history at Northwestern University. He knows about such antique matters as self-discipline and would readily offer a reminder: "Drunkenness was barbarous. You lost control, and that was not a thing to do. The Greeks thought that drinking wine straight drove you crazy. The ritualized revels were sanctioned by the gods and controlled by overseers." Funny, not an overseer in sight.

The wine-and-food crowd will adore *The Feast of Achelous* by Rubens and Jan Bruegel the Elder in the European department. Theseus and his companions, fresh from a boar hunt, dine at the cave of the river god. The setting teems with oysters and lobsters. Purists may be appalled because the god is serving red wine with fish, but the collaborators redeem themselves by putting a white on the table.

Artists work the angles. The chalice in Vermeer's contemplative *Allegory of the Faith* is predictably vertical, that is, upright, complementing an adjacent woman personifying Faith. Nearby, a glass of luminous pinkish wine held aloft by a roisterer in Steen's riotous *Merry Company on a Terrace* is slightly canted, implying that the character is off-center.

A highlight of the northern European decorative arts is a 17th-century German cabinet with a partly gilt silver panel in relief showing Bacchus hoisting a cup while seated on a barrel from which wine issues from a spout.

The museum's artifacts bring wine down to earth, even if they have heaven in mind.

The liturgical silver Attarouthi Treasure is the centerpiece of the aisle to the south of the grand staircase. Its nine huge chalices, we're told, "were made for offering the Eucharistic wine to entire congregations," probably in two churches in a thriving merchant town in northern Syria in the sixth and seventh centuries; a strainer used to prepare wine is a curious sidelight. The early Christian Antioch Chalice, a plain inner cup (once erroneously thought to be the Holy Grail) inside an ornate openwork cup, lies a few feet away. In the opposite aisle, a golden Greek libation bowl, perhaps from the fourth century B.C., is a standout, as are six darling sixth-century silver Cypriot wine jugs, all under an inch high.

Few millet-wine artifacts fuse the spiritual and material worlds as movingly as the elaborate set of 13 bronze ritual altar objects—containers, vessels, cups, beakers and a ladle—dating from the 11th century B.C. The set is featured in the gallery of ancient Chinese art. A monumental covered bronze wine container from the ninth to the eighth century B.C. is another standout. Among the especially rich Asian rice-wine implements is a stark, sharply formed bronze vessel (just north of the grand staircase) that has inlaid gold, silver and brass, and dates to the Ming dynasty. The Korean storage jars, bottles and ewers in stoneware and porcelain invite leisurely inspection.

In the Rockefeller Wing, four ornate wooden cups carved by the Kuba people of Zaire were intended not only for palm wine but also as status symbols, as were a carved animal horn and an elaborately decorated storage gourd from Cameroon. All date from the late 19th or early 20th centuries.

Ancient Egypt was lotus land for wine drinkers, especially aristocrats. Tomb paintings and reliefs and storage amphoras document virtually everything about winemaking and consumption habits. Throughout the galleries, endless processions of slaves bear black and green grapes and other fare to banquets. Grape bunches in crisp relief are notably vivid in a wall of the chapel of Ramses I at Abydos, in the Sackler Wing.

A visit would be incomplete without seeing the trellised arbor wall painting from a villa buried by the Vesuvius eruption in A.D. 79, off the Great Hall; the Bordeaux room, a salon taken from a villa in that French city; Bernini's ecstatic vine-wreathed sculpture *Faun Teased by Children*, near the Petrie Sculpture Court; six 1830–1840 American Champagne glasses in the Baltimore Room and chalices in the Medieval Treasury. And don't miss the luminous gold *Drinking Vessel Terminating in the Forepart of a Lion* in the Iranian gallery; a manuscript painting showing two men treading grapes, in the Islamic collection (despite the religious ban on alcohol);and the bird-shaped modern claret jug designed by Archibald Knox, in the Kravis Wing.

Did Frank O'Dea, who prepares the Met's wine lists, sweet-talk the department of Greek and Roman art? Is it coincidental that not long ago a second-century Roman statue of Dionysus, described as the "god of wine and divine intoxication," was positioned near the entrance to the first-floor restaurants?

Dionysus, interviewed, recommended a split of Jean Cordier white vin ordinaire in the cafeteria ($4.75), a lunchtime 1991 Robert Mondavi white zinfandel (to keep the mind clear) in the white-tablecloth restaurant ($17 a bottle), a late-afternoon glass of 1990 Beaulieu Vineyard Rutherford cabernet sauvignon ($6.50) in the cafe and a Charles Heidsieck special brut nonvintage Champagne in the fourth floor members-only Trustees' Dining Room ($35 a bottle).

The museum's shop sells such eye-catching reproductions as a pewter version of an early Hellenistic kylix or wine cup ($42), a pewter copy of a 19th-century Moroccan kiddush cup ($38), a silver copy of a 19th-century Viennese kiddush cup ($450) and a pewter duplicate of a 19th-century English bottle coaster.

Alas, there are curatorial lapses. Who had the bright idea to put *Self-Portrait* by the British painter William Orpen in a conspicuous spot in the Wallace Wing? It features, of all retrograde things, whisky and soda! More important, the Metropolitan should deaccession the Caccini statue in the Spanish Courtyard. It is called *Temperance*.

July 1993

The Big Grape: Nouveau York City

By HOWARD G. GOLDBERG

The wine merchant William Sokolin, in a published letter commenting on how to produce good vintages, has suggested that cabernet sauvignon grapes should be planted in Central Park. In fuller bloom, that idea offers the prospect of a new New York—or, more aptly, a new Nouveau York. In short, turn Manhattan into a vineyard.

Geography offers grounds: Has no one noticed the uncanny resemblance between the Médoc, home of Bordeaux wine—made largely from cabernet sauvignon—and Manhattan? Both are roughly on a north-south axis; both are surrounded on at least two sides by water, which benefits viticulture; both lie within 4 degrees north latitude of each other; both are inundated with French restaurants—though perhaps Manhattan holds an edge.

Why buy Beaujolais Villages when you can drink Greenwich Villages (plural, of course, because of the East and West Village)? Why bother with a Rosé d'Anjou when you can enjoy a Rose of Washington Square?

In a grander vision, Fort Tryon Park is to Champagne, France's northernmost wine region, as the Battery is to the Midi, the south. That makes Central Park the equivalent of Burgundy; science thus mandates, with apologies to Mr. Sokolin, that City Hall plant pinot noir there.

Since pinot noir is a basic grape of Champagne, George Steinbrenner, the Yankees' owner, and Nelson Doubleday, the Mets' chief owner, have a stake in it. Even as a "vintage of the century" is always proclaimed, so their teams will again take a World Series. Why must so much expensive Moët & Chandon be wasted in locker rooms to shampoo the champs? Fort Tryon brut would be far cheaper.

Soil, climate and the vintner are the heart of successful winemaking. Soil quality can so vary from field to field that a path between tracts can separate celebrated from middling wine, as can the terrain's slope, drainage and exposure to sun. Centuries of trial and error have taught which grape grows best where; the trick is to find the ideal Manhattan locale for each varietal.

It should be easy. Certain wines have long histories in the city. For example, surely the 1924 notebooks of the anarchist Emma Goldman, years after her angry departure from Russia, will show these tasting notes: "Union Square

Reds—coarse, earthy, lack finesse, too much acid, unbalanced, you get a headache."

Take riesling, the noble grape of exquisite, costly German wine. Like other classic varietals, it thrives only in inhospitable soil, especially on steep terraced slopes overlooking the Rhine and Mosel. Its comparable Manhattan site would be the glass-and-marble Trump Tower. Riesling's roots, sunk deep into the glistening metal, would produce a liquid of unrivaled steeliness. The bottle label would simply say: "Qualitätswein mit Prädikat Anbaugebiet Neuyork 1984er Fifthaveneuer-und-Eastfiftysixthstreeter Schloss Trumptowerer Bonwittellerbergstein Trocken-beerenauslese Erzeugerabfüllung." Just go in and ask for it.

What to plant on Wall Street? The viognier. On the vine this rare Rhône Valley grape, like many Big Board stocks, offers a low yield. But its rich taste and bouquet are found in blue-chip whites such as Château-Grillet, whose price, the wine critic Hugh Johnson observes, equals that of Montrachet, Burgundy's regal white.

The sémillon, a fairly late ripener, is thus the scholar's grape. Its aroma in young, dry wines recalls green apples—that is, freshmen. It takes five years in the bottle—a B.A. and M.A.—to reach complexity. More important, it is the basis of renowned dessert wines like Château d'Yquem, the Sauternes.

The grape is attacked by a mold that penetrates the skin, shriveling it and enabling water to evaporate; in autumn, as in thought, the retained juice concentrates into nectar. The mold is known in Latin as *Botrytis cinerea*—in French, familiarly, as pourriture noble, or noble rot. Obviously, the sémillon qualifies for planting on campuses, particularly if mulched with discarded monographs.

Another luscious after-dinner wine would be produced at Eighth Avenue and 41st Street by the port authority.

And what would the United Nations vinify? Châteauneuf-du-Pape. This southern Rhône wine is a blend of up to 13 grapes—and no two vintners can agree on the proportions. It contains the highest minimum level of alcohol in any French wine, 12.5 percent, a degree not unknown in the North Delegates' Lounge.

The dolcetto, grape of the full and velvety red Dolcetto d'Alba in the Piedmont region of Italy, would flower in Lincoln Center, whose wine would be named Dolcetto d'Opera—or, simply, Vino Verdi. Used during the first-act drinking scene in *La Traviata*, it comes in a magnum or, some say, a magnum opus.

Wonder about chardonnay, the white mainstay of Burgundy's Côte d'Or, or

Golden Slope? Down the median strip of Park Avenue. As for Catawba, Delaware, Ives, Niagara and scuppernong grapes—along the Avenue of the Americas. On East 96th Street, psychoanalysts would spend their hours uncorking native Liebfraumilch. And, last, vins de pays, or regional wines, which don't always travel well: certainly no shipments from Chelsea to SoHo.

This river of wine, after the annual crush, would flow, for storage and aging, into the still-to-be-completed East 63rd Street subway tunnel, a chilled cave stacked floor to ceiling with oak casks and barrels stretching far into the distance, under Gothic arches, candles dripping from cast-iron chandeliers, everywhere cobwebs draping dusty racked bottles whose yellowing labels tell of ancient vintages, of a distant, nearly forgotten time when people didn't know about a Kir but only about a two-cents-plain.

Where would it all lead—the trellises, the pruning, the spigots? To a small notice in the newspaper every November: "Alternate side of the street parking will be suspended Friday and Saturday for a bacchanal."

November 1984

Jefferson on Wine:
"The Only Antidote to the Bane of Whisky"

By HOWARD G. GOLDBERG

Thomas Jefferson—wine collector, student of winemaking and merchandising, grape grower and wine adviser to the first five presidents (himself included)—pulled a decanter from his wooden traveling wine chest and poured us both an aperitif. He had granted a wide-ranging interview about foreign and domestic wines, his first in 161 years. The occasion was the 200th anniversary of his tour of French wine regions, from which he emerged the father of American connoisseurs.

During lunch in his Monticello, Va., dining room, Mr. Jefferson showed off the two wine dumbwaiters he designed. They are built into the fireplace and drop down to his cool brick wine cellar.

He displayed his meticulous bin records listing Bordeaux, Burgundy, Champagne, Chianti, Frontignan (a favorite), Hermitage, Lacryma Christi, Madeira, Malaga, malmsey, Marsala, port, Sauternes, sherry and Tokay—to name a fraction. To keep the historical record accurate, he answered my questions by quoting his own words from years of wine correspondence, diaries and other records.

Mr. President, as envoy to France from 1784 to 1789, you observed Louis XVI's wine drinking and other habits. How did you characterize them to John Jay, Secretary of State?

He hunts one-half the day, is drunk the other, and signs whatever he is bid.

You were abroad when the Constitution was written. As a rural Virginia farmer observing the wine regions of France, how did you depict, in your diary, royalty's treatment of French agricultural society?

The people of Burgundy and Beaujolais are well clothed, and have the appearance of being well fed. But they experience all the oppressions that result from the nature of the general government, and from that of their particular tenures, and of the seignorial government to which they are subject. What a cruel reflection that a rich country cannot long be a free one!

What economic conditions did you find in Burgundy?

At Pommard and Voulenay I observed them eating good wheat bread; at Meursault, rye. I asked the reason of the difference. They told me that the white wines fail in quality much oftener than the red, and remain on hand. The farmer therefore cannot afford to feed his laborers so well. At Meursault only white wines are made, because there is too much stone for the red. On such slight circumstances depends the condition of man!

Did you have any bad experiences in French wine country?

When one calls in the taverns for the vin du pays, they give what is natural and unadulterated and cheap: when *vin étrangère* is called for, it only gives a pretext for charging an extravagant price for an unwholesome stuff, very often of their own brewery.

The people you will naturally see the most of will be tavern keepers, valets de place and postilions. These are the hackneyed rascals of every country. Of course they must never be considered when we calculate the national character.

You fell in love with Sauternes, especially from Château d'Yquem, and imported a great deal. What did your first tasting notes say?

This proves a most excellent wine, and seems to have hit the palate of the Americans more than any wine I have ever seen in France.

When you encountered wine snobs, what did you tell them?

We could, in the United States, make as great a variety of wines as are made in Europe, not exactly of the same kinds, but doubtless as good.

You rated four Bordeaux vineyards "of first quality." They were "Chateau Margau," "La Tour de Segur," "Houtbrion" and "Chateau de la Fite." They are still around, and fetch celestial prices; should today's middle class pay them?

The increase of expense beyond income is an indication soliciting the employment of the pruning knife.

What did you learn in the Champagne region in 1788?

The white wines are either mousseux (sparkling) or nonmousseux. The sparkling are little drunk in France but are almost alone known and drunk in foreign countries. This makes so great a demand, and so certain a one, that they endeavor to make all the sparkling if they can.

We share a taste for German wines. When you toured Rheingau vineyards in 1788, what did you find?

Though they begin to make wine, as it has been said, at Cologne, and continue it up the river indefinitely, yet it is only from Rudesheim to Hochheim that wines of the first quality are made. What is the leading Italian wine? There are several crops under different names but that of Montepulciano is the only good, and that is equal to the best Burgundy.

Let us focus on America. Vintners in minor wine states—Tennessee, New Mexico—who try to make ends meet would agree with your words in a 1787 letter to a law instructor at William and Mary College. You said "the vine" is "the parent of misery." Please elaborate.

Those who cultivate it are always poor, and he who would employ himself with us in the culture of corn, cotton, etc. can procure in exchange for that much more wine, and better than he could raise by its direct culture.

You tried to cultivate European vinifera grapes, which make the best wines, but failed. Northerners are baffled by your love of wine from North Carolina's scuppernong, a floozy of a muscadine grape.

Her scuppernong wine, made on the south side of the Sound, would be distinguished on the best tables of Europe for its fine aroma and crystalline transparence. Unhappily that aroma, in most of the samples I have seen, has been entirely submerged in brandy. This coarse taste and practice is the peculiarity of Englishmen.

Today's wine language is pretentious. How have you described wine?

Dry, sparkling, acid, barely sensible, rough, astringent, elegant, higher flavored, delicious, excellent, delicate, silky. By our term "silky" we do not mean sweet, but sweetish in the smallest degree only.

During your first year in the White House, you spent nearly $3,000 on wines— more than on groceries. While president from 1801 to 1809, you allocated $11,000 for wines. As a free-trader, what did you tell protectionist Congressmen at your table?

No nation is drunken where wine is cheap; and none sober where the dearness of wine substitutes ardent spirits as the common beverage. It is, in truth, the only antidote to the bane of whisky. Fix but the duty at the rate of other merchandise, and we can drink wine here as cheap as we do grog, and who will not prefer it? Its extended use will carry health and comfort to a much enlarged circle.

Please recite that poetic thought you wrote to your good friend Dr. Benjamin Rush in 1811 when you were 68 years old.

I find friendship to be like wine, raw when new, ripened with age, the true old man's milk and restorative cordial.

What are you pouring to toast independence this weekend?

Vin de Nice. The crop called Bellet, of Mr. Sasterno, is the best. This is the most elegant everyday wine in the world and costs 31 cents the bottle. Not much being made, it is little known at the general markets.

(Bellet, in the hills behind Nice, still makes good red, white and rosé wines. I made a mental note to buy some. But Bellet is not easy to find in New York. What to do?)

"Mr. President," I said. "Can you recommend a good cheap hotel in Nice?"

July 1987

The Spirit of Giving

By FRANK J. PRIAL

This is not exactly a Christmas story; it's not really a wine story, either, although wine is central to it. It's a story about living and dying and the occasionally surprising nobility of the human spirit. No, it's not exactly a Christmas story but—for me—it evokes the spirit of Christmas more profoundly than a hundred recorded carols or a forest of lighted trees.

The story begins in Norway in 1908. That was the year that Peder Knutsen, then 19, immigrated to Canada to homestead on the vast western plains. Sometime later, he wandered down into North Dakota, settling in Kindred, a farming community of some 600 people that is 20 miles or so south of Fargo. He owned a bit of land, about two acres, worked as a farm laborer for his neighbors and made occasional trips back to Norway to visit a sister. He never married and, toward the end of his life, lived alone and apparently content in his small house, mostly on a $78 monthly pension from World War I. He died on Nov. 11, 1974.

Several months later, on Feb. 7, 1975, a small item appeared in *The International Herald Tribune* in Paris. It said that Peder Knutsen of Kindred, N.D., had died recently and left a will donating $30,000 to a home for the elderly in the town of his birth, Gol, in the Hallingdal Valley, about 140 miles east of Bergen. But it was no ordinary bequest. Mr. Knutsen specified that the income from his bequest must be used to buy wine for the old people in the home.

On Feb. 5, two days before the newspaper item appeared, the municipal council in Gol agreed to accept Mr. Knutsen's gift ". . . even if the donation was odd and put this alcopolitical problem on our neck," as the acting mayor at the time, Ola Storia, put it.

Mr. Storia and his fellow councilmen estimated that Mr. Knutsen's bequest would provide about 1,000 bottles of wine a year, or about three bottles a day to be shared among the 23 residents then living at the home. Assuming that there are always a couple of nondrinkers, even in a group of Scandinavians, the bequest barely came to a glass a day for each resident.

But a glass of wine is just what many physicians prescribe for their elderly patients, and even one glass of wine, shared with others at the evening meal, might serve to brighten some long Arctic nights.

Shortly after the story about Mr. Knutsen's will first appeared, a neighbor and, in fact, his landlord, spoke about him. "He was a wonderful old man," said Delice Ebsen.

"He never went to church, but he was a religious man. His Bible sustained him."

The Ebsens had bought Mr. Knutsen's two acres from him around 1970 for $3,000. They let him live on, free, in the house he had built. "He used to make rhubarb wine," Mrs. Ebsen recalled, "and he enjoyed a can of beer now and then." So far as she knew, he had had little experience with grape wine at all.

"We talked about what he would do with his money," Mrs. Ebsen said, "and he liked the idea of leaving it to a home. But we had no idea he meant to leave it to a home in Norway and, to tell the truth, we had no idea how much money he had. There was the $3,000 he got from us, and he must have saved some money after selling his land in Canada."

The story of Peder Knutsen might never have come to light had it not been passed along by another elderly gentleman, George C. Sumner, an American, now deceased, who lived in Paris at the time. A Yankee of distinguished lineage, sent forth by Harvard in the misty years before the Great War, Mr. Sumner carved out an impressive career as a wine exporter and broker in the decades following World War II.

Appended to the now crumbling clipping about Mr. Knutsen are a few lines by Mr. Sumner: "It is not hard to imagine the drab dullness of life for those whose working days are over and who are confined to the routine of a home and the same old conversation—if any—at meals.

"A few glasses of wine and the fellowship they incite can change the atmosphere of the dining room and make dinner something to look forward to.

"I believe there are some, perhaps many, who would like to leave such an endowment for those who have had their day but still have some time."

It was Mr. Sumner's idea that a fund might be raised to provide a glass of wine for other old people living out their years in days of dull routine. How well he succeeded, I have no idea. I hope he did. But even if he didn't, it's still pleasant to think, particularly at this time of the year, of Peder Knutsen and to raise a glass to him and the old people of Gol in Norway.

Surely most of the old folks who first enjoyed his largesse have joined him in another life. He lived alone with his Bible in North Dakota, but, thanks to him, succeeding generations of the elderly in a little town 5,000 miles away will, from time to time, enjoy a moment of warmth and friendship over a glass of wine.

I hope they enjoy their wine in a few days. They will help make this a true Christmas story.

December 1984

CONTRIBUTORS' BIOGRAPHIES

Liz Alderman, in Paris, writes about European economics, finance and business for *The New York Times*. Earlier, she was an assistant business editor for *The Times*. She spent five years as business editor of *The International Herald Tribune*.

R. W. Apple Jr. (1934–2006) was a correspondent and editor at *The New York Times* for more than 40 years. Apple, known as Johnny, was bureau chief in Albany, N.Y., as well as Lagos, Nairobi, Saigon, Moscow, London and Washington. He also wrote frequently about food and wine, and a collection of his articles, *Far Flung and Well Fed*, was published posthumously (2009).

Eric Asimov has been chief wine critic at *The New York Times* since 2004. Asimov created the $25 and Under restaurant reviews and wrote them through 2004. He was editor of the Living section from 1991 to 1994 and editor of Styles of The Times from 1994 to 1995. His book *How to Love Wine* is to be published in 2012.

Barry Bearak, who has reported from southern Africa for *The New York Times*, won the 2002 Pulitzer Prize for International Reporting for his "deeply affecting and illuminating coverage of daily life in war-torn Afghanistan." He is now a sports reporter.

Pam Belluck is a science reporter for *The New York Times*. She is author of the book *Island Practice: Cobblestone Rash, Underground Tom and Other Adventures of a Nantucket Doctor.*

Corie Brown is a co-founder and general manager of *Zester Daily*, an online magazine featuring news and opinion about wine and food. She was a writer and editor at *The Los Angeles Times* and is writing a book about climate change and wine.

Patricia Leigh Brown has reported for *The New York Times* since 1987, first from New York and, since 2000, from San Francisco. Alice Waters once came to her house and, she says, redesigned "my family's food life."

Frank Bruni, an Op-Ed columnist for *The New York Times*, has been its chief restaurant critic and Rome bureau chief. He is author of two *Times* best-sellers: *Born Round*, a memoir, and *Ambling Into History*, about George W. Bush's presidential campaign in 2000.

Roger Cohen, a former foreign correspondent and foreign editor of *The New York Times*, is a columnist for the *International Herald Tribune*. He is author of *Soldiers and Slaves: American POW's Trapped by the Nazis' Final Gamble*.

Florence Fabricant, who has written about food and drink for *The New York Times* since 1972, is a member of its wine panel and devises the recipes to pair with the panel's featured wines. She is the author, co-author or editor of 11 cookbooks, including *The New York Times Seafood Cookbook*, *The New York Times Restaurant Cookbook*, which contained wine suggestions for the recipes, and *The New York Times Dessert Cookbook*.

Howard G. Goldberg was an editor at *The New York Times* from 1970 to 2004. He spent 23 years at the Op-Ed page, where he was senior editor. He began contributing wine articles in the mid-1980s, and, in 1987, wrote the Wine Talk column for a period. In the 1990s he developed Wine Under $20, a feature published on Sundays for many years, and Long Island Vines, which still appears in the Long Island pages on Sundays.

William Grimes has been on the staff at *The New York Times* since 1989 and is currently a domestic correspondent. He has been the paper's restaurant critic, a book reviewer, a culture reporter, an obituary writer and an editor on *The New York Times Magazine*. He has written several books on food and drink, most recently *Appetite City: A Culinary History of New York*.

Sarah Kershaw has been a *New York Times* reporter since 2000. She has covered many beats, and specializes in feature stories

Julia Lawlor, who lives in New Jersey, writes about food and travel.

Jen Lin-Liu founded the Black Sesame Kitchen, a Beijing cooking school, and is the author of *Serve the People: A Stir-Fried Journey Through China*. She is writing a book about the food of the Silk Road.

Harold McGee, who writes the Curious Cook column in *The New York Times*'s Dining section, is the author of *On Food and Cooking: The Science and Lore of the Kitchen* and *Keys to Good Cooking: A Guide to Making the Best of Foods and Recipes*.

Jesse McKinley is the San Francisco bureau chief of *The New York Times*. Earlier, he wrote about the arts.

Daniel Patterson is chef-proprietor of both Coi, a San Francisco restaurant, and Plum, an Oakland restaurant. He also writes for food publications.

Frank J. Prial introduced wine writing in *The New York Times*. His Wine Talk column, created in 1972, continued until 2004, interrupted by his stint as a Paris-based correspondent for *The Times* from 1979 to 1983. He also had a companion column in *The New York Times Magazine*. He retired in 2005. Prial has produced three books: *Wine Talk, Companion to Wine* and *Decantations*.

Evan Rail, a freelancer in Prague, writes about food and drink in Central and Eastern Europe. He is the author of *Good Beer Guide: Prague and the Czech Republic*.

Terry Robards was a reporter, foreign correspondent and editor for *The New York Times* from 1967 to 1983 and its wine columnist from 1979 to 1983. Robards wrote for *Wine Spectator* and *Wine Enthusiast* magazines. He has operated his own wine store in Lake Placid, N.Y., since 1988.

Kirk Semple joined *The New York Times* in 2003 and has been a foreign correspondent in Iraq and Afghanistan, a national correspondent in Miami and an immigration reporter in New York.

Jeffrey E. Singer is a New York interpreter and stringer who works for *The New York Times*

Warren St. John, a former *New York Times* reporter, is the author of *Rammer Jammer Yellow Hammer: A Journey Into the Heart of Fan Mania* and *Outcasts United: An American Town, a Refugee Team, and One Woman's Quest to Make a Difference.*

John Tagliabue, a longtime foreign correspondent for *The New York Times*, continues to report periodically for the paper from Europe.

Nicholas Wade, former science reporter for *The New York Times*, is author of *The Faith Instinct*, about the evolution and endurance of religion, and *Before the Dawn*, which reconstructs human prehistory.

John Noble Wilford, who retired as senior science correspondent at *The New York Times*, won a Pulitzer Prize in 1984 for articles on science and planetary exploration, and shared a Pulitzer in 1987 with colleagues for coverage of the aftermath of the space shuttle Challenger disaster.

Alex Witchel, a staff writer for *The New York Times Magazine*, writes the Feed Me column in the Dining section.

PHOTOGRAPHY and ILLUSTRATION CREDITS

Page 1, corkscrew, photo by Tony Cenicola.

Page 9, wine glass, illustration by Luke Lucas.

Page 63, wine glass with thermometer, photo by Tony Cenicola.

Page 105, dusty bottles in Burgundy cellar, photo by Ed Alcock.

Page 171, winemaker Josko Gravner, photo by Alice Fiorilli.

Page 191, pruning with Ezequiel Rojas, photo by Jim Wilson.

Page 237, man with a piece of cake, drawing by Melinda Beck.

Page 246, Paul Draper of Ridge Vineyards, photo by Noah Berger.

Page 299, motorcyclist and road signs in Burgundy, photo by Owen Franken.

Page 311, vignerons taking a wine break, photo by Owen Franken.

Page 400, champagne winemaker Anselme Selosse, photo by Robert Caplin.

Page 409, Cédric Bouchard (top left), Bertrand Gautherot (top right), Davy Dosnon and Nicolas Laugerotte (bottom, left to right) and Dominique Moreau (bottom right), photos by Nigel Dickinson.

Page 414, François Hautekeur and Baltic Shipwreck, photos by Alex Daws. Credit: Augusto Mendes/Government of the Aland Islands.

Page 433, Laurent and Natalie Gruet, photo by Mark Holm.

Page 446, Kermit Lynch at his desk, photo by Peter DaSilva.

Page 471, Winemaker Randall Grahm, photo by Sara Remington.

Page 507, Alois Kracher, photo AFP/Getty.

INDEX

Aaron, Michael, 141
Abbanat, Stephen and Susan, 231, 232
Abbott, John, 121
Abeja Winery, 121
Accademia dei Racemi association, 344
Aged wines, 50–53, 105–108, 109–111, 443, 450, 461–462, 469
Aglianico wine, 327, 328, 329
Aguardiente drink, 138
Ahlgren Vineyard (Dexter Ahlgren), 492
A.J. Adam riesling, 363
Alamos Ridge wine, 380
Aland Island, 414, 415, 416
Albariño grapes, 349
Alevras, Colin, 525, 526
Alex Sotelo Cellars, 218
Algueira wine, 351
Alicante wine, 68
Allen, Seth, 507
Almacenista sherry, 90
Alodio wine, 351
Alois Kracher wine, 365
Along the Wine Trail column, 13
Alpert, Jeffrey, 320
Alsace wine, 372–374. See also French wine
Altos de Lanzaga Rioja wine, 354
A-Mano wine, 343, 344
Amarone wine, 10, 12, 256, 445
Ambrositsch wine, 371
Amdur, Lou, 169
American Vintage wine, 260
American wine, 102–103, 241, 263–264. See also California wine; Finger Lakes wine; Washington state wine
Ameztoi wine, 357, 359
Amontillado sherry, 89, 90
Amoroso di Torcolato wine, 138
Amphorae winemaking, 171, 174, 474
Ancher, Jean-Marie, 514–515
Ancienne Cuvée Carnot wine, 107
Ancient wine, 171, 185–190

Anderson, Burton, 140, 195–196, 335, 344
Anderson, Mark, 121
Anthill Farms wine, 240, 243, 244
Antinori, Piero, 335, 344
Antioch Chalice, 544
Aperitif wines, 20, 87, 145, 373, 430
Appellation wine shop, 169
Apulian wine, 343–346
Aranguren, Ignacio Ameztoi, 357
Araujo winery, 138
Arbois Trousseau wine, 55
Arcadian wine, 241, 243, 244
Areshian, Gregory, 189, 190
Argentine wine, 379–383, 453
Ariadne white Bordeaux, 278
Armagnac brandy, 125, 131–135, 137, 142. See also Brandy
Arnault, Bernard, 291
Arnot-Roberts wine, 250, 253, 254
Asher, Gerald, 95
Aszu wine, 153, 155, 156, 157, 158–159
Ata Rangi wine, 76
Attarouthi Treasure, 544
Aube Champagne, 409–413
Auberge de la Celle inn, 144
Au Bon Climat wine, 241, 244, 258, 473
Auction Napa Valley charity event, 235
Audouze, François, 105
Australian wine, 68, 99–100, 214, 256, 273, 445, 459, 481. See also Specific brand names
Australian Wine Research Institute, 210
Austrian wines, 71, 364–368, 507–508. See also Specific brand names
Auth, Kerin, 89
Avenue of the Americas, New York, 547
AXA Millésimes company, 157

Bacco grapes, 134
Bacigalupi pinot noir, 117

Back, Michael, 390
Badler, Virginia R., 186, 187
Baijiu drink, 80, 82
Baker, Bill, 129
Balbo, Susana, 381
Baldwin, Tim, 90
Ballance, Gillian, 527
Banderet, Albert, 437–438
Bandol wine, 68, 69, 76, 450, 530. See also specific brand names
Banfalvi, Carolyn, 154, 157
Barbeito Madeira wine, 150
Barelli Vineyard, 98
Barolo wine, 12, 280, 331–333
Baron, Christophe, 121
Barossa Valley shiraz, 251–252
Barraud, Daniel, 322
Barsac wine, 276
Barthold-Noëllat wine, 495
Basque wine, 357–360
Bastardo grapes, 152
Bastianich winery (Joseph Bastianich), 173, 346
Bâtard-Montrachet wine, 514
Bayard's restaurant, 498, 499
Beal, Norman D., 164
Beaujolais. See also French wine; specific brand names
  in a box, 100
  California, 66
  chilling, 66
  commercial, 11
  declining popularity of, 311, 314
  with food, 55, 75, 83, 97
  nouveau, 311, 312, 313
  qualities of, 7
  sweetness/savoriness of, 11, 12
Beaulieu Vineyards, 475, 476, 477, 482, 534
Beaune Burgundy, 534
Beaune Grèves Vigne de L'Enfant Jésus wine, 105, 107–108
Beckett, Fiona, 145
Beffa, Clyde, Jr., 297
Behr, Edward, 320, 321
Bel Air et Clardy Chablis, 309
Bensa, Nicolò and Giorgio, 174
Benton Lane wine, 76

Berger, Dan, 238, 239
Berk, Mannie, 151
Bernini, Gian Lorenzo, 545
Bernkasteler Doktor wine, 534
Bern's Steak House, 150
Berry Bros. & Rudd wine
    dealer, 488
Bespaloff, Alexis, 45
Best Cellars wine shops, 209
Bettane, Michel, 274, 373
Bindocci, Fabrizio, 341
Bindschedler, Thomas K., 438,
    439
Biondi Santi, Franco and
    Ferruccio, 338, 339,
    340, 341
Bisquit, Renault, 129
Bixler, Mark, 226, 228
Biyela, Ntsiki, 384–386
Bizkaiko Txakolina wine,
    359–360
Bizot, Christian, 484–486
Black Box wine, 100
Blanc de Chardonnay Vintage
    Brut Champagne, 515
Blanc de Lynch-Bages
    Bordeaux, 64
Blanc de noirs wine, 402, 429,
    434, 436, 486
Blanc, Georges, 144
Blanchots, Chablis, 489
Blanck, Georges, 407
Blandy's Madeira wine, 150
Blaufränkisch wine, 71–72, 368
Bocuse, Paul, 142
Bodegas Norton wine, 381,
    382, 383
Bodegas Riojanas wine, 356
Bodo, Judit, 157, 158
Boillot, Domaine, 495
Boingnères, Domaine, 134
Boissenot, Jacques, 215
Bollinger Champagne, 407,
    440, 441, 484
Bollinger Charter of Ethics and
    Quality, 485
Bonnard, Pierre, 543
Bonnet, Leon, 477
Bonny Doon Vineyard, 69, 250,
    254, 344, 471, 473
Bordeaux. See also French
    wine; specific brand
    names
    blanc, 96, 276
    chilling, 64
    classifications of, 285–287

corporations running, 282,
    296
declining popularity of,
    295–298
dry, 96
with food, 58–59
half bottles of, 529
Lurton family and, 288–291
mixture, 293, 294
Old World, 279–284
phylloxera affecting,
    292–293
rosé, 450
sweetness/savoriness of,
    11, 96
vintage ratings for, 455
white, 64, 276–278
Boshard, Derek, 393
Botrytis cinerea mold, 155, 156,
    161, 282, 376, 508, 547.
    See also Fungus/mold
Bott Pince winery, 157, 158
Bouchard, Cédric, 410, 412
Bouchard Père & Fils wine, 105,
    107, 108
Bouley, David, 365
Boulud, Daniel, 160–161, 525,
    530
Bourgeois, Louise, 121
Bourguignon, Claude and
    Lydia, 301
Box wines, 99–101
Braastad-Delamain, Charles,
    128–129
Bracero program, 219
Brandy, 14, 76, 125, 128, 130,
    146. See also Armagnac
    brandy; Cognac; spe-
    cific brand names
Bret, Jean-Guillaume and
    Jean-Philippe, 322, 324
Breuer, Georg, 362
Brewer, Greg, 256
Bride Valley Vineyard, 432
Brignot, Jean-Marc, 319, 320
Bristow, Daryl, 234
Brix, 230, 242, 257, 262
BRL Hardy wine, 100
Broadbent, Bartholomew, 388
Broadbent, Michael, 24–25
Brouilly Beaujolais, 66, 75
Browne, Kosta, 242
Brown, Rosa, 192–193
Brown, Thomas, 241
Bruegel the Elder, Jan, 543
Brundlmayer wine, 365, 366

Brunello di Montalcino wine,
    12, 280, 338–342, 456
Bruni, Annamaria and
    Francesca, 344
Brun, Jean-Paul, 312, 315
Brye, Barbara, Jacques and
    Alexander de, 224
Bual Madeira wine, 150, 151
Buchner, Rachel, 393
Buckler, Edward S., 183, 184
Bully Hill winery, 268, 269, 270
Bunker, Nicole, 122
Bureau National Interprofessio-
    nel du Cognac, 127
Burghound.com, 180
Burgundy. See also French
    wine; specific brand
    names
    chilling, 67
    clones, 180
    cool climate of, 242
    European rootstocks and,
        107
    mass selections in, 180
    New Zealand, 276
    red, 11, 21, 67, 299, 302,
        303, 455, 505
    rising popularity of, 296,
        297
    rising quality of, 299–303
    sweetness/savoriness of,
        11, 12
    terroir and, 505
    vintage ratings for, 455, 456
    white, 12, 303, 304
Bustos, David, 348
Butzke, Christian E., 464, 465
By-the-glass wine. See cocktails

Cabernet sauvignon. See also
    specific brand names
    alcohol content of, 256
    blending in, 213
    in a box, 99
    climate for, 212
    with food, 247
    greatness of, 246, 259
    ratings for, 233
    sweetness of, 237
Cabernet wine, 7, 12, 32, 213.
    See also specific brand
    names
Caccini, Giovanni, 545
Cadorel, Ronan, 58
Cafe Centro restaurant, 529
Caggiano, Antonio, 328

Cahors wine, 447
Cakebread wine, 75
Calera Wine Company, 196, 213, 222, 240, 244
California wine. *See also* American wine; *specific brand names*
aging, 222–223
alcohol content of, 238, 240, 255–256, 258, 445
appellations of, 266, 267
beating France in wine tasting, 259–261, 272
climate for, 242, 247–248, 253
clubs, 233–236
lighter pinot noirs and, 244–245
Mexican immigrants tending, 218–219, 221
sweet, 237–239, 240, 241–242, 257, 508
using screw caps, 459
vintage charts/ratings for, 452, 456
Camigliano wine, 340
Campania wine, 326–330
Campos, Samuel, 193–194
Camus Cognac, 127
Canadian wine, 163–166
Candido, Francesco, 346
Cannon, Christopher, 62, 463
Canora, Marco, 60, 61
Caparzo wine, 340
Capovilla, Vittorio, 139
Caravelle, La, 528
Carelli, Andrea, 336
Cartailler-Deluc corkscrew, 2
Cartier, Louis, 110
Cartwright, Cory, 296
Casanova di Neri wine, 340
Casavecchia wine, 330
Cascina Francia Barolo wine, 331, 332–333
Case Basse di Soldera wine, 339
Castelgiocondo wine, 340
Castellada Winery, La, 174
Castello di Lispida winery, 174
Castillo de Ygay Rioja wine, 355
Castris, Leone de, 346
Catena wine (Nicolás and Laura Catena), 379–382
Caubraque, Edmond, 215
Cebrián-Sagarriga, V. Dalmau, 355

Cedarville Vineyard, 69
Ceja Vineyards (Amelia Morán, Armando, Pablo and Pedro Ceja), 218–220
Cellarmasters Home Wine Club, 230, 232
Central Park, New York, 546
Cerbaiona wine, 340
Ceretto, Bruno, 138
Cesanese grapes, 502
Cetto, Agustín, 200, 201
Chablis, 308–310. *See also* French wine; *specific brand names*
chilling, 65
food with, 489, 519, 528
smokiness of, 10
soil and, 34, 39, 308, 309, 410, 431, 432
temperature of, 63, 65
Chablis Premier Cru, 75, 82
Chambers Street Wines, 450
Chambertin Burgundy, 7, 111, 300, 304, 305, 306, 534
Chambolle-Musigny Les Amoureuses wine, 514
Champagne. *See also* French wine; Sparkling wine; *specific brand names*
blended, 405–406
dry, 405
food with, 405, 429
from nineteenth century, 414–417
pinot noir, 404, 407, 410
savoriness of, 12
single-vineyard, 407, 408, 412
slimmer bottles for, 418–420
from small houses, 403–408, 410
terroir and, 400–402, 403, 406, 410
vintage, 7, 44, 150
Champs, Laurent, 403
Champs Royaux Chablis, 309
Chan, David, 504–506
Chang, Belinda, 297–298
Chanterelle restaurant, 161
Chaptalizing, 313
Charbono wine, 97
Chardonnay. *See also specific brand names*
in a box, 99, 100

California, 116, 223
Champagne, 403–404, 411
with food, 263
greatness of, 259
in oak barrels, 31, 110, 225, 227, 324, 345, 364, 443
popularity of, 473
sweetness of, 10, 238
Charmes-Chambertin burgundy, 111, 300, 304, 305, 306
Charmes-Chambertin Vieilles Vignes wine, 111
Chartogne-Taillet Champagne, 403
Château Aney, 283
Château Beauséjour, 283
Château Beychevelle, 294
Château Bonnet, 289, 290
Château Bouscaut, 290
Château Brane-Cantenac, 288, 289, 290, 534
Château Canon, 487
Château Carbonnieux, 277
Château Cheval Blanc, 111, 291, 487
Château Climens, 289
Château Clos Fourtet, 111, 289, 291
Château Cos d'Estournel, 452
Château Dauzac, 293
Château d'Yquem, 96, 109, 111, 161, 497, 534, 547, 550
Château de Beaucastel, 68
Château de Bellevue, 283
Château de Fieuzal, 277
Château de Lignières, 129
Château de Monbazillac,, 160–162
Château de Rochemorin, 290
Château de Saran, 489
Château des Jacques, 312
Château du Clos de Vougeot, 506, 534
Château Ducru-Beaucaillou, 292, 293
Château Durfort-Vivens, 289, 290
Château du Seuil, 277
Château du Trignon, 112, 114
Château-Grillet marc spirits, 144
Château "G" white wine, 7
Château Haut-Brion, 96, 276, 277, 286, 487, 533, 550
Château Haut-Nouchet, 277

Château Jean Faux, 279, 282, 283
Château Lafite-Rothschild, 50–53, 111, 458, 487, 529, 533
Château La Louvière, 289, 290
Château Lanessan, 283
Château La Peyre, 284
Château La Tour Blanche, 110, 286, 294
Château Latour (Georges de Latour), 475, 476, 487, 533
Château Lumière, 206
Château Lynch-Pontac, 488
Château Margaux, 96, 110, 111, 286, 289, 533, 534, 550
Château Montalena, 259
Château Moulin de Tricot, 279, 281, 284
Château Moulin Pey-Labrie, 279, 284
Château Mouton-Rothschild, 111, 286, 529, 533, 534
Châteauneuf-du-Pape wine, 10, 68, 280, 492, 514, 547
Château Pétrus, 111, 298, 462, 487
Château Pichon-Lalande, 110
Château Pradeaux, 68, 70
Château Prieuré-Lichine, 215, 216
Château Rayas, 514
Château Smith Haut Lafitte, 277, 278
Château St. Pierre, 293–294
Chavez, Manuel, 191, 193
Cheese, 54, 94–95, 142, 429–430, 516
Chelsea Bistro and Bar, 529
Chenin blanc wine, 31, 87–88, 212, 237, 266, 267, 376, 389. See also specific brand names
Chermette, Pierre-Marie and Martine, 314
Chevalier, Domaine de, 277, 278
Chevrier wine, 96, 97
Cheysson, Domaine, 312
Children and wine, 537–540
Chilean wine, 248, 273, 291, 364, 380, 453, 533
Chinon Les Picasses wine, 55, 57
Chiotti Vineyard, 104

Chiquet, Jean-Hervé, 415
Chiroubles Beaujolais, 7, 66
Chowhound web site, 145, 146, 149
Christian Brothers Winery, 219
Christmann, Monika, 390
Churchill, Winston, 125
Chu, Robert, 81
Cigare Volant wine, 76, 474
Cigarrera sherry, La, 91, 92
Cimarusti, Michael, 208
Cinzano, Francesco, 339
Cipresso, Roberto, 502
C.I.V.C. (Comité Interprofessionnel du Vin de Champagne), 418, 420
Cladosporium cellare mold, 155. See also Fungus/mold
Claesz, Pieter, 543
Clarence Dillon, Domaine, 277
Claret wine, 6, 19, 21, 25, 95, 276, 279, 295. See also specific brand names
Clarine Farm, La, 69
Clark, Tom, 229, 232
Clary Ranch syrah, 251
Classical Wines importers, 362
Classifications for wine, 285–287, 305, 317
Clear Creek distillers, 138
Clef du Vin, 468
Clendenen, Jim, 241, 258, 473
Clifton, Steve, 256
Clones, 179–181, 196, 257
Clos de Gilroy wine, 471
Clos de Tart wine, 274
Clos du Mesnil Champagne, 408, 426
Clos du Val wine, 260, 278
Clos Floridène, 277
Clos la Coutale wine, 447
Clos Vougeot wine, 487
Clubb, Martin and Megan, 121
Coates & Seely vineyards (Nick Coates and Christian Seely), 431–432
Coates, Claire, 127
Coates, Clive, 106, 276, 300, 305
Coche-Dury wine, 514
Cocktails, 89, 92, 93, 147, 238, 445, 488, 522–524
Code-38 wine knife, 1–4
Codorníu sparkling wine, 428
Cognac, 125–130, 132, 133, 137. See also Brandy

Col d'Orcia wine, 339, 340
Coldstream Hills wine, 76
Cole, Steven W., 186
Colgin Cellars, 235
Colheita Madeira wine, 151
Colin-Morey, Pierre-Yves, 300
Collotte, Pascal and Chrystel, 279, 282
Colman, Tyler, 419
Comiskey, Patrick, 251, 252
Comptche Ridge Vineyard, 243
Comte Armand vineyard, 299, 302
Comtes Lafon, Domain (Dominique Lafon), 303, 304, 323
Condemine, Serge, 314
Confuron, Jacky, 495
Conran, Terence, 141
Consejo Regulador, 90
Consorzio del Vino Brunello di Montalcino association, 339, 340
Conterno, Roberto, Giacomo, Giovanni and Aldo, 331–333
Contra Costa Wine Group, 230, 231
Cooke, Alistair, 479–480
Copain Wine Cellars, 240, 242, 244, 253, 254
Copper, 134, 137, 185, 468
Copper sulfate, 293
Coppola, Francis Ford, 97, 234
Corkscrews, 1–4, 490
Corney & Barrow wine merchants, 484
Cornu, Marc-André, 437, 438, 439
Corrected coffee, 136, 141
Corti, Darrell, 468
Cotarella, Riccardo, 327, 329, 330
Côte Basque, La, 528
Côte de Brouilly Beaujolais, 312
Côte des Bar Champagne, 409–413
CôteRôtie wines, 46–47, 530
Côtes du Forez wine, 66
Côtes du Rhône wine, 10, 16, 67, 75, 100, 112, 113, 114. See also French wine; specific brand names
Côtes du Ventoux wine, 67
Côtes Roannaise wine, 66

Coup restaurant, 529
Courtine, Robert J., 429, 430
Courvoisier Cognac, 127
Couvreur, Paul and François, 404
Creek Town Café, 122
Criolla grape, 379
Crispin, André, 111
Crowley, Bill, 538
Cru d'Arche-Pugneau wine, 279, 282, 283
Cruse, Dale, 29
Crush Wine Company, 511
Cuvée Sir Winston Churchill Champagne, 515

Dagorn, Roger, 94, 95, 161
Dagueneau, Didier wine, 512
Dailly, Louis, 316–317
D'Alfonso, Bruno, 257, 258
Dalmau Rioja wine, 355
Damoy, Pierre, 489
Dampt, Domaine, 309
Dancing Bull zinfandel, 104
Daney, Francis, 279, 282
Daniel, John, 97
Daniel restaurant, 530
Darcy and Huber Selections (Paul Darcy and Carlo Huber), 369–370, 371
Darroze, Jean, Francis and Marc, 131, 134–135
Dauvissat, Vincent, 309
David, Ernest, 293, 294
Davis, Alex, 241, 244
Davis, Jill, 478
Davis, Joe, 241, 243
Davis, Mike, 122
Davoren, John, 397
Day, Douglas and Mary, 224
DBGB restaurant, 525, 526
d'Angerville, Marquis, 144, 495
della Robbia, Andrea, 543
de Villaine, Aubert, 142
d'Ognoas, Domaine, 134
Dean, Richard, 464
DeCamp, Olivia, 436
Delamain Cognac, 128–129
Delhorbe, Bruno, 420
Delicious Red wine, 99
DeLissio, Joseph, 150, 151, 152, 522
Delmas, Jean, 215
De Loach, Cecil, 103
Delos, Gilbert, 125

De Maison Selections, 90, 92, 357, 359
DeMaria, Joseph, 165
De Moor, Alice and Olivier, 309
Dériaux, Nicole, 320
Derven, Daphne, 235
Despres, Jean-Paul, 144
Desseauve, Thierry, 106
Dessert wines, 136, 137, 160–162
Desvignes, Louis-Claude, 312
De Toren Fusion V wine, 394
Devinsky, Orrin, 233
Dhondt, José, 403
Dickson, Bonneau, 231, 232
Diethylene glycol, 508
Digestifs, 127, 136, 142, 143
Dine, Jim, 121
Dion, Roger, 38
Disznoko winery, 157
Dolcetto wine, 66, 83, 547
Dolman, Jessica, 163
Domaine de l'Ancienne Cure wine, La, 160, 161
Domeneghetti, Paolo, 336
Dominio do Bibei project, 348, 349, 350
Dom Pérignon Champagne, 210, 418
Dom Ruinart Champagne, 7
Doniene Gorrondona wine, 358, 359
Donkey and Goat wine, 254
Dosnon & Lepage Champagne (Davy Dosnon and Simon-Charles Lepage), 410, 411
Double curtain system, 509, 510
Double distillation, 126–127, 132
Doutrelant, Pierre-Marie, 16–18
Dragon Phoenix Wines, 80
Draper, Paul, 76, 247, 248
Draper, Richard, 464
Drappier Champagne (Michel Drappier), 410, 413
Dressner, Joe, 319, 511–512
Droin, Jean-Paul & Benoît, 309
Drouhin, Véronique and Joseph, 302, 309, 317
Dr. Thanisch German riesling, 534
Dry Creek Valley wine, 104, 116
Dry farming, 472
Duband, David, 300
Duboeuf, Franck, 314

Duboeuf, Georges, 312, 313, 317, 459–460
Dubourdieu, Denis, 206–207
Ducloux, Jean, 142
Dujac, Domaine, 142, 302
Dunn Vineyards (Randy Dunn), 258
Dutton, Joe, 192

E.&J. Gallo Winery, 458
Eater.com website, 450
Ebeler, Susan E., 238–239
Ebsen, Delice, 553–554
Echezeaux wine, 300, 514
Edmunds St. John (Steve Edmunds), 251, 253, 254
Egly-Ouriet Champagne, 401, 404
Eitelsbacher Karthäuserhofberg Auslese Trocken "S" riesling, 362
Ekstrom, Christian, 414, 415, 416
El Maestro Sierra sherry, 91, 92
Elsa's Vineyard School of the Plains wine, 176
Empson, Neil, 335, 344
Engel, René, 489
Ente, Arnaud, 300
Entre-Deux-Mers wine, 276
Époisses cheese, 143
Equipo Navazos sherry, 90, 91
Erhard, Arnaud, 319
Esposito, Sergio, 336
Esprit de Beaucastel wine, 69
Estreicher, Stefan K., 190
Ethical standards in wine industry, 484, 485
Etude Heirloom Carneros pinot noir, 239
Evans, Leonard Paul, 481–483
Eyrie Vineyards, 76

Failla Vineyards, 241, 242, 244, 250, 253, 254
Faller, Laurence, Catherine and Colette, 372–374
Fanti wine (Filippo Fanti), 339, 340
Farina Vineyards the Prince in His Caves wine, 177
Farm restaurant, 527
Father's Office restaurant, 526
Faustino Rioja wine, 356
Federspiel wine, 367
Felicia, Masseria, 328

Felluga, Livio, 137
Felton Road Block 3 wine, 76
Feudi di San Gregorio wine, 326, 327, 329, 330
Fèvre, William, 309
Figgins, Gary, 119, 120
Figuenoa, Pedro, 193
Fillastre, Jean-François, 279, 280, 283
Finger Lakes wine, 96, 163, 165, 268–270, 509. See also American wine
Fino sherry, 10, 12, 90, 91, 145
Fiorano wine, 334–337
Fleurie Beaujolais, 7, 311, 312, 314, 534
Folle blanche grapes, 134
Fonseca port, 148
Food, 161
    American wine with, 241, 263–264
    balanced wine with, 241
    barbera wine with, 32
    cabernet franc with, 32
    cabernet sauvignon with, 247
    chardonnay with, 263
    Chinese, 80–82, 95, 110, 117, 145
    gamay wine with, 32
    matching wine with, 145
    pinot noir with, 32, 237, 240
    sauvignon blanc with, 31–32
    savory, 145
    spicy, 210
    wine role with, 241
    wine societies and, 13
Forbes, Patrick, 423, 427
For the Love of Port web site, 145, 147, 148
Fortified wines, 145, 150
Fortissimo sweet wine, 155
Fort Tryon Park, New York, 546
Fougner, G. Selmer, 13–15
Fourrier, Domaine (Marie and Jean-Claude Fourrier), 301, 456
Four Seasons restaurant, 523
Fox, Peter, 482
Franciacorta wine, 74
Frank, Konstantin, 96, 269
Franzia wine, 100
Frappato grapes, 72
Fredrikson, Jon, 99, 522
Freeman Winery, 305

Freese, Phil, 387–391
Freixenet sparkling wine, 428
French appellation rules, 272, 274
French Laundry, 235
French wine. See also Alsace wine; Beaujolais; Bordeaux; Burgundy; Chablis; Champagne; Côtes du Rhône wine; Jura wines; Mâconnais wine; specific brand names
    appellations of, 37, 113, 216, 272, 273–274, 275, 276–277, 438
    cheap, 273–274, 275
    food with, 263
    half bottles of, 529
    tasting losing to California wines, 259–261, 272
    using screw caps, 459
    vintage charts for, 452–453
Frey, Nick, 192
Frishmuth, Harriet Whitney, 542
Fucci, Salvatore, 327
Fumin wine, 72
Funghini, Joseph, 464
Fungus/mold, 126, 155, 159, 161, 279, 334, 336. See also Botrytis cinerea mold; Cladosporium cellare mold; Torula compniacensis fungus
Funnels, 490
Furmint wine, 72, 156, 158, 367, 375, 376
Fusione company, 343, 344
F.X. Pichler wine, 365

Gago, Peter, 396, 398
Galardi, Fattoria, 327–328, 329
Gallagher, Patricia, 259
Gallo, Gianfranco, 137
Gallo wine, 98, 99, 100, 104
Gamay beaujolais wine, 97
Gamay de l'Ardèchen wine, 66
Ganevat, Jean-François, 320
Ganter, Alexis, 463
Garagistes, 229, 230, 231
Garner, Cam, 234
Garofano, Severino, 346
Garretson Wine Company (Mat Garretson), 258
Gasco, Thierry, 418, 420, 423

Gaspar Florido sherry, 91
Gaunoux, Michel, 144
Gautherot, Bertrand, 412
Gazagnes, Thierry, 143
Gelber muskateller wine, 371
Gemischter satz wines, 370
Geoffroy, Jean-Baptiste, 408
Geoffroy, René, 403
Geoffroy, Richard, 210
Germain-Robin distillers, 138
German wine, 125, 163, 479, 482, 529, 533, 547, 551. See also specific brand names
Getariako Txakolina wine, 358
Gevrey-Chambertin wine, 7
Gewürztraminer wine, 10, 373
Geyser Peak wine, 75
Giacomo Conterno wine, 331
Gilman, John, 528, 529
Gimonnet, Pierre, 401, 403
Giraud, Paul, 128
Givry wine, 55
Gluckstern, Willie, 31–32
Gobelsburg nonvintage reserve wine, 367
Godello grapes, 349
Godin Tepe site, 186, 187
Godmé Père Champagne, 403
Gombert, René, 126–127
González-Byass Tío Pepe sherry, 90
Goode, Jamie, 36
Gotham Bar and Grill, 528, 529
Gott, Joel and Gary, 103
Goudal, Monplaisir, 286–287
Gouges, Henri, 489
Grace Wine, 205, 206
Graf, Mary Ann, 478
Grahm, Randall, 69, 76, 250, 251, 252, 344, 471–474
Gramercy Tavern, 62, 94, 523
Grande Champagne Très Rare Cognac, 128
Grande Cuvée Champagne, 426
Grande, Dana, 191
Grange Hermitage wine, 47, 396–397, 398, 482
Granoff, Peter, 527
Grape breeding, 183, 184
Grapefields wine shop, 122
Grape genome, 183, 184
Grappa, 136–140
Graticciaia wine, 345
Graves La Louvière wine, 7

Graves, Nancy, 121
Graves wine, 7, 276–277, 278, 286, 288, 289, 295, 462
Gravner, Josko, 137, 171, 173–174
Grazia, Iano de, 341
Greek wine, 71, 364
Green practices, 418–421
Greenspan, Dorie, 54, 55, 56
Greenwashing, 168, 169
Grenache wine, 12, 68
Greno, Narcisse, 422
Grey Slate Kabinett Trocken riesling, 362
Grgich, Mike, 387
Grieco, Paul, 34, 60–62, 92, 94, 296
Grignolino grapes, 72
Grof Degenfeld Castle Hotel, 154
Gros, Louis, 489
Grosset, Jeffrey, 76
Growth categories, 285, 286, 289
GruaudLarose wine, 498, 534
Gruet Winery (Nathalie and Laurent Gruet), 433–436
Grüner veltliner wine, 81, 365, 366, 371, 507
Guenoc Ranch and Winery, 265–266
Guérard, Michel, 133
Guerin, Jamie, 122, 123
Guerra, Roberta, 345
Guffens-Heynen wine (Jean-Marie Guffens), 323, 325
Guímaro wine, 351
Gusbourne Estate sparkling wine, 432
Gustave Niebaum Collection, 96, 97
Gutenbrunner, Kurt, 365
Guthrie, Wells, 240, 242, 243, 253
Gutiérrez Colosia sherry, 91, 92

Haas, Daniel, 144
Haggblom, Bjorn, 416
Hajji Firuz site, 189
Half bottles of wine, 519, 528–530
Halliday, James, 76
Hamburger, Philip, 22

Hamilton Russell vineyard (Anthony Hamilton Russell), 389
Hanzell Vineyards, 222–224
Haraszthy, Agoston, 154
Harlan Estate winery (H. William Harlan), 233, 235
Harmelin, Robert, 208
Harrison, Timothy, 160
Harry's restaurant, 497
Hart Davis Hart auction house, 80
Haserot, Craig, 28
Haste in wine drinking, 531–532
Hautekeur, François, 415
Heidsieck & Company Monopole Champagne, 419
Heitz, Joe, 478
Helfrich riesling, 64
Helppie, Richard, 236
Hennessy, Richard, 125, 127
Henschke Hill shiraz, 398
Herederos de Argüeso, 91
Hermanos Peciña Rioja wine, 356
Herrick Vineyard, 96
Hersh, Roy, 145, 147, 148
Hersom, Ralph, 463
Hervet, Bernard, 506
Heublein winery, 97
Heymann, Hildegarde, 37
Hidalgo-La Gitana wine, 90
Hirayama, Youki, 207
Hirsch wine, 367
Home winemaking, 229–232
Hommage à Jacques Perrin wine, 68
Hondarrabi zuri grapes, 358, 360
Houillon, Emmanuel, 319
Hubau, Bénédict and Grégoire, 279
Huber, Carlo, 369–370
Hudson Vineyards, 228
Huet wine, 376
Hungarian wine, 72, 153–159, 375–377, 533
Huseby, Joel and Cynthia, 122
Hwang, Anthony, 376
Hybrid wines, 134, 206, 268, 269, 270

Ice wine, 163–166
Ilarria rosé wine, 449
Il Greppo wine, 338

Il Palazzone wine, 340
Il Poggione wine, 340, 341
Imparato, Silvia, 329
Inglenook winery, 97, 534
Inman Family Wines (Kathleen Inman), 243, 244
Inniskillin Wines, 165, 166
Insignia wine, 456
Institute of Masters of Wine, 485
Interprofessional Committee of the Wines of Champagne, 438
Iron Horse wine, 74
Irroy Champagne, 22
Italian wine, 72, 171–175, 256, 326–330, 338, 453, 529. *See also specific brand names*
I Trulli restaurant, 522

Jacquesson Champagne, 415
Jadot, Louis, 312
James, Tim, 385
Janneau wine, 134
Japanese wine, 205–208
Jaugaret, Domaine du, 279, 280, 281, 283
Jayer-Gilles, Robert, 495
Jayer, Henri, 514
Jefferson, Thomas, 286, 549–552
Jenkins, Steven, 95
Jensen, Josh, 196, 197, 213, 240
Jermann, Silvio, 138
Jobard, François, 494, 515
Johnnes, Daniel, 514, 522, 530
Johnson, Hugh, 67, 95, 186, 276, 406, 547
Jordan, Ehren, 196, 198, 200, 201, 241, 242, 250, 253
Jordan, Tom, 235
Joseph Phelps Vineyards, 456
Joseph Swan Vineyards, 244
Jouanda, Domaine de, 134
Juglar Champagne, 414, 415, 416
Juhlin, Richard, 416
Juliénas Beaujolais, 66, 311, 312, 314
Jumilla wine, 68
Jura wines, 318–321. *See also French wine*
Jutta Ambrositsch wine, 370

Kante, Edi, 172
Kanzler pinot noir, 29
Katsunuma Jyozo winery, 207
Katz, Solomon H., 185, 187
Keller, Thomas, 235
Kendall-Jackson wine, 10, 238, 382
Kesner, Jason, 225, 226, 228
Kesselstatt riesling, 363
Kienholz, Edward, 121
Kiralyudvar winery, 375
Kistler chardonnay, 110
Kistler Vineyards (Steve Kistler), 225–228
Knebel riesling, 363
Knopf, Alfred A., 487–490
Knutsen, Peder, 553–554
Kongsgaard, John, 177–178
Koshu wine, 205–208
Kracher, Alois, Jr. and Gerhard, 507–508
Kramer, Matt, 34, 35, 180
Krankl, Manfred, 365, 508
Kristancic, Ales, 35, 39, 172, 173
Krug Champagne (Rémi Krug), 7, 74, 110, 406–407, 408, 425–427, 485
Krug, Henri and Joseph, 425, 426, 427
Kurtzman, Ed, 305

Labrusca grapes, 268
Lacassagne family, 293–294
Lacima wine, 349
Lacquy, Château de, 134
Lafite Bordeaux, 534, 550
Lafitte, Marguerite and Martine, 134
Lafon, Dominique, 301, 303, 323–324, 325
Lagrein grapes, 72
La Grenouille restaurant, 528
Laguiole corkscrews, 3, 4
Lalama wine, 349
Lamb, 115, 116–117, 252
Lameloise restaurant, 144
Lane Tanner wine, 244
Lang, George, 138
Langtry, Lillie, 265–266
Lanzaga Rioja wine, 354
Lapierre, Marcel, 311
Lapierre, Mathieu, 313
Lardière, Jacques, 311
Large, Jean-Pierre, 312
L'Arlot, Domaine, 515

Larmandier-Bernier Champagne (Pierre and Sophie Larmandier), 401, 403, 407
Lassaigne, Jacques, 411
La Tour d'Argent restaurant, 429, 514
La Tour de Segur wine, 550
Laube, James, 248
Laureato wine, 344
Lavalle, Jules, 305, 306
Laville-Haut-Brion wine, 277
Lawton, Hugues, 215
Lazzari, Donato, 346
Le Bec Fin restaurant, 110
LeBrun, Patrick, 421
Le Centenaire restaurant, 160
Le Cercle des Vingt, 109
Le Chambertin burgundy, 304, 305, 306
Le Cirque restaurant, 529
L'Ecole No. 41, 121
Le Dû, Jean-Luc, 160, 530
Leeman, Pascal, 156
Leff, Jim, 145–146, 149
Leflaive, Domaine (Anne-Claude Leflaive), 323, 514
Le Mesnil Champagne, 407
Lemon, Ted, 240
Leonetti Cellar, 119–120
Leon, Patrick, 215
Léoville Barton wine, 455
Lepage, Simon-Charles, 410, 411
Le Pavillon restaurant, 518
Leroux, Benjamin, 299, 301, 302, 303
Les Amis d'Escoffier society, 13
Les Giroflées, 451
Lespinasse restaurant, 528
Les Prés d'Eugénie restaurant, 133
Les Vignes de Montgueux Champagne, 411
Lett, David, 76
Levi, Romano, 139, 140
Liang, Zai, 203
Lichine, Alexis, 46, 215, 216, 487, 489
Lichine, Sacha, 215
Liebling, Abbott Joseph, 19–22
Liger-Belair wine, 534
Lillie, David, 450
Lincoln Center, New York, 547

Lindquist, Bob, 251, 253, 256
Lisini wine, 340
Lis Neris winery, 173
Littorai Wines, 240, 244
Livio Felluga winery, 173
Loiseau, Bernard, 17
Lok, Vicky, 81, 82
Lomonaco, Michael, 77, 78
Longoria wine (Rick Longoria), 241, 244
Long, Zelma, 387–391
López de Heredia wine (Maria José, Mercedes, Julio César, Pedro and Don Rafael López de Heredia), 352–356
Lopez, Ralph I., 538
Loretz, François, 128
Lorson, Daniel, 419, 438
Losada, Ramón, 349–350
Louis/Dressner Selections, 281, 297, 319, 512
Louis-Michel Liger-Belair vineyard, 300
Lou on Vine wine bar, 169
Low-yield grapes
    affecting quality, 453, 510
    of A-Mano wine, 343
    of Joe Dressner, 511
    of López de Heredia wine, 354
    producing intense wines, 196, 199, 324, 334
    types of, 16
    of viognier, 547
Luberri Rioja wine, 356
Ludovisi, Alberico Boncompagni, 177, 334
Luele, Peppe, 500
Lukacs, Paul, 260
Luna Vineyards, 177
Lundberg, Britt, 416
Lurton, André, Denis, Dominique, François, Jacques, Lucien, Pierre and Simone, 288–291
Lustau sherry, 90
Lustig, Dave, 232
Lutèce restaurant, 529
LVMH (Louis Vuitton Moët Hennessy) Champagne, 291, 423, 426
Lynch, Kermit, 34, 281, 297, 320, 446–448
LZ Rioja wine, 354

Mabray, Paul, 27
Mabunda, Dudu, 393
Mâcon-Lugny wine, 529
Mâconnais wine, 322–325. *See also* French wine
Madeira wine, 150–152
Madrigale, Michael, 2
Maffini, Luigi, 328
Magill Estate shiraz, 398
Magnetic bottle collar, 467
Magoni, Camillo P., 199, 200
Magoon, Orville, Eaton and John Henry, 265, 266
Magrez, Bernard, 207
Maher, Sean, 235
Maime, Masseria, 346
Maison Faiveley, 506
Maison Ilan winery, 304
Maison Louis Jadot, 312
Malazzini, Giuseppe, 345
Malbec wine, 380, 381, 383
Malivoire Wine Company (Martin Malivoire), 163, 164
Maller, Michael, 89
Mallick, Kathi, 234
Mallmann, Francis, 381
Malvasia di Candia wine, 334, 336
Malvasia/malmsey Madeira wine, 151
Mandolas wine, 156
Maniec, Laura, 297
Manzanilla sherry, 89, 90, 91, 92
Marc Colin et Fils, Domaine, 300
Marchevsky, Pedro, 381
Marc spirits, 138, 141–144
Marie-Courtin Champagne, 410, 413
Marker-assisted breeding, 183, 184
Markham, Dewey, Jr., 286
Marqués de Murrieta Rioja wine, 353, 355, 356
Marqués de Riscal Rioja wine, 355
Martell Cognac, 127
Martinborough Vineyard, 82
Martini, Louis M., 534
Martin, Roger, 533
Martouret, Chateaux, 289
Mascarello, Bartolo, 280
Masero, Mike, 229, 232
Masseria, La, 500, 503

Mastroberardino, Piero and Antonio, 138, 328
Matching Food and Wine web site, 145
Matthews, Mark, 36
Maxime Magnon wine, 447
Mayer, Carlos Tizio, 382
May, Tony, 136
McCalman, Max, 94, 95
McCarthy, Steve, 143
McGovern, Patrick E., 185, 187, 188, 189
McGrath, Thomas J. and Diahn, 110
McIntyre, Dave, 168, 169
Mead, Leslie, 241
Meadows, Allen, 106, 180, 181
Melton, Charles, 76
Mencía grapes, 72, 348, 349
Mendoza wine, 379
Mennevaux, Mark and Céline, 495
Meredith, Carole, 343
Merlin, Olivier, 323, 324
Merlot wine, 7, 99, 100, 213, 390. *See also specific brand names*
Metropolitan Museum of Art, 542–545
Metzler, Stephen, 362
Meursault-Charmes wine, 105, 107
Meursault-Perriers wine, 514
Mexican-American winemakers, 218–221
Mexican wine, 198–201
Meyers, Duncan Arnot, 250–251
Michael, Aubert and Peter, 225
Michael Skurnik Wines, 364
Michelot, Domaine, 495
Michel, Rudolph H., 187
Microwaving wine, 463–466
Migrant/field workers, 218–221, 236
Miguel Merino Rioja wine, 356
Milan, Jean, 403
Mildew, 292–293
Millardet, Pierre, 292–293
Miller, Bissie and Jerry, 230, 231
Miller, Ron, 360
Minerality, 37, 55, 223, 246, 367
Miranda, Juan, 164
Misawa, Shigekazu, 205, 206

Mission Haut-Brion vineyard, La, 276
Mistral wind, 112
Moët & Chandon Champagne, 238, 382, 407, 489
Mohr, Doug, 368
Molettieri, Salvatore, 328
Monastrell wine, 68
Moncuit, Pierre, 401
Mondavi, R. Michael, 257, 380
Monfortino riserva Barolo wine, 331, 332
Monnet, Jean, 126
Monprivato wine, 456
Montbourgeau, Domaine de, 320
Monte Bello cabernet sauvignon, 246
Monteillet, Pierre-Louis and Joan, 122
Montepulciano wine, 502, 551
Montgolfier, Ghislain de, 485
Montrachet restaurant, 522, 523, 530
Montrachet wine, 94, 105, 106–107, 492
Morán, Felipe, 219
Moreau, Dominique, 413
Morelot, Dr., 34, 37
Morey-St.-Denis wine, 456
Morgon Beaujolais, 11, 55, 312
Moss, Stuart and Sandy, 432
Mottiar, Shiraz, 163
Moulin-à-Vent wine, 11, 312, 314
Mount Difficulty Target Gully riesling, 81
Mount Eden Vineyards, 222
Mourvèdre wine, 16, 68–70, 76, 82, 144, 232, 250, 389
Movia wine, 35, 173
Muga Rioja wine, 356
Mugnier wine, 534
Müller, Eberhard, 498, 529
Murray, Andrew, 255
Murray, Euan, 420
Muscadelle grapes, 160
Muscadet wine, 10, 12, 54, 56, 75, 89, 444
Muscat de Beaumes-de-Venise, 160
Myles, Sean, 182, 183

Nancy's Wines, 31
Napa Valley Reserve club, 233–236

Nardini grappa, 138
Nase, Joseph, 528
Natural wines, 168–170, 247, 279, 282, 319, 446, 511, 512. *See also* Old World wine
Neal, Charles, 133
Nebbiolo wine, 95
Negroamaro grape, 345, 346
Nevada County Wine Guild, 100
New Mexico wine, 433–436
New Mexico Wine Growers Association, 436
New York City wine, 546–548
New Zealand wine, 32, 76, 81, 82, 276, 277, 459. *See also specific brand names*
Nicks, Ben, 165
Niebaum, Gustave, 97
Nigl wine, 365, 367
Nikolaihof wines, 365
9/11 event, 77
Nine Popes wine, 76
Noah grapes, 134
Noellat, Charles, 489
Noninos, Benito and Giannola, 136, 137, 138
Normalized Differentiated Vegetative Index, 389
Normandin-Mercier Cognac, 127
Notarpanaro wine, 346
Ntshangase, Jabulani, 384
Nyetimber sparkling wine, 432

Off wine, 517–518
Oidium disease, 292
Ojai Vineyard, 241, 244, 254
O'Keeffe, Buzzy, 150
Olander, Tom, 123
Old Telegram wine, 69, 76, 471
Old Vine Red wine, 75
Old World wine, 279–284, 301, 306, 352–353, 412, 472. *See also* Natural wines; Vigneron(s)
Oliver, Jeremy, 481, 483
Oliveros, Daniel and Natalie, 500–503
Olney, Richard, 448
Oloroso sherry, 90, 91, 92, 94
Olson, Steven, 62, 89
Ordóñez, Jorge, 360, 508

Oregon wine, 76, 102, 138, 143, 213, 232, 459, 473. *See also specific brand names*
Oremus wine, 156, 157, 376
Organic grapes, 168, 301, 334
Orpen, William, 545
Oscar's Delmonico, 497
Os Kajan restaurant/hotel, 156, 157
Our Daily Red wine, 100
Overnoy, Pierre, 319
Overton, Marvin C., III, 110
Oxbow Wine Merchant, 527
Oyamada, Koki, 206

Pactor, Scott, 169
Pallières, Domaine les, 448
Park Avenue, New York, 547
Parker, Robert M., Jr.
    on Bordeaux wine, 295
    charbono and, 97
    Harlan Estate cabernet sauvignons and, 233
    impact of, 38
    koshu wine and, 206, 207
    Pax Wine Cellars syrah and, 252
    Pegau Cuvée Capo wine and, 493
    on red burgundy, 299
    Sogno Uno wine, 500
    vintage charts/ratings and, 452, 454
Paso Robles wine, 103, 253
Pataille, Sylvain, 300
Patriglione wine, 346
Patroon restaurant, 530
Pavillon Blanc, 96
Pax Wine Cellars (Mahle and Pamela Pax), 252
Peacock Alley, 529
Peay Vineyards (Nick and Andy Peay), 240, 244, 252, 253, 254
Pegau Cuvée Capo wine, 492
Penfolds wine, 396
Peninsula Ridge Estates Winery, 164
Penning-Rowsell, Edmund L., 23–25
Pepe, Emidio, 474
Pérez, Raúl, 348, 349, 350, 351
Perlman, Dan, 463
Pernin-Rossin, Domaine, 495
Pernod Ricard wine, 382

Perrier, Georges, 109, 111
Perrone, Osea, 248
Perrucci, Gregory, 344
Pessac-Léognan vineyard, 277
Pests, 183, 184. *See also* Phylloxera disease
Peter Barlow cabernet, 393
Peterson, Richard, 478
Peters, Pierre, 401
Peynaud, Émile, 38, 39, 215
Peyraud family, 69, 448
Peyrelongue, Patrick, 128
Peyrondet, Manuel, 515
Peza do Rei wine, 351
Phelps, Joseph, 251
Philipon, Jérôme, 440–441
Philippe, Claude, 489
Phylloxera disease, 69, 107, 183, 292–293, 347, 359, 389, 477. *See also* Pests
Piccolomini d'Aragona, Mastrojanni and Ciacci, 340
Picholine restaurant, 94, 95, 529
Pichon-Longueville Bordeaux, 534
Picolit grapes, 137, 138
Picq, Gilbert, 309
Pierce's disease, 473
Pineau D'Aunis grapes, 72
Pinguet, Noël, 376
Pinotage wine, 390
Pinot blanc, 365
Pinot grigio wine, 176, 177
Pinot Gris Quintessence des Grains Nobles Cuvée du Centenaire wine, 374
Pinot gris wine, 10, 367, 373, 374
Pinot noir. *See also specific brand names*
    Australian, 76–81
    blending in, 213
    Brix level in, 242
    Burgundy, 212
    California, 12, 117, 213, 237
    Champagne, 404, 407, 410
    climate for, 212
    clones, 180
    darkness of, 196
    with food, 32, 76, 81, 82, 237, 240
    Gary Vaynerchuk approving, 28, 29
    grape percentages in, 212–213

Pinot noir (*continued*)
    light, dry, 240, 243,
        244–245
    New Zealand, 76, 82
    qualities of, 7
    rosé, 81, 82
    sweetness of, 10, 12, 237,
        240, 241–242
    syrah in, 213
    water and acid added to,
        242, 243
    winespeak on, 7
Piper, Odessa, 364
Pisoni, Gary, 181
Pitiot, Sylvain, 274
Planchon Vineyard, 103
Platter, John, 387
Plotkin, Fred, 172
Poderi Aldo Conterno wine, 331
Poderina, La, 340
Poggio wine, 339, 340
Poggi, Stéphane, 193
Polidori, Filippo, 336
Polignac, Alain de, 422–424
Poli, Jacopo, 138
Polish Hill wine, 76
Pol Roger Champagne
    (Christian Pol Roger), 7,
    485, 515–516. *See also*
    Champagne
Pomace, 136, 137, 138, 139, 140,
    141, 143, 144
Pommard Rugiens Burgundy,
    534
Pommery Champagne, 418,
    419, 422, 423, 424
Pool, Robert, 509
Pornography, 500
Porta di Vertine Rosé, La, 450
Porter Creek wine, 241, 245
Port wine, 95, 145–149
Port Wine Institute, 148
Poulakakos, Harry and Peter,
    497–499
pH of wine, 54, 231
Prats, Bruno, 452
Pratt, Deborah, 166
Pratt, Phil, 147, 148
Première Cuvée Les Pargues
    Chablis, 308
Preuses, Chablis Les, 489
Primitivo grape, 102, 343
Propagating vines, 179, 180,
    182
Prosecco, 74
Prunes, 85–86

Pruning championships,
    191–194
Puffeney, Jacques, 319, 320
Puligny-Montrachet wine, 78
Pulltap's corkscrew, 2

Questa vineyard, La, 248
Qupé Vineyards, 254, 256

Racking barrels, 142
Radikon, Stanislao, 174–175
Ragg, Edward, 80, 81
Ragnaud-Sabourin Cognac, 127
Raiano, Villa, 328
Rainer Christ wine, 370
Ramonet, Claude, 489
Ramsay, Gordon, 58, 59
Rancho Escondido vineyard,
    198, 199, 200, 201
Rancho Zabaco wine, 104
Rare Wine Company, 151, 400
Rasteau wine, 114
Ratcliffe, Michael, 388
Ratings for wine, 285–287, 455
Ratzenberger riesling, 363
Ravenswood wine, 103
Ray, Cyril, 23
Raymond Vineyards (Walter
    and Roy Raymond),
    266
Récapet, Léonce, 289
Récolte Noire Champagne, 411
Red wine. *See also specific*
    brand names
    cheese with, 94–95
    chilling, 66–67
    decanting, 490
    food with, 52, 75–76, 91, 115,
        116–117, 145, 443, 444
    hues of, 195–197
    savoriness of, 10
    seafood with, 54–57, 58–59
    sweet, 10, 238
    sweetness/savoriness of, 11
Refosco wine, 173
Régnié Beaujolais, 66
Regulations, 202, 212, 214, 230,
    258, 508
Reif Estate Winery (Klaus W.
    Reif), 165, 166
Rémy Martin Cognac, 127
Renaud, Maurice, 110
Renteria Wines (Salvador and
    Oscar Renteria), 218
Réserve Spéciale Champagne,
    515

Rey, Bruno and Pascaline, 279,
    281
Reynoso, Leonardo, 198
Rhône reds, 11, 12, 67
Rhys Vineyards, 240, 245
Ribaudière restaurant, 128
Ribeira Sacra wine, 347–351
Ribolla gialla wine, 173, 174
Rice wine, 202–204
Richard Sauret Vineyard, 103
Richard Zahel gemischter satz
    wine, 370
Richebourg wine, 487
Rico, Gustavo, 193
Ridge Monte Bello wine, 260
Ridgeview Estate sparkling
    wine, 431, 432
Ridge Vineyards, 103, 222,
    246–249, 464
Riesling CuvéeSainte Catherine
    wine, 374
Riesling wine. *See also specific*
    brand names
    Austrian, 367, 507
    chilling, 64
    dry, 10, 12, 361–363
    with food, 81
    German, 11, 361–363, 534
    ice wine, 163
    New Zealand, 81
    spätlese, 64
    Summer of, 60, 62
    sweetness/savoriness of, 10,
        11, 12, 237
    terroir and, 34
Rigaux, Jacky, 106
Rijckaert, Jean, 321, 322
Ring, Brad, 230
Rioja Alta wine, La, 356
Rioja wines, 352–356
River Café, 150, 522
Rivers-Marie wine, 241, 243,
    245
Rixford, E. H., 248
Rkatsiteli wine, 96
Robert Pecota Winery, 218,
    221
Roberts, Nathan Lee, 250–251
Robinson, Jancis, 26, 27, 28,
    406
Robison Ranch, 122
Robledo Family Winery
    (Reynaldo Sr., Vanessa
    and Lorena), 218–221
Ro, Catherine, 504
Roche, Christian, 161

Rocky Hill Vineyards San Floriano del Collio wine, 177
Rodríguez, Pedro, 348, 351
Rodríguez, Telmo, 353–354, 356
Roederer Estate wine, 74
Romanée-Conti, Domaine de, 142, 300, 487, 506, 534
Romorantin grapes, 73
Rootstock winemakers, 388
Rosenbloom, David, 539
Rosenblum Cellars (Kent M. Rosenblum), 103, 230
Rosenbrand, Theo, 478
Rosenthal, Neal, 195, 196, 274, 280, 281, 297, 320
Rosette Chablis, 309
Rosé wine, 64, 68, 81, 82, 426, 449–451. *See also specific brand names*
Ross, Karen, 219
Rothbury Estates, 481
Rothman, Mitchell S., 190
Rothschild, Philippe de, 216, 286
Rotisserie du Chambertin restaurant, 495
Roulot, Guy and Jean-Marc, 143, 144
Roumier, Christophe, 301
Roumier, Georges, 514
Roussanne wine, 256
Rousseau, Armand, 300
Rouvière, Jacques, 129
Roux, André and Collette, 112–114
Roux, Michel, Jr., 432
Rovani, Pierre, 122
Royal DeMaria winery, 165
Rubens, Peter Paul, 543
Rubicon wine, 393
Ruby port, 147
Rush, Benjamin, 552
Russian River Valley wine, 74, 214, 242, 243, 244, 245, 252, 531

Saignée de Sorbée Champagne, 413
Saint-Amour Beaujolais, 66
Saint-Julien wine, 455
Saint-Pourçain wine, 66
Salon Champagne, 407
Samalens wine, 134
Sancerre wine, 10, 75, 530

San Domenico restaurant, 136
Sanford Winery, 257
Sangiovese grapes, 338, 339, 341, 478, 502
Sangre y Trabajadero sherry, 91
Sarratea, Andoni, 359
Saumur-Champigny wine, 32
Saunders, Audrey, 147
Sauternes wine. *See also specific brand names*
  food with, 95, 117, 145, 161
  popularity of, 276
  ratings for, 286
  sémillon in, 278
  sweet, 282
  Thomas Jefferson and, 549, 550
Sauvignon blanc, 31–32, 75, 160, 162, 177, 277. *See also specific brand names*
Sauvignon-sémillon blends, 96, 97
Sauzet, Domaine, 495
Savagnin wine, 319–320
Savennières wine, 530
Savory wines, 9, 10–11, 12
Saxum Vineyards, 238
Sbalchiero, Elvezia, 343
Scarbolo winery, 173
Schäfer-Fröhlich riesling, 363
Schiopetto winery (Mario Schiopetto), 137, 173
Schlansky, William, 528
Schmitt, Sonia and Carl, 122, 123
Schoener, Abe, 176–178
Scholium Project wine, 176–178, 527
Schramsberg Blanc de Noirs wine, 7
Schrock, Heidi, 367
Schubert, Max, 397
Scicolone, Charles, 522–523
Scions, 183
Scott, Peter, 163
Screw caps, 458–460, 474
Scuppernong wine, 102, 551
Seely, Christian, 431–432
Segura, Rose, 236
Selection Massale company, 296
Selosse Champagne (Anselme Selosse), 280, 330, 400–402
Sémillon wine, 96, 160, 278, 334, 335, 336

Sempé wine, 134
Sercial Madeira wine, 151
Seringer, Kellie, 236
Servin, Domaine, 308–309
Sessions, Bob and Jean Arnold, 222, 223
Seven Hills wine, 120
Seysses, Jacques and Jeremy, 142, 143, 302
Shand, P. Morton, 487
Shannon, Mark, 343, 344
Shaulis, Nelson, 509–510
Shaw, Charles H., 97
Sherry, 89–93. *See also specific brand names*
  aged, 111
  British and, 13
  cocktails, 89, 92, 93, 147, 488
  cream, 90
  Fino, 12, 145
  food with, 94
  sweet, 91, 92
  vinegar, 88
Shiraz wine, 10, 11, 47, 68, 82, 100, 252
Sibyl wine, 390–391
Sicilian wine, 72, 343–346
Siegel, Matthew, 46
Silk Road, 186
Simi Winery, 388
Simon, André, 130
Simon, François, 494
Sine Qua Non winery, 508
Singer, Ernest, 205, 206, 207
Singita Lebombo Lodge, 392–395
Single Bottle Club, 482
Single distillation, 132
Single-estate Cognac, 129
Sisk, Adam and Sarah, 122
Skelton, Stephen, 432
Skoff, Gail, 448
Small, Rick, 119, 120
Smart, Richard E., 510
Smith, Justin, 238
Smith, Park B., 491–493
Soave wine, 10
Sogno Uno wine, 500
Sohm, Aldo, 3, 507
Soil. *See also* Terroir
  chalky, 114, 125, 127, 310, 403, 404, 431, 432
  clay, 35, 323, 342, 410, 431
  fertilizing, 36, 301, 324, 353, 421

Soil (*continued*)
   granite, 34, 35, 39, 199,
      317, 347
   limestone, 34, 35, 39, 69,
      309, 323, 410, 431
Sokolin, William, 546
Sokolov, Raymond, 20
Soldera, Gianfranco, 280, 339,
      340–341
Sommeliers/wine stewards
   chilling wines, 63, 65
   ignoring Bordeaux, 296,
      297
   problems with, 517–518,
      519–521
   speaking about soil and
      wine, 34
   suggesting wines, 47, 62,
      89, 357
   using corkscrews, 1–4
   using microwaves,
      463–466
Sotelo, Alex, 219, 221
Souchons, Domaine des, 314
Soufrandière, Domaine de la,
      322
Soulé, Henri, 518
South African wine, 384–386,
      387–390, 392–395
Spanish wine. *See also specific*
      brand names
   appellations of, 358
   half bottles of, 529
   mencía, 72, 348, 349
   Rioja, 352–356
   sweet, 10, 508
   treixadura, 73
   using screw caps, 459
   vintage charts for, 452, 453
Sparkling wine. *See also*
      Champagne; *specific*
      brand names
   Champagne method for,
      435
   chilling, 64
   from England, 431–432
   from New Mexico,
      433–436
   for occasions, 428
Spätlese wine, 7, 64, 534
Sproule, Ryan, 100
Spurrier, Steven and Bella, 47,
      48, 259, 432
Stager, Lawrence, 187
Stag's Leap Wine Cellars, 176,
      228, 259, 260, 492

Stallcup, Pat, 200
St.-Amour wine, 316, 317
"Statistique de la Vigne Dans
      le Département de la
      Côte-d'Or" (Morelot),
      34
St.-Aubin, Domaine de, 76,
      135, 530
St. Charles Punch, 147
Steaks, 52, 91, 145
Ste. Chapelle chardonnay
      reserve, 110
Steele, Lockhart, 450
Steen, Jan, 544
Steinberg, Paul, 539
Stellekaya winery, 386
Stelvin screw caps, 459
St.-Émilion wine, 58–59
Stevenson, Tom, 485
Stewart, Rhoda, 200
St. Henri wine, 396, 397, 398
St. Laurent grapes, 368
Stock grappa, 136
Stoll, Craig and Anne, 527
Stone Barns Center for Food
      and Agriculture, 234
Stony Hill wine, 116, 222
Storybook Mountain wine, 103
Stover, Brennen, 200
Stratus Vineyards, 165
Street, Julian, 487
Sturgeon, Amanda Reade, 91
St. Valentine cocktail, 147
Substance Champagne, 400,
      402
Suk, Gabriel, 80, 82
Sulfur dioxide, 172, 174, 178,
      196, 247, 319, 468–469
Sullivan, Frank, 43–45
Sumner, George C., 554
Sun, Fiona, 81
Sutcliffe, Serena, 106
Sweet wine
   alcohol content of, 238
   aszu, 153, 155
   Austrian, 365, 507, 508
   California, 237–239, 240,
      241–242, 257, 508
   chilling, 64
   ice wine and, 163
   popularity of, 238–239, 243
   rosé, 451
   Spanish, 10, 508
   Tokaj, 153, 154, 155
Switzerland wine, 437–439,
      533

Syrah wine, 16, 68, 195, 197,
      213, 252, 253, 254.
      See also specific brand
      names
Szent Ilona Borhaz wine, 376
Szobonya, Ms., 156
Szobonya, Zsuzsanna, 153

Taber, George M., 273
Tablas Creek winery, 69
Tâche Champagne, La, 516
Taillevent restaurant, 94, 494,
      495, 514–515
Taittinger Comtes de Cham-
      pagne, 115–116, 485
Talley Vineyards, 241, 245
Tamers, André, 90, 92, 357,
      359
Tanner, Lane, 244
Taurino, Cosimo and Francesco,
      346
Tavel wine, 207
Tawny port, 145, 146, 147
Taylor Wine Company (Walter
      S., Greyton and Lillian
      Taylor), 268–270
TCA (trichloranisole), 458, 459,
      460, 469
Tchelistcheff, André, 475–478,
      482
Tempier, Domaine, 69, 76, 448,
      530
Tempranillo wine, 121, 348
Terblanche, Gerry, 393
Terra di Lavoro wine, 328
Terrantez grapes, 150, 152
Terre de Vertus Champagne,
      403
Terres Dorées, Domaine des,
      315
Terrien, Michael, 222, 223, 224
Terroir. *See also* soil
   Burgundy and, 505
   Champagne and, 400–402,
      403, 406, 410
   description of, 34–39
   French, 272
   music and, 505
   Neal Rosenthal and, 274
   Randall Grahm and, 472,
      473
   Ray Walker and, 307
   riesling and, 34
   vintage charts and, 453
Terroir wine bars, 60, 62, 89,
      92, 296

Tête, Michel, 312, 314
Te Tera pinot noir, 82
Theise, Terry, 362, 363, 364,
    365, 366, 367, 404
Thenard, Baron, 489
Thévenet, Jean, 323
Thomas, Chaad, 2
Thompson, Campbell, 80
Three Valleys wine, 103
Thundering Hooves Ranch, 122
Tinto Fino wineshop, 89
Tissot, Stéphane, 321
Tizio, Carlos, 382, 383
Tocai Friulano wine, 173
Toering, Jeffrey, 3–4
Tofanelli Vineyard, 97
Tokaji aszu, 153, 155, 375, 376,
    377
Tokara winery, 387
Tolmach, Adam, 241
Tonic restaurant, 529, 530
Tonnerre, Chablis Montée de,
    489
"Topping and tailing," 137
Torino, Etchart and Michel,
    381
Tormaresca wine, 344
Torrontés wine, 10, 380, 381
Torula compniacensis fungus,
    126. *See also* Fungus/
    mold
Trabucco, Nicola, 328, 329
Trama, Michel, 133
Treixadura grapes, 73
Trépout wine, 134
Troisgros restaurant, 144
Trousseau grapes, 73
Truchot, Jacky, 306
Trump Tower, New York, 547
Tsunami, 440–441
Tunnell, Doug, 76
Turley Cellars, 97, 103, 196, 197,
    198, 199, 200–201
"21" Club restaurant, 46, 146,
    148, 533–535
26 Brix restaurant, 122
Txakolina wine, 357–360
Txomin Etxaniz wine, 358, 360
Txori mahatsa grapes, 360
Txueka, Ernesto, 358

Uccelliera wine, 340
Ugni blanc grapes, 125, 134
Union Square, New York, 546
United Nations, 547
U.S. Wine Imports, 3

Vaillant, George E., 539
Valdiguié wine, 97, 98
Valentine, Saint, 316, 317
Vallone, Agricole, 345, 346
Van de Water, Lisa, 231, 232
Vaudesir, Chablis, 489
Vaynerchuk, Gary, 26–30
Vaynermedia, 27, 30
Ventura, D., 349, 351
Verdelho Madeira wine, 151
Vergeau, Matilde, 319
Verget, Maison, 323
Veritas restaurant, 276, 463,
    465, 493, 528
Vermeer, Johannes, 544
Veronelli, Luigi, 335–336, 337
Verrat, Patricia and Thierry, 128
Version Originale Champagne,
    402
Veuve Clicquot Champagne, 21,
    74, 415, 416, 484, 485
Vie di Romans winery, 173
Vieilles Vignes Françaises
    Champagne, 407
Viennese wine, 369–371
Vieux Télégraphe, Domaine
    du, 69
Vigneron(s). *See also* Old World
    wine
    Anselme Selosse as, 400,
        401
    of Bordeaux, 279, 282
    Burgundy, 301, 303
    Champagne, 401, 402
    Jacky Truchot as, 306
    Jean-François Fillastre as,
        279–280, 283
    Joe Dressner and, 511
    making Champagne, 409
    methods of, 10, 306, 314,
        400, 401, 412
    passion of, 281
    struggling, 282
Vilafonté wine, 387, 388, 389,
    390
Villaine, Aubert de, 94, 95, 506
Villas, James, 141
Vilmart & Cie wine, 403
Viña Caneiro, 349, 350
Vin de Pays de la Vallée du
    Paradis wine, 447
Vin Divino, 507
Vine Hill Vineyard, 226, 228
Vineyard Brands, 144
Vinifera Wine Cellars, 96
Vintage Brut Champagne, 515

Vintage Champagne, 7, 150
Vintage charts, 452–454
Vintage Cognac, 128, 132
Vintage Madeira, 150–152
Vintage port, 145, 146
VinTank consultants, 27
Viognier wine, 10, 12, 144, 214,
    381, 389, 393, 547
Vissoux, Domaine du, 312, 314
Visztenvelt, Pal, 154, 155
Volnay Caillerets wine, 105, 107
Volnay Clos des Ducs wine, 144
Volnay-Santenot wine, 115, 117
Von der Fels riesling, 361
Vosne-Romanée Les Suchots
    wine, 515
Vouette & Sorbée Champagne,
    410, 412
Vranken-Pommery Monopole
    Champagne, 419, 420
Vrinat, Jean-Claude, 94,
    494–496, 514

Wagner-Stempels riesling, 363
Walker, Fongyee, 80, 81
Walker, Hiram, 382
Walker, M. Andrew, 184
Walker, Ray, 304–307
Walla Walla Foundry, 121
Wall Street, New York, 547
Warwick Estate, 388
Washington state wine, 119,
    121, 122, 390. *See also*
    American wine
Wasserman, Becky, 300, 301,
    307, 404
Waterhouse, Andrew, 468, 469
Waters, Alice, 76
Watkins, Matthew, 345
Waugh, Harry, 46
Webb, Brad, 224
Webb, Gyles, 388
Wechsberg, Joseph, 46
Weeber, Andrew, 432
Wehlener Sonnenuhr wine,
    118
Weinbach, Domaine, 372–374
Wente Brothers wine, 534
Werle, Édouard, 415
Werner, Jean-François, 288
Wesson, Joshua, 209, 211
Whitehouse-Crawford
    restaurant, 122
White wine
    Apulian, 344
    Burgundy, 12

White wine (*continued*)
  cheese with, 54, 94–95
  chilling, 63–65
  dry, 375–377
  Hungarian, 375–377
  seafood with, 443, 444
  sweet, 10, 94
  winespeak on, 7
Wicka, Karl, 200
Widmer's Wine Cellars, 534
Wiemer, Hermann J., 269, 270
Wild grapes, 182
Wilson, Tracy, 434
Wind Gap wine, 252, 253, 254
Windows on the World restau-
  rant, 77–78, 529, 533
Wine artifacts, 542–545
Wine assemblage, 215–216
Wine cellar(s)
  "21" Club, 533, 534
  black mold in, 155
  brick, 549
  Harry's restaurant, 497, 498
  humidity in, 107
  Marvin C. Overton III, 110
  Park B. Smith, 491–493
  Pol Roger, 516
  seventeenth century, 155
  at Singita Lebombo Lodge,
    393
  sixteenth century, 153, 155
  stone, 153
  temperature of, 67, 516
  Tom Olander, 123
Wine clubs, 233–236, 464
Wine coolers, 542

Wine cooperatives, 16, 161, 324,
  404, 412
Wine Geek company, 89
Wine Institute, 419
Wine key, 1, 3
Wine Lab, 231, 232
Wine Library TV video blog,
  26, 27, 28, 29
Wine on tap, 525–527
Wine Republic importing
  company, 81
Wine Society, 23
Winespeak, 6–8, 40–42,
  43–44, 551
Wine steward. *See* Sommeliers/
  wine stewards
Wine tasting
  California outscoring
    French in, 259–261,
    272, 273
  at dinner parties, 115–118
  exhausting, 495
  of Fiorano wine, 336–337
  of ice wine, 164, 166
  myths of, 46–48
  ritual of, 28
Wine Wand, 467, 468
Winiarski, Warren, 228, 260,
  492
Wondrich, David, 147
Wong, Melissa, 81
Wong, Vanessa, 252
Woodward Canyon, 120

Ximénez, Pedro, 92

Yaseen, Roger, 7
Ybañez Creus, Javier, 356
Yeasts, 36, 90, 91, 227, 231, 257,
  320, 512
Yellow Tail wine, 90, 482
Yellow wine, 318
Yering Station pinot noir rosé,
  81
Yoon, Sang, 526, 527

Zagat Survey, 497
Zapata red wine, 380
Zecca, Conti, 346
Zellerbach, James and Hana,
  224
Zelphi company, 390
Zillier, Eric, 463, 465
Zinfandel. *See also specific*
  brand names
  alcohol content of, 103, 201,
    256, 343–344
  American, 102–103
  chilling, 66
  color of, 196
  old vineyards of, 199
  primitivo grape and, 343
  sweetness, 10, 12, 237, 238
  vineyard in Mexico,
    198–201
  white, 238
Zorriketa, Roberto Ibarretxe,
  359
Zraly, Kevin, 77–79
Zweigelt grapes, 368